University of Winnipeg, 515 Portage Ave., Winnipeg, MB. R3B 2E9 Canada

THE PASSING OF THE WHIGS

1832 - 1886

THE MARQUESS OF HARTINGTON
later 8th DUKE OF DEVONSHIRE
by H. Von Herkomer
National Portrait Gallery

THE PASSING OF THE WHIGS
1832 - 1886

BY

DONALD SOUTHGATE
B.A., D.Phil.

LECTURER IN MODERN POLITICAL AND CONSTITUTIONAL
HISTORY IN THE UNIVERSITY OF ST ANDREWS
(QUEEN'S COLLEGE, DUNDEE)

LONDON
MACMILLAN & CO LTD
NEW YORK · ST MARTIN'S PRESS
1962

MACMILLAN AND COMPANY LIMITED
St Martin's Street London WC 2
also Bombay Calcutta Madras Melbourne

THE MACMILLAN COMPANY OF CANADA LIMITED
Toronto

ST MARTIN'S PRESS INC
New York

PRINTED IN GREAT BRITAIN

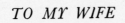

TO MY WIFE

PREFACE

THERE must be many people who, like myself, read History at a university without acquiring the means of giving a clear, short answer to the question 'What happened to the Whigs after 1832?' Writers have tended to slither from the term 'Whig' to the term 'Liberal' without explaining adequately the process implied by the substitution of the terms.

When, at Christ Church, I was advised to read for a D.Phil. rather than add a P.P.E. degree to my History Honours (London), I decided to investigate the unexplained process, and try to find how, and when, and why the Whig party 'became' or 'developed into' or 'gave way to' the Liberal party. Under the guidance of Professor Arthur Aspinall, who did much to smooth the path, I produced a thesis entitled *The Transition from Whiggism to Liberalism*. Vast, inchoate and immature, it gained only narrowly, I am sure, the approval of Sir Keith Feiling and Mr Alan Bullock. If the book has grown out of the thesis, I hope it may be thought to have grown well out of it.

The change of title to *The Passing of the Whigs* reflects a change of interest and emphasis. The theme is the decline of the unique influence exercised in the body politic by a group of people who, as the 8th Duke of Argyll said, thought of themselves as a special breed of spaniels. Their influence has gone, though, as the genealogical tables show, their descendants still figure in our affairs; the late Earl of Halifax, Sir Anthony Eden and the Earl of Home have the first Earl Grey as a common ancestor, and the wife of Mr Harold Macmillan is the grand-niece of the last Whig leader. In the House of Commons Lord Hinchingbrooke (of impeccable Tory stock, *pace* a Paget forebear) is denounced as the last adherent of 'Whig' economics. Professor Hayek, author of the *Road to Serfdom* (1945), proclaims himself the last of the Whigs and (to quote the *Economist*) extols 'that palladium of liberty the Rule of Law, in whose name [he] would deny all discretionary latitude to administration'. For students of Constitutional Law this awakens Diceian echoes. But how much do these occasional uses of the term 'Whig' in the middle of the twentieth century convey to the majority even of educated people? 'Since 1886 the word has been used in a purely historical sense, while "Tory" has still a living meaning.'[1] The study of the passing of the Whigs involves disinterment and regeneration. The labour long since became one of love, and the predominant motive became the desire to communicate, by reference to a society less remote than that of the seventeenth and eighteenth centuries, something of the inimitable flavour of Whiggery.

If the theme is the decline of an influence, it is also retention of influence. For it soon became evident that the story could not stop short of 1886, when Unionists and Home Rulers began their battle of black balls at Brooks's Club. In 1879 the *Edinburgh Review* was still performing its perennial task of presenting Whigs to the electorate as the true centre of gravity of the Liberal party, though it had been 'the fashion with shallow Liberals ever since the Reform Act to sneer at the Whigs as an obsolete party'. The premise of Labouchere's appeal to Chamberlain on 1st January, 1886 — 'the real enemies of the Radicals are the Whigs' — compels us to accept the conclusion of Hartington's biographer — '. . . Until this moment the word "Whig" was still in common use to denote a connection loosely bound together, the moderate Liberals, led by the chiefs of certain families of long standing.'[1]

The twin themes of decline and retention of power impose a broadly chronological approach, but, in attempting, primarily, to show what, as well as who, the latter-day Whigs were, how they saw themselves and how others saw them (which must be my justification for so often allowing nineteenth-century personalities to speak for themselves), I have tried not to be a slave of the narrative method. And in response to the advice of those who have read the manuscript I have included, in chapters VI–IX, a cross-section study of the policies of the last Whig governments, at the cost of suspending the action of the play.

I should add the warning that I have not attempted a balanced appraisal of various species of Liberalism and Radicalism which Whiggery collectively never accepted, though individual Whigs, excercising the prerogative of their caste, did so without necessarily forfeiting the designation 'Whig'. Nor shall I be alarmed if Mr Bullock still complains that I 'do not understand Gladstone'. For

[1] Bernard Holland, Life of the Duke of Devonshire 1833–1908, Vol. II, pp. 129–30.

my purpose it is sufficient to show that Whiggery often could not understand him, and mistrusted him (and with good reason) when it could.

By its nature this is a betwixt-and-between book. I have had to specify where others generalise, and summarise where others again itemise. But the space between the monograph and the general history is nowadays too often left vacant. If I have offered material on the basis of which some generalisations may be modified, as well as generalisations which experts in particular fields may qualify, or indeed, reject, I shall be well pleased.

I am most grateful to successive professors under whom I have worked — W. N. Medlicott (then of University College, Exeter), Michael Roberts (then of Rhodes University, South Africa) and D. F. Macdonald (of Queen's College, Dundee, in the University of St Andrews) — as well as to Mr (now Professor) Howard Warrender (then of Glasgow University) for their encouragement.

The approval and detailed criticism of a complete draft by Mr James Tumelty of Glasgow University marked the point of break-through. Mr W. D. Handcock of the University of Exeter was refreshingly and productively critical of wild assertions, and vigilant reading of the text by my colleagues Mr S. G. E. Lythe and Dr John Ward was only less helpful than their constructive conversation on many topics in which their knowledge and under-standing is greater than mine. Mr Michael Brock, of Corpus Christi College, Oxford, was kind enough to read Chapter I and make valuable suggestions which I have adopted. I acknowledge with gratitude the facilities made available by Mr David Crichton of the Dundee City Library, and the criticisms of style made by Mr A. N. Cass and Mr Roland Hall; I hasten to add that they are not responsible for the result. And last, but not least, my wife was a tower of strength in terms of moral support and forbearance. She was forbidden to empty waste-paper baskets and concealed her horror when the work flowed out of the study into the dining room. And she helped immeasurably with the chores of book-preparation. If she and my family have sometimes distracted me from my work, that is as it should be.

DONALD SOUTHGATE

October 1960

CONTENTS

ILLUSTRATIONS

INTRODUCTION

The Whigs who went Before

Dr Johnson declared that the Devil was the first Whig. Lord Acton preferred St Thomas Aquinas. There was justice in each selection. Satan was the first aristocratic rebel against absolute monarchy based on divine right. The Aristotelian scholastic propounded in philosophical terms the doctrine that no earthly sovereign has an absolute claim to the obedience of his subjects; 'tyranny' forfeits 'authority' and leaves only 'power', which may legitimately be overthrown by force. This doctrine was implicit in the feudal nature of medieval monarchy (as well as in ancient customs among the Germanic peoples), and is, of course, apt to be held, consciously or unconsciously, by any resilient aristocracy. 'No notables . . . I want no 1789' said Tsar Alexander II. The first Whigs were aristocratic rebels who would not tolerate that their lives, liberties and estates should be at the will of a (popish) prince. In the first, heroic, age, they acquired venerated martyrs — Russell, Sydney, Essex, Argyll — of whom Sydney pressed the doctrine to its full republican implications. The first phase of Whiggery ended when on 11th December, 1688 the English notables assembled at Guildhall to welcome William of Orange as 'the great Deliverer'. 'We will with our utmost endeavours', they declared, 'assist His Highness in the obtaining of [a free parliament] . . . wherein our laws, our liberties and properties may be secured, and the Church of England in particular, with a due liberty to Protestant Dissenters.'

The Revolution of 1688, though subsequently appropriated by Whiggery as its own work, was a national revulsion against popery and arbitrary power. But the Revolution Settlement, beginning with the recognition of William and Mary as King and Queen *de jure,* conditional upon their acceptance of the Declaration of Rights, was, by and large, the Whig triumph which the Whigs claimed it was. The second phase of Whiggery ended with the Hanoverian Succession, as prescribed by the Act of Settlement

1701 and the Act of Union 1707, and the failure of the Jacobite rebellion of 1715.

The Revolution Settlement was safeguarded by annual parliaments, Commons control of supply and by the developing principle of ministerial responsibility. In the third phase of Whiggery, the control of the state by a Whig oligarchy was justified on the ground that the Revolution, the Settlement and the Succession required for their maintenance the predominance of those who claimed to be their authentic guardians. But success had its penalties. In the heroic age, when the name 'Whigamoor' was transported from the covenanting regions of Strathclyde to the Palace of Westminster (as the designation, first, of a lunatic fringe and then of a great national party), everyone knew who Whigs were and what Whiggery was, and this remained sufficiently true in the reign of Anne. But when Whiggism had become the creed of the age, under the second George, it lost its significance as a term which could meaningfully be used to differentiate one set of politicians from another, and by the accession of George III in 1760 nobody knew what Whiggery was because almost everybody who was anybody in the political world claimed to be a Whig. The term did not become politically meaningful again until it could be placed in apposition to the term 'Tory', the vogue of which revived under the impact of the French Revolution. The historian of the Tory *parties*, Sir Keith Feiling, did not disguise the tenuous nature of the link between 'the first Tory party' and 'the second'. Sir Lewis Namier and his disciples have now shown us that the link between the Whigs of the earlier and those of the later eighteenth century is almost as tenuous. There is difficulty in fitting in Chatham, and Mr John Brooke casts doubt upon the validity of the traditional connection between the Pelham Whigs and the Rockingham Whigs, who belonged to a different generation. But nineteenth-century Whigs, accepting uncritically Burke's misrepresentation of the policy and tactics of George III, tended to recognise the Rockingham Whigs, whose apologist Burke was, as the repositories of the Whig faith in their day. The secession of most of Rockingham's followers, including Burke, to Pitt in the age of the French Revolution, left the faith in the devoted care of Charles James Fox.

Fox spoke in the vein of Whigs of old when he argued that 'party' — i.e. opposition to the King's government — was

essential to the maintenance of the constitution, because it prevented the 'euthanasia of absolute monarchy'. But he served the
future too, by bequeathing to nineteenth-century Whiggery the
watchwords 'Peace, Economy and Reform', though Holland
admitted in 1810 that in the past Whigs had been consistently
devoted to none of these, and it remained a matter of controversy
whether the Foxite heritage in the field of foreign policy should be
properly described as devotion to Peace or to 'the cause of nations'
(as Lord John Russell preferred). It may be argued that Canningites
and Peelites successively had equally derived these principles, not
from Fox, but from Pitt, and did as much as the Whigs to transmit
them to the Gladstonian Liberal party which, perhaps, owed them
even more to the Manchester School. But this at least made it
easier for Canningites and Peelites in turn to join and reinforce
Whiggery.

Whiggery always bore the stamp of aristocracy. The Foxites,
in adopting parliamentary reform, rejected the admonitions of
Burke. But they did not repudiate Burke's assumption that,
'Property must carry influence in every part of the public concerns . . . while the least notions exist of the means by which the
Spirit of Liberty acts . . . and by which it is preserved.' Whigs in
every age were magnates, relatives, privileged associates or clients
of magnates. Hence their power was subject to progressive
attrition as the economy and society outgrew the landed interest,
until at last it could be said:[1]

> Only a few years ago the name was a proud boast, a hereditary
> recollection, the appanage of a great party; now it is an historical
> recollection, recalling colours and cries, buff and blue, Charles
> James Fox and Mrs Crewe — pictures and figures from an indistinct
> and fading past . . . proscribed as an active intelligence. The slovenly
> and slipshod term Moderate Liberal was fixed upon to cover the
> retreat and supply the place of the old party name. At the last
> elections, Whiggism was 'suspect', the new electorate was hostile,
> did not believe that the Whigs were men and brothers, but rather
> that they had been lords and masters. . . .

Even at that last hour, Arnold Morley said that it would be worth
untold millions to the future of the country if men of the great
position and unquestionable independence of Lord Hartington

[1] *Fortnightly Review*, Mar 1886 Vol. XLV, p. 573, 'The Liberal Saturnalia'.

could become thoroughly identified with the Liberal cause. But, he added, the sympathy of dukes and earls with the claims of democracy must be spontaneous and natural or non-existent.[1] A 'Whig democrat' was a sport, not a genus. As politicians, the Whigs were congenitally undemocratic, and Whiggery could not flourish in a democratic constitution. 'In the temperate zone of our ancient Constitution,' wrote Lord John Russell in his *English Government*, the evils of despotism and democracy were alike unknown. Twelve years after the grant of household suffrage in the towns, the *Edinburgh Review* (1879) commended the Whigs for their steady adherence to principle and 'their habitual reserve' towards the people, rejoicing that they had 'never accepted the modern doctrine that legislation is to be dictated by public opinion, and in pursuing their even and consistent course for forty memorable years they have often had occasion to check the folly and extravagance of popular demands'. We shall see how they, whose spiritual ancestors (sometimes their physical ancestors as well) had started as rebels two hundred years before, ended their distinctive history as apprehensive conservatives in an age when Whiggish intellectuals complained that the new Liberalism lacked moderation and had 'insufficient sympathy with the historical way of looking at things'. Britain was 'drifting towards a type of government associated with terrible events — a single Assembly armed with full power over the constitution . . . a theoretically all-powerful Convention, governed by a practically all-powerful secret Committee of Public Safety'.[2] Then, indeed, it was time for the Whigs to be gone. We have to study how their power had progressively declined, and how for so long after 1832 their influence was maintained by virtue of their special relationship to the Liberal forces in the community.

[1] ibid., 1st Aug 1886.
[2] Fitzjames Stephen to Lytton 6th May 1880, and Sir Henry Maine (*Popular Government*, 1909 ed., p. 126) quoted by John Roach 'Liberalism and the Victorian Intelligentsia', Cambridge Historical Journal No. XI, Art IV, 1955.

CHAPTER I

The Coup d'État, 1831-2

The years 1827-9 saw the disintegration of parties. On 17th February, 1827, Lord Liverpool, an able administrator and skilled conciliator who had been prime minister longer than anyone except Walpole and Pitt, was smitten with paralysis. The appointment of Canning to succeed him split both the Tories and the Whigs. A minority of the former (but a majority of the leaders) refused to serve with or pledge support for a man who favoured the admission of Roman Catholics to public office. A majority of the latter refused to oppose Canning. The chieftain of Whiggery, Charles, Earl Grey, despised Canning for his lowly origins, had never forgiven him his anti-Jacobin journalism, laid upon him the blame for the continued denial of civil equality to Catholics,[1] and distrusted his policy as Foreign Secretary since 1822. But most Whigs, having unfairly attacked Castlereagh (Canning's predecessor at the Foreign Office) as an abettor of the repressive European Concert maintained by Metternich, regarded Canning as a hero for his sprightly repudiation of the Concert. Within a few months of his arrival at the Foreign Office it was said that he 'had knocked the Holy Alliance on the head, had saved Spain, was going to protect the Greeks against the Turks and Russians, and had nothing left to do but to save England, to which he had not yet turned his mind'.[2] Within a few weeks of his appointment as prime minister, Whigs were reserving seats behind the Treasury bench in the House of Commons, on which three of the lesser Whigs sat with liberal and moderate Tories as members of Canning's ministry, and in the Lords two of the principal Whig elders, Lansdowne and Holland, sat behind a ministerial bench which contained the Duke of Devonshire.[3] The Radical Sir John Hobhouse explained a very general Whig reaction when he wrote,

---

[1] Because he, the chief Conservative supporter of Emancipation, allowed it to remain an 'open question' and did not press it.

[2] Maxwell's *Clarendon*, 1913, p. 35.

[3] Broughton, *Recollections of a Long Life*, 1909-11, Vol. III, pp. 186-9.

'Canning was no friend of mine — he was no friend of the people; but circumstances had lately given him the power, and apparently the inclination, to be useful to the great cause of public liberty here, and more particularly on the Continent, where I knew his name was the terror of tyrants. Add to this that I felt his death would probably give a triumph to our bigots.'[1] But Grey and other patricians deplored Whig support for a man who said that he was as opposed as ever to parliamentary reform and the repeal of the Test Act, and that the Catholic question would not be a matter for government action. They held that it was an unnecessary sacrifice of the honour of the Whig party[2]— that mystical attribute, concern for which had prevented the coalition of Fox with Pitt and diverted from the Regent to the Whigs the blame for the failure of negotiations to take Whigs into government in 1811–12. Grey was particularly angry with Lansdowne, who joined Canning's cabinet, without office, and upon Canning's untimely death in August continued as Home Secretary in the administration of Lord Goderich.[3] He did not like the rumours that Holland was to be offered the Foreign Office, which Holland's uncle, Fox, had held in the months before his death in 1806, and where Grey had followed Fox. The resignation of Goderich, who had not the nerve to meet Parliament, put an end to such speculations, but the breach within Whiggery was not healed. Grey had identified the villain of the piece as Henry Brougham. This man had shown that, when opportunity offered, opposition could be rendered formidable by exploiting the prejudices of that important element in the House of Commons which was primarily landed interest and only secondarily Tory. But he was denied his due position as the official leader of the Whigs in the Commons because (like Canning) he was not a gentleman, was notoriously ambitious, and was rightly critical of the domination of Whiggery by narrow-minded oligarchs.[4]

When the Duke of Wellington succeeded Goderich as prime minister, it seemed as though parties might resume their previous

---

[1] ibid., Vol. III, p. 211.

[2] *E.C.J.R.* (*Early Correspondence of Lord John Russell*), No. 102, 13th September, 1827, (Vol. I, p. 262). See also No. 106, p. 271, for Althorp's comments.

[3] Tierney, the former Whig leader in the Commons, and Sir James Mackintosh also joined Canning's administration — see A. Aspinall *Formation of Canning's Ministry*, Camden Series LIX, 1937. Lansdowne accepted the Home Office before Canning's death.

[4] See Aspinall's *Lord Brougham and the Whig Party*, 1939, reissue.

postures. Leading Canningites accepted office under him. And of the Whigs the Marquess of Tavistock said, 'We all go into regular opposition, and may do the only good the Whigs ever can do, by acting separately and watching the Government.'[1] But such talk of opposition soon gave way to expressions of admiration. For Wellington made no opposition to the repeal of the Test and Corporation Acts[2] and then, when the Roman Catholic leader, O'Connell, was elected for Co. Clare, promoted Catholic Emancipation in order to avoid civil war within the United Kingdom. The Duke had already (in May 1828) dispensed with the Canningite ministers. And now the ultra-Protestant High Tories rebelled. Catholic Emancipation was passed with the aid of Whig and Canningite votes.

Having lost both its liberal and obscurantist wings, the cabinet was a rump and the Tory party was shattered. The tattle of politics was all of men, not of measures. The question on every lip was 'Who would the Duke get?' — and the answer was sometimes 'Lord Grey'. We now know that the Duke did not wish to offer Grey the Foreign Office. But Grey more than half expected the offer, and we cannot say that he would have refused it. 'Nothing', he said, 'could give him greater pain than to find himself in opposition to the Duke's government.'[3] In his attitude to Canning's government Grey had differed from most of his followers, but now that Wellington had become dependent on Whig support, and earned it by Whiggish measures, many a Whig agreed with the Earl. 'Why should you wish the Duke to be forced out?' asked a moderate Whig as late as July, 1830. 'That he should acquire fresh strength is indispensable. But what cause of complaint has he yet given to the public, or to any liberal-minded man?'[4] The more liberal Whigs, gathering round Viscount Althorp, were perhaps less friendly towards the Government than was Grey, but they were not hostile. When Althorp and Sir James Graham called a meeting at Albany to promote economy and administrative reform, some refused to go because it might embarrass the Duke and others because the sponsors had no such intention. The Whigs

[1] Broughton, op. cit., Vol. III, p. 237.
[2] Survivals from the seventeenth century which had no practical effect in excluding Protestant Dissenters from Parliament or public office, but were of symbolic importance.
[3] E.C.J.R., No. 126 (pp. 298–300), Grey to Russell, 13th December, 1829.
[4] Life of John, Lord Campbell, ed. Hardcastle, 1881, Vol. I, p. 473.

had advocated 'economical reform' ever since the Yorkshire county meeting and a great speech by Burke had impelled them to try to 'limit the quantity of power (i.e. patronage) that may be abused.'[1] Rockingham's government of 1782 had initiated the process; Pitt had greatly advanced it; and now the Duke of Wellington was bringing it near to completion. 'This great reduction of Taxes puts me in good humour with the Ministry, it is beyond our most sanguine hopes . . .' wrote Lord William Russell. 'I am for urging on the Ministry, without turning them out. We shall not get so good a one to replace them.'[2]

In Fox's day the Whig banner bore the legend 'Peace, Economy and Reform'. With a High Tory prime minister pursuing an unambitious foreign policy which made retrenchment possible, how could the Whigs distinguish themselves except by refurbishing the somewhat faded device of Parliamentary Reform? In 1830 reform of parliament (i.e. of the electoral system) suddenly became a burning political issue and, as a consequence, Grey became head of a government raised on the ashes of the Duke's and the small nucleus which Althorp had gathered in the early months of 1830 swelled by the middle of 1831 into a great House of Commons majority. But these dramatic changes were not the fruit of Whig strategy. The official Whig attitude to parliamentary reform remained, until *after* it had become a current issue, what it had been when Tierney expounded it in the House of Commons in May 1824 and when Grey reiterated it in the House of Lords in 1827. Explaining why he could not support Canning, Grey had said that Reform was not the reason — '. . . that is not a question to which they (the Whigs) are pledged, nor on which the party to which they belong are agreed. . . . The question of parliamentary reform is not so uniformly supported, nor has it at present the public opinion so strongly in its favour, as that it should be made a sine qua non in forming an administration'. Grey had not given up hope of office, but he had given up hope of seeing Reform achieved in his time. In February, 1830 he advised his heir, Lord Howick, not to 'hamper' himself with a question which the Crown would always oppose and which the people could not be relied on to support. Evidently he had not moved from the position of 1820 — 'though I think it highly desirable to endeavour to raise the

---

[1] Burke's Speech on Economical Reform, 11th February, 1780.
[2] *E.C.J.R.*, No. 129, 1st April, 1830.

character of the House of Commons in the opinion of the public, by uniting the representative more closely with the constituent body, I would have that pursued individually by those who are favourable to it, in such a manner as may neither divide the Whig party, nor pledge them to it in such a way as may make their acceptance of office — if so improbable an event as its being offered to them should occur — a reproach to them without it'.[1] In accordance with those views, Lord John Russell and John George Lambton had been given by the party chiefs a somewhat grudging licence to raise the question, provided they were careful to dissociate themselves from Radicals both *Philosophical* and demagogic.

Russell was still moving resolutions in favour of parliamentary reform in 1830, but they were defeated by the usual comfortable majorities.[2] The Whigs were as surprised as the Tories when, at the end of the general election necessitated by the death of George IV, they realised that Reform had arrived at the forefront of the political stage. It is not easy to explain how it came to be there, except in terms of the proposition that when something is inevitable, it becomes more imminent with each passing year.

Of the inevitability of a change in the representative system — at least if one rules out the alternative of a move towards autocracy — there can be no doubt. This provides the true answer to Disraeli's allegation that when the spiritual descendants of the architects of the eighteenth-century 'Venetian' constitution and of the Peerage Bill of 1719 destroyed that constitution and were prepared to swamp the Lords in order to destroy it, they displayed a disgracefully utilitarian approach to a sacred subject, making the constitution the plaything of an unscrupulous oligarchy.[3] The converse of such opportunism was an obscurantism which attributed to the existing mechanics of representation a mystical sanctity, and implied that man was made for the state, not the state

---

[1] Quoted by J. R. M. Butler, *The Passing of the Great Reform Bill*, p. 36.

[2] e.g. 213:117 on the resolution to find seats for large towns and extra seats for large counties by taking up to 60 away from boroughs of less than 2,500 inhabitants, with annuities as compensation for loss of privilege (28th May). This was the Whig answer to O'Connell's manhood suffrage motion. On 23rd February Russell's motion to enfranchise three large cities had been defeated by 188:140 despite Huskisson's support.

[3] See both *Vindication of the English Constitution* and *Coningsby*. By the term 'Venetian' Disraeli meant to convey the usurpation of monarchical power by an oligarchy. The Peerage Bill, if passed, would have set a rigid limit to the royal prerogative of creation of peers, to prevent a repetition of the 'packing' which had been necessary to secure the passage of the Treaty of Utrecht.

for man. 'My Lords', cried the aged Eldon, during the debates on the Whig Reform Bill, 'sacrifice one atom of our glorious constitution, and all the rest is gone.' Reform, he predicted, would reduce 'this which has hitherto been the most glorious of all the nations upon the earth to that state of misery which now affects all the nations'.[1] This alarmism gained a spurious plausibility from the fact that Burke himself had 'dared not rub off venerable rust' and defended the defects of the constitution as though they were its principal virtues, and in so doing on the morrow of the French Revolution had set the tone of official thought for more than a generation. But such fundamentalism had been rendered obsolete by the Revolution of 1688, for it is appropriate, if at all, only to some absolute proposition such as the divine right of kings to reign, or at least to inherit the throne — the proposition which the original Whigs had denied. Moreover, the fundamentalist approach to the problem of Reform was vitiated by the fact that the details of electoral right and practice had been subject to considerable modification by Commons' rulings in the eighteenth century (many of which assisted the 'closing' of boroughs)[2] and the conventional relationships between the various branches of the constitution were the products of ceaseless change. The constitution which Eldon defended was not that of 1689 or 1714 or even of 1784. Its laws were broadly the same as in 1714, but not its conventions,[3] and to the forging of these conventions out of the raw material of political practice there is no end. So the contention of the obscurantists, when reduced to its essentials, was that the constitution, though subject to *conventional* development, ought to be exempt from *legislative* process. Only a proposition of that order could justify the argument that the constituency list must remain frozen in its seventeenth-century form.[4]

Even if the propositions of the obscurantists had been more defensible in logical terms, they would still have been untenable as the basis of mid-nineteenth-century British politics. The old Tory, Sir Robert Inglis, parroted Burke's protest that 'he did not

[1] H. of L., 7th October, 1831.

[2] i.e. control by patrons — see Porritt, *The Unreformed House of Commons*.

[3] The most prominent changes had been the development of cabinet government and ministerial responsibility, and of the premiership; the transfer of all governmental expenses from the Civil List to the Consolidated Fund which was completed in the reign of William IV, was, of course, a statutory process.

[4] Until the reign of Charles II new constituencies were created by royal writ or, occasionally, legislation. None had been created since.

desire to be a better Whig than Lord Somers' and claimed that in defending 'the constitution' the Tory party was the true successor of the great Whigs of the Revolution.[1] But Lord Somers had long been dead[2] and Britain had changed. What satisfied the eighteenth century could not content the nineteenth because, as Macaulay patiently explained during the Reform Bill debates, the distribution of wealth and intelligence had altered. Free institutions cannot work efficiently unless they command a minimum of assent from the community. To command such assent they must give due scope to changes in public opinion which result from changes in social and economic reality. Constitutional provisions establish the machinery through which power may lawfully be exercised. But power itself, unless it is mere force, can come only from the community which lives under the law.[3] This is as true where full participation in the free institutions is the privilege of a minority, as in a fully democratic system of government. Such a system is merely more vulnerable to revolt against the constitutional order itself, for it may come to pass that the majority of the population, as well as a minority of the political élite, is dissatisfied and has, by definition, inadequate means of securing changes of policy through the normal constitutional processes. It was not beyond an intelligent Whig who had read his Locke to understand all this, and apply it to the situation in 1830. The first formative phase of what we call 'the Industrial Revolution' had produced powerful classes, possessed collectively of great wealth, and making a key contribution to the country's economy, who were discontented with the existing constitutional order. And beneath them, and also discontented, were on the one hand a new working class in the industrial towns, which economic change had produced, and on the other classes of artisans in the older centres of production whose livelihood was threatened by technological advance. Both were disenchanted with political arrangements under which their dissatisfaction with their economic conditions seemed to be regarded by the authorities as posing a police problem rather than a challenge to creative legislation. The prospect of continuing, and probably increasing, mass discontent, made it all the more

---

[1] H. of C., 17th December, 1831.   [2] His dates were 1652–1716.

[3] This is not to deny that there is a *vis inertiae* in consitutional provisions (e.g. the American constitution), not only because they sometimes prescribe special and cumbrous machinery for amendment, but also because they themselves help to mould public opinion.

necessary to rally to the régime the classes to whom wealth gave a claim to power which the constitution did not recognise.

The champions of the existing régime would not be allowed indefinitely to go on pleading its legal competence when the interaction of economic progress and persistent propaganda had produced a state of public opinion which signified that the régime lacked the genuine authority which can only come from communal assent. This propaganda, over more than forty years, among differing strata of the population, had been directed either towards discrediting the representative system itself as a mockery and abuse or towards mobilising public demand for reforms of all kinds which it was idle to expect an unreformed House of Commons to grant. Bentham and the Mills, with their *Westminster Review*, had appealed to what a Radical historian called 'reading and thinking people'.[1] But there were avid readers (and more numerous listeners) among humbler classes than this middle-class phrase implies. Despite all official attempts to check it, Cobbett's *Political Register* had long been a potent instrument of agitation. This varied propaganda had done its work, and, since men cannot continue indefinitely under the spell of inhibitions acquired by a previous generation, the baleful influence of the great revulsion of 1792, which economic depression and social stress in the post-war years had helped prolong not only in the governing class but in men of substance who desired admission to it, had at last lost much of its efficacy.

The time was therefore ripe for the removal of that impediment which prevented the constitution from being adapted to contemporary pressures and practical convenience. Macaulay begged the obscurantists to understand that a government might become intolerable simply because it had failed to change with the times, until at last it was no longer a question of *whether* there should be change, but whether it should be peaceful and moderate or violent and drastic. 'In peace or in convulsion; by the law or in spite of the law; through Parliament or over the Parliament, Reform must be carried. Therefore be content to guide the movement which you cannot stop.'[2]

The excesses of the French Revolution — represented by Burke in his influential *Reflections* as the inevitable result of a departure

---

[1] Harris, *History of the Radical Party in Parliament*, 1885, p. 151.
[2] H. of C., 16th December, 1831.

from 'prescription' — had doomed the cause of parliamentary reform in Britain for a generation. But in July 1830 a new French Revolution, without excesses, stimulated an interest in Reform which had already been shown in the elections.[1] Men were at hand to say that in substituting for Charles X and Polignac a 'citizen king' dependent on the upper bourgeoisie the French had set the British an example which could safely be followed and could not safely be ignored. In the debate on the Address, on 2nd November, 1830, Grey said that with the spirit of liberty breaking out all around, it would be wise, and even necessary, to safeguard British institutions by 'the temperate, gradual, and judicious' correction of defects which time had produced, and that at no time had he been disposed to go further than he now was. He realised that, contrary to his recent expectation, the advocacy of Reform had become seasonable. It was generally expected that Wellington would understand this too, especially when the cabinet decided that it would be unwise for the King to go to dinner at the Guild-hall because of the danger of disturbances *en route*. But instead of treating Reform as he had treated Catholic Emancipation, and doing a thing he hated because it must be done, the Duke made the cardinal error of closing the door on a Tory Reform Bill. Sir Thomas Acland could find no one to defend or even palliate the Duke's declaration, and so staunch an anti-Reformer as Lord Grenville, who a quarter of a century before had been the last Whig prime minister, confessed that 'absolute resistance, *in limine*, to *any* reform' was manifestly no longer practicable.[2]

The Duke's declaration automatically admitted Lord Grey to No. 10 Downing Street, to form a government which would stand or fall by Reform. Whether it stood or fell mattered more to the country than the fate of any other peacetime ministry in its history. For it carried on its shoulders the hopes of millions, and had to work under the suspicious and hostile eyes of Radical propagandists who did not much, if at all, prefer Whigs to Tories. The shoulders were aristocratic, as though the cabinet had been designed as a mannequin parade of rank and property.[3] Besides

---

[1] Professor Gash, in *Essays Presented to Sir Lewis Namier*, has shown that the news from France arrived too late to influence most of the elections.

[2] *Memoirs and Letters of Rt Hon. Sir T. D. Acland* (son of the member referred to), p. 35, 27th November, 1830; *Courts and Cabinets* (D. of Buckingham), p. 146, 21st November, 1830.

[3] Grey admitted this design.

eleven peers and baronets and close relatives of such were only two others, Charles Grant and Henry Brougham[1] and on the threshold of the cabinet stood Lord Auckland, Lord John Russell, Edward Stanley (eldest son of the heir of the Earl of Derby) and Viscount Duncannon. Of four cabinet ministers in the Commons, Althorp was the heir of Earl Spencer, Palmerston an Irish peer and Sir James Graham a broad-acred Border baronet. And, of course, the Whigs were all cousins. Lansdowne was the first cousin, and Richmond the second cousin, of Holland. The wife of Carlisle, and her brother the Duke of Devonshire (Lord Chamberlain)[2] were first cousins of Althorp and all three were first cousins of Duncannon and *his* sister, the notorious Caroline who had wed and worried William Lamb, now Home Secretary (as Viscount Melbourne). William's own sister, Emily, awaited only the death of her husband, Earl Cowper, to render conjugal her affection for the Foreign Secretary, Palmerston. Duncannon belonged, like Lady Grey, to the Ponsonby family. Grey's son-in-law, Durham, was Lord Privy Seal and his brother-in-law Edward Ellice was preferred to Lady Grey's cousin, Duncannon, as Chief Whip. Nor did the ministerial personnel fail to recall the legendary laxity of the eighteenth-century aristocracy which had peopled the great houses with 'so many children of the mist'. Grey had had a child by Devonshire's mother, the fabulous Georgiana. Melbourne inherited the estates and titles of his lawful father, and was bequeathed the wealth and property of his reputed progenitor, Lord Egremont. An illegitimate Russell figured among the lesser lovers of Caroline Lamb after her affair with Byron.

The 'Whig' government was not wholly Whig. No Whig had more than a few months' experience of cabinet office, and parliamentary aid had to be sought from many who had given more or less discriminating support to successive Tory governments. Since in 1829 some of the diehard Protestants had decided that there was nothing to be said for a representative system which allowed Wellington to emancipate the Catholics in defiance of massive national prejudice,[3] Grey was able to include in the cabinet the

---

[1] Brougham, his prestige advanced by his election for Yorkshire, foolishly allowed himself to be shifted to the Woolsack.

[2] Deafness disabled the Duke from pursuing an active political career.

[3] Gladstone in a draft of 1855 in Add. MSS 44745 opined that a reformed Parliament would have been less likely to grant Catholic Emancipation.

ultra-Tory Duke of Richmond. The Canningites, who had long ministerial experience, obtained three Secretaryships of State and the Board of Control. Not all the men who had been politically associated with Canning were to support the Whig Reform Bill, but the closest of his collaborators now abandoned as archaic their master's specific of obviating the need for constitutional reform by improvements in administration, taxation and commercial regulation which would appeal to the middle classes. It had been on a question of whether the members to be taken from the corrupt borough of Retford should go to Birmingham or be 'thrown into the county' that Huskisson and his friends parted from the Duke in 1828, and in February 1830 they approved Russell's motion to enfranchise Leeds, Manchester and Birmingham. Whiggery had no objection to the absorption of Canningites; what Grey had objected to was Canningites absorbing Whigs. It was of some importance that the head of the Canningite group, the industrious Huskisson, was killed by a steam locomotive just before Parliament met, on the eve of reconciliation with the Duke. He might have persuaded Wellington to undertake Reform.[1] His death facilitated the union of Canningites with Whigs, for Grey had disliked him even more than Wellington did, and only less than Grey had disliked Canning. After Huskisson the leading spokesman of the Canningites was Melbourne, who had been reared a Foxite Whig,[2] and only drifted into the moderate outworks of the Tory camp because he thought that during and at the end of the Napoleonic Wars the Whig attitude on foreign policy was deficient in patriotism and realism. He told the Duke that the Canningites would not rejoin him without bringing in Whigs as well. The leading Canningite in the Commons, Palmerston, gave the same answer — he roundly blamed the 'stupid old Tory party' for the crisis which necessitated Reform.[3]

The administration represented, if not in due proportion, all the streams of sentiment and judgement among public men which

[1] But in Huskisson's election manifesto (30th July, 1830, see Add. MSS 38753) a classic expostion of what Dr W. R. Brock called 'Liberal Toryism' (see *Lord Liverpool and Liberal Toryism*, 1939) there was no hint of concession on Reform.

[2] See Lord David Cecil's *The Young Melbourne*. He remarks that William Lamb, prematurely disillusioned, 'was cheerfully convinced that idealists — *excepting always the Foxite Whigs* (my italics) — were fools or hypocrites' (p. 70).

[3] The experiences and judgement which led Palmerston to change his allegiance are well treated of in Sir Charles Webster's *magnum opus*.

flowed to swell the reforming tide in Parliament. Since virtually the whole political class had rallied to Pitt, it was well-nigh inevitable that most of the cabinet should be the sons of men who on the national or local stage had supported that minister from either 1784 or 1794. Pitt, as ministers and other 'Reformers' who had spent their careers as Tories now hastened to recall, had early advocated parliamentary reform in the days when it was an open question in the Rockingham Whig party of which Fox was the leading light. Grey[1] and Holland, and Durham and John Russell by inheritance, represented the tradition of Fox and the *Friends of the People*. Lansdowne was the son of Shelburne, the Chathamite who sponsored the rise of the younger Pitt but became, during the Revolutionary War, a collaborator of Fox, despite the fact that it was to expel Shelburne from office that the Fox-North coalition had been formed in 1783. Shelburne's son, as Lord Henry Petty, rejected the overtures of Pitt and adhered to Fox, becoming in 1806, at the age of twenty-five, Chancellor of the Exchequer. He took to the Treasury as junior minister his contemporary, cousin and friend, Althorp. This young man had been brought up to 'beware all Whigs' by a father who had been one of the first to turn with Burke from Fox to Pitt in revulsion against the French Revolution.[2] The admonition was vain, for Althorp became associated with Whitbread in the so-called *Mountain*, which in modern times would have been called 'the left' of Whiggery. In November 1830 Grey gave Althorp the task of leading the Commons. The fact that he was a supporter of the ballot was no doubt some comfort to Radicals, earnest or wild, who deprecated the general character of the ministry. But their highest hope must rest in John George Lambton, now Lord Durham (for, having become by virtue of generations of coal royalties the richest commoner in England — and the most arrogant — Lambton had accepted in 1827 a peerage). It was good news to them that the most radical of the ministers was to preside over the sub-committee appointed to prepare a draft Reform Bill for the consideration of the Prime Minister and cabinet. The other members of this committee were Lord John Russell, Sir James Graham (who was in close contact with Althorp)

---

[1] Grey's own father was a Pittite, and was ennobled by Pitt.
[2] There is a *Memoir* by Le Marchant, 1876. Old Earl Spencer had become the colleague of Fox, Grey, Petty and Holland in the 1806 administration, but he had never recovered his pre-1792 Whiggism.

and Viscount Duncannon, who had long been the principal whip of the Whig Opposition.

The Bill, as approved by the cabinet, reached its final draft in February 1831. It was not at all the measure that these ministers in normal times would have agreed upon or their supporters accepted. In other circumstances the Whig oligarchy would have emasculated it at birth. When in 1810 the eighteen-year old Russell protested against an admission by Grey that he had lost both his ardour and his assurance of the efficacy of the proposals for Reform which he had made in the 'nineties, a sceptical Holland told his young friend that all that was required of a good Whig was 'a certain disposition to Reform of Parliament and no alarm at it if the present mode be found inadequate to secure the confidence and enforce the will of the people'.[1] This was not a very exigent test, and the Whig oligarchs further eroded its significance by their conclusions (the fruit of the experience of 1792–4) that a time of distress and agitation such as the post-war years 1815–21 was unseasonable for the advocacy of Reform. Since only unrest and agitation could shift the complacency with which the majority of the political nation viewed the existing representative arrangements, it was to be presumed that only an imminent threat of violent revolution could induce the Whigs as a whole actively to promote Reform. Though overt opposition to it in the highest circles of Whiggery had been reduced by the conversion of Earl Fitzwilliam[2] and the Duke of Devonshire and the defection of the old-world place-hunting Grenville connection[3] and of the Marquess of Cleveland,[4] it is fair to assume that for every avowed opponent of Reform there were a dozen noblemen who did not measure up to Holland's test. The electoral patronage at the disposal of Whiggery might be but a fraction of that employed in the Tory interest, but the hierarchs valued it and, as Brougham

---

[1] *E.C.J.R.*, No. 10, Vol. I, pp. 131 ff., 13th August, 1810.

[2] The 2nd Earl Fitzwilliam was converted by the violent break-up of the Reform meeting at 'Peterloo', Manchester, in 1819 and lost the Lord Lieutenancy of the West Riding for patronising a county meeting on the subject.

[3] The Grenvilles made their peace with Liverpool in 1823, the Marquess of Buckingham securing a dukedom and Chas. Wynn a place in the cabinet. The latter joined Grey's ministry in 1830 but resigned when the terms of the Reform Bill were known.

[4] It was said that the Earl of Darlington acquired electorial patronage in order to be made Marquess of Cleveland (he gained the title in 1827) and surrendered it (1831) to be made a duke. Mr Michael Brock has pointed out to me that according to Jenning's *Croker*, II, p. 52, Darlington had become a Reformer by February 1822. But he went over to Wellington in January, 1830.

complained,[1] often used it in the interest of relatives and friends without much heed for the Opposition's need of talented and industrious recruits in the Commons. But if the Whig party was still regarded as a sort of specialised subsidiary of the Whig caste, and the agency for the satisfaction of its appetite for offices and the exposition of its political prejudices, Whiggery as a caste had a certain loyalty to (as well as proprietary interest in) the party, and could be persuaded to accept policies, and even sacrifice interests, if it could be shown that a substantial gain in political influence, with access to official patronage, was likely as a result to accrue to the party and hence to the caste. A brute fact about the acceptance of Reform by Whiggery is that, as Charles Villiers said, 'the Whigs obtained and retained power by reforming the House of Commons'.[2] It looked as though, if a Reform Bill were passed, the loaves and fishes would remain indefinitely in the gift of the Whig leaders, and, within limits, the more thorough the Reform the surer the prospect of long retention of office.

Nevertheless, considerations of class, as well as of party advantage, needed to be pleaded if Whiggery was to be induced to accept a bill more drastic than most of the magnates, and, indeed, most of the ministers, really liked. Grey was able to persuade them that such a measure was necessary to make the country safe for Property and for their order, with which, he had told the Lords in 1827, he was resolved to stand or fall. Men who had not been prepared to press any Reform because times were unquiet and the subject unpopular with the existing electorate, were now persuaded that the subject was so popular and the times so threatening that the safety of the social order depended on the promotion of a substantial measure. No bill which could pass could meet the full aspirations of the leaders of the 'political unions' whose formation in large towns was a feature of 1830, but there must be a measure which would mollify their hostility to the establishment and thus have some prospect of 'finality'. A meagre proposal, such as Wellington might have framed in 1830, would be received by the public as an insult and would never be accepted as a settlement of

[1] See Aspinall, op. cit. Brougham could not find a seat in the 1812 Parliament. He had in 1810 succeeded Petty as member for Bedford's borough of Camelford, but that was then sold out of Whiggery. In 1816 Grey secured for him Darlington's borough of Winchelsea whence on his patron's defection he moved to Devonshire's Knaresborough, before being returned for Yorkshire in the 1830 general election.

[2] *Clarendon*, op. cit., Vol. I, p. 107.

the question. Safety lay in boldness. Because they were brought to appreciate this, conservative-minded ministers (Richmond, Melbourne, Palmerston, Lansdowne, to name but a few) accepted a plan the scope of which would have horrified them only a few months before. They prayed for 'finality', and all the cabinet except Durham accepted it as the prime objective. The main credit for the general proposals may lie with Durham and Russell, but it was Grey who, in his instruction to the sub-committee, laid down this major objective. It involved a departure from the position he had adopted as recently as the debate on the Address, for he had then spoken of the 'gradual' correction of defects. The change is explained by the alteration in the political temperature produced by Wellington's refusal to consider Reform.

'Finality' was an essentially conservative aim, and neither Radicals at the time nor the shrewder among later commentators on the Reform Bill failed to stress that it was a conservative measure, if only because it was framed and defended within the limits of Whig constitutional doctrine. Russell argued that there was a historical right of men with a substantial stake in the country (the old freeholders) to be represented.[1] But Whiggery absolutely rejected all notions or an abstract or historical 'right' to the franchise of all men, or all taxpayers, or all householders. The Whig approach to the constitution was based on the maxim *Salus Populi suprema lex*. The purpose of a constitution, Russell said in his book, was to ensure 'good government, the freedom of the people within the state and their security from without'. What was required of the electoral body was that it should be of average intelligence, 'not as a mass tainted with corruption', form upon the whole a security for the protection of property, and be 'identified with the general sense of the community'.[2] The existing electorial system did not meet these requirements; associated with corruption, it was itself an affront to the 'general sense of the community'. There must be a widening of the franchise and a re-distribution of seats. But there was no thought of destroying the general rule that each constituency should return two knights of the shire or two burgesses, no wish to overturn or undermine the ancient, traditional conception (which probably gave the Commons

---

[1] This argument was based on the reputed statute (in fact a petition never accepted by the King) *De Tallagio Concedendo* — see speech of 1st March, 1831.
[2] *Essay on the English Government and Constitution.* Cf. Palmerston's remarks to Gladstone, p. 300.

its name) that representation in parliament was the representation of *communites*,[1] and certainly no idea of dividing the country as a geographical area into constituencies with broadly equal electorates. For by 'the general sense of the community' or 'public opinion of the time' the Whigs did not mean the opinion of the majority of the people. It was not numbers that ought to be represented, but a selection of the community, including all parts and classes of it.[2] It was not citizenship which conferred a right to vote, but the judgement of Parliament as to which citizens comprised the men of substance and 'respectability' whom it was expedient should be represented. The representatives themselves ought, of course, not to be mere delegates, but men of independent judgement; not the slaves of public opinion but its directors.

At its highest level (which it rarely reached) the argument about the Reform Bill in 1831–2 between a Lord John Russell and a Sir Robert Peel was whether the measure would produce the situation described by Russell as ideal or whether it would make the House of Commons too subservient to *vox populi*, as Peel feared, and thus open the floodgates to democracy. Everybody knew that the Whigs desired the latter as little as the Tories. Indeed, it is easy to be cynical, and sum up the Whig ideal as a constitution which would allow Whiggery, through the Whig party, to govern at its discretion. In the days of Lord Liverpool, John Campbell had remarked that, though Grey and Grenville had more enlarged and liberal views on all matters of policy, they were 'greater aristocrats than any of the present Ministers. They would centre the whole power of the State in a few great families and they would have no sympathy with the body of the people'.[3] Radicals might sometimes make a distinction between Tories and Whigs by saying that the former regarded themselves as owners of the realm and the latter saw themselves as trustees,[4] but 'government of the people, for the people, by the privileged class' might have been taken as a motto by either. Consequently, the only valid Reform, in Whig eyes, was one which attacked the grievances and anomalies which made the existing arrangements unpopular — especially the spread

---

[1] The name 'Commons' arose before the evolution of the modern conception of 'peerage' as contrasted with 'commonalty'.

[2] But not yet, it appeared from the Bill, the working class.

[3] Campbell, op. cit., Vol. I, p. 254.

[4] *vide*, for example, Martineau, *History of the Thirty Years' Peace*, Vol. I, p. 555, and Harris, *History of the Radical Party in Parliament*, p. 25.

of nomination and corruption and the maldistribution of seats
which denied representation to Manchester, Leeds and Birmingham but gave it to Old Sarum, Gatton and Beeralston (or rather
to the owners thereof) — but stopped far short of household
suffrage,[1] equal electoral districts and a stiff and rigidly enforced
corrupt practice law, because the effect of these would be altogether destructive of the constitution.

The Whigs in 1831-2 played for high stakes. Success would
mean the settlement of a vital issue, avoidance of revolution, and,
they hoped, a predominance in the state such as the Whigs had
held under the early Georges and the Tories since the time of Pitt.
Failure would mean grave social turmoil, possibly social catas-
trophe, and loss of party prestige and prospects. Their best men,
conscious of the opportunity and the hazard, rose to the level of
events. 1st March, 1831, the date when Lord John Russell rose to
reveal the surprisingly well-kept secret of the contents of the Bill,
was to be remembered as a *dies mirabilis* in Whig history. Since no
one believed that the Whigs would go far in the direction of mass
enfranchisement, the key question was — how many seats were
to be taken from the existing parliamentary boroughs, of which
many were decayed to the point where an exiguous electorate was
absolutely at the command of a patron, a command which could be
traded on the open market? When Russell gave the answer — 160
— there were startled murmurs from behind ministers and a great
Tory roar. For this was nearly a third of all the English seats.
In the Tory reaction were compounded ridicule, relief, perhaps a
little grudging admiration. For here, surely, was a desperate
gambler's throw, a reckless, irresponsible proposal which lost its
power to alarm because there was no prospect whatever of the
House of Commons accepting it. But the Tories miscalculated.
They allowed a mammoth debate, instead of forcing an immediate division. And in the ensuing weeks public opinion
wrought a powerful influence. The diary of a moderate Whig tells
the tale:[2]

> 27th Feb. — Anything which amounts to the formation of a new
> Constitution I shall oppose. . . .

---

[1] Russell said on 1st March that the Government anticipated that the total
number of electors would increase by about half a million under the provisions
of the Bill.

[2] Campbell, op. cit., pp. 503-10.

2nd March — We are quite appalled. There is not the remotest chance of such a Bill being passed by this or any House of Commons. . . . This really is a revolution. . . . It is unquestionably a new constitution.

The general sentiment is that the measure goes a good deal too far. It is applauded by the Radicals and by *some* Whigs, but is very distasteful to a great part of the Whig party.

3rd March — The general belief is that the Bill must be thrown out on the second reading. I expect Ministers will then resign and anarchy begin. . . . I feel inclined as a choice of evils to support and even speak in favour of the Bill.

5th March — The measure takes very much with the country.

8th March — I still consider the Bill dangerously violent, but apprehend less danger from passing than rejecting it.

27th March — The *chance* of the Bill being carried by the present Parliament is the *certainty* that it would be carried by the new Parliament.

What saved the Bill was its calculated appeal to people outside Parliament. Its popularity was sufficient to secure it a second reading in the House of Commons by a majority of one, but not to prevent its mutilation immediately the committee stage was reached. There had, therefore, to be an election, if the Bill was to pass, and there was no constitutional difficulty in having it within a year of the previous one, because George III had in 1784 and 1807 triumphantly violated the eighteenth-century convention that a parliament should last for most of its septennial span.[1] Kings, and ministers who asked for a dissolution, had always regarded general elections as occasions for the return of a favourable majority and had strained every resource to secure it. Nobody could remember a ministry being defeated at a general election.[2] The usual apparatus of ministerial influence was systematically employed in 1831, under the able direction of Ellice, and the Whig magnates were levied in aid of the purchase of close boroughs and of votes in

[1] See Betty Kemp, *King and Commons 1660–1832*, for this convention. Both in 1784 and 1807 the King appealed to the electors to uphold a new ministry against the majority in the Parliament being dissolved. The previous elections had been in 1780 and 1806.

[2] The cases that came nearest were 1741 and 1830. But the law made an election necessary in both years and the materials for a Wellington majority were present after the 1830 elections if the Duke had been prepared to use them.

rotten boroughs. The King's name was freely used on behalf of ministers. What was new about the dissolution of 1831 was that it was not merely an appeal to the electorates to return a House to support the King's ministers, but an avowed request for the return of a House committed to a great, specific, measure of reform. And what was new about the election was that public opinion in its widest sense played a part it had never played before, operating through the narrow *pays légal* with such effect that almost every constituency which had any independence (as well as those dependent on Whig magnates), except some of the boroughs due to be disfranchised, returned men committed to 'the Bill, the whole Bill and nothing but the Bill'. Honourable men who saw the need for Reform, but could not stomach the Bill — such as Sir Thomas Acland in Devon — were swept aside. The verdict of the old electorate in favour of the creation of the new, of the old constituencies in favour of the creation of new constituencies, was a misted reflection of the popular will, but not a distorted one. In the new Parliament the second reading was granted by 367 : 231 and on 22nd September, 1831 the Bill passed by 345 : 236 and was ready to be carried up to the Lords by Lord John Russell.

Because the measure was large enough to please 'the Radicals and some Whigs', the oligarchs enjoyed a temporary popularity in circles where they were usually contemned. Radicals would not be satisfied with anything obtainable in the political context of 1831, but they were sufficiently impressed to further the success of the Whig enterprise without stressing too much that for them the Bill was only a first instalment. More important than the fleeting enthusiasm of the agitator Carlile in his prison and the brief muting of the plaints of Orator Hunt (until he pondered what the Bill would do to his constituency of Preston) was the response of solid, respectable elements in the community whose disenchantment with the old régime was the real source of its weakness. As Althorp said, 'if the middling classes in this or any other country were hostile to the form of government under which they lived, the government would never be safe'.[1] The Bill went far enough to give ground for hope that they would be attracted to the defence of the reformed constitution, and thus ensure its stability. A year before the Bill came out the *Westminster Review*, organ of the Benthamite Radicals, had hardly flinched from the prospect of a

[1] Speech of 1st March, 1831 as reported in *Annual Register*, pp. 20–1.

short, sharp convulsion ushering in the reign of Demos (a monster whom these intellectuals, after the fashion of British middle-class Radicals, were sure they could tame). But after the Bill was published, the *Westminster Review* declared that the Whigs were now, as in 1688, the acknowledged leaders of the community, having by one energetic step removed the estrangement between themselves and the 'community at large'.[1]

The estrangement was due to the aristocratic and propertied composition of Whiggery, and its tendency in a time of social unrest to identify itself with the establishment of which it was part, lest its criticism of abuses be taken, as in 1792, to indicate either sympathy with or a foolish indifference to the designs of social revolutionaries. Inhibited by the dreadful warning of 1792, the Whig leaders tended to confine their ambition to the hopeless objective of wooing the privileged political nation from its Tory allegiance. The same error — that of clinging to moderation so that actual or potential goodwill among those debarred from the *pays légal* is lost while increased support from the privileged minority is not gained — has been made in the mid-twentieth century by the United Party Opposition to the Nationalists in South Africa. It is a natural attitude for a class-conscious oligarchical côterie, even a benign one, to adopt in an age of social strife and striving, the product of educational advance and economic revolution. The Whigs could not bring themselves to try for office the hard way, by offering leadership to the emerging interests which sought political influence. They would not parley with the besiegers, and they found themselves distrusted among the besieged. Men more in contact with the common world had warned them of their folly. Francis Jeffrey, of the *Edinburgh Review*, as early as 1809 remarked:[2]

If the Whigs do not make some sort of coalition with Democrats, they are nobody, and the nation is ruined. . . . There are but two parties in the nation — the Tories, who are almost for tyranny, and the Democrats, who are almost for rebellion. The Whigs stand powerless and unpopular between them, and must side with, and infuse their spirit into, one or other of them before they can do the least good. Now the Tories will not coalesce with them, and the Democrats will;

[1] Issues of January, 1830 and April, 1831.
[2] Cockburn's *Life of Lord Jeffrey*, 1852, Vol. II, pp. 126–7, 22nd December, 1809.

and therefore it is the duty of the Whigs to take advantage of this, and to strengthen themselves by the alliance of those who will otherwise overwhelm both them and their antagonists.

Twelve years later, the Whig outlook not having changed, Jeffrey, while fearing the worst, thought the best that could be hoped for was that, to avoid revolution, the Tories would introduce some elements of liberalism into their policy.[1] This did occur, and it looked for some time as though the Liberal Conservative prescription for avoiding not only revolution but parliamentary reform was succeeding and that the Whig contribution to the public weal would consist of giving more or less assistance to the Canningites. When at last, in 1831, the Whigs heeded Jeffrey's admonition to find in 'the opulence, intelligence and morality of our middling people a sufficient quarry of materials to make or to repair a free constitution',[2] they were taking their last chance. They had always accepted, in principle, that the whole governing class was endangered by the refusal to broaden the representative system, and now they took the Radical propagandists, who said that the game was up unless the aristocracy hastened to conciliate the people,[3] at their word. As a consequence Francis Baring was able a few years afterwards to describe Whiggery as:[4]

A BODY OF MEN CONNECTED WITH HIGH RANK AND PROPERTY, BOUND TOGETHER BY HEREDITARY FEELINGS, PARTY TIES, AS WELL AS HIGHER MOTIVES, WHO IN BAD TIMES KEEP ALIVE THE SACRED FLAME OF FREE-DOM, AND WHEN THE PEOPLE ARE ROUSED STAND BETWEEN THE CON-STITUTION AND REVOLUTION AND GO WITH THE PEOPLE, BUT NOT TO EXTREMITIES.

The only argument for extensive Reform, perhaps the only argument for *any* Reform, which all Grey's ministers could conscientiously utter in unison was that it was necessary for the safety, influence and reputation of the governing class. Convinced that their task was essentially conservative, a rescue operation on behalf of rank and property, the authors of the Bill were able to

---

[1] ibid., p. 195, 15th April, 1821.   [2] ibid., p. 110, 18th September, 1809.
[3] *Political Register*, 13th June, 1829. Cf. speech of D. Whittle Harvey on the fourth day of the hustings at Chelmsford 1830. (Essex Record Office papers) — 'a contest between the pride of the artistocracy of both parties and the power of the people . . . if the Whigs and Tories should now succeed, they will succeed for ever . . .'.
[4] Mallet's *Northbrook*, pp. 32–3.

play the rôle which Whig hagiography ascribed to heroes of old. Here, they announced, was a crisis of the classical kind which Whiggery was pre-ordained to resolve, a challenge between a nation enraged and an aristocracy discredited by obscurantism and selfishness. They thought of themselves as fulfilling the mediatorial role which Burke had taught them to undertake in the American and Irish questions. They were endeavouring to detach from the ranks of those opposed to the constitution the middle classes, a large, inchoate body of people distinguished from 'mere mechanics' and labourers by wealth, property, education, by 'respectability', and therefore qualified to enter the *pays légal*. To the masses the Reform Bill offered nothing. It was an undemocractic, and anti-democratic, measure. It actually reduced the working class element in the electorate.[1] Russell told the House that of the thousands employed by Marshall of Leeds, 140 were householders, but only two would be enfranchised. In the shopping centre, all house-holders would acquire the vote; in the industrial district of Holbeck only 150 of 11,000.[2] The electorate was being widened to include 'the people', not 'the populace'. Lord Chancellor Brougham made this very clear:[3]

> ... If there is the mob, there is the people also. I speak now of the middle classes — of those hundreds of thousands of respectable persons — the most numerous and by far the most wealthy order in the community; for if all your Lordships' castles, manors, rights of warren and rights of chase, with all your broad acres, were brought to the hammer and sold at fifty years' purchase, the price would fly up and hit the beam when counter-poised by the vast and solid riches of these middle classes, who are also the genuine depositories of sober, rational, intelligent and honest English feeling. Unable though they be to round a phrase or point an epigram, they are solid, right-judging men, and, above all, not given to change. . . . Their support must be sought, if Government would endure — *the support of the people as distinguished from the populace*, who look up to them as their kind and natural protectors. The middle class, indeed, forms the link which connects the upper and lower orders, and links even Your Lordships with the populace, whom some of you are wont to despise. . . .

[1] It would be difficult to decide whether the actual number of working-class electors was reduced. But the proportion of the electorate that was working-class must have fallen, and in few constituencies after 1832 can this element have had much weight.

[2] H. of C., 17th December, 1831.   [3] H. of L., 7th October, 1831.

If we turn from the clever lawyer who, sprung from the class of
lesser landowners, now bore the style of Baron Brougham and
Vaux in memory of a mythical medieval ancestor, to one of the
splendid orations which qualified the member returned by Lord
Lansdowne at Calne to appear in the next parliament as member
for Leeds (with a Marshall as his colleague) we find that
Macaulay's theme was the same as Brougham's:[1]

> . . . a narrow oligarchy above — an infuriated multitude below; on
> the one side the vices engendered by power — on the other the vices
> engendered by distress; the one party blindly adverse to improve-
> ment — the other party blindly clamouring for destruction; the one
> party ascribing to political abuses the sanctity of property — the
> other party crying out against property as a political abuse. . . . God
> forbid that the state should ever be at the mercy of either or should
> ever experience the calamities which must result from a collision
> between them. . . .

It is always difficult, when the danger is past, to appreciate the
strength of apprehensions whose validity was never tested by
disaster. The idea of a social war, a war of classes, resulting either
in despotism or democracy, was not conjured up in 1831 as a novel
bogey to frighten faint hearts. Whigs had often enough in the
previous forty years seen it as the logical outcome of social stresses,
and abused the Tories for a purely negative and repressive response
to discontent. They had themselves no constructive proposals for
relief, but they saw that social discontent fed on and fostered
disloyalty to the constitution, and argued that an archaic electoral
system which brought disrepute on the whole governing class
(nor merely the party which profited most from its maintenance)
was a standing grievance and incentive to revolution. Sydney
Smith had said that whether despotism or democracy was the
outcome mattered no more to him than from which tube of a
double-barrelled pistol he met his death. If the reverend gentleman
stood in this peril in the 1820s, there could be no doubt that he
stood in more by 1831, for how else can one explain the virtual
unanimity of the belief in November 1830 that there must be some
Reform? But the Whigs found themselves at last in a position to
prescribe a heroic remedy for dissatisfaction with the constitution,
if not for social distress. Let Macaulay continue:

[1] H. of C., December, 1831.

... Between the two parties stands a third party, infinitely more powerful than both the others put together, attacked by both, vilified by both, but destined, I trust, to save both from the fatal effects of their own folly.... That party is the middle class of England, with the flower of the aristocracy at its head and the flower of the working classes bringing up its rear....

The social 'grand strategy' of the Reform Bill received its vindication in the Chartist fiasco of 1848, when Britain with her reformed constitution rode the storm unleashed by a new revolution in Paris. The middle classes, admitted to a share of political privileges without destroying aristocratic leadership, found that they could secure material advantages and legal facilities by pressure in and on the Legislature, and provided a solid bastion against political revolution and social subversion. Many of their prominent politicians, and most of the large urban electorates, were Radical and more or less dissatisfied with the settlement of 1832, and its harvest. But the great majority of Radicals never dreamed of acting unconstitutionally. After the Reform Bill there was, even among those who wished to democratise the constitution, the degree of loyalty to its processes required for its security.

If the resilience of the reformed constitution was revealed by the weakness of the revolutionary movement after 1832, it was the opinion of Charles Villiers that the survival of public institutions after the stormy struggle for the Bill was evidence of an extraordinary steadiness in the British people. 'The Whigs, to destroy their old opponents, carried a measure in a manner that, in any other country, would have irrevocably shaken to its base every institution by which an old community was held together.'[1] To the Tories, the means of carrying the Bill were worse than the Bill itself, and they prophesied that the Bill and the means, taken together, would have catastrophic results. For in the crisis of the Reform Bill 'the mob' as well as 'the people' had its place. After the Lords at 6.15 on the morning of Saturday, 8th October, 1831, refused the Bill a second reading (by 199 : 158), mobs wrought havoc in Derby, Nottingham and Bristol. The Tories pointed out, with glee, that all these were already parliamentary boroughs, in which the electorate was not to be greatly increased. It was more to the point that in none of them were there strong, well-organised

[1] *Clarendon*, op. cit., Vol. I, p. 123, 17th November, 1836 to Clarendon.

political unions which acted as powerful pressure groups but were held in check by 'respectable', moderate leadership. No one hoped more devoutly than ministers that the mob would keep its place. All was lost if reactionaries ceased to fear the mob; all was lost if mob action became general. No minister, save Durham, liked the political unions, but they were the best police forces available and a strong, moderate union leader was worth a troop of horse. That was the true lesson of the riots — for the mob had raged unchecked at Nottingham while the cavalry were restoring order at Derby, and at Bristol there was confusion and weakness on the side of lawful authority and ominous differences of morale between various units. A simultaneous outbreak in London and a dozen other large centres of population was not to be apprehended with equanimity even by those who thought solely in terms of military repression. The cabinet contrived to act as though it understood that, after 1st March, 1831, persecution of the unions was unnecessary, and that if it had become necessary it would have been ineffective. It would, indeed, have been provocative, for as long as ministers showed resolution in their task of passing the Bill, the unions held popular passion in check and showed themselves amenable to ministerial persuasion when they contemplated demonstrations likely to produce disorder. Althorp struck the right note when, after the Lords had rejected the Bill, he said that he would not remain in office a single hour unless he felt a reasonable hope that a measure equally efficient would be carried, and that 'there was only one chance of failure — if their disappointment led them to acts of violence, or to unconstitutional measures of resistance'.[1] There was a monster meeting at Birmingham, where Attwood led the prototype union, but it contented itself with a message of gratitude to and support for Althorp and Russell. Those ministers were allowed to thank Attwood for the address. It is not likely that the Prime Minister approved of Russell's reply, for, referring to the action of the Lords, Lord John said that the whisper of a faction would not be allowed to prevail against the voice of the nation. But it can only have done good at Birmingham.

As one reads the correspondence of ministers, it seems almost a miracle that they acted as though they appreciated that in willing the end they had willed the means — their bill could not become a statute without popular pressure which must in the last resort

[1] H. of C., 10th October, 1831.

amount to the menace of imminent uprising. The Home Office was repressive in outlook, and not given to the fine distinctions between trade unions, against which (especially in the agricultural districts) it was waging war with the advice of the Duke of Wellington, and political unions, which Grey himself thought more revolutionary than mere riots. Le Marchant, who was close to ministers, thought that no minister should have noticed the Birmingham mass-meeting except to censure it.[1] The Whigs felt the force of the Tory accusation that it was a dreadful precedent to connive at agitation, backed by ill-disguised threats of force, whose purpose was to overbear the mature judgement of one branch of the Legislature (if not both). They made clear that if the legal limits of agitation were exceeded — for example, by arming or drilling, conspiracy to withhold taxes, or the organisation of a *national* body acting as a para-parliament to coerce the sovereign legislature — the law would be invoked. This it was their duty to do; it would not have been safe for them to do more. They had not called the unions into being. They were very worried at the possibility of their slipping the leash. They appear to have been within an ace of provoking them into doing so, but wiser counsels prevailed.

The short answer to the Tory charges in respect of ministerial tolerance of organs of agitation was that the crisis was unique and the whole purpose of the Bill was to ensure that it remained unique. Sir Robert Peel complained of the assumption that 'to the pressure of external force we must give way, and that we had no alternative but that of satisfying the craving of the people'.[2] He feared that under the proposed electoral arrangements the *vis inertiae* of the constitution would be sacrificed.[3] How could it be otherwise, if it was ineffective now, *before* Reform? But the popular craving was violent because under the unreformed system the *vis inertiae* was so strong that only a quite exceptional unanimity of popular sentiment could sway legislators much more amenable to the influence of vested interests than popular aspirations. If it was right for Wellington, with Peel's concurrence, to emancipate Catholics because the alternative was rebellion in Ireland, why was it wrong for Grey to concede a more popular representation because the

---

[1] Le Marchant's *Althorp*, pp. 361–3. He was Brougham's secretary.
[2] H. of C., 17th December, 1831.
[3] H. of C., 22nd March, 1832.

alternative was rebellion in England? Diehard anti-Reformers, like diehard anti-Catholics, had the political vice of consistency. They were prepared to resist, at any cost, the will of a nation. But once it was conceded that *some* Reform was necessary, it became perverse to make an additional argument against the Bill out of the fact that it seized the imagination of the public, who insisted that it be passed. The Whigs had no desire to see the exceptional medicine of the constitution become its daily bread. They did not wish to see sober, responsible ministers and legislators continually overawed by *vox populi*; had not Burke said that the people were often outrageously wrong? But they contended that a parliament freed from the disrepute attaching to its unreformed predecessors would have powers of resistance to the passions of the moment which those predecessors culminatively had forfeited — and they devoutly hoped that they were right.

Viewed in the round, the Whigs of 1831-2 rose to a high level of statesmanship, displaying boldness of conception and patience, firmness and industry, and no little dexterity, in execution. But if this was so, it was small thanks to half the cabinet. While Brougham (who did not like the Bill) vacillated, the ex-Tory ministers and Lansdowne and Carlisle, at first carried along by Grey and Althorp and the current of popular favour to the point of asking and getting a Commons dedicated to 'the whole Bill', recoiled when they saw what was involved in the way of strife between Commons and Lords, public unrest and coercion of the King. They did not understand that there could be no retreat with honour to themselves, security to their order and safety to the state. When, two days after the Lords struck at the Bill, the Commons on the motion of Lord Ebrington reasserted (by 329 : 198) its 'firm adherence to the principles and leading provisions of that great measure and . . . its unabated confidence in the integrity, perseverance and ability of those ministers who, in introducing and conducting it, so well consulted the best interests of the country', it rebuked, impliedly if not intentionally, those ministers who had not been conspicuous in public commendation of the Bill and were now seeking in private an accommodation with the peers at the expense of the Bill. The more conservative ministers may almost have hoped, with the Tories, that the return of Lord Ashley in the Dorset by-election heralded a revulsion against the Bill on the part of the established political classes, which the tale of gutted buildings in three provincial cities would intensify. Palmerston alleged that the enthusiasts for the Bill induced their colleagues to agree to present a third version of it to Parliament early in December because by January public interest would have waned. But if delay had favoured the conservative wing by giving scope for leisurely discussions with the peers known as 'the Waverers' (led by Harrowby and Wharncliffe, men of Canningite associations) it is probable that the cabinet would have been broken up by those who could not condone a retreat which they would regard as a dangerous betrayal of popular hopes. Althorp suspected that only a Tory government could pass the Bill he had been conducting, but that there must be no Whig backsliding seemed to him crucial.

Somehow the front was maintained and no minister resigned over the decision to proceed before Christmas. But the cabinet had not yet faced the question of how the Lords were to be forced to accept their measure. They drifted, because of the fear that even one resignation would be fatal. Grey and Althorp thought that if a decision to ask the King for a large creation of peers would lose them Palmerston, Melbourne, Richmond, Lansdowne and possibly Stanley, a refusal to do so would lose them Durham and Graham. But on 13th January, 1832 the cabinet approved a minute which, in effect, required the King to place his prerogative of creation of peers at the disposal of his ministers. It was understood that a large creation would be asked for only in the last extremity. At the end of March, having survived threats of resignation from each of the most liberal ministers,[1] Grey was optimistic about the second reading, provided the Waverers declared in its favour, as they had agreed to do.[2] The Prime Minister knew only too well the difficulties which would arise with the King and with colleagues if a large creation was proposed, and thought the step itself 'a certain evil . . . very uncertain of success', for it might lose the vote of an affronted peer for every vote it added. He was concerned for 'the constitutional character and efficiency' of the House of Lords in the future. A large creation would be an act of 'extreme violence . . . dangerous . . . as a precedent'.[3] Of all the

---

[1] Graham, Durham, Hobhouse, Althorp, Russell.

[2] The Bill passed the Commons on 22nd March, 1832, by 355:239 (compared with 324:162 on the second reading in December).

[3] See Grey's long letter to Althorp, 11th March, 1832, Le Marchant, op. cit., pp. 407–13. Le Marchant is a first-rate authority for the divisions in the cabinet at this time.

principal architects of the Bill Grey was most tender towards the Lords. But he also understood better than most that the whole matter of peer-creation was an involved game of bluff. In the event, the Lords passed the second reading, but there was immediate obstruction in committee. The cabinet then agreed to give the King the choice between guaranteeing the passage of the Bill and finding a new administration. The King chose the latter, and sent for the Duke of Wellington.

Eighteen months earlier, the Duke could have carried with comparative ease a measure far more moderate than the Whig Bill, but now he could not make a ministry on such a basis, and his attempt to do so was regarded as an insult to the nation. Once more Lord Ebrington carried (by a majority of 80) a motion of confidence in the Whig ministers and their bill. There were excited scenes at Brooks's, but Stanley joined Althorp in pleading for restraint,[1] and it was resolved that there should be no factious resistance to the Duke, no appeal to the Commons to ask the King for their reinstatement of the Whigs, least of all any appeal to the nation to coerce the King. The nation needed no asking; revolution was nearer than at any time since 1688. While the Whigs were in office there was a link, oft-strained but adequate, between the cabinet, through Durham, and the Reformers out of doors, amongst whom Francis Place, 'the Radical tailor of Charing Cross', acted as broker between the more 'respectable' and the more proletarian political associations of the metropolis. The King had snapped the link at its Whitehall end, by reducing the Whigs to the status of ministerial caretakers, and Place concerted the plans of the London men and deputations from the provinces. On 18th May Hobhouse conveyed to a Whig conclave grave news of projects for a run on the banks ('To stop the Duke, go for gold'), resistance to taxes, armed drilling and worse. Lord Milton then proposed in the Commons an address to the King for the recall of the Whigs, but during the debate the cry 'It is settled' drifted into the chamber. Nine days after the King had made the wrong choice between alternatives, he had to recall Lord Grey. Everybody knew that as many peers as might be necessary would be created, and on 7th June, fifteen and a half months after the first act of the drama on 1st March, 1831, 2 William IV C 45 became law.

[1] Though in a speech of great violence — Aspinall, *Three Diaries*, p. 251, n. 3, citing Le Marchant at the time.

A 'not very murderous instrument', Professor Gash calls it, and the title of his book, 'Politics in the Age of *Peel*' is vivid proof of his assertion that the 'political fibre was tough enough to withstand' it. Old political attitudes and electoral manners survived, and, with them, aristocratic leadership. Posterity tends to view the legislation of 1832 as merely the first in a series which ended in broadly equal electoral districts and universal suffrage. There were optimistic Radicals who hailed it as such at the time, and Tory pessimists who murmured *Facilis descensus Averno*. But the Whigs, who knew that democracy would be the death of them, made an intelligent effort to frame a settlement that would last, and it is entirely probable that they delayed the arrival of the critical stage in the approach to democracy which, on the superficial view, they initiated.

It would be naive to imagine that the Whigs framed their bills without consideration of their own party interests. The Reform-hating Duke of Buckingham wrote — 'Ministers had three objects in view — to weaken their rivals, to secure the support of their Radical associates and to maintain their own possession of power; and no measure could have been better adapted for the attainment of such objects.'[1] Disraeli wrote that 'there existed . . . a prevalent conviction that the Whig party, by a great stroke of state, similar in magnitude and effect to that which in the previous century had changed the dynasty, had secured to themselves the government of the country for at least the lives of the present generation'.[2] To this day suspicion is always voiced, as a matter of routine, of the good faith of ministers responsible for electoral changes.[3] The

---

[1] *Courts and Cabinets*, p. 245.

[2] *Coningsby* (Bradenham edition 1927), p. 67.

[3] In 1948 Mr Winston Churchill moved a reasoned amendment for the rejection of the Representation of the People Bill on the ground, *inter alia*, that Labour had departed, for partisan reasons, from the recommendations of the Boundary Commissioners. In 1955 the Labour Opposition accused the Conservative government of partisan reasons for refusing to depart from the recommendations of the Boundary Commissioners. In 1959 Labour spokesmen were as sure that the abolition of restrictions on the use of cars at elections was a partisan measure as the Tories had been that the abolition of University seats in 1948 was a partisan measure. Incredulous laughter greeted in February 1931 Sir Herbert Samuel's claim that the Liberals were not concerned with the effect of the Electoral Reform Bill on their electoral fortunes. This party, at the time of its last electoral majority, had missed the opportunity for Electoral Reform because it had not read the writing on the wall; it changed its mind a little too late. In 1884 it was well understood why Tories, Whigs and Radicals had different criteria for the redistribution of seats. The element of minority representation introduced by Disraeli in 1867 was intended to benefit his party. Russell in

Whigs, reared in the political morality of Georgian England, were certainly no purists in these matters, nor immune from the natural desire of a party administration to weaken its rivals and improve its own electoral prospects. The will to derive partisan benefit from Reform is not likely to have been absent from the leaders of a sect which had not had a working majority in living memory. It is altogether necessary, when considering the Bill in terms of high strategy, national conciliation, judicious adjustment of the constitutional balance in response to current pressures, and the search for constitutional stability and social order, to remember the lesser lights by which politicians move. If, for instance, one takes seriously Lord Malmesbury's allegation that Durham and Ellice in Northumberland in 1830 were full of talk of 'the rearrangement of the boroughs and the franchise, their great object being to "cook" them (as they themselves called it) so as to expel as much as possible all local interests belonging to the Tories',[1] and associates it with the verdict of the American scholar Seymour, that 'the legerdemain which they practised in constructing and altering the schedules certainly arouses our distrust . . . but . . . if they had been invariably severely honest, their own party would have deserted them',[2] one sees the Whig Reform seriously disfigured. But Seymour says, elsewhere, that there is no prima facie case for a charge of 'wholesale gerrymandering',[3] which cancels Malmesbury's allegation and reduces the problem to its proper proportions — the prima facie case for a charge of fairly widespread partisan contrivance *within* the broad outlines of the scheme of Reform which, as a whole, is to be regarded rather as a product of statesmanship than of partisanship.

The prima facie case based on the 'legerdemain' which 'arouses our distrust' is greatly weakened by closer examination, for it rests in large part upon the disingenuous nature of ministerial argument in the debates on the second Reform Bill, which was the first to be

the 'fifties was concerned to concoct constituencies likely to return moderate Liberals.

[1] *Memoirs of an ex-Minister* (1885 ed.), p. 29. I had thought that Malmesbury was referring to the period just after the formation of the Grey government, but Mr Michael Brock has convinced me that the reference is to late summer or early autumn. It is therefore quite worthless as evidence, and doubtless, in any case, the young Tory was being 'ragged'. He was staying with his father-in-law, Tankerville, whom he describes as a Whig opposed to Reform; Mr Brock calls my attention to Greville's remark (*July* 1830) that he had become an ultra-Tory.

[2] *Electoral Reform*, Yale, 1915, p. 74.   [3] ibid., p. 67.

debated in detail. Having set up a mathematical basis for the inclusion of boroughs in Schedules A and B (those that were to lose
both or one of their two members respectively), ministers allowed
themselves to be drawn into argument on the relative merits of
particular boroughs, during which they tended to describe a place
as a decayed and inconsiderable nomination borough or a place
capable of providing a respectable constituency, according to the
fate proposed for it by the Bill. This was the result of their admission that some of the 1821 census returns misrepresented the situation of boroughs, and their willingness to consider petitions on
that ground; they had then to defend their refusal to accept many
of the petitions. There was a deep Tory conviction that ministers
were not altogether impartial in deciding between rival statistics
where the interests of some Whig magnate, a Lansdowne or
Carlisle, were involved, and that there were 'bargains' with
Calcraft of Wareham, Lopes of Westbury, Smith of Midhurst and
another Smith (Lord Carrington) of Aylesbury, to preserve their
boroughs in return for their support. We must agree with Seymour
that the Whigs sometimes gave themselves the benefit of the doubt;
it may be that in regard to Calne they even connived at the creation
of doubt in order to give Lansdowne the benefit of it. But it seems
likely that in these debates the Whigs did themselves less than
justice. However that may be, the fate of all the boroughs went into
the melting pot again after the rejection of the Bill by the Lords.
The test for disfranchisement was made to depend, as the Tories
had urged, on the 1831 census, and instead of mere population (it
had been proposed to put all boroughs of less than 2,000 in
Schedule A) a combination of houses and assessed taxes was to be
decisive. Thus any bargain incompatible with the new standard for
disfranchisement — unless it depended principally upon which
boundary was taken as constituting the parliamentary borough —
was automatically cancelled. Midhurst and Wareham remained
outside Schedule A, but Westbury and Morpeth reappeared
in Schedule B and Calne and Horsham entered it for the first
time.

One may accept every word of the Duke of Buckingham's
indictment, and yet misjudge the Whigs if one persists, as the Duke
did, in admitting no *national* grounds for Reform. For the Whigs
were in the happy position of finding that what was popular, and,
in the view of their wisest leaders, requisite in the national

interest, was bound to be electorally profitable, and perhaps more profitable than any other conceivable arrangement. They could not achieve their national and class purposes without detaching from the constituency list some 150 seats overwhelmingly Tory; without transferring some of them (less than half) to newly enfranchised towns which would probably be overwhelmingly Liberal and more to the landed interest which would not be Radical and might be Whig; without conferring the vote on the 'shopocracy' which was the provincial strength of Whiggery. 'The great point', said Buckingham, 'was the annihilation of the close boroughs. . . . That gained, they did not question their ability to deal with the Radical interest in the House, should it run counter to their own.' But the Whigs would never have obtained a majority for their proposals if Reform had not been urgent, and once it had become urgent the annihilation of the close boroughs was essential if there was to be 'finality'. The Whigs said that the object of their schedules A and B was to strike at nomination.[1] If we measure their proposals against the yardstick of Oldfield's list of boroughs wholly or partially controlled in 1816,[2] the coincidence between proposals and professed purpose is impressive. Oldfield thought that 207 members from 108 boroughs were nominated. Schedule A as finally enacted removed 105 of them from 53 boroughs and Schedule B affected 30 boroughs returning 58 of these nominees. So only 44 seats (21%) in 25 boroughs (23%) escaped punishment. But only 24 (13%) in 14 boroughs ($11\frac{1}{2}$%) failed to be included at some time or another in Schedule A or B. It is difficult to imagine that any statistical test could have been more effective in segregating the nomination boroughs from those that were not. The reprieve of 8% was the net effect of the acceptance of a petition seeking to substitute another boundary for that taken in the first Bill, the change of test, and the reduction of the numbers of Schedule B first from 47 to 40 and then to 30[3]— concessions

---

[1] The distinction between the treatment of boroughs under Schedule A and Schedule B was of course illogical, but the line had to be drawn somewhere, and it was reasonable to suppose that the B boroughs, being more populous and wealthy, would be able to provide more of the new £10 electors than the smaller ones.

[2] This list is not free from inaccuracies, and there had been changes between 1816 and 1831, but it is the best that was current at the time.

[3] Schedule A was held at 56 boroughs (counting the loss of two members by Weymouth and Melcombe Regis as equivalent to the disfranchisement of a borough). The reduction of Schedule B to 40 took place in two stages April–

about which the Tories had no right to complain, since they demanded the abolition of Schedule B altogether. It is, however, true that the majority of the reprieved boroughs remained free from Tory control, so that the Whigs as a body had no reason to object to the concessions and certain Whig magnates had cause to bless them.[1]

The small boroughs left with one or two members would be subject to the new £10 franchise, the extinction of the votes of non-resident freemen, and often to boundary extension as well, so that the character of some of them as constituencies was changed overnight. Magnates (like the Duke of Somerset in competition with the Tory corporation at Totnes) set about changing others by the creation of 'faggot' voters. It is, therefore, difficult to know how far in each case the future electoral history of a borough could be correctly forecast,[2] especially where there were a large number of (highly corruptible) resident freemen. The increase in voters was not as great as the Whigs prophesied. The test for disfranchisement bore no relation to the size or independence of the *future* electorate. (The principle of determining the fate of a parliamentary borough by statistics relating to its *existing* population or resources, and not to its prospective electorate and boundaries was followed again in 1867 and 1885.) As a result of this irrational approach, the commissioners, headed by Lieutenant Drummond (Althorp's secretary, and later Under-Secretary in Ireland) were compelled to scour country parishes for handfuls of electors to make up the prescribed minimum of 300. Sometimes, as at Arundel, their proposals were very convenient for a Whig

June 1830; at the same time the original Schedule A of 60 boroughs was amended to 55 and then 57.

[1] By the concessions of April 1831 Malmesbury escaped from Schedule A and Morpeth, Westbury and Wycombe escaped altogether. All might be expected to be Whig pocket boroughs. The change of test restored Morpeth and Westbury to Schedule B, but not Wycombe, which Seymour thought should have suffered. The change of December 1831 to a Schedule B of only 30 appeared to benefit only one Whig magnate (Lord Dundas at Richmond) to the extent of leaving two members for a threatened borough in his control. But at Marlborough the heir of the Bruces and at Thetford the Fitzroys were Whig; both had a sharing arrangement with the (now Tory) Barings.

[2] The suicide of Calcraft, patron at Wareham, had been attributed to the ostracism of his friends consequent on a supposed bargain with the Government as a result of which he was returned as a Whig county member. In December 1831 Wareham escaped into Schedule B, but the borough was so extended that a long battle between the Calcrafts and Draxes ensued. Who could foretell the fortune of battle? Lopes turned out to be speaking the truth when he said his family would not in future control Westbury. But might they not have done so if his heir had not gone Tory?

magnate.[1] Sometimes, as at Windsor, their failure to recommend a fairly obvious means of increasing the electorate by the addition of a neighbouring place suited Whig partisans.[2] In two cases, on the second Bill, ministers avowedly departed from their own rules, and sentenced Downton and St Germans to extinction on the ground that a respectable constituency could not be found. Downton was a Whig nomination borough sacrificed by the will of its Radical patron, Lord Radnor. The treatment of Tory St Germans seemed partisan. Members did not like these departures from the tests and they were not repeated, although the commissioners by no means always succeeded in finding the mystical number of 300. There is room for suspicion that Whig interests were favoured in drawing up boundaries, with marginal effect on future elections. But Tory as well as Whig preserves are found among the smallest surviving boroughs. The case of Arundel shows that not every partisan choice of boundary could survive local criticism.[1] And it would not be just to assume that every failure to find a 'respectable' constituency was deliberate.

The conclusion must be that partisan contrivance did exist, but that it was peripheral to the general scheme of Reform. To give the Whigs bright electoral prospects it did not need to be more than peripheral. For they could not save the nation without saving themselves. Their main advantage flowed from the broad scope and general features of the Bill, which were defensible on the ground that a larger measure would not be 'safe' and a smaller one could not be 'final'. Of course, a project which obliterated scores of Tory seats, with only modest Whig sacrifice (borne mainly by a very few magnates) and yet preserved, with some Tory boroughs, nearly as many seats which Whig patrons might hope to dominate, was very attractive from a party point of view, and won support on that account. But the scheme was more basically the project

---

[1] This case, discussed by Gash, in *Politics in the Age of Peel*, was described by Lord Dudley Stuart in the debate in the House of Commons on Russell's Reform Bill of 1852. He, as their member, in 1832 championed the citizens of Arundel in their resistance to the plan to add to the borough for parliamentary purposes the Howard preserve of Littlehampton. They were successful and in the restricted area the Duke of Norfolk did not succeed in ejecting Stuart till 1837.

[2] Mr Brock has called my attention to an entry in the diary of E. J. Littleton, a boundary commissioner (soon to be a Whig minister), 29th December, 1831, to the effect that Grey would not allow Eton to be added to Windsor — 'The real cause of the objection is with Mr Stanley, the Member, who very wisely suspects that the Eton Parsons are not with the Govt' (quoted by permission of Lord Hatherton).

of a landed oligarchy than of a partisan clique. The class view of what constituted the national interest fixed the Reform Bill within limits which gave the Whigs *as opposed to the Radicals* the same advantage that a relatively extensive disfranchisement gave the Whigs as opposed to the Tories.

It has rightly been remarked that the Whigs merely recognised a situation and were not so much the creators of Reform as the instruments of its enactment.[1] But they were the creators of the Bill, and they knew what they were about. Subject individually to second thoughts, intellectual confusion, irresolution and apprehension and (even the best of them) to sheer battle-fatigue, they proved, collectively, that they were not to be deterred by the Tory parade of King Charles's head and Louis Capet's or by the invocation of Whig ghosts. If heads had fallen after initial concessions, they knew it was because concessions had been obstinately denied and too late, too grudgingly, often too insincerely, granted. If they had hearkened to Lord Eldon and Sir Robert Inglis they would have been emulating not Lord Somers but James II and Marie Antoinette and they might have involved their whole order in the fate of the Bourbon court. Events were to show that the Whigs had a truer appreciation than their opponents of the relative unimportance of constitutional forms and the limited effect of constitutional reforms. The Tories were quite right to see in the Reform Bill the first of a series which would lead Britain to democratic institutions. But the next step did not come till 1867, and could have been postponed. The change after 1832 in the distribution of power between classes was gradual. The change in the general character of the personnel of politics was more gradual still. Had it been otherwise, this book would never have been written, for the Whigs would have had no future. The Tories predicted Hell and feared a savage Purgatory. The Radicals hoped for Paradise. They emerged into a workaday political world not essentially different from the old.

[1] Gash, op. cit.

CHAPTER II

The Coach Upset, 1834

To pass the Reform Bill was not enough. Unless the settlement could be consolidated, Whig laurels might go to make a Radical bonfire. The authors of the Bill might see their objectives discarded, their admonitions ignored, their interest ruined and the gloomiest forebodings of the Tories fulfilled. The Whig ministers knew that they were on trial, no less in 1833 than in 1831 and 1832. They awaited the election results under the new registers with trepidation, and received them with relief. For the elections generally, and notably in London, passed off quietly.[1] During the battle for Reform, Althorp had predicted that the same sort of men would be returned as before, and now the Solicitor-General could say 'the machinery has worked beyond our most sanguine hopes and almost universally the very men have been returned that would have been wished for',[2] except in Ireland. More borough members were 'persons of consideration' and less of 'the Blackguard Interest' than Melbourne had feared.[3] Graham's prediction, under the motto 'Breakers Ahead', that the Radicals would be stronger than ministers had imagined and 'the Destructives' would overpower 'the Conservatives'[4] now seemed unduly alarmist. But the first session of the new Parliament would be of critical importance. For, as Althorp had foreseen, the difference between the members of the new House and their predecessors lay in the increased susceptibility of representatives to influence from their constituencies. Melbourne had grown grave as reports reached him of violent talk at election meetings and pledges asked and made 'in a very positive manner'. The Home Office was still obsessed by the menace of labourers' unions, corresponding societies and seditious speech and writing. Expectations of reform were manifold and exaggerated and, in the main, doomed to disappointment.

[1] *Corr. of Pss. Lieven & Earl Grey*, Vol. II, pp. 428–9.
[2] Campbell, op. cit., Vol. II, p. 23.
[3] *Melbourne*, Vol. I, p. 146. [4] *E.C.J.R.*, No. 165, 5th December, 1832.

Given time, no doubt, the pressure groups which had arisen during the Reform struggle would wane, and parliamentary traditions, together with the exertions of the Patronage Secretary, would do their work of moderation. But, if the Radical Stooks Smith could find only two dozen dyed-in-the-wool Radicals in the new House of Commons, the droves of 'Reformers' faced by less than 150 avowed Tories in a House of 658 were a motley crew. Unlike the Labour-Socialist host which sang 'the Red Flag' in 1945, they lacked an anthem. But strident and discordant voices would sound on the ministerialist side. Revolt by many more than two dozen must be accounted likely. Ministers would need the gifts of luck, judgement and leadership. The need for efficient leadership in the House of Commons had been understood for generations. The striking disparity, until Lord Liverpool's day, between the length of tenure of the premiership by peers and members of the Commons emphasised it. Patronage had never been enough of itself to secure the management of the Commons, and there was less of it now. The more effective bond of 'party' was already taking its place. But party was very far from being the omnipotent machine it has since become, and many of those returned to the first reformed Parliament had little or no experience of such party discipline as did exist. In those days Government did not engross most of the time of the House of Commons. Private members had ample opportunity to express themselves in the service of a cause or an interest, or for the delectation of readers of local newspapers controlled by their sympathisers.[1] These opportunities provided a safety valve.[2] But their existence meant that ministers were constantly exposed to criticism and even abuse from their own side, which more developed techniques of management confine to party meetings behind closed doors. Althorp was no alarmist, but on New Year's Day he informed the Prime Minister that if ministers could weather the session without mischief being done, things would settle down and they would be

[1] Not till 1835 did Mondays and Fridays become Government days 'by the courtesy of the House' and not till 1837 were amendments to particular Orders of the Day forbidden. (See P. Fraser, 'The Growth of Ministerial Control in the Nineteenth-Century House of Commons', *E.H.R.*, LXXV, No. 296, July 1960.) He accepts contemporary criticisms of the loquacity of members and notes that in 1833 the discussion of petitions during regular hours of business was abandoned, as it threatened to monopolise the time of the House.

[2] Both in the sense that Radicals were able to 'blow off steam' and in the sense that the arrangements were not adapted to the passage of a large legislative programme.

known as national benefactors, but that, if the House slipped out of their hands and ran wild, Reform would lead to revolution and they would always be considered as destroyers of their country.[1]

Ministers, then, had to win time. They had, as Graham said, 'to steady the direction and check the velocity of the irresistable machine'. They must try to preserve the status quo in all its essentials, and yet maintain a minimal hold on a heterogeneous concatenation of 'Reformers', variously described, and describing themselves, as 'conservative', 'Whig', 'moderate', 'constitutional', 'liberal', 'convinced', 'Radical', 'thorough-going' and 'advanced' — the motley which was to be called 'the Liberal party'. There would be demands for triennial, even for annual, elections, for the ballot, for the abolition of the Lords, for the disestablishment of the Irish Church and the exemption of necessities from taxation — all of them things that ministers were not prepared to concede. Althorp saw that there must be a loose rein, and urged that there should be a liberal policy. Ministers, he said, could win command only by 'taking the lead in Popular Measures'. From 'the largest constituent body in the Empire' (the West Riding) his friend Morpeth told him what the electors, in a moderate and sensible mood, and unimpressed by hostile demonstrations from political unions, wanted. All they required was the abolition of slavery, 'a full measure of Church Reform' embracing tithes and rates, economy and reduced taxation, especially of corn, malt and soap.[2]

The ministers had luck. The harvest of 1832 was good, so that only the farmers were complaining and there was no irresistable demand for interference with the protection accorded to the landed interest. But their judgement was less good. The King's Speech offered a meagre bag of game for ambitious sportsmen. The omission of the abolition of slavery, for which there was a demand from people far from Radical, was an error of Grey's which had to be rectified. A bill was passed, after much amendment, which gave the West Indian planters and South African slavemasters £20 million, most of which flowed back to their British creditors. Russell and Lansdowne secured £20,000 p.a. for education at home. The revision of the charter of the Bank of England, giving

---

[1] Buckley's *Parkes*, p. 114.
[2] Le Marchant's *Althorp*, pp. 447–8, Morpeth to Althorp, 26th December, 1832.

new legal facilities to private banks, and of the charter of the East India Company, opening the China trade, represented triumphs for the provincial moneyed classes. But if the budget exempted tradesmen's windows, it disappointed urban householders by retaining the house tax and it disappointed the rural interests by making no concession on malt. It became evident, moreover, that there was to be no widespread administrative reform, and that the foreign policy of Lord Palmerston could not be relied upon to be cheap. While two major projects, the reform of municipal corporations and of the poor law, awaited the results of elaborate inquiry, relatively minor proposals of Church reform in England belied Peel's jibe that the Reform Bill would prove 'a charter of Dissent'. They showed that the Whigs, like the Tories, were prepared to attack the evils of pluralism and non-residence which impaired the efficiency and reputation of the established Church but were not over-eager to remedy the grievances of Dissenters. The abolition of compulsory Church rates (postponed by the Lords till 1868) was not offered till 1834 when it was accompanied by commutation of tithes, marriage in Dissenting chapels and the abolition of University tests. All these were offered on terms that irritated Noncomformists, and showed that the expediency of concession, rather than the justice of the claim, was the motive force. None was enacted. 'What would the Whigs have done without the Dissenters? And how could the Dissenters be worse without the Whigs?' asked the member for Wolverhampton.[1]

Within a few months of the general election there began a sharp reaction against the Whigs in the country, and by February 1834 three ministers had been defeated in by-elections. In April 1833 Capt. Berkeley lost a third of his votes and the representation of Gloucester to a Tory. In May Sir John Cam Hobhouse, Chief Secretary for Ireland, dropped 1,700 votes, and with a Conservative intervening and taking 738, found himself 192 behind the obstreperous Radical Colonel de Lacy Evans, who thus became member for Westminster. In the general election Hobhouse had beaten Evans by two to one.[2] Grey found himself confronted by demonstrations such as the opponents of the Reform Bill had said

---

[1] *Clarendon*, op. cit., p. 107, Chas. to Geo. Villiers, 1836.

[2] These elections were necessitated by the rule that ministers (with a few exceptions) must stand for re-election upon appointment. Capt. Berkeley had become a Lord of the Admiralty and the third defeat was that of Campbell at Dudley on his promotion to the Attorney-Generalship.

CHARLES, 2nd EARL GREY
by J. Lawrence
National Portrait Gallery

would be a natural consequence of the Bill and the means of passing it. Grey's letters to Melbourne about the need to find means of checking public meetings avowedly designed to coerce the Legislature, and his hope that 'a good jury' would find seditious content, might have been written by Castlereagh or Sidmouth, the Tory ministers of the post-war repression whom the Whigs had execrated. There were very strong demands for old-fashioned 'economical reform' by way of abolishing paid sinecures and offices performed by deputy, reversions and grants for several lives, and strictly limiting pensions. The Government was compelled to submit to the House of Commons voluminous information on these matters, and on the details of the civil and military establishments of the country. On 18th April, 1833 Althorp accepted resolutions moved by Hume that no future vacancies in sinecure offices or remunerated offices performed by deputy should be filled, and produced legislation to that effect. Nevertheless, on 16th July Ruthven carried by 88 : 79 a resolution that the reduction of taxation and of the public burdens were of paramount importance, and that all sinecures not merited by public service should be abolished throughout the British Empire. The Government declined to deprive living persons of their emoluments or pensions or to confiscate without compensation hereditary or legally conferred expectations. As to pensions, it insisted that as much had been done as could justly be done; under its legislation the Pension List (£203,058 in 1820, £180,744 in 1830, and currently £168,595) would fall to £75,000 as pensioners died off. This progress was too slow for Daniel Whittle Harvey and Joseph Hume, who on 18th February, 1834 moved for a select committee to examine each pension individually; the Government's amendment asserting the duty of the King's advisers to recommend (only) deserving persons for grants was carried by a majority of only eight (190 : 182). On the night of 5th–6th May Althorp was again under heavy fire. The House by 390 : 148 preferred a Liberal amendment for a select committee into abuses in the Pension List to Harvey and Hume's motion for an inquiry into each pension to see whether it was merited,[1] but defeated the amended motion by only 311 : 230. It was on this occasion that Althorp admitted that 'he had not the support of the great majority out of doors'. He stated that, in defence of their refusal to hack the pensions of living beneficiaries,

[1] The Liberal amendment was proposed by Strutt and Romilly.

ministers were prepared to 'risk all the reputation that they had won'. He was at the same time resisting the strenuous demands of the agriculturists for relief from malt tax. But it was the house tax which was the cause of the most serious unrest in the country, and the Government decided that it must yield to urban agitation. Not disguising that he did so against his judgement, the Chancellor of the Exchequer included the repeal of the tax in his 1834 budget.

Across St George's Channel too the ministry encountered agitation and resistance to authority. O'Connell described his country as insulted and trampled on by 'the insanity of a wretched old man with a childish hatred and maniacal contempt for the people of Ireland, interested, apart from his hostility to Ireland, only in procuring for his family and relations the greatest possible quantity of the public spoil'.[1] Grey, Melbourne and Edward Stanley (Chief Secretary for Ireland 1830–3) were as insistent as any Tory that the first duty of government is to maintain law and order, life and property, and they did not shrink from Draconian measures, suited to a rebellious colony, in John Bull's other island. The prestige of O'Connell, enhanced by his achievement of Catholic Emancipation, rendered resistance to tithe, and disorder which he did not discountenance, more respectable than obedience to laws not supported by public opinion. Even Althorp had admitted, when ministers first came into office, that O'Connell must be put down, whatever the means necessary. But the importance of having O'Connell's support in the Reform struggle inhibited ministers from proceeding with the prosecution which was to have tested whether 'the Liberator' or the King's Lieutenant was governor of Ireland. And then the results of the first general election in Ireland under the reformed system proved hardly less disconcerting to Whitehall than the Nationalist successes were to be in 1880. Although the Irish Reform Act left the franchise heavily weighted in favour of property, which was largely Protestant and almost wholly unionist, the Repealers overhauled the Tories and there seemed little prospect of building up a strong middle group of Irish Whigs.[2]

---

[1] *Address to the Reformers of England and Ireland*, spring 1834. It was Grey whom O'Connell was abusing.

[2] A reasonable estimate of the Irish returns would be — Repealers 41, Tories 37, Others 27, some of whom were nearly Tories, while others agreed with O'Connell except on Repeal. The 'Others' included seven noblemen, several great landowners (of whom R. S. Carew and Dominick Browne were subse-

The Irish legislation for 1833 had already been decided when these results became known. At a cabinet at Grey's house at East Sheen on 19th October, 1832 Althorp, Russell and Durham, who deemed it essential to try to conciliate O'Connell by reasonable concessions, failed to modify the mixture of coercion and concession (in that order) prescribed by Grey, Melbourne and Stanley. There was blood and thunder in the Irish part of the King's Speech, and before a Church Bill, which was acceptable to O'Connell as a first instalment, the House was presented with a measure described by an Irish Protestant, son of the great Grattan, as one which 'swept away the liberty of Ireland and annihilated the Constitution, repealed the Habeas Corpus Act, abolished trial by jury, established military tribunals and created an arbitrary dictator'.[1] The eloquence of Macaulay was called in aid to protest against O'Connell's famous indictment of the Whigs as 'base, brutal and bloody'. 'The loudest clamour which the Hon. and learned gentleman can excite against Lord Grey', he said, 'will be trifling when compared with the clamour which Lord Grey withstood in order to place the Hon. and learned gentleman where he now sits.' The Whigs had endured much 'rather than that he should be less than a British subject'. They would never suffer him to be more.[2]

This was stout talk. But Althorp's Whig soul flinched, and the House knew it. Althorp left a great reputation as Leader of the House. His handling of the Reform Bill deserves high praise, and after its enactment moderates knew that (despite his personal belief in the ballot) they could rely on him to maintain the settlement as 'final' and the less moderate understood that the resignation of Durham in April 1833 left him as the most liberal member of the cabinet. In May 1834 206 members of his following, representing all shades of opinion, memorialised him, begging him to remain Leader. They respected him for his integrity, his transparent honesty and disinterestedness. That he was a plodder, with no pretension to brilliance, halting in speech and tentative

quently ennobled by the Whigs), a few nominees of Whig magnates such as Fitzwilliam and Devonshire, and a lawyer or two. They had neither the unanimity nor the calibre to form a strong Irish Whig contingent. The only minister returned in Ireland was George Lamb (Under-Secretary at the Home Office under his brother), who was returned for the Duke of Devonshire's tiny fief of Dungarvan. Duncannon and Spring Rice fled from Cos. Kilkenny and Limerick to Nottingham and Cambridge respectively.

[1] H. of C., 25th April, 1834.   [2] H. of C., 29th January, 1833.

in debate, inspired confidence in many who mistrusted cleverness and eloquence. He would resist demands he thought wrong. His frank admissions, when making concessions which he disapproved but thought expedient, were persuasive. But it is a question whether a government is well served when its chief advocate adopts an apologetic tone, and this Althorp, having been overruled in cabinet by less liberal colleagues, often had to do, because it was not in his nature to do otherwise.

The testimonial to which reference has been made at least proved that for two sessions after the Reform Bill Althorp succeeded in his main task of keeping the variegated following together, even though the ministry had not been as positively liberal as he advised. It was not thought that anyone else could do as well. A rising competitor, Edward Stanley, who scored notable triumphs in the House, would have been a dividing sword. Althorp was homely, rural, retiring and prematurely old. Stanley was a glittering young man, an ornament of the sporting and social worlds, and 'the Rupert of debate'. But he was already suspected of lacking balance and seriousness and perhaps integrity. Believing with many of his colleagues, and certainly Grey, who greatly favoured him, that the Reform Bill had made the Whigs *the* conservative party, Stanley concluded that the awkward squad in the party would respond to rough handling. After all, the thirty or so extreme Radicals and their fellow-travellers, including the Irish, did not together exceed one quarter of the House of Commons or one third of the ministerialists, and need not be feared unless the Government flattered their importance. Stanley believed that in these difficult days Government should lead, not in the sense in which Althorp would have it lead, but in the sense that it should firmly fix the limits of what it was prepared to do in the way of reform and adhere to them without retreat which, whether premeditated or not, was bad for ministerial prestige and party morale.[1] This attitude was an implied reproach against Althorp, though from the point of view of keeping the party together it made his labours the more necessary.

Stanley was in the thick of the fray in 1833, first as Chief Secretary and then as Secretary for War and Colonies, in charge of the Slave Bill. Twice in February he delivered intrepid defences of the executive power which drew applause for magnificent

[1] But Stanley was usually ready to make what concessions he could to Tories.

parliamentary performance and would, a Scottish listener said, before 1832 have made him prime minister for as long as he liked to govern on the Tory principles which animated them.[1] He exploited with consummate skill what another Scotsman described as 'the common notion prevailing among Liberals in England that Ireland is wholly incapable of laws and liberty and must be governed by the sword'.[2] The House responded with votes of 466 : 89 and 363 : 84.[3] Thus fortified, Stanley accepted amendments to the Church Bill to make it more palatable to the Lords. Despairing of the fate of the Bill there Althorp wanted the Government to resign before it ever got to the Lords and when his colleagues declined to agree, hoped the peers would force a crisis. But the cabinet held on (losing only Durham) until in 1834, on the question of the Church, it was rent asunder.

The Irish Church was a statutory establishment whose administration might be reformed and its property redistributed, despite the terms of the Act of Union,[4] by Parliament. Stanley's own legislation involved the abolition of Church cess,[5] the extinction of sinecures, the amalgamation of sees, a graduated tax on the richer benefices for the benefit of the poorer, and tithe commutation. But he held that the mere fact that the state had chosen to support a certain church gave it no moral right to *confiscate* its property, and he would not hear of 'the lay appropriation of surplus revenues', especially as what was proposed was the diversion of revenues to uses not only exterior to the Church but repugnant to it, to wit, the education of Roman Catholics. Like old Lord Spencer, he thought that if corporate property could be confiscated by statute 'no property can thereafter be considered safe'.[6] These views were anathema to one who entered the cabinet on the same day as Stanley, and was seven years his senior. Lord John Russell, after introducing the Reform Bill, and acting as Althorp's chief lieutenant during its passage, had lapsed into obscurity in an office (that of Paymaster General) which gave him little work, no

---

[1] Abercromby's comment, quoted, in Le Marchant's *Althorp*, p. 455.
[2] Campbell, op. cit., Vol. II, p. 7, 18th April, 1832.
[3] For first reading, a.m. 6th March and second reading, a.m. 12th March, respectively.
[4] The Act of Union 1800 united the Churches of England and Ireland and said that 'the doctrine, worship, discipline and government of the said united church shall be, and shall remain in full force for ever, as the same are now by law established for the Church of England . . .'.
[5] The Irish equivalent of church rates.
[6] Le Marchant's *Althorp*, Vol. I, p. 492.

great measure to frame and pilot, and too much time to brood. He brooded over the declining reputation of Whiggery, of whose fame he felt himself the destined guardian by right of inheritance and dedication; he saw it tarnished by illiberality. He brooded, we may be sure, on the ill-health of Lord Spencer, which rendered imminent the removal of Althorp from the Commons, and on the rising influence of a rival with all the panache and eloquence which Russell lacked — a rival who seemed to enjoy suspending in Ireland liberties for which a Russell had died on the scaffold. The son of a viceroy whose appearance in Ireland in 1806 had been hailed as the beginning of a 'new deal' for the Catholics, Russell believed that Britain owed Ireland a debt of reparation which Catholic Emancipation alone was insufficient to discharge. A fervent anti-papist, but an Erastian to the bone, Russell thought that if the Irish would not be conciliated except at the expense of the unpopular ecclesiastical establishment, and that establishment was shown to have more resources than were needed to cover its legitimate activities, it was the statesman's duty to divert part of them to the benefit of the majority faith.

Eighteenth-century governments were primarily concerned with administration, defence and foreign policy. Twentieth-century governments are expected annually to produce a considerable, or considerable-looking, legislative programme. The nineteenth century was a period of transition between the two concepts of government and rather nearer the eighteenth than the twentieth-century view. But Grey's ministry more nearly resembled a twentieth-century one than did many which followed it, for it *was* expected to produce a considerable body of legislation, and to deal among other matters with the Irish Church. Russell may therefore be pardoned for deeming it improper that 'lay appropriation' should remain an 'open question'— as slavery, Parliamentary Reform and Catholic Emancipation were for so long — because of the *current* importance of the question, and the great present opportunity to change tepid acceptance of the measure into warm welcome. He must therefore seriously consider resignation. If he did not resign, he might enter a formal dissent on a cabinet minute, but he must support the ministerial measure; he need not disguise, but ought not to parade, his opinion that it did not go far enough. This was the basis on which he stayed in the cabinet from October 1832, and when the Tithe Bill of 1834 was introduced he adhered to it. The Bill evaded the issue; lay appropriation had to remain an 'open question' because the cabinet could not agree on it. Then on 6th May, 1834, without warning, Russell made in public the challenge he had been dissuaded from making in cabinet. Here again we have to remember the transitional character of the nineteenth century with regard to cabinet conventions. Eighteenth-century ministries were constructed on the principle that the King's government must be carried on and were composed of individuals chosen, generally seriatim, on grounds of experience, competence, executive-mindedness, aristocratic connection, electoral or parliamentary weight or royal favour. They were not supposed to be a 'team' in the modern sense or animated by collective principles closely related to a wide range of problems requiring attention. Twentieth-century peacetime governments, a projection of party, are formed of persons expected to be of one mind upon a party programme. In the nineteenth century the doctrine of the unity of the cabinet under the leadership of the prime minister (which owed much to Pitt), and of collective responsibility, made gradual progress. It left a minister less free than in earlier times to air his differences with his colleagues on matters of proximate government policy, and it was outraged by Russell's behaviour on 6th May. The debate that day had been good-humoured. Stanley had teased O'Connell's henchman, Sheil, and said he intended to adhere to his views on Church revenues. It was not a belligerent speech, and if Russell himself could not find in *Hansard* the words which he said he thought would be taken to indicate that the ministry was positively committed to the maintenance of the Church revenues unimpaired, no one else can.[1] Stanley was simply doing what Russell himself had done often enough — he was restating views he was known to hold. But Russell rose and said that for him 'justice to Ireland' meant lay appropriation; that if ever a nation had a right to complain of grievances, it was the people of Ireland of the Church of Ireland; and that when the property in tithes had been vindicated he would assert his opinion even to the point of separation from his colleagues.

In such dramatic manner Lord John Russell shed his load of chagrin, frustration and jealously. He explained that he had felt that it was one of those occasions when 'one must express one's

[1] *Recollections and Suggestions*, p. 120.

own feelings or sink into contempt'. Brougham said it was 'a
mere effusion of senseless vanity'. But it could not be dismissed as
such. In vain did Althorp and Littleton, the Chief Secretary,
assert that nothing was changed and that the matter remained one
for discussion and that any settlement of it lay in the future. This
view was, strictly speaking, compatible with what Russell had said.
But Stanley had passed to Graham the famous note 'John Russell
has upset the coach' (*not* 'Johnny', as Russell says in his *Recollections*). And the Irish had roared applause for a speech which the
Catholic squire, Barron, said would do more good than the
legislation of years and win millions of Irish hearts. It would search
the heart of the cabinet to the very core, said Sheil. When Grey
refused to accept Stanley's resignation, a Mr Ward[1] appeared to
widen the crack which Russell had made, by tabling a motion in
favour of lay appropriation. This the cabinet could evade either
by the device of 'the previous question' or by promising an
inquiry into the revenues of the Irish Church. But the latter was
objectionable to Stanley as constituting a modification of the
cabinet's position as a concession to Russell. Since, in the event,
the cabinet let Stanley and Graham and two other ministers go,
Stanley had grounds for the view that his colleagues, under
pressure from the 'movement' party of which Russell now made
himself the protagonist, were moving towards the subversion of the
church establishment in Ireland. That establishment was, in
theory if not in practice, a mainstay of the social and political order
and it was certainly a symbol of British and Protestant ascendancy
in Ireland. In England itself the Church was menaced, Graham
said, by 'the growth and boldness of Dissent', and there can have
been few decades when the hierarchy was as unpopular with
important elements in the political nation as in the 'thirties.[2] To
certain earnest Churchmen in Oxford it was apparent that the
cause of this unpopularity — the close association of the Church
with the State — was also the cause of the Church's ineffectiveness
as the principal organ of religion, and that the answer was an
assertion of the Church's spiritual independence. But this new,

[1] For Henry George Ward, see *infra*, p. 199. It seems likely that at this juncture he was in league with Durham and Ellice.
[2] Because the dignitaries of the Church, and most prominently the bishops in
the House of Lords, lacked spiritual earnestness and largely figured as champions
of political reaction, opposing not only the repeal of the Tests and Catholic
Emancipation but also Parliamentary Reform.

Catholic, High Churchmanship had nothing in common with what had passed for High Churchmanship in the first quarter of the nineteenth century, of which the views of Stanley and Graham (though the latter had some Evangelical leanings) were a political projection. That 'high and dry' Churchmanship meant little more than support for a mutually advantageous alliance of the hierarchies in Church and State for the preservation of their respective privileges. Graham saw 'danger inevitable to all our institutions if the Church be overthrown'. The Repealers who attacked the Church of Ireland were determined to undo the Union. The Radicals who attacked ecclesiastical establishments also attacked secular establishments such as the House of Lords. The Irish Church stood as a symbol of the national institutions which the Reform had been intended to preserve. Let it be reformed, by all means, like the Church of England, in order to strengthen it by the excision of scandals such as pluralism, non-residence and gross inequality of emoluments, and by the conversion into taxes or rent-charges of the dues it exacted from persons outside its communion. But lay appropriation was to be regarded not as a reform of 'but as an attack upon' the Church — that is why O'Connell so relished it.

Lay appropriation could win support among Whigs and Liberals who did not usually vote with Radicals, and was to be adopted as official Whig policy, partly because the endowment of Roman Catholicism in Ireland (concurrently with the existing endowment of the Church of Ireland and the *Regium Donum* to the Presbyterians of Ulster) as a means of cementing the Union was not a new idea to Whiggery.[1] The Whigs, though far from willing to surrender Anglican establishment in Ireland, were now coming to consider it an embarrassment rather than an asset. This seemed to Stanley very wrong-headed. All that was required to preserve the Church of Ireland inviolate was to bring into play the potent anti-popery of England and Scotland, strong in the very sects which attacked the Church of England. There was no need to lose a battle in which the assailants were so easy to divide.

In Graham's letters we find two key propositions — that the Protestant establishment was essential to the Union, and that 'firm maintenance of the established Protestant religion . . . which the

---

[1] See especially Michael Roberts, *The Whig Party* 1807–12, 1939, for the negotiations with Lord Fingall, a leading Irish Roman Catholic layman, after the fall of the Whig ministry in 1807.

E

Revolution of 1688 bore triumphant over Popery and royal tyranny' was not incompatible with 'genuine Whig principles' But Auckland shrewdly said that he was sorry for the loss of Stanley, 'the more so as the time is not far off when he is in danger of becoming high churchman and high Tory'.[1] And within a decade the heir-presumptive of Grey as leader of the Whig party[2] had become the heir-presumptive of Peel as leader of the Conservative party, and then, as leader of the Protectionists, was thrice prime minister, though never with a majority in the House of Commons. Richmond, a Tory till 1830, went with him both in 1834 and 1846. But Graham, who became Peel's right-hand man in the House of Commons, 1841-6, drifted via Peelism back into association with the Whigs in 1852.[3]

Russell's outbursts, even when they appeared unpremeditated, were very often opportune. The stroke of 6th May, 1834, was as nicely timed as that of November 1845.[4] It knocked Stanley out of the competition while Earl Spencer still lived. It is inconceivable that Russell should have been preferred to Stanley as successor to Althorp; the King was not the only person who thought him unfitted to lead the Commons. In the course of nature Stanley need not have gone to the Lords till 1851, when Russell was nearly sixty. Only by a liberal revolt, cleaving Whiggery in twain, could Russell have risen to the top. It was of supreme importance for Russell's career that at a stroke he removed Stanley from his path and established himself as a man of consequence to whom reformers might look and the strongest candidate for the leadership of the Commons. Until his retirement from active politics in 1867 Russell was to be the chief Whig politician.

[1] *Clarendon*, op. cit., p. 84.
[2] That Grey looked upon Stanley as destined shortly to become Leader of the House of Commons is shown by his explanation of why he put him in the cabinet in 1831, quoted by Professor Aspinall in his British Academy lecture on the cabinet 1783–1835.
[3] Lord Ripon, the spent-out colleague of Liverpool and Canning, who (as Goderich) had failed to maintain the premiership in 1827, also resigned. He too served in Peel's administration.
[4] See *infra*, p. 127.

CHAPTER III

Stalemate, 1834–9

The departure of the four ministers in May 1834 left the morale of the cabinet low. The replacements whom Lansdowne, virtually, was allowed to nominate did not compensate for the loss of Stanley's eloquence and drive and of Graham's reputation as an administrative reformer.[1]

Radicals hoped that parliamentary reform would be followed by wide administrative reforms. With some, the great object was retrenchment; with others rationalisation; with others, purity. We have noted that throughout 1833 and 1834 Althorp was under pressure for spectacular instalments of 'economical Reform'. But large economies were not possible without affronting what he called 'gentlemanly considerations'. Legitimate expectations partook of the nature of property, and were not to be confiscated. There was, in truth, little scope for immediate savings when the last committee on sinecures could find hardly any left which had not been sentenced to extinction. Something could, however, be achieved by the reorganisation of departments so that work could be done more efficiently by fewer persons at less cost. The new Audit department, employing thirteen people at £6,800 p.a., replaced the old Exchequer, where 59 cost £40,000. The pooling of the Stamp Office and the Tax Commission saved £18,000. As a further earnest of the politicians' rectitude the Secretaries to the Treasury each lost £1,000 of their salaries.[2] The Government completed in 1831 the long process by which all governmental expenditure was transferred from the Civil List to parliamentary appropriation and hence parliamentary 'control'. It also framed the first statutory acknowledgement of the principle of Treasury

---

[1] The replacements were Auckland, Ellice, Abercromby and Spring Rice. The last two were protégés of Lansdowne and had been respectively Judge Advocate and Under-Secretary at the Home Office under the Canningite-Whig coalition of 1827.

[2] Sir John Craig, *A History of Red Tape*, 1955, pp. 41, 84, 107.

control over the civil estimates.[1] It might have passed into history with a momentous achievement to its name if it had generalised the reform introduced by Graham at the Admiralty, which became the first department to submit annually to Parliament an audited account of its expenditure. But 'Treasury control' as transmitted by the nineteenth century to the twentieth awaited the arrival of Gladstone and Trevelyan, and effective procedures for informing the House of Commons how the money it voted was spent waited for Gladstone and Robert Lowe. The Whigs missed the opportunity to blend their traditional championship of the supremacy of the House of Commons with an appeal to the business instincts of the middle classes.

Among men attacked by Hume and Daniel Whittle Harvey for nepotism and partisan patronage, Graham stood out as one who rated efficiency and economy in the public service as highly in office as he had professed to do in opposition. Twenty years later, as emerged during the discussions of civil service reform in the 'fifties, even he could not understand how the wheels of parliamentary government could turn without their traditional lubrication of patronage. But while Brougham bewailed (as Wellington had done before) the absence of 'thick-and-thin men' in the old sense — the Crown servants who in the House of Commons supported the Government of the day with a civil service type of loyalty — Graham declined to use the patronage of the Navy List and Dockyards to win friends and influence people. His concern for efficiency extended to personnel as well as organisation,[2] and the Chief Whip complained that friends were murmuring and enemies jeering because he did not seem able to 'discover meritorious individuals of our own caste'. The Patronage Secretary had no such criticism to make of Graham's successor, Minto, one of the many Whig grandees who 'liked doing things for people'. Minto gained the Admiralty a reputation for nepotism. The Whigs had been 'out' for a very long while, and so the pressure of demand on a limited supply of places, high and low, was intense. Whiggery was very slow to abandon the assumption that relatives and friends should have a cut out of the public purse. It does not, of course,

[1] In the Act of 1834 the auditors were required to compel the departments to apply for Treasury sanction of expenditure.
[2] Graham amalgamated the Admiralty, the Navy Board and the Victualling Board into one unit — the Board of Admiralty — responsible for all the activities concerned.

follow from the filling of places by nomination that those appointed will be inefficient. The connections of Lord and Lady Grey, to whom primacy was accorded among successful place-hunters in the higher echelons, were in general men of ability, sometimes of conspicuous ability. But there were those who thought it wrong that persons of possibly equal merit were not considered because they were not so well-connected. It handicapped Grey's heir, trying, in the later 'thirties, on sound public grounds, to secure the subordination of the Horse Guards to civilian control, that it should be said that one knew *whose* relatives would benefit if he succeeded.

There were few vacancies, and likely to be few, at the cabinet level, because of Grey's loyalty to his chosen colleagues. Indeed, it was made a matter of complaint that 'he will not dismiss a colleague who has not offended; he will not even accept the resignation of an attached friend'. He bore wonderfully with Durham, an impossible colleague who was at times unbelievably offensive to his father-in-law. When Durham insisted on resigning, Grey took the opportunity to remove Goderich (as Earl of Ripon) from the Colonies, weeping at the loss of the department, to the Privy Seal. But then Goderich, because of the events of 1827, was hardly an 'attached friend'. Grey insisted on retaining in the cabinet his contemporary, Carlisle, though he was a sick man and often unable to attend cabinet meetings. Rather than lose him, Grey raised the numbers of the cabinet from 13 to 15, admitting Stanley and Russell — the former because he was destined to become Leader of the House of Commons, the latter because the Duke of Bedford asked it. The cabinet was too big for efficiency. 'I know not what things we might have done with the people and the House of Commons heartily on our side, had we been 8 instead of 14,' said Brougham. Neither administration nor cabinet was well-directed. 'Every member of the Cabinet, old or young, able or decrepit, thought himself at liberty to discuss the whole state of Europe,' said Durham. The laxity of control was in part the product of constitutional outlook. 'Having carefully chosen ministers with an eye to their aptitude for their particular posts,' said Grey, he would 'leave to each full latitude to manage his Department in accordance with his own judgement'. And he desired that 'counsel of the Cabinet' shoud be 'a veritable counsel', 'the Dictatorship [being] abolished' (a reference to criticisms of Wellington's 'one-man' government).[1] In part, however, it was temperamental. Always of a retiring disposition, Grey after the exertions of 1831–2 was a weary old man, eager to leave active politics, the more so as he did not relish this hectic post-Reform world — he was 'unprepared to govern the country under the new régime', said Campbell.[2] On occasion, at least half-consciously, Grey played upon the reluctance of colleagues to 'give him his release' in order to force on them Stanleyite or Palmerstonian policies which they did not relish, and he took advantage of Althorp's loyalty and sense of duty to keep this principal colleague, who also longed for retirement, in office as long as he stayed himself.[3] But strain developed between the two men, principally because the Prime Minister did not consider with imaginative insight the difficulties of the Leader of the House of Commons. There was no breach between them. But there was a lack of political accord, revealed by differences as to parliamentary tactics and enhanced by policy differences over Ireland. Very soon after the reconstruction of the cabinet these differences coalesced with fatal effect.

Although Russell told the Commons he would not be a minister to carry on a system of bigotry and prejudice, the cabinet was not ready to face up to lay appropriation. The appointment of a commission to inquire into the revenues of the Irish Church enabled the issue to be postponed. But Stanley's Coercion Act was due to expire, and ministers had to decide how much of it should be renewed. On 23rd June the Marquess Wellesley, who a year before had succeeded Anglesey as Lord Lieutenant, reported to Grey that he could dispense with those clauses most repugnant to Althorp and Russell. But Grey insisted on the general renewal of the Act, as Wellesley had originally advised. When this news was given to the House of Commons, O'Connell revealed a meeting between him and Chief Secretary Littleton. Grey and Althorp, each in honesty but with an incomplete knowledge of the facts, gave the two Houses contrary explanations of what had occurred. Grey had not known of the meeting; Althorp, though privy to it, did not know that instead of telling the Irish leader that the liberal

[1] The quotations in this paragraph are from Professor Arthur Aspinall's Raleigh Lecture on 'The Cabinet Council 1783–1835', *British Academy Proceedings*, XXXVIII, p. 209 ff.

[2] Campbell, Vol. II, p. 49.

[3] Grey said he would go if Althorp did. Unlike Grey, Althorp had no happy family circle to go to, but he longed for peace and agricultural pursuits, including the rehabilitation of a mismanaged estate.

element in the cabinet might yet carry the day, Littleton left him with the impression that the liberal element *had* triumphed. When Grey discovered that this had been going on without his knowledge, and that it was Brougham who, with the cognisance of Althorp, had prevailed upon the Lord Lieutenant, through Littleton (Wellesley's son-in-law), to reverse his previous advice, he stumped out of office, murmuring of conspiracy. Althorp said he too must resign, because his honour was impugned.

The Whig cabinet, the first for a quarter of a century, had maintained its unity through the most crucial parliamentary struggle of modern times, and reformed the electoral system, only to fall asunder under the impact of that *damnosa hereditas*, the Irish Question. Even the fear that if they broke up, Armageddon, the reign of Radicalism, would begin was not enough to produce among the ministers the unity of outlook and sense of collective purpose which may enable a government to win through in a time of trouble but not of supreme crisis. 'Men's crotchets', said Auckland, 'were so much stronger than their reasons.' Of course, the questions 'When does a policy rank as a principle? Where does strategy give place to tactics?' will be argued whenever a minister resigns or a government breaks up on a political issue, and it is hazardous to try to measure the parts played in political crises by principles, 'crotchets' and ambitions. But it will generally be thought undesirable that a minister should take himself too seriously (as Russell was prone to do), lest he fail to make his proper contribution to the coherence of a cabinet with whose general line of policy he agrees. And it is obviously inconvenient that the advice given by a viceroy to a prime minister as to what powers are required for the maintenance of law and order should be tainted by unavowed considerations of party expediency pressed upon him by ministers without the cognisance of their chief. Brougham, on this occasion, was not playing the part of a villain; he was trying to keep the ministry together.[1] Littleton had been foolish and Althorp, his judgement clouded by the conviction that the conciliation of O'Connell was vital, had been less careful and less frank with Grey than the latter had a right to require.

Reared in no common political school, but brought together by

[1] Brougham was to make his unique contribution to the fall of the next administration — that of Melbourne — in the form of what Disraeli called 'the vagrant and grotesque apocalypse of the Lord Chancellor', a speaking tour in which he indulged in delusions of grandeur at the expense of his colleagues.

the pressure of the unusual events of 1830, the Grey cabinet fell because the ministers had not learned to subordinate their differing degrees of liberalism, their differing senses of proportion, their different temperaments, to the development of a team spirit. It was still too early to say whether they, who had sowed the wind, had averted the whirlwind. Some at least of them doubted it.[1] Others were perhaps too experienced, too cynical, to view the future with quite the apprehension they professed. They had everything to gain by confirming the general belief that a Tory administration was not feasible. But if it was not, then the rump of the Reform Bill cabinet — a clear majority had resigned[2]— must carry on, supplemented by members of the second eleven. Althorp was persuaded to return, and Melbourne succeeded Grey in his usual mood of fearing the worst but hoping for the best. He remained prime minister for a few months only until Lord Spencer died, and then accepted from the King his *congé* and even acted as messenger to the Duke of Wellington.

'We have buried the Tories and if the Whigs will not do right the sexton must be called out again,' Joseph Parkes had written.[3] But the King solved the problem posed by Melbourne in November 1834 — how to resist the 'movement' party without Althorp as Leader of the House — by installing as prime minister Sir Robert Peel and dissolving the first reformed Parliament, in whose House of Commons Peel had commanded not a quarter. It was now a subject of speculation, not whether the Tories would survive, but whether the Whigs had any future — especially after the elections, for these doubled Peel's force. The Tories had begun to call themselves 'Conservatives' to indicate a breach with the past and Peel in the Tamworth Manifesto accepted Reform as the basis of the political order and offered a staunch but intelligent defence of the *Conservative Cause* by recognition of the need for reforms. He thus pre-empted the ground which it had commonly been thought the Whigs would occupy as a result of the Reform Bill. The 'organised hypocrisy', as Disraeli called the Conservative party, Tory men peddling Whig measures, extracted at the

---

[1] e.g. Brougham (Le Marchant's *Althorp*, p. 510), Auckland (*Clarendon*, Vol. I, p. 84).
[2] Durham, Stanley, Graham, Ripon, Richmond, Grey, Carlisle (who resigned with Grey) and Althorp. That left three Canningites, Brougham, Lansdowne, Holland and Russell.
[3] op. cit., p. 114.

WILLIAM LAMB, 2nd VISCOUNT MELBOURNE
by J. Partridge
National Portrait Gallery

elections the last ounce of strength that could be squeezed from
official influence and royal support, from the organisation of registration and the absence of the ballot and any effective safeguards
against corruption. Peel then challenged the Whigs to accept
exclusion from office or purchase readmission as the slaves of
Radicals and Repealers. For the 'miscellaneous multitude', as
Stanley called the opponents of Peel, not now much more numerous than his supporters, could not, without finding some basis of
agreement, turn him out. It was not certain that the basis could be
found. Althorp and Grey both feared a Radical government,
and preferred a Tory one, though the former thought Peel must
be ousted because his coming into office was constitutionally
objectionable.[1] Grey, Melbourne, Lansdowne and Holland
desired reconciliation with Stanley. What they wanted, said
Russell bitterly, was the ministry as it existed before 6th May,
1834, with appropriation an open question. But Duncannon told
them that if they looked to Whigs only they would be a very small
party. Matters could not proceed upon the old basis of a meeting
of a few magnates, as in the days of Pelham and Rockingham,
as if politics was concerned not with policy but simply with places.
If Russell was to contend with Peel he must have Radicals and
Repealers with him.

Whatever men who had retired or men who feared Radicalism
more than they loved place might say, the natural wish of a party
to get into office was bound to prevail, even though it meant closer
association with Radicals and Repealers, and a party meeting to
seal it. Russell's advocacy of lay appropriation made possible a
démarche between the Whigs and the Repealers. Its strongest
advocate was Duncannon, in 1832 O'Connell's most distinguished
scalp, but now his 'Noble Friend', whose appointment to the Home
Office under Melbourne had been hailed by the Liberator as a
pledge that Ireland was to have the enlightened, liberal government which Grey and Stanley had denied it.[2] Duncannon had
long wanted accommodation with O'Connell in the interests of
Ireland; now he wanted it because he thought the only alternative

---

[1] *E.C.J.R.*, No. 193, 18th January, 1835.
[2] H. of C., 17th July, 1834. Duncannon in 1831 scraped in for his family
county of Kilkenny through the exertions on his behalf of the Catholic Bishop
Doyle, but thought it wise in 1832 to transfer to Nottingham. Even there the
Radicals asked O'Connell what attitude they ought to take to him (Aspinall's
Brougham, p. 290).

to a government like Melbourne's, but going further than it had intended, was a Radical administration which would ruin the Irish Church and attack the English. Knowing the prejudices of his compeers, he spoke of co-operation rather than commitment — 'necessary communication' without 'intimate contact' was Lansdowne's formula, and, the Duke of Bedford added, 'without trust'. Hobhouse suggested that some moderate Irishman whom one knew in society, one of the Grattans, perhaps, might serve as an intermediary. But the most Radical of the whips, Warburton, sent direct to O'Connell for distribution to his 'Tail' a bundle of the circulars which were regularly addressed on behalf of leaders to those whose support they looked for, and O'Connell replied direct to Russell, promising sixty-two votes (a considerable advance on the previous Parliament) at the first challenge and steady alliance until the Tories were turned out. The so-called Lichfield House Compact is really this letter, the gist of which was made known at the party meeting at a mansion in St James's Square.

Grey abominated, and Melbourne did not at all like, the idea of such a meeting. Melbourne knew his Whigs. 'All will depend', he wrote, 'upon the number of those who may be for moderate measures. If they are considerable . . . they may possibly restrain the more violent; if they are few, and insignificant, they will only irritate and drive them further.' He added that he had never yet known them considerable.[1] He understood that in the liberal ranks the *vis inertiae* really depended on the leaders, not their like-minded followers, men of conservative temperament with no great zeal for reforms or serious interest in legislation, for whom politics was only one and not the most important of their activities and whose attendance in the House was apt to be irregular. A party meeting would only reveal how thin on the ground were conservative Whig M.P.s.[2] And the losses in the late election had fallen mainly on the conservative, moderate and nondescript elements, so that the Radicals and their associates were proportionately stronger than ever before.

In 1833 the ministry of Lord Grey dashed the enthusiasm of its mass following in the Commons by deciding that the partisan Tory Manners Sutton should be re-elected Speaker, thus em-

---

[1] Melbourne, pp. 252-3, to Grey, 11th February, 1835.
[2] Ellice (to Durham, 11th April, 1835, Aspinall's *Brougham*, p. 296) said that only 60 or 70 objected to the idea of O'Connell taking office.

phasising the continuity between pre-Reform and post-Reform
politics. In 1835 the only question was whether there should be
brought against Sutton the conservative Irish Whig Spring Rice
or the more liberal Scotsman Abercromby. The former had
infuriated Repealers by calling himself 'a West Briton' in a five
hour speech against Repeal. Abercromby was chosen, and
defeated Manners Sutton by 316 to 306.[1] A mild stricture on the
use of the royal prerogative was carried by 309 to 302,[2] as an
amendment to the Address. With majorities so small, there was
no assurance that a frontal attack to force the Government out of
office would succeed. Peel secured the 'fair trial' which he asked
for himself and which Stanley also asked for him. Men who find
themselves 'in the middle' in politics seem prone to delusions of
grandeur. Because they do, or may, hold the balance, they dream
not only of bargains but of supremacy. Parker's *Graham* records
an idea that Stanley should form a government with the co-operation of Peel and also, it was hoped, many Whigs. But the persistent
tendency towards a two-party system is, in modern British history,
much stronger than the counter-tendency of parties to break up —
a fact which advocates of electoral change forget when they seek
to bolster their case by pointing out that there have been more
often than not, more than two parties in Parliament.[3] Stanley's
effort to form a party, immortalised by O'Connell as 'the Derby
Dilly', made no headway, merely providing a brief resting place
for a few quondam Whigs passing over to Peel. Party had become
virtually all-embracing. But party required the weight of democracy to press it into its modern authoritarian mould. So there were
members who, though not prepared in general to support Peel,
disapproved of deposing a Speaker or censuring the King; there
were members who thought Peel should have a fair trial and would
be very reluctant to turn out any government; there were a few
members who had not quite decided whether to be Whigs or

[1] 19th February, 1835.   [2] a.m. 27th February.

[3] The third party is usually impotent or an auxiliary of one of the two major
parties, its nominal independence barely disguising its dependence on an
electoral pact (as was the case with the Liberal Unionists after 1886 and the
National Liberals after 1931). The Irish Nationalists, as an alien intrusion into
the two-party system, are a special case, but they were from 1886 partners in a
coalition which was regarded by electors as constituting one major party, the
Home Rule party, just as the opposing coalition was regarded as the other, the
Unionist party. Only briefly were small parties in a position to say which of the
major parties should form the government — Peelites in 1852 ff., Liberals in
1924 and 1929–31 and Irish 1885–6.

Tories.[1] What there was *not* was an appreciable body of men ready
to belong to a middle party. Parties crystallised round Peel and
Russell, and Gladstone looked back on the period 1835–45 as the
golden age of the two-party system.

Peel presented measures not inferior in range and effect to those
which a Whig ministry might expect to carry through the Lords,
and Ellice thought he might stay in office for a year if he avoided
the Irish tithe question.[2] But Peel grasped that nettle, and was
turned out on a motion insisting on lay appropriation. This marked
the triumph of Russell on the issue on which he had upset the
coach, and the defeat of Grey's hope that the question might
remain open and the Whigs recover Stanley. A ministry formed on

[1] Six weeks after the votes of 316:306 and 309:302, the Whigs forced Peel out
with votes of 322:289, 262:237 and 285:258 (3rd — 8th April) on lay appropriation. The differences in the majorities — 10, 7, 33, 25, 27, are accounted for
partly by varying absenteeism but also partly by a reluctance to give the Opposition its full nominal majority at the outset. About forty members (perhaps more
rather than less) not known in the last Parliament or (if out of it) at the elections,
as definitely Tory, appear to have voted with Peel on the Speaker and/or the
Address. Grant (*Random Recollections of the House of Commons*, 1st series, 1836)
says that *Sir G. Sinclair* was formerly of decided Whig principles but sided with
Peel on the Irish Church and afterwards, disliking the alliance with O'Connell,
while, per contra, *Sir Fras Burdett*, the erstwhile Radical, 'still makes a profession of Liberal principles but it is a profession only' — would take no step
against Peel *except* on the Irish Church. *G. F. Young* (remembered by Gladstone
as the last of the old style of independent gentry) boasted his independence but
co-operated with Stanley and more often than not voted with the Conservatives,
though supporting the Church and Tithe Bills. *John Walter* was 'the last of the
Neutral party to foresake the ministerial side' (i.e. the Whig side). In the second
series, 1838, Grant says that *John Hardy* 'until the last few years, always
identified himself with the Liberal party . . . there was not latterly a more
thorough-going Conservative' sitting behind Peel, and that *J. Richards* as a
former Liberal bitterly hostile to O'Connell was shouted down by the Radicals
without being cheered by the Tories. Of *R. Gally Knight*, Grant said that he
would not like to be called a Conservative, though, after for many years voting
and acting with the Reformers, he had lately with one or two unimportant
exceptions 'proved himself a thick-and-thin supporter of Tory principles. To
be sure, he calls himself an independent man. So, I have observed, does every
one who has apostasised from his former opinions' e.g. Stanley, Graham,
Burdett, Sinclair (a very unfair way of stating their objection to lay appropriation'). Examples such as these (and one could add others such as Sir Oswald
Mosley, spoken of as a potential Stanleyite, who with P. M. Stewart and Sir
Ralph Lopes — the latter soon regarded as a Conservative — voted for Abercromby but with Peel on the Address) show why there was briefly talk of a
Derby Dilly 40 strong. Estimates of 86 and 87 by Bentinck and Hornby respectively (see Douglas Johnson, *Birmingham Historical Journal*, Vol. IV, No. 1,
1953) were quite unrealistic, including liberals such as Lord Robt. Grosvenor
and Col. Parry on the one hand and moderate Tories like Sir Eardley Wilmot
and Emmerson Tennant on the other. The members most active in seeking support for Stanley appear to have been the brothers-in-law Ld. Geo. Bentinck and
J. E. Denison, both Canningites, the one later leader, with Stanley, of the
Protectionists and the other a Whig Speaker.

[2] Aspinall's *Brougham*, p. 294, to Durham, 19th March, 1835.

such a basis Russell had said he could support but would not join.[1] Now, provided a government could be formed, he would be Leader of the House on the basis to which he had aspired when he appealed to the Irish and the 'movement party' against Stanley. The tactics of the Opposition had been in the hands of a committee consisting of Lansdowne, Russell, Spring Rice and Hobhouse; the Radicals and Irish had dutifully accepted its plan of campaign as a result of which the Tories were ejected. O'Connell then supplemented the Lichfield House Compact with a pledge of warmest support for a Liberal government, and, when Grey, summoned by the King, referred the monarch to Melbourne and Lansdowne, all seemed plain sailing. But Rice said he could not join a government that depended on Radicals — as though any other were possible. This caused his patron, Lansdowne, to falter, especially when Grey declined the Foreign Office. 'Oh for some masculine mind to save us from the councils of these small-beer statesmen,' wrote Ellice.[2] The corner was, however, turned and soon Melbourne was writing to the King — 'Your Majesty has resorted for counsel to those by whose efforts these resolutions were placed upon the journals of the House of Commons and if Your Majesty appoints them your Ministers Your Majesty must take them pledged and bound to act upon these their recorded principles....'[3]

The King, Grey and the Tories deprecated the dependence of the second Melbourne administration (1835–41) on the Radicals and O'Connell. But it was really O'Connell who had forfeited the power of manoeuvre. He had joined with the Whigs to turn out the Tories, because in Ireland Tory rule meant Orange rule,[4] and he had promised to support a Whig government. As long as ministers were prepared, by administrative action, to clothe the dry bones of Catholic Emancipation with flesh, he must sustain them in Parliament and even command them in Ireland, for he could not expect more. He enjoyed, of course, the same licence as any other Liberal to advocate any policy he wished (in the winter of 1835 he campaigned strenuously in the north against the House of Lords) and on occasion to upbraid ministers. Thus a snationalist leader he

---

[1] *Melbourne*, op. cit., p. 254, J. R. to M., 11th February, 1835.
[2] Aspinall, op. cit., pp. 295–6, to Durham, 11th April, 1835.
[3] *Melbourne*, op. cit., p. 276, 15th April, 1835.
[4] And perhaps also because he wished to evade the dilemma with which Peel confronted him in 1843 — see *infra*, Ch. VIII, p. 188.

once said 'their incompetency to do us good almost equals their unwillingness to exert themselves for us'. But as their parliamentary ally he said, May 1838, that only time and perseverance were needed to obliterate the conviction, now for the first time diminished, that English domination worked only for mischief. The Compact condemned O'Connell to political schizophrenia, but relieved Melbourne of the anxieties which had proved fatal to Grey's ministry. If Ireland was not exactly governed under the ordinary law as understood in England, at least for five years the tendency was towards the relaxation of special powers. The Union, as conceived by Pitt and those Irishmen who accepted it for the benefit of Ireland rather than of themselves, received its first fair test in the hands of a ministry which took up the challenge to prove that Repeal was not necessary to the welfare of Ireland. A third unconventional nobleman was found to follow Anglesey and Wellesley. The opinionated but liberal Lord Mulgrave entered with enthusiasm, even with recklessness, into this Anglo-Irish honeymoon. The London clubs buzzed with the tale of his dinner invitations, his gaol deliveries and his proscription of over-articulate Orangemen. Lord Morpeth was Chief Secretary, but the real ruler of Ireland, unharassed by the passive resistance of Catholics to the tithe because neither troops nor police now assisted their collection, was the Under-Secretary, Drummond (the framer of Schedules A and B). He injected into the administration at Dublin Castle the equitable and equable temper he had admired in Althorp, purged the garrisons and police of Orange militants and admitted Catholics to them, and founded the Royal Irish Constabulary. Papists were offered patronage (and developed a taste for it). Catholic Law Officers ceased to exclude, or abet the exclusion of, their co-religionists from juries. Except for their failure to make any constructive contribution to the solution of economic problems, the Whigs under Melbourne did much to redeem England's record in Ireland. When the Tipperary justices asked for the exercise of special powers and the taking of new ones to deal with agrarian outrage, Drummond told them that this was due to evictions and that the remedy was to act on the principle that property had its duties as well as its rights. In 1839 it was possible to withdraw troops from Ireland to reinforce the garrisons in disaffected areas in the north of England.

From these good works the Whigs derived mental ease. They

were little embarrassed by dependence on O'Connell as long as he did not insist that they attempt to coerce the Lords on Irish municipal reform and franchise extension or even on lay appropriation. He made no great objection when in 1838 they concluded that to send up the Tithe Bill year after year, only to lose it because the Lords rejected, and the Commons insisted on, lay appropriation, merely wasted time, jeopardised other measures and advertised their unwillingness to force an issue with the Lords on an Irish question. So the Commons agreed with the Lords' amendments, most ministerialists abstaining when Ward and 47 other members moved to reinsert appropriation.[1] Honour was saved by reiterating (by 317 : 298) the resolution on which Peel had been turned out, to the effect that the tithe question could not be settled satisfactorily without lay appropriation.[2] The policy which had lost the Whigs Stanley and Graham, which Russell had exploited to secure the leadership, which had provided the minimum for agreement between Whig and Radical and Repealer and become the plank on which the Whigs floated back to office — that policy, having served its turn, was in practice abandoned.

Hard things have been said about the Melbourne administration, and they must be repeated here. It is therefore right and proper to emphasize that the legislative record of the two Melbourne administrations compares very favourably with that of any forerunner save Grey's. Its importance is not to be ranked below that of any ministry of the 1832–68 dispensation, unless it be Peel's government of 1841–6. But the latter, as Gladstone himself admitted, 'was not eminently distinguished for general legislation'. whereas 'the period of the Melbourne Government had witnessed the enactment of many important laws, useful in their general character and well suited to the condition of the public mind'.[3] Disraeli wrote that 'the measures of the Melbourne Government were generally moderate, well-matured and statesmanlike schemes'.[4] The Whigs themselves rated the New Poor Law as 'the most valuable, if not the most brilliant, achievement of the Whig ministry'.[5] It became the most unpopular, and the twentieth-century conscience warms to the denunciations of it by Cobbett

[1] As an instruction to the Committee, 2nd July, 1838. The voting was 270:46.
[2] 16th May, 1838.
[3] Add. MSS 44745, draft article for *Quarterly Review*, 1855.
[4] *Lord George Bentinck*, p. 11.   [5] Le Marchant's *Althorp*, p. 483.

and to those who in Yorkshire systematically frustrated the design
of Chadwick to make outdoor relief a thing of the past. But the
Whigs, having been to school with the economists, and regarding
it as a sound measure, were not prepared to abandon it, and
persisted in applying it with a firmness which we should have
regarded as admirable if we could approve the tenor of the Act.
The Municipal Corporations Act of 1835 established household
suffrage and opened local administration to the middle classes in
lieu of co-optative oligarchies. By the acts of 1836, 1838 and 1840
the administration and finances of the Church of England were
reformed. From 1836 Dissenters could marry in licensed chapels
or before a registrar (who was also charged with the new function
of recording births and deaths). The Lords declined to abolish
religious discrimination at Oxford and Cambridge, but London
University was chartered to give degrees to students of the
(Benthamite) University College and such other institutions as
might later be approved. In 1839 a committee of the Privy
Council was constituted to administer the educational grants and
provide for the inspection and training of teachers. While Russell
at the Home Office sought to improve the prisons, Peel's reform
of the criminal law was further advanced and imprisonment for
debt abolished except on legal sentence, showing that the Whigs
had not forgotten Romilly. There were even a few belated improvements in the functioning of the higher courts of justice, though the
ambitious schemes of Brougham for the wholesale rationalisation
of the court system and of important branches of the law of
England were frustrated, partly by his own unpopularity with his
former colleagues, but principally by the formidable deadweight
of tradition, prejudice and vested interest among the lawyers.[1]
Fiscal matters apart, the Melbourne legislation was not contemptible; even in that field there was a lightening of the financial burdens
on the press and a bold (and fiscally rash) innovation, the Penny Post.

All this was not far above the minimum which the country in
the decade after 1832 would accept. But it was also about the
maximum that the House of Lords, perhaps even the House of
Commons (where on 22nd May, 1837 the majority on the Church
Rates Bill was only five)[2] would stand. In the electoral context

[1] The Russell government of 1846–52 was able to establish county courts (for
small debt cases).
[2] At second reading. The measure was dropped.

f the time it is far from certain that if the Whigs had engaged the Lords in a battle royal they would have won the contest. Although individual ministers, especially Russell, wished to teach the Lords a lesson, there was no really major, non-Irish measure, on which to engage. Whiggery as a whole did not desire such a battle. Auckland had said that the whole strategy of the leadership ought to be to keep off a clash with the Lords as long as possible and yet continue on the road of rational reform.[1] And that was the policy adopted. It was assisted by Peel. As he lacked a majority in the Commons, the Lords were the instrument of his power. The Leader of the Opposition became the censor of ministerial measures, using the peers to amend them. But he restrained the Lords from rash obstruction which would have forced the ministry to face the issue or risk a breach with the Radicals. Whiggery saw no *casus belli*. The Prime Minister (himself not above suggesting to the Lords amendments which he would like them to press upon the Commons) told the Queen that when the peers altered bills they usually improved them. The nub of the situation was that Melbourne pursued his aim of avoiding revolutionary change and dangerous innovation by a half-conscious coalition with Peel concealed behind the routine strife and mutual scorn of parties. The net result was a series of measures which represented the judgement of a majority of the House of Commons as to what it was requisite to pass — a majority consisting of the Tories and the conservative Whigs, not the majority on which the Whig ministry relied to maintain it in the House.

Melbourne has been memorably guyed as 'sauntering over the destinies of a nation and lounging away the glories of an Empire'.[2] Indolent he was, and often flippant; a man of the eighteenth century, and the Regency circle, a sceptic, who had seen enough of politics for scepticism to deepen into cynicism. He remained incorrigibly pre-Victorian (as for instance in his dislike for the spread of education). But he is to be judged, like any other statesman, by the relation of his achievements to his ends. He had a sense of responsibility. He often showed firmness, and sometimes energy.[3]

---

[1] *Clarendon*, Vol. 1, p. 84.   [2] Disraeli in *Letters of Runnymede*.
[3] Parkes (Buckley p. 124) said that one day in August 1835 he left Melbourne's dressing room heartened by 'the resolution of character and acuteness' of the man who had converted the cabinet to household suffrage in the corporate towns after his colleagues had sworn they would never agree to it. In this matter, as in Parliamentary Reform, Melbourne thought that once a measure was necessary, it should be large enough to be final.

And he had convictions. The strongest of them was that th
national interest required men to serve *the Conservative Cause*
Melbourne was a Conservative before the term was isolated an
grafted on to the party which he had left because its conservatism
had become stupid, sterile and self-destructive. He believed i
the maintenance of the social and political order — that is to say
of the national institutions and the political and social supremac
of the propertied classes — to be procured by timely concession
to assuage discontent. In the later 'thirties, *the Conservative Caus*
had a majority in the House of Commons, but the Conservativ
party had not. The *Cause* had therefore to be upheld by an over
or covert coalition of Whigs and Conservatives. William IV wante
the coalition to be overt, and there were sometimes rumours tha
Melbourne's mind was turning that way.[1] It would not have seeme
strange or repugnant to Melbourne to resume official co-operatio
with Peel. Both could take the Tamworth Manifesto as thei
guide. But Whig tradition, and Whig interest, were against it
Whiggery was an archaic connection retaining its influence in the
body politic by virtue of historical associations and by the surviva
of a fiction that it *led* the liberal forces in the community, a fictio
given new verisimilitude in the crisis of 1831–2. Dissolve the
fiction, and the magic would fade. For Whiggery coalition mean
slow suicide. It would produce that division of political forces or
logical lines, Conservatives facing 'Destructives', which had been
expected to result from Reform. In the Conservative army those
Whigs who joined it (not all would have done so) would be a
minority group, their access to patronage limited, their morale and
their appeal damaged by an overt breach with the past. They must
in time have lost their identity. And on national grounds, as
Melbourne or Lansdowne or Holland understood them, it was no
more desirable than on Whig party grounds that Parliament and
the electorate should be clearly divided between supporters and
opponents of *the Conservative Cause*. The *Cause* would not have
benefited. Continuity and smoothness of constitutional development require that the real differences of opinion should not altogether coincide with party divisions, that there should always be in
the conservative ranks a liberal element and in the progressive
party a moderating wing. It is no accident that in every generation

[1] e.g. *Corr. of Lord Aberdeen & Pss. Lieven* 1832–54 (Camden Series), p. 78,
9th August, 1837.

those who wish to force the pace are tempted to conclude, when their party has been in power for some years, that their interests would best be served if it went into opposition. For it is in attack that the leadership may be most readily infected with the enthusiasm of the more advanced wing. The exercise of government naturally tilts the balance in a radical party towards the right. And so the Radical often thinks his cause would best be served if he and his friends could slough off the moderates, even at the risk of breaking up the party. The shrewder of the moderate Whigs well understood what a safeguard their association with the Radicals was from the point of view of *the Conservative Cause*.

For Melbourne the strife of Whig and Tory was not the real battle. In default of coalition between them, there had to be a liberal régime in which, as an Opposition leader testified, the inclinations of ministers were conservative but all their speeches and half their actions had to be radical. The ministerial barque necessarily proceeded by a series of tacking movements, its captain accused now of truckling subserviency to one wind, now to the other. Peel's connivance in these tactics is revealed by the care with which the Conservatives, while abusing the Whigs for staying in office on undignified terms, avoided turning them out; this Peel called 'making the Reform Bill work ... falsifying our own predictions! ... protecting the authors of the mischief from the work of their own hands'. Gladstone wrote — '... it is not to be denied that in those years great works had been achieved by both the Government and by the Opposition. On the one hand the course of administrative improvement ... commenced before the Great Epoch of the Reform Bill had become in a great degree the law of the departments of state and the tone of the Public Service had reached a higher pitch than was formerly its wont'. After his tribute to Melbourne's legislation, he continued 'On the other hand that great and firm, it might almost be said that grand, political combination, of which Sir Robert Peel ... was the centre and mainstay, had done much more than achieve a mere party triumph. It had first slackened and then assisted the feverish impetus which the convulsions of the era of the Reform Bill had imparted to the movement of public opinion and of State affairs. It was right that the Tory party whose obstinacy had provoked the Reform Bill and must stand mainly responsible to after ages for most of what was dangerous in its character, should breast and stay

the stream which they themselves had changed into a torrent'.[1]
From Melbourne's point of view the important thing was the
result, and since the electors had not commissioned the Conservative party to achieve it by itself, it had to be sought by stealth.
Meanwhile 'the King's government must be carried on'. In 1837
the accession of Victoria imparted to Melbourne a new zest for
being at the hub of affairs which belies his remark 'Nobody thinks
I want to stay in, do they?' How could it be disgraceful to hold his
office by the concurrent will of the monarch and the electorate, and,
in holding it, threaten no interest or institution which he thought it
essential to preserve and neglect no reform which he considered
it important to pass? Britain was getting the government its
electors deserved. Ireland was notably happier for it. At the
embassy in Madrid young George Villiers heard from his relatives
that there was no disturbance or agitation, no genuine hostility
between the rival parties, no danger to the House of Lords. The
country was busy, and there was little interest in politics. Only
the press was violent.[2]

To find the people passive and the Government, if not popular
or respected, at least unregarded,[3] was what all the ministers, save
Durham, who had put their hands to the Reform Bill had hoped
for. The picture was, of course, superficial, and by 1839 there was
a renewed threat of social revolution. Chartism had at the forefront
of its programme a thorough parliamentary reform. This the
parliamentary Radicals had failed to secure. It had as its real, if
ill-formulated, aspiration 'social justice' of a kind which most of
the parliamentary Radicals deemed obscurantist or utopian and
which some of them thought to outflank by an agitation against the
Corn Laws. The failure of the Radicals in Parliament was a source
of wonder to themselves. Their trumpets sounded, but the walls
stood firm. The trumpets rarely sounded in perfect concert. The
players, used to solo parts, found no one to train them for
orchestral performances. They were individualists, not lacking in
energy and zeal, but differing in their interests and emphasis, and
they had no general staff and no leader, so that they fought as
irregulars in uncoordinated skirmishes. 'Only if the people

[1] Add. MSS 44745, draft cit. supra.
[2] Clarendon, op. cit., Vol. I, pp. 122–4, letters from his uncle, the Earl of
Morley, an ex-Canningite, and his brother, Charles Villiers.
[3] Greville (1885 ed., Vol. I, p. 126), 1838, 'The country does not seem to mind
who is in or out.'

became conscious of its power and less complacement,' said Joseph Parkes, 'would the Whigs have to "raise their bids".' And that was the rub. In a parliamentary situation which was *prima facie* tailor-made for a determined Radical pressure group, the Radical M.P.s lacked both the spontaneous and the organised popular backing of 1831-2. The middle classes were 'busy' and the more aggrieved of the working classes did not recognise the Radicals as their champions.

The impotence of the parliamentary Radicals was to be chronic, and its causes persistent. An analysis of their position in 1852-3 emphasises exactly the same points we have found it necessary to make in the foregoing paragraph. 'The Radicals have been a number of men — they have never been a parliamentary party. . . . The Radicals are all clever and crotchetty. . . . The fire is insufficient for all the irons thrust in. . . . The Radicals have not carried a single point (for Free Trade was not a Radical test) in their whole history. . . . The sheerest vanity explains this non-subsidence into a practical party.[1] . . . It is useful to have politicians in advance of the age — in newspapers, in books, and on out-of-door platforms, but the truth is, such politicans have no business in the House of Commons.'[2] It is not enough to bristle with intelligence and information, even with moral indignation superadded. Houses of Commons are notoriously allergic to these when served up in unpalatable form. The Radicals failed to act on the principle that in politics the whole is greater than the sum of its parts — that individuals mobilised for common pressure achieve better results than more individuals acting without co-ordination.

In Melbourne's time the Radicals suffered from the refusal of the Prime Minister to take them seriously. He saw that it was unnecessary to negotiate with Durham, the most frustrated man in England because he was always the potential but never the actual leader of a Radical party. Arrogant, unhealthy, neuralgic and more than a trifle neurotic, Durham was sincere in his way, but more interested in himself than in any cause. If only a score of Radical M.P.s had insisted, the Whigs must have taken him back or fallen. But the ultimatum was never issued. Durham reviled the Whigs for doing without him (they sent him to Russia and then to Canada) and the Radicals for allowing them to do so. In Canada he

---

[1] *History of the Session* 1852-3, E. M. Whitby, 1854, pp. 14-18.
[2] ibid, p. 54.

immortalised his name as the author of a crucial report now rated
as the most important product of the whole Melbourne administration, which rejected most of it. But he also flouted the meagre
legal limitations on his viceregal dictatorship, and returned home
without leave, having alienated most Radicals. Sir William
Molesworth and John Stuart Mill hoped to use him yet as the
patron of an efficient Radical party. But Melbourne told the Queen
not to worry. Durham had been raised 'one hardly knows how'
into a 'factitious importance' by his extreme views, the praise
of those who wished to use him, and press campaigns, but Canada
had destroyed his reputation.[1]

Sir William Molesworth's fondest hope was to hear the death-
shriek of the Whigs, and he judged a man's Radicalism by the
virulence of his hostility to Whiggery. Early in 1835 he cherished
a scheme for a separate Radical party which he thought might be
seventy–eighty strong in the House of Commons,[2] and which was
to be connected with the Radicals of the metropolis and men up
from the provinces by a club at once cheaper, less exclusive and
more liberal than Brooks's with its aristocratic and landed traditions. But the Reform Club, when it did arise, with the best chef
in London, contained all classes of ministerialist, had a committee
of thirty-five of whom fifteen were described as Whigs, and soon
enrolled six hundred members, including a Royal Highness and
the Duke of Norfolk. This was not at all what Molesworth had
hoped; his proposed committee would have consisted of 'the best
of the Radicals and no Whigs'.[3] The Chief Whip, 'Ben' Stanley,
and his predecessor, 'Bear' Ellice, had emerged the victors from a
confabulation with the original sponsors and instead of a base
headquarters of Radicalism the Reform Club became a serviceable
extension of the whips' office. It must be understood that there
were always far more Radicals willing to bark than to bite. 'Most
Radicals', Russell said, 'were reasonable men', and would not give
much trouble unless provoked — and he did not mean only 'the
friendly section', otherwise described as Whig by party and Radicals
by opinion.[4] Melbourne was glad to hear it. For if it were so, why
was it necessary to make the ballot, which Russell disliked, an open

---

[1] *Queen's Letters SI*, Vol. I, p. 195, 7th May, 1839.
[2] T. S. Duncombe, a Radical (see *The Life*, Vol. 1, pp. 212–13) in 1836
estimated the ministerialists as 152 Whigs, 100 Liberals and 80 Radicals.
[3] Mrs Fawcett's *Molesworth*, pp. 73–4.
[4] *E.C.J.R.*, Vol. II, pp. 356–7, to Melbourne 31st August, 1839.

question, as Russell proposed? Thus rebuffed, Russell veered from urging concession to breathing defiance, and the tone of a speech at the beginning of the 1837 Parliament, which earned him the name of 'Finality Jack', reminded Charles Buller[1] of Wellington's fatal speech of November 1830 and might have drawn from Melbourne the inquiry why it was necessary to affront these reasonable men. We know that on one occasion Melbourne did write, 'I hope you have said nothing damn'd foolish. I thought you were rather teeming with some imprudence.' The serried ranks of the Opposition, 'too numerous for the existence of the Government in any respectable condition' and 'making ministers utterly powerless for legislative mischief'[2] were a better safeguard of constitutional stability than Russellite intransigence and provocation,[3] especially as it became evident that a large majority of the ministerialists, including many Whigs by party who were by no means Radicals by opinon, felt that the ballot should not be denied.[4]

The election caused by the death of William IV had made little change in party numbers.[5] But on the Jamaica Bill on 7th May, 1839 the majority sank to five, and would have been no majority at all but for the support of six Tories.[6] Even Radicals unconcerned

---

[1] Like Molesworth a Cornishman and a Radical, from a rich landed family, Buller was a Utilitarian who helped draft the Durham Report.

[2] *Aberdeen to Pss. Lieven*, p. 78, op. cit. and p. 85 (9th Aug., 1837; 30th, Nov., 1837). Peel thought it was the Tory numbers that moved Russell to speak as he did, but they were little greater than in the previous Parliament.

[3] Russell's brother, Tavistock, thought the speech did irreparable harm and that 'Johnny' could never be a popular leader. Next year Russell again offended the Radicals by a stalwart defence of the landed interest (*E.C.J.R.* II, p. 332, Duncannon to Russell). Greville, 2nd Part, 1837–52, Vol. I, pp. 190 ff. (spring 1839) reports pressure upon him to moderate his stand from 'Ellice and the out-of-door advisers, monitors and critics and his own Family, even his Father'.

[4] See *infra*, Ch. IV.

[5] The indeterminate allegiance of a few members and uncertainty as to the date of transfer of allegiance of some others makes it impossible to arrive at a firm figure either for the number of ministerialists in the Parliament of 1835–7 or for the dimensions of the Whig loss in 1837. Miss Betty Kemp, in *History*, NS XXXVII, 1952, quotes Arbuthnot's view that the Whigs lost fifteen seats, and estimates their majority in the new Parliament as 24. Duncombe (*Life*, Vol. I, pp. 212–13) accepted the *Annual Register* of 1835's estimate of 332 ministerialists; *Greville* (2nd Series Vol. I, p. 161) and a note in *Hansard* 24th June, 1839 give 331 in the next Parliament. These estimates must be too low, even allowing for vacancies. On 23rd July, 1835 the House upheld lay appropriation by 319:282 (a majority of 37) and, a.m. 4th June, 1836 by 300:261 (a majority of 39). In the new Parliament, on 16th May, 1838, a Tory motion against lay appropriation failed by 317:298 (majority 19) and on 27th May, 1839 Shaw Lefevre was elected Speaker (on the resignation of Abercromby) by 317:299 (majority 18). It looks as though Miss Kemp's estimate of the loss of seats, and of the majority in the 1837 Parliament, may both be a little high.

[6] The figures were 294:289 on the committal of the Bill.

with the fate of the emancipated slaves might legitimately doubt
whether the planter oligarchy, whose defiance of an imperial
statute was the reason for the Government's proposal to suspend
the island's constitution, was a respectable exponent of the principles of 1688 and 1776. But ten Radicals voted with the Opposition and ten abstained. Melbourne submitted the resignation of the
ministry.

Posterity has generally accepted the verdict of the Tories and
Radicals that the conditions of tenure of the second Melbourne
administration were contemptible. Disraeli depicted ministers as
reckless aristocrats stricken with palsy when confronted with a
resolute House of Lords; helpless without a mob at their back;
despoilers of property and institutions checked in their course by
what he called 'the organised hypocrisy' (Gladstone's 'grand
political combination').[1] Cobden portrayed them as destitute of the
courage and independence which principle and political honesty
alone can inspire, and thought 'truckling subservience . . . to the
menaces of the Tories' characteristic of Whiggery.[2] Joseph
Parkes dubbed them 'an unnatural party standing between the
People and the Tory aristocracy chiefly for the pecuniary value of
offices and vanity of power'.[3] And here, posterity has tended to
echo, were men who held on to place because they esteemed place
above all else, to whom dignities mattered more than prestige
and salaries were a fair substitute for success. To Parkes they were
'rickety, brainless, opinionless' mediocrities. Brougham said that
the Canadian revolt would cost Glenelg 'many a sleepless *day*'
(though 'Mr Over-Secretary Stephen' was wide enough awake).
Such censures are hardly justified if achievement is measured
against intent and if quality is estimated not by the yardstick of an
ideal but of the average level of nineteenth-century cabinets.
Ministers were not collectively, or most of them individually,
impressive, and, when so many disliked speaking, and had not the
gift for it[4] (and one who loved talking, Spring Rice, was a prize
bore) their parliamentary part was feebly played. If Russell grew
in stature, he was measured among pygmies. But of those ministers
who had not been in Grey's cabinet in 1832 only Minto and Rice
strike one as well below a realistic par. The main impression is one

---

[1] *Letters of Runnymede.*   [2] Morley's *Cobden*, Vol. I, p. 125.
[3] Buckley's *Parkes*, pp. 127–8 (1836).
[4] Campbell op. cit., and Grant's *Recollections* are the best sources for
sketches of the ministers as parliamentarians.

of insufficient energy, lack of direction and of a sense of direction.
A young Scottish duke who looked upon Melbourne as 'an excellent head of a party dying of inertia' had a point.[1] There was, in the modern slang idiom, no *future* for an administration so conducted.
It was, properly viewed, a ministry of caretakers. And that being
so, it lost its only plausible defence when, retracting its resignation,
it took advantage of 'the Bedchamber Question' to hang on to
office for another two years, although Peel, dissolving as prime
minister, would almost certainly have obtained a majority.

Nothing that the Whigs did in office became them so ill as their
return to it. The young Victoria had made herself a passionate
Whig, who could write of 'our supporters' in the House of
Commons. Tearfully she summoned Peel, and he, lacking Melbourne's finesse with young ladies, and that self-willed young lady
in particular, blundered into a position where the retention of 'a
female Court entirely Whig' became a matter of personal honour
to the Queen and of constitutional propriety to her prospective
minister. Because the Queen wished to keep about her Normanby's
wife,[2] Morpeth's sisters, Russell's sisters-in-law and Duncannon's
daughter,[3] the formation of a Conservative government was
delayed for two years. The Whig ministers (Howick dissenting)[4]
informed Her Majesty of their willingness to resume office and
framed the message with which she broke off negotiations with
Peel. That night the Queen danced happily among 'her only real
friends' — Melbourne's sister (Lady Cowper), the Duchess of
Sutherland, the Mintos and Lord Anglesey.

The late Professor Pares pointed out the ambivalence of the
attitude of the Rockingham and Foxite Whigs to the problem of
the relationship of King and cabinet.[5] They were the first party
group to claim the right to nominate their own prime minister and
the right of the prime minister to choose the cabinet, and to assert
that the monarch must accept the advice of his ministers. But they
also welcomed the prospect of the regency or accession of the

[1] Argyll, *Autobiography and Memoirs*, Vol. I, p. 151.
[2] Normanby after being Lord Lieutenant of Ireland had just succeeded
Glenelg at the Colonial Office.
[3] Peel's last terms were moderate — only the Duchess of Sutherland, Lady
Normanby and Lady Tavistock should resign (they held the chief offices in the
Bedchamber).
[4] Landsowne and Rice thought the ladies should have resigned but did not
like Howick indicate dissent on the formal recommendation to the Queen
(*Queen's Letters*, Vol. I, pp. 215-17).
[5] *George III and the Politicians*.

Prince of Wales, because they thought it would bring them into office, though they had objected to the King's nomination of Pitt as prime minister and to the appeal from the House of Commons, in which he had no majority, to the electors, who gave him one. The Whigs of 1830 rejoiced in, and fully exploited, the favour of William IV, but this was a rapidly wasting asset, and early in 1835 they condemned the King for doing for Peel what his father had done for Pitt. Melbourne became the first man to be raised to the premiership as a result of a general election, against the will of the monarch. He was also to be the last party leader who openly exploited the favour of the monarch for electoral purposes, in 1837; there was now an impressionable sovereign prepared to co-operate wholeheartedly with the Whigs. In 1839 Melbourne's feeling for the Queen, and delight in the political honeymoon they were having together, combined with the pressure of his colleagues, overbore his judgement. The Whig ministers drew a pretty picture of themselves as gallant gentlemen responding to the pleas of a maiden in distress. It was not politically proper for the Whigs to come back via the Bedchamber, but the love of place burned strong and having a monarch who thought Whigs the only safe and loyal people,[1] and read only Whig newspapers,[2] went to their heads. It was only just that in the following two years the reputation of Whiggery should reach its nadir.

In this miserable fag-end period the ministry's only triumph was Palmerston's humiliation of the French over the Eastern Question, a controversial matter which nearly wrecked the cabinet,[3] which, as Melbourne said, could not afford any resignations. The Conservatives, after the Bedchamber crisis, were angry men, who combined with some of the Radicals to humiliate the Queen's prospective consort by reducing his proposed income. Long committed by their leader to a policy of watching and waiting, they threw off the curb. Their leader, too, was now willing to strike. O'Connell, whom a diluted Municipal Corporations Act at last allowed to appear as Lord Mayor of Dublin, began to disengage from ministers and adjust his mind to the imminence of Conservative government. The cabinet did not seem to gain vigour by the recruitment of younger men.[4] And if it was relieved of its two

---

[1] *Queen's Letters*, Vol. I, p. 268, 21st January, 1840.
[2] *Clarendon*, op. cit., p. 221.   [3] See *infra*, Ch. 10.
[4] Normanby, Morpeth, Baring, Labouchere, Macaulay, Clarendon and George Grey were all about forty.

greatest liabilities, Glenelg and Spring Rice (both of whom were paid off with rich sinecures), it lost also Poulett Thomson, the minister most respected by the middle classes (he went to Canada), and Howick. The son of the Reform Bill Prime Minister rated himself too highly, was a difficult colleague and was not liked by Radicals because of his strong opposition to the ballot. But he was a positive personality, with progressive views on taxation and administrative reform, who resigned because he did not find scope for his constructive energies. He had found on joining the cabinet in 1835 that his colleagues had 'a fatal mediocrity' and was 'vexed at their indolence and inefficiency'.[1] His departure, like that of Thomson, was equivalent to a vote of no confidence in the cabinet's capacity for good.

On the Opium War with China in 1840 the Government's majority fell to ten.[2] The following year it looked as though it might be defeated even without Radical desertions or Whig abstentions, for a series of by-elections beginning with the Tory gain of the closely and corruptly contested County Carlow seat in December 1840 went disastrously for ministers. In February they lost three seats, one in a county, one in a cathedral city, and one in an industrial town.[3] And then, in alliance with the Chartists, the Tory candidate, John Walter of the *Times*, was elected for Nottingham in an election turning on the social question. This confirmed Russell's discovery that public discontents flourished on what he called 'the misrepresentation' that neither the Whigs nor the Tories 'would ever do anything for the improvement of the condition of the working classes'.[4] The middle classes too were disenchanted with Whiggery. Some desperate stroke was needed to revive Whig fortunes. The cabinet decided to brave the landed interest to which its members belonged, and assail fiscal privilege in a bid for borough seats.

[1] Howick MSS, 10th June and 16th December, 1835, cited by Aspinall, Raleigh Lecture *cit. supra*, p. 188.
[2] a.m. 10th April, 1840, motion of no confidence lost 271 : 261.
[3] Monmouthshire, Canterbury and Walsall.
[4] *Queen's Letters*, op. cit., p. 350, 16th May, 1841.

CHAPTER IV

The Whigs and The Landed Interest

During the civil wars of the seventeenth century the great bastions of the cause of the parliamentarians against the King were the centres of national commerce, and in the reign of Charles II the City of London gave refuge to Shaftesbury, the first Whig leader. But not for nothing was the expanded and temporary coalition to which Shaftesbury gave leadership called 'the Country Party'. And though in early Hanoverian times the majority of the gentry were hostile to the Whig 'oligarchy' which dominated the state, the eighteenth century made evident that the natural habitat of the Whig was the shire, among his acres and his tenants, his hunters and his neighbours with whom he governed the county through Quarter Sessions. Even when urging his aristocratic patrons to pursue with more persistence the power which arises from popularity, (the efficacy of which was demonstrated by the elder Pitt) Edmund Burke thought it entirely proper that Whig grandees should govern the country by virtue of 'power arising from property'. The best nineteenth-century definition or description of Whiggery by a Whig begins 'a body of men connected with high rank and property. . . .'[1]

There is a lesser sense in which the term 'Whig' is used, to denote moderate political opinions; it is a shorthand for 'moderate liberal'. But it was only so used because moderate liberals belonged to a party dominated by the Whigs proper, the Whigs who were part of *Whiggery*, at the head of which stood a group of noble families dubbed with affectionate humour 'the Sacred Circle of the Great-Grandmotherhood' because they were so intricately interrelated. To use the term 'Whig' simply to denote political opinions is to forfeit half the flavour and force of the word. A Whig who was part of Whiggery could hold any opinions he wished, however Radical, without forfeiting his right to the title, while a man who agreed in everything with Earl Grey or Lord John

[1] See *supra*, p. 21.

Russell might not on that account be regarded by the Whigs proper as one of themselves. The Whigs proper cannot have numbered, about 1850, much more than a thousand families owning substantial estates, a third of them titled.[1] Round them, political reflections of the great folk, clustered loyal freeholders (part of the traditional county electorate) shopkeepers, solicitors and the like, and such tenant farmers as the magnates chose to admit to the franchise.[2]

There were, indeed, men called 'Whig' outside the villages and country towns, but the term was applied to them, at least by Radicals, pejoratively, to imply that they were deficient in robust liberalism but were inhibited by material or sentimental considerations from proclaiming themselves Tories. Thus Molesworth found too many 'Whigs' in Leeds. And when discussing the project for the incorporation of Manchester, which Cobden called 'shaking off the feudal livery of Sir Oswald Mosley, to put on the democratic garb of the Municipal Reform Act', Morley says 'the Whig, as usual, was timid and uncomfortable; he went about murmuring that a charter was unnecessary, and muttered something about expense'.[3] By the middle of the century the term 'Whig' sat somewhat incongruously upon a merchant, unless he had bought an estate or been integrated by special licence into the great Whig social circles, like the Baring family which, on the profits of merchant banking and financial operations on behalf of governments, became the greatest purchasers of land in the early nineteenth century.[4] It sat even more incongruously on a manufacturer.[5] A 'Whig working man' was a creature outside the range of the most imaginative propagandist. Whiggery was not to be found at the factory gate, in the mechanics' institute or the chamber of commerce, but between the panelled walls of clubs and

[1] Author's calculation, based on an examination of the ownership of estates of 3,000 acres or g.a.v. £3,000 in the *Modern Domesday* of the 1870s.

[2] Under the Chandos clause (see *infra*, pp. 83–5) £50 tenants-at-will were given the vote in the counties in 1832.

[3] Morley's *Cobden*, Vol. I, p. 123.

[4] Only one branch of the Barings remained Whig. Alexander, the second head of the firm, was Wellington's candidate for Leader of the House in the abortive attempt of 1832, and took office under Peel as Lord Ashburton. But it was Francis Baring (later 1st Lord Northbrook) whose description of Whiggery is cited above and in full in Ch. I.

[5] I am inclined to think that the term 'Whig' was in more common use in the Yorkshire manufacturing districts than I have perhaps implied above, but by the middle of the century the politicians there were called Liberals or Radicals rather than Whigs.

libraries, on the terraces and rides of country places, at dinners and balls in Town and country, at Westminster and in Whitehall. As a prototype, Trollope's Plantagenet Palliser, Duke of Omnium, is authentic. For Whiggery was the most ostentatious and self-conscious constitutent of that potent entity which in the middle of the twentieth century has been christened 'the Establishment'. Its personnel was aristocratic. Its influence was based essentially on oligarchy. Traditional claims and a monopoly of administrative experience, and an intense tenaciousness in asserting the one and preserving the other, enabled it to maintain for many years the leadership of the Liberal party. It lacked vulgar appeal and mass support, but the restricted representative system of 1832 made it possible, by and large, to prevent the Radicals from capitalising those assets in order to break free of their self-appointed hierarchs. Whigs and Tories alike made concessions, small or large, as they deemed the case to require, in order to preserve their own importance and that of 'the Establishment' in general. The Whigs made them, perhaps, a little more readily — until the Tories learned the lesson and began leaping into the dark; they made them not to avowed opponents but to 'honourable friends', allies, 'followers'. There was no prevalent desire among the Whigs to go faster than 'public opinion' required; they deemed it no presumption that their politicians should be the judges of this, and for 'public opinon' they read 'political expediency'. They were assisted in a task which was essentially one of restraining the liberal army without breaking it up by the fact that the ranks of M.P.s labelled 'Reformers' were full of men who never approved a major reform until their ministers presented it to them for approval, and by lack of strategic and tactical skill among Radical parliamentarians. If the Radicals tolerated Whig 'leadership', restraining their impatience, it was, however, as a leading Tory said, because they had nothing to expect from the Conservatives but knew that a Whig government was composed of 'squeezable materials'.[1] The Whigs were trimmers. Their creed, if in the nineteenth century they had one at all, was to be portrayed in half-tones. To every proposition of progressive import there was a conservative caveat; to every pledge of resistance an implied indication of willingness to reconsider. Whiggism lacked political glamour, except for old-fashioned people who could feed on a highly idealised version of

---

[1] Aberdeen to Pss. Lieven, op. cit., p. 85, 30th November, 1837.

the Whig inheritance. And it often lacked relevance to the most pressing problems of a society under the stress of economic revolution. In the last resort it was apt to seem merely a series of propositions about political tactics.

The Whigs were a minority of the class to which they belonged. They commanded only a minority of the non-Radical electorates, and a minority of the House of Lords. After the brief, extraordinary, struggle for the Reform Bill, they once again lost the confidence of their own kind. Melbourne said in January 1835 that it was a serious matter for a man to decide whether he should 'at the head of a majority of the House of Commons, engage in a political warfare with the Crown, with the decided majority of the House of Peers, with almost the whole of the clergy, and I do not overstate when I add, with three parts at least of gentry of the country'. These were the classes which formed 'the Landed Interest', who, according to the Whigs as well as the Tories, were the natural bulwark of the constitution as well as comprising country society and the London world which seasonally emanated from it.

In the counties, titled magnates as of right took the political lead. The desertion of Lord Tankerville on, or before, the Reform Bill, following that of Lord Jersey not only deprived the Whigs of the second of their three foremost hostesses[1] but damaged Whig prospects in Northumberland elections by ranging the Bennets with the Percies against the Greys. The Stanleyite secession of 1834 meant the loss of the Lennox influence in Sussex and the Stanley influence in Lancashire. A Duke of Richmond, an Earl of Derby and an Earl of Carnarvon served in Disraeli's cabinets, an Earl of Tankerville and the heir of Albermarle in his government. These were but conspicuous examples of a continuing and substantial decline in aristocratic support for the Whigs, which was only briefly reversed in the 'fifties by their association with the Peelites and retarded by the supremacy of Palmerston in the decade before 1865. By 1880 the drift had reached alarming proportions, and it then became a flood. Between 1830 and 1885 Whig and Liberal nominations were responsible for the majority of a net increase of a hundred members in the

[1] Jersey veered to the Tories in the 'twenties and became Lord Chamberlain under Wellington in 1830. There are catty remarks about his wife (sister of Lady Duncannon and coheiress of the Child financial interests) in The Journal of Mrs Arbuthnot.

House of Lords, but creations and call-ups[1] were insufficient to give any Whig or Liberal government the assurance of an easy passage of its measures.[2] The way of a Whig leader in the Lords, his spiritual home, was hard. There had to be much dining of 'foolish peers, moderately dull'.[3] Lansdowne and the second Earl Granville successively had to cajole into attendance men who were their friends, even friends who as Household officials were technically members of the administration.[4] Ministers never resorted to the wholesale 'packing' threatened in 1832 or even to planned, continuous injection. This was partly because the great Whigs were not prepared to see the social distinction of the peerage further diminished for mere party convenience, as the Marquess of Westminister made plain to Russell in 1847 when he protested against the flooding of the chamber with politicians irrespective of whether they possessed large landed property.[5] But it was also because calculated recruitment might not pay dividends. A peer cannot be unmade, and there was no guarantee of gratitude, still less that it would be hereditary. The red benches proved wonderful correctors of Liberal opinions. It was not outright defection alone that had to be feared — the loss of peers to the legion commanded successively by the Duke of Wellington, Stanley (later Earl of Derby), Beaconsfield and the Marquess of Salisbury. There was in the Lords a cult of independence which included among its devotees not only hostile cavaliers like Ellenborough and Lynd-hurst but candid friends omitted from Whig governments — notably Brougham[6] and the third Earl Grey (the Howick of the 'thirties).

Extravagant claims were made in 1831–2 of the superior (Whig) virtue of peers created before the reign of George III. Professor

[1] i.e., the practice of calling up to the Lords heirs to peerages during the life of their fathers.

[2] In 1849, for instance, ambassadors were summoned home to vote for the Navigation Bill.

[3] Fitzmaurice's *Granville*, Vol. I, p. 163.

[4] ibid., pp. 240–1, *re* Lord Ailesbury, Granville's 'most intimate friend'.

[5] The Westminster peerages bear the significant dates 1761, 1784 and 1831 and bear testimony to the importance of the head of the House of Grosvenor derived from influence over relatives and clients dependent on him for election — an influence derived from property and social position. From Fitzmaurice, op. cit., Vol. I, p. 177, we learn that 'the whole Liberal party say that it is monstrous to make a Tory with no estate, and a villa near London, head of the magistracy (of Kent)'. An analysis of the policy of peer-creation 1837–1911 may be found in Mr R. E. Pumphrey's article, 'Introduction of Industrialists into the British Peerage' (*Am. His.* R., LXV, 1959).

[6] Brougham never held office after 1834.

Woodward took them at their face value; Professor Turberville subjected them to patient analysis,[1] and pointed out that only 71 of the 143 peers who owed their title to George III voted against the Reform Bill while only 60 of 111 with pre-1760 titles supported it. Pitt indeed by his creations utterly submerged the eighteenth-century aristocracy, which included the forebears of most of the great Whig families of the nineteenth century. He won the victory over the Whig aristocracy that his father had failed to achieve. But it was by the promotion of Scottish and Irish peers, country gentlemen and cadets of noble families (not, as Disraeli said, by men picked out of Lombard Street and Change Alley) that he did it, and it was not his creations but the impact of the French Revolution which transformed the Lords from a Whig to a Tory stronghold. The House was the despair of liberal Tory ministers before 1830 as of Whigs afterwards. Canning wrote 'It is a great misfortune that the Lords take so narrow a view of their present situation, that they cannot see that we are on the brink of the struggle between property and population and that such a struggle is only to be avoided by the mildest and most liberal legislation.'[2] We have seen that, when the struggle which he predicted came to a head in 1832, the Lords were forced to bow only by the joint threats of violent revolution and of wholesale 'packing'. But the temporal peers[3] divided about equally, in terms of both numbers and property, on the second reading of the Reform Bill in 1831. So did the holders of the older peerages. A score of creations by Grey and the aid of a dozen or so personal followers of Canning was sufficient, despite the long years of Tory supremacy, to produce this virtual equality among the lords of parliament who sat by right of title. It was the bishops and the representative peers for Scotland and Ireland who accounted for almost the whole of the Tory majority against the Bill. On the second reading in 1832, twelve peers (excluding prelates) reversed their votes and seven former non-voters recorded their support. The total number of peers who voted for one of the second readings (other than royal peers and prelates) was 174.

For the peers the Reform Bill was the most consequential measure on which they had to vote between the abortive Peerage

---

[1] Woodward, *The Age of Reform*; Tuberville, *The House of Lords in the Age of Reform*.
[2] Quoted by Turberville, op. cit., p. 223.   [3] Excluding royal dukes.

Bill of 1719 and the Parliament Bill of 1910–11, for a more representative House of Commons must necessarily gain in influence at
the expense of the Lords, and Reform itself shattered an elaborate
complex of influence acquired and maintained, at great cost, by
individual peers. Few welcomed it with the enthusiasm of Durham
or the Earl of Radnor, who yielded up his borough of Downton as
a sacrifice before the altar of his Radical idealism.[1] But here was a
unique challenge to that calculating adaptability by which so many
of their ancestors had accumulated and retained properties,
fortunes, honours and influence. Precisely because the challenge
was unique and the stakes so high, men swallowed the camel who
would scornfully spit out the gnats of more petty concession. The
division lists on the Reform Bill exaggerate the amount of
Whiggery in the peerage. In 1841 only 96 peers voted for the
preservation of Whig government. Within a few months of the
passage of Reform the House of Lords was passing, as is evidenced
by Dr Turberville's chapter headings, from 'survival' to 'revival'
and soon to 'counter-attack'. In 1834 the peers rejected the Jewish
Disabilities Bill by 130 : 38, the University Tests Bill by 187 : 85,
and the Irish Tithe Bill by 189 : 122. In 1835 the Lords emasculated the Municipal Corporation Bill in committee by votes of
120–30 against less than forty.[2] In 1836 the Lords destroyed the
Irish Corporations Bill by 203 : 119. They struck out lay appropriation in 1835 by 138 : 41. As we have noted, by 1838 the Whigs,
not being willing to face a collision with the peers, abandoned this
policy.

The movement of opinion among the peers on governments and
policies is ascertainable by reference to debates and divisions. A
fair idea of the trend of opinion among the freeholders may be
derived from a study of the county elections. In 1831 six (English)
knights of the shire were returned for the Bill to every one against,
and in 1832, with the county membership doubled, the Whigs did
well enough. But in 1835 they lost up to twenty-eight seats, if we
take into account the defection of 'Reform' members as well as
straight losses. The Conservatives now had an equal share of the
English county members. Having won Althorp's seat in South
Northamptonshire, they defeated Russell when, on appointment

---

[1] As Lord Folkestone, M.P. Radnor had been a member of Whitbread's
Mountain.
[2] The numbers are small because proxies were not available in committee;
they do not suggest any great enthusiasm among Whig peers for Whig measures.

as Home Secretary in 1835, he had to face a by-election.[1] They won in South Staffordshire when Littleton was shunted to the Lords and in North Northamptonshire when Lord Milton died. Whig losses in 1837 were actually heavier than they were to be in 1841, and the more conspicuous in that there was hardly any net loss in the boroughs.

The Tories owed some part of their notable gains in the counties to the influence and control which landlords were able to exercise by virtue of the provisions of the Chandos clause, an amendment to the Reform Bill accepted, reluctantly, by Althorp because Whig aristocrats and gentry joined with Tories to demand it.[2] It enabled magnates to create and manage, sometimes by mere book-keeping entries, tenant-at-will voters. Since the majority of landlords were Tory, the Whigs would clearly suffer politically from the Chandos clause if the balance of opinion among the freeholders was even or on the Whig side. But when the balance of opinion among the freeholders was on the Tory side, Whig magnates and groups of Whig landlords would derive advantage from the provision. It must be doubted whether without the Chandos clause the Whigs would have secured even a score of the 145 English county seats in 1841. The three county divisions which were most consistently Whig all contained a high proportion of tenants-at-will. North Derbyshire always returned a Cavendish and a country gentleman; it is not safe to assume that this record would have stood without the Duke of Devonshire's tenantry.[3] The liberal gentry of Cumberland tended to Radicalism, and some branches of the Howards were Roman Catholic, but it was to the Earl of Carlisle, as having 'so preponderating an influence' in the eastern division, that Graham (a great proprietor in the county) addressed himself as to retaining the seat after his breach with Grey in 1834. Approved by the Earl, he was re-elected, but when in 1836 Carlisle endorsed a Radical candidate, Graham knew he was doomed. In 1837 he was beaten by 700 and 500. But in 1841, with majorities of only 181 and 82 respectively, the Hon. Charles Howard (who sat till 1879) and his Radical colleague had reason to bless the Chandos clause. That

[1] He became member for Stroud.
[2] Radicals also supported it as increasing the electorate, and perhaps as strengthening the demand for the ballot.
[3] In North Derbyshire the Tory gained 900 votes between 1832 and 1835, compared with 500 in South Derbyshire, but in the southern division the Whigs lost 1,000, in the northern only 572 net.

year even West Cornwall, which never had a contest between 1832 and 1885, momentarily returned to Tory.[1] It is not suggested that all tenants-at-will were coerced. Russell, in opposing the ballot, avowed that it was perfectly natural for the tenant to vote as his landlord wished. And tenants-at-will were not the only voters who entertained reputable sentiments of respect for a local family and deference to the opinions of a great neighbour. It was said that Bedfordshire was Whig because the Duke of Bedford was Whig. But if Bedfordshire never rejected a Russell, it only once failed to return a Tory as well (in 1880).[2] Rutland has been regarded as in the pocket of the Noels. It sent one of that family to Westminster in eleven of the twelve parliaments elected 1832–80 and until 1865 a Heathcote as well. But the only contest in the fifty years is illuminating. On that occasion the Noel was a Whig, and he was beaten. Evidently it was not enough to be a Noel unless one was a Tory as well. The Heathcotes, another great Rutland family, found the same in Lincolnshire, though they combined Whiggism with Protectionism.

Of the views of 'the gentlemen of England' there is no measure so exact as that of the opinions of the peers or the county electorates. They were, of course, electors, often in several constituencies. They provided, with the aristocracy, practically all the county members, and a majority of every House of Commons, most of the Tory M.P.s and the vast majority of those who were fully 'Whig'. The gentry ranged in opinion, as one would expect, from Sir Robert Inglis to Sir William Molesworth, and from admirers of the Marquess of Chandos (High Tory, ultra-Protestant champion of fiscal privilege as an aid to high rents) to those who would abet Lord Fitzwilliam to transform the Corn Laws.[3] Many Whig squires returned in 1831 owed their election to the county freeholders, but in pressing the Chandos clause they were consulting

[1] Here there was no preponderant landlord but a strong, traditional Whiggism among proprietors was reinforced by marked individualism, often associated with Nonconformity, among the farmers.

[2] The Russells and Whitbreads owned 18% of the whole county. The 1841 Lord Chas. Jas. Fox Russell, being out of sympathy with his family on the Corn Laws, contested Cambridgeshire and two Tories were returned for Bedfordshire.

[3] The 5th (Irish) and 3rd British Earl, who succeeded in 1833 was the Lord Milton who attacked the Chandos clause (H. of C. 1st Feb., 1832). As Earl he was one of the Whig magnates in the West Riding (with Devonshire, Norfolk, Scarbrough) who in competition with Tory lords helped increase the largest electorate of the country by adding tenants-at-will, 1832–42, to more than 5,000 (see F. M. L. Thompson, 'Whigs and Liberals in the West Riding 1830–60' in *E.H.R.*, LXXIV, 291, April, 1959).

the interest of their own rank, not that of their electors, who, in many parts of the country, resented landlord domination. Hardly a lord or squire in the Parliament that passed the Reform Bill but insisted that 'property' should greatly influence elections. Althorp argued that the division of counties, at first disliked by the gentry, would increase the 'legitimate' influence of local families, keep out strangers relying on 'mere popularity', and reduce contests and compromises. He was thinking, not only of compromises and contests between Whig and Tory, but between magnates and 'the independent interest'. He hastened to say that 'some degree of popularity' would and should be necessary for election.[1] He disliked the Chandos clause because it would introduce *illegitimate* influence and bring on the landed class as a whole something of the discredit accumulated in the past by the special interests developed by individuals (not all of them gentlemen) in the boroughs. But he was overborne, and the amendment passed which Lord Milton said would throw county elections into the hands of a Quarter Sessions oligarchy.[2]

After 1832 a concurrence of opinion between Whig and Tory gentry was often manifest — in criticism of the malt tax, in defence of the Corn Laws, in hostility to centralisation,[3] and to urban encroachment, including, it is evident from the West Riding, urban encroachment on county representation.[4] We do not meet again quite the old style of 'independent interest' in the House of Commons, which Walpole, Newcastle, North and the younger Pitt could never render servile; which had helped raise up the older Pitt to be 'the great Commoner' and gave his son the victory over Fox; the interest which destroyed the income tax in 1816 and with

---

[1] *Annual Register*, 1831, p. 210.   [2] H. of C. 1st Feb., 1832. See note above.
[3] e.g. Sir Wm. Ingilby (S. Lincs., W.) moved the reduction of malt duty, 1833; E. S. Cayley (N. Rdg., W.) on the Royal Commission of 1836 advocated inflation to supplement the rent-raising effect of the Corn Laws; Hon. W. Portman (Dorset, W.) M.P. 1857–86 carried dislike of centralisation to the point of opposing the collection of statistics by the state (Dod).
[4] Such encroachment was possible because, amid Tory protests, the Reform Bill provided that 40s. freeholders in represented towns (as of course in unrepresented) should vote in the counties. This is discounted (e.g. by Seymour) as an important Whig electoral asset, but in 1858 a quarter of the West Riding electorate (and a predominantly Liberal part of it) derived qualification from property in parliamentary boroughs. The mayors and aldermen of Leeds, Wakefield and Bradford, running town liberal organisations, sponsored Cobden's membership for the division in 1847, rejected Fitzwilliam's son in 1849 and put up a Radical candidate without Whig support. Fitzwilliam negotiated with the Tories, although they were semi-Protectionist. (See Thompson, *E.H.R.* article mentioned above.)

whose aid alone in three decades before 1830 the Whigs could sometimes mount a formidable opposition. But there was far less disagreement, real or assumed, between the county members of the two parties than between the parties as a whole. The *County* had every interest in damping down political controversy which embarrassed social relationships. Catholic Emancipation, Reform, the Corn Laws, like Home Rule and Lloyd George's budget later, engendered bitterness within families and between neighbours. The Duke of Beaufort set up a Protectionist nephew against his Peelite brother in Monmouthshire in 1847 and in West Gloucestershire helped to victory the sitting Whig member, Grantley Fitzhardinge Berkeley, who as a Protectionist was opposed by a Free Trade Berkeley put up by his own brother, Lord Fitzhardinge. By 1852 passions had subsided and the Beaufort influence was thrown to a twenty-two old nephew of the Duke, although he was a Whig.[1] Preference of family to party interest seemed so natural that the tenants of the Trentham estate in Staffordshire could not believe that the Whig Duke of Sutherland intended them not to vote for his Conservative nephew.[2] There were, of course, settled antagonisms between rival political families. Old Earl Grey rewarded his grandchildren for notching the gates of the Duke of Northumberland with hatchets.[3] But by and large everyone was relieved when passions cooled after a crisis. Aberdeen took it as a sign that this was happening again after the Reform Bill when Whigs and Tories began marrying each other and the Fitzwilliams went up to stay at Haddo — an event which a little earlier he would have thought unlikely.[4] Nothing is more characteristic of county politics than that a transfer of representation from one party to another should occur without a contest, thus sparing the former member the chagrin of defeat among his own people and saving each side the expense of a contest and the county families the necessity of working against one another in public.[5] The grant

---

[1] Capt. (later Col. Sir) Robert Nigel Fitzhardinge Kingscote represented the division till 1885.

[2] Professor Gash adverts to this. A Howard relative of the Duke elected for Sutherland in 1837 seems to have been a Conservative.

[3] J. G. Lockhart's *Viscount Halifax*, p. 30.

[4] *Aberdeen to Pss. Lieven*, p. 112, 16th September, 1838. Lady A's niece (Lady Frances Douglas) married Lord Milton, later 6th Earl Fitzwilliam, who lived into the twentieth century.

[5] Fitzwilliam (see Thompson's article) said the 1846 by-election in the West Riding restored the representation to its proper footing — one Whig, one Tory.

of a third member to seven counties not large enough for division was popular because it permitted, and almost invited, minority representation. Thus in Dorset, where there had been a bitter and widely-publicised contest at a by-election during the Reform struggle, in which the Tory Lord Ashley defeated his Ponsonby brother-in-law, a Whig, Ponsonby was returned in 1832 and 1835 without a contest, together with Ashley and another Tory. In 1837 Lord Ilchester's son and from 1857 to 1885 Lord Portman's heir sat as representatives of the minority Whig interest in that county. Even more remarkable was the case of Buckinghamshire, where three Tories were returned as early as 1835. A vacuum was left in county politics by the bankruptcy of the Duke of Buckingham (the Chandos of the Clause) which involved the sale of the contents of Stowe and some of the estates.[1] Adjusting itself in 1847 to the altered balance the county, at the very moment that it accepted, on the morrow of the Repeal of the Corn Laws, Disraeli, the arch-champion of Protection, took also as one of its members a Cavendish, and after him his son. It did not revert to all-Tory representation until that son succeeded to the peerage in 1863.

Thus, when their popularity in the counties reached its nadir, the Whigs received some benefit from the Chandos clause, and they sometimes benefited from the convention of minority representation. In 1847 and 1857, though still very much the minority party in the counties, they enjoyed a temporary and partial revival there. But in general the tale is one of declining confidence in Whiggery, which requires explanation. Cobden's allegation that it was due to 'the base selfishness of the landlords of that party which led them to desert their colours . . . in every . . . county upon the bread question' is not acceptable as a complete explanation.[2] The Corn Law question, indeed, was always in the background when it was not in the foreground; no farmer or rural landlord was ever unaware of it. But the decline of the Whigs in the counties was cumulative, and it would not be true to say that the bread question loomed as large in 1835 or 1837 as in 1841. The example which Cobden himself chose, North Nottingham-

[1] From 'The End of a Great Estate' (F. M. L. Thompson, *Ec. Hist. R.*, 2nd Series, VIII, No. 1, Aug., 1955) it appears that sales of land began in earnest in May 1847; principal purchasers were the Barings, Rothschilds, Lord Carrington, and the banker who became Lord Overstone. Hon. C. C. Cavendish held 3,000 acres in the county and took his title (cr. 1858 Lord Chesham) from there.
[2] Morley's *Cobden*, Vol. 1, pp. 362–3, 16th February, 1846.

shire, is itself proof that deeper explanation is required.[1] The Whig decline was cumulative, presumably because Whig offences were cumulative, and the unreliability of Whiggery on the major agricultural question was only a symptom of general unreliability from the point of view of the county interests.

The old governing class and county electorates traditionally demanded of the county members that they defend the constitution, sustain cheap and efficient administration, confine to a minimum central interference in local affairs, preserve the Church as an establishment and, last but not least, defer to agricultural interests in taxation.

But for their attachment to the Church of England it is doubtful whether the country gentlemen would have tolerated Dutch and Hanoverian kings. They could not look upon the Church with detachment. Locally parish and mansion were closely connected, the living frequently in gift and the tithe impropriate, the parson and the squire deeply concerned together in local administration. Nationally the Church was an institution of the realm, an arm of the constitution. Magnates and gentry still put younger sons, brothers, nephews and cousins into orders as they put them into commissions in the army or navy. The clergy tended to be received in society rather according to their family than their ecclesiastical status. The days when a Primate of England walked with his umbrella from his palace of Lambeth to take his place at the head of the Lords Spiritual in Parliament at Westminster did not come until the death in 1848 of Archbishop Howley, who had ridden in state with a splendid equipage. Till the previous year there reigned from Bishopsthorpe His Grace the Most Reverend and Right Honourable Edward Vernon Harcourt, born of a noble family while the Duke of Newcastle shared the Government with a Pitt who was not yet Earl of Chatham, before George III was on the throne. Uncle of Lord Vernon, widower of a Levenson-Gower, heir to the estate of Nuneham Courtenay in Oxfordshire, father of members of parliament, the Archbishop would have been a great figure even if Grenville had not raised him to York in 1807. He

---

[1] Cobden said North Nottinghamshire had a small electorate and a strong Liberal party and was considered Whig until the base selfishness of the landlords caused them to desert on the bread question. But no Whig had been returned since Lord Lumley became Earl of Scarbrough in 1835. Fitzwilliam described the defeat in the West Riding in 1841 as due to 'agricultural agitation' but Thompson seems to ascribe it to superior Tory organisation.

symbolised, on a sumptuous level, the alliance of Church and State and Church and Society. But in the fourth decade of the nineteenth century most of the prelates, successors of men who had been Whig peers in lawn sleeves, were 'high and dry' Tories, and so were most of the clergy. It was not on bishops, deans and canons that Whigs relied electorally, but rather, especially in cathedral cities, upon Dissenters. Clerical opinion, which found it hard to forgive Peel the emancipation of the Catholics, gladly transferred its hostility to the party of Reform, which tampered with tithes, threatened church rates and meditated the abolition of University Tests; which lacked the power, if not the will, to prevent Nonconformists getting above themselves; which accepted lay appropriation and entered into alliance with Irish Papists, the sworn enemies of the Church of England.

Very few of the great proprietors were Dissenters.[1] In the privileged society of the *County* the Nonconformist was incongruous. This little world, indeed, was not strictly exclusive, and never had been, because it literally could not afford to be. The merchant, the banker, even the manufacturer, purchasing land, could gain an entrée, sooner or later, and sooner rather than later if there were children eligible to repair the fortune of an old family. The Barings, the Peels, the Arkwrights, the Guests, the Strutts, the Peases, the Marshals, made the grade without difficulty, and many more would follow. They had the essential qualifications, including the desire to be assimilated and the willingness to conform.[2] But if society was not closed it would have liked to be. It viewed the Dissenter and the manufacturer, and especially the man who was both, as a foreign body, an irritant. Some such came in a spirit of avowed hostility, like the Milbank of Disraeli's *Coningsby*, to flaunt their wealth, and build a great house, or, worse, to acquire and most likely to vulgarise an ancestral manor-house; some came with a fated over-eagerness to be accepted quickly. The more modest were disapproved if they kept to the chapel; others were mocked if they purchased a pew as the concomitant of an estate. County society resented infiltration from outside, and felt that it was subversion. It hated the Municipal

---

[1] The most famous exceptions were the Whitbreads. In 1806 Grey argued that his brother-in-law, Samuel Whitbread, was ineligible for the cabinet, being a Dissenter and a brewer.

[2] The progress of the Peases to social conformity may be studied in Sir Alfred E. Pease's '*Elections and Recollections*'.

Corporations Act, which abstracted power from gentlemen and gave it to townsmen who were often Nonconformist business men. There was a great outcry in 'the best circles' when Russell added landless Dissenters to commissions of the peace; this was even worse than letting them take degrees at Oxford and Cambridge. The magnates and gentry did not, of course, themselves abstain from non-agricultural business enterprise, and many owned mines or were ground landlords of industrial sites, but that was very different from being 'in trade'.

Rural society was antagonistic to experts and doctrinaires, and noted that under the Whig régime political economists and Utilitarian reformers gained increasing access to Downing Street. Men such as Nassau Senior, who boasted that the country was being 'thoroughly dug up, trenched and manured' by the new Poor Law administration and the Corporations Act[1] and Edwin Chadwick, the aggressive secretary of the Poor Law Commission, despised traditional methods of government and amateur administrators and magistrates, and extolled the virtues of centralisation and uniformity. If amateurs had to be used, they preferred them to be elected on a broad basis, as in the reformed municipalities. Under the new Poor Law, centralisation was represented by the Commission, which was not directly responsible to Parliament; rationalisation by the union of parishes for administrative purposes; democratisation by 'the network of small aristocracies in which guardians elected by owners and ratepayers are succeeding to the power and influence of the magistrates',[1] while much resistance was to be evoked by the Commission's effort to spread the workhouse system uniformly over the country, despite its manifest unsuitablity for industrial areas. Poor Law administration quickened the traditional hostility of the gentry to the intrusion of state power into the localities, although the Act had been given an easy passage through Parliament because it would reduce the burden of the poor rate and was represented as a concession to the landed interest. That interest was still denied the relief which it most militantly demanded — the abolition or reduction of the malt tax.

In retrospect, it is evident that the Corn Laws, the aspect of the fiscal system for which the landed interest cared most, were not in

[1] *Clarendon*, op. cit., Vol. 1, p. 86, N.S. to Cl., 1st December, 1835.

erious political danger in the 'thirties,[1] although it must have been
a matter of concern to the Protectionists to know that the Board of
Trade (whose ministerial head from 1835 to 1839 was Poulett
Thomson, M.P. for Manchester, an avowed Free Trader) was
staffed and assisted by doctrinaires inimical to the landed interest.[2]
There being no great danger of the repeal of the Corn Laws, and
until 1839 no serious political prospect of their alteration, it could
be argued that the danger to these Laws was indirect, via the ballot.
For the electors, if freed by secrecy from 'influence', might support
further parliamentary reform, to the peril of the Corn Laws.[3]
This furnished the county interests with an additional ground of
opposition to the ballot.

The ballot was the issue on which the Radicals came nearest
a major victory. In the first reformed House of Commons Grote
had only about a hundred supporters, but in the next nearly half
the ministerialists voted with him for the ballot. In 1837, when over
200 were with him, less than fifty Whigs could be found to vote
against it. The point was not lost on the gentry, and there seems to
have been some discrimination in the 1837 election in the English
counties against members who had supported the ballot.[4] In the
new Parliament a third of the House of Commons supported the
ballot and only a ninth of the English county members. But this
was only because of the severe reduction of Whig county members;
nearly 40% of the survivors voted with Grote. Even so the coolness
of Whig aristocrats and county members towards the ballot was
very marked by contrast with the attitude of other sorts of ministerialist. Only a third of the aristocrats voted for the ballot, while
two thirds of their party did so; nearly a third voted against it,
when only a sixth of their party did so. By 1839 all the constituencies of Wales, Scotland and Ireland, and all the English
boroughs, provided between them only thirty opponents of the

[1] There was a select committee on agriculture in 1836 which made no recommendations. The Protectionist champion on it was the Whig member for North
Riding, Cayley. The chairman, Shaw Lefevre, advocated a fixed duty, but tentatively, for he was a county member.
[2] See Lucy Brown, *The Board of Trade and the Free Trade Movement*, 1959.
[3] See Lord Worsley's account of his constituents' views, H. of C. 18th June,
1839.
[4] This is a tentative suggestion. 18 of the 25 Whig county M.P.s who had opposed the ballot were returned as county members, and only 10 of 21 who had
supported it, with 7 who had not voted on the issue (4 of these later split 2:2).
By 1839 Lord Worsley, a convert, and two new Whig county M.P.s supported
the ballot.

ballot among nearly 250 ministerialist members. English knights of
the shire formed a mere eighth of the ministerialist party, but
provided nearly half the ministerialist opponents of the ballot.

The centre of the resistance to the ballot was, however, the
cabinet. Macaulay argued that the question ought to be considered
on its merits, apart from other Radical demands for electoral
reform.[1] But the *Morning Chronicle* held that secret voting without
further parliamentary reform would be 'an unendurable anomaly'.[2]
And Russell agreed. For him the ballot was the *thick* end of the
wedge.[3] Lord John also developed the ingenious argument that the
ballot would destroy the legitimate influence of *non-electors*.
Unfitted to be legislators, administrators, judges, or even to help
elect legislators, the masses had, as it were, second-class colours.
The ballot might be a sovereign cure for the bullying of tenants by
landlords and of tradesmen by customers, and might diminish
bribery, but it would also emancipate the privileged class of electors
from the due influence of the unenfranchised.

There was plenty of evidence of improper pressure and solicita-
tion in elections. It made a mockery of the preamble of the
Reform Act — '. . . Whereas it is expedient to take effectual
Measures for correcting divers Abuses that have long prevailed in
the Choice of Members . . . and to diminish the Expense of
Elections . . .'. A standard riposte was that if things were as bad
as they were painted, the spirit of liberty must be extinct beyond
the power of legislation to revive it.[4] Another was that the remedy
would be worse than the disease, for the vote was a public trust to
be publicly exercised and George Cavendish was not prepared to
see the truth and honour that distinguished the nation imperilled
by secrecy and deceit.[3] Howick was sure the ballot would foster
the worst of evils, a want of independence of spirit, and expose the
country to the democratic tyranny which was the curse of the
United States.[5] Yet it is beyond doubt that, as Buller said, corruption and intimidation were 'the child and offspring of the
Reform Bill'.[5] Macaulay said they produced the worst of tyrannies,
one which operated by the machinery of freedom.[1] The salvation
of corruption was that it was so widespread. Electors perhaps did

---

[1] H. of C., 18th June, 1839.   [2] 25th March, 1839
[3] H. of C., 15th February, 1838.
[4] e.g. Spring Rice, H. of C., 7th March, 1837 said one could not 'arrive at
moral results by mechanical means'. Cf. Russell 15th February, 1838.
[5] H. of C., 7th March, 1837.

not like being bullied. But they did like being bribed. As the
privilege of a minority the suffrage had solid (and liquid) advantages not to be despised. It may be that the majority of the
electorate was for the ballot, but, with the great centres of population under-represented, the majority of the electorates was not.
Members of parliament may even have been more progressive than
their constituents. In 1839 Lord Worsley — whose father's
steward never canvassed freeholders but thought it his duty to
claim the votes of the tenants-at-will for the heir — agreed to
second Grote's motion. He praised his Lincolnshire constituents
for returning him despite his conversion; they, he said, were
opposed to the ballot.[1]

The electors had the power, but not the will, to destroy the evils
which the ballot was designed to cure. The majority of the elected
had no interest in destroying them.[2] It is remarkable that so many

[1] A county member, Thos. Law Hodges, West Kent, had seconded Grote in
1837. He was a schoolfriend of Althorp and Duncannon. He argued that *refusal*
of the ballot would lead to demands for universal suffrage.

[2] *The Hobhouse Papers*, especially Add. MSS 36471, furnish striking evidence
of the attitude to bribery in the Whig official circle. The three Hobhouse brothers
between 1832 and 1852 inclusive contested twenty-one times in thirteen constituencies, successfully eleven times and unsuccessfully ten. On 3rd June, 1842
(f203) Tom Hobhouse asked Sir John whether he could get Palmerston to do
anything about Redington's 'foolish motion to disfranchise Sudbury. If we had
a majority in the House of Commons the proposition would be simply ineffectual,
as the Lords would reject the bill and no worse mischief would ensue. As it is,
the motion will be amended, and after the manner of Aylesbury, Shoreham etc.
a few rural districts be added. Have we not enough counties already? . . . I know
Aylesbury by experience. No amount of corruption can be worse than the dull
torpor of its squire-ridden voters'. In the same letter he deplores Roebuck's
motion against 'compromises'. A compromise (ibid., f. 377) gained Tom the seat
at Lincoln in 1848; on Bulwer retiring, Hobhouse promised to support him next
time. It was 'the purest election ever known in Lincoln' (f. 392), the by-election
being the result of the invalidation of the previous return on grounds of corruption. Tom rather regretted the purity — he was 'sorry to add' that 'we are decidedly the low party. . . . I fear the influence of property on tradesmen and
occupiers of houses, now that the money power cannot be exerted as a counter-
balance' (f. 367). The only impact of political beliefs evident in the correspondence on Lincoln is as follows —'In one respect I am uncomfortably situated —
that the party is more radical than is consistent with my views. . . . It is useless
for me to appeal to the moderates, for this party I am in disinclines them. Hence
conciliation is impracticable, and a spice of strong radicalism necessary.' Meanwhile Sir John himself, defeated at Nottingham, was contesting the exceedingly
corrupt borough of Harwich, where the previous return had been voided; he was
advised (f. 439) not to see any voter without a witness. He was returned under the
patronage of the Eastern Counties Railway. The correspondence about Harwich
is all about bribery in various sophisticated forms — the dinner for 142 electors
at £120 14s. od. after the poll; the £50 for the regatta cup; the financial needs of
the Mechanics' Institute; the urgency of the provision of a steam-packet service
to Rotterdam. Sir John (trained in the by no means pure electoral ways of the
City of Westminster and Nottingham) took it all as a matter of course — his

of the ministerialists, and over a third of the aristocrats, were willing to vote for Grote. For with the ballot, even without any extension of the franchise, would the Whigs proper return more than a handful of members? The erosion of their strength in the counties enhanced the value of boroughs small, biddable or buyable. The experience of the Fitzwilliam family well illustrates this. According to the traditional *cursus honorum* the fifth Earl, on his succession to the title in 1833, was succeeded as member for North Northamptonshire by his heir, Lord Milton, who had been member for the quiescent family borough of Malton. When this Lord Milton died in 1835 the seat was won by a Tory and in 1837 the new Lord Milton (a younger brother) failed to capture it, and was also defeated in 1841, with Lord Morpeth, in the West Riding. Between 1835 and 1865, when the sub-division of the West Riding altered the prospects, no Fitzwilliam was elected for an English county. When Morpeth became Earl of Carlisle in 1848 Fitzwilliam promoted the candidature of his twenty-two year old son Charles, but withdrew him after he had been roughly treated by an election meeting in Leeds. In 1852 another Fitzwilliam son, George, stood for North Northamptonshire, but had to withdraw. So Lord Milton represented Malton from his coming of age in 1836 to 1841, from 1846 to 1847 and then Co. Wicklow until he succeeded his father in 1857. George Fitzwilliam was member from 1841 to 1859 for the seat which was the perquisite of the family in Peterborough, near their secondary residence of Milton. And Charles represented Malton from 1852 to 1885. George had briefly figured (1841) on the list of members for the Dundas borough of Richmond in Yorkshire, which in 1832 retained two members even though the extension of its boundaries to 8,000 acres could not produce the minimum of 300 electors for which Melbourne's letter to Drummond instructed the boundary commissioners to provide, nor maintain as many as 273. The Lord Dundas whom the Whigs in 1839 made Earl of Zetland had five sisters, three of whom married respectively his cousin, the fifth Earl Fitzwilliam, Archibald Speirs and John C. Ramsden. In fifty years Richmond accommodated five Dundases, and sons of Fitzwilliam and Speirs, while

only concern being to assure himself (by consulting Palmerston, Wortley, a Peelite, and Molesworth, a Radical) that there was no danger of the borough becoming the subject of a full-scale inquiry which might lead to its disfranchisement (the fate that had overtaken Sudbury) — see f. 436.

Malton provided for three Fitzwilliams and Mr Ramsden. The other members for Malton were J. W. Childers (the brother-in-law of the leading Whig Sir Charles Wood) and John Evelyn Denison, later Speaker, both of them expelled from the representation of counties.[1] Richmond was for many years represented by Marmaduke Wyvill of Constable Burton, descendant of the 1780 champion of economical reform. Both seats were on occasion made available to ministers — Malton to Sir Charles Pepys (later Lord Chancellor), Richmond to Henry Rich, a whip. When in 1847 Macaulay was defeated at Edinburgh, Lord Zetland offered him a seat at Richmond, but, having sat for Lansdowne's Calne while advocating one Reform Bill he did not feel he should sit for Richmond while intending to advocate another.

The prize gem in the jewel-case of the Whig magnates was Lichfield which, because of the reprieve of the freemen, had as many as 861 electors. Staffordshire's richest nobleman, the Earl of Ellesmere, though a Leveson-Gower, brother of the Duke of Sutherland, had become a Conservative.[2] But the county was littered with great houses, mainly Whig.[3] The magnates naturally nominated the Whig champions for the southern division — an Anson, a Littleton and a Paget successively — but from 1841–54 could return only one of the four members for the county.[4] As great landowners in an industrialising county they benefited from the rise of mines and potteries.[5] But the local parliamentary boroughs were either corrupt, like Stafford and Stoke, and as open to a man of mere wealth as to a man of birth, or attracted to strong liberal sentiments, which Wolverhampton found in Clarendon's brother, Charles Villiers. Edward Buller fled from the northern

[1] Evelyn Denison, described as Fitzwilliam's closest confidant, and Sir Charles Wood both figure in Thompson's aforementioned article in connection with the Whig management in the West Riding, and no doubt Wood was instrumental in getting Childers a seat from Fitzwilliam.

[2] Lord Francis Leveson-Gower took the name of Egerton on succeeding to the great land, coal and transport interests of the Duke of Bridgwater. Something of a Canningite, he joined Wellington's ministry. Peel gave him a peerage in 1846.

[3] e.g. Trentham (D. of Sutherland), three seats of the Ansons, with Shugborough as the chief, Beaudesart (M. of Anglesey), Teddesley Park (Littleton).

[4] One southern seat was lost when Littleton became Lord Hatherton in 1835 and the other when Sir John Wrottesley (later cr. a peer) was beaten in 1837. But except 1835–7 the Whigs always had one seat here. They had none in the north 1841–65, when Buller recaptured one.

[5] In the 1870s Sutherland, Lichfield, Anglesey and Hatherton were credited with 70,000 acres g.a.v. £180,000, 17,000 strategically placed acres of the Pagets accounting for half the value; Lord Granville was a large leaseholder in the county, with considerable industrial interests.

division to Stafford in 1841. An Anson sat briefly for Stoke
1836–7, before moving to the southern division and Lord Granville's brother, 'Freddy' Leveson-Gower represented the borough
in the 1852 parliament. It was Lichfield, however, which provided
the county Whig aristocracy with its safe seats. In thirty-three
years after the Reform Bill it had nine Whig members, only one of
them (the most conservative) a mere baronet; the others were not
only aristocrats but placemen or the sons of placemen — or both.[1]

A connection between the Whig aristocracy and a large popular
electorate was not very common. Between 1832 and 1865 (inclusive)
there were 258 returns, in nine general elections, of aristocrats on
the liberal side. More than a quarter of them came from boroughs
which in 1832 had less than 300 electors, and very nearly half of
them from boroughs which had lost a member in Schedule B of
1832 or would do so in Schedule B of 1868, when there was a
minor redistribution. The eleven boroughs with 1,000–2,000
electors which at some time returned a liberal nobleman become
less imposing when we find that two were virtually county seats,
two were ports responsive to official influence, and five had more
than their share of freemen, a corrupt element. Larger boroughs
were by no means free of the influence which could control a
return or the influence which, in a safe seat, could nominate the
candidate. Thus Chester, with just over 2,000 electors, asked of

---

[1] 1832–41 Gen. Sir George Anson, uncle of the first Earl of Lichfield.
     1832–7   Sir Edward Dolman Scott, Bart.
     1837–65 Lord Alfred Paget, son of 1st Marquess of Anglesey.
     1841–6   Lord Leveson, later 2nd Earl Granville.
     1846–7   Hon. E. M. L. Mostyn, later Lord Mostyn.
     1847–54 Viscount Anson, later 2nd Earl of Lichfield.
     1854–6   Lord Waterpark (an Irish peer, a Cavendish) who married the first
              Earl of Lichfield's sister.
     1856–9   Lord Sandon, later 3rd Earl of Harrowby.
     1859–68 Hon. Augustus Anson, bro. of the 2nd Earl of Lichfield.
The 1st Earl of Lichfield was Postmaster-General under Melbourne, his uncle
George was equerry to Queen Victoria's mother and groom of the Bedchamber
to Prince Albert, his heir was a précis writer at the Foreign Office. The Marquess
of Anglesey, who pickled the leg he lost at Waterloo, was Lord Lieutenant of
Ireland under Wellington and Grey and subsequently in Whig administrations,
Master-General of the Ordnance. Gen. Lord Alfred Paget was for many years
Clerk-Marshal of the Royal Household. It was of the Pagets that Melbourne
remarked that they got on very well without education. The 1st Earl Granville
was for many years Ambassador in Paris and his heir was Under-Secretary of
State at the Foreign Office at the end of Melbourne's ministry, Secretary of State
for three separate spells and a cabinet minister for twenty-five years. Lord
Waterpark was a Lord in Waiting. At the time that Lord Sandon became member for Lichfield his father was in Palmerston's cabinet; he himself was to be, as
a Tory, in Disraeli's.

ts members that they should be (*a*) of liberal persuasion, (*b*) rich
there were many freemen) and (*c*) if possible, a Grosvenor from
he family of the Marquess of Westminster at nearby Eaton Hall.
This family had dominated the representation of the cathedral city
since the Restoration, and contributed a member without inter-
mission till 1874. Opinion at Derby was very radical, but the
Duke of Devonshire was regarded as patron of one seat, and we
ind him acting as electoral relieving officer to Cavendish, Ponsonby
and Leveson-Gower relatives in turn. Sometimes the explanation
of the presence of an aristocrat in a fairly numerous borough constituency was that he was politically advanced, like Berkeley of the
ballot, member for Bristol; Viscount Duncan, member for
Southampton and Bath; Lord Dudley Stuart, member for Marylebone after his explusion from Arundel; Charles Villiers, member
for Wolverhampton. It was no disadvantage in a strong liberal
constituency for the strong liberal candidate to be an aristocrat.

The only aristocratic members for larger boroughs who opposed
he ballot in 1838–9 were ministers. A fair number of the governing
Whig circle did represent the sort of constituency which did not
usually return Whig noblemen. It was advantageous for a borough
o have a minister as its member of parliament; even back-
benchers were expected to get favours for their constituents. And
t was the plutocracy, or a mixture of the plutocracy and freeholders, that was represented. The mixture was seen to perfection
n the West Riding, for which Cobden sat as the representative of
he freeholders of less than £10 in parliamentary boroughs (such
as Halifax) and the £10 freeholders of other manufacturing and
mining towns and villages, (the latter, today, the home of immense
Socialist majorities); the adoption meetings were held at Norman-
on. When Cobden withdrew in 1857 he was succeeded by Lord
Goderich, well-connected but of advanced opinions. In 1859,
when the Tories were proposing to disfranchise the county freeholders in the parliamentary boroughs, the Liberals carried both
seats. Recognising the facts of politico-economic life, Sir Charles
Wood wrote 'I, as a landowner, in conjunction with the whole
body of the Whig landed proprietors of the Riding, am anxious to
see a manufacturer as colleague of Sir J. W. Ramsden.'[1] The

[1] F. M. L. Thompson, op. cit., Sir John Ramsden, a broad-acred baronet
whose property included the whole of Huddersfield (except one site), was the
on of the Ramsden referred to on p. 94, by his Fitzwilliam wife.

H

carpet manufacturer, Crossley, was chosen. He was, currently, Sir
Charles's colleague as member for Halifax, made a parliamentary
borough in 1832. The electorate was originally only 531. Wood
represented it for more than thirty years, but his highest poll ever
was 714. It was the plutocracy of the place which returned the local
landowner who was a purist of the *laisser-faire* school. In 1865 he
deemed it prudent to retire to Ripon, where 215 votes gave him a
comfortable victory. When Howick, rejected by his county constituents, sought refuge in Sunderland in 1841, his 706 votes gave
him a 20% margin over his adversary. When in 1847 Russell
received over 7,000 votes in the City of London (only just enough
for election)[1] he had the support of almost as many electors as
fourteen other Whig aristocrats needed between them. Sixteen
others were returned unopposed, mainly for small places. These
figures give us the proper proportions.[2] But it was not unimportant
that a representative connection with the City of London, Edinburgh, Nottingham, Northampton, Halifax, Sunderland, Stroud,
Devonport, Leeds and the West Riding[3] gave leading members of
the Whig ministerial class more direct contact with 'public opinion'
than was the common lot of their caste. Poulett Thomson, for eight
years virtual or actual head of the Board of Trade, who sat for
Manchester, came from outside that caste, being the son of a
Russia merchant. It was partly in deference to him that his colleagues in 1839 accepted Russell's advice to make the ballot an
open question in the cabinet. Thomson was the only cabinet
minister to vote with Grote, but, if Russell took with him into the
Noes' lobby (amid the host of Tories and the merest sprinkling of
Whig private members) Palmerston, Howick, Spring Rice and
the rising men Wood, Baring, Lord Seymour and the lawyer
Rolfe, Thomson had the company of Campbell, George Grey
and 'Ben' Stanley, the Chief Whip.[4] With only forty of more than

---

[1] In 1837 Grote was returned for the City by a majority of 6. In 1841 Russell,
taking his place, polled 6,221 and was elected by a majority of 9, behind a Liberal
and two Conservatives. The City had four members.

[2] See Appendixes: Introduction *infra* p. 422.

[3] Russell moved on to the City after representing Stroud (1835–41); Edinburgh was successively represented by Francis Jeffrey 1832–4; Abercromby
1832–9; John Campbell 1834–41 and Macaulay 1839–47: Macaulay having
previously sat for Leeds; Duncannon sat for Nottingham 1832–5 and Hobhouse
1835–47; Northampton was represented by the egregious and very rich Vernon
Smith; Sir George Grey sat for Devonport 1832–47 and Morpeth for the West
Riding 1832–41 and 1846–8.

[4] Hobhouse, Morpeth and Labouchere did not vote.

300 supporters of the administration voting against the ballot, it took a 90% Tory turnout to maintain the majority for the *Conservative Cause* at its previous level of 117.[1]

Russell's own opposition to the ballot had never been firmer. He seemed to close all the openings offered him for a future as well as a present change of mind, and it was fortunate that Thomson did not choose to upset the coach. Russell made it plain that making the ballot 'open', as a concession to very strong and persistent pressure from the parliamentary party, was intended only to reduce tension and facilitate *resistance* to the ballot. He was unmoved by Macaulay's plea that the Reform Bill must not be made an object of idolatory (like the old electoral system!), or by the recollection that the sub-committee which produced the first draft of the Reform Bill recommended the ballot,[2] or that he himself on the morrow of Reform had said that the ballot would come if landlords abused their power, or that he had stigmatised as very corrupt the classes of old electors exempted from disfranchisement (as a concession to the opponents of Reform). He said that the authors of the Bill were peculiarly committed to finality and that to weaken on this would be to confess that they had deceived the people or themselves.[3] This argument surprised even Graham, who said that the finality pledge meant only that the authors were bound not to *assist* a movement for further Reform, and Howick too, who said that his father and the other Reform leaders could only have meant that they *hoped* the settlement would be lasting.

Howick's speech did not seem to indicate any very firm conviction that the ballot could for ever be denied. He himself had agreed to make it an open question, he said, in order to strengthen the resistance to it, but if it ever came to be understood that the country could not have 'a liberal system of policy' without a government committed to the ballot, then such a government there would surely be. The landed interest had no ground for assurance, therefore, that Whiggery would continue to stand firm on the ballot, and, simultaneously with the first weakening on that question came signs of a change of front on the Corn Laws. Ever

[1] The figures, 15th February, 1838, were 315:198 and 18th June, 1839, 333:216, the majority including 287 Tories.
[2] As a bargaining counter to secure that the borough franchise should be as low as £10.
[3] Letter to the Electors of Stroud and speech in ballot debate of 1839.

since 1832 Whig county members presenting petitions from thei
constituents, men such as Childers and Heathcote, had professe
their confidence first that Lord Althorp, and then that Lor
Melbourne, would never allow the landed interest to be betraye
Melbourne was still staunch in their defence. He said that the rea
aim of those who asked for reconsideration of the Corn Laws wa
Repeal, and that this was the wildest and maddest scheme eve
entertained. But in the other House Russell spoke favourably c
inquiry and fixed duty and by the next year, 1840, seven member
of the cabinet had shown in divisions sympathy for some chang
in the Corn Laws,[1] and so had half the ministerial party. Th
counties therefore had ample warning before 1841 that the poli
ticians whose leadership they had already rejected were likely to b
unreliable on the matter nearest the hearts and pockets of landlord
and farmers.

The country gentlemen were not remarkable for cultivate
intelligence or political sophistication. To dramatise their passag
through the lobbies in a vain defence of fiscal privilege Disrae
judged it necessary to supplement names of interest only to th
editors and devotees of *Burke's Landed Gentry* with reference t
'the stout heart of Mr Buck and the pleasant countenance c
Walter Long'. It was of such that Stanley said, in his woundin
way, at a party meeting in connection with the attempt to form
Tory administration in 1851, that theirs were not names he coul
submit to the Queen for cabinet office. But these judges of horse
hounds and cattle were no bad judges of men from the point c
view of their aptitude to serve the landed interest. They truste
the Duke (when he was not emancipating Catholics) and Lor
George Bentinck (when he was not showing traces of his Car
ningite liberalism). They mistrusted clever men, like Canning an
Disraeli; open-minded men, like Peel; unpredictable men, lil
Russell. And now they judged that the Whigs were incompeten
even that they were mere seekers after spoils. But above all the
doubted whether they had the stamina to defend the nation
institutions, among which 'the gentlemen of England' certainl
ranked the Corn Laws.

The greater landowners in those parts of England which wer

[1] Minto, Cottenham, Hobhouse, Normanby, Clarendon, Morpeth, Macaula
of whom the last four entered the cabinet 1839–40. Thomson and Howick (bo
of whom left the cabinet in 1839) and George Grey (who entered 1841) had vot
similarly.

being transformed by the joint operation of industrial enterprise
and the development of communications did not share the limited
attitude of the landed interest proper. They sponsored, invested in
and sometimes helped direct turnpike trusts, navigation companies
and railways. They owned, and sometimes operated, mines,
quarries, ironworks, brickfields, potteries. They received royalties
and urban ground rents. We have been warned by a Canadian
scholar, Mr Spring, who shows how great was the involvement
of principal landed families in non-agricultural economic development, that they were often heavily in debt and that their incomes
from non-agricultural property were rarely a considerable part of
their revenues as early as 1846.[1] He argues convincingly that Earl
Fitzwilliam, the first great English landlord to advocate the radical
reduction of the corn duties, and preach it in and out of season,
was not directed to this course by conscious economic motive.
This magnate, whose income in the 'forties was so great that the
charges on £800,000 of debt swallowed up less than a third of it,
derived less than 10% of his revenues from coal and iron enterprises, and it is doubtful whether he made anything, on balance,
out of such enterprises, all taken together. By 1900 the return on
the Wentworth Woodhouse estate had trebled and his successor's
income from minerals had multiplied almost sevenfold.[2] The Earl
was a man of deep Evangelical piety, with a high sense of steward-
ship, and a man, too, of wide reading and curiosity, the best type of
Whig aristocrat, ready to practise the mediation between the
classes which Burke had preached.[3] On the basis of his example,
and the conspicuous fact that some great coalowners, and the heirs
of others, some great urban owners[4] and the heirs of others,[5]
remained Protectionist, and that other magnates with vast non-
agricultural interests decided, belatedly, in favour of Free Trade on
political, not economic, grounds,[6] Mr Spring thinks it 'plain . . .

---

[1] 'The English Landed Estate in the Age of Coal and Iron 1830–80', in *Journal of Economic History*, XI, I, 1951.
[2] Dr J. T. Ward 'The Earls Fitzwilliam and the Wentworth Woodhouse estate in the Nineteenth Century', in *Yorks Bulletin of Economic and Social Research*, XI, II, 1960.
[3] D. Spring, 'Earl Fitzwilliam and the Corn Laws', *Am. Hist. R.*, LIX, No. 2, January 1954.
[4] Including the Tory Duke of Portland, half of whose income came from Marylebone.
[5] Including Lord Stanley, who became Protectionist leader.
[6] e.g. the Duke of Bedford, reluctant to decide between his brothers Lord John and Lord Charles (the latter feared agricultural disaster if the Corn Laws were

that the presence of non-agricultural resources on the greatest landed estates signified less than one might expect for the dispute over the Corn Laws, and a long clear rent roll . . . little more'.

Mr Spring's conclusion is incompatible with Dr Kitson Clark's statement that Free Trade arguments 'seemed reasonable enough to great nobles whose rent rolls were comfortably supplemented by revenues from mines or docks or urban property' and also to 'those whose sources of revenue were primarily agricultural, but whose estate provided a surplus . . .',[1] though the two writers agree that Repeal is a phenomenon to be explained in terms of political sagacity. It would seem, however, that Mr Spring may have minimised unduly what Mr Kitson Clark stated a trifle too baldly. The key to the differentiation of a considerable part of the landlord body from the rest, and from the general body of smaller owners and farmers, may be the statement of a third scholar that in the West Riding '. . . in the early nineteenth century, agricultural rents had long ceased to be the *sole* sources of income for an enterprising landowner'.[2] It may be right to link a disposition to reduce agricultural protection, not with a conscious self-interest generated by heavy reliance on non-agricultural sources of income, but with a considerable *potential* income from such sources. Fitzwilliam himself began his attacks on the Corn Laws in 1825, too early for him to feel the confidence that his varied interest would buttress him against the adverse effects of Repeal on which he could rest by 1850, or even the reasonable anticipation that this might be so, to which he was entitled by about 1840. But as much cannot be said of other magnates who defaulted from the Protectionist cause later than he. Prudent landlords look ahead. When opportunities outside agriculture existed, it was not likely that they would think solely in terms of retrenchment, debt consolidation, careful management and planned investment in agricultural improvement. Under the operation of the Corn Laws, agriculture was frequently depressed. It might be argued that their repeal would make little difference, but it required much greater faith to forecast a 'golden age of British agriculture' in the 'fifties than to predict an upward surge of mineral production, iron manufacture or urban development. While the weight of debt drove some landowners into such

repealed and opposed his brother's fixed duty), and the Conservative mine owner Lord Londonderry.
    [1] 'The Repeal of the Corn Laws', in *Ec. Hist. R.*, 2nd S, Vol. IV, No. 1, 1951.
    [2] J. T. Ward, op. cit.

enterprise, Repeal would drive more, and it is really not unreasonable to attribute to those who were already well-poised, intellectu-
ally or financially, or both, for such activities a self-interest which
at least partially accounts for the softness of some of them towards
the reduction of Protection. This may especially have been true
in the north-east, where recent research shows how common and
how great was the involvement of landed families in non-agricultural development.[1] Such enterprise, and profit from urban growth,
may have yielded, with certain eminent exceptions, only a small
proportion of a man's income when compared with his receipts
from agricultural land and village property. But knowledge of, and
interest in, such development would explain how he came to take
a larger view of the national interest than the ordinary southern
rural lord or country squire. In the West Riding, progressive land-
ords who in the past had promoted canals[2] were beginning to
provide capital and sometimes leadership for the development of a
railway network which would overcome one of the two major
impediments to the profitable exploitation of mineral resources.[3]
On the eve of the Repeal of the Corn Laws the Huddersfield and
Manchester Railway Company was being formed, soon to merge
with another line into the L.N.W.R. and it was closely followed by
the South Yorkshire Company which linked up with the Lancashire and Yorkshire. Lord Derby had already begun to reap the
profits of the expansion of Liverpool's commerce and the development of industrial towns in Lancashire.[4] Lord Burlington, heir

---

[1] J. T. Ward 'The Earls Fitzwilliam and the Wentworth Estate' (*Yorks
Bulletin of Economic and Social Research*, XI, II, 1960) and 'The Squire as a
Businessman — William Aldam of Frickley Hall' (unpublished); Spring, 'The
English Landed Estate in the Age of Coal and Iron 1830–80' (*Journal of Economic
History*, XI, I, 1951) and 'The Earls of Durham and the Great Northern Coalfield
1830–80' (*Canadian Hist. R.*, XXXIII, 3, 1952). There was nothing new in such
non-agricultural enterprise — cf J. D. Chambers, 'The Vale of Trent 1670–1800'
(*Ec. Hist. R.*, Supplement 3).

[2] e.g. Ramsden's Canal at Huddersfield (1835) bought out for £46,560 by the
Huddersfield and Manchester Railway Co.; the Derwent Navigation sponsored
by Fitzwilliam to help market his agricultural produce and the Dearne and Dove
Navigations to get away his coal (see Ward op. cit.) The Duke of Norfolk and
Lord Thanet were proprietors of the Leeds and Liverpool Canal.

[3] The other impediment consisted of technical shortcomings which it was
reasonable to suppose would be overcome.

[4] The Stanleys acquired in the fifteenth century, Bury, which grew tenfold
1793–1871, and Bolton. They bought great parts of Liverpool for £12,000 in
1710; in 1843 they received £17,500 for 1,000 linear yards for dock extensions
and later £90,000 for 270,000 square yards. Spring in 'English Landed Estates',
records that the Stanley rents in Bury and Liverpool quadrupled between 1800
and 1837.

of the Duke of Devonshire, had already begun his systemati
development of the potentialities of Barrow. It needed littl
more prescience to foresee the rapid growth of Preston and Bury
Sheffield, Huddersfield, Dewsbury and Batley, or, indeed, of th
South Yorkshire coalfield than to forecast the growing profit
ability of the West End of London or of Edgbaston.[1] In the Wes
Riding there was ground for an optimism as to the general pros
pects of the area, overlaid by present anxieties as to the immediat
prospects of particular trades and concerns, anxieties whic
sometimes exploded in the form of assaults on the Corn Laws a
impediments to expansion. Fitzwilliam's contact with such emo
tions of hope and fear, and his knowledge of his own business an
that of other landlords and businessmen in the district, help explai
the language in which he warned the peers, though they might b
ignorant of the widening course of commerce and dislike the smok
and bustle of commercial towns, that they could not ignore 'th
interest that we have, as a body, in the activity of every worksho
and counting house in Birmingham and Liverpool'. They hel
explain how, while less sophisticated humanitarians defende
tariffs with the argument that they protected employment
Fitzwilliam understood that an all-round reduction of costs (bot
to producer and consumer) from the reduction of food prices migh
stimulate economic activity and increase the market for agricul
tural products.[2] Moreover, in the north, and even in the nort
midlands, politics as well as economics involved landlords an
wealthy squires in contacts with businessmen whose outlook o
politics, where politics touched economics, they were more likel
to come to share than were those of their order without suc
contacts.[3] It was not only piety and Whig adaptability — whic
he shared with Earl Fitzwilliam — that made Lord Morpeth th
politician he was; it was the fact that he was member for the Wes

[1] Peers who owned sites and market in these urban areas were among thos
who voted with Fitzwilliam (see *infra*). The Ramsdens owned nearly the whol
of Huddersfield and the Savilles much of Dewsbury and Batley.

[2] In accordance with this conception Dr Ward tells us, Fitzwilliam reduce
rents in 1850 at a cost of £3,061 per annum, less than the farmers expecte
pointing out that the cost of their purchases had fallen.

[3] Such magnates learned not to despise what Fitzwilliam called 'the hig
aristocracy' of the towns, '. . . families which have allied with some of the noble
in England', Marshalls, Becketts, Peases and Aldams (quoted by Spring in hi
Fitzwilliam article). They had in due course to come to terms with newe
families such as, in Leeds, the Baineses and Carbutts, though these were apt to b
more pushful, Radical and less deferential to the political leadership of the gentr
(see F. M. L. Thompson op. cit.).

Riding and came to understand and in many ways to share the political outlook of the textile manufacturers.[1]

It would seem that Mr Spring's evidence does not require us to abandon, but only to modify, Dr Kitson Clark's hypothesis with regard to the economic incentive of certain landlords to abandon the defence of the Corn Laws. Such men, of course, were no worse than rural landlords who clung to Protection or the manufacturers and merchants who sponsored the Anti-Corn Law League and opposed the ten hours' bills. They did not *more* consciously transpose the terms 'self-interest' and 'national interest'. One seeks not for moral judgements but for explanations, and it takes a greater weight of evidence than has yet been accumulated to smother the suspicion that peers who early leaned to Fitzwilliam had the same sort of regard for their pockets as those who were most vehement against him. Certainly self-interest was attributed to them. No doubt much of the criticism was ill-conceived. Farmers and landlords dependent on agricultural and village properties, especially the smaller and less prosperous ones, were apt to ascribe to the non-agricultural incomes of defecting magnates an importance which they did not yet in many cases possess. They tended to see something sinister in a change of political views by a progressive landlord who had the opportunity to lessen his dependence on agricultural profit and took it, when what really happened was that the magnate came to the conclusion that the Corn Laws were politically indefensible and that it would be wise to begin to adjust himself to a new régime which, because they were doomed, was in prospect. Yet Protectionists scanning the list of peers who supported Fitzwilliam's motions of 1839 for 'revision and relaxation' of the Corn Laws could be pardoned if they saw significance in the fact that very few of them had that exclusive dependence on agricultural and village property which one associates with country squires and freeholders in most of the counties of England. Of the twenty-four dissidents of 1839,[2] almost all were owners of metro-

---

[1] See *infra*, Ch. VI.
[2] Fitzwilliam's motion, 14th February, 1839, was defeated by 111 votes and 113 Proxies to 14 votes and 10 proxies. One of the 24 appears to have been a Conservative, the Lord Calthorpe who had been a *Waverer*, voting against the Reform Bill in 1831 and for its successor in 1832. In addition to 2,500 acres in Norfolk (whence came his title) and 1,400 in Hampshire (where he had his seat, and owned some urban property) he inherited the manor of Edgbaston, bought in the reign of George I by an ancestor who was an India and China merchant. Edgbaston was beginning to emerge as the 'Belgravia of Birmingham' and by the

politan or urban sites,[a] or mineral-bearing lands,[b] or estates tha
were chiefly mountain and moor[c] or mountain and bog[d] or landless
lawyers and politicians.[e] The landed interest had reason to be
alarmed that so many of the Whig hierarchs had so strong a
financial interest in the development of an expanding industria
economy, lightly taxed.

It is uncertain to what extent the Anti-League, which opposed
the Anti-Corn Law League, represented farmers who grumbled at

---

1870s the gross annual value of the 'Warwickshire' estates was reckoned at £55
per acre compared with £3 in Hampshire and 25s. in Norfolk. This peer became
a Peelite and his nephew and eventual successor (1868) a Liberal. The family
motto was 'The same way by different steps'. The 23 Whig peers' estates as
given in Bateman's *The Great Landowners of Great Britain and Ireland* (1879
edition), which in general excludes mineral as well as metropolitan values (though
sometimes giving the former separately and sometimes including them while
saying it does not), were as follows:

		acres	g.a.v.	
[a]	D. of Bedford	87,500	£141,500	Metropolitan owner
[a]	M. of Westminster	15,400	33,500	..... do................ *
[a]	E. of Radnor	24,900	42,900	..... do................ †
[a]	Lord Holland	5,800	7,500	..... do................
[a]	D. of Grafton	25,800	39,000	..... do................
[a]	E. of Albermarle	7,300	7,300	..... do................
[a]	E. of Derby	65,000	163,000	Liverpool, Preston, Bolton, Bury etc.
[a]	Lord Vernon	10,000	25,000	Derby, Stockport, etc.
[b]	E. of Durham	30,500	71,700	Durham mines and assoc. enterprises.‡
[b]	Earl Fitzwilliam	47,300§	130,500	South Yorks.
	E. of Carlisle	78,500	49,600	
[b]	Lord Hatherton	14,900	23,200	Staffs. mines and quarries and potteries.
	E. of Suffolk	11,100	14,200	
	E. of Leicester	44,100	59,600¶	

These 14 peers, their metropolitan values (including Lord Derby's in Kent
and Surrey) and mineral royalties excluded, owned 450,000 acres, a twelfth part
of all the property owned by 500 peers. Its g.a.v. was £770,000. The deserters
were Titans.

[c] The property of the Marquess of Breadalbane in Argyllshire and much of
that in Perthshire could hardly be described as agricultural.

[d] e.g. the property of the Marquess of Sligo in Connemara. Lord Cloncurry's
property lay in the cattle fattening part of Ireland.

[e] Lords Brougham, Denham and Langdale. Not accounted for in the above
analysis are Lord Seaford, whose wealth came from Jamaica, Lord Godolphin
(brother of the wealthy Duke of Leeds) and Lord Kinnaird, whose interests were
primarily agricultural though his family had banking connections.

* The Grosvenor properties in Belgravia and Pimlico, where at the time of the Reform Bill men
shot snipe, soon became the most valuable real estate in the world.

† The old Earl could be relied on to support any Radical cause.

‡ See Spring 'The Earls of Durham and the Great Northern Coalfield' (*Canadian Hist. R.*,
XXXIII, 3, 1952).

§ Includes the Northants-Huntingdon estates given by the Anti-Corn Law Earl to a younger
son. There were also nearly 100,000 acres (g.a.v. £50, 000) in Ireland.

¶ I suspect that Coke of Holkam had a great deal of money in the Funds but am unable to
verify this — DGS.

he lack of support they received from Tory magnates.[1] But there
s sense (*pace* Mr Spring) in the judgement that Free Trade views
eemed reasonable to '. . . . those whose sources of revenue were
rimarily agricultural, but whose estate provided a surplus. . . .
They did not console farmers who thought that they might be
uined by one year's drop in price, who had perhaps little capital
nd no science . . . and their opinion influenced country gentlemen,
ounty members and great magnates who valued position or with
oo little liquid capital'.[2] An investigation of the larger estates by
ounties shows that on the average peers had greater acreages than
aronets and they than untitled squires,[3] and of the three the
obleman was the most likely to have land in several counties.
The vigour of the reaction to the threat of Repeal increased the
urther down the scale from the mansion to the farmhouse one
went. Farmers and landlords are on different sides of the rent
fence, and the latter view the more optimistically the capacity of
the former, under given conditions, to pay rent. But even *qua*
landlords the peers were less representative of the rural society
they lorded than were 'the gentlemen of England'. The marginal
effect of a cut in prices increases the lower the net income, although
it is true that with great incomes come great expenses owing to the
scale on which the rich live. The great ones would feel the pinch
less acutely than their humbler neighbours if corn prices dropped.
And they stood to lose a great deal politically, as a class, from
obscurantism. In 1846 very few Whig peers refused to surrender the
Corn Laws, but six of the twenty-one Whig English county
members remained Protectionist.[4] A third of the Conservative
peers, but only 18 of 122 Conservative county members, assisted
the leader of their party to repeal the Corn Laws.

The Corn question was not only a political one. It was a constitutional question. 'The Farmers,' said Gladstone, 'looked on
Throne, Church and Peerage as so many different names for
the really great institution of the Country, namely the Corn

[1] According to Dr G. L. Mosse (in *Ec. Hist. R.*, XVII, 134, 1947), the farmers
provided the heart and soul of the movement, but this view is sharply criticised
by Mary Lawson-Tancred in the *Historical Journal*, Vol., III, No. 2, 1960.

[2] G. Kitson Clark, op.cit.

[3] That this was so emphasises the extent to which the grant of titles had been a
recognition of 'a stake in the country'.

[4] Grantley Berkeley (W. Glos.), Lord Worsley (N. Lincs.), E. S. Cayley (North
Riding), G. J. Heathcote (Rutland), W. J. Denison (W. Surrey) and K. Hoskins
(Herefordshire).

Laws.'[1] The economic arguments against those laws were, especially
in the context of the political economy of the day, very telling, even
if the assertion that food taxes constituted a burden of £50–60
million on the enterprise of the country was unproven.[2] The Corn
Laws were difficult to defend logically, for they patently failed to
achieve their professed object of securing an adequate supply of
cereals at steady prices remunerative to the producer at the existing
level of farm rents, a level inflated as a result of the existence of the
Corn Laws. Under the act of 1815 which the country gentlemen
had imposed on Lord Liverpool (following it up by abolishing the
income tax and striking at the malt tax), either the price was much
lower than the 80s. a quarter at which import was allowed, or the
ports were opened. The Act of 1828, which represented a lowering
of sights in view of the general fall in agricultural prices (and, consequently, of rents) encouraged fluctuations so that either its
opponents were complaining of its injustice or agriculturists of
its inefficacy. Sometimes both complained simultaneously.
Gracious Speeches were littered with references to the distress of
landlords, occupiers or the whole rural population. But few
agriculturists were prepared to take the risk of venturing into the
unknown waters of unrestricted competition. Some Free Traders
thought that Repeal, though in the national interest, would throw
much land out of cultivation.[3] So the dissatisfaction of the landed
interest with the Corn Laws did not incline them to jettison them.
Not all the supporters of protection in corn were merely selfish or
obscurantist. Men who admitted the general validity of Free Trade
principles were prepared to concede that cereals were a special
case. *Per contra*, men who favoured the Repeal of the Corn Laws
wanted their own interests protected.[4] Melbourne said at the
beginning of 1839 that 'the present outcry is raised evidently by
the master manufacturers, taking advantage of the present dearness
of corn, and with the object of lowering wages'.[5] For the country
gentlemen, Edward Stillingfleet Cayley, Whig member for the

---

[1] Add. MSS 44745, draft of 1855.

[2] See Lucy Brown, *The Board of Trade and the Free Trade Movement*, p. 202 ff.

[3] For disagreement on this between Board of Trade officials, see Lucy Brown,
op. cit.

[4] Ellice, who represented Coventry, had resisted Huskisson's application of
Free Trade principles to silk (*vide* H. of C., 23rd Feb., 1826) and in January 1843
was described as vehement for the Repeal of the Corn Laws but all for greater
protection for the ribbons of Coventry and 'some hideous job of his own in
Canada' (Clarendon, op. cit., p. 240).

[5] *Melbourne*, p. 289, 20th January, 1839, to Russell.

North Riding, said he would not see the country 'sacrificed for the sake of a foreign trade'.[1] This remark, made at a time when Britain was importing £30 million of raw materials and supplying the world with manufactured goods but was, according to a committee of 1833, unable to grow enough food to be self-supporting, brings us to the point where the economic becomes political. The battle over the Corn Laws was not a battle between rich and poor. It was more a battle between town and country. But it was above all a struggle between the entrepreneur and the landed interest, a struggle for power as well as for policy. The same operation of economic and social change which had brought the country to the choice between Reform and Revolution in 1831 decreed the destruction of the special economic privileges of the old governing class. This would come as soon as the interests which in 1832 secured an overt share of political power appreciated that they might destroy those privileges with advantage to themselves and earn credit with the masses by so doing. Reform therefore doomed the Corn Laws, and Whigs who argued, with sincerity, to the contrary, deceived themselves.

'The receivers of rent are a very small body. Backed by public opinion, they are almost omnipotent — in violation of public opinion, they cannot long retain an exclusive advantage.' So wrote Sir James Graham. With his usual apprehensiveness, he foresaw 'the barriers of society . . . broken down, and estates, distinctions, honours, swept away in one resistless torrent', because the contest would be decided 'on the very topic which inflames to madness' and 'that hunger which breaks through walls will be arrayed against them'.[2] When politicians began to think like that, the landed interest had reason for alarm at Lord Fitzwilliam's condemnation of the Corn Laws as in their present tendency no ancient institution but a device to maintain in peacetime the swollen rents of war and his argument that rents which had so regularly to be in part remitted must be too high.[3] Far more disturbing was the support which his motion of 1839 secured from Colossi such as the Duke of Bedford, the Marquess of Westminster, the Earls of Carlisle, Derby and Leicester (who was Coke of Holkham) as well

[1] H. of C., speech on Villiers' motion, 1839.
[2] Graham in his Address to Landowners, 1828, had advocated reduced duties as a measure of class conciliation, but in 1834 he made 'the chief landlord speech' against his colleague Poulett Thomson.
[3] Addresses to Landlords, 1832, 1835, 1839.

as the Earl of Durham — from 23 peers who thirty years late
were credited with land worth £1 million g.a.v., half a million acre
of it in England, six of whom together owned one fifteenth of al
the English land owned by peers and 1% of that owned by any
body. Next year Fitzwilliam's lobby swelled to 41, and in th
following year he expected the support of 50–60, but his motion
was anticipated by the Government's acceptance of a relatively
low fixed duty.

The Whig ministers (as we shall see) were impressed, but no
impelled, by economic arguments against the Corn Laws. Thei
gradual weakening on the Corn Laws was the response o
politicians to pressure. Pressure for Repeal varied according to
corn prices. Wheat stood in 1834–5 at 49s. a quarter (25% belov
what the authors of the 1828 Act had aimed at); in 1836 it some
times reached 60s. and Clay's motion in 1837 received 90 votes
in 1838 prices reached 73s. and Villiers in 1839 mustered 173
half the ministerialists in the House of Commons. Melbourne':
reaction to the increased pressure (which coincided with that for
the ballot) was at first all the landed interest could desire. The
question must remain an open one (as Poulett Thomson's presence
in the cabinet had made it). The Government would make no proposals, and Russell should not reveal that he favoured a fixed duty
because if he did it would be impossible either to oppose or retain
it. Repeal was not only undesirable in itself but could only be
carried 'by the same means as we carried the Reform Bill, and I
am not for being the instrument or among the instruments of
another similar performance'. He doubted whether the property or
institutions of the country could stand it.[1] But the Government had
to grant an inquiry, and the Prime Minister used an ominous
phrase (privately) about winning time 'to see what the real feeling
is — both in and out of Parliament'. Here was the rub. Fitzwilliam
was telling his fellow-magnates that the hallmark of the success of
a governing class was its ability to promote the national interest and
conciliate the articulate; six years ago he had told them that
landlords did not deserve special regard any more than weavers
or chimney sweeps. Opinion was now becoming articulate; the
formation of the Anti-Corn Law League at Manchester in 1839,
though not immediately important, was symptomatic. Strong
middle class backing for working class discontents was a pheno-

---

[1] *Melbourne*, pp. 389–90, letters of 18th and 20th January, 1839.

menon reminiscent of 1831–2; Melbourne's analogy with the Reform Bill could be taken more than one way. Graham feared social revolution coming out of political controversy — but this was, surely, likely only if the aristocracy resisted reform. Would it not be wise to emulate the ministry of Lord Grey, and grant the reform? Repeal, when it came, says Dr Kitson Clark, was as much a concession by the aristocracy as a victory of the middle class. And of Fitzwilliam, the forerunner of his party, Mr Spring says 'the Whig politician, preaching the gospel of practical expediency to the English aristocracy . . . tells us much, perhaps most of all, about the making of a Corn Law reformer out of an aristocrat'.

It was to be no salvation to the landed interest that it turned to the Conservative party, led by Peel. '. . . The final repeal of the Corn Laws in 1846', says Dr Kitson Clark, 'was . . . only the culmination of a series of desertions and betrayals, in many of which Sir Robert Peel had been the main figure'.[1] But turn it did, for want of a better course, convinced that the Whig conception of statesmanship consisted of gradual concession to interests inimical to it. Gloomy Tory predictions in 1831 that the Commons were meeting for the last time as 'an assembly of English gentlemen connected with the land and enabled to speak the sentiments and wants of that most important of all the interests in the country'[2] had not been fulfilled. But defeat on the Corn Laws would indicate unmistakeably that the landed interest had ceased to predominate. 'Of a sudden the Conservative party as they crowded the benches of the new House of Commons' (in 1841), says Gladstone, 'found themselves Protectionists.'[3] And Peel, to his great embarrassment, found himself' the leader of the gentlemen of England'.

[1] e.g. the resumption of cash payments (many agriculturalists as well as Thomas Attwood and some businessmen blamed economic depression on deflation); Catholic Emancipation; general acceptance of and imitation of Whig measures — to say nothing of budgets to come and the increase in the Maynooth grant (see *infra*, pp. 123–4, 127).
[2] Sir Edward Sugden, H. of C., 16th December, 1831.
[3] Add. MSS 44745, *cit. supra.*

CHAPTER V

The Whigs and the Corn Law Crisis

The first statesman to proclaim that 'if there is any nation under Heaven, who ought to be the first to reject monopoly, it is the English', was Shelburne. 'Situated as we are between the old world and the new, between southern and northern Europe,' he said, 'all that we ought to covet upon earth was free trade and fair equality. With more industry, with more enterprise, with more capital than any other trading nation upon earth, it ought to be our constant cry "let every market be open, let us meet our rivals fairly, and we ask no more".'[1] Disraeli always insisted that Shelburne was a Fair Trader, not a Free Trader, but it was nearly half a century before many of the official leaders of Whiggery had progressed even that far. It was Pitt who said that Adam Smith's studies furnished the best solution to every question connected with the history of commerce or with the system of political economy.[2] About 1820 the leading politicians whom the economist Ricardo found most enlightened in political economy were, apart from Shelburne's son Landsdowne, all out of Pitt's stable — Liverpool, Huskisson, Robinson (later Goderich and Ripon) and Lord Grenville. The Whigs during the debates on the Reform Bills in 1831–2 had to bear caustic reminders that Fox had been obscurantist in these matters and that Burke had (unfairly) criticised Adam Smith as an armchair philosopher who expected too much of 'legislators . . . impeded . . . in their course by the friction of interest and the friction of prejudice'.[3] Both Fox and

[1] Shelburne, H. of L., 17th February, 1783 (*Parliamentary Register*, Vol. XI).

[2] In the Stanhope Miscellanies there is a letter from Cornewall Lewis 2nd April, 1864 saying that Lord Grenville had told Sir Frankland Lewis that but for the French wars Pitt had proposed to abolish all customs duties, and that this had been quite feasible.

[3] See H. of C. 22nd March, 1832, speeches of Sir R. Inglis and Stanley. The latter said 'It was well-known that Mr Fox . . . was not well read in political economy nor was familiar with the doctrines of free trade.' On 26th May, 1820, H. of L., Lansdowne quoted Burke as saying 'You, Dr Smith, from your Professor's chair may send forth theories upon freedom of commerce as if you were lecturing on pure mathematics; but legislators must proceed by slow degrees, impeded. . . .'

Burke had shamelessly fostered and exploited the opposition of vested interests to Pitt's plans for free trade with Ireland and freer trade with France, Fox attacking the French treaty of 1786 as dictated by 'those dirty commercial considerations which entirely shut out higher motives of policy . . . England must have nothing to do with France'.

Fox viewed political economy with contempt. 'One of my grand objections to this most nonsensical of all sciences,' he wrote to Lauderdale,[1] 'is that none of its definitions are to me intelligible. . . . Your notions . . . of value seem to me to be stark nonsense.'[2] Two generations after Adam Smith wrote, the reporters could not make sense of Ricardo's parliamentary speeches. It was easy for a politician to hold up political economists to ridicule or contumely, as when Lord John Russell, in a speech which might have been made by Cobbett (the Radical of Tory origins who hated political economists even more than he hated Whigs) told a Huntingdon audience in 1822 that 'there was a party among us distinguished in what is called political economy [who] wish to substitute the corn of Poland and Russia for our own'. This was at a time when Ricardo was helping Tory ministers repel the demands of agriculturists for extended protection or currency inflation. Russell has sometimes been called a political 'intellectual' (almost as though he were his grandson),[3] and it is true that he inherited opinions with an intellectual foundation which he loved to elaborate. But he had no more aptitude than Fox for abstruse speculation, whether in the field of philosophy or 'the dismal science' of political economy, against which he shared Fox's prejudices. He required to be converted to the doctrine of Free Trade by that subtle process of inhalation by which politicians assimilate the lessons of books they do not read (which in our day has led to wide acceptance of Keynesian principles) and by the pressure of political expediency. He did not reach the Damascus road till 1845. Not until three generations after Adam Smith published *The Wealth of Nations* was it natural for a young Whig aspirant to accept Free Trade as a platitude and even then it is difficult to believe that all such made

[1] A leading member of the *Friends of the People*, James Maitland, 8th Earl of Lauderdale (1759–1839) was one of the few Whigs who sought to understand and promote the doctrines of Adam Smith, but from the second decade of the nineteenth century he developed into a prominent Protectionist and opposed the Reform Bill.

[2] Russell's *Life and Times of Chas. Jas. Fox*, IV, p. 27, 25th April, 1800.

[3] Bertrand Russell.

I

the same effort as T. G. Baring to master the details of the argu
ment. The impetus to his studies came from the victory of classical
economics in politics, a victory towards which the Whigs until
near the end of the battle made an inadequate contribution. His
researches induced in him the wish that he had been born a Tory
— 'the fallacies on that side are much prettier'. But, he sighed
'unfortunately free trade is true and we must all use our efforts to
give our manufacturers the means of underselling the world'.
Only when Whig cadets entered politics with the conviction that
Free Trade was 'true' could it justly be said that Whig govern
ment would mean 'a liberal system of policy . . . such . . . as is
indicated by the opinions of the old Whig party of England
improved and enlarged by modern speculation particularly in ques
tions of public economy and jurisprudence'.[2] One must not, of
course, be too hard on the politicians. Not till 1820 were the leading
London merchants willing to commit themselves to a wholesale
denunciation of the traditional principles of mercantile policy.[3]
A recent study of the advocacy of tariff reform by the officials of
the Board of Trade in the 'thirties suggests that the traders and
manufacturers in general were far less convinced of the applic
ability of Free Trade principles to their own interests than is
sometimes assumed.[4] The fair comparison is between one set of
politicians and another, and between the professions of politi
cians and their readiness to take risks to translate them into
practice. The Whigs of the 'thirties have always suffered in reputa
tion by comparison with the Liberal Tories of the 'twenties and the
Peel administration of the 'forties. To what extent is the traditional
assessment justified?

The Tories in the 'twenties had a prime minister who was
theroetically convinced by the principles of Free Trade and the

[1] Malet's *Northbrook*, pp. 37–9. Baring's letters from Florence intersperse
comments on art, literature and Italian politics with news that he was working
at political economy, which he found made unnecessarily difficult by 'conceited
phraseology and would-be wise acredness'. McCulloch he found superficial and
J. S. Mill had an animus against landlords, so the heir of Stratton Park turned to
Say and other Frenchmen 'who cannot write for or against any English party'.
After being private secretary to three relatives — Labouchere, Sir G. Grey, Sir
C. Wood — Baring entered Parliament in 1857 and at once got office.
[2] *Edinburgh Review*, January 1848, Art IV, pp. 138 ff.
[3] Ricardo (see *Letters of David Ricardo to Trower 1811–23*, Bonar and Hol
lander, 1899, no. xxxv, 13th March, 1820) attached great importance to the
Merchants' Petition introduced by Alexander Baring.
[4] See Lucy Brown, *The Board of Trade and the Free Trade Movement*, esp.,
pp. 180–4.

prescription of *laisser-faire*; Liverpool believed that Britain had grown rich not because of tariffs but in spite of them. What Mr Brock has called 'an economic cabinet'[1] within Liverpool's cabinet began the process which enabled Ricardo, on the eve of his death to say, 'We shall, I hope, go on from session to session getting rid of some of the absurd regulations which fetter commerce till all shackles are removed.'[2] There was a consolidation of the customs regulations by the official, Deacon Hume; there were provisions for reciprocity agreements with regard to shipping dues; there was a relaxation of the Navigation Acts in favour of colonial shippers; there were reductions of bounties and of duties on raw materials — coal, iron ore, wool, silk, hemp — and on silks (a bold blow bitterly opposed by an industry regarded as especially in need of protection) and certain articles of consumption such as coffee, cocoa and wines. Although a Fair Trader rather than a Free Trader, Huskisson's last word was that it was essential to 'lighten the pressure upon the springs of our productive industry . . . by getting rid as speedily as possible of all the monopolies affecting commerce and the free agency of the community in their capital and labour'. Taxation must be diminished and the industrious classes aided by substituting moderate for heavy duties.[3] Huskisson wished to penalise capital not engaged in industry and commerce, and saw in an income tax a means of diminishing taxes which obstructed industry.[4] Years earlier, Liverpool had wished that he could increase direct taxes by £2 million in order to relieve indirect to the tune of £4–5 million.[5] The Wellington cabinet in 1830, when proposing to remit £4 million of indirect taxation, considered a property tax, but some of the ministers, including the Duke, objected to it, and the others could not agree upon whom increased direct taxation should fall. Here was a cabinet seriously discussing the distribution of taxation between the various classes,[6] in terms very acceptable to some leading Opposition spokesmen, especially Sir Henry Parnell and Poulett Thomson. Parnell has been called 'the centre of the movement for financial reform';[7] he had presided over the Finance Committee of 1828 (one of the consequences

---

[1] *Lord Liverpool and Liberal Toryism*, pp. 191–2 ff.
[2] *Letters to Trower*, LXIII, 24th July, 1823.
[3] Address to the Electors of Liverpool 30th July, 1830, Add. MSS 38753.
[4] Lucy Brown, op. cit., p. 10.
[5] Brock, op. cit., p. 195, quoting Liverpool to Canning.
[6] Lucy Brown, op. cit., pp. 9–10.   [7] ibid., p. 15.

of which was the abolition of Pitt's Sinking Fund as uneconomical
and in February 1830 published a book which advocated the aboli
tion of duties which it was uneconomical to collect, a drastic
reduction in customs and excise duties which diminished consump
tion, and an income tax.[1] The message of this volume was cogently
expounded by Poulett Thomson in a noted parliamentary speech in
March. Here was an ambitious and comprehensive programme
for a government with the will and nerve to attempt one. But
after the Commons emasculated his budget of 1831, which was
rash rather than bold, and might have been contrived with the aim
of offending as many diverse interests as possible, Althorp, the
Chancellor of the Exchequer, professedly a Parnellite, seemed to
lose heart, and Spring Rice, the Chancellor from 1835 to 1839,
was supine. The latest study of Whig fiscal policy concludes
'Between 1830 and 1840 the original momentum of the Whigs
financial and commercial policy slackened and finally disappeared.
The traditional account of their paralysis in the face of economic
problems appears to be entirely correct'.[2] All that the author can
find to say in palliation of the Whig record is that 'the kind of
reorganising work for which Huskisson and later Peel drew much
credit was also carried out by the Whigs'.[3] There were tariff
changes directed towards lower duties and smaller imperial preferences but they were 'not fundamental'.[4] There was 'no definite
change in the structure of taxation and little extension of the reciprocity system',[5] though for the latter ministers can be blamed only
to the extent that they were unwilling to offer major tariff concessions as bait.

Dr Brown, like Gladstone,[6] regards the Whigs as Free Traders
who lost heart. But it appears that by 'Free Trade' Gladstone
meant the Huskissonian policy, for he says 'during the years of its
prosperity from 1835 to 1839 [the Melbourne administration] never
lifted so much as a finger for free trade. The traditions of Mr
Huskisson appeared to be utterly forgotten'. And while one may
agree that 'between 1828 and 1830 ... the Whig Opposition
became increasingly associated with the economic policy which
derived ultimately from Ricardo',[7] Dr Brown is surely misleading
when she claims that 'the Whigs of 1830 were more closely

---

[1] *Financial Reform.*   [2] Lucy Brown, op. cit., p. 69.   [3] ibid., p. 53.
[4] ibid., p. 52.   [5] ibid., p. 33.
[6] Add. MSS 44745, memo of 1855.   [7] Lucy Brown, op. cit., p. 12.

ssociated with a definite economic policy than the Tories of the
twenties had been'.[1] Liverpool and Huskisson had a policy, even
f it was a Fair Trade rather than a Free Trade one. This policy
he Whigs pursued with declining momentum. Parnell and
Thomson by 1830 were more thorough Free Traders than the
Liberal Tories had been, but neither of them were put in the
abinet, and the fact that these two favoured lower duties and an
ncome tax does not mean that the Whigs had been converted to
Free Trade principles, or that as a whole they repented helping the
Tory gentry abolish the income tax against the will of the Tory
ministers in 1816, or that the Whig cabinet had progressed any
urther (if as far) as the Wellington cabinet. Dr Brown herself cites
as one of the adverse circumstances which explain the Whig
ailure to pursue the Parnellite policy the fact that the Free Traders
were not prominent in cabinet counsels. Althorp, she says, was
popular, but not respected as Chancellor of the Exchequer. His
biographer tells us that at one time he read some divinity to do
himself good and political economy to do good to others,[2] and he
said that Parnell's book would inspire his policy. But we look in
vain in the Whig cabinet for any sense of mission in the economic
field or anything in the nature of 'an economic cabinet'. If the
cabinet as a whole was a Free Trade body, which is difficult to
believe, then the inadequacy of its contribution to the fulfilment of
the policy inaugurated by Huskisson is the more discreditable. It
is, of course, true that there were many other important reforms to
engage the attention of the ministry and parliament, especially
during the period of a large majority, 1832–4; that the Huskissonian
policy was steadily under attack at a time of economic distress
during which interests antipathetic to the recent trend of official
policy were militant and strong in the House of Commons;[3]
that after 1835 the smallness of the majority gave as much importance to potential obstructionists on the right as to potential
mutineers on the left of the ministerial party; that the economic
problems of the country became more serious and intractable as
the political circumstances of the ministry became more unfavourable. But the fact remains that, apart from 1832, there was a
budget surplus till 1837, and generally declining estimates. It is

[1] ibid., p. 18.   [2] Le Marchant, op. cit., Vol. 1, pp. 168–9.
[3] Dr Brown calls attention especially to the demands of the agriculturists for
the reduction of their burdens, and Attwood's campaign for inflation of the
currency; against these the Government was on the defensive.

hard to sympathise with a Spring Rice paralysed by deficits because he had not grasped earlier opportunities. The deficits, a reflection of economic depression, might well have been regarded by a Huskisson or Peel as a challenge.[1] It is very difficult to quarrel with Gladstone's verdict — 'Upon one great subject . . . the Whigs showed their hereditary infirmity. Their finance, usually indifferent, was never so discreditable as in the time of Lord Monteagle. . . . In 1839, when the revenue was already deficient, he executed the unexampled juggle of abandoning the Post Office Revenue and recording by Resolution a promise to find a substitute for it in the following year. Before that following year arrived he had worked himself by a most discreditable process into the office he now holds[2] and had bequeathed an embarrassed Exchequer to the hands of Mr Baring.' The office had been refused by Poulett Thomson, who after eight years at the Board of Trade and four in the cabinet declared that he would be able to do little except 'get through some BAD tax', for party and private interests would prevent a majority for any 'great commercial measures, timber, corn, sugar, etc . . .'[3] and preferred to become Governor-General of Canada as Lord Sydenham.

Melbourne offered the Treasury to Thomson because he admired his administrative experience and capacity, his lucid mind and his lack of 'crotchets' — which means among other things that he had not embarrassed his colleagues by demanding that they become active Free Traders. The offer did not mean that the Prime Minister had resolved on any new departure in fiscal policy. The Whigs do not seem to have grasped until well into 1840 that the intractability of the country's economic problems called for such a departure. The concessions of 1839 — making the ballot an open question, deciding on the penny post, beginning to thaw on the revision of the Corn Laws — these were *political* concessions. All the new Chancellor could suggest for 1840 was an *increase* in all taxation, direct and indirect. The result was a larger deficit than before. And so, for 1841, he posed the alternatives of an income tax or a radical reduction of the duty on foreign sugar

[1] Peel in opposition did not preach what he was to practice in office; but can it be assumed that he would have opposed a firm lead by the Government to take the Huskissonian process much further?

[2] Like Glenelg, Spring Rice was rewarded for his ejection from office by a rich sinecure, the Tellership of the Exchequer, *and* the elevation to the peerage as Lord Monteagle.

[3] G. P. Scrope's *Memoir*, p. 98.

and a revenue-producing readjustment of the timber duties.[1] The cabinet opted for the latter, which Baring preferred, and added, largely at the behest of Russell, a considerable alteration in the Corn Laws.

It is evident that the cabinet took this project from the propagandist Select Committee on Import Duties — 'the child of the Board of Trade officials and of the Anti-Corn Law League'[2] — which named sugar and timber, with coffee, as articles whose consumption would increase if the duties were reduced. The committee also proposed to attack many minor duties which it was administratively difficult and costly to collect; this was to be a main feature of the much-praised budget of Peel in 1842. But the Government programme aimed at revenue and popularity, rather than 'lightening the springs of industry', unless one supposes that the ministry, like the Board of Trade, accepted a subsistence theory of wages, a supposition hardly borne out by Melbourne's celebrated query to his colleagues as to whether they were to say it would raise or lower the price of corn — 'It don't much matter, as long as we all say the same thing.' It is difficult to accept that the cabinet's project was a piece of 'long-term strategy'.[3] Ministers knew they could not pass it through Parliament, but they had not decided to resign if it was defeated, nor to go to the country on it, and it is altogether out of keeping with their character to imagine that they envisaged themselves campaigning steadily for its adoption in the coming years. The financial proposals were tactics, not strategy. The authors hoped to limit Peel's freedom of action as a minister[4] and, by restoring their prestige with the Radicals and public opinion, limit their losses in the election which could not be long delayed. The Whigs put forward their programme 'in the utter decadence of their power and for want of anything else to fill their sails'.[5] It was, to quote Gladstone, 'no more than a death-bed vow and gave them no more claim to credit than such vows commonly confer'.[6] The fact that the income tax and reduced

---

[1] See letter quoted by Lucy Brown, op. cit., p. 221. The duty on foreign sugar was to fall from 63s. to 36s. while that on colonial remained at 24s.; the duty on foreign timber was to fall from 55s. to 50s. and that on colonial to rise from 10s. to 20s.

[2] Lucy Brown, ibid., p. 73.

[3] This is what Dr Brown calls it, op. cit., p. 221.

[4] *Letters of Queen Victoria*, 1st Series, Vol. I, p. 336. Russell thought that Peel might commit himself and thus cause serious dissensions in his party (see also, ibid., pp. 349–51).

[5] Argyll's *Autobiography*, Vol. 1, p. 159.   [6] Add. MSS 44745, draft of 1855.

indirect taxation were regarded as *alternatives* makes it impossible to regard the scheme as a notable advance upon Huskissonianism. The difficulty of estimating the yield of indirect taxation in times of economic uncertainty ought to have taught the Whigs that there could be no systematic advance towards freedom of trade without recourse to higher direct taxation. Liverpool, Canning, Parnell and Poulett Thomson had all understood this. The Whigs failed to stake their claim to the ground Peel was shortly to occupy.

In assailing three of the greatest protected interests in the country, the Whigs were turning at bay. Their proposals with regard to sugar were beaten by thirty-six. Melbourne said that, with the anti-slave lobby as well as the West and East Indian interests affronted, this was not more than expected.[1] But the cabinet had no idea what to do next. The Prime Minister said it could hardly acquiesce in the defeat of the main points of the budget, nor propose other taxes when it thought the necessary revenue could be raised without them.[2] This, surely, indicated resignation, for, Russell said, defeat at an election would be 'final and irreparable'.[3] But the ministers could decide neither to resign nor to dissolve, and so it was announced that they would make do with the existing taxes. Peel then intervened with a direct vote of no confidence. During the mammoth debate that followed everyone knew that every vote counted; there was uproar when Lord Worsley, who had opposed the Government on sugar, said he would vote with it on confidence.[4] When at 3 a.m. on 5th June, 1841, in a House of 628, the result was known, Peel's majority was one. Four Whigs had voted with Peel, but the vote of the member just elected for Sandwich against a great weight of official pressure was decisive.

The ministers had decided on 19th May to request a dissolution if they were defeated. The Queen readily granted the request, although Melbourne warned her of the undesirability of the Crown having a majority for the first time returned 'smack against it'.[5] Victoria made a round of Whig houses — 'so like her',

---

[1] The vote was 317:281, am 19th May, 1841. For Melbourne's comment see *Queen's Letters*, Vol. I, p. 340 and pp. 353-4.
[2] ibid., p. 340.
[3] ibid., p. 336, to the Queen 4th May. On 8th only three ministers (Palmerston, Hobhouse and Cottenham) favoured resignation (ibid., pp. 340-1).
[4] ibid., p. 360.   [5] ibid., pp. 347-8, 15th May.

said Emily Eden in India.[1] She was unable to believe that her chosen servants would be rejected by the country, and they, of course, once their path was fixed, buoyed themselves up with false hopes. Surely public opinion would work their way — was there not enthusiasm in the northern towns? Would not persons susceptible to Chartism see that the Whigs were prepared to do something for the people? Radical zeal would be harnessed to the official waggon, and middle-class elements, not excluding Radicals, who had begun to look to Peel for business-like administration, would be regained. But people did not take the stroke as seriously as the Whigs expected. 'Disgust at Whig rule' (Halévy's phrase) was not to be obliterated at a blow. It is difficult to say whether the Whig *volte-face* prevented a worse electoral disaster, if only because of the uncertainty of generalisations upon results in boroughs which varied so greatly in size and character, independence and corruptibility (it was a very venal election), where local interest often overbore national.[2] Obviously the proposal to tamper with the Corn Laws — to which the Whigs gave prominence — was no asset in counties and country boroughs. Every county south of the Humber where the Whigs had seats to lose showed Whig loss — except Hampshire (where the Whig member was the Speaker), Middlesex (where Fox's friend George Byng celebrated fifty years as member), Surrey (where the Whig returned was a Protectionist millionaire), the Cavendish stronghold in North Derbyshire and one seat in South Staffordshire. The two Whigs, one of them Ben Stanley, were swept out of Cheshire and Howick lost his seat in South Northumberland. The Conservatives took both Lancashire divisions unopposed and the largest constituency in the country obliterated Whig-Radical majorities of 1,100 and 400 — the West Riding figures were —

Hon J. S. Wortley	13,165
E. B. Denison	12,780
Lord Milton	12,080
Lord Morpeth	12,061

[1] *Clarendon*, op. cit., p. 234, 19th September, 1841. Emily was acting as hostess for her brother Auckland, the Governor-General. The Queen stayed with Archbishop Harcourt, the Duke of Bedford, the Cowpers, Melbourne, the Duke of Devonshire and the (Tory) Lord Salisbury.

[2] e.g. at Bristol and Liverpool the West Indian interest was strong, and there were many corrupt freemen, and in the latter the anti-popery cry was potent.

Only Durham, giving three seats out of four to the Whigs, showed no decline. Only Derbyshire and Cumberland returned two Whigs among four members. It we take the counties of England and Wales and the clergy-dominated Universities as peculiarly representing the landed interest, we find 141 Conservatives elected and 21 Whigs, of whom 6 were to remain Protectionist in 1846. The ministerial loss in the English counties was 23; in the English boroughs the net loss was only 15. In the more prominent industrial boroughs the results were oddly inconclusive. Two Free Trade propagandists, Cobden and Dr Bowring, won seats at Stockport and Bolton, Nottingham was regained from the Tory-Chartist alliance[1] and the Liberals gained a seat on a low poll at Preston. But the Liberal majorities slumped at Manchester and Salford, and seats were lost to Tories at Leeds (where Joseph Hume was beaten), Blackburn and Wigan. On the corn issue, many Conservative candidates, including the two businessmen returned for the City of London (where Russell held the fourth seat by a single-figure majority) and the young lord who gained a seat for Westminster, and, indeed, Peel himself, were unclear.[2] In Yorkshire especially the anti-Poor Law cry was potent. But in many a constituency the gist of the Conservative appeal was simply that Sir Robert could provide more efficient management of the national affairs than Lord Melbourne.

The achievement of almost exact parity with the Reformers in the returns from the English boroughs was a remarkable tribute to Peel's moderation and empiricism, as well as to his reputation as an administrator and his supremacy as a parliamentarian. Whatever united the 'organised hypocrisy' it was not dogma, when Protectionists and men evasive on the broad question, supporters and opponents of the Poor Law sheltered under the 'Conservative' umbrella, receiving electoral assistance on the one hand from Chartists and on the other (though indirectly) from Free Traders like Perronet Thompson who denounced the Whig proposal for a low fixed duty as the worst impediment to the Repeal of the Corn Laws.[3] Oblivious of the dissensions in the ranks of 'Reformers', some Whigs predicted Conservative disruption. This indeed

[1] But similar alliances won Pontefract and Knaresborough and, almost, Salford.

[2] All three of these members supported Peel on Repeal in 1846.

[3] See Betty Kemp, 'The General Election of 1841' in *History*, N.S., XXXVII, June 1952.

occurred in 1846 when the landed interest found itself 'sold', as
Lord George Bentinck said in righteous wrath, by the leader to
whom it had turned because it suspected the Whigs of intending to
sell it. The rancorous indignation then displayed against Peel had
a reasonable cause, for though the counties and country districts
together could never have given Peel a working majority,[1] they
provided the bulk of his parliamentary support, and their electors
cared most about the Corn Laws. The landed interest had perhaps
imagined that this would weigh with Peel as much as with a normal
party leader, not understanding that, in addition to caring for the
goodwill of the middle class and for the overall national interest as
he conceived it, Peel was more susceptible than the Whig leaders to
genuine 'education', so that his conception of the national interest
rapidly came to be completely at variance with that of the landed
interest.

Predictions of Conservative disruption proved prescient, but to
offset our after-knowledge it must be stressed that talk of a brief
interregnum followed by Whig restoration was merely wishful
thinking. For four years there was no sign of the cataclysm which
circumstances precipitated at the end of 1845. After their condemnation by the new House of Commons, by a majority of 91, on
28th August, 1841 the Whigs were left 'demoralized and shocked
— in a kind of apathetic acquiescence ... which looks as if all
energy and intention were extinct', said an ex-minister.[2] Another
thought the Tories would be in for ten years; some said twenty.[3]
In mid-1845 it still seemed that Peel was 'worshipped ... by all
parties as a Heaven-sent minister', and Campbell had 'given up
all thought of political changes'.[4] The constructive boldness of
Peel's great budget of 1842 threw into sharp relief both Whig
paralysis and Whig desperation. Adopting the income tax as the
means of emancipating commerce without bankrupting the
Treasury, he swept away or reduced most of the duties which
fettered production and trade, and thus attacked 'the Condition of
England Question' by the tactic of 'making the country cheap for
living'. The Corn Laws were adjusted by a new sliding scale
designed to check fluctuations and the fraud which contributed to
them. The Duke of Buckingham (Chandos of the Clause) left the

[1] Statistically they could have done, but in the conditions which existed a
clean sweep by one party was not feasible.
[2] *Clarendon*, op. cit., p. 223, 31st December, 1841, Cl. to Granville.
[3] Campbell, op. cit., II, p. 161.   [4] ibid., p. 193.

THE LAST PINCH.

cabinet, but in general the landed interest acquiesced in a policy which showed that one could keep the Corn Laws and yet pursue a liberal commercial policy (though there was a Protectionist revolt in the lobbies when in 1843 Peel and Stanley tampered with the Canadian corn preference). The Commons had accepted the income tax with surprising ease, in view of the antipathy of Free Trade Radicals as well as Whigs and Tories. The fiscal field proved an unpromising venue of battle for the Opposition, Russell's motion on the Corn Laws (which Peel's censure had prevented him bringing on as a minister) was rejected in February 1842 by 123, and in 1843 another one secured only 145 votes. From the end of that year the country began to reap in terms of prosperity and business confidence the fruits of Peel's tax reliefs (and kind weather) while the income tax extinguished deficits.

Russell must have been conscious that he did not command the whole Opposition, although the Radicals had suffered equally with Whigs at the election[1] and almost a fifth of the 289 Opposition M.P.s were aristocrats. There was mutual suspicion and jealousy between the two wings of the Opposition. Only five peers gave their

[1] Hume, Molesworth, de Lacy Evans, Warburton and a number of O'Connellites were defeated.

votes for free trade in corn.[1] Without Bright's urban impatience
with countrymen or his democratic predilections, Cobden nevertheless would say that the sooner power was transferred from a
landed aristocracy which misused it and placed 'absolutely' in the
hands of 'the intelligent and industrious classes' the better for the
country. He was not prepared to play the part of an auxiliary to the
Whig nobility. On 8th July, 1842 he told the House of Commons
that he believed Peel to be as liberal as Russell — 'If the Noble
Lord is my leader, I can only say that I believe that in four out
of five divisions I have voted against him. He must be an odd kind
of leader who thus votes against those he leads.' To the men of
Brooks's this must seem an odd and ominous conception of
leadership, involving the maxim that Sir Winston Churchill once
woundingly applied to Mr Attlee: 'I am their leader. I must follow
them.' They were not prepared to follow Cobden. When the
official Whig policy on the Corn Laws was tested in the Lords on a
motion for an inquiry moved by Lord Monteagle (Spring Rice)
on 14th March, 1843, only 31 peers present supported, against 82
opposing, and only 47 sent proxies, against 118 on the other side.
Mutual criticisms flowed thick and fast. The Whigs resented the
fact that business people, who, as Bagehot said, for all their
snobbery, 'wished to see the government administered according
to the notions familiar to them in their business life' could warm
toward 'the most intelligent Conservative government that this
country has ever seen';[2] that Cobden did not conceive it the duty
of the Radicals to try to turn the Government out, but only to
influence the House of Commons;[3] that, as Vernon Smith said, the
session of 1842 raised Free Trade principles to their zenith and
reduced the Whigs to their nadir;[4] that Cobden should think the
worst danger was that of the Whigs coming in again too soon: 'The
hacks would be up on their hind legs, and at their old prancing
tricks again, immediately they smelt the Treasury crib.'[5] The
Whigs were unable to understand how any Liberal could be

---

[1] On the second reading of the Corn Import Bill 18th April, 1842, seventeen
peers including two Whig Protectionists (Yarborough and Western) and several
Free Traders (including Clanricarde and Kinnaird) voted against 119. Brougham's Free Trade amendment was supported by Clanricarde, Kinnaird, Radnor
and Vivian.
[2] *Biographical Studies*, 1856 — 'Sir Robert Peel'.
[3] Morley's *Cobden*, p. 209, letter of 12th October, 1841.
[4] Quoted in Walpole's *Russell*, I, p. 385 — Smith to Russell.
[5] Morley's *Cobden*, p. 241, letter of 22nd March, 1842.

indifferent to whether the Whigs were in or out, still less how he could prefer a Conservative government. Cobden was fighting the battle of Free Trade versus Monopoly, not the battle of outs versus ins. 'There is no way so certain of bringing the Whigs to our ranks', he wrote, 'as by showing them that they will not be allowed to make a sham fight against the Tories at our expense. Depend on it, the Whigs are now plotting how they can use us and throw us aside. The more we show our honesty in refusing to be made the tools of a party, the more we shall have the confidence of the moderate and honest Tories.'[1] That was apropos the City of London by-election in autumn 1843, when the victory of the former member over Thomas Baring by 165 votes was hailed by the League as a victory for its ostentatious campaign. But in May 1844 the Free Trade candidate secured only 45% of the votes in the county division which embraced Manchester, Liverpool, Salford, Wigan, Bolton, Oldham and Rochdale, and the League made its decision to organise the systematic penetration of marginal county constituencies, especially the West Riding, by the creation of voting qualifications. Fitzwilliam resented the invasion of his preserves, lost to Tories, as he said, by 'agricultural agitation', or, as the urban Liberals said, by 'the apathy of the Whig gentlemen as a body'. In 1847 Cobden was returned in absentia *because* Fitzwilliam preferred a Protectionist.[2] But it may well be that the League's invasion of counties forfeited more votes from the landed interest than it created. It certainly exacerbated the Whig dislike for the Leaguers.

By 1844 nobody was very interested in Whig fortunes, except Whigs, and they, as a body, had no idea how to revive them. O'Connell trenchantly condemned them as well below the level of the times they lived in;[3] Sydney Smith said he should be sorry to see Peel out, for, unlike the Whigs, he knew 'how to disguise liberal ideas, and to make them look less terrible to the Foolery of a country';[4] Campbell, after a dinner at which he tried in vain to secure a plan of campaign, thought the party had never been in a more dilapidated and ruinous condition.[5] Whatever was proved

[1] ibid., p. 289, letter of 24th October, 1843.
[2] See F. M. L. Thompson, *E.H.R.*, LXXIV, April 1959, 'Whigs and Liberals in the West Riding 1830–60'.
[3] Campbell, op. cit., II, p. 179, 9th September, 1843.
[4] Sydney Smith's *Memoirs*, p. 591, 19th August, 1843, to Sir George Philips.
[5] Campbell, op. cit., II, p. 184, January 1844.

by the by-elections which raised Peel's majority from 90 in 1842 to nearly 100 by late 1845, they showed no signs of recovery by the Opposition.[1] There were obvious strains within the ministerial ranks too, caused by Peel's aloofness and overbearing leadership and by his development of liberal policies. The ministry was twice defeated, on their Factory Bill (Ashley's ten-hour amendment) and on the sugar duties, in 1844. In 1845, eighty Protectionists voted against another great budget, and Tory Protestants raged at Peel's increase in the grant to the Catholic college at Maynooth, which Russell very properly supported. But no one knew that Peel's personal conversion to Free Trade in corn had reached the point of meditating the gradual preparation of his party for surrender when 'the damn'd rain' which, Wellington said, washed away the Corn Laws washed away also the Conservative party which Peel had built. A shocking harvest being followed by potato blight in Ireland, Peel was struggling in secrecy to convince his cabinet that the ports must be opened and could never be closed again, when Russell made a bid for power which precipitated a political crisis.

From the Scottish capital, where forty years before he had been sent to the University, to the imperial capital, centre of Britain's commerce and of international finance, and his own constituency, Lord John on 22nd November, 1845 addressed a momentous open letter announcing his conversion to the view that the Corn Laws were 'the blight of commerce . . . and . . . the bane of agriculture', a source of 'penury, fever, mortality and crime' and of 'bitter divisions among classes'. The removal of restrictions on the main articles of food and clothing used by the mass of the people was necessary to 'all great interests' and indispensable to national progress.

We need not question the sincerity of these sentiments, but their avowal was wonderfully opportune — 'a most dexterous move', Peel called it, for whatever he now did would appear to be dictated by the Opposition.[2] Cobden said the Edinburgh Letter

---

[1] The best representation of the general election result at which the author can arrive is Conservatives 367 (+41), Liberals 291, which became 372:284 after settlement of disputed returns and replay of voided ones. By December 1845 it was 377:279. Opposition votes were often split by the candidature of militant Dissenters and Free Kirk men, and there were Chartist interventions. The Nonconformist leader Miall, by splitting the vote, allowed a Tory to win Birmingham in 1843. Conservatives won seats at Bradford, Brighton and Nottingham in 1842, but the last was lost on a replay in 1843.

[2] *Queen's Letters*, S. I, Vol. II, p. 58, Prince's Memo, 7th December, 1845.

CONFIDENCE AND DIFFIDENCE.

transformed Russell 'from the most obscure into the most popular
and prominent man of the day'.[1] On a Scottish railway station
Lord John received the plaudits of John Bright. Whiggery was
again to be cast, by its leader, in the role of the saviour of the
country, the conciliator of class discords, saving the landed interest
from itself, saving the constitution from jeopardy, yielding much
to save more, but yielding nothing essential, and displaying a gift
for right timing which, it was hoped, would, inter alia, reduce
Cobden to the status of Vice-President of the Board of Trade in a
Whig administration.

But Whiggery had not been consulted, and Whiggery was aghast.
The magnates must have known that they had no choice but to
concur, especially when it became evident that Peel agreed with
Russell. But when their leader arrived in London as prime
minister designate he found them full of doubts and fears. Some
opposed acceptance of office;[2] others thought that Russell had made
it their duty to try. Russell accepted the commission on 18th

---

[1] Speech 17th December quoted Morley, op. cit., p. 341.
[2] e.g. Add. MSS 34626 (*Macvey Napier Papers*), f. 31, Monteagle to Napier
9th January, 1846, 'I was against the experiment from first to last.'

LORD JOHN (1st EARL) RUSSELL
by Sir Francis Grant (1854)
National Portrait Gallery

December and resigned it on the 20th. The Whigs failed to form a government because they were not sure it was their interest to succeed.[1] But the explanation given the Queen — that the new Earl Grey, of all the prospective ministers the most through-going Free Trader,[2] would not serve if Palmerston was at the Foreign Office[3] and that Palmerston would not go anywhere else, was discreditable because it seemed either a thin excuse or a sign of quite excessive deference to one magnate.[4] At least, said Le Marchant, it would show 'the Whigs are not so greedy after office', but Macaulay said 'It may only increase the blame. We stayed in when we ought to have gone out, and now we stay out when we ought to have gone in.'[1]

It may well have been for the best, from the point of view of repealing the Corn Laws, that Peel should return to power, for the Whigs would have needed the support of 70–80 Conservatives in *each* House for a slim working majority, without allowing for any Whig defections, and Peel stood more chance of commanding this support as a minister than as a private member assisting ministers. But Whig relief at Russell's failure[5] was a recognition that, as Disraeli said, the chalice he handed back to Peel was *poisoned*. The formidable Conservative party was sundered, and the passing of Repeal through Parliament must accentuate its division. Whig prospects were thus transformed by the events of November and December 1845.

The Radicals had no doubt as to their course. They would propose an amendment for immediate free trade in corn, and then

---

[1] ibid., f. 102, Senior to Napier 17th February, 1846 quoted Macaulay as saying, 'We were then only patching up an administration to carry a question and then be turned out.'

[2] 'all for extreme measures, immediate repeal, no compensation, trampling on adversaries', *Greville*, II, p. 2); cf. *Queen's Letters*, S. I, Vol. II, pp. 69–71, where we learn that Grey wanted Cobden in the cabinet.

[3] See *infra*, Ch. XI.

[4] Add. MSS 34626, f. 31 ff., Monteagle wrote 'Here the liberal party in all its ramifications, from an old Foxite Whig like myself to Rochdale and the Radicals condemn Grey's conduct most loudly. . . . I think it was a great mistake that this obstinate wilfulness was submitted to. . . . It has . . . exhibited our party as humbled at the feet of a spoiled child.' Nassau Senior wrote, ibid., f. 53, '. . . scarcely anyone defends or rather excuses Lord Grey for having been the most ardent supporter of the assumption of office by the Whigs, and of its unanimous assumption, when he kept in reserve an obstacle which he must have known to be great and which was in fact unsurmountable'.

[5] op. cit., Senior, 'Everybody rejoices that the attempt to form a Whig ministry has been abandoned. Such a Ministry must have depended on Peel on one side and O'Connell on the other, and could have had little power or permanence.'

K

support Peel's bill for gradual abolition over three years. Meanwhile the League, conscious that Russell had acted on his own at Edinburgh, would carefully watch not only Protectionists but Whigs, looking 'to the conduct of the Whigs in the counties as the test of their honesty on our question. Hitherto they have done nothing except to revile and oppose us. . . . You will perhaps tell me', wrote Cobden, 'that the leaders of the Whig party can't control their old friends in the counties upon the Corn question. But then what a bold farce it is now to attempt to build up [the] ruined popularity [of the Whig party] upon a question in which the Whig aristocracy and proprietors in the counties either take no interest, or, if so, only to resist it'.[1] The clubs buzzed with rumours of Whig disunity and backsliding. The first hurdle was passed when in a large carpetless room at Russell's house the Opposition M.P.s 'as one man' accepted advice to support the Bill. 'Even old Dan O'Connell and his Tail grumbled forth their "Hear, Hear".'[2] The first reading was granted on 2nd March by a majority of 97, the second on 27th by 88 and the Bill passed the Commons on 15th May by 327 to 229. Two thirds of its supporters were party opponents of the minister, and virtually all its opponents his nominal supporters. Only eleven Whigs opposed it — all of them landed.[3] But what of the peers? As we have noted, only 78 of them had voted for an official Whig motion which implied approval of a lower, fixed duty, and only five for Free Trade. A few Whig peers were out and out Protectionists, like the Earl of Yarborough,[4] a trustee of the Agricultural Protection Society formed by the Dukes of Richmond and Buckingham. But the general feeling was Melbourne's, that the status quo was indefensible but Repeal too radical,[5] and that there should be a fixed duty of 12s., 10s., or 8s., or, if Repeal, substantial relief of local taxation of real estate. In the upper circle of Whiggery Landsdowne and Palmerston were most insistent on such relief, for which both Russell and Peel had left a loophole.[6] Even Fitzwilliam thought Repeal an imprudent sacrifice of revenue and as the farmer's friend demanded a great reduc-

---

[1] Morley's *Cobden*, pp. 362–3, C. to Jos. Parkes, 16th February, 1846.
[2] *Napier Papers*, Add. MSS 34626, f. 71, 7th February, 1846.
[3] Five county members, five members for rural boroughs and one Irish member.
[4] Father of Lord Worsley.
[5] *Queen's Letters*, S. I, Vol. II, p. 61, 9th December, 1845.
[6] ibid, p. 70, 'Mr Baring thought he could arrange a financial scheme which would satisfy Lord Lansdowne's demands for relief of the landed interest.'

:ion of the 'oppressive and unequal' malt tax. He was asked by certain noble lords' to lead a party for a small fixed duty[1] and Cobden thought it might be necessary to resume agitation, because not a hundred men in the Commons or twenty in the Lords at heart wanted total Repeal.[2] Might not the Whig moderates negotiate with the Protectionists to salvage something from the wreck? It was supposed that Bessborough (formerly Duncannon) and de Mauley (another Ponsonby) favoured this course. But the danger of Whigs joining with Protectionists in committee was avoided by the meeting of magnates at Lansdowne's house on 23rd May; Melbourne, speaking the general sentiment, agreed to 'assist in doing the mischief'. In fact the shadow cabinet had been committed to total Repeal since December,[3] and in the debate on the second reading in the Lords the Bill had been commended not only by Brougham, Grey, Granville, Normanby and Clarendon, all of whom had admitted for some time that corn should not be excepted from the progress to Free Trade, but also, with effective advocacy pitched in a minor key, by Lansdowne, the first of them all to embrace the general principles of Free Trade, but tardy in applying them to corn. He was no party to the Edinburgh Letter; he would have preferred a fixed duty, for revenue and also out of regard for the sentiments and prejudices which one should consult when making great changes. But a fixed duty was impossible now; no satisfactory Corn Law had ever been evolved; experience and political necessity justified the change; proprietors would not suffer much, and the measure would have absolutely no effect on the power of the Lords, aristocracy or gentry.[4] The vital second reading was carried by 211 to 164, with 115 Whigs in the majority and 15 in the minority.

On the very night that the Lords passed Repeal, the Commons defeated the Government. The Irish Coercion Bill had met with general approval except from the Radicals or Irish, but, with 70 Protectionists resolved to hound Peel at every opportunity, it occurred to Whig partisans that by opposing vital parts of the Bill they could turn out the minister. Peel declined a Radical offer to abstain in order to save him. He also declined a far more ambitious

---

[1] Fitzwilliam's speech, H. of L., 25 April, 1846.
[2] Morley's *Cobden*, p. 370, letter of 12th March, 1846.
[3] ibid., p. 345, J.R. to Cobden, 19th December, 1845.
[4] H. of L., 28th April, 1846. In three days' debate no Whig who was not an ex-minister, except Fitzwilliam, spoke.

course which Cobden besought him to follow. Instead of bowing to 'a chance medley of factions in the Legislature' let him appeal to the country as the representative of 'the IDEA OF THE AGE', with a mission to solve 'the Condition of England Question'. This appeal would cut across parties, already in disorder, and enable Peel to govern the country through her middle class, as the Reform Bill had decreed she must be governed.[1] But Peel was too careful of his reputation thus to violate party ties. He was sick of party, which had broken in his hand, and weary of office. He agreed with the Radicals only on Free Trade and was not at all convinced of the result of Cobden's hypothetical appeal to the country. It was left to his disciple, Gladstone, to assume the rôle twenty years later. Meanwhile the split in the Conservative party let into office a highly aristocratic government headed by Lord John Russell.

The return of the Whigs to office was the result of the 'singular *coup d'état*', as Gladstone called the Edinburgh Letter in a phrase which recalls Disraeli's verdict on the Reform Bill. The *coups d'état* of 1831–2 and 1845 each rehabilitated the political prospects of Whiggery and each was assimilated into its historical mythology as a capital asset on which the Whigs very soon found themselves living in lieu of adequate returns from current enterprise. Peelites, indeed, suspected the Whigs of a wish to backslide on Free Trade in corn. They were angry when in 1847 they thought they discerned an informal agreement between Russell and Bentinck against Peel and the Radicals,[2] a poor return for Sir Robert's resolve to keep in the Whigs because of the need to keep out the Protectionists. In the next decade the most brilliant of Peel's Kindergarten, Gladstone, indicted Peel for a supreme misjudgement, saying that Peel ought to have put the Protectionists in, so as to prove the unreality of their reactionary designs. He saw in the Whigs the real villains of the piece.[3]

They are as a party tenacious of their opinions. What those opinions were, before the letter of Lord John Russell to the electors of London, is well known. That singular *coup d'état*, which had not even as many confidants as that of the Emperor of the French, appalled them, left

[1] Morley's *Cobden*, pp. 390–7 (letter of 23rd June, 1846) and Peel's reply ff.
[2] Add. MSS 40481 (Peel Papers), Lincoln to Peel, 23rd January, 1847.
[3] Long draft article for *Quarterly* in Add. MSS 44745 (Gladstone Papers). My italics, D.G.S.

them no choice, and carried them away. *Now if there was any danger to the Act of* 1845 *it lay in this quarter.* If the Act could have been overturned, none but a Whig government could possibly be in a position to effect its ruin. . . . So that *Sir Robert Peel, by upholding the Whigs, while he believed he was averting did in fact keep alive the only serious danger to which the Act of* 1846 *could be exposed.*

This very hypothetical proposition was the product of Gladstone's chagrin at the continuance of the divorce between Peelites and Protectionists. It did less than justice both to Peel and the Whigs. Sir Charles Wood, the Whig Chancellor of the Exchequer, regretted that total repeal of major duties had been preferred to duties for revenue, and Peel thought there might be need, early in 1849, to indicate to the cabinet that he would oppose, even if to do so meant alliance with the Radicals, any retreat from Repeal. But to the message, passed via Ellice, Wood made reply, via Lord Villiers, Peel's son-in-law, that the Corn Laws had not been mentioned in the recent cabinets, although agriculture was depressed. The Chancellor had decided a year before that it was 'totally impossible' to go back on 1846 even to an extent that would be 'felt by nobody'. To do so, Bedford said, would mean a war of classes. Peel felt sure that Russell thought so too and that he and 'many at least of his colleagues, would prefer the alternative of breaking up twenty Governments'.[1]

The Whigs knew better than to put back the clocks. Nothing could more surely imperil their slowly diminishing influence in the body politic. The most they would do was to encourage the idea that the *fait accompli* was in danger, in order to keep the Peelites from relaxing their defence of the ministry and the Radicals from pressing too hard on other matters.[2] In January 1850 the Whig ministers framed a Gracious Speech which, one of them said, 'now identified [our Government] with the Free Trade cause',[3] and asked Charles Villiers to move the address in reply. It was at a moment when Protectionists were angling for Conservative reunion on a basis of compensation for agriculturalists in return for the general recognition that Repeal was irreversible. The ministry adopted the standpoint of Peel and Graham that,

[1] *Greville Journal*, Part II, 1885, pp. 237-8 (Nov. 1848) and Parker's *Graham*, Vol. II, pp. 87-90. The apprehensive Graham believed it was the secret desire of Whigs to have a 5s. duty if they dared.
[2] This was Gladstone's real conclusion in the draft in Add. MSS 44745.
[3] Campbell, Vol. II, p. 269, 6th February, 1850.

because it was proposed by Protectionists, relief to the landed interest was treachery to Repeal — a view certainly not held by most Whig magnates in 1846 and too extreme for Gladstone to accept now. To this proposition the Russell government remained staunchly committed, against the speeches and votes of a few Whig Protectionists,[1] of independent conservatives who were virtually supporters of Whig rule,[2] and a growing number of Peelites. There was no retreat even though they were pressed to the brink of parliamentary defeat[3] and stood to lose in the next election many county seats which, strangely, they had gained in 1847. Lord John had committed Whiggery to a historic political decision, and it stubbornly adhered to the commitment, even at the cost of further narrowing the slender basis of support for Whigs as opposed to Liberals which existed outside the aristocratic circle.

[1] e.g. E. S. Cayley, Grantley Berkeley, Sir G. Heathcote, Sir Montagu Cholmeley.
[2] e.g. Philip Pusey and George Granville Harcourt.
[3] e.g. majority of 21 on 21st February, 1850, of 14 (in a House of 552) on 13th February, 1851 and 13 on 11th April, 1851.

CHAPTER VI

The Whigs and the Condition
of England

Peel had become convinced that the best contribution the statesman could make to the well-being of society, to the solution of what contemporaries called 'the Condition of England Question', was to abolish taxes upon raw materials and necessities, and to encourage, by lower duties, an increase in the consumption of commodities which, though not strictly necessities, would be widely used if cheaper. He had provided, with Whig support, for the disappearance by 1849 of duties on cereals and meat, and greatly lowered the tax on sugar not grown on slave plantations. But he did not abandon the principle of colonial preference, which was anathema to doctrinaire Free Traders as protective and an impediment to the international division of labour.[1] In this he remained Huskissonian. Russell, on his assumption of office, received sharp notice from Cobden that February 1849 must be the doomsday of all Protectionists, and that if there were any delay, especially with regard to sugar, Bright thought the Radicals could get better terms at the hustings. On sugar the Whigs did indeed make haste, providing that by mid-1851 the duty on foreign and colonial sugar should be equalised.[2] They may have felt that they had a score to settle with the planter interest from 1841. But they were Free Traders now, and sugar was a modest comfort in the homes of the poor, likely to make up in increased consumption any temporary loss of revenue. And they probably wished to strike an independent blow at the tariff

---

[1] The duty on foreign sugar had been 63s., on colonial 24s., when the Whigs in 1841 proposed to reduce the former to 36s. Peel in 1844 reduced the rate on foreign *free-grown* sugar to 34s. and in 1845 to 23s. 4d., when the colonial duty fell to 14s. Coffee was reduced in 1842 from 1s. 3d. and 6d. to 8d. and 4d., timber from 55s. and 10s. to 25s. and 1s.

[2] It was also provided that the duties on British and colonial spirits be equalised and that prohibitive duties on the import of refined sugar should be abolished, with the ban on the use of sugar in distilleries.

system — one not prompted by Peel (who deplored it) — and to strike it at a time when another change of government was not to be thought of.

If there be a distinctively Whig feature in nineteenth-century fiscal policy it is the repudiation of colonial preferences. The Russell government did not confine its attention to sugar. The differential against slave-grown coffee was abolished in 1851 and the timber preference further reduced. In partial compensation, restrictions on colonial trade, diminished but not abolished by Huskisson, disappeared. The Navigation Act of 1849 virtually repealed what was left of the long series of enactments originating with Cromwell.[1] For this the Peelites denied the Whigs credit, saying that it was the result of pressure from Peel.[2] Certainly in 1848 the Navigation Bill received a low priority among ministerial measures — it was well behind a Jewish Disabilities Bill and a Bribery Bill, neither of which was likely to pass, but which reflected Russell's principal interests.

It is due to the Whigs to say that they exerted themselves to secure the hazardous passage of the Navigation Bill through the Lords in 1849. But in 1848 they suffered much in the Commons on account of their handling of the sugar question and lack of enthusiasm for the Navigation Bill. Sugar was again a question because it proved impossible to maintain the 1846 timetable for the progressive, and progressively rapid, disappearance of the preference. The Protectionists received such aid from the Peelites, rebelling against Peel's leadership,[3] that a motion for a fixed duty against foreign sugar was defeated by a majority of only fifteen. A select committee found that the Act of 1846 had aggravated in the West Indies and Mauritius the effects of the London financial crisis of 1847. The equalisation of the sugar duties was postponed until 1854, the differential being *increased* for the period 1848–51. Disraeli made much of this in a celebrated indictment of the Russell government at the end of the session, during which very little legislation passed, and a series of retreats on the fiscal front enabled the most articulate of Protectionists to jibe at 'the govern-

[1] It preserved for a season the British monopoly of the coastal trade and the rule that two thirds of the crews of British ships must be British subjects.
[2] e.g. Gladstone, Add. MSS 44745, draft *cit. supra.*
[3] 29th June, 1848. Of all the Peelite ex-ministers, senior and junior, in the Commons only Graham and the former Chief Whip and his deputy voted with Peel and Russell.

ıent of all the budgets'. But 1847–8 were years of turmoil. The
ıral interests, sullen at their great defeat, suffered distress. Trade
nionists struggled with masters seeking to deny them the effective
mitation of hours. To the urban masses whom the business men
ad sought to persuade that Repeal was *their* victory the Chartists
reached that by 'free contract' the champions of Free Trade
ıeant low wages and long hours. Agitators still exploited the
hronic dislike of the Poor Law, machine industry and factory
rganisation among those whom new techniques must prole-
ırianise. The business classes were themselves uncertain, for the
ailway boom and the interlocking reactions of British and
ımerican finance disorganised and threatened credit. The session
egan prematurely, before Christmas 1847, because it was
ıecessary for ministers and the Court of the Bank of England to
ecure an indemnity for acting in breach of Peel's Bank Act. This
vas no time to impose new burdens on the country. But the Duke
f Wellington discovered that at a time when Palmerston's rela-
ions with Louis Philippe were very bad, the coasts lay open to
'rench invasion. There was a cry for an armaments programme.
The Whig attitude to the income tax was not clear. Leading
Vhigs had criticised it in 1814–16 and the cabinet in 1841 had
ejected it as an instrument for tariff reform. But some Whigs
ıad favoured it, and there is no evidence that Melbourne's
;overnment rejected it on *dogmatic* grounds. The Whigs would in
ıny case have had to decide in 1848 whether they were going to
ry to do without the tax that Peel had used as a *temporary*
xpedient to clear off deficits and tide the country over the period
Ietween the reduction of taxes and the recovery of their yield by
ncreased consumption and business activity. The Duke rescued
hem from the quandary. They were patriots, and who on such a
natter as the defence of the Channel coasts should gainsay the
victor of Waterloo, now nearing eighty, an institution of the realm
ıs well as Commander-in-Chief? Sir Charles Wood proposed an
ncome tax of a shilling for three years and of sevenpence for three
nore, and Russell expounded the defence predicament and com-
nended the remedy in a speech of great cogency. But the House of
Commons became mutinous. After six months of contention, the
ninistry thought itself lucky to get sevenpence and power to borrow.
By this time Louis Philippe had fled and in the European com-
motion of 1848 it was perhaps more likely than ever that the

A GREAT DEMONSTRATION.

Mob-Orator. TELL ME, MINION! IS IT THE INTENTION OF YOUR PROUD MASTERS AT ALL HAZARDS TO PREVENT OUR DEMONSTRATION?
Magistrate (blandly). "YES, SIR."
Mob-Orator. "THEN KNOW, OH MYRMIDON OF THE BRUTAL WHIGS, THAT I SHALL GO HOME TO MY TEA, AND ADVISE MY COMRADES TO DO THE SAME!"

French armies would march, but much less likely that they would be unleashed upon Britain. It should be noted that during the session insurrection in Ireland was precipitated and crushed and that the Chartist challenge was met firmly by Her Majesty's ministers in concert with the Duke and the middle classes of London who turned out as special constables to man the Thames bridges and the Whitehall barricades.

It may be that the effect on the public mind of the budgets of 1848 was underservedly bad. But it subsequently appeared that, while Spring Rice and Baring had not known what to do about recurring deficits, Wood was paralysed by the spectre of recurring surpluses. That of 1849 was small, that of 1850 larger, that of 1851 larger still. The budget of 1849 marked time, that of 1850 provided for minor changes, that of 1851 at last made considerable changes in indirect taxation, involving timber, coffee, tobacco and paper, as well as offering the rural interests the peculiarly offensive boon of free import of foreign seed. But Wood still proposed to keep half the surplus in hand, and to cushion himself against the fall in revenue from the tax reductions by continuing the income tax at its existing rate for another three years. And while he would repeal the tax on the windows of larger houses, he proposed to revive that very house tax which Althorp had removed under *force majeure* in 1834. If this was a bid for county votes, the gentry and the freeholders would rather have had less income tax than more Free Trade. The budget, says Lord Campbell, proved to be 'the most unpopular ever proposed'. It was a major political blunder. The foes of the income tax, Tory and Radical; the Canadian interest; the anti-slave lobby; the urban interests who disliked even a temporary house tax and had heard of 'temporary' taxes before (this would be the tenth year of peace-time income tax) — all were aroused. Nobody regarded the proposals as a well-thought-out solution to the crucial fiscal question of the day — whether the Treasury was to rely principally upon indirect taxes or adopt a combination of these with considerable direct taxation, and if the latter, what the nature, structure and incidence of the direct taxes were to be. No one in tune with 'the spirit of the age' thought that this was a budget worthy of the year of the Great Exhibition, when Britain was on show at the Crystal Palace, and it was possible at last to look to her economic future with buoyant confidence. For fear of defeat on the budget, the ministry resigned, but was compelled to return to office. As in 1848, Wood was forced to mutilate his budget. Gladstone, the Peelite, joined with Disraeli, the Protectionist, to demand special relief for agriculture, and they came within thirteen of victory. They also joined to condemn the house tax. A motion to take fourpence off income tax was defeated by forty-eight, but Protectionists, Peelites and Radicals combined to confine the tax to a year while parliamentary inquiry was made into its structure. Gladstone made clear his view that the tax could only be justified as an instrument for substantial relief to industry, and his lucid analysis of Wood's defects made men sigh for his arrival in office as, with less indications of what to expect, they had sighed for Peel's. The surplus, Gladstone later remarked, with scorn, 'which should have formed the groundwork of another great reconstruction of the tariff, was thrown in what professed to be the commutation, but was really, as to two thirds of its amount, the repeal of the window tax'.[1]

Ministers can hardly have regretted that the end, as it had to come, preceded budget day, 1852. Sir Charles Wood was an industrious and conscientious public servant, and was to prove a competent President of the Board of Control. But his name was for ever associated with inept finance and a failure to pursue imaginatively and constructively the policy of Free Trade to which the Whigs had now adhered. Reasons may be assigned for the fact that under his tenancy at the Treasury 'commercial reform proceeded at a slackened rate'.[1] The years 1846–50 were of uncertain prospect, when industry and agriculture had not begun the forward surge which facilitated Gladstone's further advance. Every fiscal reform threatened an interest, and where there was no clear party majority interests had more than usual influence in Parliament. Whigs were prone to believe, as well as to say (though the theme is characteristically Conservative), that after stirring combat and great reforms the country needed a pause for consolidation and assimilation — and after all, the tariff reforms of 1846 did not become fully operative till 1849. It was the Chancellor's prime duty to balance the budget; to a cautious man, this inhibited experiment, especially as raising the income tax was so unpopular. Cobden thought that 'feebleness and incapacity' were inadequate explanations of 'their failure as administrators'. Russell, he said, allowed himself to be baffled, bullied and obstructed by the Protectionists because the Whigs 'are the allies of the aristocracy rather than of the people, and they fight their opponents, not meaning to hurt them'.[2] There is something in this, and more in his complaint that, though superior to Peel in moral sentiment, and 'great upon questions of a constitutional character . . . [with a]

[1] Add. MSS 44745, 1855, *cit. supra.*
[2] Morley's *Cobden*, Vol. II, p. 23, 23rd July, 1848.

THE SLEEPING BEAUTY. *(Freely Translated from Maclise.)*

reditary leaning towards a popular and liberal interpretation of
e Constitution', Russell did not so well as Peel understand
onomic questions, attached inferior importance to them, and
eighed the forces of public opinion less accurately.[1] There was
so, no doubt, a natural reluctance among high-born Whigs to have
eir policy dictated by Peel, Cobden and Bright. But nothing
in remove the impression of infirmity and over-caution, varied
y panic in 1848 and political folly in 1851, which is derived from a
udy of Wood's budgets. As they had failed to profit notably by
xample of Huskisson, and left the field open to Peel, so they failed
profit by the example of Peel, and left the field to Gladstone.
he Whigs were the Bourbons of the Fisc, not because they were
nable to assimilate new doctrines of economic policy, but be-
use they consistently failed to apply them with maximum effect
the circumstances of the day, which always seemed adverse.
ence to the historian, and especially one whose theme is the
rvival of Whiggery as a political force, their financial policy is,
y and large, of more political than economic interest. One does

[1] ibid, Vol. 1, p. 386, 7th March, 1846.

not know of 'great' Whig budgets, and one perforce dwells upo
policy decisions like that of 1841 and the Edinburgh Letter, be
cause of their political repercussions.

These policy decisions showed that the champions of politic:
economy conquered, through the traders and manufacturers; th
middle class conquered, through the League. The policy of th
nation was being set, and aristocrats who desired the governanc
of the nation were conforming to it. Circumstances appeared t
conspire with propaganda to show that Free Trade was 'true', an
it sank into the national consciousness — and, broadly speakin;
into the opinions of the aristocracy, especially its Whig section -
as a dogma fully as hard to shake as it had been to establish.

We must now examine to what extent the Whigs succumbed t
the whole gospel and mood of *laisser-faire*, of which Free Trad
was a prominent constituent. This doctrine began to predominat
in Britain at a time when it became increasingly evident that th
public authorities had been failing to fulfil their traditional func
tion of controlling the economy and that the methods applied fc
the discharge of their social responsibilities were both uneconom:
cal and ill-adapted to secure national economic progress.[1]]
provided a justification, or an excuse, for a policy of abstentio
from interference with what was unregulated by law and c
abdication of responsibilities not efficiently discharged. Politic:
economy, concerned with production, exchange and profit, an
with human beings only in so far as they were the agents an
beneficiaries of economic progress, taught that the condition of th
people depended on economic prosperity and expansion, and tha
these depended on the free flow of labour, the free flow of capita
and freedom of contract between the two. It became enlightened t
assert that well-intentioned efforts to do what Christian charit
and common humanity demanded could have no beneficial overa
effect. That was the doleful message of Dr Malthus, who thougl
that the law of population condemned the mass of the people t
misery. It was said to be folly to interfere with the free action c
entrepreneurs in the interest of those they employed, and that onl
considerations of public order, and tradition, could justify th
provision of public relief for those who could not find employ
ment, for they were the reserve in the labour market, whos

[1] The 'old' Poor Law, and the law of settlement associated with it, were cor
spicuous examples of this ill-adaptation.

numbers determined the wages of the employed and hence vitally affected costs, and their support at the public expense was an uneconomic use of resources.

The student of Victorian Britain must bow in humility before its infinite complexity and many-sidedness, which inhibit glib generalisation and, still more, the patronising retrospect which was once fashionable. The principle of *laisser-faire* had its greatest sway in Britain at about the middle of the nineteenth century and in the United States a little later. It is no accident that this was so. Those who preached it were the products of an industrialising society and those who maintained it were the leaders in the process of capitalist development. But if one supported *laisser-faire* because it paid, one was entitled to make exceptions where it did not pay. In the case of the United States, the exceptions were very large indeed — high tariff walls, a rigidly pegged currency, enormous land grants and other forms of financial aid to railways. In Britain, too, it was never feasible, or desirable, that state abstention and abdication should be complete. The changes in company and mercantile law dictated by the recognition of competitive capitalism as the agent of economic expansion were not merely liberationist. Some banks had to be deterred, or barred, from issuing notes at will; a limited liability law was essential if enough capital was to be employed at risk.[1] The state could not altogether confine its relationship to the railways to the grant of legislative facilities; there had to be supervision, and even regulation, of the new form of communication and carriage which transformed the country's economic prospects, and, less patently and immediately, but no less surely, its social and political character, bringing to it that startling contraction which a century later air transport and wireless reproduced on the worldwide scale. The Victorian state interfered in these matters because it was Utilitarian, and for the same reason it could never stand altogether aloof from the social problems which industrial revolution brought in its train. But Victorian Britain also had a conscience. It inherited a conscience which had already dictated the abolition by Whig governments of the slave trade and of slavery. At a time when colonies were increasingly regarded as a burden and a relic

---

[1] The Act of 1856 of course 'freed' the use of capital, and it may be argued that it was perfectly compatible with *laisser-faire*. But from the other point of view it was protective.

of the age of economic pre-enlightenment, the Colonial Offic
functioned largely as a welfare office on behalf of coloured peoples
We need not dwell upon the hoary jibe that the British publi
conscience was unduly selective; let the age that is without si
cast the first stone. Nor need we linger over the allegation tha
conscience was simply a cover for conscious self-interest.
Victorian people were much like their grandparents and grand
children. If they were more complacent, they were richer and mor
knowledgeable than their forebears, and had a more reasonabl
prospect of the secure enjoyment and pursuit of further wealt
and understanding than their descendants. They were a good dea
more worried than they used to be given credit for by the evils i
the midst of their society, and what has been caricatured a
callousness or hypocrisy was an uncertainty as to the validity c
remedies which a later generation, in its wisdom, unhesitatingl
prescribes. The freer a capitalist economy in rapid expansion, th
greater the human problems, the more pressing the challenge of th
casualties of material progress. Conditions of work in factories an
of life and health in the great, haphazard, jerry-built conurbations
the care of human, and the disposal of industrial, waste; the mor
condition of the masses — all demanded attention. And in the ver
heyday of *laisser-faire*, and of private charity, there began a pain
ful, hesitant, empirical, unsystematic advance of official action i
such fields.

In these complex and controversial matters Whiggery had n
traditional interest, and its only asset was the Burkite principle o
the reconciliation of interests sufficiently articulate (as the te
hours' advocates were) to threaten the commonwealth if thei
grievances were not attended to. Whig aristocrats had a wide –
too wide — acquaintance with the mortgage[2] and a detailed know
ledge of farm leases. In every generation their caste produce
owners skilled in the management of estates,[3] occasionally of ver
diverse enterprises together forming a mixed economy. They kne
the ways of a rural community. Many of them had, by virtue c
ground-rents, an interest in urban development. But they did nc

[1] See *British Imperial Trusteeship, 1783–1850* by G. R. Mellor (1951), a ripost
to *Capitalism and Slavery* by Eric Williams.
[2] See D. Spring, *The English Landed Estate in the Age of Coal and Iron* f
the huge debts of Durham, Devonshire, Fitzwilliam, Bedford etc.
[3] e.g. 'Turnip' Townshend, Coke of Holkham, Rockingham (the Whi
leader), Earl Spencer (the Althorp of Chs. I and II), the 3rd and 5th Ea
Fitzwilliam, the 7th Duke of Devonshire, the 9th Duke of Bedford.

utomatically have imaginative understanding of the counting-
ouse, the problems of industrial finance, or the anticipation of
narket conditions where miscalculation might spell ruin. They did
ot know very much of the 'dark, Satanic mills' and the urban
nderworld of slums and lodging houses, the haunts of cholera.
gnorance was one handicap to decisive action, but not perhaps so
reat a one as Dogma; the prevalent political economy decreed
nat they should intervene as little as possible, and admonished
nem to remember that Conscience was a treacherous guide.
Iow often', said Lord Morpeth, 'had Charity to weep over her
wn work? In such a complicated society as ours all the depart-
nents of labour have such a close relation to each other that we
annot calculate the effect of any disturbing cause we may intro-
uce.'[1] This was the man who could not, while the Corn Laws
emained, find it in his conscience to pray 'Give us this day our
aily bread.' The savants had placed in the way of the social
eformer potent intellectual impediments. They induced in Sir
harles Wood, a charitable and ultra-conscientious Christian,[2] a
niformly negative attitude to state interference. They dominated
abouchere, a scrupulous man who, when he found that the
onstruction of a railway across his estate did not inconvenience
im, returned his share of the excessive compensation which
romoters had to pay landlords for rights of way. He said that the
vorking classes deserved consideration *above* all others, because
ne Creator had decreed that the majority should earn their liveli-
ood by the sweat of their brow. As to the legal limitation of hours
n textile factories, if he could separate the commercial part of the
uestion 'from what is called the part relating to humanity . . . if . . .
could believe that their condition, physical and moral, would be
ermanently raised, no desire for national aggrandisement, or to
ee wealth accumulated, would stand in my way. . . . BUT we should
e cautious how we interfere with that which every writer on the
ubject tells us is as unsafe a matter as the Legislature can interfere
vith — I mean the labour market of the country'.[1] A writer in the
:dinburgh Review in January 1846 stigmatised those who urged
nterference as obscurantist and short-sighted — their plan 'to
ransplant into our modern societies the beneficial part of slavery',

[1] Speeches in H. of C. debate on Ten Hours' Bill 13th–22nd May, 1846.
[2] See the tribute to the sense of duty and good-heartedness of the Erastian
nd Low Church father in Lockhart's life of the great Anglican Catholic son,
ne 2nd Lord Halifax.

L

to make the employer a slave owner deprived of his whip, was sel·
contradictory and absurd. The activity, energy and independenc
of freemen would be destroyed if they were kept in the tutelage ϲ
the state. Against these exponents of intervention stood the part
of long-sighted humanity, which recognised the working classes ϲ
citizens, adults, free moral agents. 'We do not believe that the
condition will ever be materially improved by a Poor Law or
Ten Hours' Bill.'[1]

It is too easy to write off such pontifications as hypocritical anϲ
to give to the detailed arguments and predictions used in suppoϲ
of them less weight than one would to evidence mustered by pol·
ticians of other times and creeds in support of their hypotheseϲ
The temptation to do so is great when all one's sympathies lie witϲ
the men who forced the Legislature to grant a ten hours' bill aftϲ
sixteen years of equivocation. As one reads of Morpeth respondiϲ
to Ashley's notice of a ten hours' bill in 1833 with an announcϲ
ment of an eleven hours bill to come on sooner, one spontaneousϲ
applauds Oastler's bitter comment — 'The sleek and oily Morpeϲ
like Judas enters, and at his season too — the midnight hour -
supported like his great and wicked prototype by bands of muϲ
derers (mill owners) and would betray the infants' sacred cause -
like Judas, with a kiss.'[2] There had to be legislation, because aftϲ
the 982-page report of that select committee by whose appointmeϲ
Althorp had in 1832 killed Sadler's ten-hour bill, the economiϲ
McCulloch said the facts disclosed were 'most disgraceful to thϲ
nation', Sir James Mackintosh said that 'he would not allow eveϲ
the principles of Political Economy to be accessory to the inflictioϲ
of torture', and even the younger Baines, of the *Leeds Mercurϲ*
said the facts 'seemed to call imperatively for legislative inteϲ
ference'. It was Morpeth's design, the ten-hour men believed, ϲ
facilitate relay systems and thus *lengthen* the hours of adult workeϲ
(the Lancashire factory reformers aimed from the first at limitiϲ
adult hours). It seems an entirely discreditable design, unless orϲ
accepts that Morpeth believed the assurances of mill-owners thϲ
eleven hours was the utmost limit of concession compatible witϲ
prosperity. A decent man could believe that, though the hours thϲ
children worked were disgraceful, both their masters and theϲ

[1] Article IV
[2] Published 9th February, 1833. Quoted by Driver, '*Tory Radical — T*
Life of Richard Oastler', 1946, pp. 214–15, for which also see the quotatioϲ
immediately following.

parents were dependent upon their doing it, that whole communities depended on child labour. It is true that this argument had been rejected in the case of negro slavery. But it was one thing to stake the fortune of the declining West India interest (even though one also thereby risked the future of the emancipated negroes), another to prejudice the goose which was relied on to lay the golden eggs of British prosperity, a bird in the 'thirties rather egg-bound. Politicians not personally involved in industry were liable to be accused, by men who were, of well-meaning but dangerous 'ignorance' and lack of 'practical experience'. Hobhouse, who had promoted two bills in 1831, only to emasculate them under the pressure of strenuous lobbying by the affected interests, was obviously deterred from further ventures by these charges.[1] Publicists on behalf of the masters disarmingly accepted the proposition that children were not free agents. But they firmly plugged the gap thus made in the principles of political economy as a barrier to legislative interference by prophecies of disaster if such interference occurred. These prophecies seemed the more authoritative because of the concession of principle, and some of the ten hours' men themselves (e.g. Charles Hindley) were known to have their doubts as to the commercial safety of the step they advocated.[2] We have to accept the probability that Labouchere, who denied that he was 'a bigot in favour of non-interference', and supported the Mines Act and the principle of the 1844 Factory Act, though continuing to vote against ten hours' bills, really did believe the fallacy that a reduction of hours by one sixth would diminish productive power sufficiently to take the profit out of textiles ('a man is up to his neck in the river and you tell him to go deeper'), that it would lead to lower wages and bitter industrial strife, and divert the protected children into unprotected trades where conditions were even more onerous.

In 1833 Morpeth had the grace to withdraw his bill, leaving the field to Ashley. When the mill-owners responded with a motion for a royal commission, Sir George Strickland[3] said it could not overturn the evidence of the select committee and Althorp asked the movers not to persist. He, who had appeared, *ex officio*, as 'the villain of the parliamentary drama' in 1832, now accepted an

---

[1] See Morpeth's explanation of Hobhouse's attitude, and the latter's letter, *Driver*, pp. 95–7. Hobhouse also thought the ten hours' movement a Tory trick.
[2] ibid., p. 312.
[3] Whig member for the West Riding.

eight-hour day for children under fourteen as desirable. But the
motion for a royal commission was carried, and the commissioners, devotees of the principles of political economy, turned not
humanitarian but Utilitarian lights upon the northern scene, pronounced that grave physical and moral effects resulted from
excessive child labour, and agreed with Althorp that eight hours
maximum and no night work ought to be prescribed for children
between nine and thirteen, the age which Nature had set. The
Government then sponsored a bill, which rapidly became law. It
established important principles. Labour was forbidden under the
age of nine in all textiles;[1] two classes of protected persons were
created, aged nine to thirteen and thirteen to eighteen respectively,
for whom maximum hours (48 hrs and 69 hrs per week) were
prescribed and night work proscribed; compulsory schooling was
enjoined; and quite drastic powers were given to inspectors.
Unfortunately the Act was very widely evaded. Yet the mill-
owners thought it worth their while to campaign for its modification, finding an enthusiastic supporter in Poulett Thomson, who
had described it as 'an evil forced upon the Government'. He
secured permission to introduce a ministerial bill bringing down
the age of the sixty-nine-hour class to eleven.[2] Hobhouse said this
was 'a cruel measure', and with the north up in protest, and a
majority of only two, Thomson had to withdraw the bill. Upon
the presentation of another ten hours' bill by the Radical, Hindley,
Russell promised steps to improve the enforcement of Althorp's
Act. Northern resistance to the Government turned to the Poor
Law field until in 1839 Chartism obtruded itself.

In 1839 the Whig Fox Maule introduced a bill to take Althorp's
Act a little further. In 1843 Peel and Graham sponsored a similar
measure, which would include women among the protected
persons and attempt to counter the relay system, which not only
involved very long hours for adults but made the inspectors' work
impossible. Reintroduced in 1844,[3] it was the occasion of con-
flicting votes, one of which adopted Ashley's ten-hour amendment, while the other declined to incorporate this in the bill. When

[1] The age for silk was lower. Previous Factory Acts (Peel's) had applied only
to cotton. In petitions presented by Morpeth, Bradford employers said that wool
was by contrast with cotton 'wholesome and comfortable employment' — *Driver*
pp. 91–2.
[2] 16th March, 1836. The figures on the vote were 178:176.
[3] It had to be withdrawn in 1843 because of controversy on the education
clauses, which in 1844 were omitted.

Peel threatened to resign unless the Government had its way, the House came to heel. But Russell, Palmerston and Macaulay were now on record as regarding the law as inadequate, though it reduced the hours of the younger children as well as protecting women. In 1846 and 1847 Fielden pressed Ashley's ten-hour bill; defeated on the second reading by ten votes in 1846, it passed comfortably in 1847, becoming law on 1st June. Only a dozen peers accompanied Brougham in his usual stand against 'misguided and perverted humanity'. It needs to be emphasised that though the Whig record with regard to the Factory Acts is not a noble one, the Ten Hours' Bill could not have become law in 1847 if the Whigs had been as hostile as the Peelites. It was carried by the mass 'brute' votes of Tory Protectionists[1] marching with humanitarian Radicals (some of them mill-owners) and some of the Whigs and Liberals, with the Peelites abstaining. In 1846 the Peelites were 77 to 6 against it; the Protectionists two to one in its favour; many Whigs and Liberals did not vote, but those who did were equally divided, and so were the thirty-two Liberal aristocrats who participated in the division. Wood, Labouchere, Morpeth and Baring opposed the second reading; Russell, Palmerston, Macaulay and George Grey supported it.

By now all Whigs agreed that *laisser-faire* should be honoured save in very exceptional cases, but that it should be a rigid canon instead of a rule of thumb was vigorously denied by Macaulay in a speech which made some belated amends for his defeating the Tory humanitarian Michael Sadler at Leeds in 1832. He did not say anything that had not been said in the early 'thirties by Tories and a few Radicals, and his main source was obviously the report of the select committee of 1832. But the platitude derived from Locke (and through Locke from Aquinas) that government exists for the common good, that the welfare of the governed is the end of government (commonly called in aid by the Whigs when attacking Tory governments as careless of the common weal or when explaining why the masses had no right to the franchise) was now brought a little more in tune with the conditions of the 1840s by Whiggery's most imposing apologist. 'WHERE THE HEALTH OF

---

[1] The slick view that the Protectionists voted for factory regulation as a 'tit-for-tat' for the Repeal of the Corn Laws, while containing some truth, overlooks the fact that the 'protection of labour', as Col. Sibthorp said, marched very well with the protection of land. There had been nothing anomalous in Tory-Chartist co-operation.

THE COMMUNITY IS CONCERNED THE PRINCIPLE OF NON-INTER-
FERENCE DOES NOT APPLY WITHOUT VERY GREAT RESTRICTIONS,' the
Commons were told. 'WHERE PUBLIC HEALTH AND PUBLIC MORALITY
ARE CONCERNED . . . THE STATE MAY INTERVENE . . . EVEN WITH THE
CONTRACTS OF ADULTS.' The state, indeed, should not infringe the
contracts of persons of ripe age and sound mind *touching matter
purely commercial*. But it was ludicrous to pretend that children
entered into free contracts and hypocritical to argue that they were
responsible citizens when the state would not allow a rich minor to
sign away his property. 'The property of the poor and young lies in
his health, and strength, and skill,' and these should not be
wasted. Society, as well as the victim, suffered if the free labourer
of England was treated like 'a mere wheel or pulley', or worse, for
industrial equipment, and indeed beasts of burden, were cherished
Macaulay brushed aside Labouchere's complaint that, in logic
the interfering state would have to follow the victims of harsh
terms of employment from one industry to another until a third
of the population was acting as commissioners to watch the rest
'You do what you can,' he said, 'you strike what you can strike'.

When Whig leaders went into different lobbies on the Factory
Bill they differed only in emphasis. There was little between
Morpeth's view and George Grey's. The former decided, rather
against conscience, to oppose the second reading; the latter, like
Russell, frankly said that though he would support it he hoped for
an eleven-hour compromise. After the act had passed, Grey, as
Home Secretary, was responsible for the activities of the inspectors, upon whom its enforcement depended. And we soon find
Ashley denouncing him as 'fearful, vacillating and showing no
principle'.[1] There are two ways of looking at Victorian morality as
contrasted with eighteenth century and Georgian laxity. One
school, lately fortified by the publication of unexpurgated Victorian diaries, roundly asserts that the only difference was the
superior discretion and decorum of the Victorians. But it may be
felt that the Whig political leaders were on the whole better, if
duller, men than their more boisterous forebears, and that the
influence of Evangelicalism (to which some of them were exposed
in the homes of their youth)[2] and earnest Utilitarianism had

---

[1] Wesley Bready's *Shaftesbury*, p. 242.
[2] Sir Charles Wood's mother wrote in 1834 of 'the gospel so precious to our
hearts' (Lockhart, op. cit., Vol. 1, p. 76). For the simple piety of Sir Charles

brought to their standards of personal conduct and even more
generally to their sense of public duty not a false veneer but an
improving varnish. And of them all, Sir George Grey was perhaps
the most estimable. His father, brother of old Earl Grey, had been
the close associate of Wilberforce and Simeon, 'Saints' whom the
Foxite circle, reproved by them in their manners and morals,
regarded as Puritan kill-joys and political hypocrites.[1] His mother
was a Whitbread and his wife was the daughter of the first Evangelical bishop, Ryder of Lichfield. He himself had wondered
whether he might not have a vocation in the Church, and as a
cabinet minister he supplemented the patronage of foreign
missions with Sunday afternoon slumming. It is not easy to see him
as the pious Victorian hypocrite, prolific of charitable donations
but lacking in *caritas*. Like Wood, he sought to do what was right,
whether as a public or a private man. How came it that he facilitated the evasion of the spirit, and even the letter, of the Act of
1847? George Grey was a man of generous spirit, as is shown by
his tribute to Ashley when the latter brought to the attention of
the House the report of the commission on the mines (1843), a
report which Peel and Graham, the ministers, had tried to sup-
press, so horrific an exposure was it of man's inhumanity to women
and children.[2] There were not lacking Whigs to oppose state
interference in the mines — a Lambton in the Commons[3] and in
the Lords Hatherton, who allowed himself to be used as a front
by the Londonderry interest.[4] But George Grey said he would
rather have made Ashley's speech than any he had ever heard.
And in the ten hours' debate of 1846 he had said that securing

and Lady Mary, the daughter of old Earl Grey, see ibid., pp. 25, 41–3, 78, 257,
266–8. For the religious strain in the Barings of Stratton (Sir Francis married
George Grey's sister), see *Northbrook*, pp. 6–7, 16–17, 26–7.

[1] If Fox had walked into Brooks's in the last days of his old cronies Adair and
George Byng, who died in 1847, he might well have inquired whether the Saints
had captured the committee. A betting book alone survived to recall the all-night
gambling for mammoth stakes. But see Trollope's political novels, and the recent
publications of Clarendon's and Chichester Fortescue's diaries for less worthy
aspects of high Victorian life.

[2] Even Cobden was converted by Ashley's speech, but in 1846 the chief
spokesmen against the Ten Hours' Bill, apart from Peelites, were Cobden, Bright,
Ward and Lord Duncan.

[3] Sir Hedworth, uncle of the Earl of Durham, for whose interests see Spring,
'The Earls of Durham and the Great Northern Coalfield 1830–80', *Canadian
Hist. R.*, XXXIII, 3, 1952.

[4] Hatherton, as E. J. Littleton, had promoted the Truck Bill which passed in
1831. Ineffective, it was a measure to protect the larger employers from the cut-
throat competition of the lesser.

'the goodwill and cordial co-operation of the operative body' was even more important than commercial considerations. This man by approving 'intermittent' work for protected persons, so that their statutory ten hours' maximum could be combined with longer hours for those not protected, made the enforcement of the protection impossible. The only explanation reconcilable with Grey's character is that he attached importance to Nassau Senior's view that the manufacturer's profit came out of the last hours of labour, and wished to facilitate the shift systems and relays (which were the employers' response to the Act). The Act did not cover adult men, although the champions of it were known to aim at such protection and to hope that it would be an indirect effect of the limitation of hours of women and young persons. It seems a fair conclusion that this good man was trying to do what was right by all parties, and combine the protection of the women and children with the least possible interference with production, and that in doing so he in fact rendered the Act nugatory. The *coup de grace* was given in February 1850 by the Whig judge, Chief Baron Parke, who drove a coach through the statute by his dictum that Parliament could not have intended to deprive the mill-owner of the free use of his capital and the operative of his labour.[1] There followed an amending act, in terms a little less liberal than the ten-hour men thought they had obtained in 1847, but representing a substantial victory for them.[2] Brotherton, a manufacturer who had once been a 'poor, half-starved factory boy', said it was the most beneficial measure over enacted.

The passing of the Ten Hours' Act of 1847 marked a crisis, for the victory of the principle of public responsibility for the weakest of the workers in the strongest modern industry must lead to its gradual extension to other trades and to other matters than hours of labour. This occurred in the 'fifties and 'sixties and was taken

---

[1] *Ryder v Mills*, a test case, 8th February, 1850. With regard to relays, Parke said — 'The act imposes a penalty . . . and according to the established rule, must be construed strictly. . . . It is not enough that we conjecture, even strongly, that it was the intention of the Legislature to have prohibited the act. There must be words indicating plainly and clearly that it has done so. . . .' (The Law Officers had agreed with those inspectors who instituted prosecutions — sometimes successfully — that the Act *had* outlawed relays, but Parke's ratio decidendi is convincing.)

[2] Grey resisted successfully Ashley's amendment to insert a 'normal' and uniform working day between 6 a.m. and 6 p.m. for protected workers, making relays impossible. This was enacted by Palmerston's Act of 1853 — Ashley was his stepson-in-law.

much further by Disraeli. No doubt Victorian achievements in
this field were rudimentary and inadequate, but here, at the very
moment that the Free Trade tide approached its flood, the tide of
laisser-faire was checked in at least one of its channels, though
even here it was to recede only slowly. The Whigs played no
glorious part in the story. But by and large their leaders were
decent men, conscious of responsibility for 'the condition of
England', though bewildered by the jangling interchange of
embattled enthusiasts and doctrinaires and by the novelty and
intricacy of the socio-economic problems. They were not all mere
slaves of the professors, the entrepreneurs or even of the narrowest
views of party interest. It was not, for instance, the fault of the
Russell government that the permissive powers of local authorities
in matters of sanitation (i.e. public health) were insufficient until
the 'seventies, and that their statutory obligations were not more
considerable. One would, indeed, hardly gather this from the
jeremiad of one of Russell's ministers, Lord Seymour, writing in
1880 as twelfth Duke of Somerset:[1]

> ... the practice of modern ministers is to revert to a system of
> interference tending to control and regulate the whole life and free-
> dom of the subject. ... The Government is now required to inter-
> fere in almost every industrial occupation. The State is appointed to
> act as the guardian of the feeble, the protector of the poor, the
> instructor of the ignorant. Freedom of contract is no longer the
> ruling principle between the employer and the employed. Men are
> not allowed to manage their own business in their own way. Parents
> are not entrusted to bring up their own children. The hours of
> instruction and the hours of labour are regulated by law, and made a
> matter of report to Parliament.
>
> To secure the health of the people is now the duty of the state.
> The food which they eat, the water they drink (if they do drink water),
> and the air they breathe, must be freed from contamination. Their
> dwellings must be inspected, cleansed and overcrowding prevented.
> The recreation of the people also occupies the attention of a benevo-
> lent legislature; but even in their holidays they must be treated as if
> they were children, and guarded against temptations which they are
> powerless to resist.
>
> New departments are created, or old departments reorganized
> with scientific inspectors, for the due performance of these multi-
> farious functions. ...

[1] *Letters and Memoirs of 12th Duke of Somerset*, pp. 480-1.

The Duke deplored that 'the spirit of modern legislation has departed from the general principles propounded by Adam Smith' and he repeated the admonition that 'laws restricting labour, however favourable they may at first sight seem to the health and happiness of the workman, tend inevitably to increase the cost of production, and to diminish the profits of business', and then competition transfers the trade 'to a community content with harder work and lower wages. . . . Then the enactments intended to benefit the working class have the effect of closing the workshop and depriving the workman of employment'. Moreover, 'continued interference by the State undermines and destroys the habit of self-reliance, which is essential to the independence and mental energy of man'. This is a prime example of the chronic habit of British politicians, supposedly so empirical, of tracing to their logical conclusion tendencies which they deplore, making mountains out of molehills and indulging in alarmist predictions. Sir Winston Churchill's 'Gestapo' broadcast in 1945 (a Whig speech if ever there was one) was in the same vein as His Grace of Somerset's ruminations in 1880. The salvation of the body politic is that politicians do not *act* in office in the fundamentalist way so often implied by their speeches in opposition, and it is therefore no bad thing that they should point out, however dogmatically, the danger of slipping unawares into a governmental or social order which they deplore. This duke through a long life preserved a consistent approach to state intervention, and sometimes receives brief mention as an obstructor of efficient sanitary legislation. Yet even he admitted that 'a rigid adherence to Adam Smith's principles of government would have occasioned intolerable suffering to a large class of the population'. And many of the state interventions which he condemned were initiated by or supported by his Whig colleagues.

The question of housing and health had been first taken up in a systematic way by the Health of Towns Association, of which Normanby was first president, and as early as 1841 he persuaded the Lords to accept a power of compulsory acquisition by local authorities of property needed for street extensions. The Society for Improving the Condition of the Labouring Classes was patronised by Prince Albert. On such a matter the Utilitarian, hating waste and untidiness,[1] could be at one with the Christian

[1] — and perhaps remembering that the original Benthamite idea was not the Smithian natural harmony of interests but their artificial harmonisation by a purposeful public authority.

SANATORY MEASURES.
Lord Morpeth Throwing Pearls before ——— Aldermen.

philanthropist moved by human misery,[1] while outbreaks of cholera
added salutary affrights. And so there came a day when Lord
Morpeth carried the second reading of the Health of Towns Bill,
saying 'I CLAIM FOR BRITISH LABOUR AND ITS AGENTS ALL THE
ASSISTANCE AND APPLIANCES WHICH OUR FOSTERING CARE, OUR
ADVANCING KNOWLEDGE, CAN SUGGEST.'[2] This was the one important
reform of the 1847–8 session, but it underwent grotesque amendment during five months of growing parliamentary misery for its
ministerial sponsor, providing a classic example of Disraeli's taunt
that measures were 'altered, remodelled, patched, cobbled, painted,
veneered and varnished'. The bill was too bold and comprehensive,
too far ahead of public opinion. Despite the failure of Lord
Lincoln's bill in 1845 and of their own in 1847, ministers still sought
to confer upon authorities all over the country the *obligation* to
make sewers, clean streets, dispose of refuse, supply water, cover
offensive ditches, require private drainage, and inspect lodging

[1] It was Dr Southwood Smith, who after being a Dissenting minister became
Bentham's secretary and pioneer of public health, who first introduced Ashley,
the Tory Evangelical, to the London slums in which he later laboured.
[2] H. of C., 21st February, 1848.

houses[1] and slaughter-houses, as well as *powers* by which an able, progressive authority might have worked miracles. But municipalities did not wish to feel the hand of Whitehall, owners of slum property (notoriously profitable) did not wish to be investigated, ratepayers resented expense and rural interests objected to the spread of municipal tentacles and to centralisation. The Government had accepted the view of the Health of Towns Association, anathema to the Manchester School,[2] that there should be an active, authoritative central authority, and wished to prescribe that this authority have power to extend municipal boundaries for sanitation purposes and that, where there was no suitable local council, health authorities, only in part elective, should be created. It was certainly an error to follow the advice of Chadwick and model the proposed authority upon the Poor Law Commission which was at this very time wound up because it had become odious. And so the scheme was emasculated.[3] The Board of Health was left with power to harry and expose, but rarely to act; in 1853 its powers were actually reduced[4] and in 1858 it was wound up.[5] Not for twenty years did the authorities get the powers which Birmingham used in such an exemplary fashion under Joseph Chamberlain.

It was beginning to be understood that ignorance and bad housing were sources of crime and improvidence, that moral as well as physical disease lurked amid dirt and squalor. The masculine intelligence of Palmerston, played upon, no doubt, by his Evangelical relatives, Ashley and William Cowper, responded brusquely to the Edinburgh Presbytery's petition for a day of national penance at the onset of the cholera. God, he was sure, helped those who helped themselves, and they should improve the housing of the poor.[6] When in 1852 the Foreign Office was barred

---

[1] In 1851 there became law a provision for the registration and inspection of common lodging houses of which Dickens spoke in terms reminiscent of Brotherton's panegyric on the Ten Hours' Bill.

[2] The more rigid politicians of this school were only prepared to go so far as to grant permissive powers to local authorities.

[3] London was excluded; only corporate towns were put under very limited obligations; elsewhere an authority could be set up only on requisition of the inhabitants or in certain special circumstances.

[4] And it shed Chadwick and Southwood Smith. Its ministerial head was the humane William Cowper, son of Lady Palmerston and brother of Lady Ashley.

[5] Its functions were distributed among other departments; some of them were conferred in 1871 on the Local Government Board.

[6] Ashley's *Palmerston*, Vol. II, pp. 265–6. The Under-Secretary, Henry Fitzroy, was instructed to inform the Moderator (Oct. 1853) that the weal or woe of mankind depended on observance or neglect of the laws of nature.

to him he chose the Home Office, partly because it carried the
prestige of the senior secretaryship of state, but partly because of
an interest in river pollution, smoke abatement and other social
questions. This interest arose from neither a spiritual nor a
philosophical source. Palmerston, a child of the eighteenth century, with its rationalism, optimism and scepticism (the intellectual environment in which Utilitarianism was born and against
which the Evangelical movement protested) showed that a strong
common sense is always contemporary.[1]

Liberals who thought in terms of 'rights' and 'freedom' had a
creed which was at base anarchistic, and Utilitarians a creed which
was at base authoritarian — they differed as widely as the Guild
Socialists from the Webbs. They were able to coexist in the same
Liberal movement because there was a multitude of things both
wished to abolish, because the practising politician was rarely all
of one and none of the other, and because the Benthamite acceptance of *laisser-faire* as the rule in matters purely commercial confined their bickering to the relatively narrow field between areas
agreed to belong to public authority and areas preserved for
private freedom, the no-man's land into which the state began
tentatively to advance. The key to the understanding of Victorian
England is surely that there was so much on which all could agree.
Between Ashley and Chadwick or Ashley and Bright, there was a
complete antithesis of approach to social problems — where the
Tory philanthropist was led by the spirit of compassion the
Benthamite came armed with a system of administrative reform
directed to the greatest 'good' of the greatest number and the
Liberal with a faith in a formal 'freedom' which for the miner or
mill-worker meant in theory an opportunity for self-improvement
and self-advancement but often in practice all the disadvantages of
slavery without its advantages. Yet all three agreed that society
needed profound improvement, and that this meant the improvement of individuals. We see the controversy between them in its
proper proportions if we note that Bright could never get beyond
the point that 'the increase in intelligence, civilisation and good
feeling' could do more than any act of Parliament, while Ashley

---

[1] See ibid., Vol. II, p. 246 for the view that the dirt of the town ought to be on
the fields; II, pp. 263–4 for projects to divert metropolitan sewage and drainage
from the Thames; 'I am shutting up all the graveyards in London . . . I shall
try to compel at least the tall chimneys to burn their own smoke and I should
like to put down beershops.'

argued that until working and living conditions were improved all hope of moral and social improvement was utterly vain (an assertion which through his 'ragged schools' he endeavoured to refute). Arguments about specific state interventions should never delude us into thinking that the issue was whether the state should remain liberal and lethargic or become democratic, bureaucratic, authoritarian. Only the lunatic fringe of the *laisser-faire* school thought that was the issue. The question was whether the spread of education, which was credited with an almost miraculous power to create a prosperous and enlightened community, required firing charges of public assistance and social legislation to give it momentum. Should Parliament provide for the education of the poor? Should it prescribe minimum standards of life and labour so that educative influences could operate with advantage? There was even substantial agreement as to the ideal product of education. Those who regarded a man as an interesting, predictable, psychological phenomenon, those who spoke of him as though he were merely an agent or instrument of economic processes, those who saw him as the child of God and heir of Heaven (but in mortal peril of Hell) could all agree to commend Samuel Smiles's *Self-Help* published in the late 'fifties. The ideal product of Victorian England, whether Tory or democrat, agnostic or Puritan, would have the middle-class virtues of sobriety, industry, thrift, self-reliance and self-respect, for of such was the kingdom of Man as well as of Heaven. Those very stringencies which Nassau Senior had written into the new Poor Law, against which the voices of obscurantism and compassion cried aloud, were intended to discourage sloth, fecklessness, idleness and improvidence, the very vices which the protagonists of education, religious or irreligious, strove to eradicate. It was more fashionable for a politician to advocate shorter hours for factory children in order that they might have time to be educated rather than because the hours were themselves too onerous.

Where did the Whigs stand in these controversies? They were, as a group, influenced by all and committed wholly to none of the rival pressure groups. Somewhat tardily they came into line with the Free Traders, but they never accepted the rigid concepts of the *laisser-faire* extremists. When the leader of the Anti-Corn Law League was writing to him of sugar, ships, timber and coffee, Lord John Russell linked the Repeal of the Corn Laws and the Ten Hours' Act as joint contributions to the solution of 'the Condition

of England Question' and told the electors of London that great
social improvements were required, including public education,
better treatment of criminals, sanitary reform and comprehensive
measures in Ireland.[1] The susceptibility of Whigs to Utilitarian
influence was, as we have seen, the cause of many complaints from
the landed interest — under that influence they framed the new
Poor Law, renovated municipal government and ventured as far
into the field of public health as Parliament would allow. And they
were certainly not indifferent to the social implications of Christianity. It is fair to say that while the economists and the Manchester School persuaded and bludgeoned Whiggery into a sense
of the folly of trying to control the economy, Utilitarians and
Evangelicals separately contrived to impress upon them new
standards of public responsibility and claims which men of good
intentions, however convinced of the general validity of *laisser-
faire*, however worn into the grooves of official routine, however
lacking in imaginative depth, could not ignore.

In the field of national education the Whigs' record is good.
It was never given to Russell to establish the comprehensive
system he desired, though he lived to see it come. But it was Grey's
ministry which obtained the first public subsidies for private
schools, and Melbourne's which established the Committee of the
Privy Council to administer them. And in 1846 Russell as prime
minister and Lansdowne as President of the Council thought it so
shameful that the active secretary of the committee, Kay-Shuttle-
worth, should command less than the total of the salaries of the
political ministers or the resources of the royal stables, that they
took, just before Christmas, the courageous step of authorising the
minute which provided for improvement of standards on the
assumption that Parliament would raise the grant from £40,000
to £100,000 p.a. The courage lay in the fact that an election could
not be long delayed, and Graham's experience in 1843–4 had
shown the perils of educational legislation.[2] It was not the obstruction of Tory obscurantists or purblind industrialists which delayed
the achievement of a national system of education, so much as the
disagreements of its advocates. Voluntarists, who found their
strength in Dissent, and a well-connected spokesman in Edward

[1] Walpole's *Russell*, Vol. 1, pp. 428–9.
[2] See J. T. Ward, 'A Lost Opportunity in Education, 1843' (*Researches and
Studies*, xx, October, 1959.)

Baines, the powerful north-country 'Whig' newspaper proprietor, who did so much for education in Yorkshire, argued that the state had no part in the business at all. But they could agree with the Utilitarians, who wanted a national, comprehensive, public scheme, in insisting that aided education should be purely secular or at least non-sectarian. These views were anathema to the great Anglican interest, having the House of Lords as its political citadel, which objected to the endowment of Dissent but joined the Dissenters in objecting to the endowment of Popery. Any advance in state assistance to education was politically impracticable except on existing lines, which meant that the subsidies went mainly to Anglican schools. Such is the nature of party that the Whigs, in whose parliamentary following were to be found the foes of the establishment, were better able than the Tories to carry a pro-Anglican measure, just as the Tories were better able than the Whigs to carry a pro-Catholic measure such as the extension of the Maynooth Grant. But it was bold in an election year to confront Whig and Liberal and Radical members, some of them already in trouble with their Nonconformist supporters by virtue of their votes for the Maynooth Grant, with a pro-Anglican policy, especially as Nonconformist protest was raised to the point of apoplexy by Russell's known desire to extend aid to Roman Catholic schools. We may agree with Palmerston that the vote of 372 to 47 did great honour to the House of Commons,[1] even though it was a predominantly Anglican assembly. It showed that ministerial resolution could pay dividends. The 1847 elections saw mighty efforts to punish supporters of the Maynooth Grant and the Education Grant — they figured more prominently as issues than the Corn Laws. Macaulay fell at Edinburgh and Hawes, a leading Dissenter and voluntarist, but a member of the administration, was defeated at Lambeth.[2]

[1] Ashley, ibid, Vol. II, p. 35, P. to Normanby, 23rd April, 1847.
[2] cf. Reid's *Houghton*, Vol. I, p. 380 where Monckton Milnes, a Conservative Free Trader just returned for Pontefract as an independent Russellite writes, 'The Clergy and the Methodists entered into a holy league against me, and spared neither truth nor money to turn me out for what the fools call my Popery.' Of Hawes, the soap manufacturer, he writes '. . . it is a poor encouragement to any Government to go and take Ministers out of the great middle class when such as he are thrown over. I understand Macaulay with his Whig religion being very unacceptable to the Edinburghians, but Hawes kept up so completely the type of the respectable and intelligent bourgeois that I should have thought it a great prize for them to have a representative in whose success they themselves are honoured'.

It may seem that the Whigs developed a genius for offending powerful interests without satisfying enthusiasts and for affronting doctrinaires to the advantage of vested interests. This was because they were very moderate reformers. No one could say that all these matters were wisely handled, or that the Whigs displayed any sense of compelling mission such as Peel's mission to 'make the country cheap for living' or Gladstone's 'to pacify Ireland'. But they do not merit such censure for their conduct in relation to the extension of state responsibilities as they rightly incurred for the timidity and maladroitness of their contributions to fiscal reform, of which they professed to be supporters.

CHAPTER VII

The Whigs and the Colonies

I t is to the credit of mid-nineteenth century Whiggery that the constitutional conditions were created for the development of Commonwealth out of Empire. Pitt, appreciating the lesson of the loss of the American colonies, had said, when commending the Canada Act of 1791 (which gave the colonists control of all internal taxation) that it was intended to 'bring the constitution of the province as nearly as the nature and situation of it will admit to the British Constitution'. But the doctrine of assimilation which Pitt proclaimed was an early victim of the French Revolution.[1] Ministers were bewildered when the Earl of Durham, in his famous report on Canada, argued that assimilation could go all the way, the sovereignty of the Queen being exercised by a governor who, except in reserved matters, would follow the advice of a local and locally responsible cabinet, — the sovereignty of Parliament being (presumably) in practice suspended in that field in which the colonial cabinet was responsible to a local legislature. Russell, who was Colonial Secretary, could not grasp this momentous proposition that the circle should be squared by the device of 'dualism' or 'dyarchy' and the governor's official personality split. His attitude was summed up thus: 'Can the colonial council be advisers to the Crown of England?... Evidently not, for the Crown has other advisers, for the same functions, and with superior authority.'[2] Up to 1846 it seemed that the Whigs were as blind as the Tories to the fact that settler colonies could not be held in subjection to the mother country (which was not the mother country of the people of Quebec) and that in the last resort the only choice, in default of the acceptance of Durham's advice, was between military occupation and abdication. Perhaps they were not so much blind as fatalistic. They suspected that separation was inevitable. They did not share Durham's

[1] Sir Reginald Coupland, *The Durham Report*, 1945, p. 111.
[2] Quoted by Chester Martin, *Empire and Commonwealth*, 1929, p. 182.

faith that political freedom would cement the connection with Britain.

Russell's position of 1840 was abandoned in practice without him or his Conservative successor, Stanley, realising the implications of their own tactical decisions.[1] Governors in Canada understood what was happening — 'whether the doctrine of responsible Government is openly acknowledged, or is only tacitly acquiesced in, virtually it exists' wrote Bagot.[2] But it is doubtful whether the crucial abandonment of principle would have taken place as early as it did if the Colonial Secretary under Russell had been anyone other than the third Earl Grey. The Durham Report would not have been the first or last such document to moulder in a pigeon-hole, with only its less valuable recommendations (in this case the union of the Canadas) implemented and its larger lessons resisted or ignored. Grey is at least as entitled to the epithet 'principal founder of the British Commonwealth of Nations' as Durham.

Russell had refused to submit to the Queen a resolution of the assembly of Nova Scotia expressing no confidence in the executive council, and had banned Joseph Howe, leader of the Reform party from the latter because of his demand that it be responsible to the assembly. Russell and Stanley tried to put the governors of North America in the position of George III in relation to the House of Commons and thereby resist the establishment of what Sydenham called 'this objectionable principle'. Governors were given freedom to change the executive council according to political convenience (i.e. according to the local election results) and to try to avoid deadlock with the assembly by having executive councillors in it to expound and defend policy. Able governors loyally played the part assigned to them,[3] but the more they succeeded the more

---

[1] Glenelg, under pressure from the assembly of Nova Scotia, had forced the governor to separate the legislative and executive councils and admit assemblymen to the latter. When the Assembly rejected the Civil List, Russell agreed that executive councillors be removeable, at the discretion of the governor. The assembly then voted no confidence in the executive council and demanded the recall of the governor. Russell refused to lay these resolutions before the Queen, but accepted that the governor must go, and that four assembleymen, including Howe, should be admitted to the executive council because the assembly had confidence in them.

[2] 18th October, 1842. Quoted by Martin, op. cit., p. 341.

[3] Sydenham in Canada (he died 1841) and after him Sir Charles Bagot and 'Old Squaretoes' Metcalfe and in Nova Scotia the Whig Lord Falkland, all pursued the Russell-Stanley policy of 'divide and rule' ('government, not self-government' Sydenham called it) with fair success. But Metcalfe, like Bagot,

they became party leaders, and it was inevitable that elections should become tests of strength between the governor's party and an Opposition standing for the principle of responsible government. To the governor of Nova Scotia, Lord Falkland, the leader of the Reform party thus came to stand in the position of Charles James Fox facing George III. Durham had written:

> ... It needs no change in the principles of government, no invention of a new constitutional theory. ... It needs but to follow out consistently the principles of the British Constitution, and introduce into the Government of these great Colonies those wise provisions by which alone the working of the representative system in any country be rendered harmonious and efficient. ...

He pointed out that 'this change might be effected by a single despatch'. On 3rd November, 1846, Grey, the brother-in-law of the deceased Durham, handed to the Peelite Lord Elgin, Durham's son-in-law, a despatch sanctioning 'the fullest adoption of the principle of Responsible Government', saying that it was 'of general application to all colonies having a similar form of government'. To the governor in Nova Scotia went a despatch informing him that he, and the Home Government, belonged to no party and had nothing to do with party contests, and that 'this principle must be completely established in order long to preserve our connection with the Colony'.[1] When on 24th January, 1848 the new assembly voted no confidence in the executive, the governor called on the leader of the Opposition, Uniacke, to form 'the first formally responsible ministry overseas'. Seven weeks later, after a Radical election victory, Elgin called on M. La Fontaine and Mr Baldwin to form a government in Canada.

It is by no means clear that Grey and Elgin understood what are to us obvious implications of their own principles.[2] And in

---

concluded that responsible government was inevitable. Falkland thought that perhaps a new written constitution could prevent the governor becoming merely 'the recording clerk' of the assembly, but Howe, in his 2nd series of 'Letters to Lord John Russell' pointed out that what was needed was not an Act 'to define the duty of the Sovereign when ministers are in a minority' but 'a rigid enforcement of British practice'.

[1] 31st March, 1847.

[2] Grey and Elgin approved the break-up of parties in Canada after the achievement of self-government, because this gave an astute governor the power to act as a political mentor. But when Elgin's successors were steadily edged out of this position, the absence of a stable party system was sorely felt.

LORD JOHN TAKING THE MEASURE OF THE COLONIES.

Australasia Grey achieved only indifferent success in his efforts to impose on the colonists constitutional safeguards which their political immaturity fully warranted.[1] But these qualifications cannot detract from the profound debt the Commonwealth owes to the doctrinaire statesman whose political character was such a curious compound of enlightenment and 'crotchets'. Grey repudiated Melbourne's cynical verdict that if a colony was not materially valuable to the United Kingdom, only national prestige and the fact that the government which lost it would fall from office stood in the way of separation.[2] Though fearful of American designs on Canada,[3] Grey shared Durham's faith that political

[1] e.g. provisions for indirect election to assemblies, insistence on upper houses and reserved powers.

[2] This was in July 1837 when Durham was first asked to go to Canada; he did not accept until after the rebellions in the two Canadas which, on his advice, were united into one colony.

[3] Elgin shared Grey's apprehensions of annexation by the U.S., to prevent which it was necessary in 1867 to have Confederation as Durham had originally suggested before, out of distrust of the French in Quebec, he opted for an attempt to assimilate them to the British by creating one political unit instead of two. At Confederation, Quebec again became a separate province.

freedom could cement the British connection. What was more important, colonists came to share it too — and when in 1850 Russell said in the House of Commons (8th February) that at some future time 'our colonies might with propriety be severed from us and formed into a separate and distinct state', Baldwin replied '. . . Is it not hard upon us while we are labouring through good and evil report to thwart the designs of those who would dismember the Empire, that our adversaries should be informed that the difference between them and the Prime Minister of England is only one of time?'[1]

The way of the colonial liberator is hard. The emancipated rarely behave as the sponsor of their emancipation would wish. By the end of his tenure of the Colonial Office, Grey was involved in an imbroglio with the Government of Nova Scotia over railway development, and he saw with pain the negotiation of a commercial treaty with the United States,[2] and, with even greater displeasure, the establishment of a Canadian tariff in 1859. It was not possible, once self-government was granted, to set limits to it. Crown lands and land revenues, which Durham would have reserved to the British Government, passed to the colonies as the first-fruits of responsible government. And it soon became clear that, just as the first British Empire had perished as a result of the attempt to impose a mercantilist policy agreeable to the metropolitan power, so the self-governing colonies of the second Empire would strain at the leash if the imperial authorities endeavoured to hold them to a policy of Free Trade which was not *prima facie* applicable to nascent colonial economies. So the Duke of Newcastle, at the Colonial Office 1859–64, was informed that the people of Canada were resolved to determine the mode and extent of taxation and could only be prevented by the assumption by Britain of the administration of the affairs of the colony irrespective of the views of its inhabitants. Britain had to learn that the freedom she had granted would be extended progressively beyond the limits originally set; any attempt to fix limits would drive a colony to independence. And so 'freedom slowly broadened out from precedent to precedent' until in 1926 it was accepted by the British Government that the element of subordination had entirely disappeared and

[1] Quoted Martin, p. 317.
[2] This treaty was negotiated by Elgin who, unlike Grey, believed that reciprocity arrangements would lessen the chance of the U.S. absorbing Canada. As a doctrinaire Free Trader Grey objected in principle to commercial treaties.

that, so far as was possible, this should receive legislative recognition at Westminster.

Grey's policy in Australasia was to a great extent dominated by his acceptance of Edward Gibbon Wakefield's view that the process by which Britain had developed her economy should in these virgin territories be telescoped by provision for an economy based not on a society of smallholders but on a society of employers and workers in which capital would accumulate more quickly. This would tend to reproduce, *mutatis mutandis*, the hierarchical social organisation of the mother country, with political effects which, to Grey, a considerable critic of American democracy, could only appear beneficial. Grey had been under-secretary at the Colonial Office when in 1831 Wakefield's plans for systematic colonisation, with immigration financed by land sales, were given their first limited application.[1] But a policy of regulated and assisted emigration of free settlers was self-destructive in this sense, that as soon as the free settlers became sufficiently numerous, politicians in Australia demanded the transfer to a local government of land sales and revenues, as part of the application of the principles of the Durham Report.[2] A Tory Colonial Secretary accepted the inevitable in December 1852 and the grant of responsible government to the established colonies followed rapidly.

Both in Australasia and South Africa British governments were confronted with the problem of the juxtaposition of aggressive European settlers and coloured peoples upon whom, through the mouth of successive colonial secretaries, Whig and Tory, the dominant civil servant James Stephen, 'Mr Over-Secretary Stephen', declared the effect of European settlement to be disastrous. Men in Whitehall could not turn back tides which flowed with an appearance of irresistibility thousands of miles away, and their efforts to stay them did not always work in the interest of those they sought to protect. But it is a fact of cardinal importance that the Colonial Office consistently sought to protect backward races beset by colonial incursion. In South Africa the prime source of Liberalism was to be Whitehall; the wheel has come full circle when in the Coloured Voters Act of the 1950s the

---

[1] In 1834 the S. Australia Act set up commissioners, who in 1840 were absorbed by the Commissioners of Colonial Land and Emigration; in 1842 Stanley promoted the Australian Land Sales Act.

[2] e.g. resolutions of the committees of the Legislative Council of New South Wales 1844.

Nationalist Government thumbs its nose at the splendid Hottentot Charter of 1828 to which a Tory Colonial Secretary appended an explanatory memorandum 'All Hottentots and other free persons of colour, lawfully residing within the said Colony, are and shall be . . . entitled to all and every the rights privileges and benefits of the law, to which any other His Majesty's subjects . . . . are or can be entitled.' Soon all persons of colour within the dominions of the Crown were free, and Russell approved the Masters and Servants' Ordinance of 1840 which applied to all regardless of colour. The Boers, whose long-continuing trek to escape from the British Empire had been accentuated by the abolition of slavery, were diverted from Natal by British occupation. Stanley laid it down that there should be no distinction or disqualification whatever based on colour, origin or creed, no private aggression beyond the colony's borders and no slavery or any modified form of slavery, and Grey confirmed that 'it is mainly for the benefit of the native inhabitants of Africa that the colony [Natal] is to be maintained'.[1] Glenelg's despatch to Sir Benjamin D'Urban of 26th December, 1835 was hailed by the Aborigines' Protection Society as 'the most comprehensive, the most statesmanlike, the most British, the most Christian document of all on this great subject'.[2] It proceeded from the hypothesis that 'no greater real calamity could befall Great Britain than that of adding Southern Africa to the list of the regions which have seen their aboriginal inhabitants disappear under the withering influence of European neighbourhood'. The despatch accepted the missionaries' view that the attack on the white settlements which began the Sixth Kaffir War was justified by White provocation, revoked the governor's annexation of Kaffirland, declared that warfare could only be justified by the need to protect British subjects, denounced the European method of waging war as barbarous, and announced that power would be taken to punish British subjects for offences committed in native territories outside the King's dominions. D'Urban was dismissed for protesting that the Colonial Office regarded too lightly the dangers to which the colony was exposed from 'the savages upon its borders'. This, in retrospect, seemed over-quixotic. There was no possibility of keeping the peace between Bantu and Europeans on the frontier of the British

---

[1] 4th December, 1846, cit. Mellor, pp. 261–2.
[2] 1st Annual Report of the Society.

dominions. Under Grey British Kaffraria became a colony to be held by the chiefs under the Queen's representative as Great Chief, and even that did not work; Grey had no hesitation in blaming the Bantu for a new war (1850–3). But colonial secretaries of one party and the other consistently tried to impose upon the white and black peoples who had milled into South Africa a peaceful co-existence for which neither was ready, and it was the desire to protect the weaker party which led inexorably to the extension of British territory.

In New Zealand sovereignty was assumed, reluctantly, because there was no choice between settlement and no settlement, only between extra-legal, uncontrolled settlement and lawful, regulated settlement. Normanby, Colonial Secretary for a few months in 1839, refused to countenance the expedition of the New Zealand Land Company (promoted by Durham and the Wakefields). It was vigorously opposed by the Church Missionary Society of which Glenelg, like Wilberforce, Buxton and the elder Stephen, was a vice-president; George Grey (Parliamentary Under-Secretary to the Colonial Office) and 'Mr Over-Secretary Stephen' were on the committee. When the expedition sailed, Normanby, a Utilitarian rather than an Evangelical, authorised the negotiation of the cession of the North Island and instructed the lieutenant-governor in terms reminiscent of Glenelg's despatches to D'Urban. An increase in national wealth and power would be inadequate compensation for the injury flowing from the injustice of the act and the calamity to the numerous and inoffensive people who had a recognised title to the soil and to sovereignty.[1] 'It is impossible that the Government should forget that the original aggression was our own,' wrote Russell to the Governor of New South Wales.[2]

We see here no glorification of imperialism, not even a note of self-congratulation at the assumption of a civilising and Christianising mission, though such a mission was acknowledged. There was only regret that situations arose which made the assumption of obligations a moral duty, together with a resolve to fulfil such obligations as well as possible. If the continuity and consistency of the attempt to do so is to be attributed in a very high degree to

---

[1] Instructions 14th August, 1839. In May 1840 British sovereignty, by cession (T. of Waitangi) was proclaimed over North Island, and elsewhere by right of discovery.
[2] 21st December, 1839 — see Mellor, op. cit., p. 293.

Stephen — 'Mr Mother Country' as white colonists impatient o
Colonial Office intervention and ideologists who insisted on th
repudiation of colonial involvements called him — it should sti
be remembered that ministers of both parties gave their names t
the documents he wrote. For sixteen years between 1830 and 185
Whig ministers, increasingly committed to the general doctrine o
laisser-faire, sought by all manner of regulations interfering wit
freedom of contract (whether for the sale of land or of labour) t
protect coloured peoples from the natural results of white incur
sion, asked Parliament for money to provide physical protectio
and advance the intellectual and economic prospects of 'natives'
emancipated slaves and coloured immigrants, and regarded suc
activity as incumbent on a state forced by history and the enterpris
of its citizens, rather than by any will of its own, to be imperialist
They took seriously the Glenelg prescription that contact wit
native tribes ought to be marked by systematic and persevering
adherence to justice, conciliation and forbearance and the encouragement of the honest arts by which civilisation and Christianity might be advanced among them. They took it seriously
though they hardly hoped it could prevail, and though they
involved themselves in the dilemma of how the aborigines could
be protected without a form of apartheid which was hardly consistent with the development of the multi-racial community which
was accepted as the ideal.[1] They were, of course, attacked not only
by colonists who regarded them as interfering busybodies, but by
missionary and humanitarian societies by whose principles their
own efforts were informed.[2] They deserved the attacks of the
perfectionists a good deal less than they merited criticism for their
imposition of the new Poor Law on industrial England and
indigent Ireland or their reluctance to promote effective protection
of the children in the textile factories. We must agree that 'in
spite of sins of commission and omission, these records of something attempted, something done, can be read, not with complacency, but with some satisfaction'.[3]

To Sadler, Ferrand, Oastler, 'Parson' Bull and other 'Tory

[1] In Natal Grey suggested an interspersion of white settlement and native
reserves to accustom the Bantu to settled labour but also to prepare for the day
when taxes and laws and rights could be the same for all races.

[2] e.g. Bishop Selwyn's attack on Grey for restricting (1846) the area of land
previously regarded as acknowledged by the Treaty of Waitangi to be under
Maori proprietorship.

[3] Mellor, op. cit., p. 416.

Radicals' the Whigs, like Wilberforce himself, were hypocrites whose zeal for the abolition of slavery was not matched by enthusiasm for the legislative protection of the factory worker and humane provision for the unemployed. The point may be thought a fair one. But it does not detract from such merit as would otherwise attach to the abolition of the slave trade and of slavery. It was not Whigs who first promoted these causes and brought them into public prominence, and, like the Catholic Question, they did not clearly divide the two parties one from another. But in face of obstruction from the Lords,[1] all Pitt could do was secure legislation to improve the conditions of the voyage from Africa and recommend to the colonies which had representative government legislation to improve the conditions of slavery such as was applied to the Crown colonies. It was a predominantly Whig ministry which carried the abolition of the slave trade in 1807 and stoutly resisted Tory attempts to delete the reference to slavery as 'inconsistent with the principles of justice and humanity'. Sir James Mackintosh and Brougham, as vice-presidents, were active in bringing the objectives of the Anti-Slavery Society before Parliament; together with Buxton and Lushington they took over the management of the cause from the ageing Wilberforce. By 1824 the House of Commons passed a resolution which envisaged the eventual emancipation of the slaves. The coming to power of the Whig ministry in 1830 resulted in a stiffening of tone towards the recalcitrant colonial legislatures. Where Canning was content to rely on 'the slow and silent course of temperate, but authoritative, admonition' to secure better treatment of slaves, Goderich advanced towards the alternative course which Canning had said he hoped would never be necessary — the harassment of the colonies by the exercise of imperial powers of legislation and regulation. A new and stricter code was enjoined, and the colonies which had failed to act in the spirit of Bathurst's circulars were threatened with financial disadvantages if they did not conform to it.[2] There was some hesitation in proceeding in 1833 to emancipation by imperial law, but the plunge was taken, and the Under-

---

[1] The Lords obstructed action on the Commons' resolutions for gradual abolition of the Trade (e.g. that carried by Pitt's colleague Dundas in 1793) and even a bill to prohibit supply of slaves to foreign territories carried in the Commons by Wilberforce in 1794. Pitt said he could not continue in cabinet with opponents of Dolben's Bill of 1788 to improve voyaging conditions.

[2] Orders in Council of November 1831.

Secretary, Howick (the Earl Grey of this chapter), in commending it, remarked that the political liberty which the Poles were admired for pursuing was 'a mere speculative advantage' compared with the fundamental right of the negroes to enjoy the fruits of their industry.[1] Thus the Whigs took their championship of civil liberties to a logical conclusion. But they did not leave masters and slaves to face the perils of abrupt transition to a free labour market. The slaves were bound as apprentices till 1838 (1840 in the case of predials);[2] their hours of labour were regulated and stipendiary magistrates appointed to protect them. The Government refused to accept the Jamaican Police Act of 1837, which under the guise of provision for public order was held to reintroduce a disguised slavery, and this legislation was overriden by an Amending Act which, *inter alia*, removed the prisons from the island authorities. It was the refusal of the Jamaican assembly to fulfil its functions while this imperial legislation was in force which led to the Jamaica Bill of 1839 (to suspend the constitution) on which the Whigs were driven to resign. At the end of the apprenticeship period a new code was ready, regulating the contracts of ex-slaves to prevent their unjust exploitation. But in the colonies with representative government, Colonial Office admonitions tended to be increasingly ignored, being regarded as coming from a hostile source, and the power of harassment diminished as fiscal protection was gradually removed by laws themselves regarded by the governing classes in the islands as harassment. Owing to the economic decline of the islands, little local money could have been spared for the enhancement of the condition of the negro even if the will to employ it had been there. It was therefore not creditable to the British Parliament that imperial generosity gradually petered out. From 1835–41 the grant in aid of schoolhouses for negroes equalled the English education subsidy, but Russell in 1841 reduced it from £30,000 to £6,000 and it soon ceased altogether. In 1850 Grey reluctantly discontinued the appointment of stipendiary magistrates.

As the plantations would need extra labour after the slaves were freed, facilities were provided for the migration to the West Indies of West Africans and slaves liberated (under treaty provisions) from foreign ships and to Mauritius of indentured Indians. But

[1] H. of C. 14th May, 1833.
[2] i.e. field-slaves.

neither Tory nor Whig ministers would allow this movement to be uncontrolled. Care was taken to ensure that departures from Sierra Leone were voluntary (the movement was canalised there to prevent African chiefs from conducting slave hunts to find emigrants for West Indian interests), and to see that, as far as possible, undesirables were not admitted to British colonies. The Emigration Agent at Freetown was instructed 'always to keep uppermost in his mind that, besides procuring for the West India colonies a supply of useful labourers, the great object is the improvement of the condition of the negro population'.[1] Emigration of contract labourers from India to Mauritius was prohibited in 1839 because of abuses and resumed only on strict conditions. When half the staple export of Trinidad was produced by African or coolie labour and the Indians became the cornerstone of the Mauritian economy the planters could not justly complain that they were entirely neglected. But the protecting care of British officialdom followed the immigrant labourer with considerable effect, especially in Mauritius.

The highest ideals of British colonial policy are no inventions of the twentieth century. The spirit of the Hottentot charter remained dominant. 'It cannot be too strongly impressed upon every European within your government that the lives of the natives must be considered as equally valuable and entitled to the same protection as those of any European settlers,' a governor of western Australia was told.[2] Coloured men were to become assimilated to the Europeans by the diffusion of 'civilisation' (including Christianity) as well as by integration into an economy inevitably dominated by Europeans. But a thousand practical problems confronted the Colonial Office to which general propositions and enlightened aspirations did not supply an automatic answer. Legal equality with the white man under a law of general application to all races was seen to be a cruel gift to an ex-slave, a contract labourer or an aboriginal; special protective regulations were required to see that land transfers and labour contracts were voluntary and fair. The full rigour of European criminal law could not justly be applied to tribesmen who were total strangers to its ethos; special courts must sometimes be created, not to emphasise the coloured man's inferiority but his need of special securities

---

[1] Mellor, op. cit., pp. 190–3.
[2] By Glenelg, see ibid., p. 302.

for equitable treatment. It was often considered expedient, and just, to acquiesce in indirect rule, preserving the power of chiefs and native laws and usages (except to the extent that they were wholly repellent to the Western conscience), though this was bound to delay assimilation. *Per contra*, taxes were imposed which did not burden unduly the white settler, but seemed a grievance to the native — because of the Victorian aspiration to inculcate the habit of continuous labour among peoples unused to it (like the Bantu pastoralists)[1] or having no natural incentive to it because mere subsistence was easy (as was the case with ex-slaves, especially in Mauritius). The problem of vagrancy was one which could not be evaded by the disallowance of police regulations and vagrancy ordinances on the ground that they brought back elements of slavery. Often, in the end, laws which seem harsh were allowed. They have to be read in the context of the age as well as the local conditions. The British working man could still be imprisoned for breach of contract; the Poor Law Commissioners had power to move paupers to districts of high employment, and the infamous workhouse, where conditions were such that no self-respecting labourer would prefer them to earning an honest living, was regarded as a civilising agency because it discouraged sloth and improvidence.

Mr Mellor has fairly drawn a parallel between 'the problems of the backward classes of Britain and the problems of the backward races of the Empire'. In the absence of guiding precedents and adequate administrative machinery, he says, new problems on a vast scale were met by 'groping, floundering, experiment, trial and error', and anticipations were not fully realised because 'solutions on trial at home' were applied, very naturally, to problems which were only superficially similar abroad.[2] It may be added that it was politically impossible to secure enough money to pursue in depth the policy of raising material conditions and imparting the elements of religious and secular education so as to stimulate self-help and material self-improvement. The parliamentary tide flowed very firmly away from such expenditure of public money in the colonies. In Australasia, moreover, the progress towards representative

---

[1] It was desirable, Grey wrote, that the Africans in Natal should be so taxed as 'to render a mere subsistence difficult to be obtained without exertion' (quoted Mellor, p. 266).
[2] Mellor, op. cit., pp. 418–19.

overnment set a term to the activities of the imperial government n defence of the natives. But if the efforts of the Colonial Office, nspired by the spirit of trusteeship, wrought no miracles, they are ot to be sneered at.

CHAPTER VIII

The Whigs and the Condition
of Ireland

Assessment of British policy in Ireland under the Union is bedevilled by knowledge of its utter failure. Based on a denial to the Irish of the self-determination which was granted to settlers, including Irish settlers, in Canada, Australasia and South Africa, it had few of the redeeming features which an Indian or Nigerian nationalist may now concede to the supplanted imperium. It could not even assure law and order, and the groundworks of future prosperity were not laid. It was not able to accomplish the consolidation of the land and the introduction of machinery which in England displaced or impoverished many humble villagers but was beneficial in terms of agricultural efficiency. Unionist governments were eventually driven to the creation of a peasant proprietary. Whiggery is therefore bound to appear in the light of a landlord oligarchy which struggled against the logic of Irish traditions and social realities to create in Erin the image of the English land system. One's natural sympathies are with the struggling and often starving tenantry rather than with often feckless and sometimes harsh landlords, to understand whose perplexities requires special knowledge and an effort of the imagination. Everything conspires to the discredit of those who fought against the future.

No period of British rule in Ireland since Cromwell's massacres and the clearances of the seventeenth century has attracted more condemnation than the time of the Famine, and it is remembered against the government of Lord John Russell that its efforts to keep people alive were reluctant, the means perversely tortuous, the conditions of relief harsh and that it did virtually nothing to improve the means of supporting the population in the future. If the pressure of population on resources slackened, this was due to starvation and private emigration.[1] Can there be any appeal

[1] The population of Ireland in 1851 was only just over six million. Without the Famine, the Pestilence and the Exodus it would have been nine million.

against the coroners' juries who returned verdicts of murder against Russell?

The ministerial approach was stated clearly by Clarendon as President of the Board of Trade before he succeeded Bessborough as Lord Lieutenant. 'Sound principles were clearly laid down by the Government and Treasury at the beginning of the crisis . . . they well understood their duty and the necessity of non-interference,' he wrote, but they had to 'answer to the humanity and generosity of England for the mortality of Ireland'.[1] 'Sound principles' and moral duty met in headlong collision. According to Malthus, increase of population renders inevitable the widespread action of misery, which no charity, public or private, can in real terms, or at least in the long term, reduce. The theory is, of course, as fallacious as the Marxist doctrine that the development of Capitalism involves increasing misery for the masses, and for the same reason, that it overlooks the possibility of the constructive augmentation of resources and the beneficent redistribution of incomes. But on a government which had assimilated as a dogma the proposition that the state ought not to interfere in 'matters purely commercial' and was impelled by political pressures towards retrenchment and the reduction of taxation, the need by extraordinary interventions and subventions to keep millions of people alive had a traumatic impact. Russell, in saying that nothing could prevent widespread suffering and even death in Ireland, and O'Connell, in echoing him, after a meeting with Bessborough, thought they were stating a truism. Trollope, a civil servant in Ireland at the time, could write '. . . The Famine — the Pestilence — the Exodus . . . three wonderful events following each other, were the blessings coming from Omniscience and Omnipotence by which the black clouds were driven from the Irish firmament. . . . His mercy endureth for ever'.[2] Here was Providence, or Nature, majestically enforcing iron laws in cruel kindness. That good man, Sir Charles Wood, at the Treasury, was inclined to let Nature take its course, and had to be reminded by Russell that this was 'no ordinary calamity'. Russell told Lansdowne that he could not imagine any Poor Law which did not acknowledge the traditional duty of the public authority to see that

[1] Emilie Barrington's *Servant of All*, 1927, pp. 109–10, Clarendon to James Wilson, 8th March, 1847.
[2] *Castle Richmond*, 1860, Vol. III, p. 160.

the destitute did not perish. He appreciated that efforts had to be made to counter the Famine on a scale for which the machinery of the Poor Law could not suffice. Pressed by Bessborough, he forced his colleagues to depart from a rigid *laisser-faire* attitude.[1] But they were conscious of unwisdom and even impiety in checking Nature's operation, and laid themselves open to the charge that 'Lord John Russell seemed more concerned with maintaining the principles of trade and of orthodox political economy than with preventing wholesale starvation'.[2]

It was because it was thought important to infringe 'sound principles' as little as possible that relief measures only slowly became adequate and were brought to an end too hurriedly. Food was not to be made available to the able-bodied and their families by way of doles or supplements in aid of wages, but was to be earned by special task-works. And the actual supply of food to the consumer was to be left to the 'ordinary channels'. As these channels continued to carry food, sometimes under armed guard, out of Ireland to the industrial districts of England,[3] Bernard Shaw said one should talk not of 'the Famine' but of 'the Starvation'. And there were no 'ordinary' channels for carrying food to the worst-hit parts of Ireland. In many districts cash transactions were comparatively rare. The cottier and the smaller tenant-at-will went short of food even in the best years, and in losing his harvest he lost his only possible source of purchasing power. The private supplier of food in 1846 and 1847 came not as an 'ordinary channel' but as a profiteer. At the end of the winter of 1846–7 the Government was employing three quarters of a million Irishmen and supporting in one way or another some three million people.[4] It cannot be an exaggeration to conclude that during two awful winters the ministry succeeded in keeping alive at least a million who must otherwise have perished. That it was its simple duty to do so does not alter the labour required to do it. But because of

[1] Add. MSS 40481, Lincoln to Peel, 12th October, 1846, '. . . If he [Bessborough] told the truth to a friend of mine some ten days ago he has met with great opposition from the cabinet at home, the majority being rigid adherents to the ordinary rules of political economy, tho' J. Russell was willing to relax them. . . .'

[2] O'Hegarty, *A History of Ireland under the Union*, 1952, p. 305.

[3] The Government feared disturbances in the English industrial districts, was understandably reluctant to go back on the celebrated decision to 'open the ports' and thought that if it did the whole price structure in the British food market would be deranged.

[4] See Pomfret, *The Struggle for the Land in Ireland*, 1930.

ideological and financial inhibitions which precluded a direct approach to the major emergency operation required, ministers laid themselves open simultaneously to attack for the inadequacy of their arrangements and for their extravagance. The Peelites were severe in their strictures. Lord Lincoln told Peel that 'the most lavish application of money' was going on everywhere, and that 'the old-stagers' were 'bewildered at the liberality' and the Treasury clerks amazed 'at the utter abolition of purse-strings'.[1] 'The financial arrangements merit the severest animadversion,' wrote Gladstone later. 'Many public officers went through Herculean labour; but the ministerial part was feebly conceived and feebly played. Under circumstances so extraordinary, much mismanagement was to be expected, but the Russell Government left no signs of mental vigour applied to the subject, and were considered to have come back from such imperfect experience as their predecessors had realized in the earliest stage of the crisis.'[2]

The task-works were not resumed in the winter of 1847, and, when the workhouses filled up, outdoor relief (that feature of the *old* Poor Law which the Whigs had been trying to eradicate)[3] was resorted to on a large scale. By the first week in December half a million were on relief, and in fourteen unions that week the mortality exceeded eight per thousand.[4] Since some landlords chose this time to carry out evictions, there were disturbances and growing demands for coercion. But Russell himself declined to intervene on one side only in an eighty-year old civil war conducted with barbarity on both sides; murder, he said, was atrocious, but so were evictions. He was sufficiently impressed by the wretchedness of the Irish tenantry to propose, at least for the poorer ones, not only compensation for improvements but something striking 'deeper and wider . . . something like the tenant right of Ulster', an element of legal security of tenure.[5] Even compensation for improvements, the lack of which deterred the farmer outside

[1] Add. MSS 40481, Lincoln to Peel, 10th December, 1846.
[2] Add. MSS 44745, draft *cit. supra*.
[3] The workhouse system was as inappropriate to rural Ireland, with its mass want when harvests failed, as to the industrial districts of England, where the commissioners had to give up their efforts to end outdoor relief. The new Poor Law system was imposed in Ireland in 1838 against the advice of the commission which had reported on the subject.
[4] Barrington, op. cit., Vol. 1, pp. 129–32, Clarendon to Wilson, 25th December, 1847.
[5] For this, and what follows, see Walpole's *Russell*, pp. 462–4, Russell's correspondence with Clarendon.

Ulster from developing his holding, would be condemned as 'Communism' by the Earl of Roden, a leading Orangeman, when a Tory government proposed it in 1852. And Russell admitted that what he had in mind meant 'a transfer of property'. The estates of the Russells in Befordshire and adjoining counties, and in Devonshire, came to them via the expropriation of abbey lands in the sixteenth century, and Covent Garden had been the 'convent garden'. The English landowners had in the eighteenth and early nineteenth centuries increased and rounded off their properties by enclosure, often at the expense of customary rights for which the poor were inadequately compensated. But a transfer of property was a fearful thing for a Whig to contemplate, 'objectionable in the extreme', Russell admitted. Whigs (though not all of them) for generations paid a faltering lip-service to the principle of facilitation of voluntary transfer, applying to land the principles of political economy. But they belonged to a class which had entrenched entail as a means of maintaining family grandeur and political influence. They came in Ireland to the establishment of an official court to transfer land from owners so 'encumbered' as to be incapable of extricating themselves from their web of debt. But they could not bring themselves to admit of legislative interference between landlords and tenants in the interests of the latter. The tendency since the Union had been all the other way. In vain did Russell plead that the evil was 'deep-seated and by ordinary means irremediable'. Lansdowne was against him, as well as the Greys, and his proposals were stifled in a select committee.

It is easy to dismiss Russell's suggestions of land legislation as mere bargaining counters with which to resist demands for coercion in the interest of landlords. But it remains true that, more than twenty years before Gladstone added lustre to his name by passing the Land Act of 1870, Russell, as Prime Minister, projected its essential features. This might have merited a footnote in Halévy, and is to be set against an admiring biographer's complaint that Russell did not apply to Irish problems the generosity and sympathy of his nature.[1] Of course, his tentative proposals, even if they had passed into law, must have failed in the end, as Gladstone's failed speedily, without provision for fair rents. In Ireland tenants were so thick on the ground that the owner who sought a profit by economic management was frustrated and the

[1] A. Wyatt Tilby, *Lord John Russell*, 1930, p. 91.

class of improving farmer was almost absent. Much of the country was suitable only for grazing. A few landlords came to accept the view that a legal 'tenant right' was the best solution to the problem, because it would induce the tenant to use his labour, often the only capital he had, more productively. But this policy appealed less naturally to landlords than to those who had an animus against landlords, and was open to the objection that the real trouble was the uneconomic distribution of holdings. The only relatively uncontroversial measure which seemed indicated, there-fore, was one which would rescue some at least of the land from the impasse which made it unprofitable and, in bulk, unsaleable (despite the intense pressure for holdings, which had led to gross sub-division). Such a measure was the Government's — or Peel's[1] — Encumbered Estates Act, described by Mill as 'the greatest boon ever conferred on Ireland by any government'. It brought into being on some estates a new, capitalist proprietary. As for the rest of the country, the Greys and Wood hoped that a fall in land values would attract the capital which Ireland so sorely needed.[2] But, as Clarendon saw, capital and agriculture would never have a decent chance of success in Ireland without deple-tion of population.[3] By their failure to prevent evictions, by their rule (from mid-1847) that no one with more than a quarter acre could get relief (which compelled the surrender of temporarily worthless smallholdings), by the importation under the Encum-bered Estates Act of new proprietors contemptuous of custom, the Whigs did a little towards increasing the national income at the expense of leaving for themselves an odious memory. Profit-seeking landlords benefited, at the expense of the poor. And, indeed, at the expense of the public, for every eviction, every clearance of land for grazing, increased congestion on other land and the demand on the poor rate. What was 'economically sound' was socially dis-astrous and, when the level of poor rates deterred purchasers and hampered development, hardly even economically advantageous.

Of the various means of adjusting population to the resources available to maintain it, emigration was the simplest. Everyone knew that it offered the best chance of better days for the popula-tion of Ireland. The economic pressure, the stimulus to go, was

[1] Gladstone, Add. MSS 44745, draft cit. supra, claimed for Peel the credit of securing the passage of the Act.
[2] e.g., Wood's views quoted by Greville, S. II, Vol. III, p. 237, October, 1848.
[3] Barrington, Vol. I, pp. 129–32, 25th December, 1847, to Wilson.

not lacking. Reception areas — the United States, Canada, Australasia, southern Africa — were open. Of the various courses open to Government for the solution of the Land Question as an economic problem, a subsistence problem, assisting emigration was less objectionable to nineteenth-century orthodoxy than subsidising the development of alternative sources of employment and wealth in Ireland or the utilisation of unproductive or under-productive land. Compared with the cost of maintaining paupers at home, the cost of their export, at a time when the Government was still forcing unwanted felons on the colonies, was a bargain. But the official response to the need to decant Ireland's surplus labour was less than half-hearted. The limited powers and re-sources of the Commissioners of Colonial Land and Emigration did not operate in Ireland. In the face of 'helpless, hopeless, in-creasing destitution', Clarendon urged that there was no form under which relief could be given 'with such permanent utility, and as paving the way for profitable investment, as Emigration ...'. Who, he asked, would buy land in the Ballina Poor Law Union, with rates of 42s. in the £? It was not only humanity but interest that called for assistance of this kind.[1] Pressed by Clarendon, Russell at the end of 1848 propounded a scheme for the expendi-ture of up to £5 million on emigration from the United Kingdom as a whole, the principal to be a public issue of stock, the interest to be met by ratepayers. Unions heavily burdened with paupers would be empowered to pay the passage of families overseas. Wood and the Greys, with Lansdowne, were adamant. Russell threatened to resign, but Clarendon said he did not think emigra-tion a sufficient cause for such a step; the policy would be useful, but not 'absolutely indispensable', nor a complete remedy. The cabinet decided that it favoured emigration in principle,[2] but there the matter rested.

For the woes of Ireland the Whigs provided no remedy. The strongest ground for their indictment is that they considered all the main lines of action, but did not follow any of them to any great extent. The twentieth century sees as the solution to the problem

[1] Barrington, Vol. I, pp. 129–32. Clarendon sent the report of Under-Secretary Redington, which showed that the legal powers were inoperative, and a scheme of Monteagle's, to Wilson, with these comments.

[2] Walpole, Vol. II, pp. 76–81. The writer seems to transpose the rejection of the plan and the acceptance of the principle; on his own evidence — the partici-pation of Sir F. Baring in a division of nine to four on the principle — the latter decision must have come after mid-January 1849.

f raising the standard of living in an underdeveloped country a
large programme of development which usually has to be financed
mainly from outside by public agencies or at least under public
guarantee. A hundred years ago it was well understood that
Ireland's chief need was an injection of capital. The Protectionist
leader, Lord George Bentinck, proposed £16 million for railways.
Ten years before, Lord Morpeth, as Chief Secretary, had advocated a railway programme. But a meeting of ministerialists was
called to make sure that Bentinck was defeated. Peel suggested £5
million for reclamation and the establishment of economic farms.
His project perished less ostentatiously than Bentinck's. The
Whigs refused to spend any large sum of money productively, but
proceeded as though illegitimate offspring were less objectionable
if they were very little ones. They were not consistent in their
negativism. They did offer money for emigration, for railways, for
fisheries, and, under the Land Improvement Act, for useful
private works as well as public works. But the total sum expended
was insignificant when compared with the sum spent on relief and
when compared with the need. And they damned themselves
by disingenuous argument. One can understand their reluctance
to become involved in railway finance at the height of a speculative
boom.[1] But it was silly to say that railway enterprise in the more
backward parts of Ireland must be left to private entrepreneurs
when everyone knew how little likelihood there was of private
capital being so employed. The argument against Bentinck, that
railway construction employed only skilled labour, was flatly con-
tradicted by the spectacle of large gangs of Irish navvies engaged
in connection with railway development in England on very much
the same works of cutting and embankment as Irishmen at home
were doing, for no productive purpose at all, in the task-works.
And when ministers proposed to employ Irish labour, partly at
the cost of the British consumer, on railways in *Canada*, they
convicted themselves of either hypocrisy or intellectual anarchy.
This project was approved by Sir Charles Wood because it originated with his brother-in-law, Earl Grey, who always sustained
Wood's objections to any imaginative use of public funds in Ireland.

The Famine and its aftermath deepened the gulf between
Britain and Ireland. Even those Whigs who felt most strongly that

[1] English manufacturers complained that the railway boom abstracted capital
unduly from manufacture and mining.

Britain owed Ireland a debt for depriving her of her independence and delaying Catholic Emancipation failed to take serious account of the arguments that the Union had ruined Ireland economically, because those arguments were put forward as part of the case for Repeal of the Union. The Irish nation could hardly expect sympathetic and imaginative understanding from high-born statesmen whose outlook was English and who sat surrounded by reports of commissions and committees galore but without real knowledge of the Irish scene.[1] This criticism applies even though several of the ministers owned large Irish estates and Bessborough was partially resident in Ireland even when not Lord Lieutenant. Lansdowne and Palmerston, and, for that matter, Bessborough, had the outlook of English landlords. They denied the communities in which their mansions lay the conspicuous consumption which was part of the service a resident aristocracy rendered. But they ploughed back rents, Lansdowne into vast drainage works in Co. Kerry, Palmerston into the economic and social regeneration of farms and villages (and into assisted emigration from Co. Sligo). Dufferin, an Oxford undergraduate brought into the Lords by Russell, created extra employment for his tenants in Co. Down in hard times and spoke in scathing terms of landlords who evicted. The behaviour of these men of the Whig upper circle led to a serious misjudgement of resident landlords who did not in general behave like the better type of English gentleman in lesser emergencies or like Lansdowne and Palmerston. Why were some so cruel, and others so supine? Why did they not help themselves? Why were they always trying to dip their fingers in the public till? There were, indeed, landlords who tried to maintain an over-pretentious standard of living on incomes drastically diminished by mortgage payments, subdivisions of holdings and failure of rents — 'the scourge of Ireland', Trollope called these improvidents.[2] But there

---

[1] Russell visited Ireland in 1834, 1838, and 1848. (Gladstone went only once.) But in 1848 Russell stayed only a fortnight before a five weeks holiday in Scotland, and though he visited the Ludlow property at Ardsalla, Co. Meath, settled on him by his brother, he did not visit the really stricken parts of Ireland. The Peelite Sidney Herbert gave up visiting his Irish estates because the conditions depressed him so.

[2] *Castle Richmond*, Vol. 1, p. 123 '. . . It was not the absence of the absentees that did the damage, but the presence of those they left behind them on the soil. The scourge of Ireland was the existence of a class that looked to be gentlemen living on their property, but who should have earned their bread by the work of their brain, or, failing that, by the sweat of their brow.' In this indictment he included lesser owners and larger tenants too pretentious to be active farmers.

were many landlords who in times of crisis appeared without
resource simply because they were without resources. When the
blight and the rain which produced famine destroyed income, even
solvent owners must think rather in terms of retrenchment than
extraordinary expenditure, especially as the cost of relief was being
chalked up against them.[1] Who could blame them if they asked
subventions in aid of improvements on their properties, on which
they could have employed some of the destitute? The Government
gave them a dusty answer and insisted that the relief works should
benefit no private proprietor. It was a simple fact for many an
owner that the long-headed course of action was a hard-hearted
one, that of taking advantage of inability to pay rent to consolidate
holdings and 'clear' land for grazing. Notorious evictors like the
Marquess of Westmeath, Lord Lucan and the Earl of Leitrim
(whose murder was to inaugurate a new phase of the Land War in
1879), more dependent than Lansdowne or Palmerston on a good
return from Irish land, added callousness to the Irish landlords'
reputation for improvidence and fecklessness. With O'Connell and
Edward Bouverie proposing penal taxation of absentees,[2] and the
principal Anglo-Irish landlords in the Whig hierarchy unsympa-
thetic to, or at least not fully comprehending, the predicament of
the residents, the basic solidarity of the British with the Irish
landlords who formed the Unionist 'garrison' was obscured by
present discontents.

If Irish landlords were regarded as shiftless, when not inhumane,

[1] Lansdowne opposed the provision that a national rate-in-aid should be
levied in Ireland to subsidise poor relief in the worst areas and succeeded in
confining it to two years and 6d. in £ (see *Walpole*, Vol. II, pp. 82–4 — this was
in 1849). Much of the money spent on relief was nominally a loan, though most
of it had to be written off.

[2] Bouverie, Whig son of Lord Radnor, proposed a 50% tax on absentee
revenues for the duration of the emergency. Trollope, though aware that some
of the criticism of absentees was misconceived, has a splendid passage portraying
the absentee of common conception in *The Macdermotts of Ballycloran*, p. 74 —
'. . . Lord Birmingham is . . . a kind, good man, a most charitable man! Look
at his name on all the lists of gifts for unfortunates of every description. Is he not
the presiding genius of the company for relieving the Poles? A vice-presiding
genius for relieving destitute authors, destitute actors, destitute clergymen's
widows, destitute half-pay officers' widows? Is he not patron of the Mendicity
Society, patron of the Lying-in, Small Pox, Lock and Fever Hospitals? Is his
name not down for large amounts in aid of funds of every description for lessen-
ing human wants and pangs? How conspicuous and eager a part he took in giving
the poor Blacks their liberty! Was not his aid strongly and gratefully felt by the
friends of Catholic Emancipation? . . . Tis true he lives in England, was rarely
in his life in Ireland, never in Mohill. . . . Would the world have benefited had
he left the Parliament and the cabinet, to whitewash Irish cabins, and assist in the
distribution of meal? . . .'

"MY LORD ASSASSIN" CLARENDON MURDERING THE IRISH.

Vide "THE IRISH FELON," No. 1.

what was to be thought of peasants whose traditions and living conditions had hardly accustomed them to sustained industry or self-improvement, the cardinal virtues which the Victorians commended to the poor? The conditions of relief, stringent, complex, changing, grudging, evoked no gratitude, and the events of 1845–9 confirmed a British dislike for the Irish which those who have enjoyed Irish hospitality and humour may find it difficult to credit. Among the working-classes it was nourished by the entry of Irish labour into the English and Scottish markets, and it was strongest in the ports of entry and areas of congregation, and especially at Liverpool. The middle classes despised a country without a respectable middle class; the professional men scorned a nation without an intelligentsia. Both the aristocracy and the middle classes condemned a people prone to crimes of violence. Tales of the Famine gave English and Scots plenty of fuel to feed their prejudices against the Irish. If ever a people had excuse for dishonesty, discontent, ingratitude and violence it was the Irish in those dreadful years. But little account was taken of many acts of devotion, of examples of co-operation between priest and parson in works of humanity. Little allowance was made for the bewildered helplessness of the starving poor. People remembered that philanthropy was greeted with a stunned and querulous apathy, that there was imposture and fraud, and that there were assaults on foremen at the task-works (by men unused to working under orders and physically unfit for labour which was visibly pointless). A cabinet minister recorded that people were 'exasperated and disgusted by the ingratitude and folly of the Irish' after the British had 'drained their resources for them'.[1] People remembered also the rebellion of 1848. And the character of the Irish M.P.s in the fifties confirmed British prejudices. 'As silly, as broguey, as useless, as quarrelsome and as contemptible as ever,' a Radical called them after the election of 1852. 'Mr Duffy, Mr Moore and their little party have two Irish reforms to effect — first to make the Irish Catholic members honest, next to make them respectable.'[2] The notion gained ground that Irishmen went in for politics to an unusual extent for what they could get out of them. A recent writer says that the Irish M.P.s of the 'fifties introduced the British to the gombeen man and the land shark.[3]

The Whigs had been rash enough to attack Peel's coercion bills as though they were peculiarly the product of Tory authoritarianism. Having come into office as a result of Peel's defeat on the 'Assassination Bill', Russell's ministers nevertheless recommended to Parliament an Arms Bill. Liberal members, recalling their criticism of Peel's Arms Bill of 1843 (which he had skilfully modelled on a Whig one of 1838) forced its withdrawal. But by the end of 1847 Clarendon, who said he felt like a state prisoner in a conquered country, asked, *inter alia*, for curfew provisions like those which had served as a pretext for defeating Peel. It constantly troubled British ministers that the Queen's representative in Dublin, if he did not fall a victim to the mysterious lure of Erin, developed a thirst for special powers or simply lost his nerve. Russell feared that the Whigs would 'justly lose their character as regards Ireland', called the curfew 'tyranny without purpose' and countered with proposals for 'large measures of redress'. He contrived to moderate coercion. But when continental revolution threatened to ignite combustible material in Ireland it was Downing Street that considered Dublin Castle's proposals for the maintenance of order inadequate. Acts of 1796 and 1817, anathematised

[1] Campbell, op. cit., Vol. II, p. 243.
[2] Whitby, *History of the Session* 1852–3, London, 1854.
[3] K. H. Connell, 'The Land Legislation and Irish Social Life' (*Ec. Hist. R.*, 2nd Series, XI, No. 1, 1958).

in Whig legend, were extended to Ireland, though with the vital mitigation that what had then been treason in England was now to be felony in Ireland.[1] The resultant trials provided field days for Tory lawyers, Whiteside and Butt, acting as defence counsel for nationalist editors. When O'Connell had been prosecuted by Peel's government, Russell in Parliament solemnly denounced the exclusion of Catholic jurymen and requisitions for public meetings of protest were signed by Messrs Sheil, Redington and Monahan. O'Connell's conviction was quashed on a technicality by a partisan majority of three against two in the Lords. Two of the majority, Cottenham and Campbell, sat in Russell's cabinet, which promoted the statute under which the publicists were prosecuted. Juries were rigged as in 1843. Sheil was a member of the administration, Redington was Under-Secretary for Ireland and Monahan prosecuted as Attorney-General.

In mid-1848 the Irish prospect was so grim that the christening of Russell's son was postponed. On Saturday 22nd July Parliament rushed through a bill suspending Habeas Corpus in Ireland. The rebellion went off at half-cock, a gesture of despair. Apathy ensued. For twenty years the nationalism which had threatened to boil over barely simmered. Since it required a crisis to force through any major concession of 'justice to Ireland', England neglected Ireland when she ceased to trouble England. The only explosion of feeling in Ireland between 1848 and 1867 was caused by an outburst of anti-popery in England.

Anti-popery lay at the root of the English and Scottish distrust for and dislike of the Irish, and burned with a steady flame within Whiggery, although British adherents to the Roman communion were Whigs because the Whigs had fought for their political emancipation and civil equality with Protestants. Yet even the Conservative government had made it a major aim to break down the walls of partition between Protestant and Catholic in civil matters. Peel had faced the political issue in Ireland with his wonted authority. By exposing O'Connell's unwillingness to use physical force to achieve Repeal, he had reduced 'the Liberator' to that rather pathetic figure, the nationalist leader whose bluff has been called. But Peel then issued, from strength, 'a message of peace' which would serve as a prescription for Lord Salisbury in

---

[1] The substitution of transportation for death made it possible to qualify for assisted emigration by preaching separation or preparing armed rebellion.

886. Conservative government was to mean stout resistance to
constitutional change but, in Ireland as in Britain, Tory men and
Whig', not Orange, measures. The Whigs could only applaud
(at the risk of offending Nonconformity) the further endowment
of Maynooth. Catholic participation on the Board of Bequests was
regarded as a promising omen for negotiations upon the 'godless
colleges' at which Catholics and Protestants might receive higher
education together. The Whigs came into office with a fair hope
that they might take the rapprochement further and perhaps even
secure 'concurrent endowment'. In March 1848 Russell proposed
a Catholic endowment of £400,000;[1] in the late summer, a little
more.[2] Redington, however, advised that the Presbyterians would
never consent to be taxed for such a purpose and that the money
had better come out of the surplus funds of the Church of Ireland.
But only Earl Grey was prepared to burn his hands by resurrecting
an attack on the establishment as ministerial policy.

It appears that Russell drafted a letter to the Pope on Catholic
endowment, but recent experience of Roman policy made it very
unlikely that, if sent, it would have been well received. For Britain
was now confronted, in Ireland, with the problem of ultramon-
anism. Many of the Catholic hierarchy in Ireland were disposed
to limited collaboration with the infidel government. But against the
pragmatical 'Gallican' policy of Archbishop Murray arose Archbishop McHale, who had the ear of Rome, and there issued from
the Vatican a rescript discountenancing the 'godless colleges'. This
was a bitter blow to the Whig government, which had in mind the
possibility of regular diplomatic relations with the Holy See and
hoped that the Pope might be induced to condemn turbulent
priests who, it was alleged, incited to crime, even to murder, from
the pulpits. Palmerston said that the priests had a prime responsibility for a state of crime unknown in modern times outside
Central Africa and that he would like to see some of them strung
up.[3] All these matters a Scottish Presbyterian, the Earl of Minto, a
member of the cabinet and father-in-law of Lord John Russell, was
instructed to take up when, in the course of a tour of Italy, he
reached Rome. It is curious that anti-papist ministers, accustomed

[1] Walpole, Vol. II, p. 65. Russell's programme of 30th March combined
Catholic endowment with a bill to control evictions and £1 m of Exchequer bills
or useful works.
[2] ibid., pp. 76–8, correspondence with Redington.
[3] Ashley's Palmerston, Vol. II, pp. 49–50. P. to Minto, 3rd December, 1847.

to ascribe all manner of evils to the Romish religion and its authoritarian overtones, should have imagined that their own politica
tolerance would be reciprocated and that a Pope would consent t
Catholics becoming Erastians in a Protestant-dominated state
From the papal point of view there was no case for a concordat
The conditions for it were absent. There was in Ireland neither ;
masterful Catholic government demanding rights the Pope woulc
fain have kept, nor a hostile government with whom it was neces
sary to negotiate a basic minimum of freedom for the Roman
Church. The Protestant state allowed Catholics full political free
dom and civil equality. It abstained from interference with th
Church and actually subsidised, without controlling, the principa
seminary for the training of priests, which turned out a stream o
ultramontanes with whose aid the Pope could hope to break dow
the traditional insularity of the Irish Church and render it sub
servient to Rome. To assume that the Pope was thwarting Whig
good intentions simply because he was misinformed, and that a tall
with Lord Minto would alter Roman policy, was naive. Why shoulc
the Papacy weaken its growing authority in Ireland by affronting
anti-British sentiment and try to separate the parish priests from
the peasantry whose prejudices they shared, sometimes to the poin
of criminal incitement? The unfounded optimism of the Britisl
cabinet was strengthened by the reputation of Pius IX as 'th
liberal pontiff', symbol of Italian national aspirations, which ha
led to his being thoroughly misunderstood by foreign constitu
tionalists as well as by undiscerning Italians. Minto was discon
certed to find His Holiness obsessed with some newly discovere
relics and totally unwilling to respond to arguments that the re
script was 'a hostile, ill-judged and unnecessary act . . . a
unkind and mischievous measure'.[1] It had issued from the Sacre
College for the Propagation of the Faith, a bureau whose missio
it was, *inter alia*, to be hostile, unkind and mischievous to Protes
tant interests.

It seems that Minto was shown a document which may hav
been an early draft of the bull to re-establish, after an interval c
three hundred years, the Roman hierarchy in England. If so, h
entirely failed to comprehend the nature of what was later to b
called the 'papal aggression'. The missive was delayed until th
Pope's return, under the shield of foreign bayonets, from his exil

---

[1] ibid., p. 47, Clarendon's memo. and p.46, P. to Minto, 29th October, 1847

at Gaeta, but was unleashed in 1850 with a verbal fanfare from Wiseman, Archbishop-designate of Westminster, from the Flaminian Gate. Whereupon Lord John Russell in a letter to his friend, the Bishop of Durham, bared to the world an ancestral anti-popery as virulent as if this was the morrow of the 'Popish Plot' which the first Whigs trumped up in 1679. A passionate Protestantism burst out of the placid rationalist ethic in which it was cocooned. Russell the tolerationist was submerged in the scion of the house that had sponsored Pym when Charles I was arraigned as a friend of the Catholics. The Prime Minister's wrath was, as we shall stress in the next chapter, directed rather against Oxford than against Rome. But this did not comfort Roman Catholics who read hard words about their faith, their Church and their supreme pastor. The Roman Catholic nobles and gentry of England had a Gallican tradition, and no alternative political home. The Earl of Arundel and Surrey repudiated Russell's leadership and, quarrelling with the Duke of Norfolk, an Erastian Catholic,[1] resigned the representation of the family borough and was returned for Limerick. He was not widely emulated. But what of Ireland? There the bull did not apply.[2] Nor did the Ecclesiastical Titles Bill, the legislative sequel to the Durham Letter. It is probable, though barely credible, that in penning his epistle to the bishop. the Prime Minister gave Ireland no thought. But the harm was there. Clarendon said 'the agitators were sorely put to it for a lever with which to stir up hatred against England' until Russell's 'mummeries' proved 'a godsend to the disaffected'.[3] He was 'irritable and dispirited' at the blow given to his hopes of establishing national education 'in the teeth of the Synod of Thurles' (and of the Pope).[4] For, with England and Scotland given over to anti-papist agitation countenanced by the head of the Government,[5] the Irish masses provided prime combustible material for the Roman

---

[1] The Duke shortly afterwards joined the Church of England.
[2] Irish bishops and archbishops already bore territorial titles which were generally recognised semi-officially and sometimes officially by the state authorities.
[3] *Clarendon*, Vol. I, p. 316, 27th November, 1850, to Cornewall Lewis and p. 317, 29th November to Wood.
[4] Stanmore's *Herbert*, Vol. i, p. 135.
[5] Clarendon distinguished between spontaneous anti-popery evoked by the bull ('It is high time to resist the encroachments of Rome and to let his Holiness know that we are still Protestants,' to Lewis 29th October, *Clarendon*, p. 314) and Russell's action in exacerbating it ('I fear we are going to have a regular phase of sectarian bitterness,' to Lady Caledon, 26th November, ibid., p. 315.)

party. 'The Pope's Brass Band' began to march, and to its accom-
paniment heads rolled at the general election of 1852.[1] It was
important that after the Durham Letter a number of Irish M.P.s
were not prepared to act as Russellites, some of them, though
Catholic, preferring Lord Derby even as late as 1859. Irish hostility
played its part in keeping Russell from the premiership for more
than a decade after 1852. It was even more important that the 'Brass
Band' provided the raucous overture to the long-sustained policy
of a new ultramontane archbishop, Cullen. Subtle and tenacious
where McHale would be aggressive, he set his face equally against
movements of the *Young Ireland* ilk,[2] and against co-operation
between the hierarchy and the Castle. The whole purpose of the
'godless colleges' was frustrated, and there could be no thought of
concurrent endowment. Whig policy in Ireland perished in dust
and ashes. Sir James Graham damned the Durham Letter as
defeating by the rashness of a day the consolidation of the Union
'the grand object of the policy of the greatest men of the last half
century'.[3]

[1] The politicians of the Band were all sworn to abjure British gifts. But in
December 1852 three of them became ministers — Sadleir (who proved the most
plausible swindler ever to achieve ministerial rank and died a suicide), O'Flaherty
(who later fled abroad to escape British justice) and Keogh (who on attaining the
Bench came as near as any judge has done to having passed against him the
parliamentary addresses which are the legal prerequisite for the removal of a
judge). Their conduct deepened the unfortunate impression of the quality of
Irish members referred to above.

[2] In 1846 it was still important, from the parliamentary point of view, that 'old
Dan and his friends have given in their cordial adhesion to Lord John', so that
'the cry for *Repeal* and other extreme measures will henceforth be confined to
Smith O'Brien and Young Ireland'. (Add. MSS 34626, f. 316, 2nd August,
1846.) But the Whig government, on the principle of 'divide and rule', relished
the bitter disputes between O'Connell and *Young Ireland* which darkened the
last years of 'the Liberator' (who died in Italy in 1847). These disputes were
partly concerned with the use, or rather the repudiation or non-repudiation of,
physical force, partly with O'Connell's Whig alliance, but partly with the ultramontane tendencies observable in O'Connell under the influence of his son John.
Young Ireland was a revolutionary nationalist group which had much in common
with those of the Continent. Some of its leaders were Protestants and others were
anti-clerical. It might be thought to be an asset to Britain that the hierarchy
therefore discountenanced it, and, as a result, was inclined in the coming years
to discourage its resurgence, thereby imposing a certain restraint on the parish
priests. But if *Young Ireland* was more anti-British and anti-Whig than O'Connell,
its realistic, utilitarian approach to the problem of liberating Ireland made it
ready to use British gifts like the godless colleges as weapons in the furtherance
of the national struggle.

[3] Stanmore's *Herbert*, Vol. 1, p. 133.

CHAPTER IX

Whiggery is not enough

'Considered as a mere party combination — as resting merely on the ancient Whig connexion — the support of a few prominent and historical families, the present government stands on too narrow a base to survive the first parliamentary storm,' said a writer in the *Edinburgh Review* in 1848. Yet 'the Liberal party ... through the events of 1845–6 gained an advantage which, if properly improved, must, for some time to come, ensure its preponderance in the state'.[1] The 'Liberal party' did, indeed, preponderate as long as the electoral system of 1832 endured. But Liberal forces strained within the historic Whig tailoring, which was found not to provide adequately for growth. And so the ministry of Lord John Russell was the last to be formed on a designedly Whig basis.

Russell himself expressed to Cobden his desire to 'place in office those who have maintained in *our* recent struggle the principles of Free Trade against Monopoly'.[2] And there were not lacking advisers to stress the regret which many of his followers would feel 'if you were to enter on power without the full confidence and support of the commercial interests which it is yet in your power to command'.[3] Clarendon, the former civil servant and diplomat of Tory origins who lived long with Whiggery but was perhaps too candid a friend ever to be quite a Whig, gave shrewd counsel in strong terms. Whiggery, he said, was aristocratic, exclusive, historical and almost effete, and its roots in the country had withered. Great care should be taken in naming the cabinet, for its composition would show the extent of Whig appreciation that all future governments must depend on the middle class.[4] Macaulay agreed that 'the distribution of posts in Lord John's

[1] Vol. 87, January, 1848, Article V, pp. 138 ff.
[2] Morley's *Cobden*, Vol. I, p. 403, 2nd July, 1846. Present writer's italics.
[3] Walpole, Vol. I, p. 425, Horsman's letter. Horsman was not invited to return to office.
[4] *Clarendon*, Vol. I, pp. 265–6, memo. of June 1846.

late scheme of a government' (i.e., in December 1845) 'was a very
bad one — aristocratic, exclusive and factious' and that 'next time
the Cabinet must be constructed on a scheme better calculated for
permanency'.[1] Russell's comment on such advice was to form an
administration which bore on its face no sign that anything had
changed since 1841, no mark of the recent stirring events, of the
importance of the middle classes, of the impact of 'the Condition of
England Question'. He was not so much offering a gesture of
aristocratic defiance as simply giving rein to his own sense of what
was fitting. It can hardly be true that, asked by the Queen at
intervals of twenty years who was the most promising young man
in the party, he replied on both occasions 'George Byng, Ma'am'.[2]
But such stories have their significance, and this one gained currency as a criticism of the implicit Whig proposition that the
business of government was the concern, ideally, of a permanent
council of Whiggery, or, as a second best, of rival groups of
aristocratic politicians belonging to the *Establishment* and looking
for new talent among their own kind. Whigs would bow, when they
judged it opportune, to the demands of the middle classes,
trenchantly expressed, and also make concessions less forcefully
required by public opinion if they were pressed by important
parliamentary groups. They thus preserved in Radical eyes the
one saving grace that they were 'susceptible of education', and 'of
squeezable materials'. To avoid crisis was their desire, their
instinct, their interest, their technique. But if they were safe
because they were squeezable, they were safer because they did not
respond over-readily to the squeeze. They could retain their
influence — by preserving the sort of régime in which their influence could effectively be felt — only if resistance was habitual
and concession occasional. Concessions were represented as contributions to the greater glory of Whiggery. But too much concession would be self-destructive. It was therefore of great importance that at a time when policy was apt to be dictated by others, by
Peel or Cobden, public administration and parliamentary manage-

[1] Add. MSS 34626, f. 102, Nassau Senior to Macvey Napier, 17th February,
1846 —'. . . I told Macaulay the other day that I thought the distribution of
posts . . . a very bad one. . . . He said "We were then only patching up an administration to carry a question and then be turned out. Next time . . . etc." '

[2] This gentleman, 1806–86, Joint Secretary at the Board of Control under
Russell, had a son, 1830–98, of the same name who held several junior offices and
became First Civil Service Commissioner. It is possible that Russell on the two
occasions meant not the former, but first the father and then the son.

ment should be in Whig hands. It promoted the importance, and the self-importance, of Whiggery to man the control room. It is only fair to Russell to say that he invited into his cabinet three of the younger Peelites, all aristocrats.[1] This was a wise move, as the Peelites, if they stood together, could hold the balance in the House of Commons, and Russell wanted the aid of men of 'sound and temperate liberality', to avoid having to rest on 'the support of any extreme party'.[2] And it was an obvious tactic to try to break up Peel's formidable general staff. Yet one doubts whether Russell's colleagues were sorry when Peel refused to speak the word which would have enabled his lieutenants to accept. It was more pleasant to have their cabinet conclaves 'on their own'. Because of the disintegration of the Conservative party, Whig participation in government was indispensable. Whig monopoly was not, but to secure such monopoly, even *faute de mieux*, enabled the Whigs to pretend to themselves that they held it in the natural order of politics.

Russell's administration was the mixture as before. Of the men of 1841 all who were, in the American sense of the word, 'available', returned to the cabinet except Normanby who went as ambassador to Paris, Duncannon, who went to Dublin Castle, and Baring. Minto became Lord Privy Seal and was replaced at the Admiralty by his cousin Auckland, back from India. With his cousin, Sir George Grey, at the Home Office and his brother-in-law, Charles Wood, given the Treasury,[3] Earl Grey discovered that he could take the Colonial Office even though Palmerston resumed his old post. Lord Campbell and the Marquess of Clanricarde, morally disreputable and politically negligible, completed the team. Later entrants, besides Sir Francis Baring (who was cousin and brother-in-law of Labouchere and brother-in-law of George Grey), were the second Earl Granville, Lord Seymour and the Hon. Fox Maule. The lists of Russell's cabinet contain twenty-one ministers. Of these, twelve were the sons of aristocrats and five inherited baronetcies.[4] The exceptions were Campbell,

---

[1] The Earl of Dalhousie (cousin of the Whig Fox Maule), the Earl of Lincoln, and Sidney Herbert.

[2] *Walpole*, Vol. I, p. 423, n. i, to Bessborough, 11th April, 1846.

[3] Wood had resigned his junior office when Grey (then Howick) left the cabinet in 1839. He now urged the claims of his brother-in-law.

[4] The twelve — Russell, Lansdowne, Palmerston, Auckland, Minto, Clarendon, Morpeth, Grey, Clanricarde, Granville, Seymour, Maule. The five — Hobhouse, Wood, George Grey, Baring, Lord Chancellor Cottenham.

the lawyer who had risen by diligence; Truro, another lawyer who reached the cabinet only through a dearth of good candidates for the Woolsack; Macaulay, who rose by oratory and literary reputation, so much the Whig historian that Whiggery did not notice how discriminating was his reverence for the Whigs of the past; and Labouchere, who owed his position to charm and connections.

Macaulay and Labouchere were exceptions which proved to the hilt the aristocratic rule. Of the former G. W. E. Russell wrote that he was 'probably the only man who, being born outside the privileged enclosure, ever penetrated to its heart and assimilated its spirit'.[1] How to define a 'Whig' in terms which do not create more difficulties than they solve may well defeat us when, according to George Russell, Whigs were born and not made and it was as difficult to become a Whig as to become a Jew. It is a fair presumption that a man of aristocratic or landowning family, not of Tory affiliation, was a Whig unless like Molesworth he repudiated the appellation or in some way sharply differentiated himself from his kind. But these were only general rules. Whiggery was a law unto itself. Birth, property, party affiliation, attachment to the conservative wing of political Liberalism — Palmerston had all these characteristics of Whiggery, and yet the purists denied that he was properly steeped in the Whig pickle.[2] Labouchere, on the other hand, the French-looking son of a Dutchman of Huguenot descent by his marriage to a Baring, was accepted in youth as a Whig, although his uncles were Tories or renegades. He became a Whig minister before he married, *en secondes noces*, a Howard of Carlisle. It was this son of the counting-house of Hope of Amsterdam who first revealed to a Duke of Argyll, whose ancestors died on Stewart scaffolds, 'the extreme narrowness of the old Whig party, and the almost irrational exclusiveness of the conceptions entertained by them of what constituted a Whig. This was the more remarkable since, of course, Labouchere himself was not a member of the Whig aristicracy but only a recruit from the middle classes. Yet I found him as restricted in this matter as if he had been a Howard or Fitzwilliam'.[3] It never occurred to anyone to deny that Labouchere was a Whig, or to claim that his more famous nephew and namesake, inheritor of his funded property,

---

[1] *Prime Ministers and Some Others*, 1918, p. 124.   [2] ibid, pp. 17–18.
[3] Argyll, *Autobiography*, Vol. I, pp. 594–5.

was a Whig. A man was a Whig if Whiggery accepted him as such, and there is no more to be said.

The Russell administration was ostentatiously representative of Whiggery's political *élite*. Of all the aristocratic families which between 1832 and 1885 contributed three or more lordlings to the House of Commons,[1] two-thirds were represented in cabinet, junior (non-legal) ministerial office or among the great offices of state and of the Household which changed hands with governments. More obviously than ever the Whigs were all cousins. The influence of the Grand Whiggery, the inner circle of its aristocracy, was hardly 'behind the scenes' when the Duchess of Sutherland was Mistress of the Robes, her brother, Lord Morpeth, in the cabinet, and her brothers-in-law, the Duke of Norfolk and the Marquess of Westminster, the Duke's son and son-in-law and the Marquess's brother all in Court appointments. There were in the ministry no Cavendishes or Fitzwilliams, but they would only have had to ask to receive. Althorp's successor as Earl Spencer, and Duncannon's successor as Earl of Bessborough, did not aspire to the cabinet rank achieved by those notables, but became respectively Lord Chamberlain and Master of the Buckhounds. Lansdowne's heir, Shelburne, in politics rather by his father's will than his own, found himself a whip.[2] The politically ambitious Lord Leveson, who united the blood of the Gowers and the Cavendishes, was disappointed to be offered only the Buckhounds in 1846 (perhaps because Palmerston had found him idle when he was under-secretary at the Foreign Office). He was minded to refuse, but Lansdowne said he had never known it go against a man to have something to give up![3] In due course, to the indignation of the men of Manchester, the Master of the Buckhounds was chosen to succeed their hero, Milner Gibson, as Vice-President of the Board of Trade. In a very few years Leveson, having become second Earl Granville, and being courtly and admired at Court, succeeded Palmerston (who was neither) as Foreign Secretary at the age of thirty-six. It was a great thing to be everyone's cousin and nobody's enemy.

[1] See Appendix II, Section 1, *infra* pp. 438 ff.
[2] A decade later Shelburne returned to office, as Foreign Under-Secretary; his industry, even when suffering from tennis-elbow, was admired by the great ladies who watched with avid interest the young hopefuls of the party. He again withdrew from politics, but returned in 1866 to resist Reform.
[3] Contrast this attitude with that of Granville's dilettante brother 'Freddy' Leveson-Gower who twice refused office from Gladstone lest it be called 'a job' — see G. W. E. Russell, op. cit.

In junior ministerial offices the survival rate from 1841 was not quite so high as in the cabinet. In the (non-legal) working offices were five aristocrats and four others. Four of the five aristocrats were to reach the cabinet (three of them under Russell).[1] None of the others did so,[2] though Henry Tufnell became Chief Whip. On the face of it he was simply the cadet of an East Anglian landed family who reached the fringes of politics by marrying the daughter of a Canningite politician and was lucky enough to become private secretary to Minto as First Lord of the Admiralty, and was thus enabled to sit for Devonport and become a junior whip in 1840. But he was the son, grandson and great-grandson of M.P.s, and his second marriage in 1844 inserted him well and truly into Whiggery. For his wife was the half-sister of the George Byng, who in 1846 became Secretary to the Board of Control.[3] Byng's wife was the daughter of old Anglesey, who now became Master General of the Ordnance; her half-brothers, Lord Clarence and Lord Alfred Paget, became respectively Secretary of the Ordnance and Clerk-Marshall at Court. She was the sister of Lady Conyngham, whose husband had been Postmaster-General in 1834. Conyngham's own sister had been the wife of Sir William Somerville, fifth Bart, who in 1846 became Under-Secretary of State at the Home Office and in 1847 Chief Secretary for Ireland. Somerville's step-father, Lord Fortescue, who had been Lord Lieutenant of Ireland 1839–41, now became Lord Steward, and his heir, Lord Ebrington, entered the whips' office under Tufnell. To complete the record one may add that in 1848 Tufnell married again, this time the daughter of Lord Rosebery. Her half-brother had been a Lord of the Admiralty under Melbourne and her mother was an Anson, whose brother, Lord Lichfield, had been Melbourne's Postmaster-General and whose brother George became in 1846 Clerk of the Ordnance.

In 1846 six new junior ministers were taken from outside the aristocracy, though only one from the middle classes. This was

[1] Seymour, Fox Maule and Lord Leveson were promoted to cabinet 1851–2; Stanley of Alderley (till 1848 known as Lord Eddisbury) reached it in 1855; Hon. W. F. Cowper (Palmerston's step-son) had a long ministerial career but never crossed the threshold.

[2] They were two Irishmen, Sheil and Wyse (a Roman Catholic but a leading supporter of national education in Ireland), and Tufnell and Parker, M.P. for Sheffield.

[3] Byng's father, the Field-Marshal, was created Lord Strafford in 1835 and Earl of Strafford in 1847, when his heir took the courtesy title of Lord Enfield.

Hawes, one of three with some sort of a Radical past, the others being H. G. Ward (whose fatal amendment had prevented the righting of the coach in 1834) and Milner Gibson, the third man of the Anti-Corn Law League.[1] One of the six was a great industrialist, Edward Strutt, but he was the grandson of the founder of the firm and its fortunes, and a considerable enough landowner to qualify for a peerage.[2] Henry George Ward was owner-editor of the *Weekly Chronicle*, but no *arriviste*. His father had been a Tory junior minister, he was the first cousin of Normanby, and his wife's mother, a baronet's lady, was the first cousin of three successive Dukes of Northumberland, of the mother of a Duke of Atholl, of a countess, of the twenty-first Lord Willoughby de Eresby, of a bishop, an ambassador, two admirals etc. Thirteen later comers to working, non-legal offices under Russell's premiership ranged socially from Lansdowne's heir and Minto's brother, a son of Lord Radnor and a brother of Lord Bellew, through Clarendon's brother-in-law (Cornewall Lewis) and the well-connected Charles Buller (a Utilitarian Radical who was made first parliamentary President of the Poor Law Board)[3] to two men of the middle class, James Wilson and Matthew Talbot Baines. Hawes was a soap manufacturer, who owed his elevation to his standing with Dissenters, which he forfeited as a minister because of the Government's educational policy; his defeat in the general election of 1847 was, wrote Monckton Milnes, 'a poor encouragement to any Government to go and take Ministers out of the great middle class'.[4] Baines was a successful barrister on the northern circuit, and one of the newspaper dynasty of Leeds to whom the Whigs were much indebted. Wilson, son of a Quaker business man in Scotland, was not known in society like Buller or Lewis, did not represent a powerful pressure group like Hawes,[5] and had no proven nuisance value as a Radical M.P., and so the rapidity of

---

[1] The six were Strutt, Hawes, Ward, Milner Gibson, Henry Rich (son of an admiral), and Gibson Craig, an eminent Edinburgh advocate, heir to a baronetcy (cr. 1831) and married to the niece of Lord Vivian (Master General of the Ordnance under Melbourne), who became Scottish Whip.

[2] Chancellor of the Duchy of Lancaster 1853–4, he was created Lord Belper in 1856 and was credited in the '70s with 5,226 acres, g.a.v. £11,302. From 1846–8 he was Chief Railway Commissioner.

[3] Buller came from a great Tory borough-owning landed family.

[4] Reid's *Houghton*, Vol. I, p. 380 (see *supra*, p. 160, n. 3). Hawes took refuge in the Irish borough of Kinsale.

[5] As editor of the *Economist* Wilson was an ally rather than an organ of the Manchester School.

his adoption and utilisation by the Whigs is remarkable. He came
to their notice after he had founded the *Economist* with the help
of Lord Radnor who, with other Wiltshire magnates, assisted his
return for Westbury in 1847. These magnates included Lansdowne
and Hobhouse, and in 1848 Wilson became Secretary to the Board
of Control under the latter. He was almost permanently in office
till his premature death in India in 1860. But though he was
readily taken up, Wilson was kept in his place. The Queen acknowledged that he was 'one of our best men' but would not hear of him
becoming governor of the colony that bore her name.[1] Probably
no prime minister before Gladstone would have considered
admitting him to the cabinet; yet Cornewall Lewis, first given office
in 1847 and Chancellor of the Exchequer by 1855, said of his
subordinate 'He is animal, while I am only vegetable.' But Lewis
came of a territorial family. His father, an ex-Canningite M.P.
had given long service in administration to both Whig and Conservative governments, and took his baronetcy from Peel. Lewis
had worked for the Poor Law Commission since 1839. He was well-
liked in society, brother-in-law of Clarendon, and a gifted writer
who from 1852 to 1855 edited the *Edinburgh Review*. The elevation
of the *Edinburgh Review* over the *Economist* may be thought
symbolic.

The one source by which, traditionally, the humbly born might
rise to political eminence was the Law. But, in our period, the only
nineteenth-century Whig lawyer of surpassing talents was
Brougham, who, because the Whigs would not make him their
leader, became a great nuisance to them. Between him and Westbury, thirty years later, and no Whig, there was no active, reforming Lord Chancellor. Campbell, with a zest for political combat,
was not allowed to reach the Woolsack till his eightieth year. In
1846 he was included in the cabinet as Chancellor of the Duchy.
Grit and industry, rather than any superlative talents, had carried
him from a Scottish manse to reap, in 1859, the visible tokens of a
successful career — the Woolsack and a son who was heir to two
peerages and two estates (one in Scotland and one in Ireland)

---

[1] *Queen's Letters*, 1st Series, Vol. II, pp. 241–2, to Labouchere, 14th May,
1856 — '. . . The Queen hastens to express her opinion that Mr Wilson would
not be at all a proper person to be Governor of so large and important a colony
as Victoria. It ought to be a man of higher position and standing, and who could
represent his Sovereign adequately.' There is a pious, but not very scholarly
Life, by his daughter Mrs Emilie Barrington, called *The Servant of All*.

and a member of parliament. Other Whig lawyers made little contribution to the political fortunes of their party,[1] though W. G. Hayter, a leading Chancery lawyer, was given office in 1847 and by 1850 was Chief Whip.

'But for the old Whig leaven of three Pagets, three Howards, three Greys and some dandies,' wrote Monckton Milnes woundingly, 'it would be the ablest Administration collected for many years.'[2] 'Prizes, which are of importance to all parties, are air, light, heat, electricity, meat and drink and everything else to that which meets at Brooks's. . . . The [lower] regions inhabited by expectants . . . are infinitely more densely populated in that party than in any other,' jeered Gladstone in 1855. And he added 'When they argued that the Peelites were fifty and the Whigs and Radicals 270 they forgot that Whig selections were not made from among the 270 but from a narrower circle and with a more close and marked preference for the claims of consanguinity and affinity than is to be found among other politicians.'[3] Men who went to the House of Commons, as they had been to Oxford or Cambridge, to see whether there were any letters for them in the rack were apt to find themselves in the running for office, by virtue of their social position,[4] while men more able, articulate and even more ambitious, but not out of the top drawer, must have been overlooked. Oddly enough, a Radical, especially a slightly *ci-devant* Radical, stood a

---

[1] A due sense of the vicissitudes of political life led lawyers to look to the cursus honorum of judicial offices leading to the Bench. This, for instance, was the objective of Cockburn, whose impressive speech in the Don Pacifico debate in 1850 delighted his leaders. Campbell was embarrassed by the uncertainty of his financial prospects because he was so serviceable in the House of Commons; not till the eve of the fall of the ministry in 1841 was he made Lord Chancellor of Ireland, thus qualifying for a pension. Parliamentary success often evades those who triumph at the bar, and because of their Whiggism Pepys (later Lord Cottenham) and Wilde (later Lord Truro) were, like Campbell, well into middle age before they won seats. Cottenham, Truro and Cranworth (the lawyer Rolfe whom the Whigs imposed as Lord Chancellor on the Coalition of 1852) were without weight in cabinet and without power in the Lords, where peers learned in the law — and especially Brougham, Lyndhurst and Ellenborough — snapped and snarled round the Woolsack. Cottenham was a good judge, but nothing more; when, as Lord Chancellor, he was too feeble to perform his duties, Russell found him difficult to oust and more difficult to replace. Truro had been a brilliant pleader, but to Campbell his chief significance was that he was as great an opponent of judicial and legal reforms as Eldon had been (see Campbell, op. cit., Vol. II, esp. pp. 242, 292). Cranworth attracted epithets such as 'amiable', 'worthy', 'much-respected' which eloquently convey the standing of a certain type of cabinet minister.
[2] Reid's *Houghton*, Vol. I, p. 375, 15th July, 1846.
[3] Add. MSS 44745, draft *cit. supra*.
[4] e.g. Shelburne and 'Freddy' Leveson-Gower.

better chance of office than a Liberal who was neither highly-connected nor a successful barrister. For the Whigs had seen the utility of offering office to an occasional Radical, giving him responsibility without power or much influence. Buller by premature death, Ward by appointment as Commissioner in the Ionian Isles, Sheil by becoming diplomatic representative at the grand-ducal court of Florence, Hawes by appointment as a permanent official were lost to politics after being lost to Radicalism. Radicals preferred to have Milner Gibson back amongst them, though complaining that the Master of the Buckhounds succeeded him.[1] They did not really like the Whigs skimming off their cream, the more so as it weakened the force of their complaints about Whig exclusiveness.

A Radical or two in the cabinet, however, was a different proposition, and one to be viewed more seriously by Whiggery until experience taught it that Milner Gibson, Charles Villiers and even Sir William Molesworth could become harmless appendages of aristocratic councils. (They were, of course, all gentlemen born.) Even Bright by taking office added no lustre to his name. Administration was not their metier, though Villiers at least was competent. Perhaps the Whigs were right to recognise Cobden as of a different stamp, and this, rather than the allegation that the failure of his business was evidence of lack of capacity, or that there was a presumption against a man rescued from embarrassment by public subscription, explains the relief which was felt by most ministers when his departure on a missionary tour of the Continent provided an excuse for not inviting him to join them. Only Earl Grey and Clarendon wished to have him, in order that Russell might seem to occupy something of the position Cobden had proffered to Peel. Cobden's eminence, enhanced, if possible, by Peel's tribute to him, in his resignation speech, as the real author of Repeal,[2] made it impossible for Russell to renew the offer, made in December 1845, of the Vice-Presidency of the Board of Trade under Clarendon. It had to be the cabinet or nothing. But what a dreadful precedent to elevate a man from the back benches on the

---

[1] Gibson resigned in 1848 because he found office a trammel, and Clarendon had been succeeded as head of the department by Labouchere, who was in the Commons. (Clarendon had accepted the principle of Free Trade earlier than most of the political leaders but he was not interested in detailed work *re* tariffs and railways — see Campbell, Vol. II, p. 212.)

[2] The Whigs were deeply offended by this speech, which they thought a gratuitous attempt to embarrass the incoming ministers.

strength of successful agitation outside Parliament. Was it not the sort of thing that Peel had predicted would happen as a result of Reform, a forecast at which the Whigs (the hope being father to the thought) had scoffed? When Cobden returned, Russell proposed to invite him into the cabinet, as head of the Poor Law Board, balancing an appointment which was bound to be very unpopular with landlords by admitting also the Duke of Bedford, who had assented to Repeal only to prevent a strife of classes which must have proved damaging to the landed interest. The Queen demurred. She did not mind Cobden having the department — '... it will be advantageous to the Government and the Country that his talents should be secured to the service of the State'. But ought one to raise up a man straight from Covent Garden, the London platform of the League? (Did she remember that the Duke of Bedford owned Covent Garden?) Let Cobden work his way up, like a Fox Maule or a Vernon Smith.[1] So the viper was not asked into the bosom of the family party, and the Duke remained a wise adviser of his brother from outside.

In their later claims to places in coalition governments, Gladstone would argue, the Whigs 'forgot [their] altered position ... in regard to the Liberal party. They have long been its leaders, but not of late years without a great and growing impatience on the part of the led'. And, in partial explanation of this impatience he said that 'the large body called independent Liberals ... [though] connected with the Whigs by party organization' were increasingly willing to take any course which they thought would 'improve the chance of securing more efficient administration and greater real progress in improving the institutions of the country'.[2] And so we pass from consideration of Whig exclusiveness to the criticisms of Whig administrative capacity, which cannot be regarded as entirely a separate matter. But before we accept the Whig reputation for administrative ineptitude as deserved it is fair to inquire into its origin. Nothing is easier than to expose the faults of an administrative system and the faults of those who worked it, when it has been reformed on grounds which *a priori* seem to posterity a conclusive indictment of previous practice. The Whig reputation has been transmitted by Radicals and Peelites. Radicals did not judge a minister in terms of routine

[1] *Queen's Letters*, 1st Series, Vol. II, pp. 153–5, October 1847.
[2] Add. MSS 44745, draft *cit. supra*.

competence, but by his attitude to administrative *reform*. The
Peelites had everything to gain from writing off their Whig competitors as 'good for nothing . . . decrepit . . . crotchety . . . slaves
of routine . . . worthless . . . rubbish . . . lumber'.[1] As soon as they
found themselves detached from the Conservative ranks —
'Alexander's generals without troops' and forbidden to recruit
them, for Peel refused to form a party in the true sense of a body of
men seeking to win power[2]— the Peelites began to boost their own
administrative reputations. They had no market value except as an
official cadre. Their verdict on their rivals has won acceptance
principally for two reasons. Firstly, civil service reform is inseparably associated with Gladstone, who commissioned the Northcote-
Trevelyan report and was to practice its tenets. The fact that
Trevelyan was a Whig, appointed to his high office at the Treasury
by Whigs, and that Northcote was only briefly a Peelite before
becoming a Tory, is sometimes forgotten, when it is remembered
that Russell associated himself with the officials who criticised the
report and resisted its implementation. And secondly, the later
eminence of Gladstone, his longevity, and Morley's *Life*, conspired
to concentrate favourable publicity on his reforms as Chancellor
and as prime minister in the reforming period 1868–74. Gladstone
transmitted, with his own reputation, the verdict that Peel was a
pre-eminent administrator and educator of administrators. Hence
all the departments of state between 1846 and 1868, excepting the
Treasury when Gladstone was there, are plunged into shadows of
which the darkness is enhanced by the floodlighting of the areas
on either side, and a biassed imagination has peopled this darkness
with Whig dwarfs.

Trevelyan was 'a keen whig with no leaning towards the
radicals', but it was his ambition to 'improve the spirit and
character of the public service', so that 'the present period will be
distinguished above all others in this country for practical executive improvements'.[3] He was able, when Russell was prime

---

[1] Add. MSS 44745, Gladstone's draft *cit. supra*. These harsh epithets were
applied to Tories as well as Whigs. '. . . At this time [1855] when there is a cry
for new men in the Government, we are overstocked as we never before were,
with old ones' — enough P.C.s to stock three cabinets, 62 in all (only 17 of them
Tories) including 13 ex-Colonial Secretaries. Then Gladstone goes on to talk of
Whig resentment at Peelite interlopers carrying off the prizes.
[2] Add. MSS 40455, fs. 442–7, Aberdeen to Peel, 18th September, 1847.
[3] Jenifer Hart, 'Sir Charles Trevelyan at the Treasury', *E.H.R.*, LXXV, No.
294, 1960, pp. 15–17, Trevelyan's correspondence with Russell 1848–9.

minister, to secure a series of departmental inquiries, but they did not lead to great results, and so he took advantage of the general inquiry commissioned by Gladstone in 1853 to produce a report which was the fruit less of judicial and systematic inquiry and balanced appraisal than zeal for reform. It was handled as a propagandist document, sent to leading educationalists (most of whom praised it warmly) and 'leaked' to the *Times* before it was given to heads of departments for comment. The fact that the departments had a vested interest in repudiating the harsh criticism of the existing services does not mean that their comments should be rejected out of hand. And the fact that the principles of open competition conducted by commissioners, and division into grades, have become distinctive features of British arrangements is not proof that it was reasonable to expect the politicians of the day to accept the report as divinely inspired. It was not only the sceptical sinecurist, Monteagle, who described the survey as incomplete . . . partial and *ex parte*'; a leading supporter of reform, John Wood, of the Excise, agreed.[1] Russell, in his opposition to the proposals of the report, was no doubt influenced by considerations of *amour propre*, as one who had had much to do with patronage, and of loyalty to officials whom he had appointed, promoted or worked with. But Trevelyan's propositions were not self-evident truths, and they had political and constitutional implications. Graham, no lover of the chores of patronage, and no party hack, doubted whether parliamentary government could be conducted without patronage as 'the regulator of the machine'. Trevelyan argued that free and unrestricted competition for appointments would be a means of 'strengthening our aristocratical institutions', and Gladstone that it would strengthen and multiply the ties between the higher classes (Baring said bluntly 'the rich') and the possession of administrative power. But Gladstone also said that the reforms were his contribution to 'the picnic of parliamentary reform' and a modern commentator can write that in the long run the abolition of patronage was a more fundamental political revolution than the reform of Parliament.[2] It was reasonable, therefore, to agree with Edward Romilly, a moderate reformer who became one of the Civil Service Com-

[1] For all this one is much indebted to Professor Edward Hughes' article 'Civil Service Reform' in *History*, N.S., XXVII, 1942.
[2] Hughes, op. cit., p. 59.

missioners. In his book *Promotion in the Civil Service* (1848) he
had pointed to the anomaly of 'a democratical Civil Service, side
by side with an aristocratical Legislature'.

The adoption of open competition for entry to the civil service
more naturally followed than preceded the extension of the
franchise which occurred in 1867, and no government before tha
date accepted either the indiscriminate strictures or the principa
proposals of the report. Most of those politicians and public
servants who admitted a case for improvements thought it best to
retain departmental control of nomination, appointment, promo
tion and dismissal.[1] This avoided constitutional difficulties and
made it legitimate to proceed with the appointment of Civil
Service Commissioners by Order in Council of 21st May, 1855,
after Lewis (whose experience did not support the strictures on the
existing service) had replaced Gladstone at the Treasury. The
change, Gladstone said, 'introduced no new principle', for the
commissioners were given only the limited task of authenticating
candidates presented to them by the departments for examination
on lines agreed by the departments. Many offices already had
entrance tests (though of varying character) and virtually all
insisted on a probationary period. The commissioners' examina
tions merely established minimum, though not very high, standard
for entrance to a wide range of intermediate appointments. That
large number were 'plucked' only proves that statistics 'prove
nothing. It may be evidence that departments presented 'dummy
candidates in order to get their real selections accepted. If it mean
that people were rejected who would previously have been
appointed, then the change, promoted by a Whig government
which 'introduced no new principle', was obviously an important

---

[1] Trevelyan aspired to cement Treasury control over the departments an
abstained from recommending it only because this would be sure to provok
strong resistance from the departments and imperil the scheme for open compe
tition conducted centrally. Montalambert had recently warned Britain that sh
was in danger of sliding into the continental error of over-centralisation. Intell
gent men did not believe that, with such strong departmental traditions, th
civil servants of the Crown could ever be made 'a Service', were by no mean
sure that this would be a good thing, and doubted whether a common test woul
produce persons fit and proper for an infinite variety of tasks. Especially the
doubted whether proof of academic ability would produce the sort of men th
public service needed. The report admitted that other considerations should b
taken into account, but its prime hypothesis seemed to discount the need f
moral worth and personal merits (stressed by Graham), commonsense (to Haw
the chief requisite), discretion and trustworthiness (the importance of whic
was emphasised by Lewis). Romilly and Lewis argued that *promotion* by mer
instead of seniority was the key to efficiency.

reform. But some of the examinations under the old system had been exacting; Peel had abandoned the tests for Treasury clerk-ships introduced by Baring in 1840. Palmerston's standards of efficiency at the Foreign office had been very high. Contrary to a general impression, Clarendon as Foreign Secretary 1855–8 co-operated with the Civil Service Commissioners and instituted a second, internal, examination as a safeguard to secure efficient paid attachés. At the Board of Trade Labouchere at once instituted 'limited competition', presenting to the examiners competitors (usually three) for each appointment. In 1857 the Palmerston government directed that this system be used in all departments dependent on the Treasury. In the same year the Home Office and the Office of Works progressed to open examinations for clerkships. A Whig government was therefore responsible for cautious experimentation in reform of the civil service. And when that middle-class minister, James Wilson, extolled the virtues of 'limited competition', saying that the open competition among all comers, which Gladstone and Trevelyan wanted, 'would be pro-ductive of an enormous amount of mischief',[1] we are warned not to denigrate a cautious approach simply because the propositions of the Trevelyan-Northcote report have become familiar.

It is certain that the reputation of Whiggery has suffered by the victory of its opponents at the end of the day, just as the repute of the Stewarts and of George III has suffered at the hands of historians called 'Whig' as a pseudonym for 'Gladstonian Liberal'. *Per contra*, the Peelites have gained unduly in reputation through the spread of the Gladstonian cult. The grossest example of multiple mismanagement in this whole period was the breakdown of the supply services during the Crimean campaign of 1854. The ministers primarily responsible were all Peelites. Aberdeen was prime minister. Newcastle, who as Lincoln had been so scathing about Whig maladministration of relief in Ireland (an emergency operation on a scale never foreseen), was at the War Office. Sidney Herbert was Secretary at War. The Treasury had not clean hands, and Gladstone must share blame with Trevelyan.[2] There is much

---

[1] Hughes, op. cit., p. 83.

[2] 'It would undoubtedly be wrong to assign a large share of the responsibility for the disasters to [Trevelyan], but the correspondence does not add to his reputation' (J. Hart, op. cit., p. 102). Trevelyan told Raglan he would have 'as efficient a department as ever accompanied a British army into the field' and continued to fight the transfer of the Commissariat to the War Office, saying the

to be said in extenuation. These problems of military supply over such a vast distance were unique. The disastrous results of inadequate planning and provision were magnified by the narrow failure to snatch the citadel of Sebastopol before the winter and by a great storm in the Black Sea. Peelite ministers began, before they left office, to repair the deficiencies, and their Whig successors gained the credit. But really superlative administrators might perhaps have been a little more far-seeing, and any defence which blames 'the system' rather than the men gives blanket indemnity to Whigs as well as to Peelites. The Peelite wing, so influential in the coalition cabinet, had not seen the urgency of changing 'the system', or, rather, of making a system out of chaos. The men of ministerial rank who *had* pressed for reforms were Earl Grey and Fox Maule, two former Whig Secretaries at War and, in the cabinet, Russell.[1]

If Gladstone has the credit for instituting in the early 'sixties efficient parliamentary control of public accounts, the ministerial pioneer in this field had been Graham while he was still a Whig and in the 'fifties the pressure for the generalisation of the system he had introduced at the Admiralty came from another Whig ex-First Lord, Baring,[2] who was Chairman of the Public Monies Committee 1856-7 and became first chairman of the Public Accounts Committee which has existed (except during the 1939-1945 war) since 1861. It is not contended that the Whigs were either great administrators or dedicated administrative reformers. Like most politicians before and since, they went to their offices to see what work was waiting on their desks. They felt no mission to 'rationalise' administration. They lost no sleep over arrangements which were often unsystematic, cumbrous and uneconomical, with pockets of sinecurism and under-work and, as the Crimean War revealed, areas of overlapping responsibility where co-ordination was wanting. But Whig administrations were responsible, willy-nilly, for much administrative experiment, which was a by-product of the need to extend the state's sphere of interest or

practice had worked well on the whole. The Treasury is to be blamed for this complacency and for a parsimony which was incompatible with due provision for the army.

[1] Though it is fair to say that Maule was not sure that it was right to carry out radical administrative rearrangements during the campaign.

[2] 'He was a good Whig, but superior to party. Every one knows that at the Admiralty he was the fairest First Lord who ever administered that department' (Sir Erskine May, quoted in Malet's *Northbrook*, p. 13).

alter radically the treatment of old problems. Leaning heavily on the advice of the Utilitarians, they created the Poor Law Commission and the later Board; the Ecclesiastical Commissioners (for the management of Church property); the Tithe Commissioners; the Commissioners for Colonial Land and Emigration; the Committee of the Privy Council for Education; the factory inspectorate; the Board of Health — to say nothing of new sub-departments in, for instance, the Board of Trade. All this was part of a process of trial and error which vastly increased the untidiness of the administrative pattern until, later in the century, the very untidiness created its own demand for systematisation.

Administrative *reform* apart, there seems no reason to think that Russell's ministers, man for man, were inferior in administrative capacity to their Conservative predecessors or, indeed, most of their Peelite supplanters. Palmerston, Earl Grey, Sir Charles Wood, Sir George Grey, Sir Francis Baring were the reverse of dilettante in the management of their departments. From the same 'technical' point of view that Lord Attlee was a superb Prime Minister, Sir George Grey was a 'heaven-sent' Home Secretary; his diligence, intelligence and calm were impressively conjoined in his preparations for handling the Chartist demonstrations in 1848. These men earned criticism as statesmen, not as administrators, because their policies, or means of carrying them out, were controversial, in Wood's case because his policy lacked constructive purpose. When Peel formed his administration in 1841 it was attacked, not unfairly, though by a jaundiced witness, as drawn too exclusively from men of long experience (Goulburns, Ripons and Clerks) and the aristocracy.[1] In course of time it was freshened by youth, but it was not rendered less aristocratic, the recruits to the cabinet being three noblemen and Gladstone, the brilliant protégé of a monumentally stupid duke. The sources of supply were very much the same as the Whig. Except for Gladstone, Peel's colleagues, *seriatim*, were not more able than Russell's. And yet the Russell administration is open to unfavourable comparison with Peel's. Gladstone gives us the explanation. The Russell government, he says, was weak, though some of the departments were 'well and properly administered', while Peel's cabinet

---

[1] Reid's *Houghton*, Vol. I, pp. 270–2. Monckton Milnes became disenchanted with Peel, who would not give him the offices he wanted, preferring aristocrats to this landowning litterateur.

P

was 'admirably disciplined' though 'it did not contain a very large
number of men distinguished for administrative energy'.[1] Pee
provided energy and direction from the top, and Russell did not
Peel's Chancellor of the Exchequer, Goulburn, was hardly more
than an experienced clerk,[2] in no way superior to Wood, whose
chief fault was over-attention to detail. But the budgets of 1847–
1851 are remembered as Wood's (though Russell introduced one
of them) and the budgets of 1842–6 are *not* remembered as
Goulburn's, but as Peel's. At the Board of Trade Peel instituted
a significant system of dual control. His correspondence with the
President, the exhausted Ripon, is about departmental management; his correspondence with Gladstone, the Vice-President, is
about policy and the acquisition of information on which to base
it.[3] A man of purpose, whose influence was all-pervasive, Pee
provided 'discipline', training for the younger minister, and a guiding intelligence. 'The office of the Prime Minister received its
modern stamp from the capacity of Sir Robert Peel,' says Professor
Smellie.[4] The statement is misleading, for Peel was perhaps the
last prime minister enabled by unusual capacity and industry to
maintain a genuine supervision over the departments.[5] But it is
essentially true. The tendency for governmental responsibility to
expand made the systematic influence of a commanding personality
ever more necessary. Peel provided such a personality and Russell
did not.

If it is the duty of a government to *govern*, and not merely to
administer, then Russell's ministry was not a *government* as Peel's
second or Gladstone's first ministry was a government. Peel's
ministers were not a body of 'yes-men'. If they had been he, not
Russell, would have been the first party leader to declare for
Repeal. He had to persuade his colleagues. But his cabinet was, as
Professor Smellie says, 'a real unity' as compared with Grey's or
Melbourne's 'complete republic [in which the] ostensible head has
no overruling authority'.[6] Russell reintroduced 'republicanism' into
cabinet government after Peel had practised monarchy. Of course,

---

[1] Add. MSS 44745, draft *cit. supra.*
[2] His subordinate was Clerk by name as well as nature.
[3] See Lucy Brown, *The Board of Trade and the Free Trade Movement*, last
chapter.
[4] K. B. Smellie, *A Hundred Years of English Government*, p. 54 (1950 ed.).
[5] As the functions of the state became more varied, such supervision as Peel's
became impracticable; only Gladstone in his first premiership approached it.
[6] op. cit., p. 54, quoting, *re* Melbourne, Greville, 1840.

it is true even today that a prime minister is limited by his colleagues, though he chooses them and may dismiss them and has the
prerogative of deciding what the sense of the cabinet is on any
issue. He is still to some extent first among equals, though the
primacy is more marked than the equality. But Peel and Gladstone
were *premiers* in a way that Russell was not, and that is why their
administrations were *governments* in a way that Russell's was not.
When Lord John was in Downing Street, government was by
departments and policy-making by conclave, by a sort of select
committee of Brooks's Club. As with Grey and Melbourne,
temperament and constitutional principle conspired to produce
this effect. 'The great Whig families', writes Professor Aspinall,
'had always regarded power as something to be shared amongst
themselves rather than monopolised by an individual'.[1] Russell,
consciously reacting against Peel's techniques of management,
reflected a Whig tradition from which Pitt, Liverpool, Wellington
and Peel had all to some extent deviated; there perhaps remained
traces of the prejudice expressed by Holland as late as 1806, when
he said that the constitution abhorred the idea of a prime minister.[2]
But character as well as dogma played its part. Russell was more
interested in principles and lines of policy than in details and practical applications. He was prolific of 'heads of measures', often
intelligent and liberal ones. But unless deeply roused or committed, he lacked the drive and stamina (perhaps, basically, the
will) to impose them first on the cabinet and then on the Commons.
Both as head of government and as party leader he had insufficient
motive power and self-assurance. He was also physically unequal
to the strain of managing both an administration and the House of
Commons. As he had ideological inhibitions about the propriety of
managing either, it is not surprising that he lost his grip on both.

In cabinet, Russell's own wishes were often frustrated by
passive resistance or procrastination, while strong men like
Palmerston and Earl Grey went their separate ways with scant
regard for the spirit or even the letter of cabinet decisions. The
administration was not informed by any administrative genius
on the part of its chief nor made by him the instrument of a constructive and coherent policy. The diligent management of departments, combined with an attitude of somewhat bewildered good-

---

[1] Raleigh Lecture, *cit. supra*. For Grey's attitude, see Ch. III above.
[2] H. of L., 3rd March, 1806.

will towards many reasonable (but often mutually incompatible) demands for action, was not enough to compensate for the lack of a galvanic and a strong, guiding intelligence. The Russell government unfortunately lacked a Peel who was master of the present and a Gladstone who would be master of the future and thereby mould the picture of the past. Lord John's conception of the constitutional context in which he worked was, judging by the demands of the time upon the state, archaic. This is especially seen in his attitude towards the House of Commons, which seems to have been based on a literal acceptance of Bagehot's statement that the cabinet was a select committee of the House. Upon the mind of Russell, the amateur constitutional historian, the imprint of seventeenth-century strife of King and Parliament, and of the reign of George III (Whig version) was so deep that he never could understand that Parliament has been through the ages generally the servant of the Executive and that it may be necessary that this be so. The heroic period in which the Commons achieved supremacy over the King and regarded itself as a sort of standing opposition to the Executive was immensely significant, and of lasting effect. Much of the effect has been beneficial. But the period was short and uncharacteristic. Russell was applying an eighteenth-century eye-glass to a nineteenth-century constitution. He extolled the supremacy of Parliament, meaning not the sovereignty of the King-in-Parliament, which Dicey was to expound as a predominant characteristic of the British constitution, but the supremacy of the Commons, as the foundation of the nation's liberties. He felt in his bones that the House ought to be, in more than form, the grand inquest of the nation, the source of supply and the master of the Executive. He did not feel that the convention of ministerial responsibility for acts done in the name of the Crown rendered legitimate the use of Parliament as an instrument of ministerial will. Of course, the attitude of dominance can go too far, and become oppressive, and we must not expect of the nineteenth century a control by party to which many educated and sensible people in the twentieth are not yet reconciled. But Gladstone, a great House of Commons man as well as a skilled administrator, thought the power of the Executive needed to be increased rather than diminished, and this was appropriate in the mid-nineteenth century context of many calls on Parliament's consideration and of relaxed party ties.

"THE FARCE" OF THE SESSION.

The fragmentation of parties may be pleaded in extenuation of ministerial failures, but it really emphasised the challenge which the Russell administration was not equipped to meet. When special interests are strong and party weak, a government owes the country, and, indeed, the legislature itself, a habit of direction and a steady pressure to pass ministerial bills. There was justice in Disraeli's jibe that 'we have a cabinet who, in preparing their measures, have no conviction that those measures will be carried'.[1] A member of the cabinet (Campbell) testified that Russell lost control of the new House in its first session. Unfortunately Russell's deficiencies as Leader of the Commons were accentuated

[1] H. of C., 30th August, 1848. At that late date of the session which began before Christmas 1847 thirty Government bills had failed to become law.

by the successes of the leadership in the Lords. Parliamentary leadership requires authority, resolution, a clear sense of objectives and tactical skill. It requires also tact and sociability, especially when discipline cannot be relied on. For leader in the Lords the Whigs had a Trollopian figure, Henry Petty-Fitzmaurice, third Marquess of Lansdowne, Earl of Wycombe, Viscount Calne and Calstone and fourth Baron Wycombe in the peerage of Great Britain, fourth Earl of Shelburne, Viscount Fitzmaurice and Baron Dunkerron and fourth Earl of Kerry and Viscount Clanmaurice and twenty-fourth Baron of Kerry and Lixnaw in the peerage of Ireland. Born the year Pitt came of age (1780), he died the year Lloyd George was born (1863). He first entered the cabinet in 1806 and last left it in 1858. He inherited neither the suspect originality nor the ambition of his father;[1] he spent a good deal of time avoiding the premiership. But he did like wielding influence. In the 'twenties, willy-nilly, a faction leader, he became after 1832 a leading Whig councillor and at last the Nestor of Whiggery. He owed his influence to a classic combination of birth and titles and great estates with *noblesse oblige*, hospitality and sagacity, all matured by a long experience. He found, in the 'thirties, most in common with the ex-Canningites, Melbourne and Palmerston, and showed in the 'fifties a far less narrow regard for Whig monopoly of office than the Russellite circle, which was more liberal in political opinion. His influence was always exerted to keep the Whigs together, lest Radicals gain by their disunion, and to keep them conservative to maintain the constitutional settlement of 1832 and perpetuate the power of the aristocracy, which must diminish with every Radical triumph even if Whig aristocrats brought the triumph into being. Loyal to this principle, his son was to emerge in 1866 to lead the Opposition to the extension of the franchise and his grandson in 1909 to bid defiance to Lloyd George. His conservative inclinations made him exactly suited to his task in the Lords, for they rendered impressive his advocacy of change, as when he advised the peers to accept the Repeal of the Corn Laws (a measure which he disapproved), with the prediction that it would not affect the power of the aristocracy. Campbell doubted

[1] Bagehot in his *Biographical Studies* summed up the rather mysterious unpopularity of Shelburne by saying that he was 'like the reputed thief that policemen talk of'. Shelburne was rather antiquated in his notions of the relative roles of King, ministers and Parliament, but unconventional and forward-looking in his views on policy.

HENRY, 3rd MARQUESS OF LANSDOWNE
by J. Linnell
By courtesy of the Most Hon. The Marquess of Lansdowne

whether he would be a successful leader, for his air was lethargic and his grandiloquence rather old-fashioned and Melbourne had taken his task in the Lords so lightly that the peers had no experience even of such minimal discipline as they could be expected to bear. But Campbell soon had to admit that the Marquess showed 'energy and discretion in managing the peers, and earnestly tried to carry though measures which he did not entirely relish'.[1] Wooing the waverers, he 'made very man who approached him dearer to himself'. And among the upper strata of Whiggery Lansdowne did much to assuage passions and prejudices aroused by Russell's indiscretions and to mitigate the suspicion that the Whigs could not be relied upon to remain conservative.

What the Whigs needed in the Commons was a man of authority, tact and charm, leaning to the liberal side as Lansdowne leaned to the conservative. Such a man could have outshone Peel as a party leader, for Peel was aloof and socially awkward, and these traits contributed more than is sometimes realised to the break-up of his party. But then Peel had a great reputation as a minister, and could 'play on the House of Commons as on an old fiddle'. Russell lacked these advantages. Where the Marquess was composed, patient, even-tempered (though prone to gout), affable and, above all discreet, Lord John was moody, impetuous, frail, nervous, inclined to pettishness and prone to rash initiatives. Lansdowne was the grandee, but sociable, tactful, a sceptic, taking human nature as he found it; Russell was earnest, egotistical, with pride in his bearing if not, as he avowed on his deathbed, in his heart. The House of Commons may be led successfully by one who towers over his contemporaries, but best of all by a man who seems (but is not) ordinary, like Baldwin, or by an ordinary man who is trusted, like Althorp and W. H. Smith. Russell neither seemed nor was ordinary, but he was neither very great nor very clever. He idealised the House of Commons, but was not happy in managing a flesh-and-blood one. 'Country gentlemen, merchants and lawyers who are well-affected to the party he drives into the opposition lobby by witholding from them a nod and a smile.'[1] He was his own worst enemy, for he seemed 'proud and insolent', cold and indifferent, where he was only shy and husbanding limited energies. Unbent, he was very likeable, but, like old Earl Grey, he did not unbend easily outside a limited circle of family

[1] Campbell, Vol. II, p. 242, 28th July, 1848.

and friends. The narrowness of this circle, as well as the narrowness of the field from which his appointments were made, accentuated the restlessness of his followers. Here was a national as well as a personal tragedy. Russell was liberal, if not a Liberal. His seventeenth-century philosophy could expand, under the pressure of a generous spirit, to embrace successive schemes of reform in almost every field of policy. A man of such views and sympathies and unwhiggish urge to be up and doing might, if of more fortunate temperament, have renovated Whiggery and created a moderate Liberal party guided from above like Peel's Conservative party. He might, by 'educating' his own circle, have broadened its base in the country. Instead, Russell allowed his colleagues to stifle many a generous impulse, and yet incurred their suspicion by an unconcerted initiative all too reminiscent of May 1834 and November 1845 — his proposal, in 1849, of further parliamentary reform.[1]

From 1846 Whiggery was living on its capital in a market in which the stocks in its portfolio were depreciating. Russell himself was all too apt to recoil from matters of grave difficulty and little political promise, concerning economic relationships and social welfare, to questions of civil liberty and constitutional reform.[2] It was fitting enough that Whiggery, through its leader, should maintain its consistency by trying to extend to Jews the civic equality secured for Papists and admit imperfections in the Reform of 1832. But these questions were not urgent or ripe for solution. To those who demanded administrative, judicial and fiscal reforms Russell's sense of priorities seemed all wrong, and criticism of the programme and tenor of the ministry merged with criticism of its composition and capacity and its lack of leadership. Unrooted in popular feeling, the Government failed to acquire parliamentary prestige. It staggered from session to session, sustained only by horror at the prospect of an unrepentant Protectionist ministry, and in the last resort sustained by Peel. 'The Abdication of Peel and the incompetency of the Tories may . . . force our party once more together,' Monteagle had

[1] See *infra*, Ch. XII.

[2] This tendency was observable in the parliamentary timetable of government business in 1847–8. After 1848 Russell's plans for Ireland, in the absence of Catholic endowment, largely consisted of the extension of the franchise (in which, in 1851, he had a moderate success) and a project for the abolition of the Lord Lieutenancy.

opined in the spring of 1846, 'But this will be under circumstances in which their future relations with Peel become of the most vital importance.'[1] The Russell government could have been broken at any time by Peel, if he had been eager to return to power. Ministers were slow to understand that he had cast away all ambition except to see the Repeal of the Corn Laws put beyond dispute and the emancipation of trade proceed, that all he required from them was a decent deference to his views as the foremost man in the Commons. Peel's mastery over the fate of the Whig ministry, which he preserved in office from calculation, without love or respect,[2] was cold, contemptuous and, inevitably, patronising. And this made it very galling to Whiggery. Yet it was their salvation, and the death of Peel was harmful to Whig prospects,[3] for it was bound to start a thaw in the Peelite ice-pack. The only hope for Whiggery was that the inevitable drift of the Peelite rank-and-file back to Toryism, which had already begun, would be offset by the accession to the ministry of some of the leading Peelites. If they could be got as individuals, the Government might remain predominantly 'Whig'. But even Sir James Graham, who accepted, in principle, that his political future lay in alliance with Whiggery, had no mind to join a sinking ship. And his position was unique. The other Peelites did not yet accept where their future lay, though they chafed at having been kept by Peel suspended (as Gladstone said) between Earth and Heaven, wind and water. If they could ever bring themselves to union with the Whigs, it would not be on the basis of piecemeal absorption.

Whig control of government was therefore doomed. But how the *coup de grace* was to be administered did not yet appear. Was the ministry to linger on till it died of inanition? What seemed its end came, with appropriate bathos, upon the failure of enough members to attend the House of Commons to vote down, in February 1851, Locke King's latest attempt to extend the county franchise. But resignation solved no problems. Stanley failed to

---

[1] Add. MSS 34626, f. 140, 13th April, 1846, to Macvey Napier.

[2] '. . . I wish that Peel and Lord John were not the two repelling bodies that they are and that they would cordially confer together on the common weal. . . . But I am afraid it will never be a romance of real life, and even if Peel were inclined he would find no response in J.R.' (*Clarendon*, Vol. I, p. 291, to Cornewall Lewis, 2nd July, 1848).

[3] Campbell, Vol. II, p. 281, 'His death is a very heavy blow to the Whigs.' *Clarendon*, Vol. I, p. 313, Clarendon to Lewis, 5th July, 1850 — 'I can think of nothing but Peel's death and its evil consequences to all parties: but to none more so than to the Government. . . .'

form a government, frankly acknowledging his want of suitable materials, and that his inability to get Peelites or Palmerston to join him was fatal to his prospects. And when the Palace attempted to secure the co-operation of Aberdeen and Graham with Russell in establishing a ministry, the Peelites were able to discover an 'insuperable difficulty', namely the Ecclesiastical Titles Bill.

It is necessary at this point to explain the Whig attitude to the Church, without some understanding of which the full flavour of Whiggery cannot be savoured. Whig statesmen, individually, ranged in religious outlook from a cultured eighteenth-century agnosticism, through a seemly Victorian conformity, to a sincere Evangelical Protestantism. But when men spoke of 'the Whig religion',[1] in terms which suggested a collective outlook, they implied a creed intensely protestant but bereft of three of the principle characteristics of seventeenth-century Puritanism — zeal, dogma, and anti-popish politics. A product of eighteenth-century rationalism, basically more tolerant of agnosticism than of dogmatic assurance, because the latter tends to produce intolerance and discrimination, it assumed that human progress depended on the free play of ideas between educated minds without bar of official censorship. This 'optimistic' scepticism marched well with an open indifference to conventional morality, which has not been uncommon in dominant aristocracies. But it could coexist with high standards of conduct and duty, and even with a sincere religious faith, provided that this did not prove destructive of tolerance. It did not involve any conscious disloyalty to Christianity, which Whiggery regarded as one of the blessings of Western civilisation, to be taught to the heathen in lands under British rule or protection. Whigs might differ as to whether the state should subsidise denominational education, but most agreed that it should, and all agreed that the Christian ethic formed an important part of the curriculum. But many of them thought of Christianity as essentially uncontroversial, made a matter of controversy only by human perversity and vested interest and due to be liberated from its disorders by intellectual progress. Thus Russell 'had himself never been confirmed, but did not trouble his mind about the petty superstition which would have made this an obstacle to

---

[1] e.g. Reid's *Houghton*, Vol. I, p. 380, Monckton Milnes, 15th August, 1847 '... I understand Macaulay with his Whig religion being very unacceptable to the Edinburghians. ...'

his joining in the Lord's Supper. . . . He deplored the earthly and sectarian trappings by which man has disfigured Christianity — the multiplication of creeds, dogmas, ceremonies in the Church of England; her assumption of sanctity as the special depositary of truth. . . . He thought the English Catechism wholly unfitted for children, and vehemently disliked the dogmatic parts of it. . . . He looked forward to a day when there would be no priests, or rather when every man would be his own priest, and all superstitious notions — such as is implied in the notion that only clergymen ought to perform certain offices of religion — should be cast aside by Christian men for ever'.[1]

This concept of Christianity was eloquently elaborated by Russell's colleague, Lord Seymour, who as Duke of Somerset in 1871 published a pamphlet called *Christian Theology and Modern Scepticism*. The following extract sums up the whole:[2]

> . . . It is humiliating to be obliged to confess that after eighteen hundred years of Christian teaching, man has made no advance in certainty of religious knowledge. . . . In every other branch of knowledge assiduous study and persevering industry have been rewarded with at least partial success. Some progress has been made and some results obtained, which, while they have contributed to the convenience or to the happiness of mankind, have encouraged fresh exertions and opened a prospect of future acquisitions. . . . It is now obvious that the theology of former ages cannot be permanently maintained. . . . The progress of civilisation has not been favourable to faith. All other Christian virtues — justice, benevolence, temperance, patience, self-denial — are strengthened by education, and the advancement of religion is here in harmony with the moral improvement of society. . . . [But] the innumerable influences of our existing civilisation operating through the channels of science, of literature and of social intercourse . . . alter our preconceived notions, and faith is gradually losing her empire over the mind. . . . There is, however, one unassailable fortress to which she may retire — faith in God. . . . Here, at last, the natural and supernatural will be merged in one harmonious universe under one Supreme Intelligence. . . . [But] is faith in God the faith which Jesus taught? . . . Every man must at last seek the solution in his own mind or his own heart. Theology cannot aid him. . . .
>
> We may hope . . . that by the continued progress of learning and

[1] *Walpole*, Vol. II, p. 468, Lady Russell's account of her husband's beliefs.
[2] From *Letters, Remains and Memoirs* of Edward Adolphus Seymour, 12th Duke of Somerset, ed. Mallock and Ramsden, pp. 325–84.

liberty, Christianity . . . will be better understood. The ministers of religion will again become the teachers of the people, and the open Bible will irresistibly lead to the open church. Religious and secular instruction will then be in unison, the distinctions of Protestant sects will be obliterated and forgotten, and the Church would, without any violent convulsions, become the Church of the whole Protestant people.

In the Duke of Somerset's opinion, what was wanted for 'the moral improvement of society' was 'a view of Christianity unencumbered with the prescriptive phrases belonging to another state of civilisation', and only the influence over the least educated classes of society of 'vigorous but narrow-minded men' prevented the public from, as yet, entertaining such a view. This was both very eighteenth century and very Victorian, a vision of a Utopia to be attained by the enlarging of the human understanding. Some Whig notables, we may sure, had doubts which Somerset brushed aside; they regretted the extent to which, both in fact and potentially, scientific discoveries and philosophical systems undermined Christian belief. But, by the same token that they repudiated the ethos of Rome, they must repudiate the Anglican Catholicism, to them obscurantist, which in the 'thirties emanated from Oxford.

It was Whig politicians, Broad and Low churchmen, who all unconsciously liberated from the womb of Ecclesia Anglicana the new race of High churchmen. The Whigs remained in the nineteenth century what they had become in the eighteenth, convinced Erastians. If they did not precisely regard the Church of England as a department of state and a valuable field of patronage, they saw it as, at best, a subordinate ally of the state. It was, indeed, a part of the state by virtue of its constitutional subjection both to the royal supremacy (exercised on the advice of the cabinet) and to the sovereignty of Parliament. But to Keble, Newman and Pusey the only valid extenuation of parliamentary supremacy over the Church was the proposition that Parliament represented the laity of the Church, and the formal admission of non-Anglicans to Parliament stripped this away. That the purposes for which Whig governments employed Parliament's legislative sovereignty were reforming purposes seemed irrelevant to men who denied that the Church could properly be subordinated to the state, and Keble's sermon on 'National Apostasy', delivered at St Mary's, Oxford, on Assize Sunday 1833, which is usually taken as the inauguration of the Oxford Movement, was an attack on the Government's legislation for the Irish Church. That Church property should be put at the disposal of Ecclesiastical Commissioners; that there should be no opportunity for churchmen to challenge the consecration of bishops allegedly unsound in faith;[1] that the final word on the discipline and even the faith of the Church should be vested in a Privy Council committee;[2] that the organic institutions of the Church should be prevented from functioning even in an advisory and subordinate capacity[3]— all this was abhorrent to the men of Oxford. Between them and Whiggery there was natural antipathy, for they represented two radically divergent conceptions of the Church. It distressed the Whigs that in the late eighteenth and early nineteenth centuries the Church should be so bigoted, so far from reflecting the enlightenment of 'Whig religion'. It distressed them even more that a new form of 'bigotry', raising up new walls of partition within the Church as well as between the Church and the Protestant sects, and smacking of Popery, should begin to make way. The Tractarians, as the Oxford apologists were called, decisively rejected the notion that the Church was a sort of department for the propagation of ethics and morality. They insisted that it was the local presence of the Holy Catholic Church, existing by divine commission and acknowledging, in the last resort, no sovereignty but God's. They reminded men that parsons were priests and that bishops were by divine institution and apostolic succession fathers-in-God 'though unworthy'. They extolled the sacraments above the Articles of Religion and taught

---

[1] This was demonstrated when Hampden, appointed to a Regius Chair by Melbourne although his views offended High churchmen of all varieties, and Evangelicals as well, was promoted to the see of Hereford by Russell.

[2] It was Brougham, as Lord Chancellor, who procured the establishment of a special committee of the Privy Council to replace the former delegates *ad hoc* as the supreme court of appeal from the Church courts. There was little criticism at the time, for it was not foreseen that cases of spiritual and doctrinal import would come up to it. But in 1850 its decision that the Bishop of Exeter had no right to refuse to induct Mr Gorham to Bramford Speke although he deemed his views on baptism heretical, showed that the committee, though professing only to construe the Articles of Religion and the liturgy, would in fact determine that certain doctrines were or were not compatible with them and thereby, in effect, make rulings on matters of faith.

[3] Since the early eighteenth century the Convocations of Canterbury and York had not been allowed to meet for business. After the Gorham judgement, Church opinion, while admitting that they could not be summoned or pass or enforce canons save by royal licence, successfully asserted their right to *discuss* any matter and pass any resolutions they pleased. In the Catholic view they were provincial Synods and, in the absence of a General Council, the supreme legislature of the Church.

THIS IS THE BOY WHO CHALKED UP "NO POPERY!"—AND THEN RAN AWAY!!!

that the Prayer Book meant what it said (and that where it equivocated it should be understood in the most Catholic of the possible senses). And by resuming discarded ritual and ceremony they gave visual and oral testimony to their conception of the Blessed Sacrament as a prime channel of grace. All this Russell was to condemn in the Durham Letter as 'the mummeries of superstition'. A famous *Punch* cartoon depicted Russell as the naughty boy who chalked 'No Popery' on Wiseman's wall and ran away. But it was Dr Pusey's wall! A careful reading of the Durham Letter makes it clear that the papal bull and Wiseman's letter merely provided the occasion for an explosion of Erastian, and Protestant, and rationalist wrath against a movement which was a reaction against Erastianism and rationalism and also, though less fundamentally, against many of the special characteristics of the most virile form of contemporary Protestantism, the Evangelical movement.[1]

[1] An Anglican Catholic would not wish to decry the great contribution of the Evangelicals to the restoration of religion and piety, and many Evangelicals welcomed the earlier work of the Tractarians. But the Evangelicals attached little importance to the concept of the Church as a corporate entity divinely commissioned or to the priesthood in its sacramental aspect, and they tended to welcome Erastian means of checking the revival of Catholic doctrines and practices.

THE PUSEYITE MOTH AND ROMAN CANDLE.

"Fly away *Silly Moth.*"

Persecuted in Oxford, Tractarianism had spilled its converts into the parishes, and, *inter alia*, disturbed the calm of Russell's parish, St Paul's, Knightsbridge. The church there was built by W. J. E. Bennett, a Tractarian who became first vicar and enjoyed at the hands of the mob and Lord John a foretaste of the bitter contentions which in 1850–1 beset him in his new foundation of St Barnabas, Pimlico.[1] The movement was to flourish ever more strongly as the Privy Council, and later a new secular court com-

---

[1] Bennett's practices were not extreme; he followed the Prayer Book. But the choir as well as the clergy wore surplices, there were candlesticks and crosses on the altar, and the eastward position was adopted at Communion.

missioned for the purpose by Parliament,[1] persecuted it, while the
Queen and successive ministries withheld patronage from its
adherents. It made converts of some Whigs — in the 'thirties two
Greys,[2] and in the 'fifties the heir of Sir Charles Wood — and
those who embraced it were carried beyond the pale of a Whiggery
whose ethos was so incompatible with it. Sir Charles, a man of
simple piety, could not understand his son's view that a layman
might better serve God as president of the English Church Union
than as a member of Parliament and a gentleman of the Prince of
Wales's Household.[3] The Whigs had always distrusted religious
enthusiasm, the crime for which Whig prelates had driven Wesley,
against his will, from the Church of England long before another
Christ Church enthusiast, Pusey, was born into a great landed
political family. They must, by hereditary impulse, particularly
distrust a movement which boasted that it was *Catholic*. Sir
Charles Wood would not have been surprised, though he would
have been distressed, to see his son engage in negotiations for the
reunion of the Anglican communion with the Roman mother. He,
and his like, were bound to do the Puseyites the injustice of regarding them as Romanists, because they had neither sympathy for
nor capacity to comprehend the premises which made men
embrace large elements of 'Romish' doctrine while remaining
loyal to the Church of England.[4] Their prejudices were confirmed
when a spate of distinguished conversions to Rome indicated that a
Tractarian who saw the Anglican communion corrupted, as he
must feel, by erroneous opinions and lay interference at which the
hierarchy of the Church often connived, might come to prefer the
Roman, corrupted though he had held that also to be. Rome itself
misunderstood the significance of the Oxford Movement, from

[1] 'Lord Penzance's court', established under Disraelian legislation. This Whig
judge, who declined to qualify as an ecclesiastical judge under canon law, sent
priests to prison for contempt of his orders.
[2] Canon the Hon. John Grey, rector of Houghton-le-Spring, and Canon the
Hon. Francis Richard Grey, rector of Morpeth, sons of the Prime Minister and
brothers of Russell's Colonial Secretary and of Lady Mary Wood, wife of Sir
Charles. Wood's brother, Samuel, who died in 1843, was 'a layman of saintly
life, whose early death was deeply mourned by Pusey and Newman'.
[3] Lockhart's *Halifax*, Vol. I, pp. 143–52.
[4] Vide Wood's letter to his son (*Lockhart*, pp. 130–2, 19th February, 1867) —
'. . . The Ritualists seem to me to have arrived at opinions which have in the case
of the Roman Church progressed into grievous errors; I believe them to have
departed from what the Church of England holds to have been the early doctrine
of the Church, and now holds as her own; and I cannot but see the gradual process of Development going on amongst them. Remember where the Roman
Catholics have pushed their Development. . . .'

which it derived much benefit, and was encouraged to believe that England might be restored to its bosom. Russell and his colleagues were indignant at 'an assumption of power . . . a pretension of supremacy over the realm of England', for that, according to the Durham Letter, was what the bull involved. 'It is high time to resist the encroachments of Rome and to let his Holiness know that we are still Protestants,' wrote Clarendon.[1] But they were not really alarmed by the papal 'aggression'. 'The liberty of Protestantism has been enjoyed too long in England to allow of any successful attempt to impose a foreign yoke upon our minds and consciences.' The danger was 'within the gates, from the unworthy sons of the Church of England' herself, the clergy who were leading their flocks 'step by step to the very verge of the precipice'. It was on their account that Russell called on the nation to declare with him reverence for the glorious principles and immortal martyrs of the Reformation and its scorn for 'the laborious endeavours which are now making to confine the intellect and enslave the soul'.

If the Durham Letter is read in the context of the 'Whig religion' as expounded by Lady Russell and the Duke of Somerset, its vehemence becomes at once intelligible. The passion is the passion of the Liberal against the tyrant; the intolerance is the intolerance of the apostle of enlightenment and tolerance when confronted with what he indentifies as intolerant obscurantism. 'The most complete toleration must be expressed over and over again *usque ad nauseam*', wrote Clarendon, 'for the opposition [to the bull] should be of a purely liberal character, and the only standard to be raised should be that of the Reformation.'[2] But the wave of popular demonstrations against Rome and Oxford, which the Durham Letter raised to a flood, did not satisfy this test. Few politicians in 1851 were brave enough to oppose outright the Ecclesiastical Titles Bill, which none of them was subsequently so foolish as to try to enforce. All Russell's colleagues, whether old-fashioned sceptics like Lansdowne and Palmerston, Presbyterians like Minto or Fox Maule, Evangelicals like George Grey, pious undogmatical conformists like Charles Wood or amoral scoundrels like Clanricarde, shared his prejudices against Roman 'aggression' and 'Romish' Tractarianism. But Russell had acted without consulting them, and they thought the Letter precipitate and unwise,

[1] *Clarendon*, Vol. I, p. 314, 29th October, 1850, to Cornewall Lewis.
[2] *Clarendon*, Vol. I, p. 315, 23rd October, 1850, to Reeve.

Q

SAUCY JACK RUSSELL; OR, WHO'S TO TURN HIM OUT?

likely to give rise to all manner of mischief, which would not speedily be undone. Among the mischief they may not have counted the increased difficulty of negotiation with the Peelites, for most of them in their hearts did not yet admit that this was necessary or even desirable, unless the Peelites could be absorbed, as the Canningites had been, and this was doubtful. But Russell soon became aware that the Letter, and the Bill, were serious impediments to common action with the Peelites.

Aberdeen was a Presbyterian, but deplored the vigour of his co-religionists' feeling against Rome. Graham's reactions were primarily political; the policy of the Bill was not compatible with the policy which had passed the Bequests Act and the Maynooth Grant, to which he was resolved to adhere even though it meant that he must find a new seat.[1] But the leading Peelites of the younger generation were nearly all inclined to the Tractarians, whom Whiggery branded 'unworthy sons of the Church of England'. Gladstone and Lincoln, indeed, had lately been discussing, whether, in view of Privy Council 'aggression' in the case of Mr Gorham, it might not be necessary to envisage the Church having to demand disestablishment in order to secure its spiritual autonomy.[2] The Durham Letter repelled from association with the Whigs men who, in any case, despite the frustration of their ambitions as a result of their detachment from the two major party groupings, were, as yet, not even in principle ready for union with the Whigs. And so, for the moment, the Whigs must return to office, unreinforced, simply in default of any alternative ministry. They came back, Campbell was 'grieved to say', exciting 'the contempt of their friends and the compassion of their opponents'.[3] It was clear even to some of themselves that Whiggery was not enough and that, if they had a future, it lay in participation with men of other political stock in governments which would not call themselves Whig.

[1] Parker's *Graham*, Vol. II, pp. 124–35; Stanmore's *Herbert*, Vol. I, p. 133. Lord de Grey, the patron of Ripon, informed Graham that his support would be withdrawn at the next election in the borough.

[2] *Newcastle*, Vol. I, pp. 91–2, 19th May, 1850. Lincoln's letter from Mount Carmel to Gladstone.

[3] Campbell, Vol. II, p. 289.

CHAPTER X

Coalition 1852-5

The Whig monopoly of office, conceived in 1831 of a mésalliance with the Radicals, ailing since 1834, stricken in 1841, had received a new lease of life in 1846. But it did not thrive, and by 1851 the Palace was preparing for the obsequies.

Prince Albert desired to put the Whigs and Peelites in double harness. There had been many predictions, in and since 1846, of Whig-Peelite amalgamation. But these were over-optimistic. A great many of the Peelites, even some in the first rank, desired the reunion of the Conservative party, if only Protection could be disposed of. This was still Gladstone's hope in 1852, and it was doomed, in the last resort, only by Stanley's refusal to abandon the defeated policy until after another general election. This refusal was deplored by Disraeli, but the brilliant Jew was himself a formidable obstacle to reunion. He professed to be willing to take a subordinate place in the highest counsels of a reunited party, but the leading Peelites could not forgive his merciless, and memorable, attacks on Peel. Nevertheless, by 1850 hardly a Peelite had come to be regarded as a Liberal, and some Peelites had drifted back into Tory ranks. Peel himself vetoed all negotiations with the Protectionists, and all 'compensations' which would make them fruitful. He also refused to form a party, or to allow anyone else to organise one under his name. It was his policy to keep Russell in office, and to hold himself available to advise ministers when they desired assistance — as increasingly they did. But he refused to countenance any negotiations with them, and the majority of his followers would have been very displeased if he had done so.[1] Their attitude was summed up by Sir John Young, in his last effort during Peel's lifetime to secure the organisation of the Peelites.[2] He told Peel that the men who held the balance in the

[1] Professor Gash treats of Peel's attitude in 'Peel and the Party System' (*Tr. R. Hist. Soc.*, 5th Series, 1, 47) and Dr Connacher of his relations with his colleagues in 'Peel and the Peelites 1846-50' (*E.H.R.*, July 1958).

[2] Young had been Chief Whip when Peel was in Office. He had been prevented by Peel from organising the Peelites as a party in 1847.

House, Conservatives who favoured Free Trade, had 'no sympathies with and no confidence in the present Government. They
are with you, not with Lord J. Russell . . . they will not make
sacrifices and risk their seats night after night and year after year for
those whom they cannot help regarding as political opponents . . .
support will no doubt be withheld and without such support the
Whigs have no command of a majority'. He also said that thirty
Radicals were rumoured to desire the defeat of the ministry and a
dissolution of Parliament. His conclusion was that the Whigs were
so weak that only Peel, by raising a standard to which Young
believed a quarter of the House would rally, could prevent a
Protectionist government and 'secure fair play for your Commercial policy for some years to come'.[1]

The Whigs were certainly so weak that the death of Peel later
in 1850 was a serious blow to them. For it loosened the restraints
upon 'those who are usually termed your [i.e. Peel's] friends'.[1] Few
of these had faced the prospect of union with the Whigs. Graham,
indeed, Peel's closest confidant, was already looking to the resumption of political alliance with former Whig colleagues (*pace*
Palmerston). But he did not claim to lead the Peelites, or to be
representative of them. The only other leading Peelite who from
the first had closed his mind to all reunion with the Tories who
had 'deserted' Peel was Lord Lincoln, who in 1851 succeeded as
Duke of Newcastle. But he was distinguished for his 'equal' hatred
of Protectionists and Whigs. His central position between the
parties was to the left of that of the main body of the Peelites, more
truly represented by Gladstone. The resignation of Russell early
in 1851 showed that the principal Peelites would not join Stanley
till the ghost of Protection was authoritatively exorcised from the
Carlton Club, but also that they were not ready to join hands with
Russell. These negotiations between Russell and the Peelites
Aberdeen and Graham would probably have been abortive even if
the Titles Bill had not obtruded. The Peelite ex-ministers were not
psychologically prepared for the final abandonment of Conservatism, although their two negotiators found few matters of
political principle dividing them from the Whigs. On their side,
the Whigs were impelled to negotiate only by a royal initiative
taken in the context of their own desperate weakness. The pour-
parlers strengthened Whig suspicion of the Peelites. Whig

[1] Add MSS 40603 (Peel Papers), fs. 91-6, 22nd February, 1850.

simultaneously resented the Peelite refusal to come to their aid
and rejoiced that they were left on their own. When Russell, on
resuming office, a prime minister by default, told his colleagues
that new approaches to the Peelites might be made when the Titles
Bill was disposed of, they answered that they did not mean to be
warming pans.[1] They could not help sensing the potential bargaining power of the Peelites, which was due to their administrative
experience, the reflected glory of Peel's reputation, and the lack
of any party majority in the House of Commons. This power was
not yet fully deployed, but only because so few of the Peelite *élite*
had yet acknowledged freedom to choose between Tory alliance
and Whig alliance.[2] The fact that negotiations had taken place,
however, was calculated to incline Peelite minds, if not Peelite
hearts, to the idea of a junction which even Lord Stanley had
suggested as the natural solution to the instability of party government.[3] And Russell too, if not all his colleagues, had admitted that
'Coalition sooner or later with the Peel Party . . . appears the most
natural' of three courses — more natural than admitting to office
some of the 'Radical supporters' of the Whigs or seeking Tory aid.
'The present Ministers', he said, were 'agreed with the adherents
of Sir Robert Peel on Free Trade, and on the policy which has
regulated our finances of late years. The difference between them
is of a temporary nature.'[4] In the knowledge, however, that 'the
Whig party in the House of Commons would not be cordial
supporters of the junction', Russell carried on for nearly a year
without reopening negotiations with Aberdeen, although he made
approaches to other Peelites individually.[5] Even Graham declined
to join the ministry. The others were determined to avoid piecemeal absorption, remembering, no doubt, the ease with which the
Whigs had assimilated the Canningites. The Queen shrewdly
inquired whether these offers were made simply in order that it

[1] *Queen's Letters*, 1st Series, Vol. II, p. 376, Albert's memo. on Russell's
interview, 3rd March, 1851. Earl Grey, Wood and Baring are cited as expressing
this view.
[2] There was also the point that Peelite dislike of the Titles Bill made the group
temporarily unpopular, a point which Aberdeen and Graham made to the Queen,
25th February, 1851, ibid., p. 361.
[3] ibid., pp. 350–1.
[4] ibid, p. 378, 3rd March, 1851.
[5] Graham was offered a cabinet post January, 1849, September 1851, January,
1852 (see Parker, Vol. II, pp. 72–5, 132–5, 150 ff.); Newcastle was offered Ireland,
December, 1851 (*Newcastle*, pp. 108–11); Cardwell was approached at the same
time (Parker, p. 151); the Duke of Argyll also received an offer (*Argyll*, I, p. 342).

might be known that they had been made. She told Russell squarely that he was unlikely to effect the *absorption* of the Peelites into the Whig government, though she believed (a little prematurely) that they were 'quite ready' for a *fusion*. Fusion would mean the treatment of the Peelites as a political party, and the resultant party and government could not be emphatically Whig.[1]

Coalition, if inescapable, would come upon the Whigs as a judgement, a verdict that they were unable to reign alone and that the high hopes engendered in 1831-2 and revived in 1845-6 could not be fulfilled. Realists knew that Whiggery was more likely to submit to this verdict when out of office, to get back to office. And that was how coalition came in December 1852, by which time all the cards were in the hands of the Peelites. Tory gains had given the Derby administration more seats than all the other groups in the House together without the Peelites. It was, moreover, clearer than ever that Radicals and Irish and 'independent Liberals' looked for something other than a mere Whig administration. And to crown all, the Whigs were divided. They were divided between those who did not want Russell to be prime minister, those who (whether they wanted him or not) saw that it was impossible that he should be, and those who could not understand this simple fact. This friction, and threatened fission, within Whiggery was due partly to the recognition of how Peelites, Radicals and Irish regarded Lord John, and partly to Whig dislike of his insistence on further parliamentary reform. Russell's repudiation of 'finality' in 1849 seems to have been, like his concession on the ballot in 1839, a bid to appease the Radicals. His colleagues, once again taken by surprise, 'looked grave' when he suggested a Reform Bill for 1850.[2] Their obstruction prevented the presentation of proposals till 1852. Lansdowne, assisted by Palmerston, led the resistance in cabinet, and only withdrew his resignation when Russell saddled him squarely with responsibility for the fate of the ministry. His known objections in any case sealed the Bill's fate.[3] The Radicals, who had not taken at its face value Russell's ill-concealed vexation at the delay,[4] did not know whether to praise

---

[1] *Queen's Letters*, op. cit., pp. 434-5, 15th January, 1852.
[2] Walpole's Russell, Vol. II, p. 102.
[3] For Lansdowne's resistance see *Walpole*, II, pp. 129-30.
[4] Hume insisted on dividing the House on Locke King's motion, February 1851, despite Russell's promise (made without telling the cabinet) of a Government bill in 1852.

the measure as better than nothing or attack it as worse. A few Whigs lavished upon it an extravagant and pharisaical praise.[1] But the only question was whether the Bill would die before the Government or the Government before the Bill. Palmerston, just dismissed for his unauthorised recognition of the *coup d'état* in France,[2] provided the answer. He had what he called 'his tit-for-tat' with Russell, inducing the House to refuse the Prime Minister leave to bring in the Militia Bill. Stanley, who had just become Earl of Derby, formed an administration. Russell, in opposition, was made aware that Whigs who wished to avoid Reform were looking hopefully towards Lansdowne. He muttered of 'intrigue'. Clarendon, personally favourable to Russell, protested that a man could think Russell unsuited to be prime minister at that particular juncture without being an intriguer.[3] Peelites too felt there was 'an intrigue . . . for the salvation of the old system of Whig Cliquery'[4] or a more sinister design for a Lansdowne-Palmerston administration drawing support from Whigs, Peelites and Tories, but not all of any of the three groups.[5]

It may be that a project, nurtured behind the back of the accredited Whig leader, for the selective union of men of three political communions, to his exclusion, deserved to be stigmatised as an 'intrigue', although its object would have been to sustain, substantially unchanged, the Reform settlement of 1832, to which the majority of parliamentarians were loyal and against which there was no active public agitation. But as a *substitute* for a Tory administration such an enterprise was crude and impracticable.[6] The same result could be achieved more easily by the adhesion of Palmerston and some of the Peelite leaders to Derby. If the Tories had accepted *before* the general election Herbert's invitation to 'cross over without a taunt or a reproach' from Protectionist ground,[7] it is possible that Derby might have found

[1] H. of C., 9th February, 1852. Speeches of P. H. Howard, E. B. Roche, Lord Harry Vane.
[2] See *infra*, Ch. XI.
[3] *Clarendon*, I, p. 346, 1st September, 1852.
[4] Add. MSS 43197, 21st August, Newcastle to Aberdeen, fs. 27ff. (cf. fs. 37ff., 4th September).
[5] Parker, Vol. II, pp. 172–3, Graham's letters of 5th–11th August. Graham thought this project would exclude Russell and himself; that its purpose was to resist democracy; and that its only effect would be to assure and hasten the progress it was intended to avert.
[6] ibid., p. 172, Graham to Aberdeen, 5th August called it 'crude' and reported the Duke of Bedford (6th) as saying it was bound to fail.
[7] Stanmore's *Herbert*, p. 148, 22nd March.

himself presiding over a triumvirate of Palmerston, Gladstone and
Disraeli, with a Commons majority at his back.[1] But it was not
until the new Parliament met that Protection was ceremonially
interred in the grave of lost causes by a vote of 468 to 53 which
implicated the majority of the Tories in the admission that 'the
principle of unrestricted competition' should be the future rule.[2]
And in the meantime the election campaign had deepened the cleft
between Tories and Peelites. Only in their hostility to Peelites, said
Aberdeen, were the Tories agreed; they did not fight as a party for
Protection, and they exploited religious bigotry in constituencies
where they thought it would pay. The Peelites stigmatised such
conduct as very unprincipled.[3] Even Gladstone and Herbert
recoiled from the defiling pitch of Derbyism, and Aberdeen and
Newcastle put the thought of Tory reunion finally behind them,[4]
and so when Russell began a correspondence with Aberdeen on
21st July, the old colleague of Peel felt 'the time is come when we
ought to act in cordial concert with Lord John and the Whigs'.[5]
Free trade was now safe; differences in education and Church
questions were 'perhaps theoretical rather than practical (it is to be
hoped, that after the lesson of last year, that we shall have nothing
to apprehend from any hostile interference on the part of the Whigs
with religious freedom)'; he himself did not object to parliamentary reform.

The main plot of the drama of 1852 has never been better
summarised than by the Duke of Argyll:[6]

> The year 1852 was a highly critical one among Parliamentary
> parties, and yet a year singularly destitute of the nobler interests which
> ought to belong to them ... The moment it became certain that all

[1] Aberdeen, Canning, Gladstone and Goulburn all refused Derby's invitation
to join a Tory government early in 1851. Palmerston refused a similar invitation
in February, 1852. On 25th November, 1852, after the abandonment of Protetc-
tion, the Queen authorised Derby to try for the Peelites and Palmerston, but the
effort was abortive.

[2] Villiers' wording, which declared that Repeal was 'just, wise and beneficent'
was abandoned by 336 to 256 in favour of a milder alternative, of Peelite origin,
moved by Palmerston and accepted by Disraeli.

[3] Add. MSS 43197, 25th July, Aberdeen to Newcastle (cf. *Queen's Letters*
p. 519, Aberdeen's conversation of 28th Dec.); ibid., f.11, Newcastle to Aberdeen, 2nd August; Parker, p. 167, Graham to Russell, *re* Gladstone and Herbert,
22nd July.

[4] *Queen's Letters*, p. 519, 28th December. Newcastle wrote that he could not
join Derby without a sense of moral and political degradation, Add. MSS 43197,
f. 11, 2nd August.

[5] Add. MSS 43197, 25th July, to Newcastle.

[6] *Autobiography and Memoirs*, Vol. I, p. 360-3.

danger of a return to Protection was a thing of the past, there remained nothing but personal feelings and the associations of long antagonism to prevent all the Free Trade sections from uniting to form a new and a strong Government. The whole year was spent in attempts, by endless interviews and correspondence, to realize this aspiration, which, indeed, was the strong and just desire of the people. But personal and party feelings, intensified by hereditary traditions, ran so high that, till the close of the year, little or no progress was made. There were two or three dominant facts in the situation. The first was that the leadership of Lord John Russell had become invincibly distasteful to everybody except a small personal and family clique. The second was that Lord John Russell could not be got to see this. . . . On the other hand . . . there was no one of [the Peelite party] entitled as a matter of course to step into the shoes of their great leader. . . . During the course of 1852 there were two men . . . towards whom many eyes were directed with a wandering hope. . . . Lansdowne . . . [and] the Earl of Aberdeen. . . .

That Russell could not be prime minister at this juncture was evident not only to Peelites and Palmerston, but also to men personally favourable to Lord John, such as his brother, Bedford, and Clarendon, and to men trained to keep their thumb on the Liberal pulse — Ellice and Tufnell.[1] Newcastle wrote — 'In my opinion Lord John Russell cannot undertake it with the smallest prospect of success. . . . Many of Lord John's own *warm* and *sincere* friends have told me that it could not be done. Many of ours have said they will go over to Lord Derby if we take office under him. The English Radicals deprecate his being again Prime Minister because they say, whoever may join him, his being so would stamp his Government as a *Whig* Administration. The Irishmen . . . vow they will pursue to the death any Government of which Lord John is the Head.'[2] Newcastle had always been very hostile to Russell. He resented the ambition which Russell was (not unnaturally) reputed to share with Derby, 'to extirpate the Peelites',[3] and had very high-flown notions of an entirely new party gathering round the Peelite *élite* and dominating the state, perhaps with the Duke of Newcastle as prime minister.[4] He was determined that if this was not possible, Aberdeen should lead the projected

[1] *Re* Tufnell (a protégé of Lansdowne) see Parker's *Graham*, pp. 169–70 (early Aug.) and Ellice see Fitzmaurice's *Granville*, Vol. 1, p. 80.
[2] Add. MSS 43197, 2nd August, to Aberdeen.
[3] *Newcastle*, p. 113 (8th March, 1852) cf. pp. 104–5.
[1]. M SS 44778, fs. 30ff. (Gladstone Memo., 25th March).

coalition.¹ His comment on Russell's position was merely an expansion of Aberdeen's own analysis.² The same verdict was conveyed, in less hostile terms, to Russell himself by Clarendon, in seeking to convince him that, although Lansdowne's name was used by the 'intriguers', the proposition that Lansdowne, and not Lord John, should lead a coalition could be made by people well inclined to Russell who saw that he could not be prime minister and that some one else would have to be found. Clarendon wrote:³

... it is quite impossible for any man to be First Minister of this country during six not ordinary but critical years without making himself enemies; it is equally impossible, too, that during that period some errors should not have been committed and remembered. In the Liberal party there are wide differences of opinion. ... Some people think you disposed to go too far; others think you stop short of the mark; the Roman Catholics as a body are still bitter about the Durham letter; many Protestants think that letter was not boldly acted upon; the ambition of many is disappointed; some complain about the distribution of patronage; others consider they have met with discourtesy, etc; and each one of these knots of complainants becomes a centre of fresh discontent, which swells for want of any-thing of countervailing character. Now all this, be it just or unjust, is sufficient to account for the existing state of feeling without explaining it by intrigue. ...

'All this' was gall and wormwood to Russell. If he half-admitted the indictment, he was not convinced that anybody else stood a better chance of uniting Whigs and Peelites. 'I shall be quite ready out of office to support a Liberal Ministry, if it is found, as may be the case, that the Radicals and Irish members would be gratified by my exclusion,' he wrote, but he could not consent to lead the Commons under a peer as prime minister — 'the Radicals, the Irish Brigade and some of the Whigs would prefer anyone else to me; so that my personal degradation would be a sacrifice to no purpose'.⁴ Graham thought this decisive — 'it is not possible to press on a gentleman what beforehand he declares to be "personal

¹ He pointed him out as the man, rather than Lansdowne, in his letter of 2nd August (Add. MSS 43197, fs. 11ff.) and 3rd (ibid. 19 ff.). Aberdeen disclaimed ambition (ibid., 25th July and 12th Aug.); he said he might be willing to be prime minister if Russell would join; otherwise perhaps the Duke might be.
² ibid., 25th July, 1852.
³ 31st August, reproduced in Walpole, Vol. II, pp. 152–3.
⁴ See 21st July, to Aberdeen, ibid., p. 155 and 23rd July, to Graham (Parker, p. 168).

degradation" '.[1] Russell had admitted the difficulties in the way of his leading a coalition, but only to make it impossible for anyone else on the Liberal side to form a majority administration. More than a promise of support from Russell for a government headed by a peer was needed; his participation was essential. As Palmerston said, if Russell's 'title by *conquête*' had been somewhat shaken, he was the leader of the Whigs '*par droit de naissance* . . . he cannot be dealt with as if he were not'.[2]

It was irritating enough to Russell to find his personal position so weak. He was equally offended as the guardian of the 'honour' and pretensions of Whiggery. For his correspondence with Aberdeen, who sent everything to Newcastle, revealed that the Peelites had their own brand of arrogance, not inferior to the Whigs' own. They displayed an assumption of superiority, a conviction that Peel had set the mark of divinity upon certain favoured mortals, and that Destiny would soon beckon them to save the nation. Peel's policy of keeping them in suspense and isolation had nourished this Messianic strain in Peelite thinking, of which the Duke of Newcastle was the incarnation. Although the great problem to be surmounted was the reluctance of Russell to assist any combination of which he was not the head, Newcastle wrote, for the eye of the Whig leader, a letter which put with wounding bluntness the point about 'fusion', as opposed to 'absorption' which the Queen had made at the beginning of the year. The Duke said that 'those who *call themselves Whigs* [were] as few as the *Peelites* in the present Parliament, the great numerical loss having fallen upon them'. This ignored the elaborate hierarchical establishment known as Whiggery, whose direct representation in the House of Commons was only a feeble reflection of its political status, as though it had no existence or importance. And it ignored the historic position of the Whigs as the leaders of the Liberal host, weakened though this position now was. The Duke suggested that the term 'Whig', for two hundred years so forward in many a stern (and many a sham) political battle, should be jettisoned, not because names were *un*important, but because they were important, and the term had become a handicap to those who used it and those proposing to associate with them. The most outrageous part of the letter read:[3]

---

[1] Parker, p. 169, Graham to Aberdeen.
[2] Ashley's *Palmerston*, Vol. II, p. 234, 23rd May, to Wm. Cowper.
[3] Add. MSS 43197, f. 19, 3rd August, to Aberdeen.

It strikes me forcibly that with a view to a real fusion of all Liberals in one Party the name of *Whig* as well as *Peelite* should as far as possible be abandoned. In the ears of the public names are things. . . . The change of Party nickname (for as such alone, writing familiarly, I must consider all these appellations) had a very great effect in drawing to Sir Robert Peel's standard many who would never have joined a *Tory* Opposition. It is impossible that Lord John Russell should part without regret from an hereditary designation which he and his Ancestors have done so much to distinguish, but I have a strong conviction that its day of influence is over and whilst it has no longer any features of superiority over other classes of 'Liberals' it has re-miniscences which are unpopular in the Country. Thus, absurd as it seems, I am convinced there are many men in Parliament who would repudiate with indignation 'joining the Whigs' yet who would willingly support a Government of which Ld J. Russell, Ld Clarendon or Sir G. Grey were Members under some other name. . . . If a New Liberal Party is to be constituted (and it is what the Country wants) it must be upon a new basis — not by one Party *joining* another. With this view all old names as well as old jealousies must be abandoned. . . .

After sending this to Russell, Aberdeen admitted that it was rather a strong proceeding to suggest to him, of all men, the expediency of sinking the title of Whig! But were they not all Liberal Conservatives now?[1] (this being the designation of Peelites and some who lived in a hazy no-man's land to the right of Whiggery and the left of the Protectionists). The implied suggestion, that he take the Tamworth Manifesto for his credo, Russell countered very neatly, with the proposition that the Liberal Conservatives should admit that they were Conservative Liberals and call themselves Whigs for short. 'The term Whig has the convenience of expressing in one syllable what Conservative Liberal expresses in seven; and Whiggism, in two syllables, means what Conservative Progress means in six.'[2] If Russell also indulged in recriminations against the Peelites, they were not unprovoked. But the Duke complained of 'a petulance, a spirit of prejudice and injustice, a tone of soreness . . . *a littleness* of mind prevading every line'.[3] As to the name, the Duke was 'ready to refer this

---

[1] To Russell, 16th September, quoted Walpole, Vol. II, p. 156, n. 1.
[2] ibid. If Walpole's terminology is right, the letter of 16th September was a reply to Russell's first riposte, and Russell's remarks about the convenience of the term Whig a reply to the letter of 16th.
[3] Add. MSS 43197, f. 27, 21st August, obviously a comment on Russell's first riposte. It is clear from Newcastle to Aberdeen, f. 37, 4th September that Aberdeen told the Duke he was unduly prejudiced against Russell.

question to our mutual *Whig* friend Mr Ellice, who will tell him Whiggery is a fossil. The Whigs are buried with Mr Fox and "Mr Pitt" (save the Mark!) but alas the spirit of Whig Oligarchical Cliquery, it is too clear, still lives'. Russell, on the other hand, reasoned that 'as the Whig party has always been the party of steady progress, that party can never become extinct till no further progress is required — and that time seems a good way off'.[1]

It is no wonder that in October Herbert could not see that matters had advanced at all during the summer,[2] and that the opinion was growing that the Tories might stay in for some time for want of unity in the Opposition[3] — a possibility that by no means all Whigs deplored.[4] But there had been some productive developments. After a speech which he delivered at Perth at the end of September had been well received even by Newcastle, Russell's morale and good humour rose.[5] He told his father-in-law that he did not feel so strongly that the taking office under a peer would be a degradation. 'As leader in the House of Commons my place would be sufficiently high.'[6] Clarendon's epistles may well have had some influence, and the Duke of Bedford had told Russell it was impossible for Palmerston to serve under him. By 22nd October Russell had 'distinctly' told Lansdowne that he would be prepared to take office in any ministry at the head of which the Marquess consented to be placed.[7]

The obstacle to this solution was the Marquess — old and ill and semi-retired, willing to be prime minister only if assured of a majority of a hundred (which was out of the question).[8] Palmerston thought that if the Queen appealed to him he would give way.[9]

---

[1] Barrington's *Servant of All*, Vol. I, p. 208, Russell to Jas. Wilson, 14th July.

[2] Add. MSS 43197, Herbert to Aberdeen, 22nd October, fs. 101 ff.

[3] ibid. and Add. MSS 43197, f. 41, Newcastle, 30th September, 'everybody now says let Disraeli cut his fingers first . . .'. cf. ibid., f. 101, Herbert, 22nd Oct.

[4] e.g. Fitzwilliam and Palmerston—see Ashley's *Palmerston*, Vol. II, pp. 251–2, late September. Tory government insulated them against genuine Parliamentary Reform.

[5] Add. MSS 43197, f., 41, 30th September, Newcastle to Aberdeen — '. . . Russell's good-humoured letter. . . .' '. . . I think his Perth speech very judicious.' Russell said at Perth that Whiggism meant 'Conservative Progress' (on which Aberdeen had insisted in his letter of 16th September as the motto of coalition).

[6] To Minto, 3rd October, quoted by Walpole, p. 158, n. 1.

[7] Lansdowne to Palmerston, 22nd October, quoted ibid., pp. 158–9.

[8] Add. MSS 43197, f .101, Herbert to Aberdeen, 22nd October.

[9] Ashley's *Palmerston*, p. 255, to Wm. Cowper, 17th November.

The Peelites, however, were not anxious to serve under him,[1] and when the Derby administration fell and the Queen sent for Lansdowne and Aberdeen jointly, the Marquess pleaded his inability, through gout, to go to Osborne, and sent off Aberdeen to receive the commission.[2] A couple of days before the vote in which Gladstone's motion against Disraeli's budget was carried by a majority of nineteen, Bedford and Clarendon acted as brokers in a meeting at Woburn between Russell and Aberdeen. Russell said he thought the Queen should send for Lansdowne and Aberdeen; Clarendon thought so too, and Bedford, who did not tell his brother that he was taking soundings on behalf of the Queen, advised Her Majesty accordingly.[3] Aberdeen, before going to Osborne, saw Lansdowne and the principal Peelites and, meeting Russell in the park, gained the impression that Lord John would act under him as Foreign Secretary and Leader of the House of Commons.[4]

Lansdowne's advice to the Queen was that she should desire Russell and Aberdeen 'to determine what arrangement of persons and situations would be best with the double view of official aptitude and of selecting those whose appointments would be most gratifying to the feeling of the friends and supporters of both parties'.[5] But Graham, who knew the Whigs of old, and being detached from the Peelites[6] was about to spend the most uncomfortable week of his life[7] in the midst of one of the most unabashed place-hunting rat races since the eighteenth century, thought it essential that there should be no joint commission of Aberdeen and Russell,[8] and the latter was informed by the Queen that she had

[1] Aberdeen told the Queen (*Letters*, p. 503), 19th December, that they would not have served under Lansdowne.

[2] *Queen's Letters*, pp. 502-3.

[3] Greville's account of this is substantially confirmed by Walpole, p. 160, and Barrington, op. cit., pp. 214-15 (citing Greville).

[4] *Queen's Letters*, p. 503; the account of the meeting in the park was given by Herbert to Graham (Parker, pp. 192-3).

[5] Quoted, Walpole, p. 160.

[6] Graham's agreement to stand at Carlisle in harness with a Radical and his speech there had led to his unofficial excommunication by the other Peelites (Stanmore's *Herbert*, pp. 149-51, Morley's *Gladstone*, pp. 420-1, Parker's *Graham*, p. 167, 179—82, where Aberdeen says 'You may fall back upon Whiggism, in which you were bred, but I was bred at the feet of Gamaliel. . . .'). But the Whigs disliked Graham's refusal to attend Russell's pre-session political dinner (Parker, 183-5).

[7] Parker, p. 202, 28th December, 1852.

[8] ibid., p. 190, 18th December. Aberdeen thoroughly agreed (*Queen's Letters*, p. 503).

charged Aberdeen with the duty of forming an administration.[1] It soon appeared that Aberdeen's conception of his task was a characteristically Peelite one. 'Bred at the feet of Gamaliel . . . he must always regard Mr Pitt as the first of statesmen,'[2] and he clearly saw it as his mission to form a Peel-like government dominated by Peelites. It was most important, he told the Queen, that the new government should be 'not a revival of the old Whig Cabinet with an addition of some Peelites' but '*a Liberal Conservative government in the sense of that of Sir Robert Peel*'.[3] It was evident that he did not think much of the 'fitness' of anybody but Peelites. On 22nd December his cabinet list embraced eight Peelites,[4] six Whigs[5] and Palmerston. 'Of 330 members of the House of Commons 270 are whig and radical . . . thirty are Peelites. To this party of thirty you propose to give seven seats in the cabinet, to the whigs and radicals five, to Lord Palmerston one,' protested Russell.[6] Peelites sometimes inflated the 'thirty' as far as fifty, and deflated the 270 to 250.[7] But there were only thirty Peelites among the 307 who brought down the Derby government.[8] Aberdeen's cabinet as finally constituted consisted of six Peelites, five Whigs, Palmerston and the Radical Sir William Molesworth. Sir George Grey was excluded in favour of a Peelite duke aged thirty, who was to take up the cudgels against Derby in the Lords.[9] Gladstone was able to produce a list of the political administration showing fifteen in a column headed by Aberdeen and nineteen in a column headed by Lansdowne, and if two of the former were not Peelites, seven of the latter were not pure Whigs.[10] Widening the survey a little to include Household officials, we find

[1] Quoted Walpole, p. 161, 19th December. Reply *Queen's Letters*, pp. 505–6.
[2] See n. 6, p. 239.　　　　　　[3] *Queen's Letters*, p. 503, 19th December.
[4] ibid., pp. 510–12. Peelites — Aberdeen, Newcastle, Argyll, Graham, Herbert, Gladstone, Cardwell, Canning. The two last had to be left out of the cabinet.
[5] Cranworth, Russell, Wood, Granville, Clarendon, Baring. The last was not included, nor Clarendon for a month or two. No doubt it was hoped that Lansdowne would consent to join, as he did, but it was thought Granville might go to Ireland, so it seems fair to say 'six Whigs'.
[6] Quoted Morley's *Gladstone*, Vol. 1, p. 446.
[7] '50' (Aberdeen to Queen, *Letters*, p. 516), '40' (Gladstone, quoted Morley, p. 448), '30' *Argyll*, p. 374 but apparently quoting Russell). The Tory Malmesbury said 46 before the vote on the budget (*Memoirs*, p. 286) and 30 afterwards (p. 287) and Derby accepted the latter number (*Queen's Letters*, p. 501).
[8] I cannot by any manner of means make it more than 32 or 33, *D.G.S.*
[9] *Argyll*, p. 371. When he told Aberdeen Canning had a better claim, Aberdeen answered that the Duke's place (the Privy Seal) had been settled from the first (p. 374).
[10] Add. MSS 44745f65

that in the whole administration eight Peelite peers and twelve Peelite M.P.s found places, but only sixteen of forty-six holders of political offices in the last months of the Russell government, and by no means all of these were Whigs.[1] Not one of the men new to office was out of the Whig top drawer. There were even more Peelite *aristocrats* in office than Whig ones. Whigs were given charge of only two of the great departments of state — the Foreign Office and the Board of Control, while the Peelites had the Treasury, War and Colonies, the Admiralty, and the Secretary-ship at War as well as, outside the cabinet, the Board of Trade and the Post Office. Palmerston took the Home Office and Molesworth Works.

The Whig discomfiture was not due to lack of effort. During the negotiations, the Whigs were attacked as superlatively grasping, and those describing the proceedings have naturally resorted to the language of appetite. 'The cake is too small,' said Disraeli. Morley was reminded of the carp at Fontainebleau.[2] Graham, pestered from all sides, complained that 'the Whigs disregarded fitness for the public service altogether. They fought for their men as parti-sans, and all other considerations, as well as consequences, were disregarded'.[3] They went back on their engagements. At first Russell insisted that the Lord Chancellor be a Whig, and that Wood and Baring should be in the cabinet.[4] He gained two of these three points, and the exclusion of two Peelite heads of departments from the cabinet.[5] But on Christmas Eve he 'sent in such a list of persons whom he required in the Cabinet' (Baring again and, for the first time — and this is a reproach to Russell — George Grey) . . . 'that having been very yielding hitherto, Lord Aberdeen was obliged to be peremptory in his refusal'.[6] 'It became necessary to make a stand', wrote Graham, 'and to bring the Whigs to their ultimatum.' But Granville's place in the cabinet was rendered secure, and Lansdowne included. The Marquess brought Russell to an 'unwilling assent'.[7] On 25th Aberdeen was at last able to take the Queen the final list. But there was still trouble about the Irish places, which were not settled until 28th. The Peelites, strong in

---

[1] These Peelites do not include Lord Hardinge, who had succeeded Welling-ton as Commander-in-Chief.
[2] Morley's *Gladstone*, Vol. I, p. 446.   [3] Parker, p. 200, 28th December.
[4] The Peelites had wanted the Tory Lord St Leonards to retain the Woolsack. See *Queen's Letters*, pp. 510, 512.
[5] Cardwell and Canning.   [6] *Queen's Letters*, p. 516, 25th December.
[7] Parker, p. 198, 24th December.

the approval of the Pope's Brass Band (three members of which struck official oil)[1] insisted that the old Whig policy of conciliation in Ireland required the exclusion of Whigs from Dublin Castle. The Peelite Lord St Germans, not the Whig Earl of Carlisle, was to be Viceroy; Peel's former Chief Whip was to be Chief Secretary. The Whigs met a firm refusal when Russell and Clarendon asked that Redington, the Catholic supporter of the Titles Bill, should return to his old office of Under-Secretary,[2] and the only Irish office they gained was the Lord Chancellorship. 'It was of more consequence to conciliate that large part of the Empire than to provide for the Ansons and Pagets.'[3] Such was the disconcerting effect of the Durham Letter and the Titles Bill.

Simultaneously with the battle about the Irish places there was war about the junior offices, in the disposition of which Newcastle assisted Aberdeen.[4] On the evening of Boxing Day Russell and the Whig whip Hayter met Peelite leaders at Aberdeen's residence, Argyll House, and 'finally settled the list of subordinate members of the Government and the Household'. But next day 'the whole arrangement was on the point of being broken off', Wood delivering an ultimatum to that effect. It was only when Graham threatened to tell the House what occurred that Hayter was directed to proceed with the moving of writs for by-elections caused by the appointments of departmental chiefs. But the battle continued into the next day.

The great clan-system called Whiggery, which could have provided enough men blooded in place to form an administration on their own, and abounded in expectants, was now, by and large, disinherited. No Peelite with any good claim was omitted from the cabinet or its threshold, while no room was found for George Grey, Baring, Labouchere, Carlisle, Fox Maule, Minto, Seymour, Clanricarde, Normanby, or for Earl Grey, whose exclusion Russell did not mourn. It seemed that the Peelites had made a successful take-over bid for the Liberal party. There were those, indeed, who professed to see in the coalition a Whig administration. The Tory ex-Peelite, Londonderry, said that Aberdeen had 'harnessed himself to the car of the Whig party',[5] and Sir William Heathcote declined to assist Gladstone's election campaign at Oxford

---

[1] See *supra*, p. 192 n. 1.   [2] Parker, pp.198–200, 24th–28th December.
[3] *Greville*, III, I, p. 26, quoting Graham.
[4] See Newcastle's letter to Wilson, Barrington's *Servant of All*, p. 216.
[5] *Clarendon*, Vol. I, p. 354, 26th December.

University 'on the specific ground of Lord John Russell, Lord
Cranworth and Hayter. He says the head of the Commons and
the disposition of the patronage show that this is to be really a
Whig government...'.[1] But this was all moonshine. Brougham
hit the nail on the head when he remarked 'As for the Whigs, a man
must be very revengeful indeed not to be satisfied with their
present prostration.... A very tiny party has entirely swallowed
up the great Whig party.'[2] And this was Russell's own verdict.
The ministry, he said, was one in which 'he himself holds a subordinate situation, from which nearly all his dearest political
friends are excluded, and which is held by some to extinguish the
party which for eighteen years he has led'.[3]

One has read much criticism (often well-deserved) of Russell's
behaviour just before, and during, and in the years after the formation of the Aberdeen administration, and the weight of criticism
in discussions of the unseemly struggle for places has been against
the Whigs. We read of Russell's vacillations with regard to his own
position — how, for instance, the day after the meeting in the park
he retracted his acceptance of office and returned to his pre-
October stance of 'best support' from outside, which must be
ruinous to Aberdeen's project. We learn that 'consultation with
some of his friends had convinced him that the act of submission
was not consistent with his honour'.[4] There was an affecting
scene in Lansdowne's library where, after the ailing Marquess had
urged the public interest, Macaulay, happening to call (most
opportunely), invoked the newly liberated ghost of the Duke of
Wellington (with shrewd and flattering references to Russell's
speech at Perth). The Queen's government must be carried on.
'Now is the time for you to make a sacrifice,' pleaded the famous
orator — 'your past services and your name give us a right to
expect it.'[5] Russell then agreed to lead the Commons, though
without office. All this was before the Whig leader could have had
much inkling of Aberdeen's proposals, and is clearly a relapse from
the grace he had received in October. But the difficulties which he
subsequently made about offices for his friends are really in a

[1] Iddesleigh MSS (by courtesy of the Earl of Iddesleigh), J. D. Coleridge to
Northcote, 29th December, 1852.
[2] *Clarendon*, p. 357, 1st January, 1853.
[3] *Queen's Letters*, pp. 533-4, 13th February, 1853.
[4] Parker's *Graham*, Vol. II, p. 193, 20th December. *Queen's Letters*, p. 505.
[5] Walpole, Vol. II, pp. 161-2.

different category. He was the leader of Whiggery, and if not all Whigs wanted him for prime minister, even if that were possible, he was, as leader, bound to advance for consideration the claims which he deemed his old colleagues and subordinates to have. One can say this without approving his particular judgement of the merits of any individual. It was very difficult for a Whig to believe that Aberdeen's judgement of fitness was not a biassed one. Nor need we qualify this extenuation of Russell by attaching too much importance to Graham's testimony, which confirms the traditionally unfavourable view of Whig place-hunting. Graham liked Lord John, and welcomed the opportunity of working again with Whigs as well as Peelites, but he did not much care, at any time, for Whig exclusiveness,[1] and he was much pestered by Whigs because he was a middle man between them and the Peelites.[2] He admitted that on 27th December Russell was 'more amenable to reason' than Wood and Hayter.[3] And his diary, at one point, reads 'It is melancholy to see how little fitness for office is regarded *on all sides*' (present writer's italics) 'and how much the public employments are treated as booty to be divided among the successful combatants'.[4] The fault was not all on one side. Aberdeen obviously regarded Russell as a party leader to be negotiated with, although not jointly commissioned, and he clearly did not regard as altogether unreasonable the Whig view that the size of the parliamentary following should be considered, for a royal memorandum of Christmas Day reads 'Now that the Cabinet was formed on a due proportion, he was inclined to let Lord John have his own way pretty much with regard to the minor Offices, considering that he brought 250 followers, and he (Lord Aberdeen) only 50.'[5] It is not *prima facie* evident that effect was given to this 'inclination', though the Prince obviously feared that Russell had been given *carte blanche*, for he wrote on 26th that 'the "Whig party" ought not to be allowed to "deal out places" (in the Household) without the Queen's pleasure being taken'.[6]

Aberdeen's opinion that the cabinet was formed 'on a due proportion' indicates the Prime Minister's belief that the Peelites,

---

[1] Parker, p. 185, 12th November, where Graham says his refusal to go to the Whig political dinner 'has rekindled the old sentiments towards me in the bosom of the Whigs, in which love is not the largest ingredient'.

[2] ibid., p. 199, 27th December, where he says that Wood and Hayter tried 'to shake me individually in my opinion'.

[3] ibid., p. 199.

[4] ibid., pp. 198–9, 25th December.

[5] *Queen's Letters*, p. 516.

[6] ibid., p. 516.

despite their parliamentary weakness, should have half the places. His concession about the minor offices reveals a consciousness that the principle of 'equality' ought not to be carried too far. Whiggery can hardly be blamed if it judged that the principle was carried to the point where Peelites were 'more equal than others'. The Whigs, with a hereditary reputation as place-hunters, were bound to seem unduly appetitive when Whig aspirants were so numerous and so unsuccessful and Peelites had no just ground for complaint. Gladstone made a valid point when he said that Whig selections were not made from the 270, but from a much more restricted circle.[1] The Whigs, he said, forgot this. But the Peelites forgot, in stressing that mere numbers gave no claim, that lack of numbers was not a positive virtue. Earlier in the year, Aberdeen himself had said that it was slightly ridiculous for a score of peers and forty M.P.s to set up as a party.[2] There was much to be said for large Peelite participation. The country, or at least the middle classes, wanted a government that was Liberal and not Whig. Liberal, Irish and even Radical members were looking away from the Whigs and to the Peelites.[3] The Peelites not only held the balance between opposing forces, but could expect to bring to the coalition the parliamentary advantage of a degree of toleration from Derbyites which would not be accorded to a Liberal government in which they were not conspicuous.[4] But in their effort to make it clear that the coalition was no Whig administration, the Peelites may be deemed to have been over-generous to themselves. The diarist Greville thought so — 'they can only hope to keep their places at all by the zealous support of the whole Whig force', he said.[5] For Whigs could hold the balance too! 'As regards the proportion borne to Parliamentary parties, there was much to excuse

---

[1] Add. MSS 44745, draft *cit. supra*.   [2] *Herbert*, Vol. 1, p. 144.
[3] '. . . political differences no longer lie between parties but within parties. The most conservative Liberal and the most liberal Conservative not only are near one another but probably the one of these two parties . . . which retains the Conservative designation is for any practical purposes. . . the more liberal of the two. Indeed, on some great questions, such as for instance Political Economy and Colonial Policy, the Peelites. . . are much more in harmony with the strong or advanced Liberal party than the Whigs' (Gladstone Add. MSS 44745, 12th April, 1855).
[4] Derby would not recommend Aberdeen as prime minister in case 'many of his party' went over to him (*Queen's Letters*, p. 501, 18th December). Russell said that some Conservatives would vote for the Government (ibid., p. 520, 28th December). Gladstone said that the coalition survived because of the support of 'the choice of rare men' of Derby's party (Add. MSS 44745, source cit.).
[5] *Greville*, III, I, p. 27.

the Whigs in the discontent they felt and did not conceal,' says
Argyll.[1] Clarendon, who honestly wished the coalition to succeed,
accused the Peelites of trying to 'kick down the Whig ladder by
which *alone* they have climbed to power', and thought they 'should
have been more self-denying, and have remembered that the best
generals are helpless without troops'.[2]

Gladstone was not justified in saying that the charge that the
Peelites were given an undue share of offices sprang 'entirely from
the lower regions of the Whig party'. Emily Eden recorded that
Wood's wife called 'in the last stage of Grey pee-waw-ishness — a
rigid, despairing peevishness which, in many people, would imply
confirmed bad health with loss of friends and fortune, but with her
meant that all the Greys had not got places'.[3] Carlisle and Clanricarde were very disappointed;[4] when Vernon Smith told Disraeli
that Fitzwilliam wanted to meet him surreptitiously, the Tory
leader asked 'Is he to convert me, or the reverse. Or is he an old
Whig disgusted as V.S. himself?'[5] The gentlemanly Labouchere
thought that Russell had 'sacrificed the honour of his friends'.[6]
These were not the 'lower regions' of Whiggery, and the consciousness that he was thought not to have obtained for the Whigs their
due share of offices and influence,[7] and his belief that this was so
(though it was not for want of trying), fatally reinforced Russell's
discontent at his own position. Physical infirmity — which, if it
did not have a psychological origin, certainly accentuated his defects
of character and deepened his moods of depression — and a wife
who, though a devoted companion and nurse, had neither sense of
humour nor of proportion, conspired to produce a hyper-sensitivity
to slights, real or supposed, upon his personal honour as a politician
and leader. Lady John's family, to which he was absurdly

[1] *Argyll*, Vol. 1, p. 374.
[2] *Clarendon*, Vol. 1, pp. 355–56, 26th December, 1852, to Reeve of the *Times*.
Granville agreed (see *Newcastle*, pp. 256—8, Granville to N., 17th April, 1855).
[3] *Clarendon*, p. 311, to Clarendon, January 1853.
[4] *Greville*, III, I, p. 45 is confirmed by *Queen's Letters*, pp. 519–20. Lansdowne
(ibid). said that Carlisle's annoyance was the only thing that personally grieved
him. *Greville* (ibid., p. 21) said that in his desire for office Clanricarde had his
wife spread the story that the Irish members sought a gentleman to lead them
and had fixed on him.
[5] Reid's *Houghton*, Vol. 1, p. 479, 4th March, 1853, Disraeli to Milnes. Fitzwilliam's object was almost certainly to sound Disraeli on his attitude to the
Peterborough election petition.
[6] *Argyll*, p. 595.
[7] Emily Eden's letter, cit. n. 1 — 'When (Lady Mary) said if Lord John went
on in *that* way he would lose all his followers, I said I thought that *then* he might
have a chance. . . .'

deferential,[1] fed the fires of discontent. The Elliots, and Lady John especially, doubted Russell's capacity to stand the strain of the Foreign Office as well as the leadership of the Commons (he gave up the department after less than two months) or even the Home Office, but had no doubt that he ought to be prime minister. And the thought that he soon would resume the premiership was all he had to buoy him up. In the December days of decision, the pill of demotion had been sweetened by unwise assurances that his ineligibility for the highest office was temporary and fortuitous and that his chance of resuming that position was very high. Within four months Aberdeen talked of going at the end of the session;[2] he was still of this mind in the summer, and spoke to Russell about it;[3] in October the Queen chided him for again talking to Lord John of his desire to leave office.[4] But Aberdeen had no intention of resigning if it would break up the Government; Russell could only succeed him if the rest of the cabinet favoured such a course, and it never did. Whether Lord John was also given the idea that Aberdeen, who had shown little interest in domestic politics, was to be, except perhaps in foreign policy, a *roi fainéant*, with Russell as Mayor of the Palace, is an open question; Lady John certainly thought that this was so.[5] We can admire Aberdeen's imperturbability in the face of provocation from Russell, and his crisp firmness — 'You know perfectly well that it is not my fault that you do not now occupy the position in which I am placed. . . . I am quite sure the sooner this kind of correspondence is brought to an end the better'[6]— and yet agree with the Queen that his tantalising references to their respective positions fed the flames of discontent in Russell's home at Pembroke Lodge.

Russell had 'summoned up enough of magnanimity to join a Government in which he was not to hold the first place, but he had

---

[1] The Earl of Minto is described as a Jewish-looking broad-accented Scot to whom public speech was a torment. The *DNB* article says he was 'undistinguished by administrative capacity' but 'possessed considerable influence in affairs of state'. That influence was mainly via Russell.

[2] Walpole's *Russell*, Vol. II, p. 171.

[3] ibid., p. 163 n. 1, citing Aberdeen's account to Bedford, December 1856.

[4] *Queen's Letters*, 19th, op. cit., pp. 557–8.

[5] Walpole thought she was mistaken (op. cit., p. 163, n. 1) and Fitzmaurice in his *Granville* says (Vol. 1, p. 85) that Russell never claimed to arrogate to himself any of the Prime Minister's functions — 'he simply desired to have a firm hold on the business of the House of Commons'.

[6] Walpole, op. cit., pp. 168–9, 21st January, 1853.

not magnanimity enough to face the difficulties which this position involved'.[1] It was not a good arrangement that he should lead the Commons without office.[2] He had too much time to brood, and it was his task to be the chief apologist for a government to which he was never able to give a fundamental loyalty, because its formation involved his 'degradation',[3] in a House which contained political friends murmuring at a ministry from which they were excluded and malicious tongues ever ready to make odious comparisons between Peelite and Whig performance. Gladstone at the Treasury commissioned Trevelyan and Northcote to make that survey of the civil service which Russell and Wood had not authorised.[4] Meanwhile Wood (the only Whig cabinet minister besides Russell on the Treasury Bench) introduced an India Bill which, *inter alia*, threw the Indian service open to free competitive examination. But the credit for this was given to the junior minister at the Board of Control, Robert Lowe, no lover of Whigs, who 'not being married into the Greys . . . is made a subordinate to cram Wood'.[5] Towards the end of the session a move by Vernon Smith to raise Wood's salary was defeated.[6] And the wretched record of Whig finance was grievously exposed when Gladstone presented his first budget, the great event of the year. Argyll has left it on record that the cabinet sat spell-bound for three hours when Gladstone propounded his scheme to them in 'by far the most wonderful intellectual effort that I have ever listened to from the lips of man'.[7] Similarly appreciative tributes were paid to the five-hour speech to the Committee of Ways and Means. Russell himself told the Queen that 'Mr Pitt in the days of his glory might have been more imposing, but he could not have been more persuasive' (the Prince sent this letter to Gladstone).[8] Members could not help contrasting both the plan and its presentation with the pitiful performances of Wood.[9]

---

[1] *Argyll*, Vol. 1, p. 463.

[2] There were doubts as to whether it was constitutional for him to do so.

[3] Walpole, op. cit., p. 191, Russell to Clarendon, 23rd September, 1853 — 'You have made me feel my degradation more than I have ever felt it before.'

[4] For Trevelyan's letters to Russell, 1848–9, on this subject see Jenifer Hart 'Sir Charles Trevelyan at the Treasury' *E.H.R.*, LXXV, No. 294, pp. 16–17.

[5] *History of the Session* 1852–3, E. M. Whitby, 1854, p. 151. Lowe had been a 'crammer' in private practice in Oxford.

[6] *History of the Session*, p. 208.   [7] *Argyll*, Vol. 1, p. 423.

[8] *Queen's Letters*, op. cit., pp. 542–3.

[9] Wood had basically a good voice but prolixity of style combined with a very rapid utterance and some sort of impediment to clarity made him painful to listen to.

Gladstone had been brilliant and merciless in his exposure of the budgets of Wood and Disraeli. He now faced the sterner test of showing his constructive ability in a context which, as Disraeli had remarked, revealed only that the Commons, and the public, disapproved of both indirect and direct taxes. Pressure for the reconstruction of the income tax, if it was to be retained, was so strong that Aberdeen said that if concessions were not made to it ministers might as well pack their portmanteaux.[1] But Gladstone, in proposing to keep the income tax for seven years, refused to assist trade and the professions at the expense of mortgages and the Funds by differentiating in favour of 'precarious' as opposed to fixed incomes. And he extended the incidence of the tax, and applied it to Ireland, also raising the duties on Irish spirits. There were ministers who said that this would doom the Government, which would fall before a Tory-Irish assault.[2] The Tories would surely fight hard, for the extension of legacy duty to all successions, whether of personal or real property, was hailed as a great symbolic blow at the landed interest; the whole cabinet disliked it, and Palmerston vehemently.[3] It was taken as proof that 'the middle classes now overmatch, or are at least fully equal to, the aristocratic classes in the House of Commons' (though not in numbers), and had as much of their own way as they were entitled to.[4] The assessed taxes were reformed and the customs recast. In reducing indirect taxation by £5 million (equal to the current product of the income tax) Gladstone gave expression to his belief that while the income tax was an obnoxious, inquisitorial impost which ought not to be a permanent feature of the fiscal system (he hoped it would cease in 1860) it was proper to use it in peacetime as a powerful engine for the relief of taxes which pressed on industry and consumption.

Gladstone was fallible. He gravely over-estimated the revenue from the succession duties, and his funding operation was a failure owing to misjudgement of the money market. He could not avoid occasional defeat in the House, and had to abandon, instead of merely reducing, the advertisement duty. But he established his

---

[1] *Argyll*, Vol. 1, p. 385.
[2] The main critics (see Morley's *Gladstone*, Book IV, Ch. 2) were the Anglo-Irish landlords Palmerston, Lansdowne and Herbert, and Wood, Graham and Granville. Clarendon (Add. MSS 43188 14th April, 1853) wrote that the proposals were not 'justice to Ireland' and would ruin the whole scheme, either by causing the resignation of Wood or defeat in the House. As a concession £4½ million of Irish loans were written off.
[3] See *infra*, p. 294 and n. 1.   [4] *History of the Session*, p. 219.

authority in the House, and in the country. The Government, thanks to his boldness,[1] which astonished both cabinet and public, passed what was thought to be its severest parliamentary test (for the Crimean War was not foreseen). Gladstone cleft the pack-ice in which Wood had become jammed, and determined a main feature of the fiscal system, i.e. reliance (as far as indirect taxes were concerned) on a relatively few revenue duties. He was hailed as a worthy disciple of Peel, who had 'taken his business country-men by storm'.[2] Odious comparisons were made not only with Wood, but with Russell. 'Peel won his Premiership by his practical grasp of the material business — the management of the taxes . . . ; the great deficiency in Lord John Russell's career is that his spirited generalisations about great principles have been unaccompanied by striking conceptions of finance,' said the *Leader*.[2] Gladstone now stood high above all his colleagues, making Russell's 'technical "leading". . . not only ridiculous but offensive'. 'The Whigs, generally, are not pleased that the coup . . . should have been made by the Peelite portion of the Ministry, and that Mr Gladstone himself should so prominently present the Cabinet as taking up the work of Sir Robert Peel.'[3]

With regard to the budget Russell behaved most handsomely. In cabinet, though doubtful whether the main point (the undifferentiated income tax) could pass, he did not join in the protests of most of the Whig ministers (Wood almost resigned). In contrast to Lansdowne and Palmerston, he agreed that the whole scheme should be presented to the House and made, if necessary, an issue of confidence, and even an issue at a general election.[4] He thus accepted Aberdeen's dictum that the mission of the Government was a financial one, and he told the Queen that it rejoiced him 'to be a party to a large plan, and to do with a man who seeks to benefit the country'.[5] But Russell's attitude can hardly have been one of unalloyed delight, for he must have known of the comparisons in men's minds, and he had to sit in the Commons beside Wood

---

[1] It frightened Cardwell; it was too much for Graham; Aberdeen thought it would be very unpopular; Lansdowne and Palmerston were sure it could not pass and were against making a confidence issue of it (Morley, cap. cit.). Argyll says, 'Ultimately. . . all the members of the cabinet became willing to take the leap together, although some of them, I know, thought it was a leap into the shambles' (p. 429).

[2] *History of the Session*, pp. 101–2.   [3] ibid., p. 111.   [4] Morley, cap. cit.

[5] *Queen's Letters*, op. cit., p. 542. The side-kick was directed against Disraeli, not Wood.

while Baring, whom he had failed to get into the cabinet, voiced (for the malicious pleasure of about six people left out of the cabinet — the Greys, Labouchere etc. — said the *Leader*)[1] all the objections to the budget, especially its Irish provisions, which had been made by Whig ministers in the cabinet.

Russell had himself little to show in comparison to Gladstone. There was soon to be an Oxford University Reform Bill, arising out of the report of a commission which Russell had set up when prime minister, but Gladstone was drafting the measure. Meanwhile Radicals grumbled that Russell stood to his point that the Bill should not enter into the question of the removal of religious tests. Russell presented an Education Bill, but it was a puny measure, of which the biographer of Granville (the Lord President) seems unaware, while the biographer of Russell leaves it unclear whether it failed to pass or merely failed to work. It was not, of course, Russell's fault that the time was not ripe for a comprehensive, and highly contentious, measure of national education; he and Granville did what they could by administrative action.[2] But for Russell the session was fruitless (the admission of Jews to Parliament was still held up by the Lords). He had, however, ample scope for his 'spirited generalisation'. For it was a session of bribery committees. They entirely failed to shock a House aptly described as 'a club, composed principally of members of the governing classes, tolerably honest, but intensely prejudiced, and managing to combine what they regard as public good with an immense amount of private-family-class profit'.[3] Members heard with interest, not indignation, of the mysterious veiled lady who distributed bribes at Cambridge. It was, of course, a little embarrassing for the Whigs that Fitzwilliam's proceedings at Peterborough should be impugned. But they treated these matters as men of the world. One must wait for the constituency to become less degraded, said Vernon Smith, and Labouchere was described as thinking that 'as the people is rather scoundrel, and business must be carried on, why, they must be bought'. Russell took a more serious view of corruption than most other Whig leaders, partly because it invited slurs on 1832, partly because it led men to say that a Purity Bill or a Ballot Bill, not a Reform Bill, was needed, and partly because it was argued that to make the franchise

---

[1] *History of the Session*, p. 114.   [2] The bill was dropped.
[3] *History of the Session*, p. 19.

only a little wider, as Russell proposed, would increase corruption.[1] Waiting eagerly for the opportunity to produce his Reform Bill in 1854 (having agreed not to disturb the new Government's first session with it) he determined to accompany it by a Bribery Bill. Meanwhile he continued to oppose the ballot — 'trotted out Sydney from that eternal scaffold, mentioned Sir John Elliot . . . invoked vigour, candour and openness in public affairs and public trusts', and, amid loud Whig cheers, bade the House pause, as even Massachusetts had not yet made up its mind.[2] In consequence of revelations of impropriety by a Tory junior minister in the Dockyards during the late election (the *Times* did not agree with Graham that the minister's personal honour was not impeached), and illegalities at Chatham (which led to the unseating of a Peelite recruit), Russell introduced a bill for the disfranchisement of dockyard officials, but there was no steam to pass it. The outlook for any kind of electoral reform was bleak when the popular journals praised the work of the session, and a Radical could say 'the source is villainous but the flow is pure', that the sort of reform bills the middle class public wanted were Gladstone's operations upon the customs and succession duties, and Cardwell's bills on pilotage and the merchant marine,[3] and that the 'great intelligent wealthy working-man class' (the discovery of whom was Russell's excuse for a new Reform Bill), so far from demanding the franchise, took little interest in public affairs and had lost faith in the benefits of state interference.[4]

Aberdeen recognised an obligation to Russell to allow him to introduce a Reform Bill as a government measure, and was prepared, in December 1853, to lose Palmerston, and probably Lansdowne, rather than lose Russell. But the great majority of the members were not prepared to persist in a bill which the onset of war provided a plausible case for postponing *sine die*. It was only with difficulty that Lord John was induced to give up the Bill and stay in the Government. He wept when making the announcement. Argyll crisply comments — 'It is surely unreasonable that any one man should so identify himself with a great public measure, which

---

[1] The Queen pointed this out (*Letters*, 1st Series, Vol. III, p. 10, 21st January, 1854), saying that the success of the Reform Bill would partly depend on the Bribery Bill. It passed into law, so mangled in both Houses as to be worthless.

[2] *History of the Session*, p. 174.

[3] ibid. pp. 218–20 and ff. In 1854 Cardwell passed an act which finally repealed the long series of Navigation Acts.

[4] *History of the Session*, pp. 218–20.

is disliked by a majority of his own colleagues, and notoriously by a great majority of the House of Commons, that he is to claim credit for some special magnanimity in consenting not to press it down their throats. Yet this was what Lord John seemed to claim for himself, and what, strange to say, many of his colleagues and other politicians conceded to him.'[1] Although the disputes in the cabinet on the Bill temporarily brought Russell nearer to Aberdeen,[2] Russell did not even pretend any longer that he was happy in the House (as contrasted with the cabinet).[3] An injudicious echo of the Durham Letter, gratuitously introduced into a reply to an Irish motion on ecclesiastical endowments, had in 1853 led the Catholic members of the administration to submit their resignations. To keep them in the Government (as Russell's resignation, which he offered, could not be accepted), Aberdeen had to repudiate the speech.[4] And in 1854 proceedings on the Oxford Bill cast a cloud over Russell's reputation as a champion of religious liberty and involved the Government in defeats by margins which the Leader and the whips had not anticipated. Russell was personally prepared to introduce a separate bill reducing the disabilities of non-Anglicans — a bill which the Peelite High Churchmen did not relish — but adhered to his ground that the Oxford Bill should not deal with this matter, thinking, with Gladstone, that the inclusion of a relaxation of the tests would doom the highly controversial measure. But twelve ministers, headed by Molesworth, sent a round-robin to the Prime Minister, for submission to the cabinet, 'strongly and urgently' requesting that the insertion of amendments dealing with tests be made an open question for ministers. 'Professing to be the advocates of Religious freedom and equality', they said, 'we feel that we shall be seriously compromising our political principles and our position as public men by withholding our assent from the proposed enactment. We also feel that we shall be departing from the professions of opinion by which we have hitherto secured the

---

[1] *Argyll*, Vol. I, pp. 478–9
[2] *Queen's Letters*, Vol. III, p. 26, 9th April, 1854, Russell said only Aberdeen had behaved 'with due regard to the honour of the Administration'.
[3] cf. *Queen's Letters*, Vol. II, p. 558 where, 16th October, 1853, Aberdeen quoted Russell as saying, 'Oh *there* I am quite happy.'
[4] Russell said the Roman Church aimed at political power and was 'at variance with a due attachment to the Crown of this country and to the general cause of liberty' and that its clergy would not favour 'that general freedom of discussion, and that activity and energy of the human mind, that belong to the spirit of the constitution'.

confidence of our respective constituencies.'[1] They were given permission to abstain. On 22nd June an amendment to admit Dissenters to matriculation was carried by a majority of ninety-one. The Government conceded not only this, but their admission to the degree of B.A. Only administration and teaching in the University remained Anglican monopolies.

Russell was not able to carry the House with him on any of the matters on which he had taken a firm stand — Reform, bribery, procedure as to the relaxation of tests. The House, was, by nature, unmanageable, and Russell had not the arts of management.[2] He blamed the indiscipline of the Commons on the withdrawal of the Reform Bill, 'by which it was shown that hostile attacks might be made with impunity'.[3] More reasonably, he asked to be relieved of the leadership on the ground that 'the weakness of the Government lies in the House of Commons, and a change of leader may remedy the defect'.[4] This was after a caustic resumé by Disraeli of the parliamentary setbacks of the Government, in the same vein as that of August 1848, which struck cruelly at Russell's most sensitive point by predicting that the Government would last until 'every member of it is, as a public character, irretrievably injured'. But Aberdeen dare not let Russell go; in September 1853 he had told him to his face that by 'supporting' the Government from outside he meant he would not turn it out till he had an opportunity.[5] The immediate 'solution' was to call a meeting of ministerialists at the Foreign Office to ask for better support,[6] an expedient which was to be adopted again in this same Parliament by the next administration.[7] But Russell's heart was now less than ever in his work.[8] He decided to resign as soon as Sebastopol fell.[9]

But Sebastopol did not fall. The Government fell instead, as a

---

[1] Add. MSS 43200, letter to Aberdeen, 16th June, 1854, signed by Molesworth, M. Baines, Bernal Osborne, Cockburn, Moncrieff, Lowe, Grenville Berkeley, Lord Mulgrave, Henry Fitzroy, Robert Boyle, Keogh and Lord Elcho. Fitzroy and Elcho were Peelites — the rest Whigs, Liberals and Radicals.
[2] *History of the Session*, p. 133 (criticism of neglect of details in 1853).
[3] *Queen's Letters*, Vol. III, p. 73, Aberdeen's report, 7th December, 1854.
[4] Walpole, Vol. II, p. 225, Russell to Aberdeen, 14th July, 1854.
[5] *Clarendon*, Vol. II, p. 21, Lady C's Journal, 12th September, 1853.
[6] 17th July. Only 180 attended.   [7] 24th May, 1855, at No. 10. 203 attended.
[8] Stanmore's *Herbert*, Vol. 1, pp. 233–43.
[9] Walpole, p. 227 — Clarendon's reply of 25th September, 1854 is quoted, and a memo. of Russell's, 18th October, in which he spoke of his own handicaps — 'Many of his opinions are old-fashioned and out of date. He has offended some by his zeal for Parliamentary Reform; others because their private interests have not received from him the attention they thought their due; add to this the

result of the revelations by William Howard Russell in the *Times*
of what the failure to take the bastion and with it the isthmus of
Perekop, where winter quarters were available, meant in terms of
suffering and privation to the men in the field. A storm of criticism
burst upon an administration already distracted by Russell's
recurring threats of resignation. Lord John had been highly
critical of the diplomacy which, as the Foreign Secretary admitted
both in private and in public, involved the country 'drifting' into
war. When war came, Russell was critical of its conduct. 'Had I
full confidence in the Administration of which you are the head,' he
wrote to Aberdeen in May 1854, 'I should not scruple to take
office under you. But the late meetings of the Cabinet have shown
so much indecision, and there is so much reluctance to adopt those
measures which would force the Emperor of Russia to consent to a
speedy peace, that I can feel no such confidence.'[1] He had no doubt
of the root cause of the lack of vigour — 'the great want of all is a
head of the English Cabinet';[2] 'the Government . . . wants direction;
and, in wanting direction, wants everything that is essential'.[3]
But such criticisms made no impact on his colleagues, being
written off as further signs that Russell wanted Aberdeen's place.
The Prime Minister himself, skilful at keeping together the able
men in his cabinet, thought it his duty to carry on till the end of the
war. But his heart was not in the fight, and the gift for compromise
which had militated against resolute diplomacy was not what was
required in a wartime prime minister. Assuming, however, that
Aberdeen was a fixture, all that Russell could do was press for
administrative reforms and changes in personnel which might go
part of the way to meeting the lack of active leadership. He would
have liked to see the co-ordination of all the military services
(including the office of Commander-in-Chief) under a Secretary of
State. This had long been pressed by Earl Grey, and was being
currently moved in the House of Commons by Henry Rich.
Aberdeen did not even mention to the cabinet Russell's memorandum on this subject and if Russell was able to secure the
appointment of a further Secretary of State to relieve Newcastle
of his responsibility for the colonies, leaving him as Secretary of

extreme divergence of views entertained by supporters of Government and the
certainty of offending some of them by the line adopted or the language held. . .'
[1] Walpole, p. 217, Russell to Aberdeen, 5th May.
[2] ibid., p. 218; *Clarendon*, Vol. II, p. 44, to Clarendon, 12th May.
[3] Walpole, p. 218, to Lansdowne, 28th May.

State for War, this was 'carried by storm' only as a result of Russell's threatening to go down and vote with Rich.[1] Newcastle was given no new powers at all — not even control of the Commissariat.[2] Sir George Grey was made Colonial Secretary and Russell Lord President of the Council.

It became increasingly obvious that Newcastle was insufficiently active, and that the case for taking the Commissariat from Treasury control, and putting both it and the functions of the Secretary at War under the Secretary of State, was overwhelming. But only Russell was willing to say so, and he not until November, when he proposed that Palmerston should become Secretary of State with extended functions. He also required that Parliament be summoned to make provision for every possible means of releasing as many men as possible for the war theatre. The latter he achieved, but Aberdeen said that the administrative reform would cause 'a dislocation of the Government', that Palmerston was too old to do the work of both Newcastle and Herbert, that any change would weaken the ministry and would not be fair and just to the Duke.[3] Russell, hearing that Panmure (Fox Maule) did not think the time ripe for administrative changes, desisted, and rejoined the cabinet which he was understood to have left. Aberdeen told the Queen that he 'received Lord John's change without resentment or displeasure', boasting that he had 'yielded nothing whatever' to Russell.[4] His colleagues had dismissed Russell's proposals as untenable.[5] They made such a point of mutual loyalty that they thought more of keeping together than of what they were together for; they discounted Russell's plans because they knew he had never been loyal to the administration. Russell was in a tragic predicament of his own making. He had complained so often, and sent in so many resignations, that his complaints did not receive the attention they merited and his resignations were regarded simply as signs of chronic discontent. In making definite propositions for more effective diplomacy; for the raising of troops; for

[1] *Queen's Letters*, Vol. III, pp. 42–3, 8th June; Walpole, pp. 217–19.

[2] Newcastle himself asked for control of the Commissariat, but did not get i till December (Newcastle p. 133).

[3] *Queen's Letters*, pp. 67–8, 23rd November; Walpole pp. 229–31.

[4] *Queen's Letters*, pp. 77–8, 16th December.

[5] Granville, in a letter of 12th December, 1854 (printed in *Fitzmaurice*, Vol. 1 pp. 88–9) pointed out that Russell did not take enough trouble in insisting on information, forcing the cabinet to decide and making sure decisions had been acted on. He was not good at persistently pressing one point, and arming himself with accurate evidence of his contentions.

the adoption and purposeful pursuit of a definite strategy; for changes in administration and personnel which in the absence of a more effective prime minister were the minimum requisite for imparting vigour to the conduct of the war, Russell deserved well of his country. But he, and the country, paid the penalty of his pride and his ambition. His colleagues strove to keep him only because his going would weaken them; he carried no positive weight. In the cabinet crisis of December, everybody was against him, and he allowed himself to be goaded into remarks which seemed to justify Aberdeen's determination to represent everything he said as amounting simply to a demand that Russell succeed him. Poor Russell could not deny that he thought Aberdeen incapable. If he felt that the war had not been, and would not be, carried on with sufficient vigour with Aberdeen as prime minister, he was perfectly entitled, perhaps bound, to resign. But when he said he would support the Government from outside, he was brutally told by Palmerston that he would 'support it at the head of a very virulent Opposition'. 'Will you say,' asked Palmerston, 'Here I am. I have triumphed, and have displaced, in the midst of most hazardous operations, all the ablest men the Country has produced; but I shall take their place with Mr Vernon Smith, Lord Seymour, Lord Minto and others . . . ?'.[1] The forecast may have been quite correct, but Russell had not formulated any plan of virulent opposition, and the implication that his *sole* aim was personal and partisan was unjustified; even the knowledge that it was Minto who, by a letter of 16th November, in which he said 'We are playing for too great a stake to allow any personal scruples or considerations to lose us the game,' stirred Russell to his latest initiative,[2] does not entitle us to support such an implication. But Russell had a knack of putting himself in the worst possible light. He allowed himself, for instance, to be incited by Palmerston into wild remarks about bringing in another Reform Bill at once.[1] And so he incurred, from Whig as well as Peelite colleagues, a mixture of disparagement and indignation. To Clarendon it was, at first, a case of 'Johnny preparing another breeze'.[3] Wood insisted throughout that he knew Russell and that 'it would all blow over'.[4]

[1] *Queen's Letters*, pp. 74-6, Aberdeen's account of cabinet of 8th December.
[2] Quoted in Walpole, p. 228. From Fitzmaurice's *Granville*, p. 88, it is evident that Russell sent Minto's letter to Granville.
[3] *Clarendon*, Vol. II, pp. 53-4.
[4] *Queen's Letters*, pp. 74-6, Aberdeen's account of cabinet of 8th December.

Lansdowne said 'It is wearisome to strive continually against the recurrence of the same causes and effects' and bade Russell remember that the cabinet was founded 'on an abnegation principle'.[1] Clarendon felt 'profound disgust' at Russell's 'selfish and unpatriotic conduct'[2] and Lansdowne 'quite a necessity to speak out'.[3] 'Everybody was dead against him, though some said nothing.'[2]

Russell had submitted resignation after resignation, only to withdraw. He finally resigned in circumstances highly discreditable to himself. He returned from escorting his wife to join her dying sister in Paris to find that Roebuck, one of the War Radicals, had tabled a motion for a parliamentary inquiry into the conduct of the war. The Leader of the House at once wrote to the Prime Minister saying that he must resign, as he could not resist the motion. Perhaps in conscience he could not. It was a motion of no confidence in a government in which he felt no confidence — 'the worst Government I have ever known'. It was a demand for a parliamentary inquest, and with his quaint views on the relation of parliament to the executive he could not feel the same constitutional objections to the proposed procedure as, for instance, Gladstone. But this was a vote of censure, and most ministers, even if on the the point of resignation because they felt they could not defend the administration any longer, would have stood with their colleagues to face a censure upon actions for which they bore as much constitutional responsibility as those colleagues. For a Leader of the House to run away from a motion of censure which was in any case likely to be carried, and thus inevitably reveal that he thought the censure justified, and utterly doom the Government, was, until Russell did it, unimaginable. What to him was honest scruple was bound to seem to others base desertion. That he should have believed that the result would be to make him prime minister argues an almost megalomaniacal insensitivity to common opinion. Had he adhered to his resignation of September or to those of 6th and 8th December, or even if he had sent and adhered to the letter he wrote on 1st January before going to Paris, he might have convinced Parliament that he was the honourable and frustrated champion of military efficiency. His colleagues would have been hampered in self-defence by their Privy Councillors' oaths. But he had failed to take the cue offered by Russell of the *Times*, and he now seemed to exploit,

---

[1] *Clarendon*, p. 54; Walpole, p. 232.   [2] *Clarendon*, Vol. II, pp. 53–4.
[3] *Queen's Letters*, pp. 74–6, Aberdeen's account of cabinet of 8th December.

from personal pique and ambition, a situation he had not created.

It was the opinion of Russell's colleagues that, though he was not active in, he was cognisant of intrigues for a pure Whig government and did not take such active steps against them as he should have done.[1] It is therefore proper to insist that, though the Roebuck motion was carried by the crushing majority of 305 : 148, the vote cannot be interpreted as a partisan Whig assault upon a ministry whose formation and existence was an affront to Whiggery. Whether we look for Whigs in terms of noble birth and proprietorial family, or of conservative opinions, or a realistic mixture of the two, we are bound to say that they did not leap to take advantage of Russell's treachery. They did not refrain from criticism, and some of them made rather a point of relating their loyalty to Lansdowne and Palmerston rather than Aberdeen or the ministry as a whole.[2] Yet, after hearing Russell castigate his colleagues for inefficiency and neglect, not only ministers and their relatives, but displaced cabinet ministers and placemen — Baring, Labouchere, Seymour, Ellice, Vernon Smith, Lord Robert Grosvenor, Bouverie — and *their* relatives — brothers of Minto and Carlisle, a nephew of Russell — and a Cavendish and other aristocratic members, besides Whig country gentlemen,[3] contributed their votes to the Government's 150. Three former junior ministers — Ebrington, Rich and Horsman — three Fitzwilliams, one Cavendish, the heirs of Sutherland, Anglesey and Cork, and some Whig-Radicals[4] cast their lot with Roebuck. But when only eighty-eight non-Peelite private members regarded as ministerialists supported the Government, and nearly as many joined the bulk of the Tory Opposition against it,[5] there is no ground for ascribing the opposition of most of those Whigs who did go with Roebuck

---

[1] Stanmore's *Herbert*, Vol. 1, p. 233. Cf. *Clarendon*, Vol. II, p. 21 where, 12th. September, 1853, Russell is quoted as saying that 'his friends were very kind' and seemed to think the obstacles to his forming a government not insuperable.

[2] e.g. speech of Vernon Smith, who said (26th Jan.) that he could not imagine anyone with sufficient credulity to have confidence in the administration; he had given it independent, though critical support, because of his confidence in Lansdowne, to whom he owed 'every species of allegiance', Russell and Palmerston. Palmerston should go to the War Office — that would sway votes.

[3] e.g. Adair, Bonham Carter, J. E. Denison, Foley, Sheridan, Whitbread, Winnington, Wrightson, Wyvill.

[4] e.g. Locke King, Lord Duncan, Lord Goderich, Hon. A. F. Kinnaird, Sir George Strickland, Hon. F. H. F. Berkeley.

[5] Of the minority of 150, 30 were ministers and 32 Peelites, Liberal Conservatives or Tories. The bulk of the ministerialists who voted against the Government were War Radicals. About half the ministerialists abstained.

to mere faction. Lord Minto had been quite right to draw to his son-in-law's attention in November 'the clamour and indignation gathering against the Government for its neglect of timely and sufficient exertion in the conduct of this war'. There were strong, popular grounds for condemning the ministry.

There was a basic misunderstanding between Russell and his colleagues in the Aberdeen administration. He imagined that there was no obstacle to his forming a government, and therefore had little scruples about breaking up the existing one; they could not see how any government could be formed as strong as the existing one, the maintenance of which therefore became virtually their chief article of faith. But they did not see how the coalition could survive without Lord John, partly because he 'was not without large following amongst the Whigs'[1] and partly because it was almost certain that 'support' from outside would soon turn into 'virulent opposition'. Because of this, though a little perhaps out of a lingering loyalty to their party, the Whig ministers, on Russell's resignation, opted for the resignation of the whole Government; only Clarendon suggested that Newcastle should retire and Russell be invited back, which the Peelites would not hear of. The Queen refused to accept the resignation, and Sir George Grey, who had initiated it, took the lead in agreeing to stay on to meet the Roebuck motion.[2] 'His (Russell's) own friends having remained in the Cabinet, is his practical condemnation,' said Aberdeen.[3] 'It is due to the Whig party to add that no leading member of that body has attempted to palliate Lord John Russell's fault or followed his example,' said the *Times*.[4] But when Derby had failed to form a government, because Palmerston would join him only as part of a coalition and the Peelites would promise only 'support', it became evident that the only solution to the impasse was a government on the lines of the previous one. It was as true as ever that if Russell were not in it he could do much mischief, and if his inclusion was not possible, because the Peelites would not serve with him, then it was important to expose to him his own inability to form a government, which he had not in his heart accepted either in 1852 or since, and did not grasp even now. Lansdowne advised the Queen that, until Russell saw that he could

[1] *Queen's Letters*, p. 109, Lansdowne, 2nd February, 1855, in interview with the Queen.
[2] Add. MSS 44745 (Gladstone Papers), memo of 9th March.
[3] *Queen's Letters*, p. 97, 27th January.   [4] *Times*, 3rd February.

"I'M AFRAID YOU'RE NOT STRONG ENOUGH FOR THE
PLACE, JOHN."

This cartoon was published in connection with Russell's failure to form a government
in December 1845, but (with the figure of Peel excluded) seems even more appropriate
to 1855.

not succeed, no strong government was possible. Asked to form a
government himself, the Marquess said that Russell had often told
him that if he (Lansdowne) had headed the coalition, his (Russell's)
position would have been quite different, but 'he felt sure Lord
John would soon be tired of him and impatient to see him gone'.[1]
There was really no point in trying to put Lansdowne in the place
of Aberdeen, even with Palmerston as Leader of the Commons and
Russell a minister in the Lords, if Russell was still going to aspire
to succeed to a premiership which his colleagues would not grant

[1] *Queen's Letters*, pp. 108–9 ff. from which primarily the following account of
Russell's attempt to form a government is taken.

him. So it was decided to go through the 'ceremony' of an attempt
by Russell to form an administration.

The result was tragi-comedy. On 2nd February Russell became
prime minister designate, intending to become a peer and have
Palmerston as Leader. He foresaw no great difficulty — Panmure
could have the War Office and (if Gladstone would not serve)
Labouchere the Exchequer and (if Graham would not serve)
Baring could return to the Admiralty. But Palmerston said he
would not help unless Clarendon kept the Foreign Office, and
Clarendon said, to Russell's amazement, that he did not think he
could carry on without the Peelites, and they said they could not
join a Russell government. There was, of course, Russell told the
Queen, no doubt that 'his own friends' (Grey, Wood, Lansdowne,
Granville) would cordially co-operate with him. Bitter disillusion-
ment followed. When the Whig ex-ministers were invited to go to
Russell's house, Lansdowne declined, having no mind to form
part of the arrangement. Wood said he had no business where
Lansdowne would not go. Grey was very averse to a purely Whig
government and said it could not stand. Clarendon administered
the *coup de grâce*, and summed the matter up with biting clarity
to the Queen:[1]

> He must really say that he thought he could do no good in joining
> Lord John; his Government would be 'a stillborn Government' which
> 'the country would tread under foot the first day', composed as it
> would be of the same men who had been bankrupt in 1852, minus
> the two best men in it, viz. Lord Lansdowne and Lord Grey, and
> the head of it ruined in public opinion. . . . From the first day of
> Lord John's entering into Lord Aberdeen's Government, he had only
> had one idea, viz, that of tripping him up, expel the Peelites, and
> place himself at the head of an exclusive Whig Ministry. Besides, he
> felt that the conduct of all his colleagues had been most straight-
> forward and honourable towards him, and he was not prepared 'to
> step over their dead bodies to the man who had killed them'. The
> attempt of Lord John ought *not* to succeed if public morality were
> to be upheld in this country. He had avoided Lord John ever since
> his retirement, but he would now have to speak out to him, as when
> he was asked to embark his honour he had a right to count the cost.

Russell could get 'no man worth getting'.[2] On 4th February he
yielded up the commission. 'The loss of the Peelites would be a

¹ *Queen's Letters*, pp. 117–18.   ² *Argyll*, p. 526.

great blow to him,' he said, 'which might be overcome, however; but if his own particular friends ... deserted him (*sic*), he felt that he could go on no further.' His bewilderment and mortification deepened when all the Whig ex-ministers said they would serve under Palmerston, even without the Peelites, and with or without Lord John. And then the Peelites too, under pressure from Aberdeen, agreed to serve, although they had said, quite honestly, that while they could not serve under Russell they would rather see him prime minister than Palmerston.[1] He had not understood how very generally the leading Whig ministers had shared since 1852 Clarendon's desire that 'there should be no Whigs or Peelites in future, and that the Cabinet should be a real fusion of principles',[2] and that in their view much progress had been achieved towards this end, despite what Aberdeen called 'the incessant attempts of Lord John Russell to keep up Party differences'.[3] The harmony which, *pace* Russell, existed within the coalition was achieved at the expense of decisiveness in foreign policy and the conduct of war. But from the point of view of the future of the Liberal party it was important that the lines of division on important issues were not, in the cabinet, identical with those of party origin — that Russell should find the Peelites more favourable to Reform than the Whigs; that Gladstone should find Russell and Clarendon among those prepared to stand by his budget as a comprehensive scheme and Graham and Herbert among those reluctant to do so; and that if Palmerston, Russell and Lansdowne were the most 'warlike' of the cabinet, Newcastle should be with them. One of the reasons that the Peelites joined the Palmerston government was their feeling of obligation towards their Whig colleagues, and though they very shortly afterwards left it, they did so because they distrusted Palmerston himself, not because they had quarrelled with the Whigs. Nevertheless, coalition failed, in the sense that it was abandoned by the leading Peelites because the fortunes of war had made their chieftain, Aberdeen, as well as Newcastle, a 'sacrifice',[4] and without him and with Palmerston they could feel

---

[1] Herbert had said this (*Queen's Letters*, p. 115) because the Peelites sincerely dreaded Palmerston's views on foreign policy 'uncontrolled by Lord Aberdeen'.
[2] *Clarendon*, Vol. I, p. 356, to Reeve, 26th December, 1852.
[3] *Queen's Letters*, pp. 100–1, 30th January, 1855.
[4] 'Our most noble victim struck down and we set to feast over the remains. The thing is bad and the mode is worse.' Add. MSS 44745, 5th February, 1855, part of a long memo. by Gladstone written in May, on the basis of diary records which cover the cabinet crises of the early part of the year.

no security that their views on war aims would carry 'due' weight. It had to be proved that even under Palmerston the Whigs alone could not satisfactorily govern the country, any more than the Tories could, before political logic took Whigs, Peelites and Radicals to Willis's Rooms in 1859 to make a party to support a coalition which should be a 'fusion'.

CHAPTER XI

The Primacy of Palmerston

That prophet would have been accounted mad who in 1812 or 1827 foretold that of the men then in politics Viscount Palmerston would leave the name which for future generations would most readily evoke an image (however over-simplified) of a man and of a policy. He could have been Tory Chancellor of the Exchequer in 1809, but instead served for eighteen years, competently but inconspicuously, in the financial office of Secretary at War. In 1827, at the age of forty-three, he entered Canning's cabinet, but in that year it was not thought insulting to offer him the governorship of Bengal or Jamaica. He was still known chiefly as a man-about-town. He began, however, to take an interest in foreign affairs, which stemmed, perhaps, from philhellenism but developed rapidly into a support for the constitutional cause in Portugal and France. He abhorred Wellington's foreign policy. This did not worry the Duke, who rated him a sparrow, but Grey was impressed. Holland and Lansdowne, however, seemed the natural candidates for the Foreign Office under Grey, and Palmerston was earmarked for the Home Office. But both the Whig hierarchs recommended Palmerston for Foreign Secretary, and Grey made the nomination. For sixteen years (1830-4, 1835-41 and 1846-51) Foreign Secretary, and for nearly nine years (1855-8 and 1859-65) prime minister, Palmerston played a dominant rôle in British diplomacy for twenty-five of the thirty-five years 1830-65.

It is vain to try to isolate a foreign policy which may be described as characteristically 'Whig'. Eighteenth-century Whigs — and there were generations when all leading politicians considered themselves Whigs — accepted the basic propositions of the Mercantile School, which no statesman seriously disputed between Bolingbroke and Shelburne. They virtually condemned Britain to a state of chronic war, hot or cold, with her commercial competitors, and reinforced a francophobia which stemmed from the recollection of Louis XIV's design to impose autocracy and popery upon England. But there was all the difference in the world between the policy, operated within this context, of a Stanhope or a Walpole and that of Chatham. In the nineteenth century it was to be presumed that a Whig would welcome the achievement of constitutional government and even, *prima facie*, some degree of national self-determination, on the continent of Europe, while a Tory would be apt to lean towards 'legitimism' and the maintenance of the Vienna settlement. But a Whig might esteem stability and the Balance of Power above the progress of nationalism and liberalism — as Clarendon seemed to do.[1] And the Whigs were no more of one mind than the Radicals as to how active a part Britain should play in encouraging the overthrow of autocratic régimes and arbitrary frontiers and involving herself in the internal politics of countries with precarious constitutional systems.[2] Between Palmerston, Clarendon and Granville there were wide differences of approach,[3] and such differences appear on analysis to lie less in ideology or party than in temperament. The true line of division is not between Whig and Tory, but between activists like Canning, Palmerston, Russell[4] and Rosebery and passivists like Aberdeen, Malmesbury, Granville and the younger Stanley[5] whose famous dispute with Beaconsfield on the Eastern Question was only the Tory equivalent of the struggle in Whig cabinets between the passivists and Palmerston. A minister's policy cannot be considered apart from the manner of pursuing it, and it was plain that Palmerstonianism, involving the decisive repudiation of any idea of 'disengagement' from Europe's ideological battle and the refusal to allow any changes in the control of the Ottoman dominions to be brought about by the enterprise of individual Powers, meant contention, for the objectives were pursued with

[1] Russell objected to the Queen's suggestion that Clarendon become Foreign Secretary (March, 1850, *Queen's Letters*, Vol. II, p. 280) on the ground that he was too anti-French and pro-Austria and Russia.

[2] The Queen, sympathetic with foreign monarchs against whose ministers British envoys intrigued to preserve constitutionalism and 'British influence', showered upon Russell complaints of interference in Spain, Portugal and Greece (see *Letters*, Vol. II, pp. 138, 140–1, 207 and especially pp. 213 and 215).

[3] Palmerston was Foreign Secretary 1830–4, 35–41, 46–51; Granville 1851–2, 1870–4, 1880–5; Clarendon 1853–8 and 1865–6 and 1868–70.

[4] Russell was Foreign Secretary 1852–3 and 1859–65 (when Palmerston was prime minister); he was premier 1846–52 and 1865–6.

[5] Aberdeen was Foreign Secretary 1828–30, 1834–5, 1841–6, as a Conservative and coalition prime minister 1852–5; Malmesbury was Tory Foreign Secretary 1852, 1858–9 and Stanley 1866–8 and (as 15th Earl of Derby) 1874–8.

great vigour, by crisp speech and 'writings as bitter as gall'[1] and with an apparent disregard for the dangers of war as well as for diplomatic niceties. Palmerston himself drew no distinction between policy and the means of furthering it; he told Russell in March 1850 that he knew he had forfeited the Queen's confidence, but thought that this was not on *personal* grounds but merely on account of his line of policy. He thus exposed the difference between the Court, which disapproved of his going such 'a long way in taking up the side of democracy' in its struggle with despotism,[2] and the cabinet, many of whom were deeply disquieted by Palmerston's methods, but who as a body warmly approved 'his general course of policy'.[3]

It was in 1840 that Palmerston first encountered a powerful movement in Whiggery, reflected in the cabinet, to curb his masterful conduct of foreign affairs. The occasion was the second great threat to the authority of the Sultan by the Pasha of Egypt, Mehemet Ali. Palmerston, who regarded the Pasha as a protégé of France, was severely criticised by those who took a narrower view of British interests, or were predominantly philhellene or admired the Pasha, those who were by nature inclined to peace at almost any price and those who thought that the maintenance of the rickety entente with France (Palmerston's own creation) was a predominant interest or simply that where British aims clashed with French aspirations the former should be pursued so as to give as little possible offence to France. In reaction against the anti-Gallicanism of the eighteenth century, Fox and the *Mountain* had bequeathed to Whiggery a francophilism which survived the revolutionary and Napoleonic wars and the Bourbon restoration and was revitalised by the establishment of the July monarchy. The francophilism of some Whigs, such as Holland, was so un-critical that it was a heinous offence in their eyes to impair the stability of the July monarchy by seeing that British interests pre-vailed over French, and mortal sin to accompany victory by need-less humiliation of the French. In 1840 the pro-French party was willing to work for the overthrow of the Foreign Secretary rather

[1] *Queen's Letters*, Vol. II, pp. 231–3. September, 1848.
[2] ibid., p. 294, June 1850, when the Queen refused to agree that it had been British policy to let despotism and democracy fight their own battles.
[3] ibid., p. 214, 18th June 1848, Russell to the Queen, and again pp. 250–1, January, 1849 . . . 'Lord John Russell has always approved in the main of the foreign policy of Lord Palmerston.'

than shake the prestige of the Citizen King. While Palmerston plied
bluff and bluster to the brink of war (but carried the other Powers
with him against France) Holland led the opposition in the cabinet
and Ellice passed between Holland House and the French court
armed with the secrets of the British cabinet. Lansdowne shared
Holland's disquiet. From Althorp, Spencer sent stern criticisms.
The Greys were restrained only by concern for the interests of
their relative Lord Ponsonby, the Palmerstonian ambassador in
Constantinople. When Holland died, the critics mustered round
Clarendon, who was henceforth accounted a potential Foreign
Secretary. They enlisted Russell, though his francophilism was
not uncritical (nor, indeed, was Clarendon's). But Palmerston
prevailed, and provided the failing ministry with one of its few
triumphs of the year. Its break-up on the issue had been prevented
only by Melbourne's reminder that they could not stand any
resignations. It was M. Thiers, not Palmerston, who fell.[1]

The same pattern re-emerged in 1850, although the Turk was
not then involved, the victim of Palmerstonian panache being
Greece not Egypt, and, though France was once again set down,
the other Powers were also affronted. It is not just to conceive of
Palmerston as antipathetic to, or even neglectful of, the Concert of
Europe. He regarded it as a most valuable means of restraining the
private enterprise of individual Powers, and had used it to settle
the affairs of Greece and Belgium, to reverse Russia's privileged
position in Turkey and to checkmate France in 1840–1. But in
1850, when compelled in the matter of the claims on behalf of
British subjects against the Greek government (which he deemed
too pro-French)[2] to reach a settlement in concert, he sabotaged the
agreement by withholding the news of it from the British representatives in Athens until they had called in the fleet to operate against
the Piraeus. On this occasion opposition in cabinet was frustrated
by the tabling of a motion of confidence in the House of Commons
which the Government was compelled to defend, but Russell told
Prince Albert that if the vote was won he would not remain prime
minister with Palmerston as Foreign Secretary.[3] To Palmerston,

[1] For a balanced account of this episode see Sir Charles Webster's *Palmerston*
1830–41, 1951. *Greville* and *Clarendon* explain the motives and tactics of Palmerston's critics.

[2] And also too absolutist — 'King Otho is the *enfant gâté de l'absolutisme* and
therefore all the arbitrary Courts are in convulsions at what we have been doing'
(Ashley, Vol. II, p. 140, 15th February, 1850).

[3] *Queen's Letters*, Vol. II, p. 288, 18th May, 1850.

however, irremovable on the morrow of victory, the simple story was that 'there had been a great conspiracy against him', hatched up in Britain under foreign inspiration, prime movers being Clarendon, Granville, Reeve and Delane of the *Times*, Guizot (the fallen minister of the deposed July monarchy) and Princess Lieven, the fascinating international busybody who had once been intimate with both Grey and Palmerston. As in 1840, the plot had been frustrated by a diplomatic and parliamentary 'double'.[1] He did not seem to understand that there was any justification for criticisms based on the quite unique dislike and distrust which his methods engendered in foreign chanceries and the diplomatic corps in London[2] — the only element in the royal indictment of him with which Russell really sympathised. His retort to suggestions that he was 'bringing the whole of the hatred which is borne to him by all the Governments of Europe upon England'[3] was that it was quite natural that he 'should incur the momentary enmity of those states whose interests and plans he might have to cross'.[4]

When Palmerston went hunting he expected scalps. He did not appreciate the value of personal goodwill in diplomacy — he got on so well without it. Content to judge himself by results, he thought it very wrong-headed of Earl Grey (for instance) to make faults of method and the allegation that he was a menace to the peace of Europe a ground of objection to his return to the Foreign Office in 1845. 'They could not charge me with failure . . . ; they could not charge me with having involved the country in war . . . ,' he said, 'and the only thing that was left for them to say was that my policy had a *tendency* to produce war. . . .'[5] He would not then consider the Colonies because his taking another department than the Foreign Office 'would be a public recognition of the most unjust accusations that had been brought against him'.[6] And so he became Foreign Secretary for the third time in 1846, though the appointment was offensive to Peelites who held the balance in the

---

[1] ibid., pp. 313–14, conversation of 6th August, 1850 with Russell.
[2] A factor in the criticism of Palmerston was undoubtedly the inconvenience caused to the aristocratic embassy staffs in foreign capitals and to London hostesses intimate with foreign diplomats by the frequent squalls inseparable from his conduct of affairs.
[3] *Queen's Letters*, Vol. II, p. 288, Albert to Russell, 18th May, 1850.
[4] ibid., pp. 313–14, conversation of 6th August, 1850 with Russell.
[5] *Queen's Letters*, Vol. II, pp. 78–82, 26th December, 1845, a reply to Earl Grey's letter to Russell cited by *Walpole*, Vol. II, pp. 414–16, 19th December.
[6] ibid., p. 70. Russell told Grey (*Walpole*, p. 416) that Palmerston was the man best fitted for the Foreign Office and that the aspersions on him were 'unjust'.

House of Commons, as well as to Radicals of the Cobden-Bright school and to many Whigs. His conduct of the office produced a steady deterioration in his relations with the Palace and with Downing Street as well.

As early as September 1848 Russell agreed in principle with the Queen that Palmerston should leave the Foreign Office,[1] and in January 1849, when there was a furore over Palmerston's release of arms to Sicilian rebels, he would have made a change had not Palmerston unexpectedly agreed to send an apology to the Bourbon court at Naples.[2] In March 1850 Russell proposed to become a peer at the end of the session, and make Palmerston Leader of the House; in principle, at least, he yielded to the Queen's view that as she thought that Minto would not do for the Foreign Office, and he objected to Clarendon, Russell should take it himself. British political history might have been very different if Russell had left the Commons at this time, but the death of Peel (regarded as a great blow to the prospects of the Whig government) and his interest in Reform made Lord John unwilling to do so. When the Queen, at the end of the session, pressed Russell to take the Foreign Office and stay in the Commons, Palmerston declined to leave for any other office than that of Leader of the House of Commons.[3] No change could therefore be made, for Palmerston was riding a crest of popularity. His diplomatic and parliamentary 'double' checked both the Queen and the Prime Minister. On the night of the vote on Roebuck's motion of confidence in the Government's foreign policy the Peelites marched with unwonted unanimity against the Government, and they were led by Peel, who divided against the Whigs for the first time since Russell had crept unworthily into his place. A classical education bred philhellenes, like Aberdeen, and so did Anglo-Catholicism.[4] The younger Peelites had come under both influences, and, now that they were associated with the Free Trade cause, were grafting a neo-Mancunian non-interventionism on to the stock of Tory passivism. Serious, sensible, rather priggish, they shrank from seeming flippancy and irresponsibility, blunt communication, unabashed appeal to the vulgar passion and prejudice, and, be it added, from the manly contempt for 'cant' which made Palmerston

---

[1] ibid., pp. 232–3.   [2] ibid., pp. 250–1.   [3] ibid., pp. 279–82 and 309–15.
[4] Because the Tractarians developed a stronger respect for the Orthodox Church than for Rome.

at bottom an anachronism in Victorian England.[1] The 'Don
Pacifico' debate therefore gave a pre-view of the gulf between
Palmerston and Gladstone which was to result in Peelite secession
from Palmerston's first administration and to trouble his second.
In 1850 the Peelites marched in vain. In the 'Civis Romanus'
speech Palmerston's exaltation of the disproportionate use of
power (in a cause which can only be described as disreputable)[2]
as the vindication of the duty of an imperial power to protect her
subjects trading or residing abroad triumphed over the moderate
statesmanship of Peel and Gladstone's appeal to moral restraints
upon power.

Palmerston made an outstanding speech, and gave the Russell
government what Gladstone himself called its 'only marked and
brilliant triumph'.[3] Lord John could justly point out that the vote
was won only because, while the Tories did not muster their full
strength against an assertion of British power, colleagues and
supporters with varying degrees of reluctance voted for a motion of
confidence which the cabinet, being collectively responsible, could
not evade.[4] But it was a famous victory, and it was regarded as
Palmerston's own. It was more popular outside the House than
within. It was not from parties that Palmerston was to draw the
support that would make him chief minister; it was from a public,
drawn from all classes; it was from John Bull. The masses did not,
and do not, dislike a 'tough' policy; business men liked the
ostentatious assurance that British interests would be protected;
the landed interest had no objection to hearing the lion roar. In
the following months Palmerston contrived to deepen the impact
of his personality upon the classes which were naturally Radical.
In the process of enlarging his 'public' he broke all constitutional
and diplomatic niceties. He had to accept an ultimatum designed
to reinstate the supervision of the Prime Minister and the Queen
over foreign policy. Owing to the volume of business (and Palmerston's high sense of personal responsibility)[5] its terms were, in the

---

[1] In a bitter attack on Palmerston, for the eye of Aberdeen, in 1857, Gladstone
complained that a boyish bullying, levity and good humour were no substitutes
for a character devoted to truth and genuine earnestness, which was the boast
and ornament of England (Add. MSS 44747).
[2] Don Pacifico, the inaptly named Jew of Gibraltar, whose claims against the
Greek Government for riot damage were grossly inflated, was obviously a
scoundrel.
[3] Add. MSS 44745, draft cit. supra.   [4] Queen's Letters, Vol. II, p. 313.
[5] He insisted on writing all the more important despatches himself, so that it
was often urgent to get them off as soon as they were ready.

letter, impracticable, and he did not in good faith accept their spirit. Thus when General Haynau, conspicuous for the cruelty of his suppression of risings against the Habsburgs in Italy and Hungary, was manhandled at a London brewery, Palmerston's 'apology' to the Austrian ambassador contained an implied congratulation of the draymen who had carried out the assault. Palmerston had prevented the extradition from Turkey of the Hungarian refugees who sought asylum from the troops of Tsar and Kaiser, and when the most eminent of them, Kossuth, came to Britain to be fêted by Radicals and to utter violent attacks on the crowned heads of what were, officially, 'friendly Powers', the Foreign Secretary intended to invite him to his house. With the utmost difficulty restrained from so doing, he received addresses from the Radicals of Finsbury and Islington in which the Habsburg and Romanov rulers were referred to in Kossuthian terms. Public opinion was with Palmerston, and Russell did not dare dismiss him.

Palmerston retained his office because the Peelites were not yet ready for coalition, and the ministry could not afford to lose the minister whose popularity grew as that of the cabinet fell. No one imagined that if Palmerston left the Government he would be idle — he would lead either the Radicals or the Protectionists, thought Russell.[1] In such a judgement there was an implication of insincerity, a suggestion that Palmerston took political principles too lightly, and such an impression was enhanced by the apparent dichotomy between the conservative minister, ready to resign in opposition to a Reform Bill,[2] and the 'radical' Foreign Secretary. There was, in truth, no dual political personality. Those — and they were many — who thought it 'strange . . . that neither age nor power abates one jot of Palmerston's rage for Revolutions outside the range of danger to himself'[3] had not taken the trouble to understand him. Palmerston was a Constitutionalist. He liked to see foreign peoples having their 1688 and their 1832. He had an abiding belief that peoples were happier and more prosperous under representative systems and the Rule of Law,[4] and that states

[1] *Queen's Letters*, Vol. II, p. 279.   [2] December 1850.
[3] Add. MSS 43192, 27th October, 1856, Graham to Aberdeen.
[4] In a despatch to Lamb, 18th June, 1833, Palmerston said it was not true as the Absolutists believed that Britain wanted revolutions everywhere, or wanted other countries to adopt her constitution or that British institutions 'must necessarily answer *at once* everywhere else'. But in a letter to Lamb, January 1841 he said that only constitutional government could provide good government

JOHN BULL SHOWING THE FOREIGN POWERS HOW TO MAKE A
CONSTITUTIONAL PLUM-PUDDING.

so constituted were more naturally the coadjutors of Britain than
authoritarian states.[1] Few men did more to translate into a nineteenth-century idiom the already old conviction that British
institutions were an example for the world to follow, or to transmit
the proposition that an emergent and progressive society will
naturally, if it consults its best interests, frame its political system
in the British image. This the twentieth century has transmuted
into a commendation of 'Western democracy' to emancipated
communities in Asia and Africa. But Palmerston did not wish
other peoples to have a more democratic system than his own.[2]

development of natural resources, security of life, liberty and property, and in a
despatch of 19th March, 1841 he said countries were *always* better off for a constitutional system.

[1] Melbourne denied this — 'All these Chambers and Free Presses in other
countries are very fine things but.... Full as hostile to England as the old
Governments' (quoted *Webster*, p. 786).

[2] Except in the sense that, as foreign nobilities tended to be more obscurantist
than the British, a viable constitutional system in a European country might
well be more avowedly bourgeois than the British. But he was against large
republics and universal suffrage — the former were aggressive and the latter
disturbed the non-voting population in Britain (*Ashley*, p. 73, to Normanby,
28th February, 1848).

T

It was not 'Red' revolutions that he relished, and he never ceased
to warn foreign rulers, officiously as they thought, that they should
yield much to save more, like sensible Whigs or Canningites.[1]

Nor was the principle of self-determination one which Palmerston adopted with Wilsonian lack of discrimination. Austria as a
principal on the wrong side in Europe's ideological war he
abominated. Austria as an occupying power in Italy was anathema
to him. But he fully understood the value to Europe, and to
Britain, of a central power without territorial ambitions, whose
material interests did not clash directly with any of Britain's and
which shared with Britain a common concern at any prospect of
Russian expansion westwards or south-westwards. And he never
felt the qualms which beset his colleagues — and not only Peelite
ones — at the implications for the Christian nationalities of the
Balkans of the maintenance of the Ottoman Empire. It was a
British interest to preserve the two empires in Europe which were
based on a denial of the principle of nationality, and for them he
desired only more efficient and more liberal governance and an
adequate military strength,[2] not their liquidation. Radicals who
looked to Palmerston had therefore to be uncritical. They had to
forgive him his conservatism in home affairs and the limits he set
to his approval of changes in the Vienna territorial settlement.
Many contrived to do so, attracted by the support he gave to
Liberalism and Nationalism. Tories, on the other hand, if they
were to embrace Palmerston, would have to overcome their
suspicion of those very features of his policy which most appealed
to Radicals. What attracted *them* was Palmerston's conservative
opinions on domestic questions and his concern for the landed
interest. Sir Charles Webster, in explaining how Palmerston came
to be associated with the Whigs, says, very aptly, that he 'found
himself' in that section of the Tories 'which the Whigs invited to
join them in order that their own position might be secured'. For
twenty years he had drifted with the Whigs, devoted to 'finality'

[1] e.g. Instructions to Minto for his Italian mission — '*H.M.G.* are deeply
impressed with the conviction that it is wise for sovereigns and their governments
to pursue. . . a system of progressive improvement. . . to apply remedies to. . .
evils. . . and to remodel, from time to time, the ancient institutions of their
country, so as to render them more suitable to the gradual growth of intelligence
and to the increasing diffusion of political knowledge.' ibid., p. 43.

[2] Almost alone of British statesmen, Palmerston believed that 'the Sick Man of
Europe' could be galvanised, not only into spasmodic military activity, but into a
fair level of general vitality.

and always for moderate courses. He stood with Lansdowne against the Reform Bill which Russell pressed on his colleagues in 1850. He had favoured freer trade, and commercial treaties in the Huskisson tradition, but he resented the decision to repeal the Corn Laws, and it was not thought impossible in 1850–2 that he might accept a moderate fixed duty and enter into alliance with Stanley. And though the Tories in general did not care for his participation in the ideological war, attaching as they did great importance to the preservation of the Vienna settlement and friendship with Austria, they were often, being 'patriots', less averse to diplomatic victories and displays of British strength than they indicated in the division lobbies. Palmerston had far more in common with them than with Cobden or Bright, who made a moral principle of cosmopolitanism and assumed that, if only the diplomatists would go on an extended vacation, Europe, gratefully espousing Free Trade and its larger implications, would flow sweetly into a mood of mutual understanding and general disarmament. There was, in Palmerston's handling of foreign affairs, a certain arrogant insularity which the Tories could appreciate, while Radicals could warm to his championship of the cause of 'democracy' in Europe.

That Palmerston should become leader of the non-pacifist Radicals was thought possible; that he should return to his Tory associations was thought fairly probable; that he should become the key man in some arrangement cutting across parties, to prevent a genuine Reform, was in 1852 much canvassed. What only Queen Victoria hypothecated before the Crimean War was that Palmerston should become the political leader of Whiggery. Whereas in March 1850 Russell thought it safe to make Palmerston Leader of the Commons, as 'he was too old to do much in the future' (Palmerston was in his sixty-sixth year, Russell in his fifty-eighth), the Queen feared that he might emerge as a rival to Russell.[1] It was certainly clear by 1852 that Palmerston was a dark horse in the Coalition Stakes. It was an open question from which stable he would run and which colours he would carry. And after a complex concatenation of circumstances made him the political chief of Whiggery, the Sacred Circle of the Great Grand Motherhood continued to insist, with emphasis, and even with acrimony, that

---

[1] *Queen's Letters*, Vol. II, pp. 279–82. The Queen thought that, if the Whig ministry fell, Palmerston in the Commons might break with Russell in the Lords and force himself into office.

THERE'S ALWAYS SOMETHING.

"I'M VERY SORRY, PALMERSTON, THAT YOU CANNOT AGREE WITH YOUR FELLOW SERVANTS; BUT AS I DON'T FEEL
INCLINED TO PART WITH JOHN, YOU MUST GO, OF COURSE."

he was 'not a Whig'.[1] He never gave the impression of having been
decently absorbed. The political clothing did not make the man.
But he revelled in the enigma. He liked being courted for the
dowry he could bring the successful suitor — a dowry which
increased as he proved his political character to be congenial to the

[1] G. W. E. Russell, *Prime Ministers and Some Others.*

age. Cobden and Bright had regretfully to admit that the materialism and complacency of the middle classes frustrated their joint desire to transform the whole temper of British foreign and colonial policy as well as Bright's desire for a further approach to democracy. Gladstone persistently regretted the nation's willingness to pay the taxes which were the price of Palmerstonianism.

The main reason for keeping Palmerston at the Foreign Office, despite his cavalier treatment of Queen, premier and cabinet, was the fear that if he were to be turned out, he would at once turn out the ministry. And that is precisely what he did, when, at the earliest opportunity after his dismissal in December 1851, he 'had his tit-for-tat with John Russell'. It had been thought at last inevitable that he should be removed, and even that it might be safe, for his current offence was, unlike its numerous predecessors, not popular. There were good and sufficient reasons (as his colleagues admitted) why Britain should seek to stand well with Louis Napoleon, President of the French Republic since 1848, who in December 1851 carried out a *coup d'état*. But the prompt and unauthorised approval of a Buonaparte destroying a constitution by military force, of which the cabinet first heard not from the Foreign Secretary but from an aggrieved ambassador in Paris,[1] could not be tolerated. After the tit-for-tat, and the formation of a minority Tory government which Palmerston refused to join (on the ground that it would not accept Free Trade), Palmerston bore no grudges. He said, indeed, that he could not serve under Russell,[2] and he kept a door open to Derby,[3] but he made no difficulties about the formation of the coalition, committing his interests to Lord Lansdowne, and accepting the Home Office. During the coalition, though maintaining his objections to Reform, and resigning upon it,[4] he conducted himself with restraint, although he could not altogether approve the foreign policy that resulted from a persistent tug-of-war between himself and Russell on the one hand (often supported by Lansdowne and Newcastle) and the pacific and rather pro-Russian Aberdeen on the other. He did not bring forward demands in regard to foreign policy in such a

[1] Normanby, the ambassador, was in very close social relations with Orleanist magnates who were manipulating the assembly in opposition to Napoleon.

[2] Ashley, Vol. II, pp. 232, 236–7.

[3] He enjoyed the civility of both parties — from 'the Government. . . hoping I may join them' and the Whigs 'hoping that I may not leave them' ibid., p. 237.

[4] December 1853 (see *infra*, Ch. XII). He was induced to withdraw his resignation.

way as to give an impression of self-seeking. As opinion in favour of his assumption of the War Office if not the premiership grew, he made no attempt to force the pace by seconding Russell's attempts to secure more adequate personal and administrative arrangements for the management of the war effort. Hence the coalition ministers accounted Palmerston a good colleague and Russell a bad one, and when before the beginning of the session of December 1854 Russell seemed to have resigned, Palmerston's appointment as Leader of the House was agreed. He actually held that office for the brief period between Russell's desertion and the resignation of the Government after the passage of Roebuck's motion.

The competition between Russell and Palmerston which the Queen had predicted had now become reality, but with Russell still in the Commons. The weight of his disloyalty to the cabinet while he was Leader of the House brought Russell's end of the see-saw to ground level, while Palmerston's soared aloft. The mutual dissatisfaction between Russell and his colleagues, culminating in bitter recrimination at the end, conveyed itself to Parliament and the country in a manner deeply harmful to Russell's prestige and prospects. Palmerston's unwonted discretion had proved the better part of valour. His colleagues respected him; the country cried out for him. The war was popular, and the public demanded that Palmerston conduct it. He was raised up, somewhat after the manner of the elder Pitt, by national exasperation. The fact that he was a member of an unpopular government, and its chief apologist in the debate that was fatal to it, was no more held against him than against Winston Churchill in 1940. In both cases the reputation for being a 'war-monger', which had been a handicap to the statesman during peacetime, became an asset when a war-monger was visibly required. Men might argue whether the reputation, in its pejorative sense, was or was not deserved, but it would not have been won by any statesman who was not credited with a masterful and belligerent nature, with the qualities of courage, intrepidity, resourcefulness and a taste for decision. The parallel, indeed, extends further. War might have come in any case if Russia in the 1850s and Germany in the 1930s had not been adequately concerned to avoid it, but a stronger and clearer British stand in the years of uneasy peace would have made it far less likely. Palmerston could be blamed for the war only in the sense that it

SEEING THE OLD YEAR OUT AND THE NEW YEAR IN.

was he who had established the dogma that the maintenance of the integrity of the Turkish Empire was an essential British (and European) interest — the proposition which had sent the British fleet to the Dardanelles — and that it was he who originally sent to Constantinople Sir Stratford Canning, who was blamed for the Turkish assumption that British aid could be relied upon even if the Turks refused all conditions which the Powers formulated as the basis of peace. But people were no longer concerned as to whether Britain had or had not 'drifted' into war. They only knew that the same government whose Foreign Secretary used that fateful phrase and whose Prime Minister attempted a reasoned assessment of the policy of the enemy after the declaration of war, when the public was in a jingoistic mood, had not showed itself competent to direct the conflict. The war had degenerated into a long siege, causing untold suffering to the soldiers because ministers and commanders had not prepared for such a siege. And public opinion identified Palmerston as the man to win the war.

Palmerston's good behaviour as a coalition minister had rehabilitated him in the eyes of his Whig colleagues and diminished the antipathy of the Peelites. At first the Whig colleagues said they would serve under Palmerston only if the Peelites would too, but when the Peelites declined, they agreed to serve anyway. It was then intimated to the Peelites that it ill-became them to desert their Whig colleagues who, when Aberdeen and Newcastle were attacked, had stood by them even though Russell, the accredited leader of Whiggery, joined the attackers, and had refused to raise up Russell as a Whig prime minister on the ruins of the coalition. Under pressure from Aberdeen himself, the Peelite ex-ministers agreed to join a reconstructed coalition under Palmerston, and without Aberdeen and Newcastle. Gladstone, however, acquiesced in this decision with the utmost reluctance,[1] and within weeks was responsible for the secession of most of them. The nominal ground for the secession was Palmerston's view that the new Government could not resist the appointment of the committee of inquiry for which the Roebuck motion had called.[2] But the real reason, as Palmerston told Gladstone, was that 'to speak plainly and frankly, you distrust my views and intentions'[3]— the same reason that Earl Grey had resisted Palmerston's re-appointment in 1845. To Gladstone there was something immoral in the reconstitution of the cabinet without Aberdeen — 'our most noble victim struck down, and we set to feast over the remains'.[4] He could in the circumstances under which the Aberdeen administration had fallen join neither a Derby nor a Russell government, but he thought that it was round those two leaders that a party system must reconstitute itself, and preferred the former. These objections, however, could be overcome; the real difficulty was his conviction that Palmerston would prolong the war by extending the war aims. He believed that the absence of Aberdeen from the cabinet guaranteed that Palmerston would be beyond restraint, that the Peelite ministers would be

---

[1] Gladstone's reasons are detailed Add. MSS 44745, f. 4, 4th February, 1855.

[2] On 7th February (ibid.), Gladstone had noted that Hayter doubted the possibility of resistance — 'I apprehend however that we should not give way.' The Palmerston government was able to use Lord Seymour on the committee to counter Roebuck's attempts to make the report a very drastic indictment. Gladstone was partly concerned for the reputation of Aberdeen and Newcastle, but he also had constitutional objections — Argyll (*Autobiography*, Vol. I, p. 566) wrote that the Peelites 'quitted us because a useless committee of the House of Commons would put an end to the British Constitution'.

[3] Add. MSS 44271, 6th February, 1855... 'you think that I should be disposed to continue the war without necessity for the attainment of objects unreasonable... unattainable... or not worth the efforts necessary. In this you misjudge me'. Gladstone replied that the word 'distrust' did not truly describe his sentiments.

[4] Add. MSS 44745, 6th February, 1855.

'part of the mob' in the cabinet where foreign affairs were concerned.[1] He still held this view when other Peelites acknowledged
that it was erroneous. 'To make Palmerston useful or even harmless
his Ministry should have been leavened and not opposed,' said
Herbert in November 1856. But Gladstone replied, 'Was it not
quite clear that the first time he and the leaven disagreed about a
question on which he had the popular side (he was perfectly sure
to have or take the popular side of all questions) the leaven would
go to the wall?'[2]

The Peelites incurred great unpopularity by leaving the
Government and by their subsequent parliamentary conduct.
Animated by Gladstone's basic assumption that Palmerston was a
villain, some of them seemed to forget that they themselves shared
the responsibility for going to war and for going to the Crimea,
and gave the impression that they thought the war a mistake. And
in the event Palmerston was induced by the French, if not by his
colleagues, to make peace rather earlier than he would have wished,
leaving the Peelites tainted with the suspicion of factiousness and,
to boot, at sixes and sevens among themselves. Gladstone drifted
to the proposition that the Palmerston government was the worst
he had ever known, and that even if a Derby government were not
in itself better, it would 'be kept in order by the Liberal Party,
which is at present disqualified for good'.[3] He was thus well
disposed towards overtures from Derby through Northcote.[4]
Graham's view was that Palmerston was the only Liberal leader
he could not support. Herbert regretted that the Peelites had left
the Government, and Cardwell was anxious to rejoin it. When
Gladstone wanted to reconstitute a third party, Aberdeen told
him sharply that in 1852 the whole relation of parties had
changed and that an amalgamation with the Liberals had taken
place.[5]

The tragedy was that the amalgamation had not been complete.
The coalition ministers had frequently expressed their pleasure at
working together (*pace* Russell) and would do so again in retrospect. There is evidence, however, of tension between Peelites and

---

[1] Add. MSS 44745, 5th February, 1855.
[2] Stanmore, Vol. II, pp. 59–60, letters of 18th and 20th November, 1856.
[3] ibid., p. 54, to Herbert, 24th October, 1856.   [4] ibid., pp. 64–72, 76–9.
[5] Stanmore, Vol. II, pp. 85–6. It is true that he said the Peelites had 'virtually'
merged with the Liberal party and that the amalgamation was 'complete *as long
as the Government lasted*'. But, he pointed out, the ground of the Government's
resignation had nothing to do with Peelism.

Whigs just below cabinet level. Cardwell wanted to be in the cabinet, and when in September 1854 Granville met him at Carlsbad he found him discontented and dreaming of getting rid of the Whig ministers and perhaps Graham as well. 'Argyll used to say that some of the Whigs talked of themselves as if they were a particular breed of spaniels. I certainly never had an idea of what a Peelite was till I had seen much of Cardwell.'[1] Newcastle, in April 1855, complained that much that was 'very unfriendly . . . to your late colleagues and more especially myself is going on in your Government *sub rosa*', and that this was due to 'a vain notion that the *game* is to crush all Liberals who are not Whigs and that the day is come to resuscitate Whiggery pure and simple'. He had wished, he said, that the name of Peelite had been obliterated, but it had been 'kept alive by the same Clique which is now endeavouring to injure those who have acted with the Whigs with the purest honesty and patriotism but of whom they have always been — it is better to speak the simple truth — *jealous*'.[2] Granville sent him a warm reply. He (Granville) had so strongly pressed the importance of amalgamation 'that I am considered and put down as a Peelite'. He did not deny that the obstacles to a cordial junction arose chiefly from the Whigs. But the Peelites had been in error too, and it was a misfortune that in the cabinet crisis caused by the Roebuck motion the 'Peelites as such' were known to be in conclave round Graham's bed.[3] The sense of that conclave, indeed, was for going on with the Whigs, and, after the Whigs had agreed to stand by the Peelites against Lord John, Peelites felt a duty to go on with the Whigs, even under Palmerston, who, Herbert said, could be regarded from a party point of view as the neutral head of a coalition.[4] The significant thing was that the Peelites still argued from a party point of view, and, indeed, acted upon it. The Peelites went into the Palmerston government as they had gone into the Aberdeen government — as a group. And as a group they left it, Cardwell with the greatest reluctance, and Lord St Germans with the explanation 'I think it my duty to adhere to the friends and colleagues of Sir Robert Peel.'[5] Only three Peelite members of the administration stayed on — the Duke of Argyll, Lord Canning

---

[1] ibid., Vol. I, p. 173, Granville to Herbert, September 1854.
[2] *Granville Papers*, P.R.O., Gifts and Deposits 29/18, 16th April, 1855.
[3] *Newcastle*, pp. 256–8, Granville to Newcastle, 17th April, 1855.
[4] Stanmore, Vol. I, p. 253   [5] Parker's *Graham*, Vol. II, p. 267.

and Lord Ernest Bruce. Yet a few weeks before Gladstone had said that he agreed to stay in office under Palmerston because 'only Young and Lord Alfred Hervey would have held with us (of men in place) out of cabinet',[1] and Herbert wrote, 'Our friends, some few of whom I have seen, cannot even understand our doubts. They think we shall, if we do not mind, find ourselves classed with Lord John and be thought to be trying to hold the balance with a view of becoming . . . masters of the situation.'[2] The secession was proof of the failure to achieve fusion, and it really made nonsense of the later protestations of the leading Peelites that since 1852 they had all become Liberals, and that Peelites, like Whigs, had ceased to exist except as constituent elements in the Liberal party.[3]

Greville records that the secession of the Peelites was greeted with 'uproarious delight' at Brooks's.[4] Sir Charles Wood, deeply regretting that 'we have come to an end of that fusion of all the liberal bodies which has been a public object for years', continued 'The aspirants for office, the excluded from the Whig Government, may rejoice at the loaves and fishes thrown open to them. I do not deny that there may be joy in the old coterie of Brookes [sic], but the sensible and reflecting men of the party will grieve, and grieve deeply.'[5] Whiggery would not have been human if it had not relished the Peelite desertion, both for the vacancies which it made, and for the public obloquy which the Peelites brought on themselves. It even rehabilitated Lord John. He went to the Colonial Office, but only to incur a deeper humiliation than ever. As special representative to the conference at Vienna he accepted terms which the cabinet rejected and persuaded the French to reject, and then returned to defend their rejection in the House of Commons. The Austrians revealed what had happened. The French Foreign Minister resigned. Junior ministers waited on Palmerston to demand Russell's resignation, which was accepted. In the past it had been impossible for a Russell government to dispense with Palmerston lest it fall; now it was impossible for a Palmerston government to retain Russell, lest it fall. To such an

---

[1] Add. MSS 44745, 7th February, 1855.
[2] ibid., 5th February and Stanmore, Vol. I, pp. 251 ff., 4th February, 1855.
[3] Parker's *Graham*, Vol. II, p. 309 (15th April, 1857 to Herbert); Stanmore, Vol. II, p. 81, 18th March, 1857 (to his wife), p. 87, 12th April, 1857 (to Gladstone).
[4] *Greville*, III, 1, p. 246.   [5] Stanmore, Vol. I, pp. 266–7.

extent had the vogue of the two men changed that administrative reformers made excuses for Palmerston,[1] while Russell was condemned by them as obsolete. 'Can anybody remember', asked the *Times*, 'the time when Lord John Russell was not on his legs advocating civil and religious liberty, an extension of the franchise and a select circle of safe, abstract and comprehensive reforms? He has never once varied that performance. . . . Undoubtedly he did some considerable things in his day but we don't want him to be always doing them. There is a time to have done. . . . The dust of those everlasting old bills is still in your throat. It is always choking you . . . Lord John has shut himself up in a little world of his own. . . . His reforms are all in the high constitutional region. . . . It is the Revolution of 1688 in a perpetually diminishing series, Lord John is always landing at Torbay to deliver an ideal Englishman from some hypothetical bondage'.[2]

The revelations of W. H. Russell, the evidence accepted by the Roebuck Commission, and the strictures on patronage made in the Trevelyan-Northcote report, produced a considerable demand for reformed, as well as vigorous, administration, and there were strong attacks on aristocratic monopoly. Palmerston's response was to recall three ex-cabinet ministers — Lord Panmure (Fox Maule), Carlisle ('a Howard of noble birth')[3] and Labouchere, who was brother-in-law of Carlisle and hence also of Argyll — and to raise up four others of whom only Sir George Cornewall Lewis, who went to the Treasury, was even in the second rank of ability. Panmure was described by Argyll as 'a very good fellow . . . a rough, strong-headed Scotsman', but it had never occurred to him that he was 'a man to resort to in any great crisis of administrative affairs'.[4] Yet he was given the War Office, with which the office of Secretary at War was at last amalgamated. Granville described this 'Mars' as 'a Scottish divinity more fit perhaps to direct a campaign

---

[1] e.g. Raikes Currie to the Liberal Representation Society in the City, opposing the endorsement of Russell (*Times* 26th March, 1857).

[2] 24th April, 1857. The *Times* was strong for administrative reform. The writer admitted that Russell had taken up Education, but pointed to law reform, urban improvement, better 'social organisation', increased facilities for trading, land transfer etc., as contempory topics in which Russell had no interest.

[3] *Clarendon*, Vol. II, p. 296, 8th December, 1864, 'Poor Lord Carlisle. I do not think the *Times* article will be gratifying to his family, and though so much of it is true, there was a peculiar press-vulgarity about the blood-royal of the Whigs, and aristocracy, and Howards of noble birth etc. The truth was, poor man, that he had a mind capable of just so much cultivation as to yield a very pretty flower-garden; but the soil was not deep enough for forest trees. . . .'

[4] *Argyll*, Vol. I, p. 533.

in the General Assembly of the Church of Scotland than on the shores of the Black Sea'.[1] Vernon Smith, who at the Board of Control was to encounter the Indian Mutiny, was thought by the same writer 'more intelligent than Mars' but lacking in 'go' and 'tact'; the best to be said of him was that his reputation was below his 'deserts'.[2] The *Times* called his appointment a breach of faith with a country demanding strong government.[3] Yet this was no scraping of the barrel, for these ministers, with the egregious Stanley of Alderley, were among the foremost of the Whig 'disinherited'. Whatever one may think of the relative merits of Whig and Peelite ministers of 1841–55, there was nothing impressive in the quality of these second-liners whose hopes had been frustrated in 1852. Palmerston himself did not think much of them. In February he wrote 'We shall have many discontented men behind us, because the body of the Whigs are angry that the Peelites joined me, and have occupied places which the Whigs hoped to have themselves,' but the Peelites 'consisted of more able men'.[4] Forced by Peelite defection to fill many places anew, he came to Lewis only after Cardwell and Baring had declined the Treasury and to Labouchere only after Derby's independent-minded heir, Stanley, aged twenty-eight, had refused the Colonies. He raised up Baines, from the middle class, 'of more sense than genius and more industry than figure',[5] but only after his stepson Shaftesbury (the Ashley of the Factory Bills) and the Peelite Elgin had declined. He sought to avoid complete dependence on Whiggery, and captured, mainly for minor offices, a mixed bag of Peelite and crypto-Peelite game.[6] And these apart, he did not rely entirely on the 'disinherited'. But because he would not go much outside the traditional preserves, most of his nominees were out of the top drawer, many out of the Whig top drawer.[7] He would not

---

[1] Fitzmaurice, Vol. I, p. 102.   [2] ibid., p. 269.
[3] 26th February, 1855.   [4] Ashley, Vol. II, p. 307, 15th February, 1855.
[5] *Times*, 9th April, 1857, thought the appointment of men of large private fortunes and commercial origin to the Duchy of Lancaster very peculiar. For Strutt had held the office until it was needed for Granville when Russell took the Presidency of the Council in 1854.
[6] The Peelite Argyll had stayed in, and Canning had joined, the cabinet. In 1856 the Conservative Peelite Harrowby (pro-Pole and therefore anti-Russian) did so. Keogh, once reckoned a Peelite, Lord Ernest Bruce and Wellington retained office and the Peelites Viscount Monck, Stuart Wortley, H. A. Herbert and Sir Robert Peel accepted office.
[7] He retained William Cowper, Lord Wodehouse, Chichester Fortescue, and two Berkeleys and appointed Shelburne and Hon. J. K. Howard (son and son-in-law of Lansdowne), Henry Brand (later Speaker), Horsman and Bouverie.

have thought very highly of Whig talents, but he did not go out of his way to humour administrative reformers. There was no nonsense about merit when Lowe was subordinated to Ben Stanley at the Board of Trade and Wilson remained an underling. Palmerston acquiesced in the Queen's veto on the appointment of Layard as Under-Secretary for War and in 1857, gave the post, as one might have done in the eighteenth century, to Sir John Ramsden, aged twenty-five, a wealthy landed baronet closely related to Fitzwilliam and Zetland and brother-in-law of Chief Secretary Horsman. This young man's official career lasted less than a year! It would not be an exaggeration to say that Palmerston blithely defied the demand for less aristocratic government.

The parliamentary situation was chaotic, and the skilful whip, Hayter, had his work cut out. A meeting of Liberal members was called at No. 10 on 24th May, 1855 to muster support against a vote of censure by Disraeli.[1] 203 members attended. The most that the *Times* could say of this precursor of our modern meetings of parliamentary parties was that its 'tone, though by no means harmonious, was, perhaps, as favourable to the Government as could be under circumstances so little calculated to inspire confidence'. Gladstone has described the effect of the Peelites acting, or at least existing, as a section — it encouraged the formation of other sections, he said, and they themselves 'had indirect relations with others on both sides of the House'.[2] There was the chronic possibility that the Peelites and Russell and the Mancunians would form an alliance, and turn out the Government whenever the official Opposition promoted a suitable motion. The safety of Palmerston lay in the divisions among the Peelites themselves and, above all, in the fact that, apart from winning the war, there was nothing the country felt strongly about. Prime Minister and country were in tune. Palmerston allowed himself to be restrained by his colleagues in foreign affairs — the scope and purpose of naval action in Nicaragua was limited, and a proposed demonstration against Naples did not take place. But when Palmerston did

---

[1] On account of the failure of the Vienna Conference.

[2] Herbert had a poor opinion of the Manchester School personalities (especially Cobden and Bright) and tactics (they talked too much, and forgot that people were flesh and blood and had national feeling). He deprecated concert with them as encouraging the criticism that the Peelites too were 'doctrinaires' (Stanmore, Vol. I, pp. 424–6, to Aberdeen, 17th May, 1855, 430–1, to Gladstone 27th May). But Gladstone said the Mancunians had 'certain rights of priority which we cannot ignore' (p. 434).

break out in debate with his characteristic jingoism, Gladstone bitterly complained that he could make the House drunk on ginger beer.[1] Herbert explained to Gladstone that his parliamentary impotence was due to the fact that he was out of harmony with the spirit of the moment — 'the deep-seated national military spirit' — 'You must . . . make allowance for the prevailing passions and prejudices of the public. You can never lead men by reason alone.'[2] Gladstone, however, retained the view that 'the whole world is drunk about a Palmerston government and if we humour it in its drunkenness it will rightly refuse to admit the excuse when returned to soberness it condemns what we have done'.[3]

All the principal Peelites, and Russell, joined with Disraeli to defeat the Government on an issue reminiscent of the Don Pacifico affair. The slackness of the Government whips enabled Cobden to pass a condemnatory motion by 263 to 247 early in 1857, after the Government had endorsed the action of the Benthamite Bowring, who summoned the Navy to do vengeance on Canton after the minions of Commissioner Yeh had molested the *Arrow*, a vessel which was as disreputable a representative of British property as Don Pacifico of British citizenship. But what if Bowring's case was weak in justice and international law? The British public does not judge by refinements. Repudiation of Bowring, and an offer of compensation, would not assist British prestige in the Far East. Britain must not 'lose face'. And so the Mancunians and Peelites and Tories found themselves exposed to a penal dissolution of Parliament. Palmerston proffered the electors the picture of 'an insolent barbarian' affronting the flag. Half the Peelite and Liberal and Radical supporters of Cobden's motion failed to be returned.[4] Cobden himself, fleeing the West Riding, was defeated at Huddersfield and Bright and Milner Gibson at Manchester. Some Liberals, and not a few Tories, who had voted with Cobden protested that they had not meant to defeat Palmerston, and others assured the electors of their general support for the Prime Minister.[5] Russell, to the general surprise, polled

---

[1] Stanmore, Vol. II, p. 47, July 1856.
[2] ibid., p. 73, 8th March, 1857 (cf. Vol. I, p. 441, 1st June, 1855, to Graham).
[3] Add. MSS 44745, 5th February, 1855 (diary).
[4] *Times*, 30th March — 'The League has disappeared from Parliament,' on 13th April it estimated casualties as 9 Manchester School, 12 Peelites, 3 Independent Irish. The victims included W. J. Fox, Hadfield, Miall, Hon. A. Gordon, Lord A. Hervey, Sir James Hogg.
[5] See *Times*, 11th April — e.g. Lord R. Grosvenor (Middlesex), Sir F. Baring.

PAM—WINNER OF THE GREAT NATIONAL STEEPLE-CHASE.

well in the City (a project for bringing Palmerston against him had not matured).[1] But Sir Francis Baring, who generally acted on the maxim that the Queen's government must be carried on, and as a responsible elder statesman formed a valuable link between cabinet and Parliament, nearly lost his seat at Portsmouth (which he had represented since 1826) for giving a conscientious vote with Cobden.

The general election of 1857 was a Palmerstonian victory of almost plebiscitary character.[2] Candidates not irrevocably committed against him sought a foothold or an armhold on his band-waggon. Whigs were the chief beneficiaries of his popularity. Twenty-one gains in the English counties raised 'Liberal' represen-

[1] Russell's supporters held a rival meeting after the Liberal Representation Society excluded him from their slate in favour of 'Liberal and Commercial Candidates', arguing against his aristocracy, his poor attendance, and alleging insincerity in support of the admission of Jews to Parliament (but Rothschild defended him). Crawford and Currie declared themselves Reformers and Palmerstonians. It was true said Currie, that Palmerston was not a Reformer 'but never was the leader of any aristocratical party found to be a Reformer except upon compulsion'. *Times* (25th and 26th March).

[2] *Times*, 16th April, 'We see approbation of Lord Palmerston, more or less qualified, but no praise of Lord Anybody else.'

HENRY JOHN TEMPLE, 3rd VISCOUNT PALMERSTON
by F. Cruikshank
National Portrait Gallery

tation to fifty-three, the highest since 1835, so that Whigs were once more able to pass from borough to county seats; men long excluded by the Tory tide in the counties gained readmission;[1] and with rural boroughs and larger towns as well swinging over to Palmerston,[2] there were more Whiggish members in the House of Commons than perhaps since 1835. This of course was the first election for nearly twenty years in which Protection was not an issue (the *Times* thought this hit the sections that lived on it, Protectionists, Peelites and the Manchester School).[3] The Church was not in danger. There was general prosperity. But the 'Liberal' revival could never have been achieved but for Palmerston's appeal as 'a Conservative minister working with Radical tools and keeping up a show of Liberalism in his foreign policy' (as the Tory leader said),[4] 'an old-fashioned ultra-Tory leading the Liberal party' (as a Peelite said),[5] a militant defender of Britain's interests ('We hear too much of the prestige of England as distinct from its character, reputation and honour,' complained Russell in Peelite voice.) Herbert noted that Palmerston's popularity was very great with the country gentlemen, because of 'his old Protectionist leanings, his unconcealed aversion to Gladstone's financial policy, his objection to Parliamentary Reform . . . and his noisy foreign policy'. Many squires were Palmerstonian pure and simple; many of their M.P.s who sat opposite him would have liked to sit behind him (especially as they did not care for Disraeli) and did not do so only because the machinery of party was stronger than its spirit and 'the club in London and the attorneys in the country prevent them'.[6]

But Palmerston's electoral strength did not alter his parliamentary weakness. There was a considerable majority, and most of it had been returned as Palmerstonian. But, the *Times* shrewdly remarked, the majority was 'a snow giant'.[7] With Palmerston

---

[1] Briscoe, M.P. 1832–5, won West Surrey; Buller defeated at Exeter 1835 returned to the House as North Devon's first Whig member since 1839; King who lost Warwick in 1837, was the first Whig member for South Warwickshire since 1836.

[2] Sir Harry Verney recaptured Buckingham and F. J. S. Foljambe, aged twenty-seven, calling himself an 'old Whig' (*Dod*) won Retford. Lord Bury, later a Conservative, won Norwich.

[3] *Times*, 7th April, 1857.

[4] Malmesbury's *Memoirs*, p.385, 15th December, 1856, Derby to M.

[5] Stanmore, Vol. II, p. 80, 15th March, 1857.

[6] ibid., p. 69, 27th January, 1857, Herbert to Graham.

[7] *Times*, 4th April, 1857.

u

himself losing his sureness of touch,[1] it melted away. A plebis-
citary authority, unless conferred for a fixed term, disappears when
the statesman who secures it affronts public opinion. This
Palmerston did when, in response to a sharply worded note from
France, he introduced legislation at the behest of Napoleon III.[2]
Liberal chauvinists joined with Russell, Tories, Peelites and
Mancunians to pass by 234 to 215 an adverse motion of Milner
Gibson and Bright (who had been returned in by-elections).
Palmerston resigned.

The 'fifties, in many ways, resemble the pre-1830 rather than
the post-1832 dispensation. Detached politicians, like Russell,
sought a following, or were sought, like Palmerston, Graham,
Gladstone, and young Stanley, as allies. Fortuitous combinations
of men uncertain whether or how they could replace ministers
turned them out. Heads of government sought recruits from
anywhere and everywhere outside their own pledged following.
Diverse groups coalesced without sinking their separate identities.
Though of course dependent upon a minister securing a majority
in, or at least the acquiescence of, the House of Commons, the
monarch had some discretion as to whom to ask to form a government and three times granted a dissolution to a prime minister
after he had been defeated in the House of Commons. Governments lasted for a few months or a year or two by the aid of their
natural opponents and were destroyed by unnatural alliances,
though on questions of importance (budgets, conduct of the war,
foreign policy). This was the political world of Trollope, which
existed on the eve of Bagehot's famous study of the British constitution. The basic reason for the instability was the fragmentation
of the 'Liberal' forces which had been for some time held together,
first by the fear of 'Free Trade in danger' and then by the existence
of the coalition. The Peelites broke with the Whigs and could not
agree with one another. Russell became separated from his former
colleagues. The Radicals — no more effective for constructive

---

[1] The appointment to the cabinet of Clanricarde ('a man universally and justly
disesteemed', Stanmore, Vol. II, p. 105, Gladstone's comment) was said to have
caused Lansdowne to ask if Palmerston was out of his mind.

[2] Orsini had thrown a bomb of British make at Napoleon, who demanded a
Conspiracy to Murder Bill. Palmerston desired to stand well with the French
Government and sustain the Emperor against anti-British chauvinists in the
army and newspaper offices. Russell's move against the first reading of the Bill
was decisively defeated, but publication of the French despatch altered the
public temper.

purposes than in the 'thirties, and for the same reasons — were
rent in twain on the issue of chauvinism versus pacifism which was
posed by Palmerstonian diplomacy and the Crimean War. It was
useless for the Peelites (*pace* Gladstone) to protest that they had
been Liberals since 1852, that they did not exist as a separate
party, and would not again become so. That only meant that,
unlike Gladstone, they could no longer consider alliance with
Derby. If they were Liberals they were, from the point of view of
the 'Liberal' ministry of Palmerston, Dissentient Liberals. And so
it was obvious that there was no point in turning out Derby (who
succeeded Palmerston but failed to get Gladstone, Newcastle or
Earl Grey to join him) unless the members of Parliament opposed
to Tory government agreed, through their several champions, to
constitute a Liberal party not only for the purpose of expelling
a ministry, but for the purpose of sustaining its successor. When
such agreement was made at Willis's Rooms on 6th June, 1859
and ratified by a vote of 323 to 310 for the Marquess of Hartington's amendment to the Address in reply to the Gracious Speech,
the Parliament which put the second administration of Palmerston
into office lasted for six years and the ministry itself for seven
(Russell succeeding Palmerston in 1865).

There had been, before the general election of 1859, the usual
stories of intrigue by the more exclusive of the Whigs. Ellice
nursed ideas which Graham told him were preposterous because:

> ... the broken fragments of the old Whig party are so shattered that
> they cannot be pieced together again. The old stagers have known
> each other too long and too well, and they dislike each other too
> much ... I see no mutual friendships, no habits of familiar confi-
> dential intercourse, no disinterested love of the public service, which
> after all are the real cement of political combinations. ... No man
> knows the difference between the old and the new Whigs as well as
> you. You remember on what terms they once lived together; you
> see with what jealousies they now fly apart.

Graham told Herbert that Ellice wanted through the Duke of
Bedford to 'establish a Whig reunion embracing the houses of
Devonshire, Sutherland and Howard. ... But the day is gone by
when a conclave of Dukes could sway a Parliament'. Herbert
agreed — '(Ellice) and the Whigs are incurable in their super-
stitions about ducal houses. ... The aristocratic Whigs seem to be
nearly used up, and the party produces no new men, but at the

same time complains of the old ones'.[1] This was a case of Peelites having their old-fashioned fun at the expense of the Whigs. But there was point in their remarks. The old leaders of Whiggery were an ageing crew, no successors were in sight, and there *was* a decline in public spirit among them and no exercise of the arts of leadership over an increasingly heterogeneous party. Herbert could see no prospect of the formation of an efficient party, let alone government, 'out of the chaos on the Opposition benches'. Certainly, after Tory gains in the general election, restoring the Derbyite numbers to their 1852 par, there was no prospect unless all the varied sections agreed to come together and stay together. There could be no thought of Whigs 'going it alone'. Bright, with perhaps thirty-five supporters, held the balance in his hand — 'however humiliating and painful the fact may be', Graham told Russell, 'without the concurrence of John Bright you cannot succeed in overpowering Lord Derby, or in holding the Government, even conjointly with Palmerston'.[2] And Bright would want Peelites prominently in the ministry. Russell was not averse to this, as a check on the Palmerstonian element which, he knew as well as Graham, could not be exluded.[3] Everybody (including ducal houses) would have to co-operate, because the margin was so narrow. And Herbert made it quite clear that a new government would have to seek better roots in the parliamentary party than the coalition of 1852 had done. The party had become 'very independent in habits and feelings and the time is gone by when they will vote like a flock of sheep for what some half dozen men may concoct in a library'.[4] This was not to be 1852 all over again, still less 1845 or 1846. There must be something like the Lichfield House Compact, for the parliamentary situation was similar. Now, as in 1835, the fiction of automatic 'leadership' by an oligarchy remote from large elements of its parliamentary following had been exposed. The meeting at Willis's Rooms was necessary to constitute a party by registering agreement between leaders *and* mutual obligation between leaders and followers. It was a conscious effort to restore the two-party system of 1835–45, because of the incon-

[1] Parker's *Graham*, Vol. II, pp. 364–6 and Stanmore, Vol. II, p. 165, 7th–10th January, 1859.
[2] Parker's *Graham*, Vol. II, pp. 383–5, 17th–18th May, 1859.
[3] Russell had already sketched (p. 381, 7th May) a government of himself, Graham, Gladstone, Herbert, George Lewis and 'two or three of the Palmerston set'; Graham, 17th, talked of 'Palmerston and his quasi-Liberal adherents'.
[4] Fitzmaurice, Vol. I, p. 328.

venience experienced since it collapsed. That this was so was shown by some of the speeches in the debate on the Hartington amendment. Milner Gibson said that the issue before the House was simply 'the rival claims of two great parties in the country to political power'. Hartington's characteristically low-keyed style of saying the same thing was that the Liberals had learned a lesson from adversity, and perhaps from their opponents, and were not so disunited as of late. With few dissentients (but they included Gladstone) all who were not Tories voted with Hartington; after Willis's Rooms to vote against him was to opt for Toryism. Willis's Rooms is the only occasion before 1868 at which one can reasonably commence the history of the Liberal party as a continuing organisation.

Willis's Rooms did not solve the problem of the leadership, for which Russell craved; three weeks before the meeting he was said to be expressing his regret that he would have to leave out so many old friends.[1] But neither Palmerston nor Russell wanted to go to the Lords, and neither would serve under the other until the commission to Lord Granville caused them both to agree that neither could be the third man in the state and that the Queen should choose to which of them — 'the two dreadful old men' she called them — to offer the premiership. Victoria, reluctantly, chose Palmerston, and he, reluctantly, agreed that Russell should have the Foreign Office and stay in the Commons. Difficulties were eased by the prominence of the Italian Question, on which Palmerston and Russell were happily in agreement, and this provided the bridge over which Gladstone crossed to join them. Thus was formed the strange triumvirate, each of whom was to be prime minister before ten years had passed, the succession of one to another in the Liberal leadership marking major steps in its transition from a conservative to progressive posture, with critical effect on the future of Whiggery.

While Palmerston lived, Whiggery could feel safe. His primacy really meant that (*pace* Gladstone's budgets) the administration had no domestic policy at all. The Radicals, faced with the alternative of a Derby government, could only wait for the future. The Tories, faced with Palmerston's potent appeal to *Conservative Cause* men, were afraid to defeat him in the House, having no hope of defeating him in the country. Ambition apart, they were well

[1] *Greville*, III, 2. 246, 17th May, 1859.

content with a government as little offensive to Conservatives as any imaginable. Palmerston barred Parliamentary Reform. He upheld the landed interest, as in 1853 when he had first confronted Gladstonian finance in cabinet.[1] He checked both Russell and Gladstone, his destined successors. His government was not, at first, overwhelmingly Whig, and was therefore, though very aristocratic,[2] far more talented than his previous administration after the Peelites had left it. It was like Aberdeen's, 'of a very Peelite complexion'.[3] This offended the more exclusive of the Whigs, who found a spokesman in 'Ben' Stanley:[4]

> ... The rather contemptous way in which the Whigs were excluded from the Government and every Peelite crammed into every important place without bringing a single vote besides their own, will make many Whigs lukewarm and after all they are the backbone of the Liberal party. The Peelites are still a separate section, they are not members of the same clubs, they have not the same traditions or the same feelings and they view the Whigs with dislike and mistrust, which feeling is fully shared by the Whigs towards them.

Even Granville expressed 'annoyance at finding myself between Elgin and Newcastle instead of between Lord Lansdowne, Ben and Clarendon'.[5] Russell himself had at last realised that Whiggery was not enough.[6] But the hatchets between Whigs and Peelites were not buried until the Peelites disappeared from the scene. Death, however, did carry most of the Peelites away by 1864, and the cabinet became more Whiggish. 'Ben' himself entered the cabinet as Postmaster-General when Elgin went on a mission to China;[7] Granville said he found it 'the seventh Heaven'. Towards the end, Clarendon and ex-Chancellor Cranworth were brought back.

---

[1] Add MSS. 44271, 10th–12th May, 1853. Gladstone argued that his legacy duties were mild and fair and that not they, but a differential income tax, would be the true mother of land confiscation. But Palmerston said they were confiscatory, 'a great Individual oppression' and would give people the idea that the Government was hostile to the landed interest.

[2] The cabinet consisted of seven peers, the brothers of Bedford and Clarendon, the brother in-law-of Clarendon, two relatives of Grey, Gladstone and Cardwell (both now landowners) and Milner Gibson, an ex-Tory.

[3] Greville, p.253.

[4] Gifts and Deposits 29/18, to Granville, 21st Septeber, 1859.

[5] Fitzmaurice, Vol. 1, p. 344.

[6] When projecting a ministry he had proposed to include in the cabinet, of Whigs, 'only Somerset', 'possibly Baring' and 'two or three of the Palmerston set'.

[7] He subsequently became the fourth successive Peelite viceroy in India.

And Whigs crowded the junior and honorific places.[1] It was the Indian summer of Whiggery, this period when everyone was waiting for Palmerston to die:

> Ye Gods, it doth amaze me,
> A man of such a feeble temper should
> So get the start of the majestic world
> And bear the palm alone.

The ill-considered Tory hack, rising by unorthodox methods, in association with the Whigs but not by the will of Whiggery, relying not on the connection but on himself, had reached a sort of Caesarian supremacy, making the Whigs dependent on him rather than he on them. And at the last they were too apprehensive as to what would follow to grudge him that supremacy.

---

[1] A Dundas, a Pelham, an Eden and a Whitbread at the Admiralty under a Seymour; Knatchbull-Hugesson at the Treasury, Wodehouse at the Foreign Office, Chichester Fortescue at the Colonial Office and Brand Chief Whip.

CHAPTER XII

The Dishing of the Whigs

'To the last he fought as a contemporary, claiming no favour and requiring none,' said an obituary of Palmerston.[1] But could a man of eighty who rode in open cabs on wintry nights, saying that this was almost as good as walking, be accounted a 'good life'? As he prepared, fifty-eight years after first entering the Commons and also after first receiving office, after being a minister for forty-eight years, to face his seventeenth general election and his own thirtieth appeal to an electorate, the Tories were filled with foreboding. It was quite likely that he would not live to meet the new Parliament (nor did he). 'The exceptional sway of Lord Palmerston', as the *Edinburgh Review* remarked, 'could not be reproduced by any other statesman, or any combination.' But surely the obvious successor to Palmerston as champion of the *Conservative Cause* was Lord Derby. And if the electors were simply asked to 'leave it to Pam' the real issue, Radicalism versus Conservatism, would be obscured. The *Quarterly* implored the electors to understand that soon the battle for the constitution would be hard and serious work and begged them to abandon secret for open Conservatism.

The event was as the Opposition feared. As in 1857, Palmerston's appeal to the electors resulted in an increase in the ministerial majority — he was the only man ever to achieve this between 1832 and 1955,[2] and he achieved it twice. The Liberals held their own even in the small boroughs, and registered net gains in the counties.[3] And then Palmerston died. Would the new Parliament, as the *Fortnightly* feared, prove to have inherited the conserva-

---

[1] In the *Fortnightly Review*.

[2] The Conservative government formed in 1951 increased its majorities in 1955 and 1959, an unparalleled performance. But it changed its leadership just before the 1955 election and in January 1957.

[3] The Liberals did especially well in the counties subject to rapid urbanization (except East Surrey) and now held four Derbyshire and four West Riding seats (two recently created) and three out of four in Staffordshire and Durham, while Gladstone won the additional seat in South Lancashire. But, in more rural places, if the Liberals lost two seats in Wiltshire, one in East Sussex and one in North

tism and lethargy of its predecessor? Or was it, as the *Quarterly* apprehended, ready to be made the instrument of a robust Liberalism? To pose these questions was merely to say that all depended on how much *vis inertiae* Whiggery would bring into play against the progressive designs of Russell and Gladstone.

In 1859 'Ben' Stanley prophesied that the Radicals would not be conciliated 'by a nonentity like Gibson and a Tory aristocrat who happened to have been a pronounced Corn Law Repealer and who they had forgot to pay in the division of the spoils', an offensive description of Charles Villiers. That there should be two representatives of Radicalism in the cabinet was a tribute to the indispensability of Radical support. But it was to Gladstone, who seemed in 1859 to have reverted to his Tory affiliations, that Radicals were looking, rather than to Gibson or Villiers. Palmerston had wanted Cobden. Bright he would not have, for he attacked *classes*, had spoken of British diplomacy as 'a gigantic system of outdoor relief' for the aristocracy,[1] and was an uncompromising opponent of Palmerstonianism. But Gladstone too had been for nearly thirty years a political opponent of Palmerston, primarily on account of his foreign policy, and by the 'fifties had seemed to embrace all the elements of Cobdenism, with its insistence on peace, disengagement from the colonies, and retrenchment. The Mancunian concept of foreign policy was somewhat at a discount in 1859–61, because both Gladstone and Gibson were enthusiasts for Italian independence. But Gladstone fought the battle for economy in the cabinet, firing from the Treasury incessant volleys of resignations in order to check Palmerston and Russell and the two service ministers, Herbert and Somerset. He was able to secure compromises because 'they want his tongue to help and they fear it in opposition'.[2] There was a famous dispute with Palmerston over the latter's repeat performance of Wellington's 1848 campaign for rearmament. An invasion was possible, Palmerston said, unless new fortifications were built. And unless the

Essex, they won two in Berkshire, two in Norfolk and one in the North Riding. The overall result in the English counties was:

Conservatives 96 (63 unopposed)
Liberals 51 (30 unopposed).

In the thirty-seven smallest English borough constituency seats there was a Tory majority of only seven. In the eleven smallest boroughs which must be threatened by *any* redistribution, however small, as they had less than 5,000 inhabitants, eight Liberals and nine Tories were returned.

[1] Birmingham Town Hall, 29th October, 1858.
[2] *Clarendon*, Vol. II, p. 186.

navy were modernised and increased British maritime power might be paralysed for half a century and the country be reduced 'to a 3rd rate power if no worse'. 'Our colonies, our commerce and the subsistence of a large part of our Population would be at the mercy of our enemy,' he wrote,[1] counting the cost of Free Trade. That policy Gladstone advanced to its apogee by the Cobden commercial treaty with France.

The ironclads were laid down and the forts still known as 'Palmerston's follies' were raised up, but it was agreed that the programme should be financed by borrowing so that a great Gladstonian budget could proceed. But there was strife upon the budget still, for Gladstone seemed to indicate that, with Cobdenism, he had assimilated traces of its hostility towards the aristocracy, which, indeed, Palmerston had detected in 1853.[2] When reducing dutiable articles to less than fifty (at the cost of postponing the abolition of income tax *sine die* and, as it proved, for ever), Gladstone proposed to include paper. Long ago Lord Grenville had said that it was the multiplication of newspaper readers which made the old electoral system untenable. Since 1832 there had been progressive reductions of the 'taxes on knowledge', especially the crucial stamp duty, but the aristocracy appeared still to cherish the remnant, the tax on paper itself. Palmerston, supported by Wood (and Cardwell), spoke for three-quarters of an hour in cabinet, but in vain. The Paper Bill went forward, and received a majority of nine in the Commons. Palmerston (not for nothing the brother-in-law of Melbourne) made no secret of his wish that the Lords would reject it, and so they did, by 193 : 104, Monteagle taking into the Opposition lobby some thirty of the Government's nominal supporters. Russell, a House of Commons man (though soon to take his earldom) was furious, and Gladstone threatened to resign unless he got an autumn session and a threat of dissolution. He was persuaded, however, to be content with a resolution of the Commons condemning the action of the Lords as unconstitutional. Next year Gladstone put all his fiscal proposals into one Finance Bill, and they included the repeal of the paper duty. Palmerston was very angry, but he gave way, leaving 'Ben' Stanley the sole protestant on behalf of disgruntled Whiggery (and *he* was not likely to resign).

---

[1] Add. MSS 44271, 29th November and 15th December, 1859, to Gladstone.
[2] See *supra*, p. 294, n. 1.

When the Commons passed the proposal by fifteen the Lords bowed.

Gladstone had further impressed his personality on public administration by provisions for parliamentary scrutiny of accounts, by making a habit of the single, comprehensive Finance Bill, and by fastening on the departments a penny-wise Treasury control. Thereafter, having left himself little scope for further major fiscal and financial reforms, Gladstone began to turn his mind to legislative schemes of other kinds, from Cobden, as it were, to Bright. These schemes could not mature until Palmerston was dead, and the real significance of the period 1860-5 in Gladstone's career is that he was building up goodwill among Radicals and an increasing public. Early in 1861 a not unfriendly colleague noted that he was as unpopular as ever among all sections of all parties, except the Radicals.[1] Whiggery viewed him with grave mistrust. Clarendon grasped that he was potentially both a progressive politician and a popular leader, calling him 'an audacious innovator with an insatiable desire for popularity' who would be 'a far more sincere Republican than Bright, for his ungratified personal vanity makes him wish to subvert the institutions and classes that stand in the way of his ambition'.[2] Emily Eden deplored a parvenu air which reminded her of Peel, and a 'jesuitical' character.[3] Greville thought his notions the more dangerous because he was so good and conscientious a man.[4] Gladstone's cultivation of a public did not proceed without setbacks.[5] But it did proceed, and with it came auguries of a restless future whenever he should succeed Palmerston as Leader of the House. There would be an end to the attitude 'Oh, there is really nothing to be done. We cannot go on legislating for ever.'[6] As long ago as 1857, when Gladstone still desired reconciliation with the Tory party, he had made it a matter of complaint against the first Palmerston administration that, when 'full of the expansive vigour of youth, this ancient Empire demands the energetic prosecution of the work of legislation to meet its varied and

[1] Fitzmaurice's *Granville*, Vol. 1, p. 391.
[2] *Clarendon*, Vol. II, p. 331 n. (1860).   [3] ibid., p. 224.
[4] *Greville*, 3rd Series, Vol. II, p. 291.
[5] His avowal during the American Civil War that the South had made a nation was more palatable to the upper classes than anybody else, and a proposal to tax charities puzzled many who wished him well.
[6] *Lord Goschen and His Friends*, ed. Colson, p. 58, Palmerston's conversation with Goschen in 1864 on the Government's programme.

multiplying wants', Palmerston permitted sessions of 'legislative sterility and impotence'.[1] Before Palmerston died Gladstone had indicated a possibility that he would attack the Irish Church and had made, in debate on Baines's bill, on 11th March, 1864, a startling pronouncement on Reform, to which, in the past, he had seemed indifferent.

Gladstone explained to his colleagues that by this speech he meant nothing novel or revolutionary, and had in mind nothing more drastic than Russell's bill of 1860. But that was not how his audience, and the wider audience outside, understood him when he said that 'every man was morally entitled to come within the pale of the constitution' unless presumptively incapacitated by 'some consideration of personal fitness or political danger'. Through this broad escape hatch trenchant meaning might escape, leaving only platitude. But it seemed the language of democracy. Disraeli accused Gladstone of preaching the doctrine of Tom Paine. Palmerston, too, thought he had accepted, in principle, the doctrine of universal suffrage, and sent a strenuous protest to his colleague. For Gladstone had reversed the orthodox order of juxtaposition. Instead of recognising the vote as a trust, with the onus of proof that it should, or with safety could, be extended upon the Reformer, he seemed to embrace the theory that the vote was a 'right' of citizenship and 'called on the adversary to show cause' why it should not be conferred. Palmerston protested on behalf of 'all persons who value the maintenance of our institutions'. What every man, and every woman too, had a right to, was good government under just laws. They were already 'within the pale of the constitution' because they enjoyed 'the security and civil rights which the constitution provides'.[2] No wonder the *Quarterly* identified Gladstone as the first Radical candidate for the premiership.

The new Prime Minister was Earl Russell. He was no more a democrat than Palmerston, but if he was with Palmerston in principle, he rejoiced at the assurance that the most able of the ministers had become a Reformer. Russell resumed the premiership as 'an old man in a hurry'. The Queen's Speech announced a Franchise Bill. It was the fourth to be presented by a govern-

[1] Add. MSS 44747, 1857, unpublished indictment of Palmerston, apparently in the form of an open letter to Aberdeen.
[2] Palmerston's letter and Gladstone's reply are given in *Morley* (2-vol. ed. 1905) pp. 762 ff.

nent, and the fifth to be presented by a minister,[1] since Russell
n 1849 had offered a model for Gladstone to follow in 1864 and
ransformed himself from the 'Finality Jack' to the 'Fidgety
ohn' of Reform. Previous bills had foundered because, as Graham
emarked, Whig grandees were dissentient, Conservative Liberals
larmed and the middle classes at heart unwilling to share the
political power they possessed.[2] They had perished in parliaments
n which the governments which sponsored them had no majority
or only the slimmest of majorities. It had not been necessary for
Whigs outside the cabinet circle to demonstrate very ostentatiously
against them. But now the ministry which promoted Reform was
armed with a majority of seventy, and the prospects of the Bill
were assisted by the widespread feeling that the death of Palmerston marked the end of an era. Whiggery was to be faced with the
choice of acquiescing in an approach towards democracy or open
revolt against it.

The issue was not, indeed, overtly whether the country should
become a democracy. If for practical purposes Russell was with
Gladstone, he was in principle firmly with Palmerston. It was
possible to advocate Reform without transgressing the basic
Whig (and Tory) conception of representation.[3] The representation of interests, and of varied communities, as distinct from the
democratic representation of people, the counting of heads, was
compatible with the progressive extension of the franchise, at
least to the point where it could be authoritatively contended that
the whole population had become fitted to participate, and even
beyond that point if manhood suffrage was linked to very unequal
constituencies. Russell stopped far short of this ultimate. He had
said that he would never consent to 'the representation of counties
and cities alone'.[4] Like Sidney Herbert, he valued 'inequalities
and varieties in the suffrage, because the society to be represented
is composed of unequal and various materials'.[5] He had experi-
mented with 'fancy' franchises.[6] Concerned to devise 'some mode
of entrance for Liberal Tories and temperate Whigs'[7] he had
adopted, in the 1854 bill, Earl Grey's principle of 'minority

---

[1] Governments had presented bills in 1852, 1854 and 1859 and Russell had
presented a bill in 1860 which did not commit the Government.
[2] Parker's *Graham*, Vol. II, p. 171, 15th August, 1852, to Dunfermline.
[3] See Ch. 1, *supra*.   [4] H. of C., 9th February, 1852.
[5] Stanmore, Vol. 1, p. 228, 1st January, 1854.   [6] See *infra*.
[7] Parker's *Graham*, Vol. II, p. 314, 16th September, 1857.

representation'. This was very obnoxious to Radicals as 'a miserable proposal — that refuge of the half-hearted who, pre tending to trust the people, have not true confidence in them who try to evade the national will which they dare not openly contest; and who make of national politics a game of shuffling intrigue instead of honest dependence on democratic principles'. In the absence of a minority clause, Russell thought redistribution should be very limited.

The most articulate of Russell's opponents in 1866 was the middle-class Liberal, Robert Lowe. He was a doctrinaire Utilitarian, who equated Gladstone's 'moral' rights with 'the a priori rights of man which formed the terror and the ridicule of that grotesque tragedy, the French Revolution'. To him all talk of 'rights' was confusion and irrelevance. 'Government does not deal with justice, it deals with expediency,' he said. The object was to create the best machinery for the purpose in mind — i.e., to provide good government — and 'we may violate any law of symmetry, equality or distributive justice in providing the proper machinery'.[2] Foreign commentators noted that the debates in 1866-7 upon Reform were conducted upon the basis of 'utility', rather than 'rights', to an extent unlikely on the Continent.[3] This was a tribute to the power of Benthamism, and to some extent to the striking temporary prominence of Lowe. But it was also very British. The House of Commons was not ready to face the issue of manhood suffrage, and to concentrate on the ground of 'right' would have rendered the Reformers vulnerable to the exploitation of the prejudice against American democracy. During the American Civil War, the upper classes in general had sympathised with the South which, led by its aristocracy, resisted a northern protectionist plutocracy with a democratic mass at its tail.[4] The British governing class regarded democracy as a corrupting

---

[1] Harris, op. cit., p. 405. The minority clause would have allowed a substantial minority in three member constituencies to return one member and influence by selective voting the option between three candidates of the majority party for the other two seats.

[2] Lowe's H. of C. speeches were 3rd May, 1865, 13th March, 26th April and 3rd May, 1866.

[3] e.g. Boutmy, *Psychologie Politique du Peuple Anglais au XIXme Siècle*, Paris 1901.

[4] Gladstone himself had shared these sympathies. A conspicuous exception was the Stafford House Set, led by the Duchess of Sutherland, of which Argyll was a member and Shaftesbury an associate. This group was abolitionist and patronised Mrs Harriet Beecher Stowe, authoress of *Uncle Tom's Cabin*. That lady subsequently wrote an article defending the Sutherland evictions.

and levelling system, and a tyrannical one of which the British 'mixed' system was the antithesis.[1] It welcomed the anxieties of John Stuart Mill, who favoured working class representation but sought safeguards against oppressive majorities. It welcomed the witness of Lowe and Marsh, members with Australian experience, that democracy was not favourable to liberty or civilisation. Everybody knew where Lowe got his model when he denounced democracy which prostituted itself to demagogues and sold itself to millionaires, terrorised an educated minority, concentrated all powers in committees of the legislature, paralysed the executive and robbed the judges of independence and ministers of statesmanship. Reform had to be preached to a parliament in which the majority shared this view of democracy, and most Reformers had the wisdom to accept a utilitarian basis of argument. Russell himself contended that the sagacious Whig would not wait for a crisis like those of 1829, 1830–2 and 1845, but would remember his Burke and act ahead of an emergency. When he saw that a wider section of the population than had been admitted to the franchise in 1832 was qualified to vote, he would extend the franchise. Arguments on the merits of democracy were irrelevant.

According to Lowe, however, the merits of those whom it was proposed to enfranchise were also irrelevant. He denied them any legitimate grievance against the representative system which had produced 'good government'. That was not to say that like Palmerston, or the great businessman Laing, he believed that abuse after abuse had been remedied until there were no practical abuses left.[2] But if in his attitude to the aristocracy, the Church and foreign policy Lowe was poles apart from Palmerston, he was afraid that the late Prime Minister had been right in his view that an extension of the suffrage would hand over the representation of the great towns to trade unions and reduce to nullities 'all the wealthy and intelligent men in those seats of manufacture and trade, thus undoing what was one of the great merits of the Reform Bill of 1832 to do'.[3] And it seemed to him evident that the working class,

[1] Cf. Parker's *Graham*, Vol. II, p. 367, 21st January, 1859 where Graham described to Russell Bright's offence — 'Bright has avowed his purpose. He is dissatisfied with the mixed form of government under which we live... and because the second chamber is not representive he seeks to render the House of Commons purely democratic.'

[2] Laing's speech, H. of C., 12th March, 1866.

[3] *Granville Papers*, (P.R.O.) Gifts and Deposits 29/18, 26th December, 1859.

if admitted to political power, would not endorse the prime virtues of Victorian Liberalism — economy, *laisser-faire* and a pacific foreign policy — and would reject the leadership of the accomplished middle classes. As a long-term forecast, Lowe's analysis was sound. But, at the moment, to many who were not Radicals the facts and prospects seemed against Lowe, who, in his effort to impress his argument, overstated his case. For he dilated upon the depravity and stupidity of the working classes and seemed to commit himself to the proposition that the £10 line of 1832 marked (apparently for ever) the exact line between those who were swayed by reason and enlightenment and those who were ruled by emotion and ignorant prejudice. Even people who had argued, with much plausibility, that Russell in 1849 was premature in his conviction that a considerable portion of the people had since 1832 become fitted to exercise the franchise,[1] were impressed by the evidence that since that date many working class leaders had shown themselves responsible persons who accepted Victorian ideals of self-betterment and the basic assumptions of Victorian capitalism. By what logic could it be held against them that they had largely turned their backs on political agitation? Was not this a sign of maturity rather than apathy?

All the same, it was an embarrassment to the Reformers in 1866 that there was so little public agitation for Reform. Five years before Russell had been constrained to admit that 'the apathy of the nation is undeniable. Nor is it a transient humour, it seems, rather a confirmed habit of mind'.[2] Bright was hardly more successful now than then in provoking popular demonstrations. There could be no question of repeating Macaulay's warnings of 1831–2 that the alternatives were revolution by law or revolution by violence. It could only be argued that there would be trouble sooner or later, if 'the sound morals and the clear intelligence of the best of the working classes'[3] continued to be excluded from the political nation. 'If we will not admit the working-men into the

---

[1] Russell admitted that not enough of the working class had been allowed the vote in 1832. But Tories and Radicals had pointed this out at the time, and had presumed that it was deliberate. Russell naturally preferred to stress the argument that a great improvement in morals and intelligence had occurred subsequently. The force of the argument was somewhat diminished by statistics in 1866 which showed that the working class proportion of electorate was greater than either Russell or Gladstone had imagined.

[2] Walpole, Vol. II, p. 331, to Palmerston, 16th November, 1860.

[3] Russell in the reprint of his *English Government* said he would be glad to see this element represented.

great school of Public Life, we leave them to the free exercise of their instincts and their passions; if we will not teach them political wisdom, they will teach us political disaster,' wrote Lord Houghton.[1] 'If we reject what may be, in some instances, a representation of defective knowledge and short-sighted speculation, we must be prepared to encounter an organized ignorance from without, and the boundless Utopia of revolutionary expectation.' This was true, but it was tame, and it did not frighten Whig oligarchs. The arguments of the more intellectual of the Reformers in 1866 had not the bite of Macaulay's because they could only proclaim that Reform would be wise, not that it was necessary or urgent. Nor could they pretend that the working of the existing representative arrangements was as unsatisfactory as that of the pre-1832 dispensation. Houghton admitted that the peaceful and simultaneous development of national prosperity, intellectual standards, education and the political sympathy of the nation were signs that the 1832 Act had succeeded. As a result, Reformers could not afford to accept the test of beneficial results or the apparent satisfaction of the masses as conclusive. So he argued that these very symptoms of success rendered further enfranchisement inevitable, leaving statesmen only the task of deciding from time to time how to make the franchise 'co-equal with the political capacity and requirements of the country'. Hon. G. C. Brodrick, a Radical Oxford don, remarked that if the unreformed House of Commons had been as enlightened as it was obstructive, it could not have continued long after 1830. Economic, social and intellectual progress had rendered it obsolete by making it increasingly unrepresentative of those who were fitted to exercise political influence. For the same reason, periodic readjustments were required.

The central theme of Macaulay's thesis was thus as apposite as ever, and in the 'sixties it derived nourishment from the newly fashionable scientific doctrine of Evolution. Darwin had published *The Origin of Species* in 1859. There were not lacking men to seize upon its 'progressive' theme to argue by analogy from Nature to Society that there is a forward and upward thrust in human development. Bagehot, politically a conservative Liberal, published a book with the significant title *Physics and Politics*. In the year that Palmerston died, the *Fortnightly Review* began its career with a

[1] In *Essays on Reform* 1867, originally published in the *Fortnightly Review*.

X

mission, as stated in its prospectus, to 'further the cause of Progress by the illumination of many minds'. Under the leadership of John Morley, it was to become after 1867 'the best authority for the orientation of the English mind towards a more secular and scientific outlook'.[1] Scouts were sent forward by an intellectual advance which assailed obscurantism in all its forms, and could not spare political obscurantism. Among them were Lord and Lady Amberley, more recognisable as the parents of Bertrand Russell than the son of Lord John and the daughter of 'Ben' Stanley.[2] Such people affected the intellectual atmosphere that future generations would breathe. But it was of present importance that the public should begin to be told, in the currently fashionable idiom of the new science, that politics, like science, was emerging from its 'metaphysical era'; that a revolution was in the making as drastic as the substitution of the Copernican for the Ptolemaic system; that there was a tendency to a more democratic society, and that therefore there must be a more democratic constitution.

The Tories, and many of the Whigs, did not like the drift of the evolutionary argument, and for the same reason that they were not prepared to argue a Reform Bill on its merits. The bill of 1832 had been professedly 'final'. Its authors had repudiated the notion that it was the beginning of a progression ending in the representation of numbers. In 1866 even Russell, in a correspondence with Grosvenor, was not prepared to go further than express the hope that a 'settlement' might last as long as that of 1832 (which had lasted longer than he liked). It was not tenable to contend that a new bill could be 'final', and Lowe and the rebel Whigs, beginning with Earl Grey in his speech on the Address on 6th February, insisted that below £10 there was no resting place short of household, if not manhood, suffrage. The issue was therefore not the Bill, but the respective merits of a democratic and a 'mixed', or 'temperate zone', constitution. Perhaps the evolutionists were right, and the 'great social forces' moving onwards in might and majesty (to which Gladstone looked for victory, saying 'You cannot fight against the future') were, in the long term, irresistible.

[1] See *The Party of Humanity*, E. M. Everett, N. Carolina University Press, 1939. The title of this resumé of the influence of the *Fortnightly* is taken from an article in which Morley wrote that most of the parliamentary Liberals, as well as the Tories, belonged to a party of Privilege against which was enlisted the party of the Nation, of active humanity, and political initiative.

[2] They were early advocates of women's rights and birth control.

But they were not *yet* irresistible, and many Whigs were prepared to fight against a future which offered Whiggery nothing but disappointment and frustration.

It should not have surprised Russell that a part of Whiggery rose in arms against a moderate Reform Bill. Ever since 1849 Whiggery had provided the ultimately decisive part of the *vis inertiae*. After he made his pledge, his cabinet colleagues (who had not been consulted) delayed for two years its fulfilment, the production of a Government bill.[1] The measure, when it came, was greeted with Radical contempt, but even that could not endear it to Whiggery. The defeat of the Russell ministry, on the initiative of Palmerston, put an end to that bill. For its successor, sponsored by Aberdeen and Graham, with Russell, as a project for the 1854 session, Granville was the only Whig minister to show any enthusiasm. Lansdowne and Palmerston repeated their obstructive tactics of two years before.[2] Wood declined to put his name to the measure.[3] Resistance in the Commons was planned at the house of Lord Harry Vane.[4] Lord Seymour employed the argument that the eve of war was no time for Reform,[5] and a similar reasoning united Russell's colleagues in declining to consider another bill until the war was over. Aberdeen agreed with Russell that they were glad of the excuse. When Palmerston was prime minister Herbert said that he hated Reform like the Devil and only disliked peace because it would lead to it.[6] Russell was not, however, when peace came, in that ministry, and so the next Reform Bill was presented by a Tory administration, in 1859, and was the product of Disraeli's ingenuity. The conservative Whigs were divided in their attitude. Some hoped to avoid Reform altogether. Others, according to Argyll, secretly desired to 'help the Government in passing a bill less Liberal than we ourselves could have ventured to propose',[7]

---

[1] See Walpole, Vol. II, pp. 196–7 (Russell to Palmerston, 16th Nov., 1853) for an account of the insistence on postponement by Earl Grey, Hobhouse, Wood and Lansdowne. See also ibid., p. 102 and *Queen's Letters*, op. cit., Vol. II, p. 373.
[2] At the end of 1851 Lansdowne withdrew his resignation (on Reform) only when Russell said he would resign if the Marquess persisted. Palmerston was dismissed on other grounds (see Ch. XI). At the end of 1853 Palmerston resigned but was persuaded to return by formal concessions extorted by Lansdowne.
[3] This was inferred from its absence — see Somerset's *Letters and Memorials*, p. 296, 1st March, 1854.
[4] ibid., p. 295, 28th February, 1854.   [5] ibid., p. 297, 3rd March, 1854.
[6] Stanmore, Vol. II, pp. 89–90, to Aberdeen, 12th April, 1856.
[7] *Argyll*, Vol. II, p. 134, to Geo. Grey, 8th March, 1859.

and Palmerston was thought to be among them.[1] But all wanted to return to office. And so nearly all of them joined with Palmerston (and Bright and the Radicals) in voting for Russell's wrecking resolutions. The Opposition's victory in the lobbies drove the Government to a general election, and thus avoided a committee stage which could not have failed to reveal the serious difference between Palmerston, Russell and Bright on Reform. In 1860 Palmerston allowed Russell — once again Leader of the House — to bring on a bill. It perished in committee for lack of oxygen. The historian of parliamentary Radicalism says that the Radicals accepted it without enthusiasm and the Tories opposed it without bitterness; 'its fatal opponents were the Whigs'.[2] No further attempt was made by ministers in a parliament denounced by the Radical organ as 'one of the most adroit of nothing doing parliaments . . . (which) stood on the defensive for the greater part of its long existence and guarded its life by a shield of selfishness and calculation which was proof to all the assaults of passion and enthusiasm, and parried every vital question'.[3]

It was a serious question whether a new parliament, elected at great expense, would welcome or accept in its first years a measure which must lead to its dissolution. But, by the same token, in such a parliament a threat of dissolution by the Government had little force, for a 'penal' dissolution would only anticipate by some months the fate which would befall it anyway if the Bill passed. And to dissolve would be to risk the loss of the majority, as well as a confession that the majority procured by Palmerston as his last political act had refused to allow itself to be used for purposes Palmerston had not approved. It was therefore incumbent on Russell and Gladstone to do everything in their power to conciliate those whose opposition could wreck their schemes. But they did not seem to see this. They gave unnecessary affronts to Whiggery. Russell's first appointment to the cabinet prompted the remark 'Who can stand a German Jew put without trial into the cabinet?' That very elderly and Whiggish body[4] needed new blood, and in

[1] When the Government's proposals were announced however, Palmerston took strong exception to the plan to abstract from the country electorates freeholders in parliamentary boroughs.

[2] Harris, op. cit., p. 444. Mills, Tory M.P. for Taunton, said that of the forty-three speeches (twenty-five by ministerialists) in four nights of debate twenty-nine were against the Bill, twelve neutral and only two in favour.

[3] *Fortnightly Review*, Vol. I.

[4] On the eve of Palmerston's death the average age of the cabinet was over sixty. Vacancies since 1859 had been filled without admitting more than one

AN OLD HAND.

LITTLE J—CK R—SS—LL. "NOW, THEN, LOOK SHARP, OR ELSE LET ME COME!"
PAM. "DON'T YOU BE IN A HURRY, YOUNG GENTLEMAN—I KNOW THE COUNTRY!"

his selection of George Joachim Goschen, a banker who had been
returned for the City of London at thirty-two and had recently
been made, at thirty-four, Vice-President of the Board of Trade,
Russell showed an unwonted judgement of ability as well as of
basic acceptability to the Whig aristocracy. Goschen had upheld
Palmerstonian foreign policy against the Manchester School and
complained to Cobden of Bright's 'dangerous' views of 'the motives
and intentions of the governing class . . . Mr Bright believes . . . in
a degree of selfishness on the part of the governing classes which

person new to cabinet office — the refreshingly unorthodox Earl de Grey and
Ripon, formerly member for the West Riding (as Lord Goderich), prominent
champion of administrative reform, friend of trade unionism and something of a
Christian Socialist. Of Peelites, only Gladstone and Cardwell were left apart
from Argyll, who grew ever more Whiggish, as did Charles Villiers and even
Milner Gibson. Palmerston in 1864 brought back Clarendon who, after suggesting that Wodehouse merited promotion, accepted, saying he would be thought
very greedy for the sweets of office and 'Palmerston very wicked for not bringing
forward any of the latent talent that is always talked of, but never appears, as it is
withering away under the scornful pride of the Whig aristocracy'. And then he
brought back the aged ex-Chancellor Cranworth.

THE OFFICIOUS PASSENGER.

Lord John. "EXCUSE ME, FRIEND BRIGHT, BUT DO YOU COMMAND THIS SHIP, OR DO I?"

in my humble opinion is a libel on them . . .'.[1] Opposing household franchise in the counties in the 'seventies, and the 'socialism' of Joseph Chamberlain (and Lord Salisbury) in the 'eighties, Goschen was to figure as a latter-day Lowe, one of the 'Commercial Liberals' (if one may so christen them) who would stand with

[1] *Lord Goschen and His Friends*, ed. Colson, pp. 19–21, 59–60.

Whiggery in defence of the mid-Victorian order. But the 'many of our old hands' who, according to Brand, the Chief Whip, took offence at the appointment, did not consider this. They wondered why it was necessary to look beyond the Marquess of Hartington, Chichester Fortescue, Lord Wodehouse and the rest of the Whig junior ministers.[1]

Though Goschen was a sworn opponent of Bright, his appointment seemed to many a Whig symptomatic of the remoteness of Russell and Gladstone from the conservative wing of their following, the complement of which was, they alleged, an unhealthy connection between those principal ministers and Bright. The *Saturday Review* said that Bright governed, though he did not reign. Earl Grosvenor was to indict Russell for 'deserting the party' by consulting mainly and in the first instance the feelings and wishes of men below the gangway, '*disregarding the feelings and opinions of the great majority of the Whig party and foresaking the old traditions of that party*'.[2] He said that Bright used language which no gentleman would use in the House and no gentleman would tolerate outside. The Chief Whip thought there was ground for such complaints. 'You will be shocked at some of the names scored as voting against us,' he wrote to Wood (just ennobled as Lord Halifax). 'Bright has done it all by patronising us. . . . The Whigs hate Bright; moreover many distrust Gladstone. Lord Russell is very unpopular; since Palmerston died he has greater proclivities for Bright . . . the fact is, we have been resting too much on the Radical leg. Palmerston's plan was to rest upon Whigs support, and the Radicals had no choice but to follow. Russell's plan has been to rely on Radical support, and the Whigs immediately take fright and desert to the Tories.'[3] The complaint of the conservative Whigs was not confined to the matter of Reform. It extended to the manner in which the leading ministers conducted

---

[1] Gladstone (*To His Wife*, ed. Bassett, pp. 170–1) described the appointment as 'extreme and gratuitious folly. . . a serious political error', and wondered what the critics would think if they had known that Russell came to Goschen after his colleagues expressed objections to Horsman, Sir R. Peel (whose office of Chief Secretary was wanted for Fortescue), Hon. E. P. Bouverie (whose office of 2nd Church Estates Commissioner was a not usual stepping stone to cabinet) and H. A. Bruce. Of these, only Horsman and Bouverie were Whigs, and both were prone to an independence ascribed to thwarted ambition. Brand apparently first knew of the Goschen appointment from the newspapers. In advising it, George Grey was probably thinking in terms of the assistance Goschen could give Gladstone in financial business.

[2] H. of C., 12th April, 1866.   [3] *Clarendon*, Vol. II, p. 314, 21st April, 1866.

themselves and their parliamentary affairs, without due reliance or a shrewd whip who knew his Whigs better than Russell did. When the battle had been fought and lost, both George Grey and Granville felt that it had not been well managed. When Emily Eden was saying that Whigs could not die peaceably in their bed unless Bright was exterminated,[1] it would have been wise for the chief Ministers to stand ostentatiously aloof from the principal 'Americaniser', whom Palmerston had regarded as a political out law because of his attacks on *classes*. It would have been wise to soften the blow of Reform as much as possible to those who would feel it most, by careful consideration of their susceptibilities. The Opposition, mindful of the Whigs' 'weakness of conviction and . . . intense tenacity of power', of 'that lowest form of partisanship which prefers rather to change opinions than change companions',[2] noted with pleasure the failure to do so.

The Tories had hoped for a cabinet crisis, looking especially to Clarendon and Somerset, 'old Whigs' with whom they might be able subsequently to come to an agreement on a 'fusionist' ministry.[3] They were disappointed, and so must look primarily to the Whig aristocracy to provide the thirty-five House of Commons rebels needed.[4] In the debate on the Address, Earl Grey had defended the existing representative system. It might be faulty, he said, but it was not repugnant to reason or commonsense, and he appealed to the success of his father's endeavours and the principle of finality.[5] But Earl Grey was all too used to speaking for himself alone. And so the Opposition heard with pleasure that Lansdowne and Spencer were openly hostile to Reform;[6] that Halifax was said to have remarked that he feared he might end his days in opposition to his old colleagues;[7] that Cleveland (formerly Lord Harry Vane) was disgruntled.[8] Soon Lord Lansdowne came out into the open and began to frequent Tory houses. But where was his equivalent in the Commons? There was Horsman, complaining that 'Lord Palmerston would never have been weak enough to be

[1] ibid., p. 321, 23rd July, 1866.
[2] *Quarterly Review*, July 1865, Art. X, 'The Six Year Old Parliament'.
[3] *The Iddesleigh Papers* record (28th Feb.) excitement that these two ministers and de Grey were reported to have walked out of a cabinet meeting. T. H. Farrer thought that Stanley or Somerset might serve as a fusionist prime minister (ibid., 2–3rd March) and Derby and Disraeli were discussing a possible arrangement with Somerset, Clarendon, Cleveland, etc.
[4] ibid., Disraeli to Northcote, 3rd February, 1866.
[5] H. of L., 6th February, 1866.   [6] *Clarendon*, Vol. II, p. 307.
[7] *Iddesleigh Papers*, 6th February, 1866.   [8] ibid., 2–3rd March.

persuaded that England would be governed from Manchester or the Liberal party dominated over by the member for Birmingham. . . . The wise and tranquil policy of Lord Palmerston was to be reversed, the days of truce and compromise were over, and so was the reign of moderate Liberalism behind the Treasury benches'.[1] But Horsman was regarded as a man of crotchets, and a disappointed placeman. There was Lowe, the most articulate of the Liberals who would not 'trust the people'. He believed in government for the people, not by it, but he was not a Whig, or, at least, only 'an exotically or artificially produced one', for 'he differ[ed] from the true historic Whig in this, that the qualification which he would substitute for popular election would be not family influence and traditional power, but an undefined intellectual status, which his set . . . almost deified under the term "culture" '.[2] Lowe, the middle class intellectual, was one of the 'satisfied' classes some of whom, like W. H. Smith, became Conservatives on the death of Palmerston while others, like Laing and Lowe, fought for the *Conservative Cause* within the ranks of Liberalism. The Tories did not care for Lowe, who had an irritating sense of his own superiority and was noted for his 'principles of pure reason' and antipathy to the Church.[3] And they knew that he was not the man to rally Whig aristocrats. A search for such a one was conducted, with the blessing of the Tories, by a man of somewhat indeterminate political allegiance, originally a Peelite and now 'rabid against Reform'.[4] This was Lord Elcho, who brought into rebellion his brothers-in-law, Lord Lichfield and Hon. Augustus Anson, M.P. Early in March he was able to inform Lord Cranborne[5] that Earl Grosvenor, M.P. was organising Whig resistance to the Bill.[6]

There was no wholesale revolt by Whiggery. Hopes that the Dukes of Devonshire and Sutherland might patronise the rebellion[7] and Hastings Russell, nephew of the Prime Minister and heir

---

[1] H. of C., 12th March, 1866.   [2] Harris, op. cit., p. 458.
[3] Lowe had been forced out of office before Palmerston's death by Lord Robert Cecil's allegations that he had 'doctored' reports of education inspectors before laying them before the House of Commons. Granville thought Lowe might have responded to an invitation from Russell to return to office, but there is no reason to doubt the sincerity of his antipathy to Reform.
[4] *Clarendon*, Vol. II, p. 308.
[5] Formerly Lord Robert Cecil and later the great Marquess of Salisbury.
[6] Iddesleigh Papers, 8th March. Northcote noted 'Disraeli thinks this very important'.
[7] On 25th March Cairns mentioned Devonshire as a possible fusionist prime minister (*Iddesleigh Papers*). Malmesbury, *Memoirs*, p. 615, 23rd March — 'I

of the Duke of Bedford, join it;[1] were not fulfilled. But there was schism at the heart of Whiggery. Lady Grosvenor, her husband's cousin, was the sister of the Duke of Sutherland and of the Duchess of Argyll. Now it was said that the Grosvenors and Argylls were 'not speaking'. We should not overrate the normal political homogeneity of noble families. The Duchess of Sutherland, the Marchioness of Westminster and Westminister's brother, the Earl of Wilton, were all Conservatives, the last the brother-in-law of Derby. Another brother of Westminster, Lord Ebury, was a Liberal and his heir, Capt. Grosvenor, was Radical member for Westminster. But now relatives of common political profession were diverging. Argyll remained in the cabinet and Sutherland remained loyal to it, but Grosvenor led revolt against it. The Marquess of Westminister favoured the course taken by his two sons in the Commons; their cousin, Capt. Grosvenor, supported the ministry. Hartington, a cousin of Lady Argyll and Lady Grosvenor, joined the cabinet; another cousin, Hon. Leopold Agar-Ellis, went with Grosvenor. In crucial votes Clanricarde's son and heir, Lord Dunkellin, his son-in-law W. B. Beaumont, and his nephew, Lord J. T. Browne (heir of the Marquess of Sligo), rebelled. So did the cousins Charles Carrington and Gilbert Heathcoate. So did a Fitzwilliam, and Lord Ernest Bruce. Such were the names that Brand said would shock Halifax.

The Reform Bill of 1866 was a Franchise Bill, and the omission of redistribution clauses offered its opponents an obvious procedural gambit. *Prima facie*, there was much to be said for the separation of the question of the suffrage from the question of redistribution, for, while the extension of the franchise aroused general apprehensions, proposals for redistribution always produced particular grievances. In 1851 Russell had flinched from a Schedule A, and the cabinet even vetoed a Schedule B at a time when twenty-three of the twenty-seven smallest English double-member boroughs were represented by members who regularly,

---

hear the Dukes of Cleveland and Sutherland, Lord Lichfield and other Whig peers are against Gladstone's Reform Bill.' But see *Fitzmaurice*, Vol. 1, p. 501, 26th March, for Granville's assurance of Sutherland's loyalty.

[1] On 22nd February Northcote thought headway could be made with Lansdowne, Westminster, Clarendon, Hastings Russell and the Grosvenors. (*Iddesleigh Papers* — and cf. 4th February, ibid). But on 7th March Northcote noted that Hastings Russell was 'liberalising more and more' and had asked Bright to dinner.

or on occasion, supported the Whig ministry, members whose votes were required to pass a bill.[1] Because there were members of that administration, and more Whig families, and yet more M.P.s, who had a vested interest in the preservation of the *status quo*, the Russell government resorted to a device which it was hoped would avoid, or at least diminish, 'the animosity . . . which an attack on vested interests could not have failed to have produced'.[2] By a scheme stigmatised by Lansdowne as 'tying places together more or less distant and wholly unconnected with each other' the Whigs exposed themselves to Radical complaints that they preferred patronage shared to patronage abolished, and the 'grouping' plan was not revived. Russell was sufficiently impressed by Whig distaste for redistribution to say that, while there must be a Schedule B and perhaps a small Schedule A, 'the consent of the Whig party would be a *sine qua non* with me', which Graham took to mean that Calne, Arundel and Morpeth would not be disfranchised without the consent of their patrons, Lansdowne, Norfolk and Carlisle.[3] Nevertheless, the bill of 1854, while so contrived that it would probably have caused merely a game of musical chairs between Whigs and Tories, with few Radical gains,[4] proposed a redistribution of sixty-two seats. In nineteen boroughs threatened by Schedule A, two thirds of the twenty-nine seats were held by ministerialists, Whig or Peelite.[5] The seats in thirty-three boroughs (those with electorates of 300–500 or populations of 5000–10,000) menaced by Schedule B were currently held very evenly between the parties. In many cases a

[1] Two thirds of the 30 boroughs of the Schedule B of 1832 were under more or less effective patronage, and the majority of them had since 1832 been predominantly Whig in representation. Russell did not propose to touch them, but to have a new Schedule B of 20, 30 or 40 boroughs. There were 27 two-member English boroughs with electorates of under 500. Only 4 were represented by two avowed Protectionists. 6 were represented by 2 Whigs, including Zetland's Richmond, Bedford's Tavistock, Carrington's Wycombe, and Tiverton. At Thetford, Totnes and Tamworth, Grafton, Somerset and Townshend respectively returned one of the members.

[2] *Queen's Letters*, op. cit., pp. 402–3 and 436, 3rd December, 1851, 27th January, 1852.

[3] Parker's *Graham*, Vol. II, pp. 174–5.

[4] The Tories would gain by the increase of county seats and by the 'minority clause' in the boroughs, the Whigs by the minority clause in counties.

[5] These were boroughs with an electorate of less than 300 or population under 5,000, and they included Calne, Arundel, Richmond, Thetford and Totnes. Their members included Hayter, the Chief Whip (Wells), the Whig junior minister C. Berkeley (Evesham) and the Peelite Household official Lord E. Bruce (Marlborough); three Whig ex-ministers Shelburne (Calne), Rich (Richmond) and Seymour (Totnes), and the Peelite ex-minister H. Baring (Marlborough).

contest for a single seat would be a gamble, as at Hertford, where Lord Cowper returned his brother, a minister, but the other seat was usually Tory. And what of the safe Whig fiefs? Who would sit for Tiverton — Palmerston, or the great and popular local employer Heathcoat? who for Lewes — the Whig Brand or the Peelite Fitzroy? Supposing that the Anson who sat for Lichfield was given the preference by his relative, the patron, where would his Paget colleague go? What was to happen to the respected Denison (soon to be Speaker) if Fitzwilliam gave his son the preference at Malton? Would Peterborough, where, although Fitzwilliam was allowed to control one seat, his attempt to domin-ate the other was resisted, consent to be a pocket borough if there were only one seat to fill? The dislike of Whiggery at having to weigh such imponderables militated against a fair consideration of the bill of 1854.

Such was the background to the decision not to confuse the issue of the franchise by including redistribution in the bill of 1866. But the answer of conservative Whigs was to move, against the second reading, a reasoned amendment declining to proceed unless the plan of redistribution was revealed. To vote for such a motion did not inexorably commit a man against the extension of the suffrage, and seemed a wise precaution. Whiggery wanted to know where it was to stand if the Bill passed. Procedure on the suffrage, without redistribution, had been publicly recommended, years before, by Bright, who hoped to get out of a parliament elected under a wider franchise a more radical redistribution than could otherwise be obtained. Russell himself remarked that Bright had spread his nets in sight of the bird. And so, on the motion for the second reading, Grosvenor moved his amendment, seconded by Lord Stanley, and only the Government's promise to introduce a Redistribution Bill before the Franchise Bill reached committee saved ministers from defeat. Grosvenor mustered more than thirty ministerialists (fifteen of them aristocrats), and divided 315 against 320.[1] Many ministers wished the cabinet to resign, and thus put an end to the Reform project, but Russell and Gladstone decided to persevere, conceding, first, that the Redistribution Bill should come up for second reading before the Franchise Bill was discussed in

---

[1] Figures (27th April) include tellers. The usual figure given of the dissentient Liberals is thirty-three (listed in Harris, op. cit., p. 471) but at least one of these, the ex-Peelite Townshend Mainwaring, was surely a Conservative.

committee, and, later, that both bills should be discussed together in committee.

The redistribution plan was modest. No borough was to lose representation. Forty-nine seats were to be obtained (twenty-six for countries and only six for unrepresented boroughs) by the grouping of parliamentary boroughs with a population of under 8,000. But grouping was as unpopular as ever with Radicals and was not liked by many Whigs. The son of the former Chief Whip, Hayter, tabled an amendment against it, and Gladstone had to agree that it should not be regarded as vital. When the Bills at last got into committee, the Tories moved to substitute rating value for rental in the counties. The Government won by seven. But on 19th June the Whig Lord Dunkellin carried with him, on a similar motion with regard to the boroughs, most of those who had defected with Grosvenor, and ten more besides, making the total number of rebels forty-six or forty-seven. The Government was beaten by 317 to 306.

Having won the battle, the Adullamites, as Bright christened the rebels (he also called them 'the forty traitors' and 'the forty thieves') hastened to assure ministers that they did not wish them to resign, that they were ready to vote 'confidence' and even, in principle, to declare for Reform. The willingness of many ministers to accept this course was ascribed by Russell and Gladstone to their dislike of Reform. The sponsors of the Reform plan could not be satisfied with anything less than a fair majority for the principal features of it — i.e., a reversal of the adverse vote. Gladstone leaned to a dissolution. Brand, however, was strongly against this, on the ground that it would lead to disaster, not only in terms of seats, but of internecine conflict. And so Derby was invited, once again, to form a minority administration. He hoped, as on previous occasions, to gain recruits from outside his own ranks, and first approached Clarendon and Somerset. The former said that party allegiance was the only strong political feeling he had, and the latter returned a brusquer reply.[1] Both, of course, as ministers under Russell were committed to the late Bill. Derby then negotiated with Lansdowne and Grosvenor. They felt, however, that the anti-democratic front could best be maintained if there was no open coalition. Mrs Lowe told Malmesbury that the Adullamites were not prepared to join Derby, 'as they looked upon that

[1] *Queen's Letters*, S. II, Vol. I, pp. 344–52.

as ratting', but would coalesce under Stanley[1] (that very independent-minded man who had himself received overtures from Palmerston in 1855 and from Russell in 1865). But the instinct of the Whigs was to remain in the Liberal ranks, where their *vis inertiae* was needed. And so they disappointed those who from the very beginning of the Reform crisis had looked for a 'fusionist' ministry to emerge.[2]

The refusal of the Adullamites to depart from their Liberal allegiance had fateful consequences. Within a matter of months they found themselves struggling in vain, with the aid of a small Tory 'cave' under Lord Cranborne, to thwart a Reform far more drastic than that proffered by Russell and Gladstone. Disraeli performed that 'leap in the dark' (as Derby called it, leaping with him) which took by surprise Tories, Radicals and Liberals alike. It was not a matter of Disraeli 'educating' his party, but of bamboozling it. Gambling on the inability of the Liberals to agree to throw out a bill so unceremoniously as in 1859, he presented a measure purporting to confer household suffrage, but full of qualifications, limitations, restrictive technicalities, fancy franchises, minority provisions and the like. Gladstone said that the Liberals were 'bowled over by the force of a phrase' ('household suffrage') and forced to make that phrase a reality 'beyond the wants and wishes of the time'.

We have seen that Russell in 1854 endorsed 'minority representation'. 'Fancy franchises' are inseparably connected with the name of Disraeli, who contrasted them with 'vertical extension' and christened them 'lateral'. But Russell had suggested in 1851 the representation of trade and professional 'guilds', and the bill of 1854 proposed to allot members to London University and the Inns of Court and votes to graduates (where they resided), holders of Funds, Bank of England and East India stock and persons who had £50 on deposit for three years in a savings bank, persons in

---

[1] *Memoirs of an Ex-Minister* p. 620, 22nd June, 1866. In Tory circles lately Stanley had often been mentioned as an alternative to a Whig peer as head of a coalition, or as Leader of the House under a Whig peer. But many Tories did not trust him.

[2] 'If it was possible to effect a union of the moderate Whigs with the Conservatives, a strong continuous government may be formed,' wrote the Devonshire Conservative agent Wescomb to Northcote, 29th April, 1866. 'Lord Clarendon, Lord Grey, Sir George Grey, Roundell Palmer, Lowe, Horsman, Grosvenor and some others joined with the Conservatives would form a great party and I should think they would have little on which they could not act in concert' (*Iddesleigh Papers*).

receipt of a salary of £100 p.a. paid not oftener than quarterly, and men who paid 40s. of assessed taxes, income tax or licence duty. Russell had found the leading Peelites prepared to accept Reform, but not 'mere democratic infusion'. Graham especially was anxious to see 'station acquired by superior intelligence and industry' recognised as a qualification for the suffrage, and had adumbrated many of the provisions of the Bill.[1] It was a natural desire for Reformers who were not democrats, who did not admit that the franchise was a right of the citizen, but were prepared to endorse it as a privilege which could be won, without the traditional sort of 'stake in the country', by the exercise of the Victorian virtues of enterprise, industry and thrift. The fancy franchises were repugnant to Radicals because they would counteract the effect of lowering the general franchise, multiply plural voters and enfranchise not only those who rose by their exertions but every man whom a relative, patron or political manipulator chose to endow with a qualification. In 1867 the feeling that the 'fancy franchises', though no Tory monopoly, were an objectionable feature of Disraelian chicanery enabled the Liberals to strike out many of the counterweights and 'safeguards' which had commended the Bill to the Tories (but not 'minority representation'). But Gladstone could not command the House of Commons. His party had refused to challenge the second reading, and, after he had persuaded it to support a radical instruction to the committee, he was thwarted by the 'Tea-Room mutiny'. When he tried to secure a major enfranchisement, that of the compound householders (who did not pay their rates directly), twenty Liberals abstained and more than forty (twenty-five of them Adullamites) voted with the ministry to give it a majority of twenty-one.[2] So the Tories and Adullamites together had contrived to keep the proposals far short of genuine household suffrage. What was their horror when, without warning, and (it seems) without need, Disraeli accepted the amendment of an obscure Liberal back-bencher, a Mr Hodgkinson, to abolish the practice of compounding. This had the effect of admitting the compounders to the franchise. The enfranchisement would be double that proposed by Russell and Gladstone in 1866. Earl Grey

[1] In a letter to Dunfermline, 5th August, 1852 (Parker's *Graham*, Vol. II, p. 170) Graham proposed representation of all universities, possibly the Inns of Court and other chartered and scientific bodies, and the enfranchisement of proprietors of East India and Bank stock.

[2] 12th April 1867. The figures, including tellers, were 312:291.

predicted that the character of Parliament would be vulgarised; this was 'Americanisation'. And it was not only the Adullamites who were horrified. Argyll said the middle classes would be swamped, and so, added Russell, would be the skilled artisans. Good government was bound to disappear.[1] The Disraelian *coup* united, too late, virtually the whole of Whiggery in a doleful anti-democratic chorus. 'I am no more alarmist than I am Radical,' wrote Clarendon, 'but when I know that such a Radical as Bright is alarmed at the consequences of giving political power to the residuum as he calls the dregs of society, I cannot but feel uneasy about our future. There may be some exaggeration in Lowe's speech of last night; but that some of his forebodings will come to pass I have no doubt.'[2] Tories were stunned. One of their M.P.s asked how he could accept extreme Reform from a bad Jew, after having refused moderate Reform from a good Christian.

Alone of his party, Disraeli was imaginatively equipped to risk the leap into the dark. He staked his own political future, and that of his party, and of all men of property, on the hope that the lower classes, whether from deference to the upper or antipathy to the middle classes, would assist the counties and the tiny Tory boroughs to produce the Conservative majority which had been so long denied. He summoned Democracy to the aid of Aristocracy. Lowe was intelligent enough to see that Disraeli's gamble might succeed. But whether it succeeded, or whether it failed, Lowe foretold an end of a policy of peace, economy and the species of reforms of an emancipatory nature which for him constituted true Liberalism. Bright had desired to set down the aristocracy with the aid of those working class elements which to a greater or lesser degree had acquired education and assimilated the middle-class ethos. But he too flinched from the enfranchisement of the lower working classes, not so qualified. He feared, with Lowe, that they would be favourable to a robust foreign policy, high expenditures and social reforms not at all to the taste of the Manchester School. Both foresaw, in principle, the demagogic politics of Lord Randolph Churchill, who would direct against the plutocracy the sort of insults which Bright hurled at the aristocracy. And Whiggery, apart from disliking the democratic principle and pros-

[1] H. of L., 22nd July, 1867. Grey presented an amendment to reject the Bill as offering prospects neither of permanence nor good government.
[2] *Clarendon*, Vol. II, p. 332, 27th May, 1867, to Lady Salisbury.

pects of Tory government, feared the price the Tories would have to pay, and the Liberals in competition with them — the price in terms of political bid and counter-bid. In the 'moment of truth', when the full implications of Disraelian duplicity dawned on them, they glimpsed a future of professionalised politics, of party programmes, of incessant legislation, of caucuses and mandates.[1]

The *Fortnightly Review*, rejoicing that Palmerston's mantle could descend to no successor, had yet feared that he would leave many apt pupils who had learned the style of the great master of fence.[2] The conservative Whigs, with a few middle-class individualists such as Lowe and Laing, had duly fought against the future, successfully in 1866, vainly in 1867. Their defeat came not, as Gladstone had predicted it would, through the movement of 'great social forces'; there had only been a scuffle in a park. In the same 'shuffling' parliament, with the people still 'unawakened',[3] Disraeli, by sheer political manoeuvre, lead the country into democracy, which not half a dozen members of Parliament wanted. In his flippant way,[4] Derby said that the Tories 'dished the Whigs'. No doubt he meant simply that the Liberal party had been out-manoeuvred. But this was one of the true words that are spoken in jest. It was the *Conservative Cause* men who were dished, the men who had looked to Palmerston and Derby to protect them against Gladstone and Bright, men like the Devonshire Palmerstonian who wrote, 'Two years ago I fell out of the ranks, disgusted with Lord Russell's Reform Bill. Of course I like Lord Derby's even less. I should witness with pleasure the organisation of a real, bona fide Conservative Party.'[5] And above all it was Whiggery that was dished. In the competition for the favour of the masses the Conservatives, so intrepidly committed to uncharted seas, would twist and tack. Some sort of Liberalism would doubtless flourish, a Liberalism with its centre of gravity shifted towards Radicalism.

[1] cf. Somerset's pamphlet 1880 (see *supra*, p. 153) bewailing a form of government which 'repudiates and ostracises' the aristocracy and involved 'the rivalry of competing parties seeking popular support'.

[2] Vol. 1, p. 767.

[3] Gladstone wrote that a dissolution in 1866 would have been an appeal from a shuffling parliament to an unwakened people.

[4] People spoke of Derby and Disraeli as 'the Jockey and the Jew'. It was once alleged that Derby degraded political ethics to the level of Newmarket (where his colours were well known). Half his reputation for insincerity arose from his breezy cynicism.

[5] *Iddesleigh Papers*, Benson to Northcote, 21st August, 1868.

Y

Neither Whig nor Tory was surprised when in 1884 a Radical historian wrote 'The operation of the Reform Act of 1867 made an important alteration in the position and power of the Radical party. . . . During the comparatively short time in which the united Liberals have been in office, since the Reform Act increased the Radical power, every department of national life — religious, social, commercial, industrial and intellectual — has been invigorated and improved.'[1] But what future was there for Whiggery?

The essence of Whiggism was the supremacy of the territorial class acting in the spirit of ancestors who had defended the 'traditional' liberties of 'the people' against the Crown, had extended liberties and even, under pressure, broadened privileges. From Locke to Fox, Grey, Russell and Hartington, the Whigs professed to govern *for* the people, within a representative system. In the course of the nineteenth century they had learned from the Utilitarians sufficient of what was involved in governing *for* the people to preserve, if only by virtue of a restricted franchise, a great deal of influence, despite the shift of economic power from land to industry and commerce. But between Whiggery and democracy there was fundamental anthithesis. The democratisation of the representative system (which the Reform of 1867 began, and showed to be inevitable) meant the destruction of Whiggery as a political force. When the Duke of Argyll depicted the third Earl Grey as 'left almost alone to keep alive the flame of his devotion before a solitary and abandoned shrine . . . [in] the temple of the Third party . . . razed and strewn with salt'[2] he accurately conveyed the atmosphere of desolation, foreboding, apprehension and regret which surrounded Whiggery as, repelled by Disraeli's treachery to the *Conservative Cause*, it entered dolefully into its Gladstonian Captivity. Whigs did not believe in government *by* the people, whatever that might mean. They were an *élite* which upheld as its own by right of heredity, tradition, rank, property and experience the prerogative of governing the country, dispensing patronage and regulating Reform. At times of crisis they stood with 'the People' to detach it from 'the Populace', a distinction[3] which assumed that the views of the Populace were of no importance, except as imparting the element of crisis to the national affairs. But if the People and the Populace were to be-

---

[1] Harris, op. cit., conclusion.   [2] H. of L., 22nd July, 1867.
[3] Vide Ch. I.

come one and the same, if the mass was to preponderate on the ruins of the representation of interests and varied communities, Whiggery was doomed. For it was the one element in British politics so specialised that in a democratic climate it could exist only as a frail exotic.

CHAPTER XIII

The Whigs and Mr Gladstone

When in December 1867 Earl Russell indicated that he would not again be a candidate for the premiership, Whiggery knew that where Russell had scourged them with whips, Gladstone would scourge them with scorpions. Russell's Whiggism was flexible to the point of aberration, and he was, at the last, driven from office by Whig revolt. But he was a Whig to the core, 'the arch Whig of the nineteenth century' as Professor Woodward called him in the Oxford *History*. His mind harked back to 'rights that have been claimed by Hampden . . . liberties that have been vindicated by Somers', and after forty years he made no substantial change in his youthful study of *English Government*. It was his life's work to sustain, extend and refashion as he thought circumstances required the rule of law, personal liberty and representative government. He never doubted that these were the essential preconditions of moral and intellectual and, indeed, material, progress in all civilised states. And if he half-assumed, in face of mounting evidence to the contrary, that it was enough for a government to be in a state of grace, as measured by these tests, that it need not concern itself overmuch with positive action to improve material conditions, this was a characteristically Whig error. He remained the champion of the right of the aristocracy to rule, and to select a few men of merit from outside its own circle to act as colleagues and assistants. He hoped such a régime would continue, at least in the foreseeable future. But when he resigned the leadership he left Whiggery reeling under the Disraelian Reform, which made the representation of interests untenable. Russell's brother, the Duke of Bedford, had shuddered at the prospect of a future dominated by Gladstone and Disraeli. Whiggery now found itself exposed to the chill winds of their rivalry, and had to accept as its political chief the alien from the tribe of Peelites, the friend of Bright, the 'People's William'.

It had become evident that Gladstonian Liberalism would be a restless, reforming creed. To later generations, who have assimilated reformist Toryism, Radical Liberalism and Socialism, it hardly seems so. To us, even Chamberlain's Radicalism appears pallid and nebulous, a matter of ferocious barks followed by small and harmless nibbles; yet it was developed as a protest against Gladstonianism as rigid, negative and unconstructive. Gladstone's criticisms of Chamberlain's doctrine, in the 'eighties, make it clear that there was a very much wider field of agreement than of disagreement between the Whigs of the Gladstonian Captivity and their gaoler. Gladstone always insisted that his principal aim was to maintain the unity of the Liberal party, Whigs included. He delighted in the co-operation of Whig noblemen, and esteemed it the more highly as the upper class moved progressively away from Liberalism. He intended in 1885 that he should be succeeded not by Chamberlain but by the heir of the Duke of Devonshire, and so far as domestic affairs were concerned the Whigs had come to realise that, for all their dislike of much that he had done, Gladstone spoke the truth when he claimed to be a conservative influence. Yet Gladstonian Liberalism was strongish meat for the followers of Palmerston and even of Russell. If it involved no tendency towards economic equality, it did strive towards greater equality of opportunity and even of status, though in the context of a society still hierarchical. It tended to loosen the control of superiors over inferiors, to threaten established churches, to erode landlord privileges, to imperil the political predominance of the aristocracy. It was far less sharply differentiated than Whiggism from the more robust and positively democratic and decidedly anti-aristocratic creed of Bright, whom Gladstone admitted to the cabinet. Not without reason did the *avant-garde* of the intelligentsia, and working class leaders impregnated with the seeds of middle-class Radicalism, look with hope to Gladstone as the parliamentary champion of Progress.

We have already noted the facets of Gladstone's personality which Whigs criticised[1] and which, with the recent unhappy experiences over Reform, explain why early in 1868 Clarendon could find among them no 'germ of approximation to Gladstone'.[2] The new leader did not fit into any recognised political groove, certainly no Whig one. He was potentially radical. He flourished on popular acclaim. He allied to the gift of tongues a powerful

---

[1] See *supra*, Ch. XII, p. 299.
[2] *Clarendon*, Vol. II, p. 341, 4th February, to Granville.

intellect, a fervent imagination[1] and a penchant for the importation of moral passion into politics. He was unpredictable without being, like Russell, impetuous. Long and intricate intellectual processes preceded apparently sudden changes of mind, and he was adept at refusing to be drawn except at his own season (he prided himself on a gift for right timing). He made skilful use of verbal obscurities. He combined courtesy, suppleness and diplomacy with self-will, obstinacy and pertinacity, a Macchiavellian equipment with an intense belief in his own righteousness and consistency. To a plain, straightforward Whig like Hartington he was incomprehensible; the Marquess once said that he could not understand what Gladstone meant in private conversation! To men who waited and watched for premonitory warnings of new departures, or sought to elucidate verbal complexities which might conceal either platitude or portentous meaning, Gladstone seemed, as South Africans say, 'slim'. Certainly in its relations with him after he became Liberal leader Whiggery always felt itself at a disadvantage. Gladstone always saddled someone else — usually a Whig — with the potential responsiblity for a split in the party, begging the offender not to force an issue on some point that was not of critical importance or some matter of merely hypothetical significance, i.e., some matter on which Gladstone had not yet thought it opportune to declare. And for twenty years the Whigs came to heel, lest their last state be worse than their first. Once Gladstone had made himself a great popular figure, the embodiment of 'the Liberal image', it was a fearful prospect to envisage an appeal to the nation in which Gladstone might side with the Radicals against the Whigs.

Gladstone's apprenticeship as leader of the Liberals in the House of Commons was unhappy and unpropitious. To say, as Houghton did, that Gladstone's fervour for Reform had won him the attachment of 300 members and the horror of the rest was gross oversimplification.[2] Few of the party in 1866 felt any such attachment. Perhaps a majority resented the fact that Gladstone was known to have desired, not resignation, but dissolution, the annoyance, expense and (in some cases) peril of which members

---

[1] 'An audicious innovator with an insatiable desire for popularity... and a fervent imagination which furnished facts in support' (*Clarendon*, Vol. II, p. 331, to Granville 1860) 'His genius and eloquence enable him to soar high above the heads of his party, who are always suspicious of what he may devise when he gets into higher and unknown lattitudes' (ibid., p. 341).

[2] Reid's *Houghton*, Vol. II, p. 154, 13th July, 1866, to G. Von Bunsen.

were as determined to avoid. For Gladstone the great thing was Reform; for Liberal members in general it was that the Liberal government should stay in office.[1] Reform in 1866 would have stood a better chance if, as Gladstone himself suggested, not he, but Sir George Grey had succeeded Palmerston as leader in the Commons. For Grey was unassuming, widely liked and respected. He was also to the right of centre, while Gladstone was veering to the left. He would have worked closely with Brand, employing the social arts which Russell had never learned and which, as Gladstone's niece said, 'Uncle William . . . lacking in tact' neglected.[2] Gladstone did not see that if the right wing was to be induced to accept reforms it did not relish it must be treated with special courtesy. Grey understood this.[3] Gladstone might have taken over from him with a Reform Bill on the statute book, but if Grey had failed, at least the beginnings of Gladstone's career as party leader would have been happier. At the end of the session of 1866, in which he and Russell had provoked the most ostentatious revolt of right-wing Liberals yet seen, Gladstone fled abroad, 'leaving the wound of the Liberal party to the healing powers of nature'.[4] He returned conscious that 'our line ought to be great patience and quietude in opposition', unless the party could agree on the handling of Reform. As the session began, a Liberal member could find 'no leaders, no plan, no union, no sympathy. . . . What [Mr Gladstone] thinks or does, or is said to be thinking or doing, nobody seems to know'.[5] The party was, in Brand's phrase, so much 'at sixes and sevens' that the usual dinner was not held on the eve of the session.[6] Gladstone and Lowe together could not induce the party to agree to defeat the second reading of the Tory Reform Bill. 'In the singular mental condition of our party, it may be well that I should lie low for a little while,' wrote Gladstone.[7] When he did move, he encountered 'smash perhaps without

---

[1] Vide Brand's reasons against a dissolution, *Later Correspondence*, p. 351, 20th June, 1866.

[2] Lady Frederick Cavendish's journal 31st May, 1866, quoted by Magnus, p. 180, cf., *Clarendon*, Vol. II, p. 331, February, 1867, 'his ignorance of the world and of men and his want of tact'.

[3] e.g. *Later Correspondence*, pp. 345–7, Grey to Russell, 29th March, 1866.

[4] Quoted by Morley, p. 848, Gladstone to Brand.

[5] Quoted *Clarendon*, Vol. II, p. 330. The writer was Sir David Dundas (2nd Feb., 1867).

[6] Brand to Halifax, 29th January, 1867 (*Clarendon*, Vol. II, p. 329) and see ibid., p. 330. Grosvenor held a dinner for the Adullamites.

[7] *Later Correspondence*, pp. 358–9, 27th March, 1867.

example' — the so-called 'Tea-Room' mutiny. The two House of Commons Russells had not entered the Cave, but they went to the Tea-Room because, it was said, they could not bear Gladstone as their leader.[1] Gladstone's isolation and lack of authority were plain for all the world to see. The plaudits of Bright did not help to reconcile to him 'Whigs (aristocrats) who won't risk a collision with the government and hope that very little reform will be carried and want to discredit Gladstone' or, for that matter, 'a large body who care for nothing except to avoid a dissolution.'[2] In May 1867 Gladstone refused to preside at a presentation to Brand, who was retiring from the office of Liberal Chief Whip; he would not countenance the appearance of a sham union. Six months later he was still complaining of his 'crippled means of action'. He had, he said, only to speak a word, especially against Disraeli, for some Liberal to rise and protest. It seemed best to avoid all acts of leadership that could be dispensed with.[3]

To Gladstone, and to others as well, the remedy for 'the condition of things in which a nominal leader is regularly deserted by his men at the moment when he orders a charge'[4] was evident. He must appeal from the House of Commons to the country. But unless the Government could be defeated, the timing of such an appeal did not rest with Gladstone, and Argyll, in January 1868, said it would be courting defeat to fight with such troops and that Gladstone should not try to test party fidelity in the coming session. Remembering that his hold over the country was very different from his control over the House, he should wait for the next Parliament.[4] But Gladstone ignored this advice. He found a way of breaking out of the circle of frustration in which he had lived for two years, and by a decisive act of leadership forced the Tories to put to the test his appeal to the country. Ireland, so often a dissolvent in British parties, was made for once a solvent of Liberal discords.

The Irish Question had again become pressing because the Fenian movement revived the need for coercion, and this always awakened political leaders, especially on the Liberal side, to the

[1] Quoted by Morley, p. 866.
[2] Acland's description of two of three sets of people who hampered Gladstone (10th April, 1867), see Morley pp. 861-2.
[3] *Later Correspondence*, pp. 362-3, 2nd November, 1867, to Russell.
[4] *Argyll*, Vol. II, pp. 239-41, to Gladstone, 30th January, 1st and 3rd February, 1868.

DARBY AND JOHN.

(IN THE TEA-ROOM, AFTER THE DIVISION.)

Lord Derby "*I NEVER THOUGHT WE SHOULD LIVE TO SEE THIS DAY!*"
Lord John "*HA! I DID!*"

See *infra* p. 341.

need for concession. In December 1866 Russell had decided that
he must 'declare in Parliament that unless Ireland is satisfied by
some new distribution of Church revenues, there is no hope of
permanent peace in that country or real union with England'.[1]
Whiggery was reverting to its old specific of concurrent endowment.[2] The division of the revenues of the establishment among
the three communions figured large among twelve resolutions
which Earl Grey had recently submitted as the remedy for Ireland's

[1] *Clarendon*, Vol. II, p. 329.
[2] And the Ultramontanes reacted characteristically — e.g. Manning to Rome
19th January, 1868. . . 'Endowment of the Catholic clergy in Ireland. . . (is
urged). . . with the avowed intention of gaining a hold over them. It would
absolutely separate them from their flocks' (*Clarendon*, Vol. II, p. 344).

ills. This principle was approved by Chichester Fortescue (and by Russell who, on 24th June, 1867 initiated a debate in which he justified large-scale disendowment as preferable to mere payment of priests (the day for which had gone by) and to disestablishment, which would be hailed by Dissenters as a precedent. The riposte of Derby, that the Church had as much right to its property as the House of Russell to Woburn Abbey and Covent Garden, was highly reminiscent of 1834. The same gladiators, about to retire almost simultaneously from party leadership (Disraeli became prime minister at the beginning of 1868) adopted the same postures as on the day the coach upset. Thirty-eight peers, headed by the Duke of Devonshire, a great landlord in Ireland, voted for the motion.

It was not, *prima facie*, evident that political dividends would flow from an attempt to deal with the Irish Church. Clarendon thought the question would not be settled for a long time, since nothing embittered politics like religion.[1] That disendowment could provide the Liberal bond of unity seemed problematical; that disestablishment should do so might have seemed impossible. But Gladstone, who in Lancashire (where he represented a county division after defeat at Oxford University in 1865) in December 1867 had projected measures on Irish Church, Land and Education, opted, in March 1868, for disestablishment as well as disendowment. That he had succeeded in raising an umbrella of policy over the disunited Liberals was apparent when the first of the three resolutions which he introduced on 16th March was passed with the votes of virtually the whole of the nominal majority credited to Palmerston after the elections of 1865. Disraeli indicated that there would be a dissolution as soon as the registers were ready.

Disestablishment was popular in Wales, where the majority of the population were Dissenters, in Scotland[2] and in Ireland. It

[1] Stead's *M.P. for Russia*, Vol. I, p. 119, Clarendon to Mme Novikov, 10th July, 1868 — 'It will play a sinister rôle in the coming elections.' cf. Howden to Clarendon, 16th May, 1868. . . 'What I think a serious misfortune is a general election on a religious cry. People in England, while despising Southern superstition, are wonderfully and woefully bigoted about their own matters of faith. . . (*Clarendon*, Vol. II, p. 342).

[2] In the elections for Scottish universities seats, Free Kirk and United Presbyterian ministers voted 1081 to 34 for Gladstone's men, and other dissenting ministers 360:35, while Episcopalian priests were 78:4 Tory and ministers of the Established Church (Presbyterian) 1221 to 67 against the Liberals. (G. W. T. Omond, *The Lord Advocates of Scotland*, 2nd Series, London, 1914.)

also 'took' in many boroughs, though not in Lancashire. Since,
however, the Tory borough losses (due to disfranchisement as well
as change of allegiance) were nearly cancelled by gains in the
English counties, virtually the whole of the increase in the Liberal
majority from 70 to 110 was provided by the Celtic fringe. And
there, ominously for Whiggery, anti-landlordism was a potent influence, as well as hostility to Anglican establishment. In Ireland,
it is true, Whig landlords and Catholic farmers found themselves,
for the last time, allies. Even in the Welsh counties the Dissenting
electors, being a minority, could make way against Landlord and
Parson only by alliance with Whig families. But, says Dr Hanham,
if 'for tactical reasons the Dissenters denounced Toryism as their
enemy . . . in practice they were quite as concerned to overthrow
the Whigs as the Tories'. In Denbighshire, 'headquarters of terri-
torialism', the Whig colleague of the impregnable Wynns went
down in a campaign fought on Tenant Right.[1] In Merthyr, with a
trebled electorate, the Gladstonian H. A. Bruce was overthrown
by Nonconformity.[2]

In the English counties the Liberal policy of disestablishment
was a Tory asset which counterbalanced the disenchantment of
electors with Disraeli on account of his astonishing conduct in
regard to Reform. The Tories had a net gain of thirty seats, and
the Liberals a net loss of five, despite a small bonus from the
minority representation provisions of the Reform Act. It had been
hoped that, while Nonconformity would take comfort from the
fact that there was no proposal to endow Popery, High churchmen
would prove that, like Gladstone, they did not respect the Irish
Church, which was Erastian and very Low, while Evangelicals did
not care very much about establishment *per se*. No doubt Gladstone's stout Churchmanship did limit the damage done by the
'Protestant' cry.[3] But a Devonshire elector who had always voted
Liberal told Northcote he could do so no more because 'the
disestablishment of the Irish Church would be a measure unjust,

---

[1] H. J. Hanham, *Elections and Party Management 1959*, pp. 171, 175–6.
[2] ibid., pp. 173–5. There were other factors in Bruce's defeat — his connection
with the Guests of Dowlais, his hostility to the ballot and to trade unions.
[3] Gladstone, as an Anglican Catholic, was deeply opposed to 'Vaticanism',
especially the promulgation of the Infallibility Decree in 1870, But in 1868
Cardinal Manning asked that he should be treated kindly in Rome, saying 'for
a long while he has been silent about Rome and the temporal power. . . I think
he will do nothing hostile' (*Clarendon*, Vol. II, p. 345).

impolitic and fraught with danger'.[1] Brand admitted that, though the 'temper of the Public Mind' was strongly for Gladstone, there was 'in many quarters . . . apprehension that the Church and the rights of property are not safe in your hands!!! . . . Some people, even among our friends, are weak enough to believe it'.[2] The old Whig banker, Lord Overstone, declined, because of the disestablishment plan, to assist Vernon Smith's son in North Northamptonshire.[3]

Among the anxious friends to whom Brand referred — men anxious about property right in general as well as the Irish Church in particular — were many Whigs who had no reason to relish Gladstonian leadership. The five Whig dukes seemed reluctant to stir.[4] The total donations from the peers to the Chief Opposition Whip's election fund were only £4,200 (and the fund, at £14,325, was a mere seventh of its Tory counterpart).[5] The correspondence with Gladstone of Glyn, who had succeeded Brand as the principal Liberal whip, confirms that the Whig caste was lukewarm. 'The peers have done *very little*. . . . Hitherto *Brooks* Club has done what was needed, but the times are changed. . . . In former times if the "Whip's" Fund ran low a few cheques from Brooks soon set matters right. . . . The country is with you & you will win in Nov but you will not do so from the exertions of those to whom "the party" has been accustomed to look. I wish Brooks Club were shut up, it does positive harm.'[6]

The Whig share in the Liberal victory is not to be estimated solely in terms of contribution to the general fund, with its modest target of £15,000. One is grateful to Dr Hanham for the reminder that 'it is difficult to overstress the contribution of Whig land-

[1] *Iddesleigh Papers*, Mr Pye to Northcote, 12th September, 1868.

[2] Quoted by A. F. Thompson in 'Gladstone's Whips and the General Election of 1868' (*E.H.R.*, LXIII, 1948, p. 197). Cf. (ibid.) Glyn's letter of 8th October, 1868.

[3] Hanham, op. cit., p. 18.

[4] According to Hanham, of Bedford, Devonshire, Sutherland, Norfolk and Argyll, only the last contributed (£100).

[5] In 'British Party Finance 1868–80' (*Bulletin of the Institute of Historical Research*, XXVII, 1954), Dr Hanham seems not to see that the three 'Bessborough' entries and the 'Lord Bessborough-de-Grey' entry, totalling £2,700, are simply the 1868 equivalent of 1874 entries to the tune of £2,700 covering more than thirteen peers apart from Bessborough himself, who collected as Lord's Whip for the Liberal Party. His conclusion that 'only eight peers' contributed is therefore unacceptable.

[6] A. F. Thompson op. cit., Glyn to Gladstone, 4th, 12th and 22nd September, 1868.

owners to the Liberal cause in the counties even as late as the
'eighties'; they provided leadership (and money) even in industrial
counties.[1] The refusal of the Duke of Sutherland to 'give a
farthing' in South Salop in 1868 cost the Whig Jasper More the
seat, and it was said that West Surrey need not have been lost if the
Duke of Norfolk had stirred himself.[2] It seems likely, however,
that most of the Whig magnates did their local duty, though
usually without enthusiasm and certainly without impressive
results. If they did not exert themselves they were very foolish,
for now that Totnes, Thetford, Arundel and Ashburton were no
longer constituencies and Bodmin, Lewes, Richmond, Ripon,
Lichfield, Malton, Marlborough, Tavistock and Wycombe had
fallen under a new Schedule B, the avenues of entry to Parliament
for Whig territorialists were narrower than ever, and if they could
not find compensation in the increased number of county seats,
they would not find them anywhere else. It has been reckoned[3]
that up to eighteen Liberal members (as compared with up to
twenty-one Tories) were returned in 1868 for English nomination
boroughs and four (as compared with twelve Tories) for county
seats in the gift of magnates. The list of Liberal seats in gift
includes familiar names — Bedfordshire, East Cumberland, North
Derbyshire, the southern division of the West Riding, Calne,
Chester, Peterborough, Shaftesbury and most of the aforesaid
Schedule B boroughs. But Lichfield and Malmesbury figure as
Tory nomination boroughs, for the extension of the suffrage had
there been sufficient to reverse the effects of 1832. The Adullamite
Anson was beaten at Lichfield, which now had 1,100 electors, and
the voters of Malmesbury, swelled from 293 to 641, preferred an
open Conservative to the Adullamite heir of the Earl of Suffolk
and Berkshire, Viscount Andover.

It was a sad day for Whiggery when in all three kingdoms
only 26–31 seats were in gift, and when the total muster of
Liberals from the English counties was 46 out of 170. The virtual
identity of the numbers of Liberals elected for all English seats
(247 in 1865, 243 in 1868) conceals a shift in the balance.
Moderate Liberals displaced by the reduction of members from
small boroughs could rarely expect to prevail against the Tories
in county divisions or to be chosen as Liberal candidates for

[1] Hanham, *Elections and Party Management*, p. 25.
[2] A. F. Thompson, op. cit.   [3] By Hanham, op. cit.

large towns. Robert Lowe, reconciled to Gladstone by the attack on the Irish Church, was fortunate to be able to leave Calne (wanted by the new Lord Lansdowne for his brother) for the new London University seat. But other Adullamites, and some Whig loyalists, and some of the carpet baggers who had sat for small boroughs, could not rely upon a seat in future, though, as elections were more expensive than ever under the rules of 1867, money still talked, a fact which reduced the quality of the Liberal membership.

John Stuart Mill feared that the umbrella appeal would produce a House of Commons too like its predecessor. In a letter to Bouverie which was published in the *Times* (21st October) he said:

> ... The real danger, in my opinion, of the Liberal Party ... is in a renewal of the tactics which made the last House of Commons a spectacle of dissension and want of principle — showing us representatives trying to slip out of the engagements which their constituents conceived them to be bound by, and others yielding a shameful obedience when called to order by the dread of losing their seats, while in cases where this powerful motive was not in operation, men elected under the same banner proved by their conduct that there was as irreconcileable a variance in their intentions and political feelings as if they had sat on opposite sides of the House. What gave this deplorable character to the last House of Commons was that its so-called Liberal members were rallied under the cry of supporting Palmerston, as we are now told they ought to be rallied under the cry of disestablishing the Irish Church. I am not one of those who think that the political progress of England has but one step more to make before reaching its summit, where it may rest and be thankful; that if a man is ready to vote for the disestablishment of the Irish Church he is ready to do all that the staunchest Liberalism can demand of him. ... There does not appear to be any danger that Mr. Gladstone's nominal majority will not be greater than in the last Parliament. What the country has to look to is that his majority shall be more steadfast to genuine Liberal principles. ...

While the whip, Glyn, did his best to see that no seats were thrown away by Liberals fighting one another,[1] Mill argued that if a reasonable number of men of advanced opinions, or possessing the

---

[1] Apart from assistance with registration and choice of candidates (on the initiative of a constituency) and the grant of subsidies from the central fund to certain candidates, this was the principal function of the Whip in an election.

confidence of the working classes, were not to be included among
the recognised candidates of the party, they could not be blamed
if they sometimes stood against those who were. Occasionally local
feeling proved so Radical that on the intrusion of a candidate
representing it a Whig withdrew; thus, the Whig-Radical compact at Lincoln broke down and the Whig landowner, Edward
Heneage, did not go to the poll.[1] Such compacts for sharing the
representation of a two-member borough were one of the ways in
which Whigs or moderate Liberals[2] could get returned, where it
was feared that if two stalwart Liberals were chosen moderate
voters would go with the Tory. In his efforts to prevent Liberals
fighting one another, Glyn entered into surreptitious relations
with the National Reform League, endeavouring to direct its efforts
against Tory constituencies and giving it subventions on the
understanding that it would act against no Liberal except Roebuck.
Emily Eden would have been horrified if she had known of this,
for of Beales, one of the leaders of the League, she had written 'I
suppose the meekest of babies would hang that man as soon as
look at him.'[3] Such sentiments were reciprocated. George Howell,
secretary of the League, wrote '*I hate the Whigs*. They have ever
been our enemies and are now. . . . We must fight the next election
tooth and nail, and if the Whig is doubtful I personally should
prefer a Tory. . . . We must tell the professing Liberals that their
programme must be a good and bold one and their pledges must
be kept or they will not do for us.'[4] It is not surprising that Glyn
had to report to Gladstone 'the upper part of our party are so
jealous and sensitive just now'.[5] What could be expected when
Lord Henley was asked to submit himself to a meeting of electors
to determine whether he or the extreme Radical Leaguer Brad-
laugh should be candidate for Northampton, and Baron de Rothschild was asked to abandon the compact by which Aylesbury was
represented by his son and a Tory in order to assist Howell's
candidature, subsidised from the general fund to which the Baron
had subscribed £500. Feeling between Whigs and Radicals was
such that Lord Enfield (son of 'young' George Byng) openly

[1] Hanham, op. cit., p. 75.
[2] In Hanham's chapters on 'The Big Towns in 1868', 'The Early Seventies'
and 'The Rise of the Caucus' the only 'Whigs' mentioned are Edward Baines,
J. B. Smith, Milner Gibson, Sir T. Bazley, Henry Fenwick, the Leaders of
Sheffield, and T. C. Thompson. Only the last was a considerable landowner.
[3] *Clarendon*, Vol. II, p. 321, 23rd July, 1867.
[4] *Hanham*, p. 331, 11th May, 1868.   [5] ibid., p. 338, 13th November, 1868.

rejoiced when the Duke of Abercorn's Tory son was elected with him in Middlesex and the indecorous Radical, Henry Labouchere the younger, defeated.[1]

Mill himself was beaten in Westminister by W. H. Smith, who became the colleague of Capt. Grosvenor. But such defeats of stalwart Liberal members were rare, and if the Liberal majority in the new House of Commons could hardly match Mill's ideal, it was as satisfactory an instrument as Gladstone could reasonably have hoped for. 60% of the former members (on the Liberal side) who were re-elected in 1868 came from the aristocracy, gentry or parliamentary families;[2] 60% of the new entrants did not. It was a slight shift from the traditional sources of recruitment to the plutocracy, by no means all of whom were men of robust Liberalism.[3] But the process was henceforth to become progressively more distinct. The participation of the old governing class in Liberal politics declined steadily from 1868 onwards. Whiggery was told very clearly that it was a nuisance. 'We do not want men who cast reluctant looks back at the old order of things, nor men whose Liberalism consists chiefly in a warm adherence to the Liberal measures already passed,' Mill had written to Bouverie. '. . . [We want] men whose heart and soul are in the cause of progress, and are animated by that ardour which, in politics as in war, kindles the commander to his highest achievements, and makes the army at his command worth twice its numbers; men whose zeal will encourage their leader to attempt what their fidelity will give him strength to do.' Brodrick said the same. 'Just as when the old stage coaches were abandoned they did not select the coachmen to drive the steam engines, so many of the gentlemen who had been returned to Parliament under the old electoral system would be found unequal, at all events not politically "fast" enough now. The era has passed when the country's political spirit was lulled to sleep and the political conscience was deadened under Lord Palmerston. Questions of Reform, which that able statesman had

[1] Thorold's *Labouchere*, pp. 80–4.

[2] Birth in a stately home or gracious manor house, still less being the son of an M.P., was no absolute guarantee of moderate opinions. But a republican aristocrat, like Auberon Herbert, was a very rare bird, and so was Hon. E. L. Stanley (of Alderley), a League candidate. There was an undoubted tendency for 'good connections' and moderate opinions to go together.

[3] Cf. Bagehot, *The English Constitution and other Essays*, Introduction to 1872 edition — 'The middle class element has gained greatly. . . and the aristocratic element has lost greatly. . . The spirit of our present House of Commons is plutocratic, not aristocratic.'

staved off, most now come on.'[1] This sort of thing has been said often enough before. It was thirty years since Parkes had said the Whigs' hearse was ordered. Whig survival was evidence of tenacity, pertinacity and adaptability, and of the conservatism of the nation. It was due in part to mid-Victorian prosperity which, says Dr Hanham, 'sustained and invigorated the old hierarchial society which in the 'forties had seemed doomed to decay.' Men had been 'too busy taking advantage of the good times which had come to them, and sampling the pleasures of their new-found power abroad, to care much for their abstract rights'.[2] Palmerston had been fortunate, in that his temper and techniques suited the decade and a half of prosperity for both agriculture and industry following 1850. Depression did not come until the 'seventies, when it hastened political change. But already in 1868 men sensed the beginning of a new dispensation, of which household suffrage in the boroughs was as much a sympton as a cause. 'In the course of the 1868 parliament', says Dr Hanham, 'the middle classes who had enjoyed nominal power since 1832 at last came into their own.'

Whiggery was now to be asked to move faster, as the rearmost section of a Liberal host which under Gladstone's leadership would seek to win not *a* reforming victory but a series of victories, a campaign. Whigs had been induced, in the past, sometimes abruptly (as in 1831 and 1845) to accept *a* reform, even a major one. But not since 1833 had a new parliament met with the expectation of undertaking a whole programme of reforms. Since the majority was so large, even Whig secession on the scale of the Cave would be inadequate to prevent Gladstone from achieving an objective. Therefore the *vis inertiae* in the cabinet became of the utmost importance to Whiggery. But the cabinet had far more of a 'new look' than the Parliament. It did not bear much relation to Palmerston's. It was the first to represent the variety of the Liberal party. Gladstone said it consisted of three Peelites, five Whigs and seven new men. The three Peelites were Gladstone, Cardwell and Argyll, of whom the two last became progressively more Whiggish. The five Whigs were Clarendon (on whose death in 1870 Halifax returned), Granville, de Grey, Hartington and

[1] *Times*, 10th October, 1868, report of speech of Hon. G. C. Brodrick at Woodstock.
[2] op. cit., pp. xiii–xiv.

z

Chichester Fortescue.[1] Of the new men, only Childers and Lord Chancellor Hatherley came of Whig stock, though Kimberley (Wodehouse) may be called a Whig.[2] The unparalleled number of nine cabinet ministers were to sit in the Commons. And, of these, only Gladstone and Cardwell had been in a cabinet for more than six months. Hartington and Goschen had been added by Russell. Bright had never held office of any kind. His nomination to the cabinet was a sure sign that the centre of gravity of the party had moved left. Lowe had spent ten years in official apprenticeship, Fortescue rather less, H. A. Bruce under four years, Childers two. In the course of the Parliament they were joined in cabinet by Forster and Stansfeld. Of these eleven ministers only Hartington and Fortescue were Whigs born. All the others, except Bruce, who had bettered himself by his connection with Dowlais, were self-made or the sons of self-made fathers. The making had been achieved in commercial, industrial or professional life.[3]

The distribution of offices was also symbolic. To men not born in the purple went the premiership, the Treasury (Lowe), the Home Office (Bruce), the War Office (Cardwell), the Admiralty (Childers), the Board of Trade (Bright), the Local Government Board (Goschen) and the Education Department (Forster).[4] To the two aristocratic Whig M.P.s went the Post Office (Hartington) and the Chief Secretaryship for Ireland (Fortescue), and to peers the Presidency of the Council (de Grey), the Privy Seal (Kimberley), the Foreign Office (Clarendon), the Colonies (Granville) and India (Argyll). No doubt it was administratively convenient to have in the Commons the ministers responsible for internal departments, and for legislation.[5] But it had not been

[1] Halifax's Journal, 9th December, quoted *Clarendon*, Vol. II, p. 354.

[2] Asquith, in *Fifty Years of Parliament*, noted that Wodehouse came of a Tory family. op. cit., pp. xiii–xiv.

[3] Gladstone and Cardwell were the sons of Liverpool commerce, Goschen a banker, Bright and Forster manufacturers, Lowe a tutor, Stansfeld a solicitor. Childers, a parson's son from a county family, had, like Lowe, Australian experience, having acted as agent for the Barings in a railway loan to the state of Victoria. Bruce, a magistrate from a landed family, was a coal owner and trustee of the Dowlais company. The fortunes of the Cavendishes were being repaired by extensive urban and industrial development, Bagehot, *The English Constitution*, 1872, wrote — 'the most prominent statesmen [in the House of Commons] are not men of ancient or of great hereditary estate; they are men mostly of substantial means, but they are mostly, too, connected more or less closely with the new trading wealth'.

[4] Not, at first, in the cabinet.

[5] With his strong views in favour of the leadership of parliament by the Executive, Gladstone was on his guard against views such as Bright's, that

thought necessary before on such a scale, and the substitution of *arrivistes* for the usual bevy of Whigs revealed no high opinion of Whig capacities. Hartington's defeat in North Lancashire[1] was held to disqualify him for the War Office, but Bruce's defeat at Merthyr did not prevent his appointment to the senior Secretary-ship of State. Northbrook remained an under-secretary. Dufferin, Chancellor of the Duchy, denied the cabinet, was to pass into that proconsular career of which his nephew, Sir Harold Nicolson, writes so charmingly in *Helen's Tower*. One or two Whigs, such as Knatchbull-Hugessen, received junior offices, and places at the Treasury were found for the new Lord Lansdowne (aged twenty-three) and a middle-aged Vivian. Shaw-Lefevre, George Trevelyan and Arthur Peel were all well-connected, but they were not chosen principally on that account, though Gladstone had sentimental regard for the names of Trevelyan and Peel. The first two were rather radical. Gladstone looked to merit, rather than origins, connections or even opinions or indeed, as it seemed, accept-ability, for some of the middle class men and/or men of advanced opinions were less agreeable than they were able.[2]

The inauguration of the new dispensation was eased, in the constituencies, by the fact that in the course of nature one genera-tion of local Liberal politicians was giving place to another. Similarly, death had recently made a great dispersion of the 'ministerial lumber' of the 'fifties.[3] But to former ministers disposed to make trouble for the new incumbents — Grey, Clanricarde, Taunton (Labouchere), Lyveden (Vernon Smith), Westbury, Panmure (now Dalhousie) — were added Russell, who refused the cabinet without office, Somerset, who refused the cabinet, Halifax,

Commons committees, not the Treasury, should prepare the estimates (see *Queen's, Letters*, Series II, Vol. I, p. 563 and of *Clarendon*, Vol. II, p. 351, Clarendon to Russell, 14th Nov., 1868). Management would be easier if the responsible ministers were in the Commons.

[1] Gladstone and Milner Gibson were also beaten in Lancashire.

[2] Lowe was full of rough edges ('of a very angular mind', Gladstone told the Queen *Letters*, op. cit., p. 565). He had to leave the Treasury because of irregularities in 1873. Ayrton, unsociable, querulous, truculent M.P. for Tower Hamlets was moved from the Financial Secretaryship of the Treasury in 1869 to the Board of Works which he involved in such contention that he had to move again in 1873.

[3] Twenty-five non-Tory ex-cabinet ministers died 1859–69. Some of them (Ellice, Glenelg, Monteagle) had been out of office since the 'thirties; Aberdeen, Graham, Lansdowne and Palmerston died 1860, 1861, 1863 and 1865 respectively. The younger Peelites, Herbert, Newcastle, Dalhousie, Canning and Elgin also died.

who refused an offer and Stanley of Alderley who was offered nothing. There were also ex-ministers who had never reached the cabinet — Athlumney, Eversley, Belper.[1] These men were lampooned by Lord Edmond Fitzmaurice in his '*Life of Granville*'. At the bidding of the ex-premier (Russell), he says, 'the dry bones of many ancient Whig peers who in their day had been men of renown stirred again upon the battlefield . . . and executed more than one disastrous attack on the flank of their own party'.[2] No doubt these ex-ministers, the colleagues of his grandfather, seemed very *passé* to a stripling returned by his brother as member for Calne when just of age, and even to a cabinet whose average age was only fifty-one. No doubt, too, many of them, including Russell, were, in part at least, motivated by their resentments.[3] They represented the past, the Whig past, eyeing critically, and with little good will, the Liberal, the Gladstonian, present. When they conducted the assaults of which Fitzmaurice complains, they were standing for an ancient policy, approved by Pitt, Grenville, Grey, Russell, Peel and Palmerston. It was a policy that had never been popular, and had never prospered, except in the one particular of the Maynooth Grant — the policy of concurrent endowment. But it was not just taken up as a stick with which to beat Gladstone. It was a liberal policy (more liberal than mere disestablishment).[4] It was one in which the older Whig peers believed, and which many younger ones sincerely accepted. What to sectarians were the virtues of Gladstone's Irish Church scheme of 1869 appeared to many Whigs its fundamental flaws. A corporation disliked by Dissenters as a religious establishment, by Presbyterians as episcopalian, by Catholics as protestant, by secularists as a church, was to be excised from the constitution and stripped of most of its endowments — but all without any advantage to the Catholics except the satisfaction of seeing an old enemy felled.

[1] Formerly Sir William Somerville, Shaw-Lefevre (Speaker), and Strutt respectively.
[2] Vol. I, p. 10.
[3] When the Queen expressed surprise at the offer of the cabinet to Russell, Gladstone explained that he feared he might be more troublesome out of office than in (*Queen's Letters*, op. cit., p. 565). Russell told the Queen that out of office he thought he would be more use in composing differences and inducing the Lords to avoid dangerous struggles (p. 567).
[4] George Moore, 16th July, 1869, said, 'the vaunted spirit of the constituencies' claimed as the mandate for the bill was the same old spirit that had produced the Ecclesiastical Titles Act (now quietly repealed). Roundell Palmer the day before had said the Bill was 'a monument of Protestant Ascendancy'.

How, asked Whiggery, could this bill heal the social wounds of Ireland? The only answer was Argyll's, that much of the dis- affection of the Irish people was purely traditional, and that the establishment was 'a traditional remembrance of the miseries and oppressions of their former history', so that its removal would, 'to a very great extent, pacify and conciliate the thinking and moderate people of Ireland'.[1] But were they the people who needed pacifying?

Whigs did not care very much for disestablishment. Russell had wanted by some means or other to keep the Irish Church's connection with the state.[2] Clanricarde complained that he had not, last year, understood the full scope of the disestablishment.[3] Westbury violently attacked the Bill, though admitting that, in view of the election result, the peers must give it a second reading (which was done by 179 : 146). Many Whig peers thought the disendowment too sweeping, and joined with Tories to carry an amendment for the grant of free glebes to the clergy of the dis- established Church. The vote was 213 : 144, and in the majority were Russell, the Dukes of Cleveland, Grafton, Leinster and Somerset, Earl Grey, the Earls of Lichfield, Minto and Suffolk, and Lords Halifax, Eversley, Belper, Athlumney, Taunton, Vivian and Westbury.[4] In the Commons Sir George Grey and Roundell Palmer (who had refused office because of his objections to dis- endowment) pleaded in vain for acceptance of the Lords' amend- ment; they were overruled by a majority of eighty-nine. The two House of Commons Fitzwilliams were in the minority. The more reasonable of the Whig peers admitted the force of the ministerial argument that a large scheme of concurrent endowment was unacceptable to the Irish hierarchy and to British public opinion.[5] But they resented the absolute veto, stated in the preamble to the Bill, of the application of the confiscated revenues to the purposes they favoured. Earl Grey raised the battle cry of concurrent endowment.[6] With Tory aid, the Whig rebels emasculated the preamble, and in committee they tried to insert an amendment to

[1] H. of L., 29th June, 1868.
[2] *Argyll*, Vol. II, p. 245, Argyll to Gladstone, 12th September, 1868.
[3] H. of L., 29th June, 1869.
[4] 2nd July, 1869. The H. of C. debate on this was 15th July.
[5] e.g. speeches of Cleveland and Devonshire, 17th June, 1869. Cf. n. 4, p. 340, *supra*.
[6] 29th June, 1869. Grey wished to prevent the usual postponement of the preamble for consideration last, but was dissuaded by Russell as well as Cairns and Salisbury.

confer a house and ten acres on each Catholic parish priest and Presbyterian minister. They argued forcibly that this would be a measure of social benefit, standing on the same footing as the Maynooth Grant and the *Regium Donum* (both of which were now to cease). Without some measure of concurrent endowment, said Houghton (no dried-up Whig), nothing was being done for the peace of Ireland; a government with courage would risk a little for that end.[1] With ex-ministers marched the bearers of famous Whig titles, Devonshire, Cowper, Fitzwilliam, Fortescue, Ilchester, Radnor. They failed in committee by 146 to 113 (most Tories did not like endowing Catholics), but subsequently inserted the provision by 121 : 114, after a debate marked by a slashing attack on Gladstone from the Duke of Somerset.[1] In the Commons, George Grey pleaded in vain for the retention of the amendment as a small act of grace calculated to remove the most visible inequality between the three Irish religious communities. Gladstone, with the Anglican hierarchy and the paladins of Dissent at his back, stood firm, and carried the day by 346 : 222. The majority bespoke some Tory aid, for a number of Whigs revolted.[2] A constitutional crisis threatened when the Lords again struck at the preamble by a large majority, only seventy peers supporting ministers.[3] It was averted by an agreement between Granville and Cairns, the Tory lawyer. The Lords gave way, Russell protesting that they did not deserve the calumny to which they were exposed.[4]

The Liberal party (and the Lords) owed much to Granville. He combined sanity and tact in counsel with a suave firmness in public. He had not the conservative projudices which had rendered so potent old Lansdowne's advocacy of innovations, being of much more flexible opinions. But he was known to wish to save the Lords from the penal action which both Bright and Lowe desired. He was assisted in his unenviable task by the vast spread of his cousinship across all parties,[5] a sociable disposition and a gift for negotiation which, if it did not prosper

---

[1] H. of L., 12th July. Chichester Fortescue's brother (Clermont) and Gladstone's brother-in-law (Lyttelton) supported the amendment.

[2] e.g. Hon. A. F. Egerton, Hon. D. F. Fortescue, J. B. Carter, Col. North, W. Nicholson.

[3] H. of L., 20th July.   [4] H. of L., 22nd July.

[5] On 14th May, 1855 Granville, replying to an attack by Ellenborough, said, 'My Lords, I am a Gower. . . . I am also a Cavendish. . . . I am sorry to say that I am also related to some of the Howards. . . . I had better make a clean breast of it

when he was Foreign Secretary in the Europe of Bismarck, was indispensable in cabinet and Parliament. A brusque Tory sailor once complained that he was more like a Frenchman than an Englishman. But 'Pussy' was a cat that could scratch if too vigorously provoked.

In the winter and spring of 1869–70 Granville was much in demand as peacemaker in a cabinet brought to the verge of disruption by the Irish Land Bill. In September 1869 Clarendon spoke very strongly to 'Merrypebble' (his nickname for Gladstone), protesting that he did not mean to be a spoliator.[1] He continued to protest. On 4th December Granville praised the reticence and restraint of his colleagues, but added 'Clarendon talks the loudest and most indiscreetly. He has always done so and always will do so and it is no use trying to educate men out of their one particular fault when they are nearly seventy'.[2] One understands why G. W. E. Russell called Clarendon 'a typical Whig placeman' and Asquith said he was 'the last of the Whigs'.[3] But Clarendon was not alone in his doubts and fears. 'On Irish land I will *not* follow Ch. Fortescue, who seems to me a bit of a fool,' wrote Argyll. 'I would be not party to ask the House of Lords to assent to measures which Cairns or Bethell would blow to shreds on the *merits* — we having no plea in support except pure Funk and the argument of the Blunderbuss.'[4] He would rather see the Government broken up than be a party to wild schemes of tenant right, any attempt to fix rents or interfere with contracts, and he was most reluctant to give statutory effect to the tenant right of Ulster. But by the beginning of December he admitted that the Irish tenantry was so excited (Spencer, the Lord Lieutenant, was asking for coercion) that nothing reasonable would satisfy them, and so he was prepared to respond to Granville's plea to be a cement, not a dissolvent.[5] In the next few weeks he accepted the

at once; and I am obliged to admit that some of those who went before me had such quivers full of daughters who did not die old maids, that I have relations upon this side of the House, relations upon the cross benches, relations upon the opposite side of the House, and I actually had the unparalleled misfortune to have no fewer than three cousins in the Protectionist Administration by my noble friend opposite.'

[1] *Clarendon*, Vol. II, p. 361, to Lady Salisbury 1st October, 1869.
[2] *Granville Papers*, P.R.O., Gifts and Deposits 29/51, 4th December, to Argyll.
[3] *Prime Ministers and Some Others*, p. 29; Asquith, *Fifty Years of Parliament*, p. 7.
[4] Gifts and Deposits 29/51, 12th November, 1869, to Granville.
[5] Gifts and Deposits 29/51 A. to G., 1st December, G. to A., 4th December. Cf. Argyll to Gladstone, 26th November (*Argyll*, Vol. II, p. 258).

statutory recognition of Ulster Custom, and of local customs and usages, and where these were lacking, statutory compensation not only for improvements but for mere eviction (other than for non-payment of rent).[1]

It was not only from Whig and Peelite noblemen that Gladstone encountered difficulty. Bright was one of those 'Commercial Liberals' who regarded landed proprietors as privileged monopolists who insisted on the maintenance of the law because, although their property was founded in violence, they controlled the assemblies that made the land laws. He wanted, eventually, to expose Land, free of its inherited legal and customary encumbrances, to the blessings of *laisser-faire*, and argued that the parallel to land legislation of the kind he advocated was not a factory act (which he consistently deplored) but the Repeal of the Corn Laws. The state's function was emancipatory. It might properly effect, by incentives and facilities, the transfer of land from owners to occupiers, but should involve itself in landlord-tenant relationships only with the object of abolishing them. He therefore abominated, as much as Argyll, any idea of rent-fixing,[2] which was not a major issue for the cabinet in 1869-70, and he did not relish the tenant right provisions which were in train. The Bill could only be made palatable to him by the introduction of 'purchase' clauses. His colleagues humoured him, though they accepted the clauses only because they knew they would be inoperative. That other Commercial Liberal, Robert Lowe, was prepared to extend to the landlord and his rights, however acquired however exercised, the blanket immunity from state intervention which he wished to accord to the entrepreneur. His Utilitarianism was so impregnated with dogmatic adherence to *laisser-faire* principles of economic policy that he was no more willing than Sir Charles Wood in 1847 to violate absolute canons promulgated from professors' chairs simply because they proved unjust or inefficient in practice. He was reluctant to admit that it was ever socially or politically expedient to legislate what was, *a priori* unsound. As in 1865-7 in the House of Commons on the subject

---

[1] *Argyll*, Vol. II, pp. 256-8, to Cardwell, 29th December.
[2] Gifts and Deposits 29/52, Bright to Granville, 2nd January, 1870 complained of a *Fortnightly* article which 'alarms me, for he advocates the fixing of *rents* by an authority above landlord and tenant and says that this is not at variance with the true teaching of political economy. I hope Mr Lowe will read it — it will afford fine scope for his powers of criticism'.

THE 2nd EARL GRANVILLE
by George Richmond, R.A. (1876)

of Reform, so in 1869–70 in cabinet, he, who had no respect for
aristocrats as such (but as great a contempt for Irish peasants as
for the British working man), stood forth as the extreme, lucid
and pertinacious champion of class privileges. Compensation for
disturbance, he said, would involve:[1]

> ... a direct attack upon property, a direct breach of the duty of
> Government to do impartial justice between all its subjects, a pre-
> cedent under which any amount of spoliation might as far as principle
> goes be justified, the fining one class for the benefit of another, the
> transfer of money from one person to another without fault in the
> person amerced or merit in the person enriched, the forcing new
> and arbitrary terms into existing contracts, the breaking of faith
> pledged to the purchasers in the encumbered estates court and
> undermining all confidence in the justice and courage of the Govern-
> ment.

So Argyll, the Whig of Peelite origins, heir of fifty Campbell
chieftains owning vast estates on a tenure very like the Irish,[2]
received support from the academic tutor who argued landlord
right in terms of Political Economy, as well as from Cardwell,
sprung from trade but now a landowner, and, for totally different
reasons, from Bright. But Gladstone got his way, with some
concessions to Argyll and Bright.[3] Lowe had predicted that he
would, although, he said, the majority of the cabinet disapproved
of the Prime Minister's views. It was Granville's function virtually
to hold the ring until his colleagues came round to Gladstone's
way of thinking. He was to have much further experience in this
rôle.

In the Commons George Grey and Roundell Palmer did much
mischief (once lowering the majority to thirty-two) and were able
to do so, Gladstone said, because of the fear that the Land Bill
would cross the water. Clarendon had predicted that 'if he used the
Irish landlords roughly, the English ones would assuredly frater-
nise with them, which would be more injurious to the Government
than dissatisfying the agitators who are, one and all, irresponsible,

[1] Gifts and Deposits 29/66, 16th May, 21st December, 1869, 1st January,
1870.
[2] *Argyll*, Vol. II, p. 262.
[3] To Bright, the purchase clause. To Argyll, first a twenty-one year lease
exhausting the right to compensation for eviction and, subsequently, a 'free
contract line' down to £50 (ibid., pp. 263–6, 23rd April, 1870, to. Roundell
Palmer).

pennyless and dishonest'.[1] But when the Bill reached the Lords, only the rabid Earl of Leitrim attacked it outright, as another step in the policy of confiscation begun by the Church Bill. He was rebuked by the Earl of Lichfield, who, however, set the tone for the Lords debates by saying that landlords should carefully scrutinise the proposal for precedents that might be extended to England and Scotland, and that some clauses would give rise to injustice and others to discontent.[2] The restraint of the peers may seem surprising, for O'Hegarty says that this measure began the undoing of the Conquest. It marked the reversal of the attempt to rewrite Irish land tenure in the alien image and the Bright clauses, though puny, contained the germ of a vast transfer of property from landlord to tenant. The explanation is, however, fairly simple. Argyll, in wrestling with Sir Roundell Palmer, argued that there was a serious danger of agrarian revolution in Ireland, 'the anchors of opinion, on which all rights of property depend, are dragging and have lost their hold'. He further argued that no essential principle was violated, and free contract was not really interfered with. Only the existing holders were helped, because 'all tenants taking farms after the Bill is passed will have to discount all artificial advantages'. So all future holders would be free contractors. The great thing about the Bill was that it would not prevent consolidation — the landlord could evict (subject in certain cases to compensation claims) simply by raising rents. And, the Duke added, 'I dread the loss of this Bill more than I can say; and I, as a landowner, am satisfied with the concessions made.'[3] These were the considerations which dominated the discussions in the Lords. The Act would be a half-measure, trenching as little as possible on such rights as most landlords could exercise without risk of violence. It established the far-reaching principle that property in land was not absolute, but only as a recognition in law of a set of facts peculiar to Ireland. It validated existing custom and imposed rules of a similar kind where no custom was acknowledged. Dufferin, the only minister whose whole property was in Ireland, declared himself an unfailing and irreconcilable enemy of tenant right, but had approved since 1853 of retrospective compensation for improvements and in 1865 acknowledged the equity

---

[1] *Clarendon*, Vol. II, p. 361, to Lady Salisbury, 1st October, 1869.

[2] H. of L., 17th June 1870. This Lord Lichfield was one of the few aristocratic politicians who looked kindly upon trade unions.

[3] *Argyll*, Vol. II, pp. 265–6, 23rd April, 1870.

of compensation for disturbance. He showed that, despite Lowe and Bright, Whig landlords could accept legislative interference to protect tenants on the same grounds as legislative protection of factory children.[1] 'I know very well that this Bill will limit my power as a landlord but only when that power is unjustly abused,' said Chichester Fortescue.[2] Viscount Burke (brother of the deceased Dunkellin), soon to be notorious as an evicting absentee Marquess of Clanricarde, said that though it was unjust to the landlord it fairly preserved his material interests and, as for the bad landlord, 'serve him right'.[3] There was wide agreement that the effect of the Bill would be to levy a relatively light fine, determined by a local tribunal, in order to compensate a tenant evicted other than for non-payment of rent, and that it would hit only the minority of bad landlords. Lansdowne in Co. Kerry (where, he said, he had 795 tenants of under £10 p.a. for whom mere compensation for improvements was inadequate),[4] Dufferin in Co. Down and Argyll in Scotland were used to paying the sort of compensation the Bill required, which conscience required.

Thus, while Lowe, whom Morley dubs the most rigid of 'Whig economists', had to choose between his principles and his party (and his ministerial career), the Whig aristocracy, in face of the problem set by Gladstone in his 'mission to pacify Ireland', asserted its empiricism. Even Halifax advanced so far from the negativism of 1847 as to say that Irish customs which checked, restricted and burdened the landlord were bad in Political Economy, an affront to common sense, and bad for both parties, but the fact that the Irish liked them must be accepted as the only sound basis of legislation.[5] So Whiggery went on record as prepared to invade property right, though only tentatively and for good cause shown in terms of political expediency or even social justice. The choice seemed to lie between a Land Bill and a social war. But the Bill became an Act, and the land war continued, and in Westmeath and parts adjoining became more intense. And so Spencer and, in the cabinet, Hartington (who had succeeded Fortescue) found themselves involved in the usual dispute between Dublin and Downing Street on the timing and degree of coercion. The Marquess complained that the duty to maintain life and

---

[1] H. of L., 14th June, 1870.   [2] H. of C., 7th March, 1870.
[3] H. of C., 10th March, 1870.   [4] H. of L., 17th June, 1870.
[5] H. of L., 16th June, 1870.

property and the prestige of the Executive did not receive due attention. There developed between the two noblemen and Gladstone, who was old enough to be their father, a complete failure of confidence. Gladstone's approach was theoretical; the Irish grievances, he reckoned, were ecclesiastical, economic and educational, and they were to be met by a Church Bill, a Land Bill and a University Bill. Hartington shared the lukewarmness of his kind towards the Church Bill and hardly concealed his belief that the Land Act would not win over the agrarian population. He believed that it is the primary function of all government to ensure that legal privileges and liberties could be effectively exercised, by the preservation of order. He also thought that, with a new separatist movement developing, it should be made much clearer than Gladstone was willing to make it that there was no question of Home Rule. But at the same time Hartington saw that the Irish could legitimately complain that scant regard was paid to their practical needs, and he (like Fortescue) pressed for the nationalisation of the railways, as a means of cheapening rates.[1] Gladstone was committed to the end,[2] but burked the means, and Lowe, of course, could not see that Ireland should be excepted from his dogmatic denunciation of nationalisation. So Hartington's suggestion was ignored. If Hartington had had his way, the new Home Rule movement would have been met at the outset by some attempt, however inadequate, to kill it with kindness.[3] A string of Home Rule victories in by-elections showed that the Prime Minister's preconceived prescriptions had not taken in Ireland. But he proceeded with unimaginative obstinacy to produce a University Bill on which he was defeated. In the case of the Church Bill the hostility of the Catholic hierarchy towards endowment had been stated to be decisive. The hierarchy did want a state-aided Catholic university but it did not want what Gladstone offered, an unpalatable variant of the 'godless colleges'. To Protestants the bill seemed to menace Trinity and 'rob' private funds (the verb was Hartington's). As though to leave it no friends, it affronted reason in its details, which Disraeli enjoyed analysing. Whigs spoke against the measure, Radicals mocked it, Catholics con-

[1] As Postmaster General it had fallen to Hartington to manage the nationalisation of the telegraphs.

[2] In his speech of December 1867, at Southport.

[3] Hartington's views at this time are well covered in *Life of the 8th Duke of Devonshire*, Vol. I, Ch. VI.

demned it. Horsman volleyed and Harcourt thundered (he had refused office in 1868). Hartington damned the dogmatists and sectarians with all the vigour of a man who cannot understand people getting excited about religion. But he could not disguise his distaste for a bill he had condemned in the cabinet.

When the Irish University Bill was defeated by 287 : 284 on 12th March, 1873, Gladstone resigned. But Disraeli refused office, and sentenced the Liberals to a wretched fag-end period of government by accepting the advice of Northcote:[1]

... I am strongly convinced that time is required to mature the fast-ripening Conservatism of the country, and to dispel the hallucinations which have attached a great mass of moderate men to the Liberal cause. I believe that the disintegration of Gladstone's party has begun and that nothing but precipitancy on our part can arrest it. He has expended the impetuous force which brought him into office, and now is brought face to face with new, or rather old, difficulties which he can hardly surmount without alienating one or other wing of his party. If he goes on with the Extreme section, a large body of his moderate supporters will rank themselves with the Conservatives; if he quarrels with the Extreme section, they will become the Opposition while the conduct of affairs will go to the acknowledged Conservatives, who will obtain the support of the moderate Liberals. But if we appeal to the country before the breach in the Liberal ranks is fully made, and before the policy of the extreme men is fully developed, we consolidate them; and the extreme men will hold back a little, the moderates will advance a little, and there will be more confusion and confiscation.

This advice was sound. All discipline disappeared from the Liberal party in Parliament. A scandal in the Post Office discredited three ministers, and resulted in Gladstone becoming Chancellor of the Exchequer as well as prime minister. At the Treasury he bethought himself of the reiterated admonitions of Bright,[2] and although he could not reach agreement with the ministers in charge of the spending departments, he offered the electorate the abolition of the income tax. It did not prove a winning horse.

[1] *Iddesleigh Papers*, 14th March, 1873, to Disraeli.
[2] Attacks on the Government's failure to economise, especially in defence, Gifts and Deposits 29/52, 26th January, 1871, 29th May, 1871, 25th September, 1871, 2nd January, 1873 — and 19th February, 1872 '... To lessen now or to indicate the intention of getting rid of the income tax in a year or two or to reduce the income tax and repeal the rest of the sugar duty in this session, would be a great thing and would do much for the Government...' Bright had advocated 'the free breakfast table' during the general election of 1868.

It is no part of the intention of the present writer to decry the reforming achievements of the first Gladstone administration. But they were followed by what Gladstone himself called the greatest expression of public disapprobation of a Government that he ever remembered.[1] By-election victories for the Opposition began in February 1870 and became a flood. In all there were twenty-seven gains in forty-seven months to January 1874, halving the Liberal-cum-Home-Rule majority. Great county divisions in Surrey and the West Riding, which were rapidly becoming urbanised, agricultural boroughs like Shaftesbury, great industrial and commercial centres like Oldham and Hull, and Gladstone's own constituency of Greenwich all told the same tale. Tory working men appeared in force, some of them trade unionists seeking the right to use effectively by strike action the legal rights the Liberal government had given them, some of them men who liked their pint and resented the Liberal tilts at the publicans, some of them men thrown out of work by economies in the dockyards. This very plutocratic government in which *laisser-faire* doctrinaires such as Lowe, Bright, Cardwell and Bruce figured prominently (men who were no lovers of trade unions and were allergic to constructive social reform) antagonised men of the masses as well as men of the classes. With that strange, insensitive rigour and financial rectitude which in the early 'sixties had led him to try to tax charities, Gladstone supported Lowe's attempt to tax matches, which turned out a propaganda gift to his opponents. Middle-class Nonconformity, while approving much that Gladstone had done, was incensed by a major Education Bill which Bright said 'was one the Tories might have proposed, but could not have passed. A Liberal Government only could pass a measure so far wide of the Liberal line of march'.[2] Mutiny over this matter did not go the length of voting for the party of squire, parson and brewer. But it was difficult for militant Dissenters to vote for Liberals who had supported a bill which seemed so pro-Anglican, and the National Education League, the Liberation Society and other bodies were doing all they could to make Dissenters militant. Their campaign aroused the zeal, or bigotry, of Anglicans. The clergy became very active in the Tory cause, complaining of the Irish Church Bill, the abolition of University Tests, the Deceased Wife's Sister Bill,

---

[1] *Queen's Letters*, 2nd Series, Vol. II, p. 318.
[2] Gifts and Deposits 29/52, 31st August, 1873, on rejoining the Government.

the proposed rape of Trinity and the projected incursion of the Nonconformists into the churchyards which, since Disraeli's abolition of compulsory church rates in 1868, were maintained solely by Anglicans.

But this is a book about Whig attitudes, and Whig fortunes. Whiggery disapproved of many of Gladstone's achievements, though Whig M.P.s and peers had perforce to abet them. County families deprecated the abolition of the purchase of commissions (by royal warrant when the Lords proved fractious) and the effect of Cardwell's reforms on the Volunteer movement. There was aristocratic resistance to giving open competition for the civil service the full sweep that Lowe desired.[1] The Palmerstonian instinct was affronted by the submission to arbitration of American claims against Great Britain in the *Alabama* dispute. And, in addition, there was, at last, the enactment of the ballot. It would have come thirty years before but for the resistance of Melbourne and Russell and their cabinet colleagues, backed by the Great Grandmotherhood. It could not be long delayed after the grant of the franchise to so many persons in the boroughs who were economically dependent one way or another on property owners, and employers, though the by-election at Southwark early in 1870, when the trade unionist, Odger, thrust the official Liberal to the bottom of the poll and ran the Conservative hard, raised the question of whether working men did not, as Shaftesbury had prophesied they would,[2] require to be protected from their mates as much as from employers or landlords.

The final impetus to the ballot came from the revelation of scandalous practices at the 1868 elections, which resulted in 111 petitions. Hartington introduced a Government bill in 1870, which lapsed. The Bill introduced by Forster in 1871 was given so low a priority that their Lordships in August, in a thin House, ventured to vote it down, stressing the discourtesy of sending it up so late.[3] 'There is evidently grave dissent among the supporters of the Government,' Northcote had told Disraeli.[4] Lyveden,

[1] See Gifts and Deposits 29/66, 5th December, 1870 and 19th January, 1871. Lowe complained that Clarendon and Granville, supported by their officials at the Foreign and Colonial Offices, had 'one rule for the rich and another for the poor' and threw on competition 'the stigma of unfitness for the most important posts which would be filled by University men'.

[2] H. of L., 6th August, 1867.

[3] The vote was 97:48, 10th August, 1871, on the second reading.

[4] *Iddesleigh Papers*, 22nd July, 1871.

remarking that he had been a Liberal long before Gladstone, protested against the ballot being made the test of Liberalism. Russell and Somerset voted in the majority. Even Bright realised what a radical reform the ballot seemed to the old Whig peers. 'The Ballot has always been offensive to them and only recently almost all Conservatives and many Whigs have regarded it with horror,' he wrote. 'It was not perhaps wholly unreasonable for the Lords to take a little more time before consenting to so great a change. They come up rather slowly, but they do come up in time to what the nation requires'.[1] But next year his patience wore thin. 'You have a bad team to drive,' he told Granville. 'I am afraid they will neither be led nor driven and can, in the end, come only to grief. . . . To show their power and hatred of representative freedom, they insult Government, Commons and People in their insolent way of dealing with the Ballot Bill. . . . If the Lords will not pass the bill with the change which I have described, it will be best for you to let them reject it, for there can be no better question for you to go to a general election on than that of a real as against a sham Ballot.'[2] The 'sham' ballot was an optional one. Ministers objected that the provisions desired by the Lords would defeat secrecy, but the peers carried such provisions, on 17th June, 1872, on the motion of the Duke of Richmond, by 162:91, with the Dukes of Bedford, Somerset and Cleveland, Earl Russell, Earl Fortescue and, of course, the Marquess of Clanricarde in the majority. The Government stood firm, but accepted elaborate checks against personation, fear of which led an honest, and rather progressive member like Lord Frederick Cavendish to doubt whether the effect of the introduction of the ballot would not be worse than not having it. We, to whom the secret ballot is part of the natural order of political life, should make the effort to appreciate how revolutionary a change it seemed. Hartington accepted it with the utmost reluctance, hoping that it might be only temporary, and that one day voting might be free, tranquil and open as well.

Freddy Cavendish's doubts as to whether the ballot would really produce purity were well justified. Electoral manners and methods did not change overnight. An effective Corrupt Practices Act (which came in 1883) was required, and probably it was the dis-

[1] Gifts and Deposits 29/52, 25th September, 1871, to Granville.
[2] ibid., 20th June, 1872.

franchisement of 1885 which struck the fatal blow at corruption.[1] The contribution of secrecy to the first Conservative victory in thirty years, won in 1874, and to the advance of the Home Rulers in Ireland, should not be exaggerated.

If Gladstone could not claim in 1874 to represent the people against the peers, the masses against the classes, he could certainly echo Melbourne's complaint of 1835 that the Lords, the gentry and the clergy were overwhelmingly against him. Of the minority which was for him, many were lukewarm. What Fitzmaurice says of peers who 'professed Liberal opinions' may indeed stand as the general view of Whiggery. 'Even those who approved the particular measures which Mr Gladstone from time to time proposed, were growing suspicious that the ultimate aims of the new Prime Minister were not their aims, nor his mind their mind; and that the Liberal party was being gradually led by him onwards to some only as yet partially disclosed goal.'[2] They shared the apprehensions of Carnarvon, who made his way back to the Tory fold 'very much alarmed at the possibility of a great attack on the land, suspicious of Gladstone and of an attempt to set tenants against landlords'.[3] That there was some ground for their fears is apparent from a 'scrap' in Gladstone's writing, attributed by Morley to late 1873. The Prime Minister wrote 'Divisions in the liberal party are to be seriously apprehended from a factious spirit on questions of economy, on questions of education in relation to religion, on further parliamentary change, on the land laws. On these questions generally my sympathies are with what may be termed the advanced party, who on other and general grounds I certainly will never head nor lead.'[4]

In 1874 the Whig peers contributed rather more to the party's central fund than in 1868. The Whig M.P.s fought and suffered in the elections. But they did so without joy in their hearts. Many of them could not feel that the country did wrong in calling a halt to 'harassing' legislation. Yet the judgement of the country fell with unfair force on them. For more than half the Tory gains were in counties or in boroughs with less than 2,000 electors, the sort of constituencies where the Liberal candidate was most likely to be

[1] Dr Hanham's judgement to this effect seems well-founded.
[2] *Granville*, Vol. II, p. 3.
[3] *Iddesleigh Papers*, Northcote to Disraeli, 23rd September, 1872. Carnarvon had left the Tory Government in hostility to the Reform Bill.
[4] Morley, Vol. II, p. 65.

2A

a Whig. Of thirteen Liberal members seeking re-election in the counties and opposed by a Tory, only three got in; only seven Liberals were returned in full fight in the English counties. The English knights of the shire now constituted a quarter of the House of Commons, but only 15% of them were Liberals. County electors who shared the Whig view of Gladstone and Gladstonianism were not to the same extent as Whig members prisoners of a traditional allegiance which inhibited them from deserting secret for open Conservatism. The social *élite* of the Liberal party, its natural reservoir of moderation and its link with the Whig party that had gone before, took a beating at the polls. Russell still called the Liberal party 'the Whig party' and said that Gladstone and Granville had led 'the Whig party of Lord Grey to destruction and dispersion'. The meaningless remark of an old man in his dotage had its element of truth, like the phrase 'dishing the Whigs'. The first Gladstone administration revealed the full severity of the decline in Whig influence. And by frightening away from Liberalism moderate men attracted by the lure of Palmerston it accentuated that decline.

CHAPTER XIV

The Defence of 'Liberty and Property'

J. D. Coleridge found the treatment by both the country and the Liberal party of 'the greatest, noblest, purest and sincerest public man' of the century 'infinitely disgusting'.[1] Gladstone agreed with him, and resigned the Liberal leadership. He felt no great party political issue calling him to the fray, and that the party in Parliament was not worthy of him; it must learn how through its 'divisions and self-seeking' its disruption had been accomplished. The man best qualified, by ability and central position within the party, to be its leader was W. E. Forster. In the succession to the son of Liverpool commerce of a Bradford manufacturer, son of the Quaker revival, sitting in the seat of a Russell and a Temple as Leader of the Opposition, there would have been symbolical importance. But at this particular moment the appointment would have shattered the party. For though Gladstone had largely dictated the shape of the Education Act of 1870, Forster, as the minister in charge of the measure, had borne the brunt of the Dissenters' militant protest against a pro-Anglican policy which, they said, showed that the Liberal leaders still looked on the Nonconformists as their 'hewers of wood and drawers of water'.[2] And so it was to the Marquess of Hartington that Bright conveyed the news that he had been elected the party's leader in the Commons.

Since the Whigs had suffered more than any other section of the party from the national reaction against policies which, taken as a whole, they, more than any other section, deprecated, there was poetic justice in the succession of Hartington to Gladstone. But the choice of a Whig as leader was not a recognition of the *Edinburgh Review*'s claim that Gladstone had been punished by the electors, as Russell had been punished by the Adullamites, for the offence

[1] *Forty Years of Friendship*, p. 149.
[2] Joseph Chamberlain at the Manchester Delegate Conference, 22nd January, 1873 (*Speeches*, p. 14).

of reliance on Radicals instead of Whigs.[1] It was simply that, in default of the colleague extolled by the *Economist* as having raised himself above other self-made men 'mainly by the sagacity and honesty which succeed in business',[2] Hartington was chosen 'rather than any other, perhaps abler, man' because the comparison between him and Forster would not be personal. 'Constituted as English society is, there is no humiliation to any one in being led by the eldest son of the Duke of Devonshire.'[3] Whiggery had its uses after all! Gladstone and Granville thought Hartington the very man to give the 'light and negative . . . reticent and expectant' leadership which was the most the party could stand. He seemed, indeed, the very man for a dull parliament, to 'sit opposite to a Government in the anxious hope that it may make some mistake, and with little to say if it does not', and frame minute criticisms of minor measures.[4] Spencer Compton Cavendish was not prone to errant enthusiasms or sudden initiatives. He hated the sound of his own voice, yawned during his own speeches and dozed through those of others, and stayed in public life only because of *noblesse oblige*. In his maiden speech as leader, he told the House he was there to assist the course of business, and that the Government's measures generally were 'wise, salutary and beneficent' (which he could not have said of many of Gladstone's).

Expectations of a dull parliament were rudely shattered by Gladstone's return to the arena in the guise of a crusader advocating the expulsion of the Turks 'bag and baggage' from the scene of their atrocities in the Balkans. At first in pamphlets, and then on platforms and in Parliament, he poured out the vials of his indignation not only on the Turk but on Disraeli (now Lord Beaconsfield) as his accomplice, denouncing as 'perfectly fictitious and imaginary' any British interests which did not coincide with the interests of civilisation and humanity. He carried with him some of the upper class. Argyll was roused, with the rest of the Stafford House set.[5] The Duke of Westminster (the Earl Grosvenor of the Adullamite revolt) presided over a great meeting in St James's

[1] *Edinburgh Review*, CXL, October, 1874.
[2] 2nd January and 6th February, 1875.
[3] Coleridge, op. cit., p. 157, 22nd August, 1875. Cf. the *Economist*, 6th February, 1875, 'When Liberalism is popular it can prosper very well without aristocratic help. In times of adversity it is different. . . .'
[4] *Economist*, 9th January, 1875. See also, on the leadership and condition of the party, issues of 16th, 23rd, 30th January and 6th February.
[5] See *supra*, p. 302, n. 4.

Hall on 9th December, 1876 when, amid eight hours of oratory, Gladstone was lionised by churchmen (Evangelical and Anglo-Catholic), dons and literary men.[1] The Marquess of Ailesbury (formerly the Peelite and Adullamite Lord Ernest Bruce), Evelyn Ashley (heir-presumptive to the Palmerston estates), Freddy Leveson-Gower and Lord Arthur Russell assisted. Granville and even Adam, the whip, approved the demonstration.[2] But Hartington did not, and when Gladstone wanted parliamentary action, was pleased to be able to tell him that there was 'on our side of the House no disposition to raise . . . any definite issue relating to the Eastern Question, and . . . if it were considered necessary . . . the Bulgarian case would not be considered the best ground'. He added 'I should be sorry to see a state of public opinion, in which horror of the crimes of the Turkish Government would overpower every other consideration.'[3] It was precisely such a public opinion that Gladstone was striving to create. He went so far as to say that Russian intervention to expel the Turk would confer a noble boon on mankind. War to keep the Russians north of the Balkan Mountains, or even, it seemed, out of the Mediterranean, would be 'an act of utter wickedness'. No man could have carried the Liberal party in the House of Commons with him in favour of such drastic propositions. Palmerston had not lived in vain. The Eastern Question, as in the 'fifties, split Radicals as well as the right-wing. Hartington feared that Gladstonian extravaganzas would drive 'our best men, or at all events the Whigs' over to the Tories,[4] for the aristocracy in general was against Gladstone. Hartington himself was a Palmerstonian without bluff or bluster, one of the class condemned by Cobden as willing to fight to the stumps for the honour of England, narrowly patriotic enough to regard the honour of England as involved in the defence of British interests, Balance of Power etc., which to Cobden and Gladstone were 'stereotyped phrases'. The sceptical, empirical aristocrat was antipathetic to moralising and crusading, and totally unable to share Gladstone's sense of proportion. He believed these matters were best dealt with at the normal level of realism and com-

[1] Liddon, the Bishop of Oxford, Shaftesbury, Richard (of the Peace Society), Trollope, Bryce, Freeman, Fowell Buxton, the politicians Trevelyan and Fawcett, the Radical working men Howell and Broadhurst. Carlyle, Froude, Goldwin Smith and Lowe were also anti-Turk.
[2] So did old Earl Russell and the young Lord Rosebery.
[3] Holland's *Devonshire*, pp. 193-4, 3rd March, 1877.
[4] ibid., pp. 185–7, 18th December, 1876.

promise by statesmen and diplomats who saw the need to keep the Russians out of Macedonia, Thrace and Constantinople, not by public demonstrations and platform oratory. He did not deny that ministers made mistakes. But he shared their general outlook, paid them the compliment of thinking them as honourable and responsible as himself, and sought to strengthen the moderates in the cabinet and to avoid giving aid and comfort to Britain's ill-wishers. He must disapprove, with many aristocrats of both parties, of certain facets of Disraeli's character — ostentation, vulgarity, lack of scruple. But he could not see him as the incarnation of Evil. While Gladstone penned a bitter indictment of national iniquity, Hartington sent the Prime Minister grouse.

Gladstone had the grace to admit that the leaders of the party were limited by their duty to keep it together ('I, thank God, am more free'). But he behaved with an egocentricity which only the righteousness of his wrath could extenuate, and which was criticised even by some of his admirers.[1] He tried to force on the Liberal Front Bench, just after the Russian attack began, resolutions which he admitted had not 'a single approver in the upper official circle', which accused Gladstone of 'mischievous egoism and folly . . . past endurance'. The reaction of the party chiefs Gladstone found 'deplorable' and 'almost incredible'. They announced that they would move 'the previous question' on the ground that the resolutions were 'inopportune'.[2] When, with the Russian army within sight of Constantinople, the Government asked for a £6 million vote, Hartington said he could neither propose nor vote for any negative amendment. Gladstone found 144 supporters against the ministerial 330, who included a score of Liberals. Hartington and Forster walked out without voting. In many of the votes of 1878 this pattern of three-way disintegration was repeated until on 3rd August the Treaty of Berlin was approved by 338 : 133.

The importance of Gladstone's return to active politics under the spur of the Bulgarian atrocities, and his decision to harry a government which he deemed Satanic to a defeat which, besides obliterating the bitter memory of 1874, would partake of the character of a providential chastisement, was that it made him to

[1] e.g. Coleridge op. cit., p. 161. Though heart and soul with Gladstone, he thought he showed 'too little consideration for others and too much for himself'.
[2] For Hartington's justification see *Holland*, pp. 198–200, to Granville, 25th May, 1877.

an extent he had never been before the leader of Liberal and
Radical idealists (many of whom had been offended by the Education Act). It became unnecessary for him to produce a constructive
domestic policy, which would have caused divisions in the Liberal
ranks. Radicals did not ask it of him, being content to sail in his
wake. Gladstone asked himself no questions as to the designs of
men who joined in his destructive criticisms of ministers, echoed
his tirades against the aristocracy and plutocracy (so insensitive
to the woes of the Balkan Christians), and assailed the Liberal
leadership as 'shuffling, temporising, prevaricating'. The foes of
the Education Act muted their criticisms of Gladstone, while
continuing to assail 'Whig hacks and officials who creep about the
backstairs and tortuous passages of party intrigue' because they
'have no love for Nonconformity, which concerns itself with principles rather than with place or party'.[1] Prominent among these was
Joseph Chamberlain who, at the time of the breach between
Gladstone and the Front Bench, wrote 'If the Whigs adhere to
their present determination, a complete split in the party must
result. I am not certain that this will be altogether a bad thing,
since we might hope that it would be reformed upon some more
solid basis.... The future of Liberalism must come from
below.... It is evident we have no inspiration to expect from our
present official leaders.'[2]

When he spoke of 'the future of Liberalism [coming] from
below', Chamberlain had definite plans in mind. Very soon afterwards, on the last night of May, 1877, Gladstone stayed the night
in Birmingham at the house of Chamberlain, ex-mayor of the city
and now one of its M.P.s, the strong man of the Nonconformist
rebellion and architect of the National Liberal Federation. Gladstone, glad of any platform on which to denounce Turks and
Turkophiles, had consented to address the Federation in conference. Ignorant of party organisation and electoral management,
Gladstone did not discern the potential of the new body, or the
aims of its founders, and he did not fathom the force and quality
of Chamberlain. Hartington was more wary. When he was asked
to go to bless the Federation, he refused. Adam urged him to
recognise it, for it was a federation of associations the most
efficient of which were organised on the Birmingham 'caucus'

---

[1] *British Quarterly Review*, January 1879, Article IV.
[2] Stead's *M.P. for Russia*, pp. 359, 362, 4th and 24th May, 1877.

model, ward branches sending delegates to a city association whose
excecutive controlled the local party and could plan an effective
election campaign. The Marquess did not dispute that this might
be the best way of gaining Liberal victories in large towns. But
he understood that this was Chamberlain's method of ensuring
that the future of Liberalism came from below; that, in addition
to wishing to turn out the vote, the bosses of the Federation aimed
at political power, securing more radical candidates, dictating policy
to them as M.P.s and, ultimately, turning the Federation, under the
control of ambitious managers recognisable as the counterpart of
American manipulators, into a sort of Liberal Parliament impres-
sing its will on the parliamentarians. Such objectives were not
ruled out by the fact that the Federation was avowed to be
'thoroughly representative', open to every sort of Liberal. A
democratic organisation rising pyramid-like from ward to national
federation could be dominated at every level by Radical activists
who were not at all the sort of men the Whigs thought should have
much influence in public affairs. It is now fashionable to decry the
old, cataclysmic, view of 'the Caucus', and it is easy to do so with
the after-knowledge that by the end of the century the Gladstonian
parliamentarians were able to render the Federation almost as
inoccuous as a Conservative party conference.[1] But the ambitions
of the founders were certainly high, and they were what Hartington
said they were. They sought 'the chief control and direction of
the party . . . to the exclusion of the more moderate and easy-
going Liberals'. Chamberlain's letter of invitation to Hartington
took a high tone as irksome to the Marquess as Cobden's missive to
Lord John in 1846. A visit to the conference would, he said,
strengthen the leader's position in the country; a refusal would
lead the extra-parliamentary movement 'more and more to separate
from official Liberalism and to form a party within a party'.[2]
Honest Hartington said he would go only on the basis of stating
what he felt about the Federation. Its leaders preferred to be
able to complain that the leader of the party neglected their
importance.

Gladstone coasted to an easy victory in 1880 not because of the
Eastern Question, which was the principal theme of his 'pilgrimage

[1] The 'caucus' and the N.L.F. are treated of in Ostrogorski's *Democratic
Organization*, Lowell's *The Government of England*, McKenzie's *British Political
Parties* and Hanham, op. cit.

[2] For the Chamberlain-Hartington correspondence see *Holland*, Ch. XI.

of passion' in Midlothian, but because of the Depression.[1] All the circumstances were against ministers. They had become involved in war in southern Africa and in Afghanistan. The country, engulfed in a drastic industrial and agricultural depression, could not endure higher taxation. Heavy borrowing accentuated Gladstonian wrath and stimulated Bright and other Radicals to great exertions to visit on Lord Beaconsfield the condign punishment they had singularly failed to administer to Lord Palmerston. The Prime Minister was ailing and Northcote had no power of command. The reforming impetus of the Tory leadership was long spent; the Government was fully engaged in resisting demands for liberal public aid to Irish peasants and even English tenants, to say nothing of the unemployed.[2] The working classes forgot the very material concessions made to them in 1874–6. Who could blame them with unemployment at 11%, and in some places much more, and the great surge forward of trade unionism in the days of high prosperity before 1875 reversed in a plethora of desperate industrial disputes? The Liberals, though united only in criticism of the Tories, walked the course. The National Liberal Federation and the Farmers' Alliance both claimed exaggerated credit for the victory.[3] But to most people it seemed a Gladstonian triumph, and few condescended to notice that the Whig section of the party had made a contribution to it. The moderates were clearly, in the inter-party strife, on the defensive against the assailants of 'mere aristocratic pretension and antiquated delusion',[4] and Chamberlain's 'Bevanites' had publicly repudiated Hartington's leadership. But if it was not possible to accept the literal validity of Russell's prediction in 1874 that, whenever the Liberal party was reconstituted, it would be on a *Whig* basis, there was point in the *Edinburgh Review*'s election appeal to the moderate voter to appreciate that there were men of liberal but not extreme views, fervent in their attachment to freedom but not less opposed to rash and violent innovation, a left-centre standing between Tory prejudice and ignorance and Radical crotchets. 'Whig'

---

[1] *Elections and Party Management*, p. 229.

[2] See *Iddesleigh Papers*, Northcote to Beaconsfield, December 1878, 7th January and 12th October, 1879, 9th and 20th February, 1880.

[3] Chamberlain pointed out that the Liberals won 60 of 67 seats where there was a caucus, and 10 county seats. And 40 of the 60 Liberal candidates (and 2 of 3 Tory) supported by the Alliance were elected. But then the Liberals won almost all the seats held by Tories by less than 10%.

[4] Goldwin Smith, cited in the *Edinburgh Review*, CLI, January, 1880.

principles, understood as those held by Liberals who were neither Radicals nor democrats, were not only those of a great historic party; they were held by men of the highest character, ability and position, no mere clique or coterie of aristocratic statesmen, men who represented the true centre of gravity of the Liberal party. The writer claimed that they were the principles and opinions of the great mass of intelligence and liberality in the country, of the pith and marrow of the nation, and bade the electors look to Whig noblemen, to Goschen, Forster, Childers and Stansfeld as:

> men . . . perhaps less demonstrative than their neighbours; who esteem sobriety of language, dignity of demeanour and steadfastness in action as the first qualities of statesmanship; who distrust alike exuberance and power of eloquence and mysterious artifices of policy; who condemn and detest unjust, unnecessary and costly wars; who are not imposed upon by the tinsel and bombast of the present Administration, but who cling to the good old cause of constitutional progress with stability of principle and fixity of purpose. . . .

The Whig apologist warned the Radicals that to exclude such men and make them into a right centre would be an act 'worthy only of Spanish revolutionists'.[1] They were the existing official leaders of the party, and the guarantee that in office it would not behave like a rogue elephant. Neither the Tories nor the Liberal chiefs discounted the importance of their rôle in the 1880 elections. The Tories would dearly have liked an open breach between Gladstone and the party leaders, which they could have exploited. They felt against Hartington the same sense of grievance they had felt against Palmerston in 1865. The Marquess, they thought, was helping to swell a Liberal majority which would not be the instrument of *his* purposes. In a number of county and some borough seats the elector had a choice between a Tory and a moderate Liberal. When Hartington had argued, in a conclave of leaders before the election, that Gladstone should be urged to resume the official leadership, Adam demurred on the express ground that 'those who follow Mr Gladstone will all join him in following Hartington, whereas there are many who call themselves moderate Liberals who would not move a finger to support Mr Gladstone'.[2] This was the ground on which Harcourt, after the election, pressed

---

[1] *Edinburgh Review*, CLI, January 1880.
[2] Holland's *Devonshire*, Vol. I, pp. 261–2.

he Marquess to stand on his claim to the premiership. He pro-
ested against 'the notion that any one has had more to do with the
great victories of the election than yourself' and added 'Those who
have rallied to you in reliance upon your wisdom and moderation
have a right to expect that you would not deliver them over into
other hands.'[1] When Hartington was offered the premiership by
he Queen he would have liked to accept it, not from ambition, but
because of this responsibility towards the moderates and because
he felt it was only his due, who had (against his will and judgement) retained the leadership which Gladstone had discarded and
declined to resume. But he dare not do so unless Gladstone would
join the cabinet, and Gladstone, by promising 'independent
support' for a Hartington administration, in fact insisted upon and
obtained the premiership.

Gladstone had been hailed in the *Fortnightly Review* as 'the
impersonation of all that is hopeful, bold and belligerent in
Liberalism',[2] and denounced in the *Edinburgh Review* as the
purveyor of highly-seasoned dishes on which quiet people could
not live.[3] But Hartington's decision to join Gladstone's government was assisted by the discovery that Gladstone had no very
radical, indeed, no very definite, views on policy. 'No Whig
following such a leader could feel safe for a single moment,' the
Quarterly Review had said long ago.[4] That was as true as ever. But
the Whigs had given up hope of feeling 'safe' or happy in their
politics; they had only a choice of evils. Sir Henry Lucy, of *Punch*,
remarked that the Radicals and Tories were cocksure, but the
Whigs argumentative. In young Whigs especially he found a
'serious . . . unemotional, prophetic manner'.[5] Whigs had reason
to be thoughtful and argumentative, for they now had continually
to ask themselves whether it would be better for the *Conservative
Cause* if they rebelled or stayed to fight another day. For the
moment they found that if they were not to have power they were
to have place, and such security for their influence as numbers in
office could provide. Gladstone, anxious to maintain the unity of
the party, intended that the group which was weakest in the
House of Commons should be strongest in cabinet, and so, with a

---

[1] ibid., pp. 271–2.
[2] Vol. CLVII, 1st January, 1880, article by Henry Dunckley.
[3] Vol. CLI, January, 1880, art. cit.
[4] 280, X, 'The Six Year Old Parliament' (1865).
[5] *Diary of Two Parliaments* (1886), p. 176.

Parliament in which, Herbert Gladstone says, 'Whigs an Radicals fought, if not to a finish . . . yet to an advanced stage o the way to it',[1] the great posts went to patrician Whigs, say Morley, as if Mr Gladstone had been a Grey or a Russell.[2] Th only Radical in the cabinet, apart from Bright, was Chamberlain.[3]

The structure of the cabinet was some relief to Tories an pessimistic old Whigs like Somerset, but they had not much fait in the Whig ministers as champions of their class. They anticipate an attack on the landed interest, just when it was suddenly an acutely vulnerable economically. For the golden age of Britis agriculture, which, somewhat fortuitously, followed the Repeal o the Corn Laws, had ended abruptly with a succession of ba harvests and an influx of cheap American grain, and though goo harvests might return, the prairie farmer was already involved i that nightmare search for fair returns which world competitio was to deny both him and his European competitors in the absenc of tariff protection. The economic decline of the British land owner could therefore be forecast. Agriculture would never agai prosper in peacetime till the Agriculture Act of a minister who sa as a Socialist for a Yorkshire mining valley, whose colleague authorised the tearing-up of Lord Fitzwilliam's park of Went worth Woodhouse for open-cast mining. The political and socia consequences of the economic decline of the landed interest have been crucial. But it was subject to political attack simultaneously with the economic blizzard. Henry George was preaching the doctrine of land nationalisation. Charles Stewart Parnell declared that the landlord had no equitable interest in the soil except 'as the Flood left it'. Henry Labouchere amended that statement only to the extent of admitting a progessively diminishing sum for land-lord's improvements. Joseph Chamberlain developed the pro-vocative gospel that property ought to pay 'ransom' to the com-munity, on the assumption that the land had originally belonged to the community and passed into private hands by force or fraud. Chamberlain and Labouchere spoke favourably of graduated taxation and death duties, and their friend Jesse Collings of

[1] *After Thirty Years*, p. 176.
[2] op. cit., Vol. II, pp. 237–8.
[3] Gladstone had hardly seen the need to have one, and had assumed that that one would be Sir Charles Dilke, but he pressed Chamberlain in his stead. Dilke joined the cabinet in 1882 in lieu of Bright, who could not stomach the bombard-ment of Alexandria.

expropriation for the purpose of creating smallholdings. No wonder His Grace of Somerset was alarmed. 'The Democratic party,' he had said in his book, wanted to sub-divide estates, extinguish the large landowners and 'pull down "the pinnacles of Burghley and the oriels of Longleat" for the purpose of planting cabbage gardens'. 'Watch the party of revolution, a hundred strong in the new House,' cried Beaconsfield when his depleted legions gathered before him at Bridgwater House on 19th May, 1880. The first step towards any organic change in society would be a revolution in the tenure of land, for the revolutionists' first aim was 'the pulling down of the aristocracy'. At first, no doubt, the Government would resist the Ultras, and every assistance should be given to Whigs who stood on guard.

Many a landlord must now have recalled the impressive words of the great social reformer, Shaftesbury, during the debates on the 1867 Reform Bill — 'I know that a large proportion of the working classes have a deep and solemn conviction . . . that property is not distributed as property ought to be; that some checks ought to be kept upon the accumulation of property in single hands; that to take away by legislative enactments that which is in excess, with a view to bestow it on those who have insufficient means, is not a breach of any law, human or divine.' It was remembered how the merchants and manufacturers had mobilised urban opinion against the Corn Laws. Might they not respond to the recurrence of urban discontent by seeking to turn the masses against the landed interest, regarding it as expendable? Pell, the Tory agriculturist, was quick to reply to the Wolverhampton industrialist Henry Fowler, who argued that the ordinary rules of Political Economy did not apply to land because it was fixed in amount. Did this not apply equally to coal?[1] It was very important to the landed interest to establish a common front of property owners in defence of property of all kinds, and therefore very pleasant to hear Joseph Pease, much more industrialist than landlord, denouncing state intervention in property rights and contracts as mischievous and pernicious to the last degree.[2] Lack of reliance upon Whig ministers to defend the landed interest was due partly to the Whig habit of concession, partly to their alleged lack of land. To hear Somerset saying that Argyll was the only member of the cabinet who had lands and Beaconsfield predict

[1] H. of C., 29th July, 1880.   [2] H. of C., 30th July, 1880.

that he would 'kick only for his own acres'; to hear Somerset
dismissing the Devonshire estates (a quarter of a million acres in
England and Ireland) as 'mainly mineral and urban' (and Beaconsfield feared they knew the length of Hartington's foot); to be told
that Granville 'had not an acre' and Kimberley 'not much',[1] was
to be misled. Half the ministers, including Gladstone himself,
were landowners. Kimberley's 'not much' was 10,000 family acres
in Norfolk. Northbrook was a conscientious landlord on a similar
scale. Spencer had 50,000 acres (but he, said Beaconsfield, was
'weaker than water'). In 1881 Argyll was succeeded in cabinet by
Carlingford,[2] heir to an Irish estate and landlord in England
jure uxoris. In 1882 the Earl of Derby entered — the Tory Foreign
Secretary of 1874–8 who had thrown his weight to the Liberal
cause in Lancashire in the election and declined the cabinet at the
outset. The complaints of Beaconsfield and Somerset make sense
only in the light of the fear that because most of the ministers were
not wholly, or even mainly, dependent on farm rents and village
property they would sell the pass as in 1845. But this would have
been very short-sighted. No landowner could now feel safe merely
because he had extraneous interests. Why should the doctrine of
ransom stop at land? Were not mineral royalties and the 'unearned
increment' from urban sites — which made Westminister, Bedford,
Portman, Derby and Calthorpe so rich — especially vulnerable?
The minds of the property-owning class in general, and of Whig
ministers among them, turned to arguments in defence of property
in general.

It was no longer impressive to stand upon the doctrine so often
stated by Burke and Disraeli, that property was essentially
'representative', and the property-owner the natural as well as the
historic champion of the community against tyranny. But if Property was no longer the accepted guardian of Liberty, might not
Liberty be made the champion of Property? The landed interest
fled to the *locus standi* of *laisser-faire* as the bulwark of lands and
mines and stocks alike. It appealed to the dictum of the Whig
academic Dicey who, at the same time that he bequeathed to
generations of students of Constitutional Law the proposition

---

[1] Somerset's *Autobiography*, pp. 420, 520–1; *Monypenny and Buckle*, Vol. VI,
p. 581, Beaconsfield to Lady Bradford. Granville was a large lease-holder from
the Duchy of Lancaster in industrial Staffordshire.

[2] Chichester Fortescue had been raised to the peerage as Lord Carlingford on
his defeat by a Home Ruler in Co. Louth in 1874.

that the sovereignty of Parliament is a predominant characteristic of the British constitution, warned his contemporaries that with a democratic suffrage this parliamentary omnipotence exposed the Liberal society to the creeping paralysis of Socialism. For many a Liberal of means and position Liberalism was what it was to Dicey, a matter of individual freedom and competition, freedom of speech, conscience, contract and trade. 'If you once desert the solid ground of individual freedom,' he said, 'you can find no resting place till you reach the chasm of Socialism.'[1] Here was a cry which made the defence of privilege, of property 'right', sound reputable in the Victorian idiom. Dicey agreed with the Earl of Wemyss and March (as the Lord Elcho of the 1866 Reform crisis became in 1883) that measures of the Tory government, including the Merchant Shipping Act[2] and compulsory education, had set terrible precedents for Radicals to follow, and Lord Wemyss's *Socialism at St Stephens* 1869–85[3] was to continue the sorry catalogue in the doleful tones of the Duke of Somerset's book. Whether a proposal for state intervention came from Joseph Chamberlain or the Marquess of Salisbury and Queen Victoria;[4] whether it trenched on landlord right or the freedom of the industrialist to dictate conditions of work, or merely allotted public funds for purposes normally left to private enterprise, Wemyss was against it. So was Lowe (now a peer). So was Lord Cardwell. So was Goschen. (None of these were now in the cabinet.) So, in principle, was Gladstone, and we shall see him arguing the point against Chamberlain, in 1885. But at the moment Gladstone was paying out dividends to the Farmers' Alliance, which had invested in the Liberal victory and, it seemed, to the Irish Land League (which had not).

Those who remembered the Anti-Corn Law League's mobilisation of urban animosities against the landed interest remembered

[1] *Fortnightly Review*, CXXVI, 1st October, 1885.

[2] cf. *Economist*, 13th February, 1875. 'The Tories . . . wanted to abet Mr Plimsoll to injure our mercantile navy by schemes half injurious and half impracticable; they talked doctrines approaching to socialism about it being the the duty of Government to provide healthy dwellings for the poor. . . .'

[3] Originally a speech, H. of L., 31st July, 1885.

[4] The Queen was interested in the Royal Commission on the Housing of the Poor (*Queen's Letters*, S. II, Vol. III, pp. 451–3). When Salisbury moved for it, Wemyss alone demurred. On the commission, Goschen was horrified at Salisbury's easy acceptance of housing subsidies, and this 'State Socialism' was attached in debates on the Housing Bill (H. of L., 20th and 24th July, 1885, Wemyss; H. of C., 10th August, Lyulph Stanley's amendment and J. R. Hollond's speech).

also its abortive effort to split the farmers from the squires, one aspect of which had been Bright's assault on the Game Laws, which found a staunch defender in the Whig Protectionist, Grantley Berkeley. In 1880 the budget repealed the malt tax, as the landed interest had so long desired, and the Ground Game Bill proposed to give the tenant-farmer a share, with the landlord, in the disposal of the hares and rabbits which ravaged his land. The latter measure was so just that many Conservatives hesitated to attack it.[1] But their leader was in fundamentalist mood. The budget, Beaconsfield wrote, was 'another attempt to divert and separate the farmers from the gentlemen, and will be successful. I think the Game Bill, with this view, the most devilish of the A[rch] V[illain]'s schemes. In time the farmers will find that Rep[eal] of M[alt] will do them no good but they will stick to the hares and rabbits and they will be a chronic cause of warfare.'[2] In the debate on the Game Bill, James Howard, of the Farmers' Alliance, cited the Irish Land Act as a precedent,[3] an argument which was bound to provoke land-lords to root-and-branch resistance to further interferences. 'Four leading Whigs' — Henry Brand, the Speaker's son, Hon. Arthur Elliot, Stafford Howard and a Dundas — 'in concert with Lord Grey, Lord Halifax and others, as well as with Elcho, who of course considers that he has done the trick' put down an amendment against the second reading,[4] to the effect that it was 'not expedient to restrict or interfere with the freedom of contract between independent persons of full age, and under no legal disability, nor with the use and enjoyment of land as they agree'. Brand denounced the bill as a reversal of a long attempt to place the relation between owners and occupiers on the healthy, Cobdenite principle, a reactionary protectionist measure. Whig critics kept the debate going far into the night and resumed the next day, reiterating that the terms of contracts took into account circum-stances which it was now proposed to alter by law. Where would this stop?, asked Brand and Whitbread. Why not determine by law the rotation of crops? Why not fix rents? If one deprived a man with capital of £5–15,000 of the power to make bargains, why not

---

[1] *Iddesleigh Papers*, Northcote to Beaconsfield, 7th June, 1880 asking him to come up for a party meeting — 'our men will need talking to in order to avert a confusion'.

[2] Monypenny and Buckle, Vol. VI, 14th June, 1880, to Lady Bradford.

[3] H. of C., 29th July, 1880.

[4] *Iddesleigh Papers*, Northcote to Beaconsfield, 7th June, 1880.

protect the labourer in his wage contract?[1] Such were the *reductiones ad absurdum* of 1880!

Some of the supporters of the Bill said that 'free contract' was a red herring.[2] It had never existed, said Howard, the tenants' champion. Others were more concerned to try to reconcile what they felt should be done with 'sound principle'.[3] Lord Lymington said the bill would not harm free contract in its 'real and best sense'.[2] To Earl Fortescue, pillar of the Liberty and Property Defence League, such evasions were dangerous, and, as for the speeches of ministers, they were worse than the bill, which was a 'perfectly wanton little claptrap measure of petty confiscation'. Looking back two and a half years later, he portrayed it as only the first of a series of acts which showed what might be apprehended from ministers 'in the way of interference with local self-government, individual liberty and freedom of contract for adults', thus raising the old aristocratic cry against 'bureaucracy'. 'I object,' he declared, 'to needless grand and petty meddling on the part of the Government, which gradually replaces Mill's principle by a willing acquiescence in the intervention of the Executive.'[4]

For reasons of politics the Farmers' Alliance confined its demands to the modification of entail (to free the landlord), simplification of transfer, concurrent rights over game, repeal of the malt tax, and reform of local government and local taxation, thus blunting the collision of 'tenant right' with Cobdenite principle. But the appeal of Liberal candidates, endorsed by the Alliance, to farmers against landlords was a phenomenon disquieting to the Whig aristocracy, only less pernicious than the appeal of Jesse Collings, with his 'three acres and a cow', to the rural labourers who would soon be enfranchised. Would not 'tenant right' soon merge into 'ransom'? One of the Peases has recorded the part played by the activities of the Alliance in the defection of the northern Whigs. For a by-election in the North Riding a dreary and humourless farmer was adopted, in the hope that his class would support him against a Protectionist aristocrat. 'The Whigs did not like exchanging the yellow for the blue, but felt that they had come to the parting of the ways when their

[1] H. of C., 29th July, 1880 (Brand, Whitbread, Elliot) 30th (J. W. Pease M'Lagan, Elcho).
[2] H. of C., 29th July, Heneage.   [3] John Walter, 30th July.
[4] *Times*, 8th February, 1883.

party selected a farmer to seduce tenants from their loyalty to their landlords. The result was that whole families of Whigs, or their heads, which was then pretty much the same thing, went over to the enemy. This was the case with Lord Zetland, the Russells,[1] Sir Henry Beresford Peirse, the Hildyards, Cradocks, Stapyltons, Chalmers, Yeomans, the young squire of Skelton, W. H. A. Wharton and others. Some, like the old squire of Skelton, the Hon. John Dundas . . . and the Duke of Cleveland, did not change their colours but were shaken in their allegiance.'[2]

The local cause of this particular manifestation of 'the first great secession of the Whigs' was, of course, only symptomatic of a general trend against which Whiggery revolted. The Duke of Cleveland (old Lord Harry Vane) was a great landowner just across the border from the North Riding, in Co. Durham, where the Lambtons, like the Greys in Northumberland, were now dissident. So were the Fitzwilliams in the West Riding, their relative Sir John Ramsden, the Woods, and Mr Foljambe whose estates stretched down into Nottinghamshire. In January 1881 the Duke of Bedford, angry with the Government, threatened to withdraw his wife from the office of Mistress of the Robes. He had hated the Irish Land Bill of 1880, but agreed with Beaconsfield's verdict that the Whigs in the cabinet were 'indignant but pusillanimous';[3] there was no use standing up to Gladstone, he said. And so, Northcote commented, 'it seems likely to be for some time. They will swear in their beards, but they will eat any amount of leak'.[4] But at least the unofficial Whigs had begun spitting, for in the same letter in which he told Beaconsfield of Brand's revolt Northcote was able to record that Albert Grey (nephew and heir of the Earl) had given notice of opposition to the Irish Land Bill 'which gives the tenant ejected for non-payment of rent right of compensation for disturbance'.[5] Treated at first by Forster, the Chief Secretary, as a minor measure of limited currency (eighteen months) to deal with exceptional circumstances,[6] this bill of three clauses totalling thirty-five lines took thirteen sittings and a great

[1] Not, of course, the Russells of Bedford.
[2] Sir A. E. Pease, *Elections and Recollections*, 1932, pp. 59–61.
[3] Monypenny and Buckle, Vol. VI, p. 581, 4th July, 1880, to Lady Bradford.
[4] *Iddesleigh Papers*, 2nd July, 1880.
[5] ibid., 7th June — see also 19th July, 1880.
[6] The depression had hit Ireland sore, and Gladstone said that evictions at a time when so many of the population were on outdoor relief produced disorder verging on civil war.

Gladstonian oration to pass the Commons. At third reading, Charles Fitzwilliam seconded rejection, saying that outright subsidy would be better than ruining innocent and deserving subjects by a tax on their capital which infringed one of the most valuable principles of the law of contract, a main stay between man and man. Elcho said the bill repudiated the primary duties of government — the protection of life, the fulfilment of contracts, the security of property, which comprised the basis on which civilisation rested. Sir John Ramsden quoted what Gladstone said in 1870 — that 'every Irishman must be absolutely responsible for every contract into which he enters'. Eviction for non-payment of rent, said the ground landlord of Huddersfield, was not disturbance by the landlord but 'self-disturbance'. This was a pernicious bill, notoriously repugnant to many of Gladstone's steadfast supporters.[1]

In the division, Fitzwilliam was supported by his nephew Henry, by the heirs of Sutherland, Grey, Ducie and Portman, by brothers of Zetland and of Durham, by Ramsden and Rothschild and the veteran Glamorgan mineowner, Talbot of Margam, by a Guest and Kingscote, nearly twenty in all. In the Lords the Bill was rejected by 282 to 51 on the motion of Earl Grey, and would have been defeated even if no Tory had bothered to vote. Beaconsfield thought himself very astute to secure this result by leaving the initiative to the men from Brooks's.[2] But Grey needed no urging. In his ninetieth year (in 1892) he would still be writing pungent, lucid articles denouncing interference with contract and any idea of legislative protection of land, industry or labour as reminiscent of Luddism and Captain Swing and calculated to check 'that progress which . . . has by degrees raised civilised nations from barbarism, with its attendant privations and hardships, to whatever wealth and prosperity they now enjoy'. He would then attribute the vicissitudes of agriculture in considerable degree to mistrust of the security of landed property engendered by legislation from 1870 onwards, especially the Land Acts but also Disraeli's Agricultural Holdings Act and Gladstone's Ground Game Act.[3] He still believed that, as clearance was the greatest need of Ireland, any-

---

[1] H. of C., 26th July, 1880.
[2] *Queen's Letters*, S. II, Vol. III, p. 128.
[3] Earl Grey's principles were so pure that in this article of January 1892 (the reference escapes me) he vehemently denounces reciprocity treaties like the Cobden Treaty of 1860.

thing that impeded it by trying to shield the tenant from eviction was as stupid as the attempt of 'well-meaning but very unwise philanthropists' to preserve the handloom weaver from extinction had been. The Duke of Somerset of course opposed the bill and even Derby (who had sold out his Irish interests) said he would rather reject the bill than pass it as it stood. But the speeches listened to with the greatest attention were those of the Marquess of Lansdowne, because, after much hesitation, he had resigned from the Government,[1] and the Duke of Argyll, because he had not. Lansdowne complained that the Bill singled out a particular contract (relating to rent) and imposed on one party only (the landlord) losses due to act of God, while shielding the other from the natural consequences of breach of contract. Unjust to one class, it would foster mischievous hopes and opinions in the other, demoralise both and strike at public confidence and security in Ireland 'a blow the traces of which will not be effaced by volumes of remedial legislation and years of vigorous government'. Argyll, a minister defending a ministerial measure, said that it was a sudden one apparently introduced to meet partially a most unreasonable demand from a most unprincipled man (Parnell)[2] at a time when Ireland was the victim of one of the most unprincipled agitations which had ever vexed the melancholy ocean of Irish politics (a reference to the activities of the Land League).[3]

On the Compensation Bill sixty Whig peers revolted. Twenty of them were landlords in Ireland, where eleven of them had over 20,000 acres each, and Lansdowne, Fitzwilliam and Sligo were amongst the largest of all. Other great owners of Irish land, the Earls of Cork and Kenmare, who were in 'office, Bessborough (a founder of I Zingari), Devonshire, Leinster, Powerscourt, Lismore, supported the Government. But that in a House of 330 only forty unofficial peers should support the Liberal ministry entitles us to regard the vote as a rehearsal by the Whig peerage of its exit from the Liberal ranks, which so many now saw as a matter of time only. Whiggery agreed with Beaconsfield that the Bill was 'a reconnaissance against property' and, when Argyll told them it was not intended to set up any principles applicable to permanent

---

[1] *Queen's Letters*, op. cit., p. 116.
[2] The Bill had originated as a Parnellite one but was taken up by the Government, with amendments as a result of which the Parnellites abstained on the third reading so that the majority was only sixty-seven.
[3] H. of L., 2nd and 3rd August, 1880.

legislation, retorted that the Land Act of 1870 was now to be treated as 'the thin end of the wedge . . . [to] shatter the whole fabric of landlord-tenant relations by successive blows'.[1] Argyll could not, in his heart, dissent from their view. Though he said that only four of the cabinet had approved the late Bill, he saw his colleagues 'drifting' to the opinion that a new, and worse one, was needed, for which he would reserve his 'stronger action'.[2] Well might Houghton conclude that the Government would have to decide in the vacation 'whether they can govern without the Whigs or not',[3] when the heads of the families of Leveson-Gower, Fitzroy, Seymour, Lambton, Elliot, Howard, Dundas, Fortescue, Fox and Grey were in open revolt and were soon to be joined by the head of the Russells and the chief of the Campbells.

That there should be an Irish problem was something of a shock to Gladstone, for 'the Grand Old Man' had dismissed as an electioneering stunt Beaconsfield's contention that Ireland would monopolise the attention of the new Parliament. Now he found the Irish members under Parnell developing systematic obstruction, which soon compelled ministers to consider rules restricting debate, while an alliance between Home Rule politicians and the Land League mustered, out of the very genuine grievances of the Irish peasants, a formidable agitation spattered with agrarian outrage. A level-headed and liberal-minded civil servant began 'most unwillingly, to think that Ireland is not fitted for Constitutional Government . . . and that she will not be got in hand again without a return to something like a Cromwellian policy'.[4] In the winter of 1880 Hartington and Spencer, and perhaps others as well, were prepared to resign if the Chief Secretary (who was to earn in Ireland the nickname 'Buckshot Forster') were not given the special powers he asked, and Bright and Chamberlain if he were. Gladstone leaned to the Radicals, and it seems that only Forster's indecision saved the ministry. The Queen sent Hartington on 12th December an even more than usually underscored letter — 'You moderate Ministers must be firm. . . . Dont yield to SATISFY Messrs Bright and Chamberlain: let them go.' By this time, however, Gladstone was convinced of the necessity of Coercion, which would have to have priority in the new session,

[1] Ramsden's speech.   [2] *Queen's Letters*, S. II, Vol. III, p. 134.
[3] Reid, Vol. II, p. 393, 1st August 1880, to Bss Bunsen.
[4] *Blunt*, Edward Hamilton to Blunt, 22nd December, 1880.

but, of course, remedial measures must be announced, and principally a Land Bill. This, as originally drawn, seemed to Argyll 'within the main lines of the Act or at any rate the Bill of 1870', and Gladstone himself said 'the three F's (free sale, fixity of tenure and fair rents) as advocated by Lords Monck and Powerscourt meant 'considerable changes, likely to lead to expropriation' and that this 'would not do'.[1] But Forster said the Ulster Liberals were all going for the three F's; Chamberlain said that 'justice for Ireland' had never been fairly tried; Carlingford, and, it transpired, a majority of the Bessborough Commission, reported for rent-fixing. Gladstone, saying that massive discontent demanded heroic remedies, convinced himself that the peers had caused all the trouble by defeating the Compensation Bill. This Argyll repudiated.[2] He, Hartington and Spencer fought a stiff battle in the cabinet — 'weary work', he called it, because of 'such ignorance of all that landed ownership ought to be and is'.[3] (So the doleful predictions of Beaconsfield and Somerset had been right after all!)

Argyll's aim was to keep Gladstone from the substance as well as the form of the three F's, on which his view was that to concede one was to concede all.[4] He rejected the universal right of free sale, because it meant joint-ownership, 'a great statutory transfer of property from one class to another'. He could not accept that there should be no line above which contract was to be entirely free or the abandonment of the principle that time exhausted all improvements other than permanent buildings.[5] At the last he concluded that the Bill had become the three F's 'under a temporary and thin disguise'[6] and on 31st March, 1881 he resigned, protesting against the confounding of occupancy with ownership, so that the latter was put into 'commission or even . . . abeyance'.[7] He joined the Cassandras of the Cross-Benches, whence in 1886 he stretched out welcoming hands to the stream of Whig peers who then repudiated Gladstone.

In the debate on the Compensation Bill, Argyll had warned the peers to beware the doctrine of 'implied concession'. It was not right to hold that because one admitted something in limited and

---

[1] *Queen's Letters*, S. II, Vol. III, p. 164, 15th December, 1880.
[2] *Argyll*, Vol. II, p. 354, 3rd November, 1880.
[3] ibid., p. 369, to Dufferin, 23rd February, 1881.
[4] ibid., p. 361 (15th Dec.), 366 (28th Jan.).
[5] ibid., pp. 364–6, 28th January.
[6] ibid., p. 365, 7th April, to Dufferin.　　　[7] H. of L., 8th April, 1881.

exceptional cases, under strict conditions (like the consideration of rents by land courts under the 1870 Act) one was bound to support its generalisation. The Irish Land Bill of 1881 was, however, framed as an amendment to the 1870 Act, in order to catch fish with the argument that one must, or at least consistently could, support the amending bill if one had supported the Act. The bill became unnecessarily complicated as a result of this approach, and its conduct was a Gargantuan task in which the aged Premier exhausted himself. The Whigs needed Argyll's passionate prejudice and lucid intellect to reiterate that the limitations and conditions in the 1870 Act were part of the principle of the Act; it was perfectly proper to oppose the bill having voted for the Act. To say otherwise was to impose on the champions of landlord right the obligation to oppose every innovation on the ground that it contained the germs of some later concession. Some, of course, Grey, Somerset, Elcho, were prepared to do so. But, as Argyll said, legislation is not an exact science, and all institutions are full of 'germs'. What one had to decide was where to cry halt. Argyll stood by the Act of 1870. It was working well, working as people like himself had wanted it to work (had they not comforted themselves in 1870 that no impediment had been put on rack-renting)? That its working revealed 'injustices', practices with which it had not professed to deal, was no justification for assuming that those who supported the Act would, or should, support the Bill.

Between twenty and thirty Whigs, about half the number of M.P.s with which Herbert Gladstone was prepared to credit them, participated in demonstrations against parts of the Bill in the Commons. On 16th June, for instance, Heneage moved to exempt 'English-managed' estates in Ireland from the Tenant Right clauses. He was supported in debate by Charles Fitzwilliam, Dundas, and Cartwright. Sir Henry Lucy sets the scene:[1]

> ... The Whigs, those uncertain compounds of slow-moving impulse, entrées in the feast of politics which are neither fish, flesh, fowl nor good red-herring — had stirred, and the atmosphere was tremulous with excitement and doubt ... the Conservatives with a welcome shout marched forward to join their forces. It was known that twenty or thirty Whigs would go the length of voting against Ministers, and there were angry whispers going about of men who had paired for the dinner hour and were running it on to midnight. ... It was clear

[1] *Diary of Two Parliaments*, pp. 175-7.

that the Ministry would be run very close; and when Lord Richard Grosvenor, in tones that lacked their usual triumph, announced that 220 had voted for Mr Heneage's amendment and 225 against no wonder that a thunderous cheer rose from the Opposition benches. . . .

The bill spent thirty-three days in committee. But the Whigs and the Tories alike knew that, though the Duke of Somerset might call it 'one of the most discreditable measures that I remember in all my public life . . . Irish ideas have demoralised British statesmen',[1] it must be passed. Even Argyll admitted that it was necessary to appease Ireland, and that the Bill might do good to landowners (who otherwise might lose all), though he was not prepared as a minister to use 'the argument of the blunderbuss'.[2] And so, though asking one another where the process must end, if the Irish thought they could get concessions every time they agitated, and the greater concessions the greater the agitation, and every new Liberal government was thought to mean a new Land Act, the peers abstained from brave displays like those of 1880. Too many of them agreed with Spencer that, though on general principles Argyll was right, no policy had a chance of restoring law and order which did not deal with the land question or doing so, fell short of the bill.[3] But Whiggery felt, with Dufferin, the deepest gloom[4]— 'to speak plainly, the tendency of the extreme section of the Liberal party is to buy the support of the masses by distributing among them the property of their own political opponents, and it is towards a social rather than a political revolution that we are tending at least, if what is taking place in Ireland is any indication of the future, and a precedent established there is almost sure to be applied elsewhere'. Tory Front Benchers began to talk of Land Purchase, of buying out the Irish landlords.

Hartington had eaten the leeks which Lansdowne, Bedford and Argyll spat out. A man not given to mock heroics, he must have been much disturbed to say in December 1880 that in London he could not look men in the face and would rather be at his Lismore estate taking his chance of being shot.[5] It was his lot to work in a party of Liberals who could hardly bring themselves to maintain

[1] *Autobiography*, pp. 520 (6th Aug.), 521 (20th Aug.) *Nineteenth Century* September 1883.
[2] *Argyll*, pp. 369–71, 7th April, 1881. Cf. Somerset, op. cit., p. 520 'it could not have been rejected without causing violent convulsion and the re-enactment of a similar law'.
[3] ibid., p. 379, 10th April, 1881.   [4] ibid., p. 380, 19th April, 1881.
[5] *Devonshire*, Vol. 1, p. 334, 14th December, 1880, to Granville.

GEORGE DOUGLAS, 8th DUKE OF ARGYLL
by W. Wontnes (1898)

law and order if it involved the suspension of the liberties of the subject and always insisted on accompanying coercion with remedial measures to purge the impiety. They might, indeed, feel, as they did when the League tried to render the Land Act unworkable, a righteous indignation against agitators who for political purposes tried to stultify their good words. But not for long. Many Whigs, however, were not ashamed to uphold the rule of law against agitators and criminals, as they had in the past against princes. What was improper in landlords exercising the rights the Act of 1870 had left them? Hartington had opposed the decision not to renew the Conservative Coercion Act, was prepared to resign with Forster, approved only the decision (not efficiently acted on) to prosecute the Land League.[1] He had 'strongly objected' to the Compensation Bill, and when he knew of the report of the Bessborough Commission, he demanded that if it was accepted landlords should be compensated out of the public till for loss of market value.[2] Appeased by the priority given in 1881 to Coercion (Chamberlain was very annoyed), Hartington did not go with Argyll, but he declined, though a minister, to give 'active support' to the Land Bill.[3] He did not believe that when agitation had been shown to pay, the Land League would allow the landlord to collect the 'fair' rent. In fact, the League tried to prevent mass recourse to the courts to have the rents fixed. Then even Gladstone was provoked to the detention of the nationalist leaders, whereupon the Act began to work. Chamberlain asked rhetorically whether any government in the world would 'allow, in the name of liberty, the creation of a tyranny which interferes between every man and the exercise of his personal rights and legal obligations'.[4] But, even so, violence again paid dividends, for it was arranged with Parnell in Kilmainham Gaol that he should discountenance violence in return for an Arrears Act to plug the major gap in the Land Act. Lord Frederick Cavendish, Hartington's brother and Mrs Gladstone's nephew by marriage, was sent to Ireland to work the new dispensation, and assassinated in Phoenix Park. Revulsion at this crime was almost universal, and it moved the Government (though it persevered

[1] ibid., p. 335, 19th December, 1880, to Gladstone.
[2] ibid., p. 333, 9th December, 1880, to Gladstone.
[3] ibid., p. 340, 6th April, 1881, to Gladstone.
[4] C. H. D. Howard's *Chamberlain — a Political Memoir*, pp. 18–20, 18th October, 1881.

with the Arrears Bill) to institute for three years a Draconian régime presided over by Lord Spencer. Not until the end of 1884 did the question of the renewal of Coercion cast its shadow over the cabinet and produce its disintegration.

In the interval, ministers had to face the assimilation of the borough and county franchises, and with it, the redistribution of seats. Hartington had adopted this, *ex officio*, as Liberal policy in 1877, and because of it Goschen had declined to enter the cabinet. But it was not a thing to attempt at the beginning of a Parliament. It waited till 1883, and then Hartington was horrified to find that Gladstone, notwithstanding the experience of 1866, proposed to deal with the franchise separately from the redistribution. The reason for his horror was that Gladstone, visibly ailing since 1881, might resign before redistribution, and Gladstone was discovered to be rather old-fashioned on that subject, the only man who could thwart the demand of Chamberlain for 'one man, one vote' and equal electoral districts. Hartington found, to his pleasure, that Gladstone wanted to preserve the forty shilling freeholder vote and the representation of small boroughs (the havens of Whig and moderate Liberal members).[1] And though the Marquess hated the idea of household suffrage in Ireland, he felt he could not regard this objection as fatal to his continuance in the Government once Gladstone had agreed to attempt redistribution in 1885 and to hold himself bound to the general plan of distribution which he had outlined.[2] Gladstone threatened that if Hartington resigned, he, Gladstone, would resign too. Everybody saddled on Hartington the responsibility for the fate of the Government.[3] It was not the threat that he himself would be called upon to be prime minister, that deterred Hartington, but the opinion that only Gladstone could prevent Radical measures, that only Gladstone could keep franchise extension and redistribution within bounds and that it would be very dangerous to let Gladstone loose with a grievance against the Whigs as responsible for breaking up the party.[4] There was, of course, no guarantee that the ministry would still be in office in 1885, when redistribution became due, but at least, if it were not, Gladstone would be bound by his pledges.

---

[1] *Devonshire*, Vol. 1, pp. 402–4, 14th January, 1884, to his father.
[2] ibid., and also pp. 395–6 (to Gladstone, 24th Oct. 1883) and pp. 400–2. Gladstone agreed to leave the question of 'minority representation', which might be applied to Ireland, 'open'.
[3] ibid., p. 398 (Granville), p. 399 (Gladstone).   [4] ibid., pp. 402–4.

Hartington thus forced Gladstone to follow the logic of the latter's assumption that the fate of the Government and of the party depended on the Whig leader. The policy which had been decided upon without his assent (as he complained in a most unseasonable letter of Christmas Day, 1883) was sufficiently modified to preserve Whig interest in the battle of the distribution of seats. Or so it seemed. But, through a series of events which Hartington did much to bring about, the Whigs were once again 'dished'. The Tories, even if they knew of Gladstone's pledges to Hartington, could not rely on them. The whole future of their party depended on the sort of map the boundary commissioners would draw. They could not risk a dissolution under a new franchise but with the existing distribution of seats. Perhaps, also, they hoped to postpone the whole question till after a general election which, considering the low water into which the Government had drifted, they might win. The Conservatives therefore held up the Franchise Bill in the Lords, insisting, like the Adullamites in 1866, upon franchise and distribution being treated *pari passu*. And so in the summer and autumn of 1884 Chamberlain and his friends had the time of their lives assailing the Peers in the name of the People, little discouraged by Gladstone, who was determined not to yield to the Lords what he had denied to Hartington. But the Marquess said, in public as well as in private, that the demands of the Conservatives were reasonable and deplored the attacks on the aristocracy and the upper House. He went further, and at Rawtenstall sketched a possible compromise. With the ill-tempered acquiescence of their respective leaders, who were under pressure from moderates on both sides and from the Queen, Hartington and Sir Michael Hicks-Beach held cautious conversations. Eventually the leaders of the opposed parties met to discuss the principles of redistribution, the enactment of which, it was agreed, should follow closely that of the franchise extension. Gladstone gained his procedural point, but the Tories won the assurances they required. Hartington gained nothing except the satisfaction of having brought the parties together and thereby forced Chamberlain to call off his peer-baiting. No one relished the results of the tea-party at No. 10, at which was determined the electoral formation of Great Britain for thirty-three decisive years, less than Hartington, who was there with Gladstone and Dilke (the minister who was to have charge of the Bill), while

Sir Stafford Northcote accompanied the Marquess of Salisbury (22nd November, 1884). If the franchise proposals were Gladstonian (plural voting was to stay, and the regulations would prevent even all householders from having the vote) the redistribution was much nearer what Chamberlain desired than Gladstone and Hartington liked.

Hartington had contrived that there should be no election between Franchise and Redistribution, and had done more than any other man to extricate Salisbury and Gladstone from rapidly freezing postures of antagonism which endangered the House of Lords. But the Tories came to the conference with very clear ideas of their party interests, and they were by no means compatible with those of moderate Liberals. Gladstone had a tenderness for small boroughs. So had the Whigs, and for two-member boroughs as well, the homes of compromise that put a Whig in with a Tory or a Radical. The Government therefore proposed to extinguish fifty-six parliamentary boroughs with less than 10,000 inhabitants, throwing them into county divisions, and to reduce to one-member constituencies parliamentary boroughs of 10–40,000. Hicks-Beach had proposed minima of 25,000 and 80,000 and a régime of single-member constituencies in town and country based on the principle of economic and social segregation. He even proposed that this should be carried to the point of grouping small boroughs (the Liberal centres in many counties) so as to segregate them from rural districts which it was hoped would be strongholds of Conservatism. He reckoned that, in the long run, the Tories stood a good chance in straight fights with Liberals in country districts, suburbs and business centres (and in some working class areas as well).[1] As in 1867 the calculating radicalism of the Tory appalled the Whig. Gladstone was quoted as saying that it was difficult to tell who was the magistrate and who was the thief.[2] 'Black Michael's' approach was more thoroughgoing than that of most of his colleagues, but in principle they agreed, and found that their views were not far from Chamberlain's. In the event there was compromise. There was to be no grouping in England. But minima of 15,000 and 50,000 were adopted and double-barrelled constituencies were in future to be exceptional. The old distinction

---

[1] See *Life* (by his daughter 1932), pp. 217–20.

[2] H. of C., 4th December, 1884, Goschen's speech, rubbing in the Tory triumph, though, he said, it was a matter of preferring Conservative votes to Conservative principles.

between county and borough constituencies would virtually disappear, as both the counties and big cities were to be divided into several single-member constituencies. And the commissioners were instructed, not only to respect the boundaries of petty sessional areas where possible and never divide a parish,[1] but to 'have special regard to the pursuits of the population' in the division of boroughs.[2] Neither a reduction in the number of Irish members, nor minority representation for Ireland, which both Hartington and Hicks-Beach wanted, were included in the scheme. The plan was put before the House as an agreed measure, somewhat to the indignation of members, who felt that the House was being treated as a rubber stamp. It passed with only minor alterations. Attempts to secure proportional representation (by Albert Grey) or the single transferable vote (by the right-wing Liberal intellectual Sir John Lubbock)[3] were decisively defeated despite a moving appeal from Leonard Courtney (a Radical who shared Mill's fears of mass uniformity and tyranny) to preserve some means of entry for political economists.[4]

The Reform and redistribution offered Whiggery no prospects. The precious remnant of biddable boroughs — some with electorates of under a thousand — Calne, Malton, Marlborough, Newport, Richmond, Ripon, Tavistock, Wycombe remained on the constituency lists, if at all, only as places giving their names to county divisions. Chester, Peterborough, Lincoln, Scarbrough, Taunton lost a member. As the era of effective electoral corruption ended under the combined effect of the ballot, the Corrupt Practices Act of 1883 and, most important of all, the increase in the electorate; as the nomination borough or county passed from the scene (except in the sense that a patron might retain great influence on the choice of candidate), the Tories rejoiced in great gains in London and Lancashire, and rapidly recovered control of the counties. The Liberals, but not the Whigs, found compensation in the north-east. The substitution at Morpeth, once the secure preserve of the lord of Castle Howard, of the miner, Thomas Burt, for Sir George Grey in 1874 had been symbolic, though working men were always a tiny minority of the Liberal members.

---

[1] H. of C., 2nd December, 1884, Dilke answering Borlase.
[2] H. of C., 4th December, 1884, Dilke, asked by Fowler whether the division was to be class, sectional or social, answered evasively.
[3] H. of C., 2nd and 3rd March, 1885.
[4] H. of C., 4th December, 1884, 3rd March, 1885.

For a moment a revolt of the rural poor against Tory squires and farmers might benefit a Whig candidate. But the encouragement or exploitation of revolt against landlordism or farmers' tyranny was not a congenial avenue to Parliament for a Whig nobleman, and if the revolt persisted it might well extend to the choice of candidates. At the dissolution in 1885 there were in the House of Commons forty aristocrats, forming rather less than one eighth of the British Liberal members. In the next Parliament there were twenty-three, one fourteenth. Sixteen of them had sat in the previous Parliament. Only three, one of them Charles Villiers (who was an institution) were returned for borough seats. The changed times were aptly illustrated by the failure of Henry Fitzwilliam, a county member, to secure nomination as the successor of his uncle Charles at Malton: he received only 11 votes on a Liberal selection committee 74 strong.[1] John Fitzwilliam was elected at Peterborough in a straight fight against a Liberal, the Tories supporting him. John Dundas and Frederick Lambton did not stand. The swing of the pendulum in the boroughs was fatal to Northbrook's heir at Winchester. Former Whig members for Hertfordshire and Buckinghamshire, Hon. Henry Cowper and Hon. Rupert Carrington, failed to win the Hertford and Wycombe divisions. In the Isle of Wight, with a tripled electorate, Hon. Evelyn Ashley was beaten. In the Scottish Highlands the Franchise Act emancipated the crofters, and the sons of the Whig dukes were no longer returned for Sutherland and Argyll.

The general election of 1885 took place with a Conservative government in power, for the Gladstone administration fell asunder and sustained defeat in the House of Commons before the new registers were ready. The meeting of the new Parliament at the beginning of 1886 was to see the definitive divorce between the mass of Whiggery and the official Liberal party, and bring us to the end of our story.

[1] Pease's *Elections and Recollections*, p. 75, June 1884. Fitzwilliam was already virtually a Conservative. The borough disappeared under the Redistribution Act.

CHAPTER XV

The Parting of the Ways, 1886

While to conservative Liberals the legislation of 1880–2 was disturbing, to Radicals the general record of the second Gladstone administration was intensely unsatisfactory. Some of them made their main grievance the occupation of Egypt, with the resultant involvement in the Sudan, where it became necessary to send someone to secure the withdrawal of the Egyptian garrisons threatened by the Mahdi. Gordon was sent. It then became necessary to send Wolseley to rescue Gordon. 114 voted with John Morley to express regret at this decision. It seemed to the passivists only appropriate that one of the last acts of a government which had come into office in the wake of Gladstone's assaults upon Disraeli's expensive warmongering in Africa and Afghanistan should be to ask a large vote of credit in view of the probability of war with Russia over the approaches to India, appropriate because Gladstone in office had not lived up to the professions of Gladstone in opposition. There had been, between the occupation of Egypt and the expedition to the Sudan, a new intervention in southern Africa. This Bechuanaland expedition had been approved by Chamberlain. He never took the Bright view of the impiety of Imperialism and favoured the continuation of the occupation of Egypt, refusing to see in Arabi Pasha and his friends a genuine nationalist movement. And so we find Bright writing to Chamberlain to complain that he was using 'the stock-arguments of the Jingo School' by which, ever since William III, all the crimes which had built up the Debt and wasted the blood and wealth of the people had been defended, and that the best that could be said for the Egyptian adventure was that it differed from the worst doings of Palmerston and the more recent scandals of Beaconsfield in being a deplorable blunder rather than a crime.[1]

---

[1] 4th January, 1883, cited in Chamberlain — *A Political Memoir*, C. H. D. Howard, pp. 79–80.

The difference between Bright and Chamberlain was not wholly one of generations; Imperialism exposed the Liberal party to the sort of schisms induced by Palmerstonianism and the Crimean War and divided Radicals as well as others. But it was of the *failures* of the Gladstone government that Salisbury was thinking when he said that it awoke the slumbering genius of Imperialism. To many Liberals, and especially to Whigs, it was not the various decisions to intervene but weakness, indecision and procrastination which constituted the Government's crimes.[1] Ministers continued the war with the Boers, only to yield after a skirmish at Majuba. They allowed Bismarck to acquire portions of Africa, one of which Britain had pre-empted and another of which the cabinet had decided to pre-empt. Worst of all, before the relief force reached Khartoum, Gordon and his garrison had been massacred. Gladstone had long burked the need for relief, requiring to be satisfied that Gordon was not only 'surrounded' but 'hemmed in'. A flood of contumely rolled over the Government. On 28th February, 1885, a vote of no-confidence, promoted by Forster and Goschen, was beaten off by a majority of only fourteen. The Tories were able to add to the cry 'Remember Majuba' the infinitely more damaging cry 'Remember Gordon'. Dicey praised their narrow sense of honour and greatness because it would render them immune from 'the influences degrading the statesmanship of the Liberals'.[2]

While the Government's record in foreign and colonial matters satisfied no one, its record of legislative sterility after the Irish legislation of 1881–2 (*pace* the Corrupt Practices, Franchise and Redistribution Acts) was harmful to its prestige. This sterility was in part a triumph for Parnell, who had determined that if the House of Commons would not give the Irish members what they wanted, it should at least be compelled to spend so much time discussing their demands, listening to their attacks on Coercion, and suspending them from the service of the House, that it would have little left for British business. But it was also a reflection of the disunity of the Liberal party. Labouchere, in the old Radical tradition, roundly blamed Whiggery for the barrenness and perversity of the record, though also condemning the Radical members for being 'such a miserable lot' as to allow the thirty

[1] e.g. comments of A. E. Pease, *Elections and Recollections*, pp. 70, 77, 79.
[2] *Fortnightly Review*, N.S., CCXXVI, 1st October, 1885, 'Three Platforms' — No. 2. 'Plea of a Malcontent Liberal'.

or so Whigs on the back-benches to get their way by acting solidly together and influencing ministers by the back stairs.[1] In a retrospect of this Parliament, Reginald Brett, Hartington's private secretary, but a Radical, bitterly attacked 'the custom which induces a Liberal prime minister to go into the byways of the House of Lords in search of mediocrities to whom the destinies of England are to be entrusted'. This was both comical and dangerous. The old failures who had no conception of the true aims of the Liberal party must not be condoned. 'The brightest omen for a new Parliament would be to find itself presided over by a Liberal Government as little as possible resembling the last. In a new Parliament weeded of indifferent loungers, in a Liberal Government shorn of its supine and lethargic members, and in a policy grappling with the supreme social and political evil of the moment, there is hope for the future.'[2] Herbert Gladstone, invoking sympathy for his father as 'the persevering, perplexed and sometimes exasperated referee in the cabinet', complains that the Whig ministers, 'disconsolate and irritable, increased perplexity by a total want of initiative'.[3]

All these critics rate the *vis inertiae* of Whiggery high. But if, as Herbert Gladstone claimed, the bulk of the Liberal centre was 'progressive and certainly not Whig', the activity of the Government reflected equally the ineffectiveness of the Radicals (deplored by Labouchere) and the failure of the Radical ministers to force decisions to the point of schism (for which Maccoby criticises them).[4] The truth was that Gladstone, aged and ailing, had lost his effectiveness, and while he conceived it his prime duty to keep the party together, neither Hartington nor Chamberlain was prepared to take the risk of causing a split with Gladstone on the other side. The party was suffering because the desire to preserve it took precedence, even with the leading Radicals, over the desire to employ it for any particular purpose, such as the grant of local representative institutions to Ireland. Chamberlain had decided to delay the battle for control of the party until a general election could be fought with the labourers enfranchised and the constituencies recast. That is the sense in which it is true, as Reginald

---

[1] *Labouchere*, p. 206, to Chamberlain, 3rd July, 1883. Cf. speech at North Camberwell, 14th October, 1885.
[2] *Fortnightly Review*, op. cit., 'Three Platforms' — No. 1. 'New Policy and Old Failures'.
[3] *After Thirty Years*, pp. 167 ff.   [4] *Radicalism 1853–1886*, p. 275.

Brett argued, that the party was held together simply by the commitment to Reform. Once that was settled, the cabinet broke up
and the Government resigned. The occasion of its resignation was
defeat on the budget by 264 : 252[1] (at which, it is said, the whiggish
Whip, Lord Richard Grosvenor, connived) — an inglorious end to
the great majority elected in 1880. But the cabinet was in dissolution, as, indeed, it had seemed to be for months, on one issue or
another.[2] The matter currently in dispute was the Irish Question.
Ministers were quite unable to decide how much of Coercion,
Land Purchase and representative self-government should be
proffered. At the time of the budget debate it looked as though the
Whigs were winning the argument, and the Radical ministers
(with whom on this Gladstone sympathised) had submitted their
resignations.

It was on Ireland that the cabinet broke up, and it was to be on
Ireland that the party broke up. Our after-knowledge of this must
not lead us to ignore the fact that the electors had no reason to
think this would be so. In the campaign for the allegiance of four
million voters the Irish Question was muffled by a competition in
platitude and equivocation between Salisbury and Gladstone. And
the contest was so much a trial of strength between Hartington
and Chamberlain that it is sometimes an effort to remember that
the Tories were in the fray. Chamberlain's bitter sallies against the
Lords in 1884 — 'the cup is nearly full. We have been too long a
peer-ridden country'[3]— fitted neatly into a campaign which he had
already begun when, embracing the taxation of unearned increment, he reviled Salisbury as the spokesman of a class that neither
toiled nor spun, but enjoyed fortunes which originated long ago in
grants made for the sort of services courtiers render kings and
increased while the owners slept.[4] What held for a Cecil held for a
Cavendish, as Northcote perhaps hoped to underline when he
protested against Chamberlain's use of 'the language of Jack Cade'.
(The first Cavendish to cross the pages of English history was a
judge lynched by the revolting peasants at Cambridge in 1381.) To
Gladstone's suggestion that cabinet ministers had not been used to
enter so freely into questions not 'proximate', and that if other

---

[1] The Parnellites voted against whisky tax, but only four Liberals rebelled.
More than seventy did not vote.
[2] e.g. on Egyptian finance and ironclads, on which in January Hartington,
Northbrook and Childers wished to resign.
[3] Denbigh, 22nd October, 1884.   [4] Birmingham, 30th March, 1883.

ministers did likewise the Government would be weakened, Chamberlain made unrepentant reply. The customs of the past were not applicable to the new conditions of popular government; the platform was now one of the most powerful and indispensable instruments of government; the vast masses of new electors who would in future form the great majority of Liberal voters must be assured that their interests were a constant subject of concern and those 'who may be considered specially to represent the majority who are to be appealed to' could not fulfil their duty if 'confined within the narrow limits of a purely official programme'.[1]

The only curb on his vigorous tongue which Chamberlain would acknowledge was that he should not flatly contradict the leader of the party and Government in which he served. This gave him *carte blanche*, for Gladstone made no pronouncement on future domestic policy until his obscure address to the electors of Midlothian after the dissolution, by which time the *Unauthorized Programme* had been for two years unfolding in the *Fortnightly Review* and a long series of pungent speeches by Chamberlain in the country had invested it with a revolutionary air. What Chamberlain demanded, at Ipswich, for instance, 14th January, 1885, was popular county government, land for labourers, protection of the interests of the poor in commons and endowments, free education and the revision of taxation. While one Whig landlord, Foljambe, protested bitterly (earning from Chamberlain a denunciation of 'the prejudice and intolerance of a limited section of the Liberal party who claim, as the price of their support, not only to moderate and restrain the action of the majority but even to silence its voice')[2] a more radical one, Lord Carrington, rejoiced that at last the party had a programme to work on. In itself unattractive to Whiggery, the programme became anathema by reason of the bellicose language of social revolution in which it was propounded. Legislative provision of allotments or even smallholdings for labourers, for instance, which became a matter of violent controversy, might be, as Gladstone assured Hartington after communication with Chamberlain on the eve of the election, simple in form and mild in application, without wide results. It was by no means certain that Hartington and Chamberlain could not

---

[1] Correspondence of 31st January–7th February, 1885, cited by Howard, pp. 111-19
[2] Chamberlain to Gladstone, 3rd February, 1885 ibid.

agree on a measure. When, after the election, the matter was discussed in Parliament, the Marquess refused to put his objection to Jesse Collings' 'three acres and a cow' motion on the high doctrinal ground adopted by Goschen, who was now being attacked by Radicals as a Tory agent in comparison with whom 'the most solid and immobile Whig is almost a pioneer of progress'.[1] Like Gladstone, Hartington would have preferred to 'try freedom first' (and landlords were taking the hint).[2] But, admitting the object to be desirable, he denied that he had ever opposed legislation or definitively excluded the intervention of public authorities. When compulsory acquisition of land had been so often sanctioned by legislation, he could not join in a cry of 'confiscation'. What he objected to was that the question had been given far greater importance than belonged to it. Too great hopes, false hopes, had been held out, as though any appreciable or permanent improvement in the lot of the poor could come other than by their own efforts and the general increase of prosperity.[3]

Hartington's resistance to the most controversial element in the Radical programme is thus not to be judged in the light of Dilke's soothing assurance that legislation might amount to no more than a grant to local authorities of power which they perhaps possessed already, but in the light of Chamberlain's insistence (even when he was prepared to relegate free education to the realm of inquiry) that the legislation was a *sine qua non* of his joining a government. For the 'land for the labourers' was not mere electoral bait, though it was that. It was both the symbol of what Chamberlain called 'the Revolution of 1885' and the most specific element in a policy admitted by its authors to be socialistic (though they denied that it was communistic).[4] This policy was advocated on the hypothesis that property was theft — 'the birthright of the English people has been bartered away for a mess of pottage and has become the possession of private owners of property'.[5] According to this doctrine, 'ransom' was owed to the community for the

[1] *Fortnightly*, 25th September ,1885 'Home and Foreign Affairs'.
[2] While Carrington and Lord Compton were vice-presidents with Chamberlain and Dilke of the Allotments and Smallholdings Association, many owners, including Lord Tollemache (who, with the Duke of Bedford, was a respected pioneer in this field) joined the Duke of Westminster's 'Landowners' Association for the Voluntary Extension of Allotments'.
[3] H. of C., 26th January, 1886.
[4] *Fortnightly*, 1st July, 1885, Part VII of the Radical Programme.
[5] Chamberlain at Warrington, 8th September, 1885.

security of property, which the state was in any case entitled to redistribute for the common weal. When it was necessary to grapple with the mass of misery and destitution in their midst, said Chamberlain, objections based on the eternal laws of supply and demand, free contract and the sanctity of property rights were merely 'the selfish cant of power and wealth'. His friends said that the rules of Political Economy would not 'restore' to the people their 'rights' in the soil, and so there must be compulsory purchase and state credit'.[1]

The allotments policy was an attack in strength at a vulnerable point in the defences of property, by a general staff which did not conceal that a gain here would be exploited on a wider front. Chamberlain at Ipswich talked of differential and graduated taxation (at which even Hartington cried 'Socialism'),[2] steeper death duties and imposts on ground rents. Fiscal Reform was to be in part the infliction of retributive justice on landlords, in part compensatory endowment of their 'victims'. But it was also to be a means of reversing the old-fashioned policy of retrenchment. The governing class was now subjected to a renewal of the sort of attack in which Cobden and Bright had specialised, but with the object of reversing Cobdenite principles of public expenditure. Taxation, it was said, was unpopular, and against the public interest, only if, as at present, it fell unfairly on the industrious classes and was used by a small upper caste with an interest in the spending departments, war, patronage and place. Taxation was legitimate wherever the state could spend money for public advantage better than individuals, and should be regarded as in the nature of insurance or investment by the community for the common weal.[1] But indirect taxation was 'a scheme of trickery and humbug more worthy of savages than of a civilised state'.[3] Taxation should fall primarily on the property owner.

The shadow of Lloyd George's budget of 1909 was thus already visible on the horizon. The doleful prophecies of Robert Lowe; the apprehensions of Bright; Goschen's refusal in 1877 to accept household suffrage in the counties on the ground that democracy would not prove favourable to the principles of Political Economy

[1] *Fortnightly*, 1st July, 1885, Part VII of the Radical Programme.
[2] To Granville, 5th August, 1885. (All quotations of Hartington in this chapter are printed in *The Life*, unless a reference is given.)
[3] *Fortnightly* N.S., CCXXVI, 1st October, 1885 'Three Platforms' — No. 3. 'The Promised Land' (Labouchere).

— all seemed justified. And the landlords, and especially the Whig aristocrats, and their allied intellectuals, fled to the Cobdenite bastions that they had been assiduously preparing since the 'reconnaissances against property' in 1880–1. They were willing to look sourly upon entail (even upon primogeniture) and all other impediments to the free enjoyment and disposal of property, so that they might defend Property in the name of Liberty. The Duke of Argyll denounced the apostles of the new Radicalism as reactionaries who wanted to make the freedom of the individual as narrow and restricted instead of as wide and secure as possible.[1] In an article entitled 'Plea of a Malcontent Liberal', Dicey upheld true Liberalism as the advocacy and defence of the liberty of the individual, freedom of thought, religion, speech, writing, labour and trade and the assertion that there should be no interference with liberty where it did not affect the liberty of others. (This, of course, was taken almost straight from Mill.) 'Laisser-faire was our motto,' said Dicey, 'and to that motto I for one adhere still.' But latter-day Liberalism had an opposite ideal, the ideal of State Socialism, the notion that the state should control the community, albeit for its own good.[2] A writer in the Edinburgh Review, probably also Dicey, declared that the nation was approaching 'a great parting of the waters — a chasm between the past and the future — a passage from death to life or, possibly, from life to death'. He condemned the Radicals for preaching Henry George to townsmen and denouncing the game laws to people who knew nothing of game, and pretending that democratic government was cheap, when the municipalities had created £150 million of debt[3] and raised the rates, by prodigality, to the level of imperial taxation. Inequality in the conditions of human life must become more striking the more highly civilised a society became and it was very unworthy of the Radicals to exploit this progress in order to seek notoriety and power, setting class against class, raising envy, covetousness and discontent into political factors, inflaming the worst passions of democracy and deluding the masses into popular fallacies which would in the end prove fatal to themselves. 'Liberty has more to fear in this age from Democracy

[1] H. of L., 10th July, 1885.
[2] Fortnightly, 1st October, 1885, 'Three Platforms' — No. 2.
[3] Chamberlain at Birmingham had been a pioneer of municipal (or 'gas and water') Socialism in which the Webbs were to see the pattern for the gradual evolution of a socialist society.

than from any other cause.' The true issue of the election was
Liberty (with which went law, rights, patience, tolerance, enduring
order and peace) versus Democracy (with which went lawless
arrogance, impetuousness and bloody dissension).[1]

Gladstone was more or less a complete Cobdenite, and it was
reasonable to hope that he would be with the angels against the
Satanic hosts which threatened the Liberal paradise. And so, in
principle, he was, though refusing to see the issue in such cataclysmic terms as Goschen, Argyll or Dicey. 'There is,' he told
Acton in a famous letter, 'a process of slow modification and
development mainly in directions which I view with misgiving. . . .
The liberalism of today . . . is far from being good. Its pet idea is
what they call construction — that is to say, taking into the hands
of the state the business of the individual man.' But the Radicals
were not the only, or even the worst, offenders. There was the
'Tory Democracy' of Lord Randolph Churchill. That lordling,
arrogating to himself the Disraelian 'mantle of Elijah', had been
saying dreadful things about the plutocracy of Liberalism, and
about Gladstone himself (the son of a mere millionaire with the
impertinence to live in a castle)! He condemned his leader, Sir
Stafford Northcote, whose political temperature was very much
that of Hartington, as supine, antiquated and worthy to lead only
'the old men crooning over the fires at the Carlton' (language
which could only convince the old men at Brooks's that the country
was going to the dogs). Winning control of the National Union of
Conservative Associations, and crediting it with the sort of
potentialities which the Birmingham caucus attributed to the
National Liberal Federation, Churchill tried to wrest control of
the party machine from Northcote, Salisbury and Earl Percy,
forced them to compromise, and became the second man in the
party. He mocked the Whigs as prisoners of a traditional allegiance
which made them the Trojan horse of their class. He assaulted the
Birmingham citadel of Bright and Chamberlain. Late in 1884 the
Aston riots attracted national attention to the somewhat strenuous
initiation of Northcote by Churchill into the ways of urban
democracy. Lord Randolph equalled Chamberlain in rabble-
rousing demagogy and excelled him in vulgarity. 'Tory Democracy',
said Gladstone severely, was 'demagogism not ennobled by love
and appreciation of liberty . . . living on the fomentation of angry

[1] *Edinburgh Review*, July 1885.

passions, and still in secret as obstinately attached as ever to the evil principle of class interests'.

It is no accident that there was mutual respect and liking between Churchill and Chamberlain. Tory demagogy, added to recent tendencies of Tory social legislation (the Artisans' Dwelling Act, the Agricultural Holdings Act, the Housing of the Working Classes Act, Land Purchase in Ireland), placed the Whig Right in a quandary. If it recoiled from the embrace of Chamberlain, would it fare much better in association with Tories who seemed only too ready to accommodate themselves to democracy? Whiggery took it hard that Labouchere should allege that the Tory system of policy, the attempt to arrest the march of democracy by 'trickery and misrepresentation' — the 'last flicker of an expiring aristocracy' — was stolen from the Whig political arsenal.[1] Whigs feared that the Radicals were only too right when they said that Tory Democracy would give Radicalism a lift, and that the only issue for the constituencies to decide was whether a Radical policy should be carried out by those who were proud to be its friends or by its secret enemies. The Earl of Wemyss bewailed the fevered competition in the 'Socialism at St Stephens' stakes. Both parties were abandoning Liberty and Property and Political Economy.[2] Dicey could only hope that their vested interests would recall the Conservatives to sanity.

Tory Democracy no doubt repelled potential Liberal deserters, as did the memory of Disraelian and pre-Disraelian chicanery, which Gladstone, noting unscrupulous Tory-Parnellite electoral alliance, expected to see repeated on a grand scale in Irish policy. Nevertheless, Hartington saw moderate electors slipping away to the Tories, and thought they were probably right and that 'the Radicals are so forcing the pace that there will soon be no place in the party for less extreme men'.[3] He must call upon Gladstone to discountenance the *Unauthorized Programme* and to repudiate the disturbing doctrine of 'ransom'. Hartington truly represented the moderate electors. Whether he desired the unity of the party after the general election depended on what the party was likely to do, and Gladstone, as leader, was the man to declare policy.[4] It was not enough that Gladstone's private views should seem, in August,

[1] *Fortnightly*, 1st October, op. cit., 'The Promised Land'. Cf. Vol. CCXXIV, 1st August, 1885.
[2] *Times*, 8th March, 1885.   [3] To Gladstone, 9th November, 1885.
[4] To Gladstone, 6th and 10th September, 1885.

'tolerably reasonable, though vague'.[1] When Gladstone returned from a cruise at the beginning of September, the siege of Hawarden began. For to Chamberlain also what the Grand Old Man would say was important; it would never do for him to rule out the *Unauthorized Programme*.

Gladstone presented the supplicants with an initial obstacle. The only question to be settled, he said, was whether he was to lead the party for the general election. All agreed that unless he did its unity could not be preserved. Then, said Gladstone, he must 'avoid all conflict with any declared Liberal opinion entitled to weight', especially Hartington's,[2] and must do 'no act disparaging to Chamberlain's wing'.[3] His address to the electors of Midlothian would be a programme 'for the dissolution, not for a future Liberal government',[4] a 'political minimum'.[5] It would not imply that the party was ripe for action except on Procedure, Local Government, Land and Registration. On the third of these, the key one, Gladstone said that he would rejoice if Cobdenite means (legislation on entail, land transfer and registration, possibly on primogeniture) *'or other means in themselves commendable'* should lead to a large extension in the number 'directly interested in the possession and produce of the soil'. The *Edinburgh Review* took this as identical with Hartington's Rossendale platform ('which we accept as the true programme of the Liberal party and to which we cordially adhere'), and said that it offered no sort of encouragement to Radical designs.[6] This was not quite true. The clause italicised above, the Delphic references to taxation 'during life and upon death', and the proposition that 'further questions' might arise on 'the attributions and purposes' of local government, were faint genuflections in Chamberlain's direction. But were they sufficient to count as 'favourable references to our additions' without which, Chamberlain had said, the address would be taken as 'a final acceptance of Hartington's position' and a slap in the face to the Radicals?[7] As the reference to free education was, though non-committal, certainly not 'favourable', Chamberlain's reaction to the address was that it was very near to a repetition of Harting-

[1] To Granville, 8th August.   [2] To Hartington, 8th September.
[3] To Granville, 12th September.   [4] To Hartington, 11th September.
[5] To Chamberlain, 14th September.
All these letters are to be found in *Devonshire*, Morley's *Gladstone* or Howard's *Chamberlain*.
[6] October 1885, 'Plain Truths and Popular Fallacies'.
[7] To Gladstone, 12th September.

ton's speech at Waterfoot, and would be taken as a blow to the Radicals, and that he should feel dishonoured to join any administration formed on so narrow a basis.[1]

Hartington was pleased with the first reactions to the Midlothian address.[2] But within seven weeks the continuance of Radical propaganda for the *Unauthorized Programme* and Tory abuse of Hartington for playing the Radical game by staying in the party,[3] caused him to address a last appeal to Gladstone. The party could keep the moderates, he said, only if Gladstone took a strong and firm line against the Radicals.[4] But Gladstone was not to be drawn. He did not seem interested, so far as domestic affairs were concerned, in what the party was for, only in keeping it in being. He had told Chamberlain that 'for Liberals generally' there was work enough for three or four years upon which all might agree. He did not deny that a split was likely in 'the far or middle distance', but he would have 'nothing to do with it'.[5] To Hartington he replied that if they were men of sense 'the crisis will not be yet'. There was not in the allotments 'stuff enough' for a breach. Let it come, if it must come, later, and on some great issue, the Church or the Lords. But he added that if modern Radicalism was rampant and ambitious, moderate Liberals as well as Tory democracy had done much to foster Chamberlainism, and 'the gradual disintegration of the Liberal aristocracy' was especially to be deplored.[4]

The favourable effect of the Midlothian address had evidently worn off. Moderate electors deemed the *Fortnightly* correct to say that the construction of that formidable array of Gladstonian prose would depend on the unforeseen circumstances of the future. Hartington himself did not think these circumstances would be favourable. Those who were leaving were probably quite right, he said; the future would be with the Radicals and the Whigs would disappear or turn Tory.[6] It was with relief that he concluded, as the election returns came in, that the independent majority predicted by Schnadhorst (the N.L.F. pundit) had gone smash, and they would not have to try to get their miscellaneous team into harness

---

[1] To Gladstone, 20th September.   [2] To Goschen, 20th September.
[3] e.g. Churchill, 4th September *re* Harington 'If you are absolutely compelled by honesty to express these differences . . . with another section of Liberals you have no longer a right to oppose a Government and party on grounds of certain old antiquated names'.
[4] To Gladstone, 8th November; reply 10th November.
[5] To Chamberlain, 22nd September.   [6] To Granville, 3rd October.

again.[1] Gladstone's resort to verbal camouflage had achieved its modest aim. It had prevented the party leaders openly excommunicating one another during the campaign, though they made it clear that they were not of the same faith. It had prevented electoral disaster. But it could not prevent, and may have provoked, electoral setback. Labouchere wrote to Chamberlain:[2]

> We have been losing for a very clear reason. You put forward a good Radical programme. This would have taken. But no sooner had you put it forward than Hartington and others denounced it. The Grand Old Man proposed that any question should be shunted to the dim and distant future, and that all should unite to bring him back to power, with a Coalition Ministry — in fact the old game which had already resulted in shilly-shally. I think the inhabitants of the towns have shown their wisdom in preferring even the Conservatives to this. . . . Our only hope now is 'the cow' and here too I am afraid that the Whigs will have poured cold water on all enthusiasm. . . . Milk may be good for babies, but Whig milk will not do for electors. . . .

The suggestion that the Liberals would have gained, on balance, if Gladstone had endorsed the Unauthorised Programme, is probably untenable, and in any case was purely hypothetical, as Gladstone never considered doing any such thing, nor could it be imagined that Hartington would acquiesce. The Radicals made fun of Hartington's habit of 'thinking aloud' in public when he was thinking one way and going to go the other; of his tendency to yield, 'grumbling as usual, but still yielding'.[3] Hartington was very well aware of this impression, which decreased the reliance of Conservative Liberals upon his declared resistance to innovations. At this crisis the awareness stiffened his determination. He might in the end, had circumstances been other than they turned out to be, have yielded after the election, but he was certainly resolved to grumble all through it. Nor was Chamberlain sorry, for he gave it as his view (which Gladstone did not share) that the electorate was entitled to know of the differences of opinion.[4] This must mean that, pleased at the extent to which the majority of Liberal candidates adopted his line rather than Hartington's, Chamberlain was prepared to risk the adverse effect on the party's fortunes of

---

[1] To same, 29th November.   [2] *Labouchere*, p. 243, 29th November.
[3] *Dilke*, Vol. II, p. 3 (Chamberlain to Dilke, 2nd December, 1883); *Labouchere*, p. 239 (Chamberlain, 20th October, 1885).
[4] *Dilke*, Vol. II, pp. 142 ff., 21st May, 1885. But that was when the Radical ministers were considering resignation.

evident dissension between its principal men. To Chamberlain the immediate issue of the election was less important than the emergence, under his control, of a strong Radical party. He expected the Liberal party to split, either immediately after the election, or upon Gladstone's resignation, because Hartington was the heir-presumptive and Chamberlain and Dilke had long ago decided that they would serve under him only on their own terms.[1] The important thing was that Chamberlain should be able to claim a parliamentary status derived from a 'mandatory' verdict of a democratic electorate. The fact that the Radical policy was the only one before the country — 'the well-fatted unauthorised cows swallowed the newly arrived lean kine' of Midlothian[2] — might lead to such a run-off of moderate Liberals that Hartington said it did not matter whether he went too, for he would be left alone.[3] But the Liberal party would, in Chamberlain's view, only benefit from that.

The striking fact about the elections was the contrast between the counties of England, where the Conservatives were reduced to 46% of the votes and 40% of the seats, showing that the 'cow' had been very productive, and the boroughs, where the Tories won 50% of the seats with $49\frac{1}{2}$% of the votes. There was, as Labouchere said, no urban cow. Free — or as Gladstone preferred to call it — 'gratuitous' education did not fill the bill, for ratepayers counted the cost, and Disestablishment, for which (according to Brett) two-thirds of the Liberal candidates stood, hardly attracted people who would not have voted Liberal and frightened some who might have. The *Fortnightly* thought this very important, and also the appeal of some Tory candidates to 'Fair Trade' at a time when unemployment and trade depression helped the Tories as in 1880 it had helped the Liberals. To Brett it was very remarkable that there was a Liberal majority at all, in view of the play Salisbury had been able to make with Egypt, South Africa, the Sudan and Ireland, the adverse economic circumstances, the disunity of the party, the success of Tory Democracy with the working men and the solid anti-Liberal Irish vote.

It is now thought that the influence of the Roman Catholic bishops, instructing the faithful to vote Tory on the schools issue,

[1] ibid., p. 137, to Mrs Pattison, May 1885.
[2] *Fortnightly Review*, 1st January, 1886, Brett on 'Procrastination or Policy'.
[3] 8th November.

may have been, in English constituencies, as influential as Parnell's instructions, and also that the number of seats lost to the Liberals by Parnell's initiative was much exaggerated by its victims.[1] But if the number of seats given by Parnell to the Tories was anything like the twenty to twenty-five claimed,[2] that would only emphasise what is in any case clear — that Parnell was the true victor of the general election of 1885 because of all the political leaders he alone achieved his principal objective. He had decided that, unless the Liberals would go for Home Rule, he would contrive, if he could, to hold the balance between the parties. To do this, he must assist the Conservatives, as the weaker contestant. The way was easy, for the Irish had voted with the Tories to bring down the Liberal government on the budget; there was a *mariage de convenance* between Parnell and Churchill which would not be broken unless Gladstone made a satisfactory bid. Salisbury abandoned the Crimes Act and appointed as Lord Lieutenant Carnarvon, who spoke (and thought) ambiguously about Home Rule; the Tory government passed the first effective Land Purchase Act. And so, in the elections in Ulster, Orangemen and Nationalists marched together to vote down Liberals, and not a Gladstonian was returned in the whole of Ireland. The sweeping Liberal victories in Scotland and Wales were not enough to give Gladstone a clear majority in the new Parliament, though he came very near it and was correspondingly disappointed that the damage done by the Irish vote in Britain, as distinct from Ireland, had been in this sense decisive. His attitude to the Irish must indeed have been curiously ambivalent. In his own mind he had determined on Home Rule if Parnell did impressively in Ireland. But Parnell did so well that Gladstone could be accused of going for Home Rule only because Parnell's assistance was necessary to turn the Tories out and keep the Liberals in.

On 6th December Hartington wrote to Goschen that he hoped he would never have to go through 'that' again. 'That' referred to his experiences between the fall of the late Government and the polling in the general election, but especially to his relations with Gladstone during this period. For he knew the way that Glad-

---

[1] C. H. D. Howard 'Parnell and the General Election of 1885', *E.H.R.*, January 1947.
[2] Gladstone (*Morley*, Vol. II, p. 498) said 20. So did the *Fortnightly* 1st January, 1886 ('Home and Foreign'); in the same issue Arthur Arnold "The Elections and After" said 25.

stone's mind was working on Irish matters, and when on 10th September he had written to Gladstone 'My desire . . . for the unity of the party under your leadership is under present circumstances subject to very serious qualifications,' it was Ireland, not the allotments, that he had in mind. On 24th August Parnell had raised the flag of 'National Independence', declaring the auction open. On 29th Hartington, at Waterfoot, declared that England would unite to resist so fatal and mischievous a proposal as Home Rule. Chamberlain at Warrington on 8th September also ruled out national independence. Gladstone remonstrated with them. They ought not to have joined issue so pointedly. Hartington inquired why not?; as they had nothing to offer Parnell, there seemed nothing for the portion of the party with which he was 'specially connected' to do but disclose 'as early as possible an uncompromising resistance to the present demands'. Gladstone's answer, that he feared others would follow suit, was very disquieting. What could it mean but that some great design was maturing in that remarkable brain, as the Marquess had suspected when he last met him, on 7th August (they did not meet again till January) and found him 'unusually unintelligible' but 'extremely alarming'? Herbert Gladstone, in his elaborate defence of his father, complains that Hartington knew what Gladstone had in mind from 7th August but did not definitely and finally oppose Home Rule until December.[1] The truth is that Hartington publicly repudiated Home Rule on 29th August, and never in public or private deviated from his position. He did not know with any clarity what Gladstone had in mind, but feared the worst because Gladstone refused to express resistance to Parnell, or to express anything definite at all, but wrote in private deploring 'rapid announcements' which might hamper future policy. On 6th September he did not know enough of Gladstone's ideas to say whether he could accept them. Gladstone's letter of the 8th did not clarify those ideas, but increased Hartington's fear that a Liberal victory would mean the adoption of an Irish policy which he could not accept. He was, of course, bound by the confidential nature of the correspondence not to reveal to the electorate either his apprehensions as to Gladstone's intentions or the reasons for them. But Northbrook's biographer quotes evidence that Hartington was now thinking in terms of an arrangement between the moderate Liberals and the Tories to

[1] *After Thirty Years*, p. 307.

resist Parnell, and only hoped that Salisbury would not make concessions to his temporary allies which they could use as stepping-
stones. Hartington was angry and apprehensive, sworn to secrecy,
unable to get elucidation, and adjured to remain silent on one of the
major questions of the day, soon to dwarf all others — adjured
indeed to keep an open mind, so that not only a united party, but
he himself, could be free to accept the great man's vision when he
vouchsafed to reveal it. Gladstone was apt to take the view that any
Liberal of intelligence and goodwill would accept any proposals
he put before the party, provided he (Gladstone) was able to choose
the opportune moment to proclaim them, and the Liberal in
question had not hopelessly committed himself in the meantime.
Conscious of the righteousness of his designs, the Grand Old Man
felt aggrieved when colleagues pressed him for clarification,
definition and consultation. They must await the hour. They were
not even told when this would be. On 9th September Chamberlain
was informed that one of the two great reasons for maintaining the
unity of the Liberal party was that 'only the Liberal party can (if
it can) cope with the great Irish question which may arise three
months hence'. But when those three months were up, Gladstone
was saying that it was for the Conservative government to act.

The significance of the three months' wait was that Gladstone
attached momentous importance to the Irish election results,
viewing them as a democratic nationalist awaiting the verdict of a
self-determination test. He treated the Parnellite victory as proof
that Home Rule should be conceded on grounds of public morality
as well as expediency, though of course the verdict strengthened
the case on grounds of expediency too. Neither Hartington nor
Chamberlain was prepared to be impressed by Parnell's victory,
for both had expected it; it did not seem to them much to advance
the case for Home Rule, which was a question of imperial policy
to be determined on imperial grounds — a point Gladstone
admitted only to the extent that he insisted that Home Rule must
be 'compatible with the unity of the Empire'. It was to be powerfully argued against him that the imperial electorate was not
consulted, and Herbert Gladstone evidently found this telling, for
he strove in his defence of his father to argue that 'the electorate
had general knowledge . . . ; the public knew that he would deal
with Ireland, and probably on Home Rule lines'.[1] The defence

[1] *After Thirty Years*, p. 285.

is not convincing. Certainly Gladstone's address and speeches were very obscure on Irish questions, and the obscurity was framed in order to leave Gladstone free to go for Home Rule. But it was also deliberately designed to conceal his intentions, just as Salisbury's vague generalities were designed to conceal a lack of intention. The public did not know that Home Rule was to be an issue in the next Parliament, except to the extent that Parnell would demand it. Morley does not attempt to justify Gladstone on this ground. He says frankly that during the general election 'there was nothing like a general concentration on the Irish prospect. The strife of programmes and the rivalries of leaders was what engrossed the popular attention'.[1] It is no doubt possible to justify Gladstone on some higher, or at least alternative, ground, and argue that a party leader convinced of the justice and righteousness of a proposal is entitled, in certain circumstances, to conceal it from the electorate if there is not time to prepare the public for a favourable response and a felicitous conjunction of circumstances, unlikely to recur, seems imminent, and that he is entitled to do this even if the matter is fundamental and a *fait accompli* would be irreversible. It may further be argued, though less powerfully, that Gladstone had no 'proposals' or 'intentions' but only, as he said, more or less of 'opinions and ideas', and was not bound to reveal them; even that he was bound not to reveal them by a duty to preserve the unity of the party. This is not the place to assess the value of such extenuations, because it is not our function to arrive at an objective judgement upon the propriety of Gladstone's conduct. We have to try to see him as Whigs saw him, and to understand what became the majority view among them, that 'the electoral battle of 1885 was fought on sham issues and false pretences'[2] since the imperial democracy was not told that a Liberal government would mean Home Rule;[3] that policy should be at least to some extent an emanation from the party, though it was for leaders to give it shape and formulation and carry it, but that this policy represented an abrupt and radical departure for which there had been no feeling in the party;[4] that Gladstone's colleagues had been 'jockeyed' into an invidious position by inconsiderate treatment.

[1] Morley's *Gladstone*, Vol. II, p. 486.   [2] *Edinburgh Review*, July 1886.
[3] H. of C., Leatham, 13th May, 1886, Westlake, 25th May.
[4] ibid., Leatham's speech.

The first two of these propositions do not perhaps come altogether appropriately from Whig lips, except in the sense that it was the Whig way to act upon pressure from within the party only when the pressure became inconveniently strong. 'The Old Constitutional Whig' had recently been condemned by Brett for the pre-democratic view that 'the set of men once chosen, decisions must be left to them and that the verdict of the people may be taken subsequently on their conduct'.[1] Was this not the very principle on which Gladstone had now proceeded in relation to Home Rule? with the difference that he appreciated more than the Whigs Brett's point that Government now required to heed, and mould, and mobilise public opinion all the time. The Whig complaint on these matters was only valid to the extent that it was a reply to Gladstone's own emphasis upon the will of the Irish people 'shown unequivocally and constitutionally'[2] which neglected to take into account the views of the British people, so that while the Irish M.P.s were representative of the views of Ireland on National Independence, the British M.P.s were not representative of the views of the British electorate on Home Rule. But the protest against 'jockeying' was entirely valid, and justified Hartington's plaint 'Did any leader ever treat a party in the way that he has done?'[3] Gladstone for months evaded pleas for consultation and for definition. Not until November did he reveal to Hartington a preference for 'action at a stroke' and that he was thinking of 'a derivative chamber acting under imperial authority'. Not until 17th December did he forward 'the conditions of an admissable plan', but still recommending that nobody should commit himself, and assuring people who knew very well that there had been communications between Hawarden and some of the Irish politicians that he had said or done nothing which pointed in any way to negotiation or separate action, and that he had no 'intentions'.[4] This was *after* his intentions had been 'leaked' via Herbert Gladstone through the National Press Association and published in the press as Gladstone's definite plans and opinions. To colleagues who knew that the proposals were entirely congruous with the generalities with which Gladstone had favoured them, it was maddening to be told that there were still no plans or intentions,

[1] *Fortnightly Review*, CCXXVI, 1st October, 1885.
[2] H. of C., 10th May, 1886.
[3] *Devonshire*, Vol. II, p. 109, 2nd January, 1886, to Granville.
[4] To Hartington, 17th December, to Chamberlain 18th.

and that they should keep their own counsel and study the question and not commit themselves, and that they were to be 'very in-credulous as to any statements about my views and opinions'. These men had their rights, as well as Gladstone, and they had their self-respect. They could not accept that they should remain hamstrung in order to suit the convenience of a leader who pro-posed to promulgate a policy of which they could not approve. They could not agree with Herbert Gladstone that it was 'square and honest' to expect them to play Gladstone's game. Herbert Gladstone himself admitted that silence and obscurity were no longer even profitable, because both the Whigs and the Radicals were manoeuvring, the latter, he thought, with the intention of shunting both Ireland and Gladstone out of the way. That is why he flew the famous 'Hawarden Kite'.[1]

To Hartington and a circle gathering round him it did not matter whether or not Gladstone had approved the 'leak'. Gladstone's views were now public property, 'I do not know whether I can or ought to do anything but I cannot admit that he has, as he seems to imagine, done nothing,' wrote Hartington.[2] And so, in the *Times* of 21st December Hartington reaffirmed his views. Glad-stone complained that this was very unhelpful; men should look for points of agreement, actual or possible. The faithful Granville broadcast appeals to colleagues not to commit themselves. But Hartington replied that Gladstone had 'committed himself up to the chin'. There was no longer any justification for asking the Marquess to stand by while Gladstonian pressures worked upon other colleagues at present inclined to join with the Marquess against Home Rule. The Whig Unionists must mobilise — the more so as nobody trusted Hartington when he was grumbling. Dicey had predicted during the election campaign that if the Liberals entered the path of Irish self-government they would not stop and that 'Lord Hartington will protest and will then withdraw his objections in deference to Mr Gladstone's representations, and, as for the others, they will follow suit'.[3] The Queen was urging Goschen to induce Hartington to form a middle party; 'You must keep Lord Hartington up to the mark and *not* let him slide back (as so often before) into following Mr Gladstone and trying to keep

[1] *After Thirty Years*, p. 308.
[2] To Granville, 18th December.
[3] *Fortnightly*, CCXXVI, October 1885, 'Plea of a Malcontent Liberal'.

the party together.'[1] Hartington did not now need the Queen to tell him 'his duty . . . and what he owed to his Queen and country, which really goes before his allegiance to Mr Gladstone who can persuade himself that *everything* he takes up is right'. This was the parting of the ways.

On 1st January, 1886 Harcourt, Chamberlain and Dilke went to Devonshire House to discuss with Hartington 'how to bring Gladstone to book'.[2] They decided to urge Gladstone to give them, and subsequently the party, his views and intentions. Gladstone replied that he had submitted *all* his views to Hartington on 17th December, had done nothing to convert them into intentions, had no proposals to give them but would be available in London for consultations at 4 p.m. on 11th January, ten days before the Queen's Speech. They had better go *in posse comitatus*, said Harcourt, but Gladstone forestalled this by naming times to see them separately. All he then had to tell them was that he would in Parliament 'announce with reasons a policy of silence and reserve'. The Marquess told Gladstone that, for his part, he must, on the Address, (in Gladstone's words) 'proclaim a policy of absolute resistance without examination to the demand made by Ireland'. The old man was shocked at the prospect of such a 'gratuitous declaration'. Why should the Marquess want to play the Tory game of working the Irish Question to split the Liberals? 'He will make my position impossible!!!' Hartington would really have to consider whether he would lead the party himself or leave it in chaos.[3] It had not yet dawned on Gladstone that Hartington meant what he said on 10th September — 'you are, and have long been, in favour of granting to Ireland a larger measure of self-government than I think I could ever agree to' — and on 10th November — 'I am as much opposed as ever to the attempt to create a central body dealing with local government in Ireland . . . a long step in the direction of complete legislative independence'— and what he had published in the press on 21st December. Even after Hartington's declaration in the House of Commons, Gladstone hoped that he might join an administration on the basis of examining the practicability of establishing a legislative body in Ireland for purely Irish affairs without impairing 'the unity of the

[1] *Queen's Letter*, 3rd Series, Vol. II, pp. 709–17.
[2] Hartington to Granville, 28th December.
[3] 18th January, 1886, to Granville.

Empire' and with safeguards for minorities. Refusing to bandy sophistries with the master of sophistry, the Marquess replied that he was 'unable to attach great importance to a distinction between examination and the actual conception and announcement of a plan'. He could not accept the principle of Home Rule, and, the spokesman of the moderate Liberals, he could not administer such a shock to those who thought he had already too frequently surrendered his own judgement for the maintenance of unity in the party.[1]

At base, the issue between Gladstone and the Whig Unionists was the same as it had been whenever coercion and concession had been discussed in the first two Gladstone governments. Was one to concede to agitation what one would not have conceded on other grounds? Was one to flinch from the maintenance of law and order if it involved a coercive régime? It may be that the situation had so far altered, as a result of the introduction of household suffrage into Ireland (which Hartington had opposed), and more especially as a result of the importance which Gladstone attached to the election results, that half-measures, such as the Gladstone cabinet had discussed in 1882 and three-quarter measures, such as it had discussed in 1884–5, were no longer acceptable to the Irish. The acceptance of Home Rule by Earl Spencer (Lord Lieutenant during the coercive régime of 1882–5) was ascribed to his belief that 'under the system of government by party, modified by democratic change, the maintenance of a firm, consistent and vigorous administration of the law in Ireland is no longer to be hoped for'.[2] Northbrook, who became a Unionist, so feared the alternatives of absolute separation or absolute government that he was at first prepared to consider Home Rule with guarantees. But, as speaker after speaker said in the Home Rule debates, the issue was whether one could trust the Nationalist leaders.[3] What would be the use of paper checks upon the treatment of landowners and Protestants?[4] What, indeed, would be the use of paper limitations on the powers of a Dublin parliament? Was Britain prepared, in case of violation, to attempt reconquest?, asked Westlake.[5] Lord Ebrington declared that there was no reason to suspect the Nationalist politicians of any capacity for self-government, and

---

[1] 30th January, *Devonshire*, Vol. II, p. 122.   [2] *Times*, 28th March, 1886.
[3] e.g. speech of Lord Wolmer (Selborne's son), 17th May, 1886, and of Hobhouse (same night).
[4] H. of C., Lord Lymington, 25th May.   [5] H. of C., 25th May.

they would have to remain disloyal to the British connection in
order to stay in power.[1] In other words, to these Unionists the
question was not really Home Rule but Separation, and the
abandonment of all hopes of a solution other than Separation, as
well as the abandonment of the loyalist minority. Parnell went to
his ultimate aim, said Leatham, by a hop, a skip and a jump —
the expulsion of landlords,[2] a parliament in Dublin, and then
independence, and Leatham would not go with Gladstone two-
thirds of the way.[3]

Leatham, member for Huddersfield, who knew that he was
probably forfeiting his seat after twenty-four years in the House
of Commons, stated with great clarity (on Hartingtonian lines, but
more animatedly) what had been the issue between the Whig and
the Gladstonian ever since the two confronted one another on
Irish questions. To Gladstone, even the briefest suspension of
ordinary liberties was repugnant, and required atonement; the
three year Crimes Act régime after the murder of Lord Frederick
Cavendish was abhorrent. To Gladstone the discontent of Ireland
called imperatively for legislative remedies and, as he increasingly
felt, for the grant of some degree of responsibility for Ireland to
elected Irishmen. But to many a Whig the Crimes Act régime was
more creditable to the British Government than preceding
dispensations when a writ that was not the Queen's ran in Ireland
or when violence and intimidation reigned. The insubordination
of the Irish, so far from calling for the grant of self-government,
increased reluctance to consider it. Herbert Gladstone, indeed,
blames the Whigs for the necessity for Home Rule, as well as for
the failure to achieve it. 'Lack of foresight and courage brought a
great historic party to an end,' he says, condemning the cabinet's
refusal of county councils in 1882. He quotes his father as saying
'Ah, they will rue this day' when the scheme for a Central Board
was rejected in cabinet in 1884; 'the Whigs sat stolidly on the safety
valve and another golden moment passed'. What the electorate did
not know in 1885, he says, was how far 'Whig timidity and secret
Conservative advance had forced the pace'. The Whig rejection

[1] H. of C., 10th May, 1886.
[2] Earl Spencer, in 1886 as in 1885, insisted on a great Land Purchase scheme
as due to the landlords when any extensive self-government (reducing them to
political nullities) was granted. The scheme was highly controversial and
imperilled the Home Rule Bill.
[3] H. of C., 13th May, 1886.

of the local government schemes 'brought them face to face with the only alternative that remained — a Parliament in Dublin'.[1] Hartington's 'failure to form any progressive or even helpful views in the Irish troubles . . . eventually submerged the Whig party'.[2] Hartington's views may not have been progressive, but they were sincere, and they were consistent. They were the views set forth by Leatham. One of the great principles of the Liberal party was that every man should be protected, not only in his public liberties but in those individual liberties on which public liberty was founded — the liberty to do as he thought right, within the law, however unusual or unpopular the action. Such liberty was the highest product of political civilisation, the rare and splendid treasure of communities in which the law was supreme and just. But Ireland was not in that condition, and a community in which terrorism had usurped the place of law was not entitled to an autonomy which would perpetuate the trampling under foot of individual liberty, where faction, religious intolerance and the memory of past injustice all conspired. In such communities there must be a law which was just to all, but was above all parties, factions and creeds, before which all quailed. That was the road taken in 1882. A little more courage, firmness and faith and determination, and Ireland might have become a country of law. But Gladstone proposed to give faction its fling, an intolerant priesthood and a vengeful majority the upper hand, by a measure which was so notoriously a 'ship-wrecking' bill for certain classes that it was necessary to have another bill providing escape boats which were, however, too small.[3] There was an alternative, even though it meant obstruction at Westminster and coercion in Ireland. As to the former, 'there are men who think it failure if the reforming energy of generations is not compressed into a lifetime', but he (Leatham) was not one of them. As to the latter, what was called coercion was simply government, and it was because Gladstone shrank from *government* that they had a Home Rule Bill before them — a bill to coerce not the defiers of the law, but the lawful and the liberal ('Ulster', said Randolph Churchill, 'will Fight, and Ulster will be Right'). The United States had met such a crisis as this by proclaiming on a hundred battlefields that the law must be upheld. For very shame let the House take its stand upon the Union.

[1] *After Thirty Years*, pp. 278–307.   [2] ibid., p. 175.   [3] The Purchase Bill.

Thus, from the Liberal benches, was advocated what came to be known as Salisbury's prescription of 'resolute government'. The reason that Gladstone gave for continuing his 'policy of silence and reserve' even after Parnell's election triumph was known was that he conceived it the duty of the Tory government to act. He let Salisbury know, through the latter's nephew, Balfour, that if it did act he would give it all the support he could. During the election, Salisbury, like Gladstone, had equivocated upon Ireland, but his Newport speech had contained references to 'all the institutions' of England as applicable to Ireland, and had even mentioned the word 'central'. Gladstone remembered 1829 and 1846 and 1867, when the Tory leaders had turned in their tracks and repudiated the sentiments of masses of their supporters. He was keenly aware of the superior facilities the Tories had for carrying a highly controversial measure through the Lords. Gladstone did not seek honour or glory; he only aspired to see 'justice to Ireland'. He shrank from the complications which, despite his inability to understand sympathetically the difficulties which prevented Hartington (and, as it happened, Chamberlain) from following him, he knew he must encounter if he took the initiative. In the last resort the only defence of his treatment of the electorate, the party and the party leaders is that he hoped the Tories would grasp the nettle. He wished his colleagues to remain uncommitted, not only as to his own proposals, but as to whatever the Tories might propose. And this explains his bitter allegation that Hartington was playing the Tory game. The more the Government felt it could rely on moderate Liberals against a Gladstonian initiative, the less likely was it to make any bold departure itself. But this explanation of Gladstone's behaviour did not make the principal Whigs take more kindly to what seemed to them to be an unscrupulous 'jockeying'.

Gladstone was very anxious not to declare his intentions before Salisbury had revealed his, because many Liberals might vote to keep the Tories in if they proposed modest schemes unacceptable to Gladstone, and even if the Tory plans were considerable, the existence of plan and counter-plan would confuse counsel. Even when the Tory answer came — Land Purchase, Coercion, but no constitutional advance — Gladstone still wished to preserve silence until he was in office, as there would be fewer desertions if he had not committed himself to a particular plan and could form a government on the basis of the examination of the question. It was accordingly decided at a meeting of ex-cabinet ministers — which Hartington declined to attend — that the Government should be brought down on a domestic, not an Irish, issue. By a fine stroke of irony, Jesse Collings' 'three acres and a cow' amendment to the Address was selected as the battle-ground. Goschen therefore had his opportunity to deplore the consequences of a democratic franchise. On the first night of debate on the Address, he said, there had been a greater conversion towards Home Rule than he would ever have judged possible; on the second there was a large minority practically for introducing the three F's into the United Kingdom,[1] and on the third Gladstone had not stated his reservations with the firmness which one would expect if any great resistance was to be made to socialistic legislation relating to land. The next step, in logic, would be legislative provision for a fair and equitable rent for artisans. He must make his stand on behalf of those who thought that a man might be as good a Liberal if he had faith in the action of the individual as if he believed in the action of the state.[2] Gladstone had expressed his support for 'the spirit' of the amendment. Hartington could not accept its implications, and with Goschen and sixteen other Liberals voted with the Government. More than seventy Liberals abstained, and the Liberal-Irish majority was only seventy-nine.

The dissentient Liberals voted with Ireland in their minds; seventeen of the eighteen became Unionists. Goschen was the most persistent lobbyist of potential Liberal Unionists, but it was to Hartington that the Whig Right looked for leadership. 'Your abstention will make the adoption of a dangerous policy impossible . . . your acquiescence would make resistance useless,' wrote Derby.[3] In the debate on the Address, both Albert Grey and Arthur Elliot praised the Government's defence of the Union and criticised the silence of Gladstone. They called on Hartington and Chamberlain to appreciate that the country wanted outspoken, simple honesty and that the leadership of the Liberal party awaited anyone who would come forward as the Unionist champion.[4]

---

[1] On Barclay's motion (defeated 25th Jan. by 211:183) on the conditions of land tenure, urging tenant right and revision of rents, a great but (Barclay said) necessary interference with contract. For comments on debate see *Elections and Recollections* (Pease), p. 100.

[2] H. of C., 26th January, 1886.

[3] *Devonshire*, II, p. 120, 1st January, 1886, Derby to Hartington.

[4] H. of C., 21st and 22nd January, 1886.

Granville, Spencer, Harcourt, Kimberley and Ripon joined Gladstone's new government, and so did a few Irish landlords — the Earls of Morley, Cork and Kenmare. But the bulk of the Whig aristocracy was in mutinous motion and looking to Hartington, with whom stood Derby, Northbrook, Carlingford, Selborne and, of course, Argyll. Gladstone had been given an inkling of what to expect when he visited Eaton Hall, the home of his friend Westminster, on 15th December, to see Balfour. While back at Hawarden the pious Aeneas sewed the streamers on his kite, Anchises let slip to the Countess Cowper his Irish designs, and received a sharp expression of undying Unionism. On 18th January the Duke of Bedford, that beneficent landlord who was abused by Radicals for giving his daughter a wedding present of a hundred pairs of shoes,[1] pronounced, and on 25th Earl Fortescue. The Duke of Westminister resumed his Adullamite raiment, put up to auction his specially commissioned portrait of Gladstone (a relic of their intimacy during the Bulgarian Atrocities campaign) and took the chair in the Chester Music Hall at a rally of the Irish Loyal and Patriotic Union. Earl Fitzwilliam played a similar rôle at Sheffield.[2] The Earl of Fife resigned the presidency of the Scottish Liberal Association.

There could be no shadow of doubt that as a result of what Alfred Pease called 'the second great secession of the Whigs'[3] a Home Rule Bill would be defeated by an enormous majority in the House of Lords. But it would be better for the Unionists to defeat it in the Commons. This required not thirty-five rebels, as in 1866, but a hundred, and if the parting of the Whigs from the Liberals was obviously more imminent now than then, the Whig element in the Commons was less numerous. It was not enough to gather into the Unionist fold even a majority of Whig aristocrats and squires and a handful of Goschenite Commercial Liberals. 'If the worst enemy of the Liberal Party had set himself to devise a a scheme for the disintegration and disruption of it he could hardly have hit on anything so formidable or fatal' as Home Rule, said Leatham, a Unionist.[4] But that was truer of the Liberal electors than of the Liberal members, and truer of them than of the National Liberal Federation. The exertions of the whips and the

---

[1] *Fortnightly*, 1st October, Brett's article 'New Policies and Old Failures'. The Lady Ermyntrude Russell had married in March 1885 Sir Edward Malet, British Ambassador in Berlin in succession to her uncle, Lord Odo Russell.
[2] *Times*, 30th January and 11th February, 1886.
[3] *Elections and Recollections*, p. 61. [4] H. of C., 13th May, 1886.

pressure of the local organisers, and the tremendous prestige of Gladstone, which he exploited to the full in utter conviction of the righteousness of his cause (he said he would go on, if necessary, alone) — these and a whole variety of considerations less estimable conspired to keep the main body of the M.P.s together,[1] though many wavered long. It is not, indeed, suggested that Gladstone had had any chance of carrying Home Rule in the country. He did not come as near as at first sight appears to carrying it in the Commons, for if the second reading had been carried, the committee stage might well have told a different tale. Chamberlain in November thought that Gladstone imagined he could frame an Irish policy which would unite the party and 'throw into the background those minor points of difference about the schools and smallholdings which threaten to drive the Whigs into the arms of the Tories or into retirement'.[2] It is just possible that a more modest concession of limited autonomy to the Irish might have been sufficiently acceptable to pass into law. Rosebery, who went with Gladstone and in 1894 succeeded him in the premiership, thought the Irish in 1886 were offered more than was necessary to secure their cooperation. But the Liberal party could not stand Home Rule, sprung upon it without notice and without a mandate. By Christmas it was clear that whatever else the Grand Old Man did to crown his career he would break up the party.[3] All one can say is that no other man could have come within even distant sight of the goal he set himself, and no man could have held so many of the party. He was not a man to under-rate. It was perhaps unfortunate for the Unionists that they lost the services in the Commons of the former Chief Whip, Lord Richard Grosvenor,[4] though his utility would have been limited by the plethora of new members. But no effort was spared by Albert Grey and Arthur Elliot who (with Trevelyan, after he left the Government)[5] specialised in button-

---

[1] O'Hegarty, *A History of Ireland Under the Union*, 1952, says (p. 537), 'Save Gladstone himself, it was not a principle with any of them, not a moral issue. They had come to it by devious ways, because the question was always cropping up, because the Irish vote had to be considered, because they wanted to stay in office. . . .'

[2] *Labouchere*, p. 239, 20th November, 1885.

[3] ibid., p. 273, Labouchere to Chamberlain, 23rd December, 1885.

[4] Herbert Gladstone, op.cit., p. 286–7, 307 complains that after the dissolution Gladstone was ill-served by Grosvenor, who had been asked to stay on as chief party manager for the election. He was created Lord Stalbridge.

[5] Trevelyan belonged to the school of Mill rather than of Chamberlain; he was not really a 'contructionist'.

holing members and taking them off to talk to Hartington, Goschen
or Sir Henry James.[1] Alfred Pease says that too many, especially
of the younger Whigs,[2] were charmed by Grey and committed
under personal influences and in private conversations'.

But the 'too many' were not enough to defeat the second reading.
That required assistance from Chamberlain, who had joined the
third Gladstone administration on the basis of an examination of
the Irish Question within the framework of Gladstone's generalities. This is not the place to speculate upon why Chamberlain
earned from Parnell the bitter comment 'There goes the man who
killed Home Rule.' Chamberlain, and Trevelyan with him, left
the Government before the Home Rule Bill was introduced, and
efforts to secure at least sufficient understanding between him and
Gladstone to enable some of those who became Radical Unionists
to vote for, or abstain on, the second reading, failed. The pertinacious
Labouchere struggled in vain to get Chamberlain to hold to his
former ambition to rise supreme and see the Whigs submerged:[3]

> ... The real enemies of the Radicals are the Whigs, and they are
> essentially your enemies. ... They have always managed to jockey
> the Radicals. They hang together; they have, through Grosvenor,
> the machine: they dominate in Clubs and in the formation of
> Cabinets. They may ally themselves with you re Ireland, but this
> will be for their benefit, not yours. Nothing would give them greater
> pleasure than to betray you with a kiss, for you are their permanent
> bogey ... I still hold that the Radical game is to go with Mr. Glad-
> stone on Irish matters, and to use him in order to shunt them, and,
> if possible, the Whigs. ...

But Chamberlain was not convinced. He was not deceived by the
fact that the Gladstonians captured the Federation, outside his
own Midland area. The next election, he shrewdly predicted,
would be determined by the number of Liberals who stayed away
from the polls. He sensed, perhaps exaggerated, the extent of
British Nonconformist, working-class, and Scottish distaste for the
Irish, which Gladstone (perhaps misled by the precedent of the

---

[1] Pease, op. cit,. pp. 61, 76, 108, 126.

[2] 'Young Whigs' as contrasted with 'the stuffy older men who were crowning
successful business careers by being M.P.s.' Pease himself was new to Parliament.
He had fought the election as a Hartingtonian but deplored the desertion of
Gladstone by the Whigs — 'for Whigs had supported even bolder proposals than
his'.

[3] *Labouchere*, p. 278, 1st January, 1886. Cf. 23rd December, 1885, and a stream
of letters down to 5th June.

Irish Church question) underestimated. Because of this, Chamberlain believed that a Tory-Whig combination would smash an alliance of Radicals and Irish, and carry all before it.[1]

As long ago as 3rd October, Hartington had told Gladstone that, on the premise that the Radicals were capturing the party, there seemed nothing for moderates to do but turn Tory or disappear. The Queen was then urging Salisbury (3rd October and 3rd November) to a coalition of 'the best and strongest men' against 'revolutionary proposals and impracticable schemes', and Churchill favoured both an approach to Hartington and a programme designed to attract moderate Liberals. As to the latter, Salisbury preferred to bargain later; as to the former, Chamberlain thought that Hartington would not be such a fool, and he was right. Hartington in December had not moved beyond a penchant for independent support of the Tory government when it abandoned its alliance with Parnell. But the question of joint action between the Tories and the Whig Unionists against the Home Rule Government obviously did arise, and Goschen contrived on 14th April (six days after the introduction of the Bill and two days after the resignation from the Government of Heneage, Lord Morley, Kenmare and Cork) at Her Majesty's Theatre, Covent Garden, a great joint demonstration against Home Rule. Earl Cowper, presiding, flanked by Salisbury and Hartington, denounced Home Rule as desired by some as a step to separation, by others as a step to non-payment of rent, by others again as a step to the domination of an intolerant Roman Catholicism. Hartington, the main speaker, could not find in the leaders of national opinion in Ireland any indication that they adhered to the principles of civilised government — respect for law, for the rights of property, for the rights of others to labour and enjoy the fruits of their industry.

So Whiggery bid defiance to Gladstone in the name of the Union, Landlord Right, Protestantism, Individual Liberty and the Rule of Law. But the Covent Garden demonstration was not repeated, because it was important that the Liberal Unionists, who had to meet their caucuses, should do nothing to compromise their Liberalism. Their argument was that, at the least, Home Rule was a matter on which Liberals might legitimately differ, at the most that explanations were required, not of them, for they were only adhering to what they had said in the general election,

[1] ibid., see especially p. 248 (8th Dec.), 262 (24th Dec.) 278 (3rd Jan.).

but of those who had attempted a *coup d'état*. On 10th May Hartington moved the rejection of the Home Rule Bill, and although Gladstone gradually eroded the second reading of all significance, in order to get it passed, the Marquess said bluntly that the vote would really be for or against a dissolution. The decision of Chamberlain's group to vote with Hartington, Goschen and the Tories gave Unionism, at 1 a.m. on 8th June, 1886, a majority of thirty, with the unparalleled number of 656 participating in the division. 93 Liberals voted against Gladstone, the Whig Unionist Brand and the Radical Unionst Caine acting as tellers. There was drama in the divorce between Whiggery and Liberalism. For that is what it was, although some Whigs became Gladstonians and although the Whig and Radical Unionists clung for nearly twenty years to their Liberal appellation. When the fourth Gladstone administration of 1892–4 narrowly carried a Home Rule Bill in the Commons, it was rejected by the peers (8th September, 1893) by ten to one in a House of 460 (the total membership was 560). The speakers for the Government were the cabinet ministers Spencer, Ripon, Rosebery, Kimberley and Herschell (cr. 1886), other ministers Ribblesdale, Sandhurst (cr. 1871) and Brassey (cr. 1886), and, of the rest, only Thring (cr. 1886), Playfair (cr. 1892) and Swansea (cr. 1893). Against them spoke the Duke of Devonshire (i.e. Hartington), the Duke of Argyll, Northbrook and Selborne who had held office in Gladstone's cabinets, and Cowper, Zetland, Camperdown and Morley, all of whom had been in his administrations. The meagre minority — 41 — consisted of ministers, men who owed their titles to Gladstone, and only 6 others, including Russell's grandson and Granville's son. There were missing from Gladstone's ranks not only the vast majority of the Whig peerage but the holders of 38 of the 62 peerages to which he had nominated; the other 24 formed more than half his force. According to *Dod*, already in 1887 the Liberal peers were reduced to 63 of the 501 noblemen whose allegiance was noted, while the Liberal Unionists were credited with 120. When Gladstone left office for the last time he was meditating action against the Lords. He had been deserted by 'the upper and more powerful ... classes of the community', he told the Queen.[1]

---

[1] *Queen's Letters*, S. III, vol. III p. 172, 28th October, 1892. Cf. 23rd August (p.153) 'to us it matters little at what figure between thirty and forty our professed adherents are to stand'.

Gladstone said, with what justice we have seen, that the gulf between these classes and the more numerous classes of the community began before 1885–6, but that after Home Rule had been proposed the division of opinion in the Liberal party widened and hardened, some finding it an occasion and others an excuse for a separation from their former friends. Separation there was, but the Unionists claimed that they were the aggrieved and not the aggressors, that they were not 'deserters' and that the division was *in* the Liberal party. It was not a division on Home Rule alone. Dicey linked as causes of his secession his inability to trust the Liberal party to resist Socialism, to escape the 'fatuous fallacy' that Ireland must be governed by Irish ideas (when she was unfit for representative government and ought to be treated as a Crown colony), and to uphold Britain's imperial mission. The Earl of Fife laid down his office in protest against both 'Irish separation . . . and illogical and insincere tamperings with socialistic doctrines'.[1] What Home Rule did was to turn the growing trickle of seceders into a flood, by presenting a major and dramatic issue. For many Whigs would have agreed with Gladstone that in allotments there was not 'stuff' enough for a breach. As Hartington told the Eighty Club on 5th March, 1886, there had been a great debate between those:

> of whom I acknowledge I was one, who were more inclined to adhere to the steady but more vigorous prosecution of the older line of Liberal policy, who believed rather in the removal of impolitic restrictions, in the extension of popular self-government all over the country, for the improvement which we were looking forward to in the condition of the people, than in any other method,

and others who

> took a more hopeful view of newer, a more constructive, a more experimental system of legislation, who had greater confidence than I could feel in the advantages of the interference of the state or of public bodies in the concerns of private individuals, and who looked to a more rapid and in some degree a more novel extension of Liberal policy. . . .

But, he said, 'those differences are not the differences which divide us now or are likely in the coming time to divide us'.

The presentation of a clear issue made the exit of Whiggery

---

[1] *Times*, 10th February, 1886.

from Liberalism the more dramatic, and greatly facilitated its
association with the Conservative party in a common Unionism.
The maintenance of the Union was undoubtedly a conservative
cause, to which the Tories committed themselves with emphasis
and in defence of which Liberals could join them without the
doubts which beset a Goschenite or Diceyite when he came to
consider the socialistic contamination of the Tories. It was a
cause to which the Liberal Unionists could make a vital contribution because they could summon to their banner moderate
Liberals who without a burning issue of that kind would not have
deserted Gladstone, men who had not been prepared to abandon
him on the ground that 'the fundamentals of personal liberty, and
of legislative authority are now all thrown into the crucible of
discussion, and the worst heresies are taught by the men you are to
lead'[1], when no momentous measure impressed that issue upon
them. The impact of the Unionist appeal to the moderates was,
of course, immensely reinforced by Chamberlain's appeal to men
who on the issue of Liberty against 'Socialism' had not been at all
sympathetic to Hartington, Goschen and the Earl of Wemyss.

Many of the voters who opposed Home Rule were by no means
prepared to yield up the name of Liberal or to embrace the Tories,
and this was true also of M.P.s and even peers. Policy therefore
reinforced sentiment in determining Hartington to fight the election of 1886 without overt alliance with the Tories except on the
single issue of the Union[2] and to refuse the premiership when, after
the election, the Unionists held the balance between the Tories
and Home Rulers, and to refuse office again in January 1887 after
the resignation of Churchill from the Treasury (where he was
succeeded by Goschen, who joined alone). Chamberlain advised
the Marquess, now his ally, and in a sense his leader (to such a
extent do circumstances alter cases) not to head or join an administration, though he might do so and be perfectly consistent, because if he did the Hartingtonians would suffer the fate of the
Peelites — absorption — and would have to 'cease to be or call'
themselves Liberals.[3] And Hartington told Salisbury that, apart

---

[1] *Argyll*, Vol. II, p. 397, 24th October, 1885, to Gladstone (cf. p. 398, 9th Dec.
p. 404, 4th May, 1886).
[2] Hartington launched a fund on 22nd May. The Tories gave a unilateral
pledge not to oppose the Liberal Unionist M.P.s, which only six local associations
refused to honour.
[3] *Devonshire*, Vol. II, p. 168, 16th July, 1886.

from party interests, the national interest was against a step which would withdraw from the Liberal party all its most moderate elements, leaving it purely Radical and Democratic.[1] He spoke as a Liberal. But in May 1887 the Liberal Unionists were expelled from the Eighty Club (formed to commemorate the great victory of 1880)[2] and the posture of 'independent' support for a Conservative administration 'provided [it] did not play the fool either in foreign policy or in reactionary measures at home',[3] though not insincere, became to the ordinary elector indistinguishable from alliance, because the Unionists could not contemplate putting the Tories out and the Home Rulers in. To the public, except the more sophisticated members of it, politicians were either Unionists or Home Rulers. And if they were Unionists they were not regarded as Liberals. It was entirely natural that in 1895, after three years on the Opposition benches with Tory colleagues,[4] Hartington (after 1891 Duke of Devonshire) and Lansdowne (as well as James) should join Goschen as members of a Unionist government under Salisbury, of which Chamberlain at the Colonial Office was the most prominent member.

---

[1] ibid., p. 170, 24th July.   [2] Pease, op. cit., pp. 170–1.
[3] *Devonshire*, Vol. II, p. 168, 16th July, 1886.
[4] Not in itself committing them to merger, as ex-minsters often sit on the Front Bench opposite ministers, regardless of party; from 1886 to 1891 (when he went to the Lords) Hartington sat there alongside Gladstone.

Finis

Defending himself and his peers against criticism by Salisbury in 1883, Hartington had re-stated, with an assumed complacence, the traditional function of Whiggery:[1]

> I confess I am not dissatisfied with the position that the Whig party have in former times occupied, and that I believe they occupy at the present time. I admit that the Whigs are not the leaders in popular movements, but the Whigs have been able, as I think, to the great advantage of the country, to direct, and guide, and moderate those popular movements. They have formed a connecting link between the advanced party and those classes which, possessing property, power and influence, are naturally averse to change, and I think I may claim that it is greatly owing to their guidance and to their action that the great and beneficial changes, which have been made in the direction of popular reform in this country, have been made not by the shock of revolutionary agitation, but by the calm and peaceful process of constitutional acts.

The reader may judge the justice of this claim. The Radicals did not deny it; its truth exasperated them. Thus Chamberlain complained:[2]

> The business of the Radicals is to lead great popular movements and if they are fortunate enough to stir the hearts of the people . . . then it will be the high-born prerogative of the great Whig noble who has been waiting round the corner to direct and guide and moderate the movement he has done all in his power to prevent and discourage.

Our theme derives its unity from the recurrence over three generations of the same Whiggish self-justification and the same Radical vilification. If Whig influence was less in the 'eighties than half a century or a quarter of a century before, Radical impatience had never been greater —

> A distant view of the promised land, and a few grapes from it, will not suffice us. We must possess the land at once. We are not prepared to suit our pace to the heavy lumbering coach of Whiggism. The day

[1] *Devonshire*, Vol. I, pp. 402–3.   [2] *Dilke*, Vol. II, p. 3.

is over when the opinions of a few dozen respectable noblemen and gentlemen are likely to be blindly accepted by the country as though they were divine emanations. They must fall into line and march with us, or they will be left behind.

So wrote Labouchere.[1] And the Radicals now had in the democratic franchise an instrument of greater potential than was available to Hume, or Molesworth, or Bright, with which to make their words effective, and in Chamberlain a man who knew how to use it. In 1885 it seemed that Whiggery was about to be shed, as an incubus which the Liberal party would in future do without.

Then came Home Rule. The Liberal party lost its incubus, but also its practical-minded demagogue. It was diverted from its Radical mission into a political cul-de-sac, and lost its penultimate chance to become a party of the masses as distinct from one of two parties for which, *faute de mieux*, the masses must vote. It lost sight of the Condition of England in its preoccupation with the condition of Ireland, and it turned from the latter, after Gladstone's retirement, only to split asunder upon the question of Imperialism. By the time that the decay and disunity of the Unionists presented the Liberal party with power in 1905, Labour had already become a political force (though the Liberals, by electoral alliance, aggrandised it). Only then, through Lloyd George and Winston Churchill, did a Liberal government act in the spirit of Chamberlain's speeches of 1883–5. It was by no means inappropriate that the champion of the Lords when they struck at the Chamberlainite budget of 1909 should have been the fifth Marquess of Lansdowne, allied with the aged Tory Halsbury (a latter-day Lowe) who as Sir Hardinge Giffard in 1885 had denounced the *Unauthorized Programme* as 'Socialism, Violence and Infidelity'. Had not the *Edinburgh Review* boasted that the Whigs had never accepted the modern doctrine that legislation was to be dictated by public opinion?[2]

Tory jeers had been as recurrent and uniform as Radical impatience, and were recognition that Whiggery had an influence which was inconvenient to both Right and Left. On the eve of Palmerston's death Cranborne (as Salisbury then was) had

---

[1] *Fortnightly*, CCXXVI, October 1885 — 'Three Programmes'.
[2] CXLIX, April 1879, p. 256.

inveighed against 'that lowest form of partisanship which prefers rather to change opinions than change companions':[1]

> The Whigs constitute only an accidental compromise due to the matrimonial arrangements of a few great families, with the peculiarity that many of them are willing to sacrifice the interests of their class, in order to promote the personal ambitions of those who belong to their family connections. But their number diminishes at every election. It is obvious that in course of time these merely personal conditions of association must be overruled.

Unlike the Radicals, the Tories, for propaganda purposes if not from conviction (for there was a powerful argument to the contrary), reviled the Whigs as a danger to the *Conservative Cause* as well as an impediment to the Conservative party. Thus Salisbury in 1883, in an article which provoked Hartington's apologia cited above, sought by ridicule to accentuate an agonising reappraisal of Whiggery's political predicament:[2]

> The present Whig party is a mere survival kept alive by tradition after its true functions and significance have passed away. A Whig, who is a faithful member of the present Liberal party, has to submit to this peculiar fate, not only that he inherits the political opinions he professes — a lot which befalls many Englishmen — but that he also inherits a liability to be compelled to change them at the bidding of the leader whom the Radical party may have chosen for him. . . . The majority have neither the courage to abandon their Whig professions, nor to part with their Radical allies. They may often be met with helplessly lamenting their fate, for the only solution of their difficulties that has yet presented itself to them is a combination of public loyalty with private imprecation.

In 1886 the reason for this type of expatiation passed away, and Salisbury found himself the beneficiary of alliance with Whiggery and also with the less congenial, but politically valuable, Radical Unionists. By virtue of that alliance Salisbury was prime minister for thirteen years, and bequeathed the office to his nephew Balfour. The alliance, and the subsequent coalition, greatly benefited the Conservative politicians. It is, however, an open question to what extent it benefited British Conservatism. There is a sense in which, as Christopher Hollis remarks, the Conservative party became

[1] *Quarterly Review*, Vol. 118, July 1865, 'The Six Year old Parliament'. p. 295.
[2] *Quarterly Review*, October 1883, 'Disintegration'.

'sodden with Whiggery.' For when Whiggery entered into connection with the Tories, it brought in its train Commercial Liberals and their creed, which it had virtually adopted. Goschen, as well as Chamberlain, came with Hartington; the right-wing Liberal Unionists represented the plutocracy almost as much as the landed aristocracy.[1] So, *pace* Chamberlain, any gain in liberality was likely to be cancelled out by the narrow and negative conception of Liberty which these gentlemen entertained. In the absence of effective competition from the Liberals in the field of social policy, the Conservatives tended to become 'Goschenised'. The split between Hartington and Chamberlain came at last in 1903, when they were colleagues not in a Liberal but in a Unionist administration. Chamberlain tried to divert the renewed threat of social reform financed on the principles of discrimination and retributive justice by a policy uniting Protection and Imperialism. Many of the Liberal Unionists, Whig and Radical, were imperialists, but nearly all the prominent Whig Unionists clung obdurately to the Cobdenite principles so painfully assimilated by their forebears. In the 1906 election there were Whig candidates who fought as Unionist Free Traders. Partly through the Whig-cum-Commercial Liberal *vis inertiae* in the Unionist ranks, the way was left open for Lloyd George and Churchill.

These tentative interpretations must not be pressed too far, nor can a writer who has 'lived with the Whigs' for so long end upon a note of bitterness. Professor Laski in 1932 drew a picture of the old ruling class which 'controlled two hundred years of English destiny'. The 'gentleman', he was sure, picturesque in his thickheadedness and monumental in his complacency, had become a danger in an age of altered social concepts and complex economic problems and of the redistribution of national wealth,

[1] The more Whiggish section of the Unionist M.P.s as distinct from the Radicals, who were mainly business and professional men — included twelve aristocrats, thirteen baronets and seventeen untitled great landowners (or their heirs). But the tie-up of land and industry and commerce was well represented and not only by Cavendishes and Fitzwilliams. Among the baronets, Ramsden was ground landlord of Huddersfield and St Aubyn of much of Devonport; Crossley was the son of the great Halifax carpet manufacturer; Goldsmid came of a family of bankers and Jardine of the famous clan of China merchants. Among untitled landowners Willyams and Talbot leaned heavily on mineral royalties, Corbett (Droitwich) was a manufacturer and Robertson (Shrewsbury) an ironmaster and maker of locomotives. Non-landed baronets included Watkin, the railway magnate and Lubbock, banker-philanthropist-intellectual. Among other Unionist members were a Rothschild, a Bass, Currie the shipowner and the bankers Goschen, Biddulph and Leatham.

an age which required government by experts. But the gentleman, he said, was frequently tolerant, often personally gifted and a patron of the arts, capable of the generous gesture, and 'a better ruler than any of his possible rivals'. And he admitted:[1]

> It is not certain that we shall replace him by a more admirable type. . . . The leader of the future seems not unlikely to be the remorseless one-idea man, who governs us by hewing his way to his goal. He has no time for the open mind. He takes clemency for weakness and difference of opinion for crime. He has a horror of a various civilisation and he means by freedom only a stronger kind of chain. . . . The gentlemen scourged us with whips. We must beware lest our new masters drive us to our toil with scorpions.

That is a tribute a Whig would have been proud to earn and it is the warning that the latter-day Whigs so earnestly gave.

[1] H. J. Laski, *The Danger of Being a Gentleman.*

APPENDIXES

EACH of the three Appendixes is intended to be useful in itself. Appendix I, for instance, gives a complete list of the official careers of all persons who, under Whig or Liberal administrations between 1830 and 1885, reached the cabinet or a principal Household office or an office the holder of which (but not the particular person concerned) was sometimes in the cabinet, or who held junior (non-legal) political office (with membership of Parliament) for a total of about three years. The information is presented in such a way that one may read off who held a particular office at a certain time, or what office a particular person held at a certain time, or a whole political career. The writer became keenly aware during the preparation of this book how handy information presented in such a form would be.

But the appendixes are also inter-dependent, and reinforce the author's arguments as to the nature of Whiggery, its dependence on kinship and the sort of influence which flowed from rank and landed property, and its gradual decline. Thus 50 of the 80 Whig and Liberal cabinet ministers of 1830–85 appear in the three genealogical tables which form Appendix III. It is surely significant that 39 of the 52 who reached the cabinet before 1859, and 43 of the 60 who reached it before 1868, qualify for inclusion by virtue of connection with one of the leading Whig families or with other holders of high office, while only 9 of the 20 raised to the cabinet by Gladstone in 1868–74 and 1880–5 do so. Of the heads of departments who were not in the cabinet (see Section III of Appendix I), 9 appointed before 1852 are in the tables and only 4 not, and 16 of those appointed before 1868 are there and only 7 not, but of Gladstone's appointments 3 are there and 7 are not. Even Section II, the list of holders of the principal 'political' Household offices, confirms the trend. All who appear in these lists were noblemen, but while 26 of these appointed before 1852 are in the tables and only 4 are not, of Gladstone's appointments, while 11 appear, 6 do not. Appendix I, read in conjunction with Appendix III, graphically illustrate the decline of Whig influence between the 'thirties and the 'eighties.

Analysis based on the list of aristocratic M.P.s on the Liberal side, given as Appendix II, tells the same tale of decline after 1859. The aristocratic representation, measured at each general election, was as follows:

Seats for which they sat	1832	1835	1837	1841	1847	1852	1857	1859	1865	1868	1874	1880
Eng. cos	25	14	13	7	14	10	15	14	13	16	8	16
Eng. boros	30	25	30	35	33	36	30	35	24	16	11	17
Welsh cos	1	1	0	2	1	1	1	1	1	1	1	1
Welsh boros	1	0	0	1	2	2	1	1	2	3	3	2
Eng. & Wales	57	40	43	45	50	49	47	51	40	36	23	36
Sc. cos	4	2	3	4	5	7	5	2	1	3	2	3
Sc. boros	2	3	5	3	4	3	3	2	2	2	2	0
Ir. cos	8	7	9	12	8	4	4	4	9	9	3	0
Ir. boros	2	0	2	2	1	1	1	1	0	0	0	1
GRAND TOTAL	73	52	62	66	68	64	60	60	52	50	30	40
Approx. % of Lib. party in Parliament	15%	15%	18%	22½%	22%	20%	17%	18%	15%	14%	9½%	10%

A breakdown of the aristocratic representation in terms of years of service for different categories of boroughs is of interest. For this purpose I have used three categories which Professor Gash used in his *Politics in the Age of Peel* (see ibid., pp. 75–6), viz.:

Group A — Boroughs which in 1832 had less than 300 registered electors.

Group D — Boroughs which then had 1,000–2,000 electors.

Group E — Boroughs which had more than 2,000 electors.

But I have divided the 301–999 electorate boroughs into two categories:

Group B — Those which had lost a member from Schedule B in 1832 (plus the single member seats of Abingdon and Bewdley) and those which lost one or two members in the Reform of 1867–8 or by disfranchisement for corruption.

Group C — The rest.

Analysis yields the following results:

GROUP	*No. of boros*	*No. of seats*	*No. of yrs. Lib. aristocrats*	*In no. of boros*	*Approx. total yrs. Lib. repn. in those boros*	*ditto in all boros in group*
A	31	43	350	17	760	1050
B	45	74	340	17	810	1500
C	45	73	290	26	1470	2460
D	36	72	180	19	1280	2210
E	29	60	160	14	1050	2350

The years of service of aristocrats was to the total years of Liberal representation of the boroughs for which the aristocrats sat as follows:

Group A — nearly 1 in 2. B — 1 in 2½. C — 1 in 5. D — 1 in 7. E — 1 in 7.

And the years of service of aristocrats was to the total years of Liberal representation of all the boroughs in the group as follows:

Group A — 1 in 3. B — 1 in 4½. C — 1 in 8½. D — 1 in 12. E — 1 in 15.

The beautiful congruence of this picture shows the extent to which the Whig aristocrats relied for entry to the House of Commons on small electorates. Only 52% of the total Liberal years of representation in the English boroughs was provided by the boroughs with less than 1,000 electors in 1832, but these provided 74% of the total years of Liberal aristocratic representation of the English boroughs. A mere 29 populous constituencies (with over 2,000 electors in 1832) provided 24½% of the total Liberal representation in boroughs, but only 12% of the aristocratic representation of the boroughs, and much more than half of this is accounted for by the freeman borough of Chester, highly susceptible to the influence of the Grosvenors (see pp. 96-7 *supra*), the long tenure of Bristol by the Berkeley who advocated the ballot, and Lord John Russell's representation of the City of London. And of the 180 years of aristocratic representation in Group D, 50 years is accounted for by Charles Villiers's representation of Wolverhampton.

The overall picture of aristocratic representation on the Liberal side is as follows:

297 people represented for a total of about 2,800 years the following sorts of constituencies:

English counties	660 years	English boroughs	1320 years
Welsh counties	66	Welsh districts	73
Scottish counties	194	Scottish b & d	137
Irish counties	314	Irish boroughs	42
	1230 —		1570 —

The counties provided 39% of the members of the House of Commons *of all parties* (ignoring University members) and, as can be seen from the above, 44% of the *Liberal* aristocratic membership. This is remarkable, for the Tory predominance in the English counties was overwhelming. Yet the English counties provided nearly a quarter of the whole Liberal aristocratic representation, which was about 30% of the whole Liberal representation of the English counties. The English boroughs with less than 1,000 constituents in 1832 provided 35% of the Liberal aristocratic representation, but this was only about 19½% of the whole Liberal representation of such boroughs. The English boroughs with more than 1,000 constituents in 1832 provided a mere 12% of the Liberal aristocratic representation, and this was less than 7½% of the total Liberal representation of such boroughs.

Appendix II links up with the genealogical tables which form Appendix III, in that, where convenient, aristocratic members of the House of Commons are noted on those tables. Appendix II shows that 39 noble families, each providing 3 or more M.P.s in the period 1832–85 on the Liberal side, produced 162 M.P.s with a total service of some 1,720 years. The Cavendishes produced members for 138 years, the Russells for 123, the Berkeleys for 105, the Fitzwilliams for 95, the Grosvenors for 87, the Leveson-Gowers for 84, the Howards of Carlisle for 73, the Pagets for 60, the Ansons, Bouveries, Brands, Byngs, Fitzroys, Fitzmaurices, Fortescues, Fitzalan-Howards and Ponsonbys for more than 40 each, the Dundases for nearly 40, and the Cowper, Temple, Ashley-Cooper and Cowper-Temple complex for a total of 118 years. Round these families, (apart from the Berkeleys), the genealogical tables are built.

In Appendix II the definition of 'aristocrat' is strict,[1] being confined to the sons and brothers of peers, their heirs (not being sons or brothers) and the sons or brothers of the heirs, with the odd bastard, who took the name and inherited the influence of his father, added. The list therefore grievously underestimates the representation of constituencies by the relatives of peers, by excluding those without courtesy styles, and 'in-laws' who do not qualify on their own account. Where convenient, members of this kind who do not appear in Appendix II have been included in the genealogical tables, in order to provide some indication of the scope of the inter-relationships of peers, office-holders, M.P.s etc.

---

[1] But brothers of newly created peers are included, though their years of service are counted (as in the case of sons) only from the date of creation.

Symbols and References

In Appendix I and Appendix II references to the genealogical tables in Appendix III are given as follows:

> The genealogical table on which the person or family appears is indicated by a capital letter (A, B or C) and its position on that table is further indicated by the letter l, r or c, standing for 'left', 'right' and 'centre', with '$\frac{1}{2}$' standing for 'inset table'.

Thus, for example, the reference in Appendix I, Section II, to G. S. Byng, indicates that he can be found on each of the Tables A, B and C in Appendix III, without difficulty on Table A and to the right on Tables B and C. The reference (Cl$\frac{1}{2}$, Cr, Bc) to the third Earl of St Germans in Appendix I, Section III indicates that he can be found in the central section of Table B, on the right of Table C, and also on the left inset of Table C.

In the genealogical tables which form Appendix III the following symbols are used:

CAPS — ★	Cabinet minister (see App. I, S I).
CAPS — ▮	Head of department but never in cabinet (see App. I, S III).
CAPS — ◆	Household official (see App. I, S II).
Underlined	Junior minister.
▲	Lord in Waiting (which usually involved being a government whip in the Lords).
†	Peer who was Whig or Liberal M.P. before he succeeded to the peerage.

APPENDIX I

SECTION I : WHIG AND LIBER

This is a dual-purpose chart, from which it is possible to read off the composition of each cabinet by referring to the offices not in italics, and seeing who held them. The ministerial career of each minister can be read off from left to right, offices in italics

Refs. to Genealogical Tables.

	ADMINISTRATION	Nov. 1830–Nov. 1834	Apr. 1835–Aug. 1841	Jul. 1846–Feb. 1852
ABr	2nd E. Grey	Premier – vii 34/		Cl¼ Aberdeen%
BrA	2nd V. Melbourne	{ S. S. Home / Premier vii 34	Premier /	
Br	V. Palmerston	S. S. Foreign	S. S. Foreign	S. S. Foreign – xii 5...
BlCl	Ld. J. Russell	{ *Paymaster* / Paymaster vi 31	{ S. S. Home – x 39@ / S. S. Cols.@	Premier@
Br	Vt. Althorp M.P.	Exchequer@/		Br Gladstone%
A	1st B. Durham	Privy Seal – iii 33/		Cc Newcastle%
Bl½	1st B. Brougham	Woolsack/		Bl Hon. S. Herbert%
Br	Vt. Goderich"	{ S. S. Cols – iii 33 / Privy Seal – v 34/		Bc D. of Argyll%
	(E. of Ripon 33) Sir J. Graham"	Admiralty – v 34 ··········		······· % ··
CcA	D. of Richmond."	Posts – v 34/		Bc¼ Ld. Canning%
	Hon. Edwd. Stanley"	{ *Ch. Sec.* / Ch. Sec. vi 31 / S. S. Cols. – v 34/		E. Cardwell%
	Charles Grant (Ld. Glenelg 35)	P. B. Control	S. S. Cols. – ii 39/	
ClBl	3rd Ld. Holland	Duchy	Duchy – x 40 d/	
C.B.	3rd M. of Lansdowne	Council	Council	Council
Bc	6th E. of Carlisle	{ No office – vi 34 / Privy Seal – vii 34/		Bl Hon. Charles Villers
Bl½	E. of Auckland	{ *P. B. Trade* / Admiralty vi 34	{ Admiralty – viii 35 / (*Viceroy*)	Admiralty – i 49d/
	T. Spring Rice	{ *Fin. S. Try.* / S. S. Cols. vi 34	Exchequer – viii 39/	
Bl½	Hon. J. Abercromby	M. Mint vi 34/	*Speaker*	Sir W. Molesworth
ACc	Edwd. Ellice	{ *Ch. Whip – viii 32* / *S. at War iii 33* / S. at War vi 34/		
	C. Poulett Thomson	{ *V.P.B.T. – vi 34* / *P.B. Trade*	{ P. B. Trade – viii 39/ / *Canada*	Ld. Wodehouse (E. of Kimberley 66)
Br	Vt. Duncannon M.P.	{ *M. of Woods ii 31* / S. S. Home vi 34	M. of Woods (& Ld. Privy Seal – xii 39)	Ld. Lieutenant – v 47...
A	(E. of Bessbro 44)			
Cl	E. of Mulgrave (M. of Normanby 38)	Privy Seal vii 34	{ *Ld. Lieutenant - ii 39* / S. S. Cols. / S. S. Home x 39	*Ambassador*
Cr	Sir J. Hobhouse (Ld. Broughton 51)	{ *At War ii 32* / *Ch. Sec. iii – v 33* / M. of Woods vii 34	P. B. Control	P. B. Control – i 52/
A	Vt. Howick M.P. (3rd E. Grey 45)	{ *U.S.S. Cols. – 33* / *U.S.S. Home i–vi 34*	At War – ix 39	S. S. Cols./
	1st B. Cottenham (C. C. Pepys)	*Sol. Gen. ii 34*	Woolsack i 36	Woolsack – i 50/
Bl½	2nd E. of Minto	*diplomat*	Admiralty ix 35	Privy Seal/
Bc	Vt. Morpeth M.P. (E. of Carlisle 48)		{ *Ch. Sec.* / Ch. Sec. ii 39	{ M. of Woods – iii 50 / Duchy
	T. B. Macaulay	*J. S. Control, xi 32-xii 33*	At War ix 39	Paymaster – viii 47/

indicating that he was not in the cabinet.
″ indicates the ministers who resigned in May 1834. % indicates Peelites.
@ = Leader of House of Commons.
/ = did not hold office again.

. 1853–Feb 1855	Feb. 1855–Feb. 1858	Jun. 1859–Jul. 1866	1868–74	1880–5
emier – 1–ii–55		Premier – x 65d @/		
S. Home (@ i 55) emier 1–ii–55 S. Foreign–ii 53 @ o office – vi 54 @ uncil – i 55 r @	Premier @ S. S. Cols. ii 55 – vii 55	{ S. S. Foreign { Premier x 65 { (peer 1861)	{ Premier@ & also { Exchequer viii 73	{ Premier@ & also { Exchequer – xii 82
xchequer		Exchequer (@x 65)		
S. Cols. – vi 54 S. War - 1–ii–55 War		S. S. Cols. – iii 64/ S. S. War – vii 61		
rivy Seal dmiralty osts sts ii 55	{ Privy Seal – xii 55 { Posts { Posts – xi 55 { Viceroy	Privy Seal { Ch. Sec. – vii 61 { Duchy – iii 64 { S. S. Cols.	S. S. India S. S. War	Privy Seal – iv 81
B. Trade	A E. of Elgin%	{ Posts – iii 60 { Viceroy		
o office	No office/	P.P.L.B.		
Adv. Gen.	J. Adv. Gen.	{ U.S.S. War – ii 61 vii & 61 { U.S.S. Ind. i–vii 61	Council – viii 73	Viceroy
of Woods	Br E. de Grey & Ripon { Works - vii 55 { S. S. Cols. – x 55d/	S. S. War iv 63 S. S. Ind. ii 66		
S.S. Foreign	U.S.S. Foreign – iv 56	{ U.S.S. Foreign – viii 61 { U.S.S. Ind. iv 64 { Ld. Lieutenant xi 64	{ Privy Seal – vi 70 { S. S. Cols.	{ S. S. Cols. – xii 82 { S. S. India
on. T. G. Baring . Northbrook 66)	Ld. Admiralty v 57	{ U.S.S. Ind. – i 61 & vii 61 – iv 64 { U.S.S. War i–vii 61	{ U.S.S. War – 1872 { Viceroy	Admiralty
		{ U.S.S. Home iv 64 { Sec Admiralty 66		
	Bc M. o. Harting- ton, M.P.	{ Ld. Admiralty iii 63 { U.S.S. War v 63 { S. S. War ii 66	{ Posts – xii 70 { Ch. Sec.	{ S. S. India – xii 82 { S. S. War
	G. J. Goschen	{ V.P.B.T. 1865 { P.P.L.B. i 66	{ P.P.L.B. – iii 71 { Admiralty	
	Cc H. Austen Bruce (Ld. Aberdare 73) Ld. Lieutenant W. E. Forster	{ U.S.S. Home xi 62 { V.P. Educ. iv 64 Ld. Lieutenant – x 64/ U.S.S. Cols. 65	{ S. S. Home – viii 73 { Council { V.P. Educ. { V.P. Educ. vi 70	Ch. Sec. – v 82

	ADMINISTRATION	Nov. 1830–Nov. 1834	Apr. 1835–Aug. 1841	Jul. 1846–Feb. 1852
A Bc	H. Labouchere	*Ld. of Admiralty vi 32*	*V.P.B.T. – ii 39* *U.S.S. Cols.* *P. B. Trade ix 39*	*Ch. Sec. – v 47* *P. B. Trade*
A	Sir F. Baring	*Ld. of Treasury* *Fin. Sec. vi 34*	*Fin. Sec. – viii 39* *Exchequer*	*Admiralty i 49/*
Bl	E. of Clarendon	*diplomat*	*Privy Seal i 40 &* *Duchy x 40 – vi 41*	*P. B. Trade - vii 47* *Ld. Lieutenant*
A	Sir George Grey	*U.S.S. Cols. ix 34*	*U.S.S. Cols. – ii 39* *J. Adv. Gen.* *Duchy vi 41*	*S. S. Home*
A	Sir Chas. Wood (Ld. Halifax 66)	*Ch. Whip viii 32*	*Sec. Admiralty – ix 39*	*Exchequer*
	1st Ld. Campbell (M.P. 1841)	*Sol. Gen. 32* *Att. Gen. ii 34*	*Att. Gen. – vii 41* *Irish Woolsack*	*Duchy – iii 50*
	1st Ld. Truro (T. Wilde M.P.)		*Sol. Gen. 39* *Att. Gen. 41*	*Woolsack vii 50/*
Bc½	Clanricarde			Posts
Bl½	Hon. Fox Maule M.P. (Ld. Panmure 1852)		*U.S.S. Home – vi 41* *V.P.B.T.*	*At War* *At War x 51* *S. S. Cols. ii 52*
	Ld. Seymour M.P. (D. of Somerset 1855)		*Ld. of Treasury – ix 39* *J. S. Control* *U.S.S. Home vi 41*	*Paymaster iv 49* *M. of Woods iii 50* *M. of Woods x 51*
Bc	2nd E. Granville (M.P. to 1846)		*U.S.S. Foreign iii 40*	*Buckhounds* *V.P.B.T. v 48* *Paymaster x 51* *S. S. Foreign i 52*
	1st Ld. Cranworth (R.Rolfe)			
Bl	Sir George Cornewall Lewis	*Sol. Gen. 34*	*Sol. Gen. – 39*	*J. S. Control xi 47* *U.S.S. Home 48* *Fin. Sec. vii 50*
Bl	R. Vernon Smith	*Ld. of Treasury*	*J. S. Control* *U.S.S. Cols. ix 39*	*At War ii 52*
Cl	E. J. Stanley M.P. (Ld. S. of Alderley)	*U.S.S. Home vii 34*	*Ch. Whip – 41* *Paymaster*	*U.S.S. Foreign* *V.P.B.T. xi 51 & P* *master ii 52*
Bc	E. of Harrowby % (Ld. Sandon M.P. – 47)	*Jr. Cmr. of Control v 31*		
	M. Talbot Baines			*P.P.L.B. i 49*
	T. Milner Gibson 1st Ld. Westbury (R. Bethell)			*V.P.B.T. – v 48*
	Robert Lowe 1st Ld. Hatherley (W. Page Wood)			*Sol. Gen. iii 51*
Bl	Chichester Fortescue (Ld. Carlingford 74)			

...1853–Feb. 1855	Feb. 1855–Feb. 1858	Jun. 1859–Jul. 1866	1868–74	1880–5
	S. S. Cols. xi 55/ Ar½ **1st Ld. Selborne** **(R. Palmer)**	{ *Sol. Gen. vii 61* { *Att. Gen. x 63* Br **5th E. Spencer**	Woolsack x 72 *Ld. Lieutenant*	Woolsack { Council – iii 83 { Ld. Lieutenant v 82
S. Foreign ii 53	S. S. Foreign	Duchy iv 64	S. S. Foreign – vi 70d/	
S. Cols. vi 54	S. S. Home	{ Duchy – vii 61 { S. S. Home/		
B. Control	S. S. India	S. S. India – i 66	Privy Seal vi 70/	
		Woolsack – v 61d/		
....	A **H. C. E. Childers** Privy Seal xii 57/	{ *Ld. Admiralty iv 64* { *Fin. Sec. ii 66*	{ Admiralty – iii 71 { Duchy viii 72–viii 73	{ S. S. War – xiii 82 { Exchequer
		John Bright	{ P. B. Trade – xii 70 { Duchy viii 73	Duchy – vii 82
	S. S. War/	Bl **Sir W. Harcourt**	Sol. Gen. xi 73	S. S. Home
		Admiralty/	{ *V.P.B.T. 71* { *U.S.S. Home 71–1* { *Sec. Admiralty 71–4*	{ *Sec. Admiralty 80–80* { *Works – 84. Posts* { Posts ii 85
ouncil – vi 54 uchy	Council	Cl½BlAr½ **G. J.** **Shaw-Lefevre** Council	{ S. S. Cols. – vi 70 { S. S. Foreign **15th E. of Derby**	S. S. Foreign S. S. Cols. xii 82 { *U.S.S. Foreign – vii 82* { P. L. Govt. Bd.
Voolsack	Woolsack	Woolsack vii 65/	**Sir C. W. Dilke**	{ *U.S.S. Home 81–3* { *Works 1884* { Privy Seal ii 85
	Exchequer	{ S. S. Home – vii 61/ { S. S. War – iv 63d	Al½ **E. of Rosebery**	{ P. L. Govt. Bd. { – vii 82 { Duchy – x 84
	P. Control/	**J. G. Dodson** Posts iii 60/	*Fin. Sec. 73*	{ *Sec. Admiralty – v 82* { *Ch. Sec. – x 84* { Duchy
.P.B.T. & Pay- master	P. B. Trade	**G. O. Trevelyan**	*Ld. Admiralty – vii 70*	P. B. Trade
.P.L.B.	{ Duchy – xii 55 { Privy Seal – xii 57/			
....	{ *P.P.L.B.* { Duchy xii 55/	... P. B. Trade	**J. Chamberlain**	
Sol. Gen. . S. Control	{ *Sol. Gen. – xi 56* { *Att. Gen.* { *J. S. Control – viii 55* { *V.P.B.T. & Pay-* *master*	{ *Att. Gen. – vi 61* { Woolsack – vi 65/ *V.P. Educ. – iv 64*	{ Exchequer - viii 73/ { S. S. Home ....Woolsack – x 72/	
.d. Treasury i 54	{ *Ld. Treasury – iv 55* { *U.S.S. Cols. – v 57* { *Irish Under-S.* **Jas. Stansfeld**	{ *U.S.S. Cols. – iii 66* { *Ch. Sec.* { *Ld. Admiralty v 63–* { *iv 64* { *U.S.S. India ii 66*	{ Ch. Sec. – xii 70 { P. B. Trade { *Ld. Treasury – 69* { *Fin. Sec. – 71* { P. L. Govt. Bd. iii 71	{ Privy Seal iv 81 – ii { 85 { Council iii 83

APPENDIX I

SECTION II: PRINCIPA

The following is a list of the persons who held the offices of Lord Chamberlain, Lord Steward, Master of the Horse, Vice-Chamberlain, Treasurer, Comptroller, Captain of

ADMINISTRATION		Nov. 1830–Nov. 1834	Apr. 1835–Aug. 1841	Jul. 1846–Feb. 1852
Bc	D. of Devonshire VI	Chamberlain		
Cc	E. of Albermarle IV	Horse	Horse	
Cr‡Bc	Ld. Robt. Grosvenor	Comptroller		Treasurer – vii 47
	M. of Donegal (till 44 E. of Belfast M.P.)	V. Ch.		Yeomen 1848
Cc	B. Foley III	Gents. – 33d		
CcBc	B. Foley IV	Gents. 33	Gents.	Gents.
	E. of Gosford II	Ld. Waiting xi 31	Yeomen – vi 35	
CcA	D. of Argyll VI	Steward, ix 33	Steward – xi 39d	
CrABr	G. S. Byng (later E. of Strafford II)	Ld. Treasury vi 32	{ Comptroller { Treasurer vi 41	{ S. B. Control – xi 47 { S.P.L.B. ii 51
CrBc	Ld. Chas. Fitzroy		V. Ch.	
A	E. of Uxbridge (B. Paget 33, later 2nd M. of Anglesey)		{ Ld. Waiting x 37 { Chamberlain v 39	
			{ Bucks. – xi 39 { Steward	
Cl	E. of Errol XVIII	Ld. Waiting 31		
Cl	E. of Ilchester III		Yeomen – vii 41	
Bc	E. of Arundel (D. of Norfolk XIII, 42)		Treasurer vii 37	Horse
Cc	B. Kinnaird IX		{ Yeomen vii 41 { Bucks. xii 39	
	Ld. Marcus Hill (later Ld. Sandys)		Comptroller vi 41	{ Comptroller – vii 47 { Treasurer
Bc	Dss. of Sutherland II		Robes 37	Robes
Br	E. Spencer IV			Chamberlain – ix 48
Bc	Ld. Edwd. Howard			V. Ch.
Cl	V. Falkland X		Ld. Waiting vii 40	Yeomen – 48
			M. of Breadalbane II	Chamberlain ix 48
Bc			M. of Westminster II	Steward iii 50
Br			Hon. W. S. Lascelles %	Comptroller vii 47 – vii
CcABr			E. of Bessborough V	Bucks. v 48
Cl			E. of Mulgrave (later M. of Normanby II)	Comptroller vii 51
Cr½			D. of Wellington II %	
			Ld. Drumlanrig M.P.%	
			Ld. Ernest Bruce%	
Cr½			V. Sydney III (cr. % Earl 1874)	

This list does not include the M. Wellesley (Ld. Steward 30–ix 33, Ld. Chamberlain iv–v 35), the M. Conyngham (Ld. Chamberlain 35–9), the 1st E. of Lichfield (Bucks 30–4), 2nd E. Fortescue (Ld. Steward 1846–50), 3rd E. of St Germans (Ld. Stewrd. 57–8, 59–66) 7th E. Cowper (Gents. 71–4) and Ld. Rd. Grosvenor (Vice-Chamberlain 1868–74) all of whom are in SECTION III, nor the 2nd E. Granville, who is in Section I.

Ld. de Tabley

Lords in Waiting and ju political ministers are italics.

the Yeomen of the Guard, Captain of the Gentlemen at Arms, Master of the Buckhounds and Mistress of the Robes under Whig and Liberal administrations 1830–85.

853–Feb. 1855	Feb. 1855–Feb. 1858	Jun. 1859–Jul. 1866	1868–74	1880–85
	M.of Ailesbury II Cc V. Bury, M.P. (later E. of Albermarle VII) Ld. Proby M.P. (later E. of Carysfort III) Bl E. of Ducie III Gents Cl M. of Huntly XI Cc Ld. Otho Fitzgld Bc Dss. of Suther- land III Bc½ E. of Cork IX ABr D. of St Albans X Cl E. of Ilchester V Cr Dss. of Welling- ton II	Horse Treasurer – v 66 Comptroller Yeomen Gents. Treasurer v 66 Bucks. 66 Robes 61	Horse *Ld. Waiting* 70–3 Comptroller Robes 70–4 Bucks. Yeomen Gents. i 74 Robes 74	 Gents. 81–1 Bucks.
		Bc Dss. of Argyll VIII	Robes 68–70	
– i 54		Bl Dss. of Bedford IX		Robes – 83
		Bl Dss. of Rox- burghe VII		Robes 83
		B. Monson VII	Treasurer i 74	Yeomen
		BrBc D. of West- minster I		Horse
		E. of Breadal- bane VII	*Ld. Waiting* 73	Treasurer
	Robes	Robes – 61d	B. Kensington IV Ld. Chas. Bruce	Comptroller V. Ch.
rd i 54	Steward – xi 57		Cl E. of Fife VI B. Carrington III	Gents. – 81 Gents. 81
berlain	Chamberlain			
	Bucks.	Bucks.	Steward	
rer	Treasurer	*Ld. Waiting* *v–vii* 66	{ *Ld. Waiting* – *xii* 69 { Gents. – 71	
	Horse			
troller	Comptroller – 56			
en astlerosse, P. (E. of hare IV 71)	V. Ch. Yeomen Comptroller viii 56	Chamberlain V. Ch.	Chamberlain { V. Ch. – 72 { *Ld. Waiting* 72–4	Steward Chamberlain
aiting	*Ld. Waiting*	*Ld. Waiting*	Treasurer – i 74	

SECTION III: MINISTERS W

A. Holders of offices whose occupants were in the period 1830–85 sometimes in the cabinet, and of the post of Master-General of the Ordnance.

	ADMINISTRATION	Nov. 1830–Nov. 1834	Apr. 1835–Aug. 1841	Jul. 1846–Feb. 185?
	G. J. W – Ellis, Ld. Dover	Woods – ii 31		
Bl	C. W. W. Wynn	At War – iii 31		
	Sir Hy. Parnell	At War iii 31 – ii 32	Paymaster – vi 41	
ACr	M. of Anglesey I	Ld. Lieutenant – ix 33		Ordnance
Cr½	M. Wellesley I	{ Ld. Steward – ix 33 / Ld. Lieutenant	Ld. Chamberlain iv–v 35	
ACr / C	M. Conyngham II	Posts vii 34	{ Posts iv 35 / Ld. Chamberlain v 35 – viii 39	
Cr½	E. J. Littleton	Ch. Sec. v 33		
Cc½	E. of Lichfield I	Bucks.	Posts v 35	
BcBl	Ld. Ebrington (s. 41, as E. Fortescue II)		Ld. Lieutenant iii 39	Ld. Steward – iii
	Chas. Buller		*J. S. Control 1839*	{ *J. Adv. Gen.* / *P.P.L.B.* xii 47 –
	R. L. Sheil		{ *V.P.B.T. i 39 &* / *M. Mint viii 39*	{ *M. Mint – x 50* / diplomat
				E. Strutt
Cr	Sir W. Somerville			{ *U.S.S. Home* / *Ch. Sec. 47*
	Jas. Wilson			*J. S. Control 48*
Cr½	Ld. Raglan % / Sir Ben Hall			
Al½	Hon. Ed. Bouverie			*U.S.S. Home vii*
Br	W. F. Cowper		*Ld. Treasury vi 41*	*Ld. Admiralty*
Br½	Edwd. Horsman		*Ld. Treasury v 41* ·········	
Cl½CrBc				E. of St Germa… III%
				Sir John Young
Cr				Hon. Hy. Fitzro…
				W. Monsell
Cr	B. Dufferin V			*Ld. Waiting i 49*
	A. H. Layard			*U.S.S. For. i 52*

B. Chief Government Whips. For E. Ellice, C. Wood and E. J. Stanley see Cabinet lists pp. 428-31.

	R. M. O'Ferrall		{ *Ld. Treasury – ix 39* / *Sec. Admiralty – vi 41* / *Ch. Whip briefly*	
Cc½	Henry Tufnell		*Ld. Treasury xi 39*	*Ch. Whip – vii 50*
	W. G. Hayter			{ *J. Adv. Gen. xii 4?* / *Fin. Sec. v 49* / *Ch. Whip vii 50*

1853–Feb. 1855	Feb. 1855–Feb. 1858	Jun. 1859–Jul. 1866	1868–74	1880–85
	Wm. Hutt W. P. Adam	V.P.B.T. & Paymaster ii 60-65 Ld. Treasury iv 65 Lyon Playfair A. S. Ayrton G. G. Glyn (s. as Ld. Wolton 1873) Bc Ld. Fredk. Cavendish Br. E. Cowper VII H. Campbell-Bannerman	{ Ld. Treasury – 73 { Works Posts 73-4 { Works 69-73 { J. Adv. Gen. Ch. Whip – 73 Ld. Treasury 73 Gents. iv 71 Fin. Sec. War 71	{ Works 80-80 { Colonial governor Ch. Ways & Means (H. of C.1 880-3) Paymaster Fin. Sec. – v 82 Ch. Sec. v-v 82d Ld. Lieutenant – 82 { Fin. Sec. War –82 { Sec. Admiralty 82 – xi 84 { Ch. Sec.
			A. J. Mundella	Educ.
Duchy – 54				
Fin. Sec. Treasury Ordnance P. B. Health viii 54 Ch. Ctees. (H. of C.) Ld. Admiralty Ld. Lieutenant Ch. Sec. U.S.S. Home Clerk Ordnance Ld. Waiting 54 Sir Robt. Peel III	Fin. Sec. Treasury Ordnance – vi 55d Works 55 { V.P.B.T. & Paymaster ii 55 { P.P.L.B. viii 55 { U.S.S. Home P. B. Health viii 55 { & Educ. ii 57 ····Ch. Sec. v 57 Ld. Steward vii 57 { Clerk Ordnance – ii 57 { P. B. Health – ix 57 Ld. Waiting Ld. Admiralty – v 57	V.P.B.T. & Paymaster – viii 59 { V.P.B.T. & Paymaster viii 59 { Works i 60 Ld. Steward Works – xii 59d V.P.B.T. & Paymaster ii 66 { U.S.S. Ind. xi64 { U.S.S. War ii 66 U.S.S. For. viii 61 Ch. Sec. vii 61-5	{ U.S.S. Cols. – xii 70 { Posts – 73 { Duchy & Paymaster – viii 72. { Diplomat ff. Works – 69	
c Hon. Henry B. Brand G. G. Glyn (see above) Chief Whip	Ld. Treasury iv 55 Chief Whip	Chief Whip Bc Ld. Richd. Grosvenor Cr Arthur W. Peel	Speaker 1872-84 V. Chamberlain Household { S.L.G.B. – 71 { S. B. of Trade –73 { Ch. Whip	Ch. Whip U.S.S.Home xii 80 Speaker 1884.

C. Holders of political junior offices (non-legal) with total service of three years or mor

ADMINISTRATION		Nov. 1830–Nov. 1834	Apr. 1835–Aug. 1841	Jul. 1846–Feb. 1852
Bl½	Capt. Hon. G. Elliot	*Ld. Admiralty vii 32*	*Ld. Admiralty – 38*	
	Adm. Chas. Adam	*Ld. Admiralty x 34*	*Ld. Admiralty*	
	Adm. Sir J. Pechell	*Ld. Admiralty*	*Ld. Admiralty ii 39*	
BlCc	Adm. M. F. F. Berkeley	*Ld. Admiralty iii 33*	*Ld. Admiralty 38–9*	*Ld. Admiralty*
ClBl	Gen. C. R. Fox	*Surveyor Gen. Ordnance xi 32*	*Sec. Ordnance*	*Surveyor Gen.*
	Robt. Gordon	*J. S. Control ii 34*	{*J. S. Control* {*Fin. Sec. 39–41*	
	J. Parker		{*Ld. Admiralty – viii 36* {*Ld. Treasury – vi 41* {*Sec. Admiralty*	{*Fin. Sec. – v 49* {*Sec. Admiralty*
	Sir Geo. Shee	*U.S.S. Foreign – x 34*	(diplomat)	
	A. Leith Hay	*Clerk Ordnance 34*	*Clerk Ordnance – ii 38*	(Colonial governor)
	Robt. Grant	*B. Control*		
		J. Adv. Gen. – vi 34	(Colonial governor)	
	R. C. Fergusson	*J. Adv. Gen. vi 34*	*J. Adv. Gen. – xi 38*	
Bl	Adm. Jas. Whitley Deans Dundas		{*Clerk Ordnance iii 38* {*Ld. Admiralty vi 41*	*Ld. Admiralty*
Cc	Col. Hon. Geo. Anson	*Clerk Ordnance vi 41*		
	Robt. Steuart	*Ld. Treasury – vi 41*		
	Adm. Sir E. Troubridge	*Ld. Admiralty*		
Al½	Ld. Dalmeny, M.P.	*Ld. Admiralty*		
ClBl	E. of Shelburne, M.P.			*Ld. Treasury xii 47–51*
Cr	Frederick Peel			*U.S.S. Cols. xi 51* R. Bernal Osborne G. C. L. Berkeley,
	Henry Rich			*Ld. Treasury*
Bc	Ld. Ebrington (later 3rd E. Fortescue)			{*Ld. Treasury – xii 47* {*S.P.L.B. – ii 51*
	Sir W. Gibson Craig, Bt.			*Ld. Treasury*
	R. M. Bellew			*Ld. Treasury viii 47*
	Benjamin Hawes			*U.S.S. Cols. – x 51*
Bl½	Hon. J. E. Elliot			*J. S. Control*

NB. This list does not include G. S. Byng (2nd E. of Strafford) for whom see SECTION II.

D. Persons who were Lords in Waiting, or held junior office for a short while, whe

Bl	Ld. Nugent, *Ld. Treasury 1830–2*	Br	Ld. Fordwich (later 6th E. Cowper), *very bri U.S.S. Foreign late 1834*
BrA	Hon. G. Ponsonby, *Ld. Treasury 1830–3*		Ld. Elcho, M.P. %, *Ld. Treasury 1853–5*
	Hon. G. Lamb, *U.S.S. Home 31–3,* bro. of Melbourne Br.		Hon. Lauderdale Maule, *Sec. Ordnance 1853* bro. of Fox Maule, Bl½
Ar½C	C. Shaw-Lefevre, *U.S.S. Home & then Cols. 1833–4, Speaker 1839 ff.*	BcBl	Hon. Jas. Stuart Wortley %, *Sol. Gen. Nov. 5 May 57*
Bc	Sir Jas. Macdonald Bt., *Cmr. Control 30–2*	Br½	Sir J. W. Ramsden Bt., *U.S.S. War May 57–8*
		A	J. Bonham Carter, *briefly Ld. Treasury May 66*

1853–Feb. 1855	Feb. 1855–Feb. 1858	Jun. 1859–Jul. 1866	1868–74	1880–85
		Bl E. of Morley III	*Ld. Waiting*	*U.S.S. War*
		W. E. Baxter	*{ Sec. Admiralty – 71* *{ Fin. Sec. – viii 73*	
		Br W. H. Gladstone	*Ld. Treasury 69*	
		Br H. J. Gladstone		*Ld. Treasury 81*
		Cl½ClBl 5th M. of Lansdowne	*{ Ld. Treasury – iv 72* *{ U.S.S. War*	*U.S.S. Ind. – vii 80*
		Hon. J. C. Vivian	*{ Ld. Treasury – 71* *{ U.S.S. Home*	
		Bl 3rd E. of Camperdown	*{ Ld. Waiting – vii 70* *{ Ld. Admiralty*	
		M. E. Grant Duff	*U.S.S. India*	*{ U.S.S. Cols. – 81* *{ Colonial governor*
		Leonard Courtney		*{ U.S.S. Home – 81* *{ U.S.S. Cols. – 82* *{ Fin. Sec. 84* *{ Ch. Ctees (H. of C.)*
		J. T. Hibbert	*S.L.G.B. 71 – xii 73*	*{ S.L.G.B. 80–83* *{ U.S.S. Home – 84* *{ Fin. Sec.*
		A. D. Hayter		*{ Ld. Treasury – 82* *{ Fin. War*
		R. W. Duff		*Ld. Treasury 82*
		J. Holms		*Ld Treasury*
		C. C. Cotes		*Ld Treasury*
		ClBl Ld. Edmond Fitzmaurice		*U.S.S. Foreign 82*
		Br Hon. Evelyn 'Ashley		*{ S. B. of Trade – 82* *{ U.S.S. Cols.*
	U.S.S. Foreign vii 56			
S.S. Cols.	*U.S.S. War – v 57*	*Fin. Sec. 60–65*		
c. Admiralty	*Sec. Admiralty*			
P.L.B.	*S.P.L.B. – v 56*			
	E. Knatchbull-Hugesson	*{ Ld. Treasury* *{ U.S.S. Home v 66*	*{ U.S.S. Home – 71* *{ U.S.S. Cols.*	
	Sir Wm. Dunbar	*Ld. Treasury – iv 65*		
	Hon. Luke White	*Ld. Treasury ii 62 – v 66*		
	Cr Ld. Clarence Paget	*Sec. Admiralty – v 66*		
il servant ff	Ar½ Saml. Whitbread	*Ld. Admiralty – iii 63*		
	T. E. Headlam	*J. Adv. Gen.*		
	Chas. Gilpin	*S.P.L.B. – ii 65*		
	CrBc Vt. Enfield M.P. (peer 1874 & 3rd E. of Stafford)	*S.P.L.B. ii 65*	*U.S.S. Foreign i 71*	*U.S.S. India viii 80 – i 83*
	Cr Ld. John Hay	*Ld. Admiralty iv 66*	*Ld. Admiralty – 71*	

appear in the Genealogical Tables.

APPENDIX II

THE WHIG NOBILITY AND ELECTORAL CONTESTS 1832—85

N.B. Only sons and brothers and heirs of peers are included, and the sons and brothers of heirs.

* asterisk before name indicates failure of candidature;   asterisk after name indicates defeat after tenure of seat;   Bracket indicates brother of person ennobled;   % indicates Liberal ex-Peelite;   unstd = unseated;   Ref is to Genealogical Tables.

(Peelites who became Liberals are included as from 1852.)

Constituencies are in italics for boroughs, in roman for counties, except where candidate was defeated.

SECTION I FAMILIES WHICH PROVIDED THREE OR MORE M.P.S

FAMILY	REF.	MEMBERS		PEERAGE AND RELATIONSHIP TO PEER
ANSON 49 years' service as M.P.s	Cc½	(1) (Sir George) 1769–1849 (general)	*Lichfield 1832–41*	brother of 1st *Vt. Anson*
		(2) Gen. Hon. George 1797–1857	*Yarmouth 1818–35**	brother of 1st *E. of Lichfield*
			S. Staffs.* 36	nephew of (1)
			Stoke 1836–7	
		(3) Thos. George, Vt. 1825–92	S. Staffs. 1837–53	2nd E.; nephew of (2)
			Lichfield 1847–54	
		(4) Hon. Augustus 1835–1900	*Lichfield 1859–68**	son of 1st E.; brother of (3)
			Bewdley 1869–74	
BERKELEY 105	Cc, Bl	(1) Adm. Sir Maurice F.F. 1788–1867	*Gloucester 1831–3**	illeg. son of 5th *E. of Berkeley*
			1835–7, 41–57	cr *Fitzhardinge* 1861
		(2) Hon. Grantley C.F.F. 1800–81	W. Glos. 1832–52*	brother of (1) — legit.
	Cc	(3) Francis H.F. 1794–1870	*Bristol 1837–70*	brother of (1) and (2) — illeg.
	Cc	(4) Hon. Craven F. 1805–55	*Cheltenham 1832–47, 48–55*	brother of (1) (2) (3)
		(5) Capt. Hon. Fras. 1826–96	*Cheltenham 1856–65**	son of (1); s. 1867, as 2nd E.
		(6) Hon. Chas. P. b. 1830	*Gloucester 1862–5*	brother of (5); s. 1896, as 3rd B.
			W. Glos. 1874	
BOUVERIE 40	Al½	(1) Hon. Duncombe P. 1780–1850	*Salisbury 1833–5*	brother of 3rd *E. of Radnor*
		(2) Hon. Philip P. 1788–1872	*Devizes 1835,*	brother of (1)
			*W. Smst. 1847	
			Berkshire 57–65	
		(3) Hon. Edward P. 1818–89	**Salisbury 43*	brother of 4th E.; nephew of (1) (2)
			*Liskeard 1880	
			Kilmarnock 1844–74	

Family	Code	Person	Constituencies	Notes
BRAND 47	Br	(1) Hon. Thos. C. W. ... 179...	*Leaves 37* / Herts. 47–52* / *Leaves 52–68* / Cambs. 68–84	
	Arf	(2) Hon. Henry B. W. 1814–92		brother of (1); cr. *Vt. Hampden*, 1884 s. as 23rd B. 1890
	Br Arf	(3) Hon. Henry R. b. 1841	Herts. 68–74* / *Stroud 1874* unstd. / 1880–6	son of (2); s. as Vt. 1892
BYNG 52		(1) (George 1764–1847)	Middlesex 1791–1847	elder brother of 1st B. (1835) and 1st E. (1847) *of Strafford* s. 1860 as 2nd E. (called up 1853)
	BcCrAl	(2) Hon. Geo. S. (Vt. Enfield) 1806–86	*Chatham 1834–5*, 7–52 / Poole 1835–7 / Tavistock 1852–7 / Middlesex 1857–74*	heir, called up 1874
	Cr Al	(3) Hon. Geo. H. C. 1830–98 (Vt. E.)		
CARRINGTON (Smith-39) 29	(1)	Hon. Robt. J. Smith 1796–1868	*Wycombe 1831–8*	s. 1838, as 2nd *Ld. Carrington*
		(2) Hon. Chas. R. b. 1843	*Wycombe 1865–8*	s. 1868; Earl 1895
		(3) Hon. William b. 1845	*Wycombe 1868–83*	brother of (2); son of (1)
		(4) Hon. Rupert b. 1852	Bucks. 1880–5 (*76)	brother of (2) (3)
CAVENDISH 138	Ac	(1) Gen. Hon. Henry F. C. 1789–1873	*Derby 1832–5*	son of 1st E. of Burlington, cr. 1831
	Bc	(2) Hon. Chas. C. 1792–1863	E. Sussex 1832–41 / *Youghal 1841–7* / Bucks. 1847–57	brother of (1); cr. *Ld. Chesham*, 1858
	Al	(3) William, Lord C. 1808–91	N. Dbys. 32–4	nephew of (1) (2); s. as E. 1834 7th *D. of Devonshire* 1858
		(4) Ld. George 1810–80	N. Dbys. 34–80 / *Bandon 37*	brother of (3)
		(5) Hon. Wm. G. 1815–82	*Peterborough 47–52* / Bucks. 1857–63	heir of (2); s. 1863
	Al	(6) Spencer, M. of Hartington 1833–1908	N. Lancs. 57–68* / N. E. Lancs. 80–5 / *Radnor 1869–80*	heir of (3); Duke 1891
	Br	(7) Ld. Frederick 1836–82	W. Rdg. (N.) 1865–82 / E. Sussex 65–8* / N. Dbys. 80–5 / *N.E. Lancs. 1874*	brother of (6)
		(8) Ld. Edward 1838–91		brother of (6) (7)

FAMILY	REF.	MEMBERS		PEERAGE AND RELATIONSHIP TO PEER
CLEMENTS 20		(1) Robert, Ld. C. 1805-39	Leitrim 32-9	eldest son of 2nd *E. of Leitrim*
		(2) Wm. Ld. C. 1806-78	Leitrim 39-47	brother of (1); 3rd E., 1854
		(3) Hon. Chas. S. 1807-77	Leitrim 47-52*	brother of (1) (2)
CONYNGHAM & DENISON 19		(1) Ld. Albert C. (name changed to D.) 1805-60	*Canterbury 35-40, 47-50*	brother of 2nd *M. Conyngham,* cr. *Ld. Londesbro* 1850
		(2) Ld. Francis 1832-80	Clare 57-9 / 74-80 (Home Rule)	son of 2nd M. nephew of (1)
		(3) Hon. W. H. F. Denison 1834-1900	Beverley 57-9 / Scarbro 59-60	s. 1860, as 2nd B.; son of (1)
[COWPER, TEMPLE, ASHLEY, COWPER-TEMPLE (Cowpers 67 others 51)	Br	(1) Geo. Vt. Fordwich 1806-56 (Cowper)	*Canterbury 1832-5*	s. 1837, as 6th *E. Cowper*
		(2) Hon. Wm. F., 1811-88 (added -Temple)	*Hertford 1835-68* / S. Hants. 1868-80	brother of (1); cr. *Ld. Mount Temple,* 1880
		(3) *Vt. Palmerston* 1784-1865 (Temple)	S. Hants. 1832-5* / *Tiverton 1835-65*	step-father of (1) (2); estates to (2) and then to (6)
		(4) Hon. Henry F. Cowper 1836-87	Herts. 1865-85 (*64) / *Tamworth 63*	younger son of (1)
		(5) Anthony, Ld. Ashley 1831-86	*Hull 1857-9* / *Cricklade 1859-65* / *Poole 1874-80*	s. 1885, as 8th *E. of Shaftesbury* nephew of (1) (2) maternally
		(6) Hon. Evelyn Ashley b. 1836	Wight 74-80-5	nephew of (1) (2) maternally; brother of (5); inherited the Palmerston estates
DUFF 35	Cl	(1) James 1814-79	Banffshire 1837-57	s. 1857, as 5th *E. of Fife* (I)
		(2) Hon. Geo. Skene 1816-89	*Elgin Dist. 1847-57*	brother of (1)
		(3) Hon. Alex. G. 1849-1923. Ld. Macduff	Elgin & Nairn 74-9	heir of (1); cr. D., 1889
DUNDAS 39	Br½	(1) Gen. Sir Robert L. 1780-1844	*Richmond 32-5* / 39-41	son of 1st B, brother of 1st *E. of Zetland*
		(2) Thos. Ld. D. 1795-1873	York 33-5 (*32) / *Richmond 35-9*	s. 1839, as 2nd E.; nephew of (1)
		(3) Hon. John C. 1808-66	*Richmond 32-5* / 41-7, 65-6 / *N. R'd'g 57*	brother of (2)

ELLIOT 35	Bl½	(1) Adm. Hon. Sir Geo. 1784–1863	Roxburgh 1832–5*	brother of 2nd *E. of Minto*
		(2) Hon. John E. 1788–1862	Roxburgh 37–41* 47–59	brother of (1)
		(3) Wm. Vt. Melgund 1814–91	Hythe 37–41 *Rochester 41* Greenock 47–52 Clackmn. & Kinross 57–9	s. as 3rd E., 1859; nephew of (1)
		(4) Hon. Arthur R. D. b. 1846	Roxburgh 1880–5	younger son of (3)
FITZROY 43	Cr	(1) Ld. Jas. 1804–34	*Thetford 1832–4*	son of 4th *D. of Grafton*
		(2) Henry, E. of Euston 1790–1863	*Thetford 1834–42* *S. Nhts. 1841	brother of (1); s. as 5th D., 1844
		(3) Ld. Chas. 1791–1865	*Bury St E. 1832–47*	brother of (1) (2)
		(4) Wm. E. of E. 1819–82	*Thetford 1847–63*	son of (2); s. as 6th D., 1863
		(5) Ld. Fredk. b. 1823	*Thetford 1863–5* *S. Nhts. 1865, 68	brother of (4)
FITZMAURICE 40	Bl	(1) Wm. E. of Kerry 1811–36	*Calne 1832–6*	heir of 3rd *M. of Lansdowne*
		(2) Henry E. of Shelburne 1816–66	*Calne 1837–56*	brother of (1); called up 1856; 4th M., 1863
		(3) Ld. Edmond b. 1846	*Calne 1868–85*	younger son of (2)
FITZWILLIAM 95	Br½	(1) C. W., Vt. Milton 1786–1857	N. Nhts. 1832–3 Malton 1832–3	s. 1833, as 5th *E. Fitzwilliam*
		(2) W. Chas., Vt. M. 1812–35	N. Nhts. 1833–5 Malton 1837–41 Malton 1846–7	heir of (1)
		(3) W. Thos., Vt. M. 1815–1902	*N. Nhts. 1837 *W. Rdg. 1841 Wicklow 1847–57 Richmond 1841–1 *N. Nhts. 52	brother of (2); s. 1857, as 6th E.
		(4) Hon. Geo. 1817–74	*Peterborough 41–59*	brother of (2) (3)
		(5) Hon. Chas. Wm. 1826–94	*Malton 1852–85*	brother of (2) (3) (4)
		(6) Wm. Vt. M. 1839–77	W. Rdg. (S.) 65–72	heir of (3)
		(7) Hon. Wm. Hy. b. 1840	Wicklow 1868–74*	brother of (6)
		(8) Hon. Wm. John 1852–89	W. Rdg. (S.) 1880–5 *Peterborough 78–85*	brother of (6) (7)

FAMILY	REF.	MEMBERS		PEERAGE AND RELATIONSHIP TO PEER
FORTESCUE 49	Bl Bc	(1) Hugh, Vt. Ebrington 1783–1861	N. Devon 1832–9 / Plymouth 41–52 / *Barnstaple 52	c. up 1839; s. 1841, as 2nd E.
		(2) Hugh, Vt. E. 1818–1905	Marylebone 54–9 / Barnstaple 41*, 47–52 / *Youghal 52	heir; c. up 59; s. 1861, as 3rd E.
		(3) Hon. John W. 1819–59	Andover 1857–74*	brother of (2)
		(4) Hon. Dudley F. b. 1820	Tiverton 1881 — 5 ff.	brother of (2) (3)
		(5) Hugh, Vt. E. b. 1854		heir of (2); s. 1905
GORDON (-HALYBURTON) 28	Bc	(1) Ld.Douglas 1777–1841	Forfar 32–41	half brother of 5th E. of Aboyne, 9th M. of Huntley
		(2) Ld. John F. 1799–1878	Forfar 41–52	nephew of above; son of 9th M.
		(3) Ld. Douglas W. 1851–88	W. Aberdeen 76–80 / Huntington 80–5	nephew of above; son of 10th M.
LEVESON-GOWER 84		(1) Granville G. Ld. Leveson 1815–91	Morpeth 1837–40 / Lichfield 41–6 / Derby 47 unstd. / Stoke 1852–7*	s. as 2nd E. Granville 1846
		(2) Hon. Edward F. b. 1819	Bodmin 1859–85	brother of (1)
		(3) Geo.M. of Stafford 1828–92	Sutherland 52–61	s. as 3rd D. of Sutherland
		(4) Ld. Ronald b. 1845	Sutherland 67–74	brother of (3)
		(5) Cromartie, M. of S. b. 1851	Sutherland 74–86	son of (3); s. as 4th D.
		(6) Adm. Hon. Francis Egerton 1824–95	E. Dbys. 68–86	son of 1st E. of Ellesmere (c); 1st cousin of (3) (4)
GREY 22	Ac	(1) Hy. Geo. Howick 1802–94	N. Northumbd. 1832–41* / Sunderland 1841–5	s. as 3rd E. Grey
		(2) (Gen.) Hon. Chas. 1804–70	Wycombe 1832–7 / *Devonport 1863	brother of (1)
		Hon. F. W. 1805–78		brother of (1) (2)
		(3) Albert b. 1851	S. Northumbd. 1880–5	son of (2); s. 1894, as 4th E.
GROSVENOR 87	Bc	(1) Richard, Ld G. 1795–1869	S. Cheshire 1832–5 / Chester 1826–47	s. 1845, as 2nd M. of Westminster
		(2) Robert, 1801–93	Middlesex 1847–57	brother of (1); cr. 1857 Ld. Ebury
		(3) Hugh, Ld. G. 1825–89	Chester 1847–69	heir of (1); s. 1869; cr. D., 1874
		(4) Ld. Richard b. 1837	Flintshire 1861–86	brother of (3); cr.B. Stalbridge, 1886

Family		Members	Constituencies	Notes
HAY 19	Cr	(1) Rear-Adm. Ld. John 1793–1851		brother of 8th M., & [cut] heir of 8th M., who d. 1876
		(2) Geo. E. of Gifford 1822–63	Totnes 1855–62 Taunton 1865–8 *Haddington 1868 *Midlothian 1874 Haddington 1878–8	brother of (2); s. as 9th M., 1878
		(3) Ld. Wm. b. 1826		
		(4) Ld. John b. 1827 (Adm.)	Wick 1857–9 *Belfast 1865 Ripon 66–71	brother of (2) (3)
FITZALAN-HOWARD (& Talbot) 43	Bc	(1) Hy. Chas. E. of Arundel & Surrey 1791–1856	W. Sussex 1832–41	s. 1842, as 13th D. of Norfolk
		(2) Hy. Granville, E. of A. & S. 1815–1860	Arundel 1837–51	
		(3) Ld. Edward 1818–83	Limerick 1851–2 Horsham 1848–52 Arundel 1852–68 *Shoreham 41 *Preston 1868	s. 1856, as 14th D.; heir of (1) brother of (2); cr. 1869 B. Howard of Glossop
HOWARD (of Carlisle) 73	Bc	(1) Capt. Hon. Fredk. G. 1805–34	Morpeth 32–4 W. Riding 1830–41 46–8 *Dublin 1842	brother of 7th E. of Carlisle heir of 6th E.; s. as 7th E., 1848
		(2) Geo. Vt. Morpeth, 1802–64		
		(3) Hon. Edw. G. C. (Adm.) 1809–80	Morpeth 1834–7 40–53	brother of (2); cr. N. Lanerton, 1874
		(4) Hon. Chas. W. G. 1814–79	E. Cumbd. 1840–79	brother of (2) (3)
		(5) Geo. J. b. 1843	E. Cumbd. 1879–80*, 81–5	son of (4); s. 1889, as 9th E.
HOWARD (of Suffolk & Berkshire) 35		(1) Chas. J. Vt. Andover 1804–76	Malmesbury 32–41	s. 1851, as 17th E. of Suffolk and 10th of Berkshire
		(2) Hon. Henry T. 1808–51	Cricklade 1841–7, *37	brother of (1)
		(3) Hon. Jas. K. 1814–83	Malmesbury 41–52	brother of (1) (2)
		(4) Hy. Chas. Vt. A., 1833–98	Malmesbury 59–68*	heir of (1); s. 1876
LAWLEY 3	Bl	(1) Hon. Beilby R. 1818–80	Pontefract 1851–2 Beverley 1852–4 *Wenlock 74 Chester 1880 unstd.	s. as 2nd B. Wenlock
		(2) Hon. Fras. Chas. 1825–1901		brother of (1)
		(3) Hon. Beilby b. 1849		heir of (1); s. 1880

FAMILY	REF.	MEMBERS		PEERAGE AND RELATIONSHIP TO PEER
LENNOX 18	Cc	(1) Ld. John G. 1793–1873	W. Sussex 1832–41	brother of 5th D. of Richmond
		(2) Ld. Wm. Pitt 1799–1881	Lynn 1832–5	brother of (1)
		(3) Ld. Arthur 1806–64	Chichester 1832–46%	brother of (1) (2) — N.B. (3), and less definitively (1) went Cons. after 1834.
MORETON 18	Bl	(1) Hon. Hy. G. F. (Ld. Moreton) 1802–53	E. Glos. 1832–5	s. 1840, as 2nd E. of Ducie
		(2) Hon. Augustus 1804–62	W. Glos. 1832–5	brother of (1)
			E. Glos. 1835–41	
		(3) Henry, Ld. M. b. 1827	Stroud 1852–3	son of (1); s. 1853
		(4) Henry, Ld. M. b. 1857	W. Glos. 1880–5	heir of (3)
PAGET 60	Cr	(1) Capt. (R.N.) Ld. Wm. 1803–95	Andover 1841–7	son of 1st M. of Anglesey
			Sandwich 47–52	
		(2) Adm. Ld. Clarence 1811–95	57–66	brother of (1)
			*Southampton 1837	
			Lichfield 1837–65*	
		(3) Gen. Ld. Alfred 1816–88	Beaumaris 1847–57	brother of (1) (2)
			*Carnarvon 1841	brother of (1) (2) (3)
		(4) Gen. Ld. George 1818–80	S. Staffs. 1854–57	
		(5) Henry, E. of Uxbridge 1821–80		heir of 2nd M., s. 1869
ANDERSON-PELHAM 21		(1) Hon. Chas., Ld. Worsley 1809–62	N. Lincs. 1832–46	s. 1846, as 2nd E. of Yarborough
			*Wight 37	brother of (1)
		(2) Hon. Dudley 1812–51	Boston 1849–51	
		(3) Chas., Ld. Worsley 1835–75	Grimsby 1857–62	son of (1); s. as 3rd E.
PONSONBY 40	Br	(1) John, Vt. Duncannon 1781–1847	Nottingham 32–34	cd. up 34; s. 1844, as 4th E. of Bessbro
		(2) Hon. Wm. F. S. 1787–1855	Dorset 1832–7	brother of (1); cr. 1838 B. de Mauley
		(3) John, Vt. Duncannon 1809–80	Derby 1835–47	son of (1); s. as 5th E.
			*Kildare 35	
		(4) Hon. Fredk. 1815–95	*Carlow 40	brother of (3); s. as 6th E.
		(5) Hon. Chas. 1815–96	Poole 1837–47	heir of (2); s. as 2nd B.
			*Youghal 47	
			*Cirencester 48	
			Dungarvan 1851–2	
		(6) Hon. Ashley 1831–98	Cirencester 52–7*	brother of (5)
			Cirencester 50–65, 78*	

444

Family	Code	Member	Constituency	Relationship
		(2) ... 1807–54		
		(3) Ramsay, John, Ld. R. 1847–87	Liverpool 1880–80	s. 1880, as 13th E.; cousin of (1)(2)
RUSSELL 123	Bl Cl	(1) Ld. (Geo.) William (Gen.) 1790–		brother of 7th D. of Bedford
		(2) Ld. John, 1792–1878	Tavistock 1832–5	brother of (1); cr. 1861 E. Russell
		(3) Ld. Chas. Jas. Fox 1807–94	S. Devon 1832–5* Stroud 1835–41 London 1841–61 47–8, *Cambdge 41 Tavistock 1835–41	half-brother of (1)(2)
		(4) Wm., M. of Tavistock 1809–72	Beds. 1832–41	s. 1861, as 8th D.; nephew of (1)(2)
		(5) F. C. Hastings 1819–91	Beds.1847–72	son of (1); s. 1872, as 9th D.
		(6) (Ld.) Arthur 1825–92	Tavistock 1857–85	brother of (5)
		(7) John, Vt. Amberley 1842–76	Nottingham 1866–8	heir of (5)
		(8) Geo., M. of T. 1852–93	Beds. 1875–85	son of (5); s. 1891, as 10th D.
		(9) Ld. Edward, 1805–87	Tavistock 1841–52	brother of (3), half-brother of (1)(2)
SPENCER 13	Br	(1) John, Vt. Althorp 1784–1845	S. Nhts. 1832–4 Midhurst 1832–5	s. as 3rd E. Spencer
		(2) Hon. Fredk. 1798–1857	37–41	brother of (1); s. as 4th E.
		(3) John, Vt. Althorp 1835–1908	S. Nhts. 1857–7	son of (2); s. as 5th E.
		(4) Hon. Chas. Robt. b. 1857	N. Nhts. 1880–5	half-brother and heir of (3)
STANLEY (of Alderley) 42	Cl	(1) (Hon.) Edwd. J. 1802–69	N. Cheshire 1832–41* 47–8	cd. up 1848; s. 1859, as 2nd Ld. Stanley of Alderley, cr. 1839
		(2) (Hon.) Wm. Owen 1802–84	Anglesea 37–47 Chester 50–7 Beaumaris 57–74	twin brother of (1)
		(3) (Hon.) Edwd. Lyulph b. 1839	Oldham 1880–5 (*72, 74)	son of (1); s. 1903, as 4th B.
TOWNSHEND 17		(1) Ld. Chas. 1785–1863	Tamworth 1832–5	brother and heir app. of 3rd M. Townshend
		(2) Rear-Adm. John 1798–1863	Tamworth 1847–55, 41*	cousin of (1); s. 1855, as 4th M.
		(3) John, Vt. Raynham 1831–99	Tamworth 1856–63	son of (2); s. as 5th M.

FAMILY	REF.	MEMBERS		PEERAGE AND RELATIONSHIP TO PEER
VIVIAN 25		(1) (John Henry 1785–1855)	Swansea 1832–55	brother of Sir R., cr. B. Vivian, 1841
		(2) Capt. (Hon.) Chas. C. 1808–86	Bodmin 1835–42 Penrhyn 1841–7 Bodmin 57–9 Truro 65–71 (*59, 63)	s. as 2nd B., 1842
		(3) Capt. (Hon.) John C. 1818–79		brother of (2)

N.B. — Where a peerage was created after 1832, the total years' service enumerated under the name of the family are counted only from the date of ennoblement.

446

SECTION II OTHER FAMILIES WHICH HAD AN M.P. ON THE LIBERAL SIDE

For English and Welsh Seats

Ar	BARING, (Hon.) Thos. G. 1826–1904	Penrhyn 57–66 (*52)	s. 66, as 2nd B. Northbrook (cr. 66) heir of above
	——, Fras., Vt. B. b. 1850	Winchstr 80–5	
	BERTIE, Montague, Vt. Norreys 1808–84	Abingdon 52–4 Had sat as Cons. & %	s. as 6th E. of Abingdon
	(BROUGHAM, William	Southwk. 32–5*, *Leeds 35	s. brother 1868, as 2nd B. (cr. 1830) brother of above)
	(——, Jas.	Kendal 32–4	
	BRUCE, Ld. Ernest 1811–86	Marlbro. 52–78% N. Wilts. 65–74	s. 1878, as 3rd M. of Ailesbury half-brother
	——, Ld. Chas. 1834–97	Marlbro. 78–85	
	CALTHORPE, Hon. Frdk. 1826–93	E. Worcs. 59–68	s. 68, as 5th B. Calthorpe
	CAMPBELL, Hon. W. F. 1824–93	Cambridge 47–52 Harwich 59–60	s. 60, as 2nd B. Stratheden, cr. 36, & 61 as 2nd B. Campbell, cr. 41
Cc½	CAVENDISH, Henry Ld. Waterpark (I) 1793–1863	S. Derbys. 32–5*, *41 Lichfield 54–6	3rd B. in the peerage of Ireland
	PELHAM-CLINTON, Ld. Robert	N. Notts. 52–65% Newark 57–9* Nottm. *62	brother of 5th D. of Newcastle
	——, Henry, E. of Lincoln 1834–79		s. 1864, as 6th D. of Newcastle
Cc	COKE, Hon. Edwd. K. 1824–89	W. Norflk. 47–52 E. Norflk. 58–65*	sons of Coke of Holkham, 1st E. of Leicester, cr. 37
	——, Hon. Wenman b. 1828		
	COLBORNE, Hon. Wm. N. 1814–46	Richmond 41–6	heir of 1st B. Seaton, cr. 39
	DENMAN, Hon. Geo. 1819–96	Tiverton 59–65* 66–72 *Camb. Univ. 56	son of 1st B. Denman, cr. 34
	DUNCAN (peerage of Camperdown) — see under Scottish seats		
	EDWARDS, Wm., Ld. Kensington (I) 1833–96	Haverfordwest 68–85, *65	s. 1872, as 4th B. in the peerage of Ireland
Bc	ELIOT, Wm., Ld. E., 1829–81	Devonport 66–8 *Cricklade 65	called up 1870; s. 77, as 4th E. of St Germans

Bl	FELLOWES, Hon Newton 1772–1854	N. Devon 32–7	s. brother 53, as 4th E. of Portsmouth
	——, Newton, Ld. Lymington b. 1856	Barnstaple 80–5	g son of above; s. 91, as 6th E.
Cr	FITZROY, Hon. Henry 1807–59	Lewes 52–9%	brother of 3rd B. Southampton
Bc Cc	FOLEY, Hon. Thos. G. 1868–69	W. Worcs. 32–3	s. 33, as 4th B. Foley
	GLYN, (Hon.) Geo. G. 1824–87	Shaftesby 57–73	s. 73 as 2nd B. Wolverton, cr. 69
	——, Hon. Sidney b. 1835	Shaftesby 80–5	brother of above
	——, Hon. Henry 1829–84	*Chatham 80	brother of above
Cl½	GORDON, Hon. Arthur b. 1829	Beverley 54–7	son of 5th E. of Aberdeen, the Prime
		*Liskeard 57	Minister; cr. Ld. Stanmore, 1893
		Aberdeenshire 61*	
	(for brother see Scottish seats).		
	(GUEST, Montague b. 1839	Wareham 80–5	brother of Ld. Wimborne, cr. 1880)
	HARE, Wm., Ld. Listowel (I) 1801–56	St Albans 41–7	2nd E. of Listowel in the peerage of Ireland
	HEATHCOTE, Hon. Gilbt. b. 1830	Rutland 56–67	s. 1867, as 2nd B. Aveland, cr. 56 &, 1888, as
	had repd. Boston 52–6		24th Ld. Willoughby D'Eresby
	HENLEY, Anthony, Ld. H. (I) 1825–98	Northampton 59–74*	B. Henley in the peerage of Ireland; cr.
		*S. Nhts. 47 & 58	U.K. peer 1885
Br	HERBERT, Hon. Auberon b. 1838	Nottingham 70–4	brother of (C) 4th E. of Carnarvon, m. to
		*Berks 68	heiress of E. Cowper
Bl	HERBERT, Hon. Sidney	S. Wilts. 52–61%	heir of 12th E. of Pembroke; cr. 1861,
			Ld. Herbert of Lea
	HERVEY, Fdk., E. Jermyn 1800–64	Bury St E. 52–9%	s. 59, as 2nd M. of Bristol
	——, Ld. Alfred 1816–75	Brighton 52–7*%	brother of above
		Bury St E. 59–65*	
	HILL, Ld. A. Marcus 1798–1863	Evesham 38–52	brother of 3rd M. of Downshire; s. 1860, as
			B. Sandys
	HOWARD, Hy., Ld. 1806–89	Shaftesby 41–5	s. 1845, as 2nd E. of Effingham

	KEPPEL, Hon. Geo. T. 1799–1891	*Lynn 37 E. Norfolk 32–5, Lymington 47–50 41* Norwich 57–60 Wick 60–5	s. 1851, as 6th E. of Albemarle
	——, Wm. Coutts, Ld. Bury 1832–94		went C. as M.P. for Berwick, 1868 ff. s. 1891, as 7th E.
Bl	KING, Hon. P. Locke 1811–85	E. Surrey 47–74*	brother of 8th Ld. K., 1st E. of Lovelace
Al	LAMBTON, Hon. Fdk. W. b 1855	S. Durham 80–5	son of 2nd E. of Durham
	LANGDALE, Hon. Chas. 1787–1868	Beverley 32–5 Knaresbro. 37–41	brother of 18th Ld. Stourton
Bc	LASCELLES, Hon. Wm. S. 1798–1851	Knaresbro. 47–51%–L	brother of 3rd E. of Harewood (C); son-in law of 6th E. of Carlisle
Bc	LEIGH, Hon. Gilbt. 1851–84	S. Warws. 80–4	son of B. Leigh, cr. 1839
	LESLIE, Hon. Geo. 1825–1904	Hastings 64–8	uncle of 9th E. Waldegrave and husband of Ctss. of Rothes
Cr½	LITTLETON, Hon. Edw. 1815–88	Walsall 47–52 S. Staffs. 53–7	s. 1863, as 2nd B. Hatherton, cr. 1835
	LUMLEY, Vt. Jno. 1788–1856	N. Notts. 32–5	s. 1835, as 8th E. of Scarbrough
Br	LYTTELTON, Hon. Chas. b. 1842	E. Worcs. 68–74*	s. 1876, as 5th B. Lyttelton and 1889 as 8th Vt. Cobham
	MOLYNEUX, Vt. Chas. 1796–1855	S. Lancs. 32–5* S.W. Lancs. 80	s. 1838, as 3rd E. of Sefton
	——, Hon. Hy. H. b. 1842		son
	MONCK, Vt. (I) Chas. 1819–94	Portsmouth 52–7%	s. 40, as 4th Vt. (Irish); U.K., cr. 66
	MONSON, Hon. Wm. 1829–98	Reigate 58–62 *Reigate 65	s. 62, as 7th B. Monson
	——, Hon. Edmd. b. 1834		
	MOSTYN, Hon. Edw. Ll. 1805–84	Flints. 31–7,* 41–2, 7–54 Lichfield 46–7 Flints. 54–61	s. 54, as 2nd B. Mostyn
	——, Hon. Thos. E. Ll. 1830–61		heir of above
Bl	NUGENT, Ld. (I), Geo. 1789–1850	Aylesby 1847–50 *S'hmptn. 42, Aylsby 37 & 39	brother of 1st D. of Buckingham

G
449

	Name	Seats	Notes
	PELHAM, Ld., Walter 1838–1902	*Lewes 65–74*	*s. 1886, as 4th E. of Chichester*
Cl	PETRE, Hon. Robt. E. 1805–48	*York 32–5* *Bridport 47*	*half-brother of 11th B. Petre*
	PHIPPS, Geo., E. of Mulgrave 1819–90 (his uncles Hon. Sir Chas. 1801–66 Hon. Edmund 1808–57)	*Scarbro. 47–51,* *52–7* *Lincoln 35, Scarbro. 41* *Whitby 52)*	*s. 1863, as 2nd M. of Normanby*
Br½	PIERREPOINT, Chas., Vt. Newark 1805–50	*E. Retford 32–5*	*heir of 2nd E. Manvers*
	PORTMAN, Hon. Wm. H. B. b. 1829	*Shaftesby 52–7* *Dorset 57–85*	*heir of 1st Ld. Portman, cr. 1837*
	PRATT, Jno. C., E. of Brecknk. 1840–72	*Brecknk 66–6*	*s. 66, as 3rd M. Camden*
	AGAR-ROBARTES, Hon. Thos. b. 1844 (see also Agar-Ellis p. 454)	*E. Cornwl. 80–2*	*s. 1882, as 2nd B. Robartes, cr. 1869, later 6th Vt. Clifden*
Br	ROBINSON, Geo., Vt. Goderich b. 1827	*Hull 52–3* *Huddersfld. 53–7* *W. Rdg. 57–9* *Ripon 74–80*	*s. 1859, as E. de Grey and E. of Ripon, cr. M. of Ripon 1871*
	———, Fredk., E. de Grey b. 1852		*heir*
	RYDER, Dudley, Vt. Sandon 1831–1900	*Lichfield 56–9*	*later C. s. 1882, as 3rd E. of Harrowby*
	SEYMOUR, Edw. Adolphus, Ld. 1804–85	*Totnes 34–55*	*s. 1855, as 12th D. of Somerset*
	STANLEY, Edwd. G. 1799–1869 ———, Hon. Henry T. 1803–75	*N. Lancs. 32–5* *Preston 32–7*	*later E. of Derby and Tory premier brother of above*
Cl	FOX-STRANGWYS, Hon. John G. C. 1803–59	*Calne 36–7* *Dorset 37–41*	*half-brother of 3rd E. of Ilchester and father of the 5th*
	STRUTT, Hon. Henry b. 1840	*E. Derbys. 68–74* *Berwick 80–80*	*s. 1880, as 2nd B. Belper*
	CRICHTON-STUART, Ld. Dudley 1803–54 (for Ld. Patrick see Scottish seats)	*Arundel 32–7* *Marylebone 47–54*	*brother of 2nd M. of Bute (C)*
	MANNERS-SUTTON, Hon. John H. T. 1814–77		*%s. 1869, as 3rd Vt. Canterbury*

	Member	Constituencies	
	——, Hon. Fredk. b. 1848	*Montgomery 77–85*	brother of above
	VANE, Ld. Harry 1803–91	S. Durham 41–59, *Hastings 59–64*	s. 64, as 4th *D. of Cleveland*
Bl	VERNON, Hon. Geo. 1806–89 (his heir Augustus)	S. Derbys. 32–5*, **S. Derbys 1859*	s. 1838, as 5th *B. Vernon*
	VILLIERS, Hon. Chas. P. 1802–96	*Wolverhmptn. 35–96*, S. Lancs. 47, *Brecknk 69–70*, **S. Warws. 68*	brother of 4th *E. of Clarendon*
	——, Edwd., Ld. Hyde, b. 1846		nephew; s. 1870 as 5th E.
Br	WATSON, Hon. Richard 1800–52	*Canterby 32–5*, *Peterbro. 52–2*	brother of 4th *B. Sondes*
	WHITE, Col. (Hon.) Luke 1829–88 (before his father was made a peer, Luke White had represented Irish constituencies)	*Kiddmstr. 62–5*, **Carrickfergus 65*	s. 1873, as 2nd *B. Annaly*, cr. 1863
Cr½	WELLESLEY, Ld. Chas. 1808–58	Windsor 52–5%	brother of 2nd *D. of Wellington*
	YELVERTON, Hon. Wm. 1791–1884	Carmarthen 32–5	brother of 3rd *Vt. Avonmore*

For Scottish Seats

	Member	Constituencies	
Bl½	ABERCROMBY, Hon. Jas. 1776–1858	*Edinburgh 32–9*, Stirls. 38–41, **37, Clackmnn. 41–2*	son of *Bss. Abercromby*
	——, Hon. Geo. 1800–52		nephew of above; s. 1842, as 2nd *B. Abercromby*
	BOUVERIE, Hon. E. P. see English seats		
Bc½	BENTINCK, Ld. Wm. 1774–1839	*Glasgow 36–9*	brother of 4th *D. of Portland* (C)
Ac	BRUCE, Hon. Robt. P. 1851–93	Fife 80–5	brother of 9th *E. of Elgin*
Bc	CAMPBELL, Jno., M. of Lorne 1845–1923	Argyll 68–78, Argyll 78–85	s. 1900, as 9th *D. of Argyll*
	——, Ld. Colin 1853–95		brother
	CAMPBELL, Jno., E. of Ormelie, 1796–1862	Perth 32–4	s. 1834, as 2nd *M. of Breadalbane*
	CARNEGIE, Hon. Chas. b. 1833	Forfar 60–72	brother of 9th *E. of Southesk*

451

Cc½	CHARTERIS, Fras., Ld. Elcho b. 1818	Haddtns. 47 ff.%	s, 1883, 10th E. of Wemyss (C)
	DALRYMPLE, Capt. Ld. D. (Jno. H.) 1819–1903	Wigtown 41–56	s. 1864, as 10th E. of Stair
	(his heir b. 1848 his second son, Hon. North de C. D. Hamilton b. 1853	*Wigtownsh. 73, 80 *S. Ayrshire 1880	
	his third son, Hon. Hugh b. 1857	*Wigtownsh. 1885)	
	DOUGLAS, Archbld., Vt. Drumlanrig 1818–58	Dumfries 52–6% (had sat as a Cons.)	s. 1856, as 7th M. of Queensberry
	DUFF, see Part I		
	DUNCAN, Adam, Vt. 1812–67	Southhmptn. 37–41 Bath 41–52 *Bury 52 Forfar 54–9 S. Warws. 65*)	s. 1859, as 2nd E. of Camperdown
	(his heir b. 1841		
	ELLIOT, see Part I		
	FLEMING, Adm. Hon. Chas. (né Elphinstone) 1774–1840	Stirling 32–35*	uncle of 13th Ld. Elphinstone and father of 14th
Cl½	GORDON, Geo., Ld. Haddo 1816–64 (for his brother see English seats)	Aberdeen 54–60	s. as 5th E. of Aberdeen
	GORDON-HALYBURTON, see Part I		
	LEVESON-GOWER, see Part I		
	GREVILLE, see Irish seats		
	HAY, see Part I		
	KEPPEL, see English seats		
Bl	INNES-KER, Jas., M. of Bowmont 1839–92	Roxburgh 70–4	s. 1879, as 7th D. of Roxburghe
Cc	KINNAIRD, Hon. Arthur F. 1814–87	Perth 37–9, 52–78	s. brother 78, as 10th B. Kinnaird
Bl	MARJORIBANKS, (Hon.) Edwd. b. 1849	Berwick 1880 ff.	s. 1894, as 2nd B. Tweedmouth, cr. 1881

RAMSAY, see Part I

	Seats	
CRICHTON-STUART, Ld. Patrick 1794–1859	Ayr 34–52 / Ayr 57–9	brother of 2nd M. of Bute and half-nephew of Ld. D. C. C-S., see English seats

Irish Seats

		Seats	
	ACHESON, Archbld., Ld. A. 1866–64	Armagh 32–47	cd. up 48; s. 1849, as 3rd E. of Gosford
	BRABAZON, Wm., Ld. 1803–87,	Dublin 37–41, 32*	s. 1851, as 11th E. of Meath
Bc½	BROWNE, Ld. John T. 1824–1903	Mayo 57–68	s. brother 1896, as 4th M. of Sligo
	BROWNE, Hon. Wm. 1791–1876 —, Valentine, Vt. Castlerosse 1825–1905	Kerry 41–7 / Kerry 52–71	brother of 2nd and 3rd E's. of Kenmare / s. father as 4th E. of Kenmare
Bc½	BURKE, Ulick, Ld. Dunkellin 1827–67	Galway 57–65, *52 / Galway 65–7 / Galway 67–71	heir of 1st M. (14th E.) of Clanricarde
	—, Hubert, Vt. Burke b. 1832		s. father 1874 as 2nd M.
	BUTLER, Col. Hon. Pierce 1774–1846	Kilkenny 32–46	brother of E. of Kilkenny (12th Vt. Mountgarret)
	CAREW, Hon. Robt. S. 1818–81	*Co. Wexfd 52 / Waterfd. 40–7	s. 1856, as 2nd B. Carew, cr. 1834
	CAULFIELD, Jas. M. 1820–92	Armagh 47–57	s. uncle 1863, as 3rd E. of Charlemont
	CAVE, Hon. Robt. Otway d. 1844	Tipperary 37–44	son of 3rd Bss. Braye
	CAVENDISH, see Part I		
	CHICHESTER, Geo., E. of Belfast 1797–1883	Antrim 32–7 / Belfast 37–8 / *Donegal 1832)	called up 1841; s. 1844, as 3rd M. of Donegall
	(his son Ld. H. F. Chichr		
	CLEMENTS, see Part I		
	CONYNGHAM, Ld. Francis 1832–80 see Part I		

	Name	Constituency	Notes
	DAWSON, Hon. T. Vesey d. 1854	Louth 41–7 / Monaghan 47–52 / Monaghan 65–8	*brother of 1st E. of Dartrey*
	——, Vesey, Vt. Cremorne b. 1842		*s. 1897, as 2nd E. of Dartrey, nephew of above*
	AGAR-ELLIS, Hon. Leopold 1829–99	Kilkenny *52, 57–74*	*bro of 3rd V. Clifden; 5th V, 1895*
	FITZALAN-HOWARD, see Part I		
Cc	FITZGERALD, Chas., M. of Kildare, 1819–87	Kildare 47–52	*s. 1874, as 4th D. of Leinster*
	——, Ld. Otho 1827–82	Kildare 65–74	*brother of above*
Bl	FITZGIBBON, Hon Rd 1793–1864	Limerick 32–41	*s. as 3rd E. of Clare*
	FITZPATRICK, John Wilson, illegit. son of last E. of Upper Ossory, 1809–83	Queens. 37–41, 47–52, 65–9 *57	*cr. Ld. Castletown,* 1869
	——, Hon. Bernard b. 1848	Portarlington 80–3 (C?)	heir
	FITZWILLIAM, see Part I		
	FRENCH, (F. Fitzstephen French 1801–73	Roscommon 32–73	*brother of 1st B. de Freyne, cr.* 1839)
	——, Chas., b. 1851	Roscommon 73–80	(Home Ruler), illegitimate eldest son of 3rd B. and nephew of above
	GORE, Hon. Robt.	*New Ross 41–7*	*brother of the E. of Arran*
	GREVILLE (-NUGENT), Capt. Hon. A. W. F. b. 1841	Wstmeath 65–74* / Perth 78* / Longford 69 unstd. / Longford 70–74	*s. 1883, as 2nd B. Greville, cr.* 1869
	——, Hon. R. J. 1848–78		brother
	——, Hon. Geo. F. 1842–97		brother
Br	LAMB, Hon. George d. 1834	*Dungarvan 32–4*	brother of Melbourne, the Prime Minister
	LAWLESS, Hon. Cecil J. d. 1853	*Clonmel 46–53*	(Repealer), son of 2nd Ld. Cloncurry
	O'BRIEN, Wm. Smith 1803–64	Limerick 35–49	(Repealer), bro of 13th B. Inchiquin (s. 1855)
Br	O'CALLAGHAN, Hon. Cornelius 1809–49	Tipperary 32–5 / Dungarvan 37–41 / Tipperary 74–7	*heir of Vt. Lismore*
	——, Hon. W. F. d. 1877		(Home Ruler), son of 2nd Vsct, nephew of above
	O'GRADY, Hon. Standish 1792–1848	Limerick 32–5	*s. 1840, as 2nd Ld. Guillamore, cr.* 1831

Oxmantown

PONSONBY, see Part I

PROBY, Granville, Ld. P. 1824–72	Wicklow 58–68	s. 1868, as 4th *E. of Carysfort*
ST LAWRENCE, Vt. Wm. b. 1827	Galway 68–74	s. as 4th *E. of Howth*
STUART, (Capt. Wm. Villiers 1804–73	Waterfd. 35–47	brother of *Ld. Stuart de Decies,* cr. 1839)
TALBOT, Hon. Jas. 1805–83	*Athlone 32–5*	s. 1850, as 4th *Ld. T. de Malahide*
WESTENRA, Hon. Henry R. 1792–1860	Monaghan 34, 35–42	s. 1842, as 3rd *E. of Rossmore*
——, Hon. John C. 1798–1874	Kings 35–52	brother
WHITE, Capt. Hon. Chas. 1838–90	Tipperary 66–75 *Co. Dublin 1865*	(Home Ruler) son of 1st *Ld. Annaly* cr. 1863 (for his brother see English seats)

BIBLIOGRAPHY

The author wishes to thank the custodians of MSS. for their courtesy and assistance, and owners of copyright for permission to reproduce material from MSS., articles and printed books.

The following is a list only of authorities quoted or cited in the text and footnotes.

A. *Manuscript Sources*

There is a vast wealth of MSS. relevant to so wide a subject as the history of Whiggery 1830–86, which it was possible to tap only very selectively. The basis of selection, in general, was a search for information on the relations of Whigs and Peelites after 1846 and Whigs and Conservatives after 1865.

1. BRITISH MUSEUM (Additional Manuscripts)
   - Huskisson Papers 38753.
   - Hobhouse Papers 36471.
   - Macvey Napier Papers 34636.
   - Peel Papers 40455, 40481, 40603.
   - Aberdeen Papers 43188, 43192, 43197, 43200.
   - Gladstone Papers 44271, 44745, 44747, 44748.

2. PUBLIC RECORD OFFICE (Gifts and Deposits)
   - Granville Papers 29/18, 51, 52, 66.

3. PRIVATE COLLECTION (by courtesy of the Rt. Hon. the Earl of Iddesleigh)
   - Papers of Sir Stafford Northcote, 1st Earl of Iddesleigh.

I wish also to thank the ESSEX RECORD OFFICE for access to cuttings relating to the county election of 1830 and the Rt. Hon. Lord Hatherton and Mr F. B. Stitt, County Archivist of Staffordshire, for permission to publish a short passage from E. J. Littleton's diary.

B. *Diaries, Collections of Letters, Autobiographies, Biographies containing material quoted, and original works by nineteenth-century notables.*

Italics show the name by which the work is cited in the text.

Place of publication London except where otherwise stated.

Correspondence of Lord Aberdeen & Pss. Lieven 1832–54, ed. E. J. Perry—R. Hist. Soc.'s Camden Series, III, 60. 1938.

458   BIBLIOGRAPHY

Memoirs and Letters of Rt. Hon. Sir Thos. Dyke Acland, ed. A. H. D. Acland—1902.

Memoir of John Charles, Viscount Althorp, 3rd Earl Spencer, by Sir Denis *Le Marchant*—1876.

The Journal of Mrs Arbuthnot 1820–32, ed. Bamford and D. of Wellington—1950.

Autobiography and Memoirs of George Douglas, 8th Duke of *Argyll*, ed. Dwgr. Dss. of Argyll—1906.

Three Early Nineteenth Century Diaries, ed. A. Aspinall—1952.

Asquith (Earl of Oxford &), Fifty Years of Parliament—1926.

Bagehot, Walter, Biographical Studies—1856.

— Physics and Politics—1872.

— The English Constitution and Other Essays—1872 edition.

Blunt, Wilfrid Scawen, 1840–1922, by E. Finch—1939.

Memoirs of the *Courts and Cabinets* of William IV & Victoria, by Duke of Buckingham and Chandos—1861.

Lord Brougham and the Whig Party, by A. Aspinall—1939 reissue.

Life of John, Lord *Campbell*, ed. Hon. Mrs Hardcastle—1881.

Mr Chamberlain's Speeches, ed. Chas. W. Boyd—1914.

A Political Memoir 1880–92, Joseph Chamberlain, ed. C. H. D. Howard—1953.

Life and Letters of Geo. Wm. Fredk., 4th Earl of *Clarendon*, by Sir Herbert Maxwell—1913.

The Life of Richard Cobden, by John Morley—1881.

The Croker Papers, ed. L. J. Jennings—2nd ed. 1885.

The Life of Spencer Compton, 8th Duke of *Devonshire*, by Bernard Holland—1911.

A. V. Dicey's Introduction to the Study of the Law of the Constitution —1885.

Life of Rt. Hon. Sir Chas. W. *Dilke* M.P., by Stephen Gwynn & G. M. Tuckwell—1917.

B. Disraeli, Vindication of the English Constitution—1835.

— Letters of Runnymede, intr. Hitchman—1885 edition.

— Lord George Bentinck—5th ed. 1852.

— Coningsby—Bradenham Edition 1927.

Life of Benjamin Disraeli, Earl of Beaconsfield, by W. F. *Monypenny &* G. E. *Buckle*—1910–24.

The Life and Correspondence of T. S. *Duncombe*, ed. T. H. Duncombe —1868.

Viscount Milton, Earl Fitzwilliam—Address to the Landowners of England on the Corn Laws, 5th ed. 1832; 2nd Address 1835; 3rd Address 1839.

Life of William Ewart Gladstone, by John Morley—2 vols. ed. 1905.

Gladstone to his Wife, ed. A. Tilney Bassett—1936.

Gladstone, A Biography, by Sir Philip Magnus—1954.

After Thirty Years by Viscount Gladstone—1928.

Lord Goschen and His Friends (The Goschen Letters), ed. P. Colson—1946.

Sir James Graham—Address to Landowners—1828.

Life and Letters of Sir James Graham, ed. C. S. Parker—1907.

James Grant—Random Recollections of the House of Commons—1st Series (2nd edition 1836); Random Recollections of the Lords and Commons, 2nd Series 1838.

The Life of Granville George Leveson Gower, 2nd Earl Granville, by Lord Edmond Fitzmaurice—1905.

Greville's Journal, 1st Part, ed. H. Reeve 1874.

             2nd Part 1837–52   1885.

             3rd Part 1852–60   1887.

Correspondence of Pss. Lieven & Earl Grey, ed. Le Strange—1890.

Recollections of a Long Life, by John Cam Hobhouse, Lord *Broughton*, ed. Lady Dorchester—1909–11.

Charles Lindley, Viscount Halifax, by J. G. Lockhart—vol. I, 1935.

Sidney *Herbert*, Lord Herbert of Lea, A Memoir, by Lord Stanmore—1906.

Life of Sir Michael Hicks Beach, by Lady V. Hicks Beach—1932.

Life, Letters and Friendships of Richard Monckton Milnes, 1st Lord *Houghton*, by T. Wemyss Reid—1891.

Life of Lord Jeffrey, by Lord Cockburn—Edinburgh, 1852.

Life of Henry *Labouchere*, by A. L. Thorold—1913.

Lord Liverpool and Liberal Toryism, by W. R. Brock—Cambridge 1941.

Robert Lowe, Speeches and Letters on Reform—1867.

Sir Henry Lucy's Diary of Two Parliaments—1886.

Memoirs of an Ex-Minister, by the Earl of Malmesbury, 1885 edition.

Papers of William Lamb, Viscount Melbourne (*Melbourne Papers*), ed. Lloyd C. Sandars—1889.

Rt. Hon. Sir William Molesworth, Bt., M.P., by Mrs Fawcett—1901.

Life of Henry, 5th Duke of *Newcastle*, by J. Martineau—1908.

Thos. Geo., Earl of *Northbrook*, a Memoir, by Bernard Mallet—1908.

The M.P. for Russia, Reminiscences and Correspondence of Mme Novikov, ed. W. T. Stead—1909.

Tory Radical, the Life of Richard Oastler, by C. Driver—1946.

D. O'Connell—Address to the Reformers of England and Ireland—1834.

The Life of Henry John Temple, Viscount Palmerston, vol. III, by Lord Dalling, ed. E. Ashley—1874.

—— 1846–65 by E. Ashley—1876.

Joseph Parkes of Birmingham, by J. K. Buckley—1926.

Sir Henry Parnell—Financial Reform—1830.

Elections and Recollections, by Sir Alfred E. Pease—1932.

Letters of David Ricardo to John Hutches Trower 1811–23, ed. Bonar & Hollander—1899.

Early Correspondence of Lord John Russell (*E.C.J.R.*) 1805–40, ed. R. Russell—1913.

Later Correspondence 1840–78, ed. G. P. Gooch—1925.

Lord John Russell—An Essay on the History of the English Government and Constitution—2nd edition 1823 and new edition 1865.

— Letter to the Electors of Stroud—2nd ed. 1839.

— The Life and Times of Charles James Fox—1859–66.

— Recollections and Suggestions 1813–73—1875.

The Life of Lord John Russell, by Spencer Walpole—1889.

Lord John Russell, by A. Wyatt Tilby—1930.

G. W. E. Russell—Prime Ministers and Some Others—1918.

Lord Shaftesbury and Social-Industrial Progress, by J. Wesley Bready —1926.

Letters, Remains and Memoirs of Edward Adolphus Seymour, 12th Duke of *Somerset*, ed. Mallock & Ramsden—1893.

Miscellanies Collected and Edited by Earl Stanhope—1863.

Speech of C. Poulett Thomson Esq. in the House of Commons 26th Mar. 1830—1830.

Memoir of the Life of Rt. Hon. Charles, Lord Sydenham, by G. P. Scrope—1843.

The Letters of Queen Victoria (*Queen's Letters*) 1837–61, ed. Benson & Esher—1907; 2nd Series 1862–78—1926; Vol. III 1879–85—1928.

A. Trollope, The Macdermotts of Ballycloran—1847, Castle Richmond —1860.

E. M. Whitby's History of the Session 1852–3—1854.

C. *Other Printed Books*

A. Aspinall: The Formation of Canning's Ministry, R. Hist. Soc., Camden Series, III, 59—1937.

Lucy Brown: The Board of Trade and the Free Trade Movement, 1830–42—Oxford 1958.

J. R. M. Butler: The Passing of the Great Reform Bill.

John Bateman: The Great Landowners of Great Britain and Ireland, 1879 ed.

E. Boutmy: Psychologie politique du Peuple Anglais au XIXme Siècle—Paris 1901.

Lord David Cecil: The Young Melbourne—1939.

Sir John A. Craig: A History of Red Tape—1955.

Sir Reginald Coupland: The Durham Report—Oxford 1945.

E. M. Everett: The Party of Humanity—N. Carolina Univ. Press 1939.

N. Gash: Politics in the Age of Peel—1953.
English Reform and French Revolution in the General Election of 1830, in Essays Presented to Sir Lewis Namier—1956.

E. Halevy: A History of the English People in the Nineteenth Century—vols. III & IV—1950–51 edition.

W. Harris: History of the Radical Party in Parliament—1885.

H. J. Hanham: Elections and Party Management—1959.

Betty Kemp: King and Commons 1660–1832—1957.

H. J. Laski: The Danger of Being a Gentleman and Other Essays —1940.

A. L. Lowell: The Government of England—New York 1908.

S. Maccoby: Radicalism 1853–86—1938.

R. McKenzie: British Political Parties—1955.

H. Martineau: History of the Thirty Years' Peace 1816–46—1877–8 ed.

Chester Martin: Empire and Commonwealth—Oxford 1929.

G. R. Mellor: British Imperial Trusteeship 1783–1850—1951.

P. S. O'Hegarty: A History of Ireland under the Union—1952.

M. Ostrogorski: Democracy and the Organization of Political Parties —1902 ed.

J. E. Pomfret: The Struggle for the Land in Ireland—Princeton 1930.

E. & A. G. Porritt: The Unreformed House of Commons—1903.

C. Seymour: Electoral Reform in England and Wales—Yale 1915.

K. B. Smellie: A Hundred Years of English Government—1950 ed.

A. S. Turberville: The House of Lords in the Age of Reform—1958.

Sir C. Webster: The Foreign Policy of Palmerston—1951.

Sir L. Woodward: The Age of Reform 1815–70—Oxford 1954 (reprint).

The author did not have the pleasure of reading Professor Asa Briggs's *The Age of Improvement* until he had finished dealing with the period up to 1867 and, while working on this book, deliberately abstained from re-reading Mr O. F. Christie's *The Transition from Aristocracy* and *The Transition to Democracy*.

D. *Articles in Learned Journals*

ENGLISH HISTORICAL REVIEW

J. B. Conacher: Peel and the Peelites 1846–50, LXIII, 1958.

Jenifer Hart: Sir Charles Trevelyan at the Treasury,
                       LXXV, 1960.
C. H. D. Howard: The Parnell Manifesto of 21st Nov. 1885 and
                       the Schools Question, LXII, 1947.
P. Fraser: The Growth of Ministerial Control in the
                       Nineteenth Century House of Commons,
                       LXXV, 1960.
A. F. Thompson: Gladstone's Whips and the General Election
                       of 1868, LXIII, 1948.
F. M. L. Thompson: Whigs and Liberals in the West Riding,
                       LXXIV, 1959.

TRANSACTIONS OF THE ROYAL HISTORICAL SOCIETY
N. Gash: Peel and the Party System, 5th Series, i, 1947.

HISTORY (New Series)
E. Hughes: Civil Service Reform 1853–55 (Historical
                       Revision CI), XXVII, 1942.
B. Kemp: The General Election of 1841, XXXVII, 1952.

PROCEEDINGS OF THE BRITISH ACADEMY
A. Aspinall   The Cabinet Council 1783–1835 (Raleigh
                       Lecture), XXXVIII, 1952.

HISTORICAL JOURNAL (formerly CAMBRIDGE HISTORICAL JOURNAL)
John Roach: Liberalism and the Victorian Intelli-
                       gentsia, XIII, IV, 1957.
Mary Lawson-Tancred: The Anti-League and the Corn Law Crisis
                       of 1846, III, 2, 1960.

BULLETIN OF THE INSTITUTE OF HISTORICAL RESEARCH
H. J. Hanham: British Party Finance 1868–80, XXVII,
                       1954.

AMERICAN HISTORICAL REVIEW
R. E. Pumphrey: Introduction of Industrialists into the
                       British Peerage, LXV, no. 1, 1959.
D. Spring: Earl Fitzwilliam and the Corn Laws, LIX,
                       no. 2, 1954.

CANADIAN HISTORICAL REVIEW
D. Spring: The Earls of Durham and the Great
                       Northern Coalfield 1830–80, XXXIII,
                       3, 1952.

BIRMINGHAM HISTORICAL JOURNAL
D. Johnson: The Derby Dilly, IV, 1, 1953.

JOURNAL OF ECONOMIC HISTORY
D. Spring: The English Landed Estate in the Age of Coal and Iron 1830–80, XI, 1, 1951.

ECONOMIC HISTORY REVIEW
G. S. R. Kitson Clark: The Repeal of the Corn Laws and the Politics of the Forties, 2nd S. IV, 1, 1951.
K. H. Connell: The Land Legislation and Irish Social Life, 2nd S. XI, 1, 1958.
J. D. Chambers: The Vale of Trent 1670–1800, Supplement 3.
G. W. Hilton: The Truck Act of 1831, 2nd S. X, 3, 1958.
G. L. Mosse: The Anti-League 1844–46, XVII, 2, 1947.
F. M. L. Thompson: The End of a Great Estate, 2nd S. VIII, 1, 1955.

YORKSHIRE BULLETIN OF ECONOMIC AND SOCIAL RESEARCH
J. T. Ward: The Earls Fitzwilliam and the Wentworth Woodhouse Estate in the Nineteenth Century, XI, 2, 1960.

RESEARCHES AND STUDIES (published by Leeds University Institute of Education)
J. T. Ward: A Lost Opportunity in Education, 1843, XX, 1959.

TRANSACTIONS OF THE HUNTER ARCHAEOLOGICAL SOCIETY
J. T. Ward: The Squire as a Business Man — William Aldam of Frickley Hall, 1961.

E. *Newspapers and Periodicals*

The Annual Register	The British Quarterly Review
Dod's Parliamentary Companion	The Nineteenth Century
The Edinburgh Review	The Times
The Quarterly Review	The Morning Chronicle
The Fortnightly Review	(Cobbett's) Political Register
The Westminster Review	The Economist

INDEX